SIXTH EDITION

CURRICULUM IMPROVEMENT
Decision Making and Process

RONALD C. DOLL
Professor Emeritus
The City University of New York

ALLYN AND BACON, INC.   Boston   London   Sydney   Toronto

Library of Congress Cataloging in Publication Data

Doll, Ronald C.
    Curriculum improvement.

    Bibliography: p.
    Includes index.
        1. Curriculum planning—United States. .
2. Education—United States—Curricula. I. Title.
LB1570.D59   1986   375′.001   85-9834
ISBN 0-205-08500-8

Series Editor: Susanne F. Canavan
Production Coordinator: Helyn Pultz
Editorial-Production Services: Lifland et al., Bookmakers
Cover Coordinator: Linda K. Dickinson
Cover Designer: Lisa Tedeschi

10 9 8 7 6 5 4 3 2 1   89 88 87 86 85

Printed in the United States of America.

For Ruth, *whose faith in God, love for people, basic wisdom about human relationships, and realistic sense of the feasible have undergirded more than three decades of her husband's writing for publication*

Contents

Preface   xiii

PART ONE
DECISION MAKING IN CURRICULUM IMPROVEMENT

─────────────────────────   1   ─────────────────────────

Historical and Philosophical Foundations of
Curriculum Decision Making   3

The Cry for Excellence   4
The Meaning of Curriculum   6
Curriculum Concerns at the Beginning of the Third Century in
   United States History   9
      Activity 1-1: Identifying Curriculum Concerns in One's
              Own Environment   11
      Activity 1-2: Recognizing Well-Known People and
              Movements in the Curriculum Field   12
The Underpinnings: Curriculum Change in Early America   12
A Catalog of Events from 1860 to the Present   14
A Digest of Trends in the Evolution of the Curriculum   21
The Evolving Process of Curriculum Improvement   21
      Activity 1-3: Narrating the Curriculum History of One's
              Own School System   26
Two Differing Philosophical Foundations of the Curriculum   26
Schools of Philosophical Thought Affecting the Curriculum   30
      Activity 1-4: Describing the Educational Philosophy of
              One's Own School   37

Activity 1-5: Defining and Refining Your Own Curriculum
                    Philosophy   37
Educational Philosophy in a Context of Other Curriculum
    Foundations   37
Summary   38
Endnotes   39
Selected Bibliography   40

2

Psychological Bases for Curriculum Decisions   41

Learners—Their Growth and Development   41
    Situation 2-1: Judging What Use to Make of Certain
                    Characteristics and Needs   46
    Situation 2-2: Homework for an Eighth-Grade Class   52
    Activity 2-1: Diagnosing the Learning Potential of an
                    Individual   52
Understandings of the Learning Process   56
    Situation 2-3: Putting Selected Learning Principles to Work   59
    Situation 2-4: The Case of Mary Williams   70
    Situation 2-5: Identifying Basic Considerations Affecting
                    Learning Style   71
    Activity 2-2: Soliciting Pupils' Comments about Learning   75
Some Uses of Psychology in Making Decisions Cooperatively
    about the Curriculum   76
Summary   81
Endnotes   81
Selected Bibliography   85

3

Social and Cultural Forces Affecting Curriculum Decisions   87

Influences from Society and the Culture at Large   87
    Situation 3-1: Finding Traditions to Challenge   89
    Situation 3-2: Assessing the Effects of Specific Social
                    Changes   93
    Situation 3-3: What to Do about the Plight of Victimized
                    Teachers   93
    Activity 3-1: How Much Federal and State Control?   97

Influences within the Immediate Community   100
    Activity 3-2: *A Limited Study of One Community*   103
    Activity 3-3: *A More Comprehensive Study of the Same*
                  Community   104
    Situation 3-4: *When Subcultures and Social Classes Come*
                  to School   104
Culture-Based Curriculum Ideas: Two Examples   109
    Activity 3-4: *A Special Problem in Recognizing and*
                  Meeting Differences in Values   112
    Activity 3-5: *A Study of Present and Future Career*
                  Opportunities   114
Strategies for Using Social Influences   115
    Activity 3-6: *The Site at Which Political Power Should*
                  Be Applied   118
    Activity 3-7: *Which Will You Have?*   118
Summary   120
Endnotes   120
Selected Bibliography   121

4

Subject Matter: Its Role in Decision Making   123

A New Era in the Schools   124
    Activity 4-1: *Finding Reasons for Changes in*
                  Subject Matter Placement   130
Selecting Subject Matter as Learning Content   130
    Activity 4-2: *Planning Improved Selection of Subject*
                  Matter   140
    Situation 4-1: *Resolving Problems in Subject Matter*
                  Selection and Assignment-Making   142
A Closer Look at Subject Matter   143
    Activity 4-3: *Discovering What's Inside a Discipline*   149
    Activity 4-4: *Working with the Discovery Process*   150
Organizing and Reorganizing Subject Matter for Teaching
  and Learning   150
Special Problems in Organizing and Presenting Subject Matter   156
    Activity 4-5: *Becoming Acquainted with Curriculum*
                  Literature Relating to Special Problems in
                  Organizing and Presenting Subject Matter   161
    Situation 4-2: *Responding to the State's Criticisms of the*
                  Yalta Pass Curriculum   161
The Status of Subject Matter Selection and Presentation   162
Summary   168

Endnotes 169
Selected Bibliography 171

5

Making Decisions about the Design of the Curriculum 173

The Nature of Design and Designing 174
Sources of Ideas That Undergird Curriculum Designs 175
    Activity 5-1: *Thinking about Sources of Educational Philosophy* 182
    Situation 5-1: *Using Curriculum Foundations in Planning Improvement* 183
    Situation 5-2: *Making Further Use of Curriculum Foundations and Viewpoints* 183
The Tylerian Model for Creating Curriculum Designs 184
Additional Considerations Now Affecting Curriculum Designing 186
Strategies Used in Creating Curriculum Designs 190
    Activity 5-2: *Moving from Philosophical Sources to Objectives* 204
    Situation 5-3: *Selecting Evaluation Means for a Middle School Project* 204
    Activity 5-3: *Suggesting Concrete Actions in Selecting and Ordering Learning Experiences* 205
Examples of Curriculum Designing 205
The Purposes and the Nature of New Curriculum Designs 208
    Activity 5-4: *Identifying Curriculum Designs* 214
Summary 214
Endnotes 214
Selected Bibliography 216

6

Evaluation of Curriculum Programs and Projects 218

Evaluation as It Is Generally Known in Schools 219
Some Principles and Practices of Evaluation 224
Dimensions of Program and Project Evaluation 227
Development of an Evaluation Model 236
Additional Evaluation Models 240
Program and Project Evaluation in Action 243
    Situation 6-1: *Evaluating an Entire Curriculum Program* 246
    Situation 6-2: *Judging the Worth of Evaluation Means* 247

Making or Selecting an Evaluation Design — 247
Activity 6-1: Describing an Evaluation Design — 249
Activity 6-2: Selecting an Evaluation Design — 249
Reporting the Evaluation of a Program or Project — 250
The Need for Careful Evaluation of Old and New Ideas and Movements — 251
Some Commonsense Considerations — 252
Activity 6-3: Using Process Evaluation — 257
Summary — 257
Endnotes — 258
Selected Bibliography — 261

PART TWO
PROCESS IN CURRICULUM IMPROVEMENT

7

The General Process of Curriculum Change and Improvement — 265

How Decision Making Relates to Process — 265
Some Observations about the Process of Improvement — 266
How Change Occurs — 268
Situation 7-1: Resistance to Change: Trouble in a Faculty — 281
Situation 7-2: Misdirected Change: The Tendency to Move in Too Many Directions at Once — 281
Activity 7-1: Statements about Change Process That Are Open to Discussion — 282
Practical Applications of Change Process in Improving the Curriculum — 283
Activity 7-2: Teachers' View of Curriculum Change — 290
Four Actions That Facilitate Curriculum Improvement — 290
Situation 7-3: A Special Problem of Attitudes — 296
Situation 7-4: Some Common Problems in Getting and Using Instructional Materials — 296
Situation 7-5: The Emergencies in Pennsatonic — 299
Situation 7-6: Homework for the General Curriculum Committee — 302
Activity 7-3: The Prevalence of Built-in Evaluation — 304
Situation 7-7: Reducing Illiteracy—A Growing Concern of the Schools — 304
Summary — 305

Endnotes   305
Selected Bibliography   308

8

The Planning Process   310

The Bases of Curriculum Planning   311
    Activity 8-1:   *Finding Curriculum Needs and Related*
                 Problems in the Field of Moral Education   321
    Situation 8-1: *Sorting the Problems*   322
    Activity 8-2:   *Helping Participants Improve the Use of*
                 Their Competencies   325
    Situation 8-2: *Whose Concerns Should Have Priority?* 328
What Causes People to Plan   330
    Situation 8-3: *Procedures to Fit the Situation*   338
Customary Planning Modes   339
A Schema for Planning   341
    Situation 8-4: *What Was Done in the Planning Process?* 344
    Situation 8-5: *The Shortcomings of the Curriculum*
                 Steering Committee   346
The Computer as a Planning Instrument   347
    Situation 8-6: *Beginning to Use the Computer in Planning* 352
The Importance of Thoughts and Feelings   352
    Situation 8-7: *How the Teachers Felt*   354
Expectations, and an Eye to the Future   354
Summary   356
Endnotes   356
Selected Bibliography   358

9

Participants and Their Roles in Curriculum Improvement   360

Input Coming from Many Sources   361
Roles of Individuals and Organizations within Local School
    Districts   362
    Situation 9-1: *Achieving Balance in Participation*   369
    Situation 9-2: *How Much Involvement for Laypersons?* 374
    Situation 9-3: *Competency in Role Determination*   375
    Activity 9-1:   *Looking to the Future of Lay Participation* 376

Roles of Persons and Organizations outside Local School
   Districts   376
     Activity 9-2:   *Developing a Perspective Concerning
                Outside Agencies*   381
     Activity 9-3:   *Identifying New Agencies and
                Combinations of Agencies*   382
Accountability as a Determinant of Role Assignments   382
Assigning Roles and Achieving Balance among Them   387
     Activity 9-4:   *When People Are Held Accountable*   387
     Activity 9-5:   *The Conflict between Principals and
                Curriculum Coordinators*   390
Summary   391
Endnotes   391
Selected Bibliography   394

10

The Massive Problem of Communicaiton   395

Communication: A Complex Enterprise   395
     Situation 10-1: *Communication Backfire*   399
Communication through Literary and Related Media   400
     Situation 10-2: *How Can They Present It Most Effectively?* 407
Communication via Personal Contact   408
     Situation 10-3: *The Storms at Stoneham Center*   411
     Activity 10-1:   *Interpersonal Effects of Some Interpersonal
                Communications*   412
Dealing with Two Major Barriers to Good Communication   413
Organizing for Better Communication   415
     Situation 10-4: *Influencing the Eighty-Nine, Less Seven*   419
     Situation 10-5: *A Plan for Banksdale*   419
Summary   420
Endnotes   421
Selected Bibliography   423

11

Curriculum Leadership: Its Nature and Strategies   425

The Nature of Curriculum Leadership   426
     Activity 11-1: *Assigning Values to Leadership Traits*   430
     Situation 11-1: *Leadership without Equilibrium*   430

    Activity 11-2: *Finding Situational Factors That Affect*
                     Leadership   431
Factors Affecting Curriculum Leaders' Work   431
    Situation 11-2: *Choosing the Principal's Assistant*   438
    Activity 11-3: *Interrelating Human Relations and Task*
                  Performance in Curriculum Leadership   439
    Situation 11-3: *What Shall We Do to Improve Our School?*   441
    Situation 11-4: *The Curriculum Leader without Authority*   442
Leadership Strategies for Improving the Curriculum   442
    Activity 11-4: *Finding Evidence of Master Planning in a*
                  School System   447
    Activity 11-5: *Some Practical Problems in Local Planning*   450
    Activity 11-6: *Themes and Procedures for Planning*
                  Inservice and Staff Development Projects   455
    Activity 11-7: *Surveying Teachers' Needs for Supervisory*
                  Help   459
    Activity 11-8: *Getting to Know Teachers' Strengths*   460
    Activity 11-9: *An Investigation of Local Trends and*
                  Tendencies in Reorganization   462
    Situation 11-5: *Improve Curriculum Design or Change the*
                  Organization of the School?   462
    Situation 11-6: *A Guide to Research by Classroom*
                  Teachers   465
Implementing the Strategies   466
    Situation 11-7: *The Responsibilities of a New Curriculum*
                  Leader   469
    Activity 11-10: *What the Best Principals Do*   471
    Situation 11-8: *How Far Does Competency in Leadership*
                  Extend?   473
Summary   474
Endnotes   474
Selected Bibliography   477

Name Index   479

Subject Index   483

Preface

Since 1964, *Curriculum Improvement: Decision Making and Process* has been both a standard text and a practitioner's handbook on the essential elements of curriculum planning. So much has happened in the curriculum field, particularly during the last three decades, that continuing revision of the book has been necessary. Because the fundamental issues, problems, and concerns in curriculum planning have remained constant, however, the chapter themes have, in general, been preserved.

Beginning in the early 1960s with my polling of curriculum leaders about their major concerns, I have tried to keep in contact with both theoreticians and grassroots practitioners. The Sixth Edition mirrors many of the current interests of people in the field. It provides basic understanding of new developments without neglecting older, tested principles and practices of intelligent planning. It is perhaps a more stimulating edition than any of the preceding ones, partly because the longer I remain in the curriculum field, the more enthusiasm I have for it.

The Sixth Edition is divided into two parts. The first part deals with bases for decision making about what the curriculum should be, and the second part pertains to the process of improving the curriculum. Most of the chapters contain, at intervals, practical situations that call for careful analysis. I have invented few of these situations. The great majority of them originated in suggestions and anecdotes submitted by experienced practitioners. A few situations, of course, come directly from my own experience during numerous pleasant and satisfying years of service as teacher, department chairperson, principal, guidance director, curriculum coordinator, central office administrator, and consultant. Most of the situations, while adding spice to classroom discussions, should provide opportunities to simulate problem solving that occur commonly in the process of improving curriculum. Situations yield to some of the familiar methods of case analysis. The following questions may be used, if the instructor wishes, to guide the analysis:

- What are the issues or problems in this situation?
- What pertinent facts do you know?
- What seems to be left unsaid or obscure?
- What solutions or ameliorations for the situation can you suggest?
- What related issues or problems are involved in putting these solutions or ameliorations into effect?

Students need to be taught that, in educational decision making, the facts are never complete, else no issue or problem might exist.

The situations in the text are sometimes varied with student activities that call for thinking, observing, reading, and writing. I have included these learning exercises because they are valuable in teaching certain subject matter.

Curriculum Improvement: Decision Making and Process is used by thousands of college and university professors and their students in courses, seminars, and workshops in curriculum development and in educational supervision and administration. Practitioners of the helping professions have used the text as a handbook in schools, colleges, and elsewhere. Though the thrust of the book's discussion is directed toward improving elementary and secondary schools, many college and university faculties are finding it helpful in determining and monitoring the process of curriculum improvement at the post–high school level.

Sexist expressions can easily find their way into a manuscript. I have tried to eliminate from my writing these and other marks of discrimination or prejudice against any group or category of people.

I wish to recognize the contributions of the following persons: my former students at New York University, Hunter College, Richmond College, and Georgian Court College, who have helped me find errors and overstatements in previous editions of the book; the more than four dozen reviewers who have criticized the manuscripts of the various editions; Susanne F. Canavan, Series Editor at Allyn and Bacon; Hiram G. Howard, Managing Editor at Allyn and Bacon; Mary Meola, Reference Librarian at Georgian Court College; Beverly Genetta, Information Center Director at the New Jersey Vocational Education Resource Center; Cynthia A. Parker, Programmer/Analyst in the Office of Computer-Based Instruction, University of Delaware; and by no means least, Professor Robert E. Gerke, Trenton State College.

R.C.D.

PART ONE

Decision Making in Curriculum Improvement

1

Historical and Philosophical Foundations of Curriculum Decision Making

Attempts to educate children and youth in elementary and secondary schools in the United States have created at least as many questions as the education profession and the general public have been able to answer. Among those that have become perennial and pervasive are the following:

1. Who shall be educated? Is education in the United States really meant for *all* the children of *all* the people?
2. What types of educational experiences should be provided to given groups of learners? Which tasks and responsibilities are really the business of the schools? Is it possible for schools to go too far in providing educational experiences for learners? Have the schools gone far enough in offering varied experiences?
3. How much can Americans afford to spend for education? To what extent should people sacrifice to educate their own children and the children of others?
4. Are the schools as good as they used to be? What are the major virtues and defects found in schools today?
5. What shall be the organizing center of the curriculum — subject matter, learners, or what?
6. To what extent shall the curriculum be made uniform within the school district, county, state, and nation? Are there identifiable

minimum essentials to be mastered by all learners at given stages of their development?

7. How can the needs of individual learners be met? Are there feasible ways of organizing or grouping pupils to achieve individualization in teaching and learning?

8. Is improving the curriculum worth the effort? Is it not desirable to have a stable, tried and tested curriculum to utilize in educating each new generation?

During recent years, discussion and conflict about the education currently provided by elementary and secondary schools in the United States have brought all of these questions to the fore. The first question—Who shall be educated?—has probably received the least open discussion, but it has remained embedded in people's minds as they have pondered other questions. As usual, the public has been concerned about financial cost (question 3), and about both the immediate and the ultimate worth of a curriculum that is expensive because it is broad and rich (question 2). More people than ever before, perhaps, have been answering in negative terms the fourth question—Are the schools as good as they used to be? Some laypersons have tried to address matters of curriculum uniformity and the nature of minimum essentials (question 6), as well as the related matter of curriculum stability (question 8). Meanwhile the lay public remains content to let the professionals in education answer the other questions, saying, in effect, "We don't care *how* you improve the schools. Just improve them!"

THE CRY FOR EXCELLENCE

In the mid-eighties, the pressure to achieve excellence, directed particularly toward the public schools, has become intense. The years of declining scores on standardized tests, which presaged the failure of high school graduates at college and in the workplace, have brought a long-anticipated result: disappointment, frustration, and outright disgust with the schools, along with demands for change. In a society in which upward mobility is prized, the failure of a school to educate one's child "even in the fundamentals" offends the typical parent. To supplement the complaints of parents, college and university officials continue to remind the schools that the best graduation gift to youngsters is solid preparation for meeting the challenges that lie ahead.

In April 1983, the bipartisan Commission on Excellence in Education warned that the schools were endangering the United States in a "tide of mediocrity."[1] The Commission recommended that the high school curriculum include additional emphasis on the so-called new basics: English, mathematics, science, social studies, and computer science. Novel programs should highlight pupils' personal, educational, and occupational goals, as in the fine and performing arts and vocational education. In the first eight grades, pupils should gain needed background in English language development and writing, and in computational and problem-solving skills. Other elementary school subject matter should include experiences in science, the social studies, and the arts. Pupils should begin foreign language study in the elementary school and continue it for a period of four to six years.

The Commission and other national groups commented on a variety of curriculum issues, including graduation requirements, allocation of time to subject matter, foreign language teaching, textbook adoption, acquisition of study and work skills, and homework assignments. They also dealt with pupil performance and behavior, longer school days and school years, programs for special pupil populations, the nature and performance of teaching staffs, leadership and management of schools, fiscal support, and the federal role in education. Prominent national groups concerned with excellence included a twelve-member task force sponsored by the Twentieth Century Fund, which has specialized in research and policy studies, and the larger task force formed by the Education Commission of the States, a group that included fourteen governors, thirteen business leaders, and six educators.

Of the eighteen members of the Commission on Excellence in Education, only four were from the fields of elementary and secondary education. Of the twelve-member Twentieth Century Fund task force, none represented the elementary and secondary schools. Of the thirty-three-member task force of the Education Commission of the States, only six persons of varied backgrounds came from professional education.[2] These facts illuminate a circumstance that has long been acknowledged: when a crisis occurs in elementary or secondary education, most of the persons assigned to find ways of meeting it are not educators.

Signs have been appearing of movements to counter the crepe-hanging done by the national commissions. Harold Howe has referred to the schools as having a cold, rather than influenza or pneumonia. In part because of the commission reports, people's expectations of their schools have heightened. To meet these expectations, state governments and local school districts have been increasing graduation requirements and attempting to raise standards generally. In 1983, Secretary of Education Terrel Bell reported that all the states had acted to make the curriculum of elementary and secondary schools more rigorous. At that time, some educators conjectured that the low spot in quality had already been reached when the commission reports were issued.[3]

Educators have found one major encouragement in the reports issued during the eighties: the continuing preoccupation of many Americans with issues and problems of curriculum planning. Even those outside education know that every school has a curriculum, and that managing it is difficult. Usually, however, they have little notion of what the curriculum is; therefore, they cannot imagine what concrete steps might be taken to improve it.

What is a curriculum, anyway? Can it be that some of the issues discussed in the reports under noncurriculum headings are in fact curriculum issues?

THE MEANING OF CURRICULUM

Within the twentieth century, the curriculum of schools and colleges has been defined in several ways. Some people have called the curriculum the accumulated tradition of organized knowledge contained in school and college subjects. Other people have considered it to be the modes of thinking and inquiring about the phenomena of our world. Still others have called the curriculum the "experiences of the race."

More precise definitions of the curriculum emphasize (1) guided, preselected experiences to which children and youth should be exposed; (2) plans for learning; (3) ends or outcomes of being educated; and (4) systems for achieving educational production (for example, by concentrating on the attainment of behavioral objectives).[4]

Jon Schaffarzick, as Chairman of the National Institute of Education's Curriculum Development Task Force, conducted a poll of people's beliefs about what a curriculum is. The extent of uncertainty among Americans who are expected to know is reflected in the spread in meaning of the following phrases accepted by respondents in defining curriculum:

- What is taught
- How it is taught
- Teachers' materials
- Students' materials
- School experiences
- All experiences
- A combination of phrases from this list.

A Continuing Argument

As people have argued over the years about the breadth or scope of the curriculum, again and again they have become lost in arguments about the semantics of curriculum definitions. A definition commonly used during the thirties and forties was "the curriculum of a school is all the experiences that pupils have under the guidance of that school." A counter definition, generally considered to be too broad, was "a child's curriculum in a given day of his life is all that he experiences from the moment of his waking to the moment of his falling asleep."

The former definition, which survives in much of educational literature, has been modified to read "the curriculum of a school is the *engagements* that pupils have under the *auspices* of that school." The term *engagements* is thought to be more accurate than *experiences* because observers can see pupils engaging in educational activities, whereas they cannot see them experiencing the activities. Accordingly, Gordon N. Mackenzie has defined the curriculum as "the learner's engagements with various aspects of the environment which have been planned under the direction of the school."[5] More recently, the term *auspices* has been considered to be more accurate than either *guidance* or *direction* because there is a definite limit to the supervision or control that a school can exercise over the activities of the pupils who attend it. The term *auspices* suggests that the school offers general patronage or sponsorship of the experiences or engagements pupils have within it, without attempting to plan every experience.

Must, in fact, every curriculum experience or engagement be a planned experience? Many attempts at defining curriculum have foundered on this question. Pangs of conscience about what the schools should be planning in order to fulfill their distinctive mission have caused the creation of convoluted definitions like this one: The curriculum is "the planned and guided learning experiences and intended learning outcomes, formulated through the systematic reconstruction of knowledge and experience, under the auspices of the school, for the learner's continuous and willful growth in personal-social competence."[6]

The Curriculum, Both Planned and Unplanned

It is certainly true that every school has a planned, formal, acknowledged curriculum and also an unplanned, informal, or hidden one. The planned curriculum embraces content usually categorized within subjects and subject fields. The unplanned curriculum includes such varied experiences or engagements as teasing boys, pinching girls, advancing oneself inconsiderately in the cafeteria line, learning to like history, developing a prejudice against an ethnic group, protecting one's front teeth from being pushed down hard on drinking fountains, finding new ways to beat the system, and resisting pressure to smoke marijuana.[7] For children and youth today, these and similar informal experiences or engagements are sometimes the most memorable ones in their school careers. They are discussed at family dinner tables, and they obviously color parents' and other community citizens' views of the school. Every school administrator in the United States is held responsible for both the formal and the informal experiences or engagements that pupils have in his or her school.

One of the most memorable experiences of the author's years as an elementary school pupil constituted an informal lesson in physics and physiology. On a morning when the temperature hovered just above zero Fahrenheit, one of the pupils put his tongue on the steel railing leading from the ground level to the first floor entrance of the school building. Why the youngster could not remove his tongue from the railing, why water was used in the removal process, and how the tongue had been affected became discussion topics, all previously unplanned, in classrooms throughout the school building.

The Search for a Workable Definition

In the last analysis, one's definition of curriculum is a matter of one's perception. A pupil might define his curriculum as "whatever happens to me in school." A teacher might view it as "what I'm told to teach, modified by what happens as my pupils and I work together." The author perceives a workable definition to be the following: *The curriculum of a school is the formal and informal content and process by which learners gain knowledge and understanding, develop skills, and alter attitudes, appreciations, and values under the auspices of that school.* This definition includes both formal and informal aspects of schooling, what one learns (content) and how one learns (process), and products or outcomes in the forms of knowledge, understanding, skills, attitudes, appreciations, and values. The curriculum, whether planned or hidden, comes into existence under the auspices or general sponsorship of the school, which is able to legislate and control it only in part. The definition is necessarily broad.

The position taken in this book is that the curriculum, viewed in this way, is improvable, within limits, in both its formal and its informal aspects. That which is formally planned and presumably observable in the engagements of pupils can be evaluated and improved. Certain actions can also be taken to improve informal aspects of schooling. Whichever informal aspects are deemed constructive can be modified, reinforced, and supported. Pupil engagements that are considered harmful can sometimes be eliminated or reduced in number or potency. But the "hidden or unstudied curriculum," as it is now called in the literature, frequently cannot be dealt with directly. Fundamentally, the hidden curriculum is the pupil's own curriculum which he or she uses to cope with the school's bureaucratic organization and arrangements and with his or her social relationships inside the school. The hidden curriculum is substantially in the realm of unofficial opinion and unexpressed feelings, in much the same way that the hidden agenda represents an unspoken and sometimes bothersome discussion topic in a meeting of adults.

CURRICULUM CONCERNS AT
THE BEGINNING OF THE THIRD CENTURY
IN UNITED STATES HISTORY

The preceding discussion indicates that many concerns may be considered eligible for study as curriculum topics. According to standard definitions of curriculum, only traditional subject matter and established ways of treating it appear to fall within the curriculum field. In the thinking of many professionals in education, however, ways of treating subject matter have come to include the school organization within which the subject matter is taught and also the facilities and materials used in teaching it. More comprehensive and liberal definitions of curriculum admit studies of pupil attitudes, teaching practices, interpersonal relationships within the school, inservice education and development of teachers and other adults, and school staffing arrangements.

Under a broad definition of curriculum, some of the curriculum concerns in the early part of the third century in U.S. history include the following:

- To make the school a less dismal, uninspiring place in which to learn and work. To this end, alternatives to traditional education and efforts to open the school environment to make it less confining and more broadly educative are emphasized.
- To help pupils and their adult mentors make optimum use of that most valuable resource—time. Studies of pupil readiness for learning given subject matter, establishment of learning centers for study of unusual content, development of minicourses, reconsideration of pupil schedules and length of the school day and the school year, and analyses of time-on-task all attempt to optimize time usage.
- To improve teaching and learning of fundamental knowledges and skills. Decline in students' mastery of the three Rs during the seventies and early eighties has impelled a continuing search for better ways of teaching the basics of education to children whose ability to master the basics is highly variable.
- To view education comprehensively, rather than as mere schooling. Opportunities for educating children and youth are being found and utilized in the community, well beyond the confines of the school.
- To develop children's feelings, values, morals, ethics, and general citizenship behavior. (This concern is feared and deprecated by persons who oppose educating children and youth in traditional or "old-fashioned" values.) The call for affective education, as opposed

to education of the intellect exclusively, and the confusion in American society about values, morals, and ethics have opened a challenging era in the education of affect.

- To educate pupils about minority group cultures yet continue to instill in them the value of national unity. Within a context of unification, multicultural and multilingual programs sometimes help to give minority groups their due. Pupils in general are becoming more familiar with diverse cultures here and abroad.
- To make the school a more humane institution. The numbers of citizens who have been "turned off" by schools in the past provide evidence of the need to eliminate the indignities, unthinking behaviors, and even the cruelties that adults have sometimes visited upon youngsters in schools.

Some of these concerns are not new. People of earlier times in Europe and the United States faced educational issues that underlie certain of the concerns we feel most poignantly today.

During the nineteenth century, a group of related issues arose concerning the center about which learners' school experiences should be organized. Should the curriculum be adult centered or child centered? Should it consist of logically organized subject matter or, in the language of our own day, of psychologically organized subject matter? Should emphasis be placed on subject matter "set out to be learned" or on subject matter that relates closely to the interests and needs of growing learners? *These related issues are still alive today. Can you identify the relative positions of proponents of various curriculum plans on these issues?*

Prior to the nineteenth century, the assumption was generally made that subject matter should be organized logically and dispensed to children and youth under the close control and supervision of adults. Ancient and early-modern science supported this view by holding that objective reality had a logical structure that could readily be described; accordingly, the curriculum could be fixed in advance. Since the curriculum was fixed, whereas learners are by nature pliable, learners should adapt to fit the standard curriculum. *Some authors of current books and magazine articles seem to share these views.*

During the eighteenth century, these concepts were challenged by Jean Jacques Rousseau (1712–1778), who placed the nature of the child superior to the nature of the curriculum. Rousseau was succeeded in his views by Friedrich Froebel (1782–1852), who developed a curriculum centering in the nature of the child, establishing as his chief educational goal the child's "self-realization." According to Froebel, the curriculum must originate within, not outside, the learner, though the learner must draw on the culture for the substance of his or her learning. *Does this remind you of activity programs based on pupils' interests, concerns, and evident needs, and also of the "open school," which has been a more recent gesture toward educational reform?*

Somewhat later, William James (1842–1910) and Edward L. Thorndike (1874–1949) formulated a psychology of education that was used by others to support the child-centered curriculum. Soon studies of child growth and development were underway, and John Dewey was developing a curriculum that emphasized the life activities of children. Outspoken advocates of the child-centered curriculum ran into serious conflict with advocates of the adult-organized curriculum. Opponents of child centeredness accused Dewey and his supporters of providing "soft pedagogy" for pampered children. *Does this accusation sound familiar to you today?* The accusation gained strength as a consequence of certain excesses committed by teachers who came to be considered extreme progressives. Dewey himself, writing in *The Child and the Curriculum*, deprecated both the common underestimates of children's maturity and the rising sentimentality about children. But the battle between the Progressives and the Traditionalists had begun, and, though the Progressive Education Association is officially dead, the battle continues today. Much of the recent criticism of schools has centered about the issue "Shall the curriculum be set for learners by specialists in education, by specialists in subject matter fields, or by laypersons and pupils themselves?"

To deal effectively with any list of curriculum concerns, an individual planner or a group of planners needs to see what history says about earlier attempts to work with the same concerns. Where did our predecessors in planning succeed? Where did they fail? What signals and cues should we watch for in the planning process?

One of the characteristics of failed curriculum plans and programs of recent decades has been a disregard of history. An ahistorical attitude can lead planners to imagine that they have invented "the curriculum wheel."

An overview of historical events that have affected and should continue to affect curriculum planning appears in a later section of this chapter.

ACTIVITY 1-1
Identifying Curriculum Concerns
in One's Own Environment

List the names of three persons from each of the following four categories who have shown interest in the elementary and secondary schools in your community: teachers, pupils, administrators, and parents. Interview the twelve people about their curriculum concerns. Compare what they say. Tabulate the concerns they express, and then discuss your findings with your class or group.

ACTIVITY 1-2
Recognizing Well-Known People and Movements
in the Curriculum Field

Following are the names of some individuals who have influenced the movement toward curriculum improvement in the United States. How many do you recognize?

John Dewey	Robert J. Havighurst
W. W. Charters	James B. Conant
Franklin Bobbitt	Benjamin Bloom
Ralph Tyler	George S. Counts
William H. Kilpatrick	Jerome Bruner
Hollis Caswell	Jean Piaget

What was the major contribution of each of the ones you recognize?

Some educational leaders produced ideas that have had at least an indirect effect on curriculum reform. In this connection, what idea does each of the following names suggest to you?

Abraham Flexner	William H. McGuffey
Lewis Terman	B. F. Skinner
Edward L. Thorndike	James S. Coleman

THE UNDERPINNINGS: CURRICULUM CHANGE IN EARLY AMERICA

In social and educational movements, patterns of progress are often set by early events. During the initial years of curriculum reform in the United States, change occurred slowly, but it frequently proved to be deep moving and enduring.[8] The basic curriculum was developed by English-speaking peoples who settled along the Atlantic seaboard. When the British established colonies in America between 1607 and 1733, they transplanted three major types of education from Europe: the church state type, found in New England; the parochial school type, established in Catholic Maryland and Protestant Pennsylvania; and both private and charity education, commonplace in certain southern colonies, notably in Virginia. Religion dominated all three types but in quite different ways. In New England, church and state served a common purpose: to prepare a ministry capable of propagating the true faith and to educate laypersons in reading and interpreting the Bible, the sure foundation of the faith. In the middle colonies, the prevailing branches of Christianity, whether Protestant or Catholic, founded their own schools to educate children in religion and the fundamentals of literacy. In the South, those who, like Washington, had sufficient means sent their children to private schools oriented to the classics and religion, and those who lacked means shared some prospect of placing their children in charity schools to be trained for apprenticeships. Education everywhere in the colonies was designed chiefly for boys, and the chief method of learning was memorization. The curriculum for children of the privileged was heavy in intellectual studies. Practical and artistic subjects, which were said to "educate the senses," were considered suitable for training the servant class and entertaining young ladies who, because of their sex, could not then realistically aspire to leadership roles. Boys of the upper classes obtained their basic education in dame schools, or schools of reading and writing, and their secondary education in the Latin grammar school, a New England institution that had its counterpart in the other colonies. Here, Latin, Greek, the catechism, Bible, and arithmetic were the chief subjects.

Evident Need for Change

During the mid-eighteenth century, political, economic, and social changes were occurring rapidly enough to bring about at least a minor transformation of the curriculum. Commerce and trade were increasing, and students had not been prepared to engage in them. People were moving away from their original settlements, pioneer life on the frontier was beginning, urban growth was flourishing, and religion was becoming a less powerful force in society. The educational system responded by establishing district schools instead of town schools, by combining reading and writing schools into a new unit called "the school of the three Rs," and by establishing English grammar schools and academies to replace the inflexible Latin grammar school. Meanwhile, private tutors were teaching vocational subjects such as navigation, surveying, and bookkeeping. Franklin's Academy developed a new concept of schooling, extending the traditional list of subjects to include modern foreign languages and natural science, the content of which was deemed useful in educating enlightened men of affairs.

The post-Revolutionary period brought several developments that influenced anew the curricula of American schools. The Ordinance of 1785 set aside land for schools in each township in the new West, and as people moved into the territories they brought with them a dominant pattern of schooling, chiefly that of the New England district school, thus providing the basis for eventual establishment of the free public school. The 1820s and the 1830s were a time of political consciousness, when U.S. statesmen became convinced that children should be educated to love their country and to perpetuate its ideals. In order for education to reach enough children to have a favorable effect on national welfare, the masses would have to be educated. Finally, though many statesmen were espousing the principle without comprehending its full meaning, the people of a democracy were seen as having a right to education, that they might prepare themselves to their own personal advantage.

These startling ideas, so foreign to the European heritage of education for the privileged only, eventually caused curriculum reform. Horace Mann, Henry Barnard, and others spearheaded the drive toward establishment of common, tax-supported schools in which the curriculum would theoretically accommodate the abilities and interests of all learners. By 1860, arithmetic, algebra, geometry, ancient history, geography, and English grammar were being accepted by the colleges as subjects that partially fulfilled entrance requirements. The curriculum for girls, who were now being admitted much more freely to schooling, was differentiated to include music, painting, and dancing. Academies prepared, in practical subjects, those pupils who would not go to college; then these academies began to give way to public high schools.

A Unique System of Education

By the mid-nineteenth century, at least some Americans had an educational ladder on which they could climb from primary education to the university. By 1860, New England had public elementary schools which taught, at primary grade level, reading, spelling, writing, and arithmetic; at intermediate grade level, reading, arithmetic, geography, spelling, writing, and grammar; and in the "grammar school," advanced reading, advanced arithmetic, elementary algebra, spelling, word analysis, penmanship, grammar, composition, declamation, geography, United States history, and general history. (The antiquated label grammar schools is still used for elementary schools in many U.S. communities.)

The high school program in New England in 1860 included these subjects: United States history, ancient history, natural philosophy (elements of chemistry and botany), Latin, advanced algebra, geometry, bookkeeping, and surveying. Curriculum development, by which changes in society were reflected in the addition of school subjects, was underway.

A CATALOG OF EVENTS FROM 1860 TO THE PRESENT

From the 1860s to the early 1980s, a steady progression of incidents affected the curriculum of U.S. elementary and secondary schools. The events are catalogued in Table 1-1.

TABLE 1-1

PERIOD OR DATE	EVENT
1860 to 1890	A continuing struggle for establishment of free public schools was in process. The arrival of immigrants and the doubling of the population created demands for new and broadened types of schooling.
	Technical and commercial high schools were organized separately from academic high schools. Newly established normal schools assumed responsibility from the academies for preparing teachers and continued to transform schoolkeeping into schoolteaching. Manual training, which had originated in the Scandinavian countries, was introduced widely in both elementary and secondary schools.
	The elementary school curriculum broadened and became somewhat less dedicated to rote memorization. The oral instruction and object teaching proposed by Pestalozzi took root in the United States. Oral language, mental arithmetic, and teaching by demonstration resulted. The content of high school subjects was broadened to include the arithmetic of business, the English of business, American literature, general science, and family care.
	Educational experiments included those of Francis Parker in breaking down the barriers among subjects; of Batavia, New York, in providing remedial instruction; and of Santa Barbara, California, in preparing parallel courses of study.
1862 and 1890	The first and second Morrill Acts arranged for development of and aid to land-grant colleges, which accepted, in admitting their students, high school subjects that had previously been considered inferior to respected academic subjects.
1873	The first public school kindergarten was opened in St. Louis.
1874	The famous *Kalamazoo* case legalized establishment of high schools at public expense.
1880	The first manual training high school was opened (St. Louis).
1886	The first cooking and sewing high school was established (Toledo).
1890 to 1920	Herbart's view of apperception, formulated into his famous five steps (preparation, presentation, comparison and abstraction, generalization, and application), encouraged correlation of subject matter, especially in the elementary schools.
	Edward L. Thorndike and Charles Judd began studying the curriculum quantitatively and scientifically as they opened an era of mental measurement.

(cont.)

TABLE 1-1 (cont.)

PERIOD OR DATE	EVENT
	The junior high school was invented; vocational education received federal aid; and a psychology of individual differences began to develop. Also, the Progressive Movement was given its initial impetus; faculty psychology was seriously attacked; and the Gestaltist viewpoint grew up beside connectionism.
1893	The Committee of Ten on Secondary School Studies asserted that all subjects taught equally well for equal periods of time had equal educational value and that four programs of study might well be developed in high schools: the Classical, the Scientific, the Modern Language, and the English.
1895	The Committee of Fifteen on Elementary Education urged concentration and correlation of subjects taught in the elementary schools.
1896	John Dewey founded his Laboratory School at the University of Chicago, a school that had special concern for the interests and purposes of learners.
1899	The Committee on College Entrance Requirements approved "restricted election" of subjects by high school pupils, early completion of the high school program by gifted pupils, acceptance of a year's work in any subject as counting toward college entrance, and extension of the high school program to six years. The report of this committee marked the beginning of the unit system, which has dominated secondary education.
1911	The Committee on the Economy of Time in Education advocated child centeredness in learning. Partly as a consequence of the work of this committee, art, music, handicrafts, and health education became subjects in the elementary and secondary schools.
1918	The Committee on the Reorganization of Secondary Education enunciated the famous Seven Cardinal Principles of Secondary Education, thereby stating objectives that received wide though nominal acceptance.
The 1920s and 1930s	The 1920s constituted a decade during which particular attention was given to the curriculum of the elementary school, whereas in the 1930s special attention was given to the secondary school. The 1920s heralded a long era of scientific studies in education, including immediate emphasis on testing and measurement. Curriculum specialists began asking that the curriculum be made relevant to the problems and activities of contemporary life. Job analysis and career studies stemmed in part from the impact of World War I's training programs. John Dewey's Labora-

TABLE 1-1 (cont.)

PERIOD OR DATE	EVENT
	tory School at the University of Chicago continued to attract attention as an innovation in education. However, the curriculum in nearly all U.S. schools continued to be based on restricted subject matter rather than on studies either of children's learning potential or of the institutions in U.S. society.
	During the early 1930s, an increase in secondary school population and a reinforced realization that the secondary school curriculum was limited and restrictive brought new attention to the secondary schools. The Eight Year Study was an exciting if little heeded investigation into the effects of loosening the secondary school curriculum. Teachers in both elementary and secondary schools were beginning to realize that they had almost no curriculum documents on which to rely except textbooks, which might be satisfactory for skill development and for imparting basic knowledge but were deficient in preparing children for changes in attitudes, cultivation of appreciations, and the making of critical judgments.
	Several plans for reorganizing teaching and learning appeared: the project method, the Dalton Plan, the Winnetka Plan, the unit method, ability grouping, and the activity program.
The 1940s and 1950s	Recovery of the American people from the Great Depression helped to create confidence that education necessarily led to the good life. Little money was spent for curriculum study, as funds were expended for school building construction, pupil transportation, bonding and insurance costs, and attorneys' fees. The public was becoming disenchanted with education as it existed and was pushing the schools to do better. Ways of raising pupil interest levels and providing special education for the gifted proved attractive to parents and therefore became important themes for curriculum study. Work experience consumed a portion of the school day of some pupils who did not plan to attend college. Additional attention was being given to audiovisual instruction, guidance programs, functional reading, and increasing community involvement in school affairs.
	During the early 1950s, the schools were housing 33 percent more pupils and 50 percent more staff than they had a generation or so earlier. The 1950s became a time of ferment: McCarthyism was rampant, a redefinition of morality was beginning to occur, the family as an institution was allegedly declining, and complaints about alleged mathematical and scientific illiteracy in the general population were growing. The schools were ripe for the

TABLE 1-1 (cont.)

PERIOD OR DATE	EVENT
	criticisms of their programs that followed the blast-off of Sputnik I in October 1957. Shortcuts to learning were being sought as a means of meeting criticism; thus, teaching machines and simple applications of computerization moved into prominence. Part of that which came to be called "curriculum reform" was a variant of classic efforts at reform, emphasizing indirect ways of changing programs through adding facilities and materials and altering organizational plans.
The 1960s	During the 1960s, updating of subject matter under the guidance of scholars in subject fields dictated the selection of experiences for pupils. The quantity of subject matter had grown so rapidly that the teacher could no longer "cover" any subject.
	Money began to pour into curriculum study through the National Defense Education Act, the National Science Foundation, and private, tax-exempt foundations. While parents were calling for the schools to provide quality education by improving cognitive learning, the schools were continuing to serve multiple purposes, including the oft-criticized "social adjustment" of pupils. Subject matter projects grew in number until the funds to support them began to flow in other directions.
	The reforms that had taken place by this time had occurred chiefly in a minority of high schools and a few elementary schools, some of which had "toughened" learning and thereby made pupil transition into traditional college curricula somewhat easier.
	Meanwhile, organizational plans for rearranging the uses of pupil time were appearing. There was increasing call for humanization of schools, for improved methods of individualizing instruction, and for nongrading (ungrading) to remove another lockstep impeding children's development. Particular attention was being given urban education. Teacher militancy was on the ascendancy, the unions now having determined that the curriculum, like salaries and working conditions, was negotiable. In a number of communities, bond issues and annual school district budgets were not approved. The 1960s saw the beginning of the movement to make the school one of the media for social change. Desegregation had become a desire and a mandate. The means for achieving it, such as the busing of pupils, became an issue. The Civil Rights Act of 1964, followed by James S. Coleman's report on equality of educational opportunity, provided a clear rationale for school desegregation. Court decisions

TABLE 1-1 (cont.)

PERIOD OR DATE	EVENT

about prayer and Bible reading in the schools caused teachers to shy away from traditional ways of educating children in values. Multicultural education was being attempted.

The 1970s
Several significant trends developed during the 1970s. Decreased school population, accompanied by money shortages in many communities, caused a diminution of school staffs and a reduction in total expenditures for education. Furthermore, the nature of expenditures began to change. The purposes of schools as unique institutions within the entire context of education were reexamined. Objectives of teaching and learning received new attention, and performance criteria and other standards of accountability were sought and applied. Very early childhood education was deemed to deserve particular attention because of the ability of young children to profit from certain kinds of educational experiences.

Means were gradually being found for making affective and psychomotor education directly available to pupils. Mass or whole-group education was being criticized in view of the presumed virtues of several modes of individualizing teaching and learning. The isolation of special groups of children handicapped physically, mentally, and emotionally was being replaced with the mixing and mingling of handicapped children with "normal" ones under the system known as mainstreaming, or putting handicapped pupils back into the mainstream of classroom learning.

More sophisticated educational planning, using new technology and improved planning procedures, was just over the horizon. It was thought that, without destroying the school as an acknowledged, necessary institution, improved planning would help to alter its purposes and streamline its efforts. Interestingly, schools found themselves simultaneously in the process of "loosening" their programs of instruction in the open school during a revival of progressivism and tightening their programs in response to data from National Assessment, the College Entrance Examination Board, and state-wide testing, as well as to adverse publicity. Sometimes the loosening related to quests for more humane education, while some of the tightening was accomplished by trying systems approaches to solving educational problems. Finally, moral and ethical education was being restudied and implemented in novel ways.

(cont.)

TABLE 1-1 (cont.)

PERIOD OR DATE	EVENT
The 1980s	During the first half of the 1980s, a dominant trend has been toward conservatism in elementary and secondary education. Although differing and sometimes competing groups have proposed additional subject matter content for the schools (for example, human rights education, career education, death education, consumer studies, new versions of sex education, drug education, and alcohol education), the greatest pressure has been exerted by advocates of better education in the basics. One of the newer basic learnings has consisted of the development of computer skills.
	Falling Scholastic Aptitude Test scores and continuing poor performance by pupils in state-sponsored tests and in college have contributed to a demand for more rigorous teaching of the three Rs. In response, teachers have increased their efforts, through provision of drill and helpful insights, to improve pupils' reading, writing, and arithmetic skills. Economic recession has caused serious retrenchment in school budgets. Teachers have been "riffed" (reduced in force) as a natural consequence of the decline in pupil population and the prevailing fiscal climate. Teacher unions have lost some of their power and influence. Nationally known educational leaders whose efforts could have made a difference in school policies, as they did in former times, seem to have become fewer and less influential.
	The curriculum itself has been affected by rapid turnover of top school administrators; by a tendency to permit the results of minimum skills testing to determine the curriculum; by an all-too-frequent lack of curriculum balance; and by a drift toward curriculum chaos in too many school systems. Teachers, necessarily in the forefront of curriculum maintenance and change, have become preoccupied with the antics of pupil populations that are sometimes out of control and with the maladies of society, such as lowered moral standards and misuse of drugs.
	If the curriculum has become fragmented by these influences, it has received, on the affirmative side, the challenging task of making constructive use of high technology, such as the computer. For high technology to be used intelligently it must be placed within a framework that Harry Broudy calls "the symbolics of information," and within curriculum patterns that help young people learn more about the physical sciences, the universe, and human institutions and culture. As knowledge increases, more intelligent curriculum planning is needed in order to make sense of innovations in technology.

A DIGEST OF TRENDS IN THE EVOLUTION
OF THE CURRICULUM

Running through the whole panorama of U.S. education from colonial times to the present are several trends in the evolution of the curriculum:

- Ideas have often been developed in private schools and then adopted by public schools.
- Schools and school systems everywhere have frankly copied plans, procedures, and curriculum content from other schools and school systems.
- New institutions, such as the early academy, the junior high school, and the much more recent middle school, have been established to satisfy unmet needs. Alternative schools have increased in number and changed in nature as new alternatives have been sought.
- Educational principles, such as that of schooling for everyone, have been adopted in substance and modified in detail whenever they have struck a popular chord. The goal of educating all the children of all the people has been looked at critically from time to time.
- Experimentation has occurred, but it has usually been informal, and its results have remained largely untested.
- National committees have determined general objectives, policies, and programs.
- Psychological and social theories and revelations have turned the efforts of curriculum planners in new directions.
- U.S. educators have been susceptible to the use of the plans, some of them delusive, for making the difficult processes of teaching and learning easier.
- Important educational ideas that have been based on the soundest evidence have been adopted very slowly· by practitioners.
- The schools, as an instrument of American society, have been subjected to numerous public pressures, the nature of which tends to change from generation to generation, depending in part on the interests and concerns of individual groups within the society.
- Parents have become involved in schools in increasingly varied ways.
- A rising tide of immigration, chiefly Spanish and Southeast Asian in background, has altered the focus of schooling in some of our cities and rural areas.

THE EVOLVING PROCESS OF
CURRICULUM IMPROVEMENT

In preceding portions of the chapter, some of the events that have affected the curriculum during centuries of U.S. history have been noted. The present section deals with history of the *process* of curriculum improvement, a history that covers a much shorter period of time. Though curriculum improvement has obviously been occurring for generations, conscious efforts to make the process more effective have been expended only during the past half century.

The history of curriculum planning can scarcely be written in sequential order. For one thing, it has too little content to form a valid sequence. Furthermore, many of the older procedures considered largely unprofitable in sophisticated circles today are still being utilized in numerous schools of the nation. Contrariwise, the abler curriculum planners were using, during the 1920s, some of the procedures now considered by curriculum specialists to be completely acceptable. Thus, in the process of curriculum improvement, a very recent field of inquiry, there can be no clean chronological break between the antiquated and the novel, the formerly fashionable and the presently fashionable.

The process of curriculum improvement was made manifest only when it was first reported in the literature. Prior to 1920, practically nothing concerning this process was written in professional journals. A curriculum was considered by many persons to be the courses of study and other written materials that a given school system or individual school produced. Customarily, the superintendent of schools assembled several persons who were believed to be competent "to write the curriculum." In the larger school systems during the 1920s, committees of representative teachers met with one or more assistant superintendents and directors of subjects to prepare courses of study, which were then submitted to the system's board of superintendents for approval and subsequently to the board of education for authority to print them as school documents.[9] Participating teachers were selected on the basis of teaching ability, interest in curriculum work, college preparation, and ability to write.[10]

An Established Planning Process

The actual authority for curriculum planning centered strongly in superintendents and their immediate staffs, with teachers, parents, and pupils taking minor parts. Courses of study contained, from the teacher's viewpoint, precise "ground to be covered," and supervisors urged teachers to cover this ground in quantity and sequence. Most administrators in the cities reported that their programs of improvement were continuous, though they centered upon only a few recurrent problems in "revising subject matter."[11] One, two, or three subject matter areas were revised at a given time, and revision was "completed" within a few months, to be resumed by rearranging the same subject matter a few years later.

Generally, teachers were not asked what instructional problems needed attention. Decisions of this sort were made by top administrators, who tended to think of curriculum improvement as being a rewriting of courses of study and addition or elimination of subjects and course offerings. Curriculum decisions were made on the basis of individual opinion and consensus of groups, inasmuch as experimentation, research, and evaluation were relatively unknown.[12]

Newer Trends in Curriculum Planning

The last half century has brought into being several discernible trends in the process of curriculum improvement. The commonly accepted definition of the curriculum has changed from "content of courses of study and lists of subjects and courses" to "all the experiences that are offered to learners under the auspices or direction of the school." The change to a broader definition has magnified the task of curriculum improvement because *all* the experiences of learners over which the school has control may now be eligible for improvement. These experiences may occur in school buses, cafeterias, and corridors, as well as in classrooms and auditoriums. The broad definition suggested earlier in this chapter includes the formal and informal content and process by which learners gain knowledge and understanding, develop skills, and alter attitudes, appreciations, and values.

Furthermore, if pupils' experiences are to improve, teachers must likewise have new and improved experiences, since it is axiomatic that the blind cannot be expected to lead the blind. Curriculum improvement is, according to the broadened view, more than alteration or rearrangement of pupil experiences according to a simple, preconceived plan; it involves the reeducation of teachers through individualized inservice education and constructive supervision. Finally, the new conception of curriculum improvement requires that teachers *of* teachers—supervisors and administrators—be reeducated so that they may learn to identify teachers' needs and desirable ways of satisfying those needs.

An enlarged definition of curriculum improvement, application of newer findings in psychology and sociology to the process of improvement, and increased experience in attempting to improve school programs have opened the whole educational enterprise to these trends:

- Changes are being planned both in the environments within which people operate and in the individuals who occupy these environments. Changing an environment requires setting or resetting the stage for learning, and helping individuals change themselves requires deep understanding of the dynamics of human behavior. Both also demand a thorough knowledge of the best practice in education.

- Curriculum planning is being regarded as a necessary, continuing activity. There can be only incidental improvement unless we plan for it. Moreover, if teachers are not active in planning their own teaching-learning programs, ill-informed persons may soon do the planning for them.
- Today there is more and more variation in the kinds of activities that curriculum planning encompasses. These activities range from the planning of experimental projects to selection of teaching materials, to development of teaching units, to formation of study groups, to plotting of guidelines to action, and so on.
- Many activities now occur at the same time, a far cry from the one, two, or three concurrent activities of the 1920s. The number of activities, which include the large projects and the small, is determined chiefly by the energies and talents of school staffs.
- Improvement is now commonly considered to occur on a broken front. This means that "modifications in practice have small beginnings with a few teachers taking the lead in the difficult process of testing new ideas. As new practices are demonstrated to be feasible, more teachers take over their use. Thus, change in the actual curriculum is represented by a jagged line of emerging practice in response to new ideas and needs."[13]
- Curriculum planners are now demonstrating need for renewed concern about the objectives of education. Many curriculum ideas, new and old, need to be assessed in light of their contribution to achievement of accepted objectives of the school.
- Teachers are being involved in curriculum study in various ways. Some teachers contribute helpfully to group discussion; others organize programs successfully; others write and edit materials well; and still others succeed in experimentation, tryout, and evaluation. All teachers make decisions about the curriculum within their classrooms. But the present expectation of curriculum leaders is usually that teachers will work additionally in group planning and that they will involve themselves at differing levels and to differing degrees in the improvment tasks the school undertakes.
- Whereas pupils were once involved very little in curriculum planning, they are now consulted at least informally in classrooms and school activities as well as in certain minor matters of curriculum design. The learners, though they are neither experts nor professionals, sometimes provide significant clues about actions to be taken.
- Involvement of laypersons has passed through stages that began with minimal involvement and that continued with random, unplanned uses of the talents of community members. Laypersons who have been utilized beyond their depth have sometimes revolted or have created disturbances by constituting themselves rivals to boards of education

and professional staffs. Consequently, curriculum leaders have come to realize that the purposes of education and certain broad, general policy matters are suitable subjects for public discussion and that laypersons can sometimes be helpful in other direct ways, but that clear distinctions must be made between matters of lay concern and matters of professional concern.[14]

- Curriculum planning is not thought of as a series of distinct and fixed steps. No single pattern, beginning, for instance, with stating objectives, will suffice in solving all curriculum problems. The dynamics of given school situations and the resources provided by interdisciplinary study and practical experience in curriculum planning determine the ways in which problems should be attacked.

- Curriculum materials, which formed a major starting point of activity in the 1920s, are still widely produced and used. However, the course of study has given way to the less prescriptive course guide. Aids for teachers include manuals accompanying textbooks, resource units, and audiovisual lists. The focus during recent educational history has been increasingly on helping competent professional persons rather than on further limiting teachers' opportunities to make decisions. However, during the late 1960s, many teachers interpreted the insistence of school administrators on curriculum innovation and the availability of materials produced by national curriculum projects as constituting a limitation of their power to make certain fundamental curriculum decisions. Their power has scarcely been enhanced by the development of systems, programming, and packaging during the 1970s.

- The heritage of experience described in this chapter suggests that many of the important developments in the curriculum field have occurred before the past decade. For this reason, many of the references appearing in the footnotes of the chapters to follow bear dates from the 1930s to the early 1960s.

Obvious Ways to Improve Planning

Every effort at improvement can itself be improved. Without question, curriculum planning could be aided by increased and regularized expenditure of funds. Too often, the curriculum improvement process has crawled along in a state of dangerous undernourishment. Money can buy support, time, and technical aid.

Of course, effective planning requires more than money. Responsibilities for planning should be distributed according to extant levels of school government, especially state, central office, and local school levels. The responsibilities that belong to the state are quite different from those that belong to the individual school district.

Clearly, if teachers are to share and promote the goals established during planning, they must be involved in the planning operation. The planners should attend to pressing curriculum problems first, before they spend time on problems that seem much less important to teachers and other practitioners.[15]

Behind any comprehensive planning operation there lies a theory of the curriculum. One theory may serve to make the proposed curriculum rational by suggesting that the planners state aims, content, and approaches. Another theory may concentrate on procedures to be used in building the proposed curriculum. Still another may guide the planners in thinking about curriculum planning as an important educational activity—that is, about the phenomenon of curriculum development itself.[16] Some theorists have rejected the rational approach that dominated much of earlier plannning, advocating instead an open approach in which alternatives in content and method are valued. Whatever theory is accepted and followed, an important factor in the planning process is the presence of careful thinking as the predecessor of action.

ACTIVITY 1-3
Narrating the Curriculum History of One's Own School System

Every school system or school district has a curriculum history of its own. By searching school system documents and by interviewing the older administrators, identify several events that have dominated curriculum history in your school district. Determine how these events relate to the timing of developments on the national scene, as indicated in the preceding pages of history. Compare your findings with those of fellow students who have identified events in the curriculum history of their districts.

TWO DIFFERING PHILOSOPHICAL FOUNDATIONS OF THE CURRICULUM

Historical events are often direct consequences of what people believe or, in a formal sense, of their philosophical positions. Applying labels to philosophical positions sometimes proves dangerous. Nevertheless, two major positions bearing definitive labels appear in the sweep of historical data and interpretations in the preceding sections of this chapter. They are the Traditionalist position and the Progressivist position. (Note that the term Progressivist, though capitalized here, is not used to imply membership in the historic Progressive Education Association. The original progressives in education called themselves Essentialists or Fundamentalists.)

Persons who have held or now hold these two positions support differing viewpoints and practices in professional education relative to the aims of education in elementary and secondary schools, the issue of authority vs. freedom in the schools, and the uses of subject matter in schooling. Of course, the Traditionalist is not invariably a Traditionalist, nor is the Progressivist invariably a Progressivist, in responding to given ideas, issues, and problems, just as Republicans do not always react like Republicans, or Democrats like Democrats.

Among the Traditionalists are believers in the "eternal verities" of knowledge and wisdom as enunciated by outstanding men and women of the past. The Traditionalists also include persons who hold that a fixed or standard curriculum meets the needs of children and youth regardless of temporal or geographic considerations.

Among the Progressivists are Reconstructionists who would remake the curriculum and the world according to their own designs. A newly prominent group of Progressivists is made up of persons who pride themselves on their ability to provide innovation in education.

Although individual Traditionalists and Progressivists hold varied views concerning the following four typical aims of American education, the issue of authority vs. freedom, and the uses of subject matter, here are the customary positions of the Traditionalists and Progressivists.

The Aims of Education

AIM ONE: TO DEVELOP LEARNERS INTELLECTUALLY

Traditionalists	*Progressivists*
Certain subjects "train the mind" better than other subjects.	All subjects are potential contributors to intellectual development.
The liberal arts and sciences have intrinsic worth in disciplining the mind and building intellectual power.	Content selected carefully from both the liberal arts and sciences and the practical arts can help in developing effectively functioning human beings.
Pupils in school "learn with their heads." The task of education is to "educate heads."	Pupils learn with their heads, their hearts, and their hands. Education of the "whole child" is the only valid kind of education.
Much desirable education is to be had by absorbing ready-made experience as reported by the written and the spoken word.	Experience that is really worthwhile involves acting, acquiring meaning, and solving real problems.
Education may be conceived of as instruction.	Education may be conceived of as creative self-learning.

AIM TWO: TO DEVELOP LEARNERS AS FUNCTIONING CITIZENS

Traditionalists

Intellectual development makes for good citizenship.

Knowledge and discipline prepare pupils to exercise freedom.

Progressivists

Development of good morals and useful skills is the key to preparing functioning citizens.

Direct experiences in democratic living prepare pupils to exercise freedom.

AIM THREE: TO DEVELOP LEARNERS AS INDIVIDUALS IN OUR SOCIETY

Traditionalists

Learners may profitably follow modes of learning that have succeeded in the past within carefully prepared curricula.

Homogeneous grouping, tracking, and special grouping of pupils help learners to develop high levels of competence.

Individuals should be educated rigorously to accept their roles in society and to cooperate with others in performing common societal roles.

Progressivists

Learners should be invited and expected to develop their own learning modes within a flexible curriculum.

Practices that segregate learners on the basis of what may be false assumptions are undemocratic and un-American.

Individuals should be educated to nonconformity, individuality, creativeness, and development of their potential.

AIM FOUR: TO DEVELOP LEARNERS AS ACTUAL OR POTENTIAL WORKERS

Traditionalists

Learners who have acquired necessary knowledge and discipline in liberal studies may then profitably devote time to learning work skills.

Progressivists

Learners should develop abstractions and skills in both liberal and vocational studies. The vocational aspects of education should not be deferred or denigrated.

The Issue of Authority vs. Freedom

Traditionalists

Progressivists

Education involves direction, redirection, control, and restraint. Therefore it should emphasize use of authority.

Real education involves experiencing freedom from imposed authority, with full opportunity to pursue one's interests and to develop one's own potential.

Inasmuch as some knowledge and attitudes are fixed and absolute, pupils may be indoctrinated safely and correctly with this knowledge and these attitudes.

Pupils should be free to pursue knowledge and develop attitudes on the basis of observable data and the tests they apply to their knowledge and attitudes.

Human beings should learn to accept and to manage the environments in which they find themselves.

Human beings should learn to modify the environments in which they find themselves.

The Uses of Subject Matter

Traditionalists

Progressivists

Values are fixed, absolute, and objective, inhering in the things being valued.

Values are relative, subjective, and changeable, inhering in the circumstances in which they appear.

What is learned may be worthy because it is inherently good.

What is learned may be worthy because it is good for something.

Subject matter is important in itself.

Subject matter is important as a medium for teaching skills, intellectual processes, attitudes, and appreciations.

Subject matter should be taught mainly for deferred use.

Subject matter should be taught mainly for immediate use.

Because all people are basically the same, they should have basically the same curriculum.

Because individuals differ markedly from one another, they require widely differentiated curricula.

In summary, educators have long been divided into these two major groups, both of which desire for learners improved minds, constructive citizenship behaviors, and other advantages. Traditionalists would achieve desirable ends for learners by filling the human mind with information from a wealth of precious sources in the ancient and modern world. Progressivists would encourage learners to take from accumulated human knowledge the data they can use in creating learnings that serve their own purposes. Whereas Traditionalists believe in the superiority of liberal studies, Progressivists consider the liberal and the practical arts to have equal value, particularly when both of them open prospects for easy applicability. Traditionalists would differentiate curricula especially to cultivate an intellectual elite, whereas Progressivists favor widely differentiated curricula to develop the uniqueness of each human being regardless of his or her seeming lack of promise and potential. Traditionalists hold that one must accept the world as it is and then conform to it. Progressivists believe they can remake the world into an environment that approaches ideal conditions.

Conflict among curriculum planners occurs when persons who hold positions along a continuum of Traditionalist beliefs encounter persons with a range of Progressivist persuasions. Sometimes the conflict becomes so intense that curriculum study grinds to a halt. More often, perhaps, all differences except the most pronounced ones can be submerged temporarily in deference to the demands of an immediate task. Teachers and administrators who are clearly divided in philosophy, however, can seldom work together in close proximity for long periods of time.

SCHOOLS OF PHILOSOPHICAL THOUGHT AFFECTING THE CURRICULUM

The importance of philosophy in determining curriculum trends and decisions has been expressed by L. Thomas Hopkins:

> Philosophy has entered into every important decision that has ever been made about curriculum and teaching in the past and will continue to be the basis of every important decision in the future. . . . When a state office of education suggests a pupil-teacher time schedule, this is based upon philosophy, either hidden or consciously formulated. When a course of study is prepared in advance in a school system by a selected group of teachers, this represents philosophy because a course of action was selected from many choices involving different values. When high school teachers assign to pupils more homework for an evening than any one of them could possibly do satisfactorily in six hours, they are acting on philosophy although they are certainly not aware of its effects. When a teacher in an elementary school tells a child to put away his geography and study his arithmetic she is acting on philosophy for she has made a choice of values. If she had allowed the child to make the choice

she would have been operating under a different set of beliefs. . . . When teachers shift subject matter from one grade to another, they act on philosophy. When measurements experts interpret their test results to a group of teachers, they act upon philosophy, for the facts have meaning only within some basic assumptions. There is rarely a moment in a school day when a teacher is not confronted with occasions where philosophy is a vital part of action. An inventory of situations where philosophy was not used in curriculum and teaching would lead to a pile of chaff thrown out of educative experiences.[17]

Hopkins's statement reminds us that we cannot be content with the simplistic black-and-white view of educational philosophy that the conflict between Traditionalists and Progressivists suggests.

Philosophy has the multifaceted effect of helping us to (1) indicate in general what we mean, (2) make what we mean more specific and definite, and (3) develop what we mean into a useful construct. People in curriculum planning groups usually develop more comprehensive, and often clearer, meanings than individual curriculum workers. As they discuss curriculum philosophy, group members tend to become helpfully critical of their original purposes. They deal in the meanings of words, a feature of philosophy-making that parents and other laypersons often understand better than educators think they do.[18]

To refine and clarify the range of philosophical viewpoints that have influenced curriculum making, we need to look at general categories under which viewpoints can be classified. These categories include the distinctive beliefs of the Perennialists, the Idealists, the Realists, the Pragmatists, and the Reconstructionists, as well as the less certain beliefs of the Existentialists. In terms of public or private schools that might be imagined to operate according to these beliefs, educational practice in each school might be described as follows.

The School of the Perennialists

The School of the Perennialists, which holds that the cement of education is the common nature of man, wants to cultivate reason and otherwise develop children's intellectual powers. It considers the ends of education to be absolute and universal, for truth itself is absolute and universal. The liberal arts and sciences, the "Great Books," the "eternal verities" drawn from human rather than divine wisdom, and classical sources in general are fountains of truth.

The School of the Perennialists teaches subjects in their customary separate form: history as history, geography as geography, economics as economics, rather than in the combined form called social studies. Similarly, chemistry is taught as chemistry, biology as biology, and physics as physics, rather than in the combination known as general science. The teachers and patrons of this school are sure that some subject matter is too trivial to be included in the curriculum. Only subject matter that is alleged to be hard to learn is admissible. Education in the areas of feelings and emotions and of body movement is not to be classed with education to improve memory and thinking. Because the ends of education are necessarily absolute, the curriculum that serves these ends can be fixed. The children who attend the School of the Perennialists must like to study and must strive hard to be able, effective students. Ability to read the classics and other difficult materials is, of course, an absolute essential for these students.

EXAMPLE

An actual public elementary school that, in general, follows the philosophy of the Perennialists has eliminated all the "extras and frills" it can. These alleged nonessentials include drawing, dancing, and instrumental music. The principal has done everything she can think of to strengthen the teaching of the three Rs by nearly doubling the time spent on this "solid" subject matter, by forming small groups of pupils for intensive study, by extending efforts at tutoring, and by establishing prize contests and an award system for gaining proficiency in oral reading, written composition, penmanship, mental arithmetic, and spelling. She and the faculty are studying the curriculum literature of the past, including research data from the first half of the century, to discover practices that are fundamental to cognitive development, and also safe in the view of the school's more conservative patrons.

The School of the Idealists

Teachers in the School of the Idealists believe that reality exists only as it is experienced. Learning is to be pursued to benefit humanity, rather than merely to achieve self-aggrandizement. Because truth is the same today as it was yesterday, teachers are to serve as models of truth and other abiding virtues. They are to administer discipline, knowing that although interest and self-direction are important in the learning process, they need reinforcing with discipline, especially in the earlier stages of learning.

Learning, say the Idealists, is in the last analysis the realization of goodness and truth. The learned adult and the child protégé try to practice social justice, respecting the opinions of minorities. They are convinced that a curriculum that upholds goodness and truth can be fixed, for these qualities are immutable. Accepted, traditional materials of instruction, with reading as a learning medium, are suitable for implementing a fixed curriculum. In the School of the Idealists, divine control and influence are of central importance; hence this school is oriented toward religious, values-based education.

EXAMPLE

One private secondary school supported by a Protestant denomination is oriented toward Idealism. Its headmaster takes pride in the high standards of intellectual attainment the school promotes. He knows that many community members correctly say, "If a boy or a girl wants to be well prepared for college, he or she should go to that school." All students are required to attend chapel exercises daily and to participate in Bible study each Monday morning. Discipline is enforced by a system of lengthy detentions, by guard duty (carrying lead-filled muskets during forty-five-minute marches), and ultimately by suspension and expulsion. The football team is one of the most powerful in private secondary school circles, and an active intramural sports program is conducted for the benefit of all the students. The alumni office is proud of the number of graduates who, after further education, have entered the service professions and overseas missionary activity.

The School of the Realists

The School of the Realists is concerned with the world of ideas and things that are fixed within established subject matter and are generally accepted: facts, the mechanics of reading, the certainties of science and mathematics, and the fundamentals in any subject. In this school, theory and principles tend to come first in the learning experience; application or practice follows. The Realists believe that worthwhile knowledge is to be gathered, organized, and systematized in a rational form and then dispensed to the young so that the young may be truly educated, and so that knowledge itself may be preserved. A curriculum that includes only essential knowledge cannot contain fads and frills. In this school what matters is not whether children are naturally interested in the subject matter to be taught, but only that they somehow acquire interest in, or at any rate a sense of dedication to, the "right" subject matter. Textbooks and other written materials prepared by experts, laboratories, films, testing, and biographical studies are important media for helping children learn what they should learn. The keystone of preparation for further education and for all of life is basic, essential education to be gained by increasingly intensified study of fact-oriented knowledge of subjects.

In a large U.S. city, there is a public secondary school that is popularly known as "the academic high school."

"It's a no-nonsense school," says one of its supporters. "They teach you straight, and they expect you to come out well prepared." In this school, there are few school activities, but there is much after-school tutoring in subject matter that is "most worthy of attention," especially the natural sciences, mathematics, the foreign languages, English, history, and geography. No general science or social studies courses can be found in this school. According to the principal, they would, if they existed, be merely bastardized and ineffective versions of the pure subject matter one should be learning.

The dropout rate is high. Students who do not care to study facts and fundamentals without sugar coating soon transfer to other, less demanding high schools in the city. The faculty makes it clear that it is being realistic about school, subject matter, and life.

The School of the Pragmatists

Teachers in the School of the Pragmatists see themselves less as dispensers of facts than as humane moderators of learning, which one really accomplishes for oneself. For these teachers, knowledge is not at all immutable. In a world of rapid change, what the teacher teaches today may not be valid tomorrow. Taking account of the pervasive fact of change, Pragmatists want to relate what they teach to the surroundings and experiences of individual children. They wish to teach children how to think rather than what to think. Because the key test of what is taught is its practical effect on human behavior, subject matter content must encourage development of insight, understanding, and appropriate skills, which are to be acquired whenever possible in creative settings. The new technologies of learning, like the hackneyed textbooks of the past, are useful only insofar as they contribute to relatedness in what is worth learning. The curriculum, then, should be pupil centered, with subject matter geared to stimulating exploration and other practical action by learners. Among really worthy school activities are defining issues, solving problems, and conducting scientific inquiry. Accordingly, experimentation and means-to-an-end instrumental education are especially prized.

In a private elementary school in a suburb, the chief figure is a wealthy teacher called "Mr. Experimentation." He supports the school almost singlehandedly, when it is necessary, from his own inherited resources, and accordingly he has more to say in faculty meetings and the school offices than anyone else. Mr. Experimentation tries to see to it that nothing is taught in his school merely for its own sake as presumably important subject matter. He says, almost without challenge, "If what we teach isn't useful, it isn't worth teaching."

Young as many of them are, the children in this elementary school have numerous experiences in the community — observing, trying their skills, and serving other people. The field trip is an important part of their curriculum. The teachers, having been employed because they have declared themselves Pragmatists, try to judge what subject matter is utilitarian and therefore needed, and to teach it as naturally and openly as they can. Their written tests are designed to measure thinking and application of ideas.

The School of the Reconstructionists

The School of the Reconstructionists holds to an anthropological-sociological philosophy that would put schools in the forefront in remaking society. Teachers in this school will break precedents, if necessary, to rebuild the culture. They regard the human heritage as a tool to be used in further inquiry and action in the self-realization of peoples. Thus, they try to avoid indoctrinating children; rather, they seek to lead them in rational discussion and in critical analysis of issues. Reconstructionists use multiple teaching materials, and they consider subject matter to be useful chiefly in serving their central cause. Often they involve pupils, parents, and community members at large in planning to fuse the resources of formal education with social, political, and economic resources to try to better the human condition. Many Reconstructionists are convinced that group life should be a center of school experience inasmuch as groups are instrumental in achieving genuine democracy.

EXAMPLE

Several years ago, the board of education in a small city permitted the principal and an influential teacher in a public intermediate school to establish a small satellite school three blocks away. By renting a three-room warehouse, the board provided basic facilities for an attempt to "lift the educational level" of a minority population in the immediate neighborhood. The curriculum of the satellite school, created by several teachers who subscribed to Reconstructionism, centered in a number of themes, including self-concept development, relief from powerlessness, ability to work within an established system while seeking to change it, the nature of necessities for getting along, and prospects for improving the social and economic circumstances under which minority people often live. The carefully chosen faculty conducted weekly planning meetings with parents and with community members interested in reform. Resource persons who volunteered to help with the teaching were mainly labor union officials, chairpersons of minority organizations, and social workers. The subject matter chosen for concentration was, in the judgment of the teachers, most useful in alerting pupils to the acutal conditions under which they were living, and to possibilities for altering these conditions.

The School of the Existentialists

The Existentialists' School expects children to make their own choices and to reject authority that cannot justify its own existence. Thus this school tries to free learners to choose for themselves what they are to learn and to believe. In implementing this point of view, teachers in the School of the Existentialists refuse to adhere to course guides, outlines of content, and other documents and instruments of systematic learning. They work hard to help children find their own identities and set their own standards. Necessarily, then, they themselves do their own planning apart from committee or other group arrangements. They seldom talk about curriculum goals because they tend to reject universal or widely applicable standards. Of all available subject matter, the humanities are likely to appeal to them most. These teachers do not moralize, establish numbers of rules, or humiliate or ridicule pupils. The guidance they give youngsters tends to be nondirective. They share with existentialist thinkers in other fields a flexible philosophy which, because of its nebulousness, has been called a "nonphilosophy." In summary, their chief educational concern is to free the individual child "to do his own thing."

EXAMPLE

"I wanted my daughter to find out who she is and what she can do," said a mother who had just enrolled her child in a private middle school that advertised, "We are Existentialists. We teach your children to make their own choices." The school, founded ten years previously, had no fixed curriculum. The teachers prided themselves on listening to learners and on questioning but not telling. They refused to specify what was good or bad, useful or useless, desirable or undesirable. The administration was impatient with requests for information made by governments, local and remote, that seemed to be encroaching on the rights of private school students and faculties to do what they desired. The students made many decisions about what they would study and how they would proceed in their school activities program.

There may not be a school anywhere that follows any one of these educational philosophies to the letter. Actually, schools tend to draw eclectically upon more than one philosophy to create the kinds of schooling their patrons, administrators, and teaching staffs desire. However, it is desirable for curriculum planners to know the common, available educational philosophies, to recognize the philosophies that are being blended in the schools they know best, and to help their fellow planners change schools to combine the common philosophies in ways that satisfy them.

ACTIVITY 1-4
Describing the Educational Philosophy of One's Own School

Consult the preceding statements concerning educational philosophy, ranging from the Perennialist to the Existentialist. As revealed in day-to-day practice, the philosophical viewpoint of the school you know best probably represents a combination of philosophies. Write a paragraph or two expressing the particular philosophy of the school you know best.

ACTIVITY 1-5
Defining and Refining Your Own Curriculum Philosophy

A. W. Sturges, writing in the *Bulletin* of the National Association of School Principals, May 1982, presents an "ideology attitude inventory." The main themes of the inventory, adapted for the present purpose, are (1) human nature and development, (2) process and objectives of education, (3) the ideal curriculum, (4) the structure of schools, (5) the relationship between school and society, and (6) the role and function of the person in educational process.

Consider with other members of a group the possible meaning of each of these themes. What agreements develop among the members of your group? What differences appear? What implications do the agreements, the differences, and the process of your discussion have for the formulation of a curriculum philosophy by the faculty of a school?

EDUCATIONAL PHILOSOPHY IN A CONTEXT
OF OTHER CURRICULUM FOUNDATIONS

The preceding discussions of philosophical viewpoints suggest that what one thinks of people in general and what one thinks of young people in schools specifically are the first considerations in developing and changing the curriculum. Just as the history of curriculum thought forms an essential backdrop for curriculum development and change, estimates of the worth and potential of people add the human dimension to further discussion of points of view about the mission and purposes of schools. The mission and purposes of an educational institution should be thought about before consideration is given to the nature of learners and the ways they learn, to the influence of the society, the culture, and the community on curriculum decision making, and to the contributions of subject matter in achieving development and change.

Learners and learning, societal, cultural, and community influences, and subject matter constitute, with history and philosophy, the recognized foundations of curriculum. Though textbooks, including this one, treat the foundations in series, the foundations are actually integrating elements in the process of making decisions about the curriculum. Therefore educational philosophy is considered again and again, rather than merely once, in curriculum decision making. Furthermore, educational philosophy, like one's view of learners and learning and the other foundations, may change during the process of curriculum making whenever new knowledge and additional experience suggest that a change is needed.

SUMMARY

The curriculum of a school may be defined as the formal and informal content and process by which learners gain knowledge and understanding, develop skills, and alter attitudes, appreciations, and values under the auspices of that school.

People's concerns about an elementary or secondary school compel them to try to improve the school's curriculum. Much has happened to the curriculum and to the process of curriculum improvement from colonial times to the present. The private system of education that existed during colonial times and the early days of the republic has been transfigured into a fifty-state system of public education and indigenous developments in private education. Some of the informal experimentation with the curriculum that has occurred during the past three centuries has resulted in marked changes in curriculum practices. On several major occasions, national groups and the federal government have initiated change.

While trends have been appearing and developments have been occurring in curriculum matters, two major philosophical viewpoints of curriculum, one conservative and the other liberal, have emerged under the headings Traditionalism and Progressivism. Distinct, more specific philosophies of education — Perennialism, Idealism, Realism, Pragmatism, Reconstructionalism, and Existentialism — are combined in differing eclectic modes in elementary and secondary schools.

In subsequent chapters, the significance of psychological, social, and subject matter influences on decision making about the curriculum will be discussed. The relevance of these forces can be seen most clearly against the overview of historical events that this chapter has presented. The curriculum worker desperately needs knowledge and understanding of the whole curriculum movement as it is seen in historical and philosophical studies. Otherwise he or she is likely to fall prey to schemes that have been tried at intervals throughout educational history and found wanting.

ENDNOTES

1. Commission on Excellence in Education, *A Nation at Risk* (Washington, D.C.: Superintendent of Documents, U.S. Government Printing Office, 1983).

2. Phi Delta Kappa, *The Reports: Challenge and Opportunity* (Bloomington, Ind.: Phi Delta Kappa, 1983).

3. Marguerite Michaels, "What the Crisis Reports Aren't Telling Us: The Good News about Our Public Schools," *Parade*, January 1, 1984, pp. 4–6.

4. See Chapter 1 in Daniel Tanner and Laurel N. Tanner, *Curriculum Development: Theory into Practice* (New York: Macmillan, 1975).

5. Gordon N. Mackenzie, "Curriculum Change: Participants, Power, and Processes," in Matthew B. Miles, ed., *Innovations in Education* (New York: Teachers College Press, 1964), p. 402.

6. Tanner and Tanner, *Curriculum Development*, p. 45.

7. Compare Ralph Keyes, *Is There Life after High School?* (Boston: Little, Brown, 1976).

8. The sweep of curriculum change in much or all of U.S. history can be seen in books like those by Cremin and Brubacher, listed in the bibliography at the end of this chapter; in Hollis L. Caswell, *Curriculum Improvement in Public School Systems* (New York: Bureau of Publications, Teachers College, 1950); and in Mary Louise Seguel, *The Curriculum Field: Its Formative Years* (New York: Teachers College Press, 1966).

9. National Society for the Study of Education, *The Foundations and Techniques of Curriculum Construction* (Bloomington, Ill.: Public School Publishing Company, 1926).

10. C. C. Trillingham, *The Organization and Administration of Curriculum Programs* (Los Angeles: University of Southern California Press, 1934).

11. Edwin S. Lide, *Procedures in Curriculum Making*, Bulletin No. 17, National Survey of Secondary Education (Washington, D.C.: U.S. Governmment Printing Office, 1933).

12. W. W. Charters, *Curriculum Construction* (New York: Macmillan, 1923).

13. Caswell, *Curriculum Improvement*, p. 51. For an informative discussion of the work of Caswell and others during the early years of formal curriculum planning, see Seguel, *The Curriculum Field*.

14. See H. W. Hill, "Curriculum Legislation and Instructional Decsion-Makers," *Elementary School Journal* 73 (May 1973): 407–11.

15. See Ralph W. Tyler, "Curriculum Development Since 1900," *Educational Leadership* 38, no. 8 (May 1981): 598–601.

16. See Decker F. Walker, "Classifying Curriculum Theories: Implications for Educators," *Theory into Practice* 21 (Winter 1982): 62–65.

17. L. Thomas Hopkins, *Interaction: The Democratic Process* (Boston: D. C. Heath, 1941).

18. See Russell L. Hamm and Kenneth T. Henson, "Philosophy: Curriculum Source and Guide," *Contemporary Education* 51 (Spring 1980): 147–50.

SELECTED BIBLIOGRAPHY

Allison, Clinton B. *Without Consensus: Issues in American Education.* Boston: Allyn and Bacon, 1973.

Brubacher, John S. *A History of the Problems of Education.* New York: McGraw-Hill, 1947.

Butler, Donald J. *Four Philosophies and Their Practice in Education and Religion.* New York: Harper & Row, 1968.

Cremin, Lawrence A. *The American Common School: An Historical Conception.* New York: Bureau of Publications, Teachers College, 1961.

Davis, O. L., Jr., ed. *Perspectives on Curriculum Development, 1776–1976.* 1976 Yearbook. Washington, D.C.: Association for Supervision and Curriculum Development, 1976.

Dixon, Keith, ed. *Philosophy of Education and the Curriculum.* Elmsford, N.Y.: Pergamon, 1972.

Firth, Gerald, and Kimpson, Richard D. *Curriculum Continuum in Perspective.* Oakland, Calif.: Peacock, 1972.

Frymier, Jack. *A School for Tomorrow.* Berkeley, Calif.: McCutchan, 1973.

Gordon, Peter, and Lawton, Denis. *Curriculum Change in the Nineteenth and Twentieth Centuries.* New York: Holmes and Meier, 1979.

Jencks, Christopher. *Inequality: A Reassessment of the Effects of Family and Schooling in America.* New York: Basic Books, 1972.

McClure, Robert M., ed. *Curriculum, Retrospect and Prospect.* National Society for the Study of Education, Seventieth Yearbook, Part I. Chicago: University of Chicago Press, 1971.

Phenix, Phillip H., ed. *Philosophies of Education.* New York: John Wiley, 1963.

Rich, John M. *Humanistic Foundations of Education.* Worthington, Ohio: Charles A. Jones, 1971.

———. *Readings in the Philosophy of Education.* 2nd ed. Belmont, Calif.: Wadsworth, 1972.

Schiro, Michael. *Curriculum for Better Schools: The Great Ideological Debate.* Englewood Cliffs, N.J.: Educational Technology Publications, 1978.

Seguel, Mary Louise. *The Curriculum Field: Its Formative Years.* New York: Teachers College Press, 1966.

Tyack, David. *One Best Stystem: A History of American Urban Education.* Cambridge, Mass.: Harvard University Press, 1975.

Venable, Tom C. *Philosophical Foundations of the Curriculum.* Chicago: Rand McNally, 1967.

Wynne, John P. *Theories of Education.* New York: Harper & Row, 1968.

Zais, Robert S. *Curriculum: Principles and Foundations.* New York: Thomas Y. Crowell, 1976.

2

Psychological Bases
for Curriculum Decisions

How do learners grow and develop? What are some of the ways in which they learn? What does psychology say specifically to the curriculum improver?

Today psychological factors are at the root of many curriculum decisions, for psychology is one of the mother disciplines in which education finds its rationale. The present chapter treats psychological bases for curriculum decisions under three headings that relate specifically to the three questions in the first paragraph of this chapter.

LEARNERS—THEIR GROWTH AND DEVELOPMENT

In the United States and abroad, many investigations into the nature of learners have been conducted during the past half century. Much has been discovered about children's sequence in growth and development, about factors that affect growth and development, about the mental equipment that learners bring to their tasks, about the importance of individual personality and personal experiences, and about the effect of the social order on individual learners.

Learners have been studied from several points of view. Arnold Gesell and his followers have used a cross-sectional approach, which involves studying thousands of children at specified ages and then generalizing about their physical, mental, and behavioral characteristics at these ages.

41

Willard C. Olson has used a longitudinal method by which children are observed and examined at intervals during their development from childhood to adolescence, and their individual patterns of growth and development are plotted. Psychoanalysts have discussed undesirable feelings and experiences which, when present during childhood, cause young people to grow into disordered adults. The sociologist Robert Havighurst has outlined developmental tasks from infancy through later life. These four approaches, quite different in nature, often yield different findings about the growth and development of learners. But they do tend toward a view of the learner as a whole being rather than as a parcel of unrelated skills, understandings, and attitudes. As the findings from these and other approaches generally reinforce one another, the interrelatedness of growth factors becomes increasingly clear. In the physical area, researchers view *growth* as involving increase in the size of individuals and *development* as involving increase in their physical complexity. In the matters of mentality and emotionality with which curriculum workers are chiefly concerned, however, the same and other researchers regard *growth* and *development* as having generally interchangeable meanings.

To study groups of pupils comprehensively and comparatively, it is possible to learn about their audiological and ophthalmological status; their auditory, visual, tactile, motor, and visual-motor functioning; their verbal, nonverbal, and emotional functioning; their personality characteristics; and their social, work, and academic skills. Obviously this list does not exhaust the possibilities for study because human beings are so complex.

Data on Which Curriculum Planning Can Be Based

Following are two illustrations of collections of data about the growth and development of learners on which curriculum planners can base their decision making.

Conclusions of a Curriculum Planning Committee

The first illustration concerns a curriculum planning episode in a school system with which the author was formerly affiliated. After taking a long look at varied literature on child and youth development, a committee of teachers in this school system adapted Daniel Prescott's child study methodology to a study of children within the district.[1] They observed children against a collection of background data about pupils of the same age levels residing elsewhere and then stated in a course guide the characteristics and needs of the pupils they knew best. These pupils occupied age and grade brackets that classified them as follows: kindergarten and grade one, grades two and three, grades four and five, and grades six and seven. Because they lacked the time necessary to do so, the teachers were unable to proceed further into a study of the adolescent period, but they made categorizations for children in kindergarten and several of the initial grades. The following were their conclusions concerning the common characteristics and needs of children in kindergarten and grade one and also of children in grades four and five, noted here for illustration.

KINDERGARTEN AND GRADE ONE

Characteristics

1. Children begin to lose baby teeth, causing lisping, etc.
2. Right- or left-handedness is established. No change should be made without expert advice.
3. Bone structure growth is slower than in previous years.
4. Heart growth is rapid. The child should not be overtaxed physically.
5. Eyes are increasing in size. Watch reading and writing habits.
6. Feeling of tension may be evident in thumb sucking, nail biting, and mistakes in toilet habits.
7. Motor skills begin to develop; coordination may be awkward and uneven.
8. Large muscles are much more developed than smaller ones.
9. The child responds to rhythms—skips, beats time, etc.
10. The average child of these ages is full of vitality. He has good facial color, and he stands and sits erect.
11. Children are interested in an activity rather than in its outcome.
12. Self-dependence and a desire to help others are developing.
13. Children prefer activity—climbing, jumping, running—but they tire easily.

Needs

1. Short periods of activity.
2. Twelve hours of sleep.
3. Vigorous and noisy games so essential to growth.
4. Many opportunities to do things for oneself.
5. Frequent participation in organized groups—games, dramatics, rhythm.
6. Chances for the shy child to join in the routine and be important.

GRADES FOUR AND FIVE

Characteristics

1. Small muscles continue to develop, increasing manipulative skills.
2. Coordination is improving, especially hand-eye.

3. This is the period of prepubescence at which time physical growth slows down. Beginning of pubescence may appear in a very few boys and girls.
4. Overtaxing of heart needs watching.
5. Posture needs watching.
6. Eyes need to be considered. Attention now may prevent more serious trouble later.
7. This is a period of untidiness, overabundance of energy, frequent accidents.
8. Children show increased interest span in a wide range of activities.
9. This is the gang age, the age of secret clubs.
10. Children are critical of their families.
11. Relationship to group and approval of peers are important.
12. It is the age of collecting—cards, stamps, etc.

Needs

1. Opportunities to develop independence.
2. At least ten hours of sleep.
3. Physical equipment (desk, chairs, etc.) carefully adjusted to each individual.
4. Uniformity and fairness in rules and punishment.
5. Real need of regularity, as opposed to schedule changes.
6. Whole body activities.
7. Sympathy and understanding of adults.
8. Help in finding a place in the group.
9. Opportunity to learn to be a good follower as well as a good leader.[2]

The committee that prepared these lists of characteristics and needs recognized that they were directed toward physical development, with overtones of the intellectual and the emotional. The lists needed, therefore, to be supplemented with data from other findings in human growth and development with special reference to the observations made by teachers concerning the learners in their own school system. In studies of this kind, specific, crucial observations should be related to the ways particular learners master particular subject matter. Thus the committee that made the lists mentioned several applications of given characteristics and needs to the teaching of the language arts, and they requested that other teachers watch for and report additional applications on blank pages that were included with the course guide.

An example of the applications is a proposed list of activities for development of listening skills in kindergarten and the first grade: (1) hear stories of pets, news about each other, descriptions of objects; (2) recognize sounds made by animals, insects, machines; and rhythm changes in music; and (3) be alert to directions for dismissal, fire drills, rest periods, care of supplies and clothing.

The characteristics and needs of adolescents who occupy grades seven through twelve may be categorized similarly. Sometimes widely published lists of characteristics and needs are used literally in curriculum planning. This is especially true of lists concerning adolescents. The general lists can be subcategorized preadolescent, early adolescent, and later adolescent. To be genuinely useful in curriculum planning, they should be modified to take into account the nature of adolescent groups in the planners' own community. For example, the aggressiveness or assertiveness of most adolescent groups in High School A may differ from the aggressiveness or assertiveness of most groups in the same age bracket in High School B. Also, wealthy, lower income, and minority groups provide marked exceptions.

Of the three subcategories—preadolescent, early adolescent, and later adolescent—recent attention has been given mainly to the growth, development, and school environment of the early adolescent. Psychological "tasks" of the early adolescent group that have been identified during recent years are pertinent to redevelopment of the junior high school curriculum and organization of the middle school. They include the following:

1. An exploration of the youngster's uniqueness as an individual and his or her relatedness to other persons
2. A continuation of detachment from parents and of the assertion of autonomy that began at the toddler stage
3. Short-term commitment to work and its diligent performance, followed by a change to aimlessness and moodiness
4. Movement from transient, hit-and-run acquaintanceships to more stable and rewarding interpersonal relationships
5. Cognitive development that permits abstract thinking, generalizing, and ability to appreciate theorems, figures of speech, and ideologies
6. Examination of one's own and others' values
7. Comprehension of, and sometimes overemphasis on, law and order.[3]

Here, the meaning of "tasks," as used earlier by Havighurst, is close to the meaning of "characteristics that have relevance for what early adolescents should be doing in school and elsewhere in their environment." In school, early adolescents would seem to need opportunities to undertake a variety of activities, to relate to peers and adults in varied ways and settings, to be in charge of the action at times, to be challenged during bursts of effort, to get to know a few persons well, to stretch their minds with abstractions, and to explore values and valuing.

Piaget's Tasks

The second illustration concerns the work of the Swiss psychologist Jean Piaget in presenting tasks and questions to children to determine how they develop logical, sequential thought. Piaget found and reported four major levels of development: the *sensorimotor level*, the *preoperational level*, the *level of concrete operations*, and the *level of formal operations*.

At the sensorimotor level, from birth to about eighteen months, the child apparently assimilates sensations and interacts with unfamiliar objects. As the child accommodates to his or her physical environment, a system or structure for manipulating objects is developed.

From eighteen months to about seven years of age, the child exercises his or her perception. For example, the child recognizes differences in size and increases in number, and uses images and words to symbolize objects and events, but he or she operates not logically, but rather on the basis of what appears to the child to be reasonable.

Logical thinking operations begin at the concrete operations stage, extending from approximately seven to eleven years of age. The child now recognizes several factors at a time. For example, the child sees that some things can be combined in varied ways to arrive at the same result. He or she manipulates objects more insightfully, noting that whatever is manipulated remains the same in length, or area, or volume, or weight.

The level of formal operations involves using reasoning and applying rules in more abstract situations. Beginning at about age eleven, the child is able to state hypotheses, test them, and formulate conclusions. Meanwhile, he or she can consider possibilities, keep several variables in mind at once, and deal with probabilities. The child is able to answer the question "What would happen now if . . . ?" His or her logical system is steadily developing.

Piaget has commented that intellectual development is gradual and continuous, creating a merging or blurring of the four levels. Progress at these levels depends on how mature the child is, how much relevant experience the child has had, and how the child has processed information supplied by people in his or her environment.[4] Piaget has considered another factor to be important: equilibration, a search by the child for equilibrium in his or her cognition.

The last three levels of cognitive operation have real meaning for curriculum planners in nursery schools and on through high schools. In the middle grades of schooling, for instance, teachers should be spending much time in making the development of logical operations easier at the concrete level, as well as in creating readiness for formal operations. Piaget's theory provides hints about arranging subject matter sequence. It suggests that careful development of thought processes produces greater-than-usual individual differences among learners. Inasmuch as already wide-ranging differences are being treated inadequately in schools, this finding suggests an obvious need for careful curriculum planning.[5]

SITUATION 2-1
Judging What Use to Make of Certain Characteristics
and Needs

A committee of teachers of fourth- and fifth-grade children concerned itself with art experiences for children of these grades. Both the learning activities of the children and the facilities the children were to use came within the purview of the committee, which was charged with developing program facilities for a new elementary school. The committee's attention was drawn particularly to the following characteristics and needs of fourth- and fifth-grade children:

> *Characteristics.* Small muscles are developing more and more manipulative power; children are often untidy and energetic, and they have frequent accidents; children are interested in collecting items that they and other people produce.
> *Needs.* Independent creative ability should be developed; children need a wide range of activities in which to expend their energies.

Assuming that the characteristics and needs of children of these age groups as listed above are valid, what are some of the inferences you can make concerning program and facilities in art?

Focusing on the Individual Learner

Study of the growth and development of large numbers of learners yields some useful guidelines. However, exceptions to general findings about children and youth are both numerous and provocative. The challenge to education in a democracy appears much more prominently in the differences among children in youth than in their similarities. School practices tend unrealistically toward treating learners as though they were substantially alike, whereas they actually vary beyond our wildest imaginings. The following are some generally realistic statements about individual differences in pupil growth and development:

1. Many of the obvious differences among learners can be seen in five minutes in any classroom. Other, less obvious differences can be revealed only by careful study.
2. Learners differ in their ability to perform tasks. Thus a child may be good in arithmetic, poor in spelling, and fair in reading according to an arbitrary standard of quality. To complicate matters, the same child displays differing abilities in performing specific tasks within each of these school subjects.
3. Growth and development apparently occur in spurts, sometimes referred to as the thrustration involved in pushing forward, with a subsequent period of quiescence and reinforcement following each push.
4. If individual differences are really taken into account, the school cannot hope to maintain a single or minimum standard for a given group of children, comfortable though this standard might be for teachers. Education should cultivate differences rather than restrict them. If this were done, the range of differences would be even

more obvious. Though high schools often tend to teach adolescents as though they were all alike, maturation brings out more apparent differences in learners than were present or obvious when the same learners were young children.

5. Differences in rates of growth, with other factors, cause some children to be "early bloomers" and other children to be "late bloomers." One of the noticeable developmental trends during the second half of the twentieth century has been the tendency of children and youth to mature earlier, presumably because of new mores, changed expectations, and technological gains like increased flexibility and wider use of television. Earlier maturation may help to make classic lists of characteristics and needs obsolete.

6. Given desirable educational conditions, children of whom we have expected little can often give much. Teachers have shown an unfortunate tendency to write off as hopeless those children who have not succeeded well at first.

7. Since factors of growth are interrelated, the causes of learning difficulty at a given time may be found in some factor that we are not presently considering. For instance, an excellent biology student's sudden block to learning more biology may originate in a hidden emotional upset or physical illness.

Lists like this give curriculum workers pause as they begin to consider factors of growth and development that teachers fail to take into account. Every learner brings with him or her *individualized conditioners* of learning. These include personality, personal experiences, mental ability, and the effects of the social order. The nature of the learner himself or herself and of the learner's background has a marked effect on what is learned and on the style of learning. Furthermore, the personality of the learner becomes evident in the learner's emotional organization, which affects sensitivity to social and other phenomena, ties with adults, desire or lack of desire to master the environment, and the extent of preoccupation with personal problems, which may prevent learning. It appears, of course, in the quality of one's relationships with people of all sorts. The learner's insecurities may cause him or her to "show off" abilities by achieving to the maximum, or so to undervalue personal powers that he or she suffers from emotional paralysis. The learner is affected further by physical characteristics such as muscular coordination and visual and auditory acuity.

A reasonably clear relationship has now been established between the learner's self-concept and the effectiveness with which he or she learns. Findings from research studies show that individual learners perform according to their self-concepts, that high levels of self-concept correlate closely with school achievement, that achievers feel more positive about themselves and their abilities than do underachievers, and that underachievers learn poorly partly because they underestimate their ability to perform well. Obviously teachers should do much more than they are now doing to build pupils' ego strength and self-confidence.

One's past experience conditions learning in many ways. Interests developed early in life often carry into subsequent years. Sometimes they coincide with the curriculum of the school, but too often they are unknown to teachers, or they seem to have no relevance to anything people do in schools. Socially and in other ways, modern children have more opportunities for wide experience than children had a generation or two ago, and wide experience shows itself in the sophistication, whether real or artificial, that modern children often manifest.[6]

Learners bring to their tasks widely varied mental equipment, usually discussed under the heading of intelligence. *Intelligence* may be defined as that cluster of aptitudes and abilities that permits one to acquire new learnings. People have not yet succeeded in measuring intelligence directly, only in inferring intelligence from the results of certain tests that search out elements of common background in learners, the elements being drawn mainly from the world of words and other symbols. Modern intelligence tests yield a series of scores, including scores in reasoning ability, manual dexterity, spatial perception, and memory. Thus, intelligence is believed to come in varied dimensions rather than merely in the vague form of general intelligence. However, the school customarily tests, and so educates, in only a few of the possible dimensions. Without question, the human potential that is going to waste in our society and in our schools is appallingly large. A key purpose of schools in the future must be to educate intelligence within additional dimensions or else to recognize that schools have limited functions within the range of educational agencies in communities.

It seems likely that people possess "intelligences" rather than merely general intelligence. Usually, teachers and schools do not value intelligences that are nonverbal. For example, most teachers think that repairing complicated machinery is a less difficult activity than reading or writing, yet much abstract thinking is involved in it and few skilled mechanics, however verbal they may be, can describe completely what they have done in difficult repair operations.

During the sixties and seventies, the tendency of culturally deprived children to attain higher scores on intelligence tests when they have been exposed to an improved environment for even a few weeks was explored. When children have better concepts of themselves, their scores on intelligence tests are likely to improve. A significant finding for education is that, although the learners' basic intelligence remains quite constant, altering certain important conditions in their environment brings about variations in their performance. How, one wonders, might human potential conceivably be developed by further manipulation of the environment to free intelligence?

The broad effects of society on the curriculum are discussed in Chapter 3. In the present discussion, it is important to see how the social order affects the individual learner. First, it affects the learner within the dynamic of his or her social status. For instance, the worth of study and learning is keenly felt by middle- and upper-class people, but it is not always appreciated by the lower classes. Accordingly, middle- and upper-class children are often considered "good" students and conformers, whereas learners from the lower classes resist school tasks that they consider impractical. Second, the social order affects the learner with reference to the ethnic or national background from which he or she comes. One's ethnic or national group has developed certain expectations of schooling and of the status in society that a person of such a background may hope to reach. Soon the individual learner comes to share these expectations. A third source of effect from the social order is the family in which one has been reared. The interests of family members, their cultural advantages, and the extensiveness of their travel are but a few of the direct influences of family life. Other sources of effect are one's neighborhood, the occupations of the people one knows, and the cultural level and aspirations of associates. "Every child learns what he lives and he is motivated only to learn more about those things which he knows or imagines."[7]

Attending to Individual Differences

Information about individual learners should be used with care and forethought in planning curriculum. To take all the significant information into account, teachers need a comprehensive schema for attending to individual differences. Perhaps the best available schema was suggested some years ago by Virgil Herrick. Herrick said that, to deal with individual differences effectively, a teacher should make three kinds of decisions:

1. The teacher selects objectives, the topic to be studied, the organizing center for the subject matter content,[8] the instructional plan to be used, and a useful evaluation plan. This is a comprehensive educational decision.
2. The teacher decides how to recognize and respect individual children, how to interrelate teacher and pupil roles, and how to establish the interpersonal dynamics of the classroom. In plain English, this is a set of decisions in interpersonal relations and classroom climate, decisions about how people can get along best in the classroom so that learning can proceed.
3. The teacher determines how the children are to be grouped, how time and space are to be utilized, and how materials and resources of instruction are to be acquired and associated. This is a set of decisions in administrative arrangements and logistics.[9]

The three kinds of decisions are kept in mind, usually in a less well organized form, each time a major curriculum project in individualization is developed. Some of the subparts of the decisions are obviously more important than others. For example, if objectives are made to express significant generalizations and processes, the individual learner can supply the specifics that seem appropriate to support a given generalization or process. Thus, genuinely understanding the process of addition in arithmetic is to be highlighted; 148 plus 292 provides only an application of the understanding. Human beings' dependence on other human beings is an important concept; the Grand Alliance is only one instance of it, for there are numerous other instances. Obviously the learner should be expected to acquire the big idea, not the details of a single instance. Continual fact teaching, still so common in U.S. schools, will not suffice.

Similarly, the ways time is used can have a telling effect on the degree to which individualization is attained. Proper use of time should offer maximum opportunity for individuals to do that which is different from what members of the class or group commonly do.

The other subparts of the three decisions are worth thinking about in order to clarify their role in the task of attending to the individual learner.

Several strategies to be used by teachers in accommodating the educational needs of individual learners are

1. Finding the individual in the group; then giving that individual special attention
2. Varying learning activities and materials
3. Preparing new and different packages of learning materials
4. Varying the time needed to complete prescribed activities
5. Allowing learners to individualize to suit themselves, as by choosing activities and utilizing time in their own ways
6. Subgrouping learners in numbers of groups formed for differing purposes
7. Providing for independent study
8. Preparing varied evaluation instruments and test and inventory items
9. Following the procedures in mastery learning to be discussed in this chapter.

Many pupils are capable of planning their own learning experiences within the framework of their regular classroom learning. They need not start this planning at the beginning of a school term, but may wait until they have become accustomed to new subject matter. Opportunities for individualized learning may then be presented incidentally to "regular" learning, often in the form of brief episodes. The monotony of working alone will be reduced if some of the learning experiences occur in small groups.

Pupils may be encouraged to prepare individual outlines of their proposed activities, specifying the why, what, when, and how of the activities. By attaining self-direction, exceptional pupils can deepen their interests and increase their abilities to an unusual extent. These pupils include not only the gifted but also those for whom teachers previously held much less hope than they do today.[10]

SITUATION 2-2
Homework for an Eighth-Grade Class

Mr. Simpson's work as assistant principal of a junior high school took him into a number of classrooms. In most of them, he noticed homework assignments given in the following manner: "For tomorrow, read pages 145 to 153 and be ready to talk about what you have read." To Mr. Simpson, this way of assigning homework seemed oversimplified and insensitive. He found a sympathetic spirit in an eighth-grade science teacher, Miss Carey, who felt that assigning homework had become a special problem of which she was poignantly aware. On the day she assigned to all her pupils ten pages of textbook reading on the age of the earth, she came to Mr. Simpson for help.

"A single assignment for all these dozens of children whom I meet daily doesn't make sense," said Miss Carey. "But earth science is so remote from them! How can I vary my assignments to reach children of differing abilities and interests?"

If you were Mr. Simpson, what facts of human growth and development would you wish to take into account in working with Miss Carey in improving her assignment making? What assignments other than her routine one would you recommend that Miss Carey make?

ACTIVITY 2-1
Diagnosing the Learning Potential of an Individual

To see the advantages and disadvantages that individual learners possess, one should study individuals carefully. Each learner operates amid a cluster or complex of forces. Some of these forces have been noted above.

Choose an individual learner for study, or encourage a teacher whom you supervise to do so. Through interview, analysis of cumulative records, home visitation, and/or any other means at your disposal, find out all you can about this learner — the pattern of his or her development; his or her personal characteristics, talents, strengths, and weaknesses; and the social forces that impinge upon him or her. Describe your expectations concerning the individual and the extent to which these expectations are being realized. Tell what you think could be done concretely by the child's school to develop his or her potential.

Recent Changes in Learners

Children and youth, as distinctive groups in U.S. society, are continually changing in biological, intellectual, and other ways. Adults often observe that "children don't remain children as long as they used to." Physically, children and youth are taller, heavier, and healthier than they were a few decades ago. Puberty and sex drives appear at an earlier chronological age. Though adolescence begins earlier, by force of cultural mandate it also ends later. Curriculum activities formerly reserved for older adolescents are now in the educational regimen of younger persons. Older adolescents are often discontented with some of the elements of the curriculum that are prescribed for them, so the senior year in high school, for instance, becomes a trying time for teachers, parents, and pupils. Adolescents in senior high school and college are often frustrated by their superficial exposure to adult activities, privileges, and problems, especially when their actual adulthood is delayed far into the twenties.

One of the major features of the "new world" in which children and adolescents now find themselves is the prevalence of an excess of information from television, wide-ranging reading materials, and reports of technological achievements. Judging what information to process and knowing how to process it become confusing problems. The curriculum of the future will need to be maximally helpful to youngsters in suggesting ways to manage both of these problems.

The changed culture in which children grow and develop affects them in other ways. Ours is an age in which most youngsters no longer work with their parents or grandparents, and in which they tend to find parental authority arbitrary. In the words of Grant and Briggs, "us-them feelings" often characterize the relationships between youngsters and their older relatives.[11] Having to deal with an adult population that is increasingly aging is a new experience for young people.

As standards of morality in society and community move from uncertainty to deterioration, child abuse increases. With their rights increased by legal and social sanction but with moral and ethical standards for exercising those rights largely missing both at home and at school, the younger generation is confused about what is acceptable in people's relationships with one another. Abdication of responsibility by parents leads to roaming the streets, and free time out of doors leads to destructiveness, vandalism, and violence. Teachers sometimes wonder how so many of the pupil population can be as "good" as they are.[12]

Using Data about Learners Insightfully

Translating characteristics, needs, and tasks into meaningful concepts to be used in curriculum improvement is a special and difficult task for curriculum workers. They must realize, first, that characteristics, needs, and tasks overlap among the age groups, with the greatest overlap occurring when age groups are finely distinguished in groupings of two ages (six and seven, eight and nine, etc.) or three ages, rather than in broader groupings (six to twelve). Then curriculum workers must give careful thought to what a particular characteristic, need, or task means for school programs. Some inferences can be drawn immediately — about physical capabilities as they relate to learning experiences, for example. Other inferences are harder to draw, and the school experiences that seem to fit require tryout to confirm their appropriateness. Once a characteristic, need, or task has been validly identified, it must be thought about in relationship to other factors: What relative weight should be given to this particular characteristic, need, or task? Finally, evidence about the growth and development of learners should be checked against the objectives to which teachers and pupils subscribe.

One can point to a number of curriculum guides that are based, at least in part, on the developmental characteristics of children. These publications tend to classify child growth and development into four broad areas: the physical, the social, the emotional, and the mental. Each area may then be subdivided. For example, physical characteristics may be treated under growth in height, weight, and body proportions; growth of internal organs; growth of sex characteristics; development of physical abilities; and maintenance of physical health and hygiene.[13]

Curriculum materials can be prepared in such a way that all growth and developmental characteristics of learners show through them. When this is done, the materials are likely to list a wide range of experiences for learners and thus deal with human potential more adequately. In general, curriculum guides in art, home economics, and physical education have been oriented more closely toward reality in human growth and development than have the guides in other school subjects.

Sometimes a particular view of human growth and development proves especially adaptable to the work of curriculum planners. One of these is Robert Havighurst's concept of *developmental tasks* (tasks like learning to speak), with its special requirements at given times in the learner's life. Developmental tasks emerge from a combination of factors: maturation, the culture in which one is reared, and the nature of the individual child. The concept is therefore an interdisciplinary one, originating in individual psychology, human growth and development, and sociology.[14]

Teachers and other curriculum planners who want to use data about learners insightfully should:

1. Establish objectives for helping learners find their identities, create their own goals, and make attainment of their goals possible.
2. Teach with the needs, abilities, interests, and developmental levels of learners constantly in mind.
3. Make the school a personal and social institution as well as an agency for developing intellectually.
4. Help learners establish roles associated with achieving adulthood, practicing good citizenship, taking responsibility, and making wise decisions.[15]

From the broader standpoint of the whole curriculum, study centers where many different role-takers can work together are needed. Curriculum planners should work together to determine what is especially worth learning well. Higher mental process material, intensive art experiences, continuing social interaction, and engagement in peak experiences help to increase the worth of the mastery learning strategy.

A Specific Example of the Use of Data about Learners — Mainstreaming

Some of the enthusiasts for an allegedly new development in education insist that this development, called mainstreaming, is one of the great educational movements of the century. *Mainstreaming* consists of moving handicapped pupils out of the segregation of their special education classes into regular classrooms. Years ago, pupils with varied physical, emotional, and learning difficulties were assigned to regular classrooms because they had nowhere else to go. Because the needs of these pupils were special and because the time and energy classroom teachers needed to work with them proved excessive, special education classes were formed. In these classes, the environment is not always conducive to the all-round development of pupils with problems. It is estimated today that about 12 percent of pupils in the six to nineteen age range are emotionally, physically, and/or mentally handicapped, certainly a high percentage of children and adolescents to be retained in classes that isolate them from the general pupil population. Recent laws and court decisions have held that handicapped pupils have the same educational rights as other pupils. For all of these reasons, the idea of mainstreaming — or getting pupils into the main stream of the educational program — has attracted attention.[16]

Mainstreaming was officially and widely implemented in the public schools following passage of Public Law 94-142, which brought about the mainstreaming of pupils within the age range six to seventeen, inclusive. The law said, in effect: Find the handicapped and give first priority to the most severely disabled. Evaluate each child's instructional needs and develop for that child an individual instructional program. Put each child in the least restrictive environment possible. Evaluate the child's progress and, if necessary, change his or her program. Provide for complaint, appeal, and hearing when injustice in placement or treatment appears to have been done.[17]

To many teachers and administrators, the requirements of the law seemed stringent. Many classroom teachers felt discomfort at the presence of handicapped pupils, who were reassigned in large numbers from special classes to "regular" classrooms. In most school districts, little attention was given to preparing classroom teachers in the skills they needed to work effectively with the handicapped, though this specialized kind of teacher preparation has proved essential. Passage of national legislation caused orders to be given from the administrative top to persons who considered themselves to be at the instructional bottom. Meanwhile, the all-round lack of funds resulted in nonprovision of inservice programs and instructional facilities.[18]

Before pupils are mainstreamed, they should be screened and studied individually, and the logistics of their shifting about should be arranged to accord with their individual needs. In the background, their regular and special teachers should have particular inservice experiences and opportunities to participate in the mainstreaming process. Class size, scheduling, and curriculum modification should be considered in assigning individual pupils. The danger in mainstreaming is not in the idea itself but in the slipshod manner in which it is put into practice. Sensible adoption of the idea can provide important opportunities for gathering and utilizing additional data about learners.

Because learning is not a magical activity, ways of organizing pupils to learn are rarely a school's salvation. The main key to learning is the quality of the experiences individual pupils have according to their needs. Unless much is done to vary experiences for all sorts of purposes, and to accommodate varied needs, learners are likely to show too little gain.

UNDERSTANDINGS OF THE LEARNING PROCESS

Some Generally Accepted Principles of Learning

Much that has been said in the preceding pages has implied the importance of having a point of view about how learning proceeds. Schools of psychological thought are so numerous and so varied in their viewpoints about learning that a real service has been rendered by scholars who have tried to reconcile the differing viewpoints. Two of these scholars are Ernest R. Hilgard and Goodwin Watson. On the following pages, quotations and paraphrases of some of Hilgard's and Watson's statements are presented. The statements chosen have special relevance to teachers and other curriculum workers. They are, of course, subject to change as more is learned about psychology and about psychological bases for curriculum decisions.

- A motivated learner acquires what he or she learns more readily than one who is not motivated. The relevant motives include both general and specific ones—for example, desire to learn, need for achievement (general), desire for a reward or for avoidance of a threatened punishment (specific).
- Motivation that is too intense (especially pain, fear, and anxiety) may be accompanied by distracting emotional states, so excessive motivation

may be less effective than moderate motivation for learning some kinds of tasks, particularly those involving difficult discriminations.

- Learning under the control of reward is usually preferable to learning under the control of punishment. Correspondingly, learning motivated by success is preferable to learning motivated by failure. Even though the theoretical issue is still unresolved, the practical outcome must take into account the social by-products, which tend to be more favorable under reward than under punishment.
- Learning under intrinsic motivation is preferable to learning under extrinsic motivation.
- Tolerance of failure is best taught through providing a backlog of success.
- Individuals need practice in setting goals for themselves: goals that are neither so low and limited as to elicit little effort nor so high and difficult as to foreordain failure. Realistic goal setting leads to more satisfactory improvement than does unrealistic goal setting.
- The personal history of the individual—for example, his or her record of reaction to authority—may hamper or enhance the ability to learn from a given teacher.
- Active participation by learners is preferable to passive reception of the content to be learned.
- Meaningful materials are learned more readily than nonsense materials, meaningful tasks more readily than tasks not understood by the learner.
- There is no substitute for repetitive practice in the overlearning of skills or in the memorization of unrelated facts that must be automatized.
- Information about the nature of a good performance, knowledge of one's mistakes, and knowledge of successful results assist the learner.
- Transfer to new tasks will occur more smoothly if, in learning, the learner can discover relationships for himself or herself and has experience in applying principles of relationship within a variety of tasks.
- Spaced or distributed recalls are advantageous in fixing material that is to be retained a long time.[19]
- "Learners progress in any area of learning only as far as they need to in order to achieve their purpose. Often they do only well enough to 'get by'; with increased motivation they improve."[20]
- "The most effective effort is put forth by children when they attempt tasks which fall in the 'range of challenge'—not too easy and not too hard—where success seems quite possible but not certain."[21]
- Learners engage in an activity most willingly if they have helped select and plan the activity.
- When learners are grouped by ability according to any one criterion

such as age, I.Q., or reading ability, they vary over a range of several grades according to other criteria.

- Learners think when they encounter obstacles or challenges to action that interest them. In thinking, they design and test plausible ways of overcoming the obstacles or challenges.
- When pupils learn concepts, they need to have the concepts presented in varied and specific situations. Then they should try the concepts in situations different from those in which they were originally learned.
- Pupils learn a great deal from one another. When they have been together a long time, they learn from one another more rapidly than they do from peers who are strange to them.
- The problem of "isolates" appears in every school. Isolates are those children who are generally not chosen by their classmates and who are also likely to be unpopular with teachers.
- No school subject is strikingly superior to any other subject for strengthening one's mental powers.
- Pupils remember new subject matter that conforms with their previous attitudes better than they remember new subject matter that opposes their previous attitudes.
- Learning is aided by formulating and asking questions that stimulate thinking and imagination.[22]

Two High Points in Learning Theory and Practice

Motivation is so important a consideration in learning that it deserves special attention here. Motivation proceeds from within the learner. Thus, only an individual can motivate himself or herself; others merely set the stage or provide suitable conditions for his or her motivation. Motivation results from establishing and possessing goals. The goals most helpful in inspiring learning are intrinsic ones implicit in the learning itself, immediate goals as opposed to deferred ones, and major goals rather than minor ones. Goals may be set so high as to be frustrating or so low as to be unchallenging. A major problem of teaching is how to help individual learners set goals that are realistic for them. The evidence so far about teacher behavior that stimulates motivation in learners is as follows:

1. Teachers should behave flexibly: directively on some occasions, nondirectively on others.
2. They should do all they can to personalize their teaching, tailoring it to the needs of individual learners.
3. They should demonstrate their willingness to experiment and try new ideas in the classroom.

4. Teachers should display interested, appreciative attitudes toward learners.
5. They should have skill in asking questions that are interrelated and sequential and therefore "lead somewhere."
6. They should provide specific study helps.
7. They should show, by nonverbal means like nods and smiles, their appreciation of the qualities of individual learners.

The objective of these suggestions is to create a sense on the part of the pupil that he or she is achieving, is being recognized for his or her achievements, is learning something significant, is being given worthwhile responsibility, and is eligible for advancement.[23]

In addition to motivation, another high point in learning theory and practice is concept development. Authorities in learning theory are generally agreed that teaching directed toward concept development is prime teaching. They note that concept development supersedes in importance both verbal and motor learning, that processes can be learned best by concentrating on the concepts underlying the processes, that learning to think is critical in concept development, and that problem solving relies on formation of concepts. Conceptual content, carefully moderated, can be learned by young children. The fact that concept formation and concept use are interrelated makes the concept a functional medium of learning.

Teachers help pupils acquire concepts concerning structures, qualities, and processes. They may proceed in their teaching sequentially, gradually shifting their emphasis from simple concepts to advanced ones. Beginning with a broad learning field, teachers provide clues as to what to look for, thus contributing to the building of each concept, and they encourage verbalization, thus helping to make each concept an active part of learners' thinking.

The high status of concepts among the elements of learning content is discussed further in Chapter 4.

SITUATION 2-3
Putting Selected Learning Principles to Work

A central office supervisor and a building principal visited every classroom in the principal's building. As they did so, they spent most of their time observing pupils rather than teachers. They tried to ask themselves, "What are these pupils learning? What difficulties are they encountering? What principles of learning could we help teachers apply to improve the learning in this school?" They decided that the chief difficulties were these:

1. Too many items of content were being learned in isolation and without interrelationship.
2. Most of the reading material used in the school was too far above the

comprehension level of the pupils, but most of the classroom discussion, if it could be called that, was simple and repetitive.

3. Pupils were learning under threat of punishment more often than they were learning because the content seemed to them to be worthwhile.

What important principle of learning does each of the difficulties suggest? What could teachers do concretely to apply each of the principles?

Applying Learning Theory in Confronting Pressing Problems of Curriculum and Instruction

Learning theory, like other theory, is worthwhile only when it works. The learning theory available to the school practitioner covers a wide range of current and potential school activities. It soon becomes obvious to anyone studying learning in schools that no one theory can be used to undergird all school activities and experiences. A theory that emphasizes conditioning is helpful in supporting one experience, and a theory emphasizing concept development is useful in supporting another.

Curriculum workers, coming as they usually do from varied academic backgrounds and job assignments, are notoriously weak in specifying learning strategies that teachers can use in implementing curriculum plans. They should know what has happened to the older learning theories: faculty psychology, unfoldment, apperception, and psychoanalysis. They should know the current status of connectionism, behaviorism, and neobehaviorism, as well as of Gestalt-field theory. They should know the range of Piaget's work and Jerome S. Bruner's ideas about discovery. If any of the terminology in this paragraph looks unfamiliar to an aspiring curriculum leader, he or she should go immediately to sources of help in the field of psychology. One cannot work eclectically among learning theories without understanding the theories on which eclecticism is built. There is room in school programs for all kinds of learning activities, from memorization to drill, to inquiry, to creative activity. Curriculum specialists are responsible for helping teachers attain objectives expeditiously. In these days of increasing attention to objectives and performance, applications of learning theory must be made with special understanding and skill.

Perhaps the most significant research in learning conducted during recent decades has been Benjamin S. Bloom's study of human characteristics, Piaget's inquiry into the development of individuals, the work of several investigators concerning physiological approaches to learning and memory, John C. Flanagan's study of the talents of young people in Project Talent, inquiries into the relative significance of nature and nurture, and studies of the effects of environment on the continuing development of individuals. The frontier is only beginning to open, and much remains to be done in the study of the learning process and the conditions that encourage or inhibit learning. Attention is now being given, if only on a fragmentary and limited basis, to several facets of process and environment.

Providing Variety in Learning Experiences

A first instructional problem requiring interrelationship between theory and practice is providing variety in pupils' learning experiences. Robert Gagné has identified eight "learning types" representing eight different kinds of experiences for which differing learning theories provide rationale. They are signal learning, stimulus-response learning, motor chaining, verbal association, multiple discrimination, concept learning, principle learning, and problem solving.

1. *Signal learning* causes development of reflexive responses to signals by continuing repetition. Examples are clapping one's hands to get children's attention and turning lights off and on.
2. *Stimulus-response learning* is today often called *operant conditioning.* An example is learning by practice to pronounce words in a new language.
3. *Motor chaining* consists of connecting stimulus-response learnings. Examples are operating science equipment in a laboratory and putting letters together to form words.
4. *Verbal association* consists of putting words together in association. An example is reciting a poem.
5. *Multiple discrimination* is responding differently to events and objects and distinguishing among them. Examples are making distinctions among makes of automobiles or among geometrical figures.
6. *Concept learning* consists of placing objects or events in a class and responding to them as a class. Examples are identifying and responding to a family of objects and identifying and responding to a cellular structure.
7. *Principle learning* means linking concepts to form principles, which may appear as generalizations or formulas. Examples are statements of principles like "interest equals principal times rate times time" and "objects dropped from one's hand fall to the earth."
8. *Problem solving* is frequently called simply "thinking" and consists of combining two or more learned principles to create a new principle of higher order. An example is using principles of addition, subtraction, and multiplication to solve arithmetic problems.[24]

Giving Direct Instruction

A second instructional problem calling for application of learning theory has real import in our own times. The apparent decline in skill-teaching in elementary and secondary schools has led many a person in the street to say of modern-day teachers and teaching, "If teachers don't teach it, it doesn't get taught." In the thinking of the layperson, "it" refers to basic skills, or essentials for survival. Within the past quarter century, the basic skills, like almost everything else, have been taught, in the main, nondirectively. Although nondirective teaching surely has its place, evidence has been accumulating in favor of teaching "the basics" directively. When elementary school teachers watch successful athletic coaches drill their charges in the fundamentals of their respective sports, they are almost invariably impressed with the importance of concentrated, continuing direct teaching.

After a careful survey of the literature, Brophy reports that direct instruction unquestionably produces pupil learning of the basic skills. In teaching directly, teachers should focus on academic goals, plan to teach a large amount of content, keep the pupils involved, select and pursue particularized objectives, use carefully chosen materials, monitor pupil progress, structure learning activities, provide for immediate feedback, and create a classroom environment that is task oriented but relaxed. Brophy mentions additional obligations of the teacher: to "have a mind" to instruct thoroughly; to use time as a precious commodity; to teach personally rather than through surrogates; to be unafraid to use recitation, drill, and practice; to do whole-group, small-group, and individualized teaching judiciously; where necessary, to encourage overlearning to the point of mastery; and to manage the classroom well. If these responsibilities seem numerous and onerous, they may remind us that many teachers have not been "bearing down hard enough" to ensure success in the learning of fundamentals.[25] Trying hard begins with the will to try. As we shall see in Chapter 3, teachers' will to try has been broken by unfortunate influences in the society and the community.

The same general mandates for learning the basics are usable in middle schools, junior high schools, and senior high schools. At senior high school level, direct instruction may legitimately include lectures, demonstrations, and teacher-led discussions.

Peterson agrees that direct instruction should be used in teaching the basic skills. For teaching inquiry skills, the instruction properly may be more indirect.[26] Similarly, Powell points out that pupils learn what they are taught, not what they are not taught, and that the more time teachers spend in direct teaching, the more pupils are likely to learn.[27]

For problem cases in following the direct approach, precision teaching is needed. Precision teaching is a careful application of the techniques used in many a tutorial arrangement in public and private schools. It begins with screening pupils, assessing their skills, and initiating remediation. The continuing remedial program is then carried on in both classrroom and resource room.[28]

Mastery Learning

Mastery learning is what its name implies: learning to the point of mastery. It has been put to use chiefly within the context of *competency-based education* (sometimes called performance based education), an educational procedure in which the objectives of learning and the evaluation of their attainment, along with the time and circumstances required, are carefully planned. Studies of the effects of mastery learning indicate that it usually gets better results than less-disciplined learning strategies.[29] Much depends, of course, on the nature of the subject matter to be learned, and on the nature of the learners who are involved.

A major advocate of mastery learning, Benjamin Bloom, has expressed the belief that most pupils (perhaps 95 percent) become very similar in learning ability, rate of learning, and motivation for further learning when they are supplied with favorable learning conditions. The most important conditions are provision of feedback and corrective individualized help. Thus, learning characteristics often called good-poor and fast-slow become alterable when conditions are favorable. Bloom is convinced that learning can be made more effective by using mastery learning strategies in which the goal is mastery, whatever the amount of time and attention needed to achieve it in the individual case. When pupils achieve mastery, they appear to develop confidence in their capabilities, and their mental health tends to improve.

What, then, are the roles of teachers in promoting mastery learning? Bloom says that teachers need to equalize the feedback and help they give to individual pupils. Their procedure should go as follows: (1) group instruction, leading to (2) feedback by means of brief diagnostic tests, leading to (3) individual help which is usually given by an aide, a peer, a parent, or through previously prepared materials. Often, seeing how well mastery learning works for nearly all their pupils increases teachers' faith in learners' potential. In fact, teachers' strong but realistic expectations that their pupils can learn seem to inhere in the mastery learning process itself.[30] Confidence in what learners can do leads teachers to state in sequence desirable learning objectives, to know the reading abilities of their pupils, to model the skills to be learned, to watch their pupils perform, to give them helpful feedback by reinforcing and correcting what they do, and to evaluate learning with a view to modifying content and procedures in the future.[31]

Mastery learning has been criticized for putting too much emphasis on what adults do *to* learners; for restricting curriculum content to what learners can assuredly do, and to what pupil achievements can be measured; for ignoring much of the need for increased individualization in teaching and learning; and for reducing teachers' opportunities to make professional judgments. On the other hand, mastery learning seems to remove pupils from some of the damaging norm-induced competition they

experience in schools and yet make them aware of how well they have succeeded in their learning tasks. Through it, schools achieve a degree of quality control, and teachers are stimulated to improve their teaching of the
basic skills.[32]

Using Time Wisely

Efficiency in teaching and learning requires that the time pupils spend in
school be used wisely. Wise use of time does not imply that youngsters
should not have relaxation and change of pace during the school day, but
that time dedicated by plan to hard effort should not be frittered away. It has
been estimated that up to 39 percent of scheduled instructional time in classrooms is spent on noninstructional matters. These matters include disciplin-
ing, restoring attention to the subject matter content under consideration,
attending to the personal welfare of individual pupils, attending to inter-
ruptions originating in the school office and elsewhere, and providing for
transition from activity to activity. Teachers do not realize the amount of
time pupils spend merely awaiting instructions. In recent years, a squeeze
has developed between the increased quantity of subject matter to be taught
and the decreased amount of time pupils have to learn it. At one research
center, the time learners have for concentration has been called Academic
Learning Time, the three ingredients of which are allocated time, engagement rate and success rate. As might be expected, pupils who accumulate
more Academic Learning Time usually score higher on achievement tests.[33]

Persons who have studied use of time in elementary schools say that
the time spent on teaching and learning in these schools varies from about
eighteen to twenty-eight hours a week. At present, most elementary schools
have days that are not too long for children to endure and yet long enough
to accommodate all elements of needed instruction. Using time wisely does
not, therefore, relate directly to the current attempts to lengthen school
day and school year; rather, it relates to the ways in which time in school
is used consistently and constructively for work on worthwhile tasks.[34]

In addition to generalized Academic Learning Time, which embodies
the total time pupils are engaged in and experiencing success in learning,
the literature discusses three other types of time. *Allocated time* is the
amount of time actually scheduled for learning. The better-known *time-
on-task* is engaged time during which pupils are "bearing down" in serious
attempts to learn. *Time-off-task* is time when pupils are not involved in
learning, whatever the reason.[35] Critics of the schools say, "Time-off-task
is not what taxpayers are spending their dollars for." On the other hand,
countercritics argue that emphasis on time may deflect attention from the
nature of task, which is the more important curriculum matter. In truth,
both the tasks now being performed and the learning materials now being
used to aid in their performance need improving.[36]

Specific advice can be given to teachers for using scheduled time wisely:

1. Analyze how time is presently being used and misused.
2. Establish priorities in the use of scheduled time.
3. As learning proceeds, allot time with discretion.
4. Set deadlines for completing parts of the work.
5. Expect total concentration when the subject matter demands it.
6. Quarantine the classroom against outside demands.
7. Remain conscious of time expenditure.
8. Plan the work, both before and during the activities.
9. Recognize and respond to signs of fatigue.

Helping Pupils Learn to Think

Thinking, an important function of learning, needs to be understood more clearly. Louis Raths categorized the difficulties that learners encounter in thinking as impulsiveness, overdependence, rigidity, the tendency to miss meanings, dogmatism and overassertiveness, underconfidence, inadequate concentration, and unwillingness to think.[37] He and others have made a small start in helping upper elementary school children remove some of their difficulties within these categories. The school has had much to do with helping learners "think straight," but the means of doing so have been largely hit and miss. The thinking done by some learners has been misunderstood. For instance, the person who "thinks at right angles" to his or her group may be considered an eccentric or a deviate, whereas such a person might be described more accurately as being a creative thinker.

It is possible to prepare questions that give pupils practice in using the categories of thinking that appear in Bloom's *Taxonomy of Educational Objectives*: memory, comprehension in the forms of translation and interpretation, application, analysis, synthesis, and evaluation.[38] In funded programs, posing questions within each of these categories has proved helpful in teaching youngsters to learn to think. The meanings of the categories, with an example of each, are given below:

1. *Memory.* Pupils recall or recognize information. Example: Who is the chief character in the story?
2. *Translation.* Pupils change information into a different symbolic form of language. Example: Stated in your own words, what are the ideas in the second paragraph?
3. *Interpretation.* Pupils find relationships among facts, generalizations, definitions, values, and skills. Example: Is the climate of Portland different from or the same as the climate of Seattle?
4. *Application.* Pupils solve a lifelike problem, identifying the issue

and using appropriate generalizations and/or skills. Example: According to what we have studied, how would you solve the following problem?

5. *Analysis.* Pupils solve a problem in the light of conscious
   knowledge of the parts, so that they can describe the step-by-step
   process by which the problem is solved. Example: It is dangerous
   to cross the street. The candy store is on the opposite side of the
   street, so it is dangerous to go to the candy store. What can you do?

6. *Synthesis.* Pupils solve a problem requiring original, creative
   thinking. Example: Write a poem that describes excitement at
   receiving an unexpected gift. What's original and creative in what
   you have written?

7. *Evaluation.* Pupils make a choice of good or bad, right or wrong,
   according to established, known standards or criteria. Example:
   Do you think the main character in the story was punished enough?

For a long time, teaching children to think has been regarded as an
important function of schools. Before Hilda Taba developed her "thinking
strategies" and others began to search for ways of teaching thinking, no
systematized methods existed. Now any comprehensive curriculum used
in elementary or secondary schools should have within it one or more explanations of relevant ways of teaching thinking. Articles and books by
specialists in the subject fields (for example, the social studies and science)
include many helpful hints concerning ways of teaching learners to think.

Responding to Differing Learning Styles

One's learning style is a combination of one's characteristic behaviors in
responding to or interacting with learning environments. Every learner appears to have his or her own learning style, based on a variety of interrelated influences. When learning content really matters to youngsters, they
can tell other people how they learn, and they do the telling willingly.[39]

Cognitive style alone is said to involve three sets of behaviors: the
ways in which one gathers information, the ways in which one interprets
information, and the ways in which one reasons to reach a conclusion or
decision. The first, or information-gathering, set of behaviors identifies how
the learner gathers information—by reading, listening, using all the senses,
exercising sensitivity to others' feelings, interpreting staged effects, or
understanding body language. The other two sets of behaviors can also
be broken into parts.[40] Just as there are modes of learning cognitively,
there are modes of learning affectively. The latter modes have, of course,
been investigated less thoroughly than the cognitive ones.

Rita Dunn and Kenneth Dunn have identified eighteen elements within
four categories representing the ways pupils learn: (1) the environmental—

including sound, light, temperature, and casualness as compared with structure; (2) the emotional — involving motivation, persistence, responsibility, and structure; (3) the sociological — involving peers, self, pair, team, adult, and varied input; and (4) the physical — including perceptual strengths, intake, time, and mobility. These four categories provide structure for the eighteen elements or variables associated with teaching styles. The teaching styles also number four: (1) the traditional — representing minimum "grade level" standards; (2) the individualized — in which diagnosing, prescribing for, and guiding each pupil are prized; (3) the open — which permits pupils to select, within limitations, their own curriculum, resources, schedule, and pace of learning; and (4) the alternative — within which pupils presumably have maximum curriculum choice, freedom, and independence.[41] The individual's learning style profile may be matched with available programs to achieve the best possible fit. Specifically, given programs emphasize the achievement of particular skills. The skills developed in a program may be matched with the elements of learning style in which the pupil should have strength in order to function well in that program.[42]

The dimensions of learning style have been extended to include descriptions that can be matched with teaching style descriptions. For example, some learners learn incrementally, or step by step; others learn intuitively, by intuitive leaps. Some are sensory specialists, relying primarily on one sense, whereas others are sensory generalists, using many or all of the senses. Emotionally involved learners want an emotionalized classroom atmosphere; emotionally neutral learners like classroom emotional excitement to be low key. Then there are "explicitly structured" learners who need clear, unambiguous structure to enhance learning, as well as their opposite number, those who want open-ended structure that gives opportunity in the classroom for divergence and exploration. Finally, of course, there are eclectic learners who can draw on several styles, shifting them from time to time.[43]

Teaching styles that, in general, can be made to fit learning styles have been called task oriented, cooperative, child centered, subject centered, learning centered, emotionally exciting, and emotionally subdued.[44] Obviously schools need to make varied learning environments available simultaneously so that learners with differing style orientations may be distributed among them.[45]

To begin responding to differing learning styles, teachers should be given time to interview individual pupils, to note their preferred "learning modalities," and to provide methods, materials, and tests that match the style preferences. Pupils can be asked what methods of instruction they like best, the times of day they study best, how they assess their attention spans, and how much physical activity and structure they need. Interview data can be confirmed by observation. Evidences of cultural diversity should also be considered. The cultural values of pupils may affect their learning styles.[47]

Teaching Indirectly

The fact that varied learning styles exist and should be catered to makes one realize that whereas a portion of learning theory supports direct instruction, another portion supports indirect or more casual teaching. For a long time it has been known that if learners are to "blossom out," to become creative and self-fulfilling, they must be given time and space within which to operate freely. Open-space education was designed to take pupils from what were alleged to be oppressive school environments into open arenas where they could make free choices as they tried experiencing in ways that were new to them. What has been said in the preceding pages about the need for "tightening up" in the learning of basic skills is not inconsistent with the important goal of retaining in education the freedom to pursue other purposes. Purposes and objectives that require freedom and openness in the learning environment are common to the arts and to almost the whole of the humanities. In free and open environments, pupils learn to work independently and so develop self-reliance; they are not restrained from proceeding at their own rates of learning; they are encouraged to use a variety of learning resources; and their classroom and other learning areas are modified or redesigned so that there is ample space for preparing materials and fostering independent activity. Young children need more space and time for constructive play than they have usually been given.[48]

Pupils' work products can be evaluated individually with reference to the work each of them has done previously. Examples of these work products are the writings and drawings of individuals.

The role of the teacher in this more informal setting is less that of taskmaster and more that of guide, adviser, helper, comforter, and encourager. Pupils should be helped to understand why their teacher proceeds differently in performing a different teaching task.

Recognizing but Not Exaggerating Sex Differences

Much of the discussion about sex differences in learning is centered in the theme song "What you can do, I can do better." Titles in public law have emphasized the importance of having girls and boys do the same things in the formal curriculum and the activities programs of schools. In addition to emphasizing the desirability of freeing youngsters of both sexes to have worthwhile experiences in common, the new legislation has aroused interest in the relative capacities of boys and girls to profit equally at any given time from particular experiences. Learning theorists are more interested in the relative capacities of the sexes to learn than in the fairness of new social policy in equalizing human rights.

Learning theorists recognize that the culture affects what girls and boys can do by determining what they are expected to do. During most of the time they spend in the elementary school, girls show superiority over boys in verbal tasks. Boys receive more remediation in reading and the language arts, as school personnel and parents expect them to. In the elementary school, girls and boys do about equally well in arithmetic. As stereotyping concerning girls' alleged incompetence in mathematics begins, girls steer away from mathematics courses in high school.

Some differences in functioning are real. Young girls exhibit superiority in hearing; young boys, in seeing. Boys manipulate three-dimensional objects well. Girls who achieve well intellectually are often active, assertive, and outgoing, whereas intellectually inclined boys may be less active, more shy and more anxious.[49]

Given that schooling and the testing done in schools discriminate at different times against both girls and boys, teachers and administrators should do all they can to reduce discrimination. Both standardized and teacher-made tests need redesigning so that they give boys and girls equal opportunities to achieve. The curriculum should provide better balanced opportunities for seeing and listening. For hyperactive pupils (frequently boys), additional space should be made available. As boys grow into adolescence, they may be expected to be restless, to write illegibly, to want to disassemble things, and to be loud and clumsy. Girls, on the other hand, need to be accommodated with linguistic approaches to physics and other scientific subject matter. The overall need is for watchfulness in noting differences and for diligence in balancing opportunities.

Much has yet to be learned about sex differences and their effects on human learning. Two recent theories about differences and their effects have to do with growth spurts and the relative dominance of the right and left hemispheres of the brain.

Certain learning content can obviously be mastered more readily at a given chronological age by some pupils than by others. The cause has been attributed in part to increments in the development of the brain, in both brain weight and mental activity. Although states of development in intelligence have been discussed for a long time (by Vygotsky and Piaget, for example) how learners move from one state to the next has only recently come under scrutiny. Epstein and others have said that the advances occur by correlated brain growth and mind spurts, called *phrenoblysis*.[50] As measured by head circumference, brain growth is 5 to 10 percent during each of the age periods from two to four, six to eight, ten to twelve, and fourteen to sixteen. Between the ages of ten and twelve, girls experience growth at a rate approximately twice that of boys. At about the age of fifteen, boys overtake girls in rate of head growth. In most youngsters between the ages of twelve and fourteen, the brain actually ceases to grow.[51] Epstein and Toepfer have said further that the probable difference between a learner with an I.Q. of 160 and a learner with an I.Q. of 100 is the speed at which new intellectual capacities mature. A pupil should be kept occupied with challenging experiences, but at his or her own level of cognitive development. The importance of arranging appropriate experiences continues to be ignored by persons in authority in the field of education and by others who should know better.

These findings suggest that we should seek to increase the potency of cognitive experience during certain age periods and reduce it during other periods. The quiescent periods could be used for skill practice and for acquiring certain affective learnings. One wonders to what extent educators' ignorance of mind spurts has contributed to school failure and drop-out rates. Surely the commercially prepared graded materials the schools use will need total revision if findings about phrenoblysis continue to be supported.

Consideration has been given to the differences in function of the right and left hemispheres of the brain. At first, the left hemisphere was thought to be devoted to rationality, and the right hemisphere to emotionality and creativity. Subsequent study, however, has reduced the rigor of this distinction between the two hemispheres. Nevertheless, differences continue to appear. For instance, the two hemispheres differ in the contributions they make to perception; the right hemisphere apparently plays a special role in emotion; and for right-handed people, speech seems to be centered in the left hemisphere. The meanings for education of these and similar findings have yet to be explored.[52]

SITUATION 2-4
The Case of Mary Williams

Mary was the youngest child in a family of three children. Her father, a retired engineer, decided to move from the town of Bushville, the site of the plant in which he had worked during recent years, to an apartment in a nearby city. "We can attend the opera and the theater in the city," Mr. Williams said to his wife. "Mary will have a good school that will prepare her for Oberlin just as well as Bushville High School has done."

In the course of time, the Williams family, which now consisted only of the father, the mother, and Mary (the two older children having married and moved away), rented an attractive apartment in Jackson City within three blocks of El Centro High School, which Mary would attend. Fortunately for Mary, the Williams's move to Jackson City occurred when she was about to begin her junior year. If the move had come earlier or later, she might have had more difficulty at El Centro.

At first, Mary found the new school easy. Why should it not be for a girl whose I.Q. was reported to be 130? Mary regarded her peers as being rather dull and uninspired. Perhaps, she thought, this was because she had been in the experimental class at Bushville and these were ordinary students with whom she was now associating.

Then came the first report card. Mary discovered to her shock that it was possible for a student with a nearly straight A average in Bushville to receive a C in English, a B in American History, a D in Latin III, a C in Chemistry, and a C in Algebra II. "Is the work *that* much harder?" her distraught parents asked. "No," Mary replied, "but it's different."

Mary's cryptic remark led Mr. Williams to inquire of the school *how* the work was different, if it really was. After all, wasn't second-year algebra second-year algebra wherever a student took it? Perhaps Mary had changed. To investigate the possibility, Mr. Williams hurried her to a physician, who found no changes in Mary's physical condition that could account for her scholastic decline.

Mr. Williams's visit to El Centro High School resulted in varied comments by Mary's teachers, but one remark was common to all: Mary did her homework assignments well, but she could not compete, either in speed or in quality, when she tried the varied activities in which El Centro's teachers asked their students to engage. "We try to emphasize mind stretching," Mrs. Culver, the principal, told Mr. Williams. "Our teachers prepare their key questions in advance to encourage divergent thinking and imagination. We make up 'thinking exercises,' and some of our tests are like nothing you've ever seen. We favor student discussion, provided our youngsters know what they're talking about, but discussion is only one of many classroom procedures we use. The activities in most of our classrooms are really varied."

That night, Mr. Williams turned and tossed while he worried about Mary's situation. The next day he wrote Mrs. Culver: "My daughter came to your school from a good school in which she learned the fundamentals she needs. She memorized her grammar and solved her basic problems in mathematics without difficulty. I have diagnosed her present situation this way: You people are asking Mary the wrong questions and you expect her to do things she should not be doing. It is your duty to treat my daughter as she was treated previously. If you do not do so, I shall make a complaint at the offices of the city board of education."

What do you conclude about the relative worth of what Mr. Williams wanted done for Mary and what El Centro High School was trying to do for her?

Were the El Centro teachers validly using what is known about learning when they worked with students in general and Mary in particular?

SITUATION 2-5
Identifying Basic Considerations Affecting Learning Style

A curriculum leader surveyed some of the literature of psychology that she thought might relate to a study of the learning styles of children in her school system. Among the generalizations she noted were these:

1. Pupils change their attitudes by identifying with people who are their models.
2. Learning by wholes frequently works better than learning by parts.

3. A learner's success in performing a task depends significantly on the frequency and effectiveness with which his or her learning has been reinforced.

If you had been the curriculum leader, what might you have done to check the validity of these generalizations relative to the learning styles of a sample of fifteen pupils?

Views of Learning Suggested by the Comments of Pupils

Learners have remarkable insight into what functions in one's attempts to learn. Mosley and Smith reported the answers of 566 pupils in grades seven through twelve of the Little Rock (Arkansas) school district to the question "What do you like about the ways teachers help you learn?" The pupils said they wanted teachers to provide adequate explanations, with examples; constructive and relaxed learning situations; individualization of instruction; enough time for learning; and incentives and interest.[53]

A few years ago the author solicited from upper elementary school and secondary school pupils oral and written comments about their engagement in learning activities in school. The nature of the comments showed that pupils have their own valid, if unsophisticated, views of the classroom learning process. As Rush and his associates say, the final evaluation of any teaching-learning episode is accomplished by pupils, who decide what is worth listening to, trying, and remembering for subsequent use.[54] In any attempt to improve learning in classrooms and schools, the views of learners should be taken into account.

Pupil comments accumulated by the author were categorized to form four statements of view:

1. Teachers who "madly teach" without giving much thought to their teaching practices sometimes do little to encourage real learning.
2. The best teachers seem to set the stage for learning and then let learning take its course.
3. Teachers can take various concrete actions to assist learning.
4. Probably teachers do best in assisting learning when the school experiences they provide have greatest meaning for learners.

Most of the comments were related to the first and second statements. The following are sample comments relating to the first statement of view:

*View Number 1: Teachers who "madly teach" without giving
much thought to their teaching practices sometimes do little
to encourage real learning.*

A junior high school boy said:

> My teacher is a strange guy. He asks a question. You give an answer
> that takes fifteen seconds. Then he elaborates on your answer for twenty
> minutes. Maybe he's not so strange, though; he's like a good many other
> adults. Like all of them, he's lost me before he's five minutes through his
> speech.

A senior high school girl reported:

> You should have seen Mr. R today. He had this fancy physics experi-
> ment set up. Just as he was getting started with his demonstration, a
> pulley broke. He looked all through the drawers of the science table for
> another one but he never found any. So he tried using a lead pencil held
> by two clamps. At that point he cut his finger on something in one of
> the drawers and the blood began dripping on the table. He kept on with
> the demonstration and then asked me what he'd been demonstrating. For
> the life of me, I couldn't tell. I'd been too busy watching the blood drip
> from his finger.

Another senior high school student said:

> Today we were shown a ten-minute movie the teacher's sister had taken.
> It was pretty poor; all full of shadows. Mr. B kept saying, "Now if you
> could see that, it would look like a small animal crawling out of the
> bushes." After we had watched some more dim, shadowy figures doing
> something, Mr. B stopped the film and asked what we'd learned. I'm
> always putting my foot in my mouth. I said, "I've learned you should
> never show pictures taken by your sister if she's a poor photographer."

A fifth grader stated:

> Since we got our television room at school, we don't spend much time
> on any one thing. The room is in the basement and our classroom is on
> the second floor. We go downstairs for arithmetic. The arithmetic lesson
> comes on at 9:30 and lasts until 10:00. When that's over, we go back
> upstairs. The science lesson begins at 10:30 and ends at 11:00. Then we
> go back upstairs. Twice in the afternoon we go down and up, down and
> up. I guess I don't get much out of it. I could see better television if I
> could stay home and turn the dial myself. And we don't talk about what
> we've seen.

A bright ninth-grade pupil commented:

> Life in Miss J's class is wonderful. Only sometimes Miss J doesn't know
> how wonderful it is. We have free reading. We all think it's a good idea,
> especially those of us who hide better books than Miss J knows about
> behind the books she thinks we're reading. One of the fellows passes
> around the hottest paperbacks he can buy. When Miss J hands out the
> books she wants us to read, we just slip the paperbacks inside her big
> books.

Presumably the teachers whose actions were described by these
pupils believed that their methods were markedly benefiting their
pupils. Whatever their intentions, the teachers were evidently assuming that the youngsters were learning what they, the teachers, thought
they were learning. Meanwhile, the youngsters were learning other
things—that some teachers tell you more than you want to know, that
dripping blood is more attention getting than a lesson in mechanics,
that showing a dim, unclear picture is worse than showing none at
all, that poorly presented educational television can make schooling a
boring experience, and that an unsupervised experience, though
basically constructive, can be perverted.

*View Number 2: The best teachers set the stage for learning
and then let learning take its course.*

A high school senior remarked:

> I suppose there are three kinds of teachers: (1) the kind who set the
> world before you, open it, and let you see, hear, taste, feel and smell it;
> (2) the kind who give you a limited view of the world and then pull the
> string just as you're beginning to look at it; and (3) the kind who show
> you a piece of the world by putting it on the blackboard and then say,
> "Take it or leave it; you aren't going to get any help from me."

An eighth grader said:

> I like to go to science class in our school. I've never seen anything like
> it. There are lots of things in the room, most of them in cases along the
> walls. But every time we walk in, the teacher has enough stuff on the
> laboratory tables to make us curious. Before you know it, you're in-
> terested, and then sometimes you're confused, but by the end of the
> period, you've usually had enough hints from the teacher to begin mak-
> ing some sense out of all the activity that's been going on.

A sixth grader gave this reaction:

> Miss A is a lot different from Miss S, the teacher we had last year. Miss S knew all the answers. At least she said she did, and when we found her wrong a few times, she got mad. When we have a discussion with Miss A, she doesn't tell us much that she thinks. She asks us questions and they're pretty tough. The questions make us think more than any questions I've been asked before. Sometimes when I leave school at the end of the day, I find myself trying to think up answers to questions Miss A asked us during the day.

A ninth grader commented:

> I guess we have the sloppiest classroom in the whole school. Papier-mâché models, pots of paint, saws and hammers, rolled-up newspapers. You name it. We have it. But we have fun. Not that we hack around or destroy nothing. Mr. H doesn't say too much. He mostly walks around, gives a hint here and there. But that arts class goes places! You should see some of the things we've made. Next month we're having an arts exhibit for the school and the parents.

Pupil after pupil seemed to show that he or she knew what setting the stage in teaching, and then leaving the stage to let learning proceed, really means.

ACTIVITY 2-2
Soliciting Pupils' Comments about Learning

In the previous discussion, two statements of view, the third and the fourth, were left without exemplary comments by pupils.

The following question represents View Number 3: What can your teachers do in their teaching that you think would be most helpful to you in learning what you are expected to learn?

The following question represents View Number 4: What have you done in your classroom work during the past few days or weeks that has helped you most in understanding or appreciating what you were expected to learn?

Ask the pupils in one or more classes in your school to respond to either or both of these questions. If the response is oral, keep notes concerning what is said, or make a tape or cassette recording of what is said. If the response is written, keep the written records. Think what meaning the pupils' comments have for teachers in their efforts to assist learning. If possible, discuss the pupils' comments with other teachers, and invite them to try the same experiment with their own pupils, with subsequent discussion.

SOME USES OF PSYCHOLOGY IN MAKING DECISIONS
COOPERATIVELY ABOUT THE CURRICULUM

So far in this chapter, commentary about learners and learning as it relates to curriculum planning has been focused on teachers and learners in classrooms. This focus has seemed appropriate because, as we have seen, the curriculum is fundamentally made in the classroom by continuing interactive process. This is not, however, the only necessary focus in curriculum planning. What the teacher does in planning for the next day or for the next term is another important focus. Teachers do not properly teach merely to please themselves by following an instructional program of their own making or choosing. Several curriculum planners are likely to do better, wiser planning than just one. Major decisions about the curriculum and its impact on the lives of people should be made at a third level of planning—cooperative planning by groups of competent people.

The third level of planning is addressed in the following pages in three terms: the psychological basis for finding directions governing learning by children and youth, the psychological basis for selecting and organizing school experiences for pupils, and the psychological reasons for identifying school practices in particular need of reform.

Setting Psychologically Based Educational Directions
for Children and Youth

For a long time, expectations of pupil achievement have been stated against a background of goals and objectives, which sometimes have been expressed clearly and explicitly but more often have been left obscure. Whereas goals or aims guide the educational thrust of the school, objectives provide specific direction in the selection of experiences to meet pupils' educational needs. Teachers are familiar with the day-to-day objectives of their teaching and particularly with the objectives thay have written into their unit plans. They know much less about the goals or aims of the schools in which they work, partly because the schools themselves frequently have no stated goals.

Several key questions reflect the relationship of psychology to the wise selection of objectives:

- Is the objective attainable by the school?
- How long is it likely to take to attain a given objective?
- At approximately what age or ages should striving for the attainment of given objectives be initiated?
- To what extent should objectives be repeated in subsequent years of schooling?
- In what ways are objectives multiple in their effects?[55]

As soon as objectives have been accepted, means of evaluating their attainment should be sought. Many unfortunate time gaps develop between formulation of objectives and their evaluation because educators characteristically short-circuit the evaluation process, skipping directly to the experiences through which objectives may be achieved. As soon as the objectives are clear, then, the means of their evaluation should be considered, and these means will in turn suggest learning experiences. Placing the steps in this order tends to prevent teachers from becoming lost in a forest of experiences and activities, the purposes and means of evaluation of which may have been forgotten. In developing course guides and preparing units of instruction, the teacher usually should follow the order or sequence suggested.

Evaluation procedures should be designed to measure the achievement of every desired behavior the objectives express. Thus, if one of the objectives is development of appreciation, evaluation questions or other evaluation devices should be prepared to show the extent to which appreciation has been developed. Modern teachers often subscribe to several objectives at a time, but the tests they prepare continue to show their success with only one or two objectives, such as garnering of knowledge and attainment of understanding. Changes in attitudes, appreciations, and interests are difficult to evaluate. Pencil-and-paper tests frequently will not fulfill the need; therefore, more ingenious instruments must be prepared. Some of these may be both informal and semiprojective—for example, giving oral answers to thought questions, playing out a situation through sociodrama, or serving as an interview subject.

Psychology reveals that evaluation can become a powerful force for either good or evil. On the one hand, it stimulates learners to better achievement; on the other, it creates anxieties that inhibit worthwhile learning. According to Percival M. Symonds, "all of the anxiety inherent in the examination situation comes from the reactions of other individuals—parents and teachers—to examination results. Teachers have the power to make an examination a challenge, or an ordeal to be dreaded and avoided if possible, by the attitude they take toward it and toward the results that individual children achieve."[56] Tests should be used as media of learning and not merely to effect traumatic checkup. They are used by alert teachers to help pupils learn to take tests, they are sometimes given a second time so that the factor of novelty does not affect the result, and they may sometimes even be given for fun rather than "for keeps."[57]

By setting objectives and evaluating the extent to which pupils are able to attain them, teachers can determine some of the educational needs of pupils as these needs relate to the psychology of learning. As we shall see in subsequent chapters, other evidences of educational need must also be sought. Determining educational need in a comprehensive way goes well beyond evidence of learning in school to a consideration of the nature and goals of the instructional system, community influences, and other factors.

More comprehensively, educational directions for children and youth are guided by *academic press*, the extent to which all kinds of environmental forces press for pupil achievement. These forces include people's expectations, policies, practices, norms, and rewards.[58]

Selecting and Organizing School Experiences for Pupils

Findings in educational psychology suggest certain criteria that may be used in selecting educational experiences that lead to certain objectives:

1. Learning experiences should be designed to allow practice of the behaviors that the objective suggests. The pupil must believe that practice is helping him or her to learn what the objective specifies. If the opportunity for practice does not seem to the pupil to be relevant to his or her view of the objective, the student will tend to reject it.
2. Learning experiences should express what the learner believes he or she is expected to know. The learner's background and present environment suggest that some experiences are worthwhile and that other experiences are fruitless. The perceived worthwhileness of the experiences makes a significant contribution to learning.
3. Learning experiences should sometimes be of the self-activating type. Pupils need opportunities to proceed at their own rate through subject matter that suits them. Thus individual learning is justified and necessary. Obviously, keeping pupils in group situations in both elementary and secondary schools too consistently can lessen effectiveness. Invention and creativeness are often aided by the silences during which individual activity occurs.
4. Learning experiences should be fostered, whenever possible, in intimate face-to-face relationships within small groups. Desirable interaction and learning can apparently be achieved more readily in groups of five to eight members than in groups of thirty to forty. Teachers and other curriculum workers should pay more attention to this finding.
5. Learning experiences should be as varied as the objectives they represent. There has been too great a tendency to utilize a few kinds of experiences to achieve several objectives. Ingenuity is needed in devising experiences that achieve given objectives.
6. Learning experiences should be challenging without being frustrating. In recent years, many pupils have found work in their schools unchallenging. When a nation of youngsters fails for any reason to work hard in the process of acquiring an education, that nation is in danger of losing in competition with other nations.[59]

The ways in which learning experiences are put together greatly affect the achievement of objectives. Helpful organization of experiences provides for sequence where sequence is needed and for continuity where continuity is needed. It also provides for balance, so that there is not an overemphasis on one kind of experience at the expense of other kinds. At the same time, it affords enough scope of experiences to guarantee that a broad range will supply all that is needed for total educational development. Finally, organization assists with correlation of subject matter that is closely related — for instance, the history of the Westward Movement in the United States in clear relationship with the literature of the Westward Movement. The educational dimensions known as sequence, balance, scope, continuity, and correlation demand consideration by master planners of the curriculum.

At the level of operation of the classroom, where curriculum plans are put into effect, there are characteristics of functional organization of learning experiences as seen by classroom teachers:

> *The good organizing center for learning encompasses ability floors and ceilings of the group.* . . . Some kinds of content, such as mathematics and science, require the development of rigorous concepts. Solving mathematical problems demands high-level insight into concepts of quantity. Learning to read involves acquiring skill in word attack. There are very definite limits to the range of concept or skill development that can be challenged by a single organizing center for learning. When these limits are narrower than the range in group abilities in the particular skill or concept sought, the teacher must plan to make the two more comparable by dividing the class into smaller groups. The development of certain social skills, on the other hand, demands the interaction of individuals varying widely in interests, abilities and backgrounds. The best organizing center for such learning may be one that plans for inclusion of the entire class. . . .
>
> *The good organizing center for learning is comprehensive in that it permits inclusion of several ideas and several catch-hold points for differing student interests.* An organizing center of limited complexity is soon exhausted of its appeal and must be replaced by another. . . . But a truly comprehensive center invites exploration at several points and poses a variety of student appeals. . . .
>
> *The good organizing center for learning has the capacity for movement — intellectual, social, geographic, or chronological.* The class must be able to move somewhere with it. Such a capacity is almost always present in certain favorite units of study. . . .[60]

There are, then, two levels of operation in organizing learning experiences. The first of these involves seeing the curriculum as a whole and letting general curriculum objectives, reflected against a background supplied especially by psychology, determine the sequence, scope, continuity, balance, and correlation that programs of teaching and learning should have. The second involves decision making by teachers about how to organize both their pupils and the blocks of subject matter they study so that the maximum achievement of objectives can be attained. Curriculum leaders are much concerned with the first level, which requires mastery of large segments of the school program. They should be concerned also with the second level, which consists of helping teachers to do better what they have already learned to do in part. On neither level are the tasks simple, for the locus of them is a complex human being, the learner. We must, therefore, continue to study the learner's reactions to sequences, unit plans, ways of grouping him or her with others, and other strategies of organization.

As learners grow older, they move from the here and now of childhood to what David Elkind has called an extended spatial, temporal, and figurative world of adult thought.[61] Effective teachers gauge the worth of learning content and materials against the effect of these changes on pupils' learning abilities. By selecting and organizing learning experiences, teachers learn to select and organize experiences that are increasingly appropriate.

Identifying School Practices in Need of Reform

Certain practices antithetical to learning are being perpetuated in modern schools. Practices that need questioning and possible reform include:

1. Systems of marking that inspire excessive competition and comparison making among pupils
2. Use of evaluation data for rating and comparing, at the expense of its use for feedback and guidance
3. Overcrowding, with resultant heavy class loads, pupil anonymity, shallow teacher-pupil relationships, and loss of privacy
4. Curricular tracking, with the caste system it nurtures
5. Inflexible time schedules followed slavishly
6. Unreasonable pressures of all sorts
7. Single textbooks and one-way experiences, leading to conformity and boredom
8. The grade-level lockstep, resulting in single scope-and-sequence schemes
9. Misinterpretation and misuse of intelligence and achievement tests
10. Teachers' occasional unwillingness to accept even partial responsibility for pupils' failure to learn

11. Misuse of cumulative records, destroying their confidentiality and overemphasizing the messages they communicate
12. The tendency to insist on universally applicable "right" answers.

Practices that show promise of making wiser use of our knowledge of how people learn include the following:

1. Using varied methods of teaching
2. Using multiple teaching materials
3. Organizing instructional groups appropriate to given learning situations
4. Treating pupils humanely
5. Helping learners accept objectives and invent some of their own
6. Providing adequate opportunity for practicing skills
7. Prizing pupils' ability to develop ideas
8. Emphasizing interrelationships, or "ecological balance," of subjects and subject fields
9. Making the school a workshop for accomplishing concrete learning.

SUMMARY

This chapter has reported some of the influences that developmental psychology and educational psychology, when applied to decision making about the curriculum, have on the endeavors of learners, classroom teachers, and curriculum leaders. The chapter has discussed understandings of the learner's development and of the learning process, with emphasis on how what we know about learners and learning can be used in improving the curriculum. Special features have been a section on the growth and development of learners, a section on understandings of the learning process, and a section on uses of psychology in making decisions about the curriculum.

The next chapter turns from applications of psychology to applications of sociology and cultural anthropology. To be considered is how social and cultural forces help to mold the curriculum.

ENDNOTES

1. See D. A. Prescott, *The Child in the Educative Process* (New York: McGraw-Hill, 1957).
2. From *Language Arts Guide, Kindergarten and Grades One Through Seven* (Montclair, N.J.: The Public Schools of Montclair, 1956). Used with permission.
3. Joan Scheff Lipsitz, "The Age Group," in Mauritz Johnson, ed., *Toward Adolescence: The Middle School Years*, Seventy-Ninth Yearbook, Part I, National

Society for the Study of Education (Chicago: University of Chicago Press, 1980), pp. 13–20.

4. For an overview of Piaget's theory, see Jean Piaget, *The Theory of Stages in Cognitive Development* (Monterey, Calif.: McGraw-Hill, 1969).

5. Another important curriculum area for planning is moral development, which is treated in Chapter 3.

6. Association for Supervision and Curriculum Development, *Learning and the Teacher*, 1950 Yearbook (Washington, D.C.: The Association, 1959), pp. 29–32. Note also Calvin W. Taylor's proposal of "multiple talent teaching," a means of giving pupils opportunities to exercise their unused talents, reported in *Today's Educator*, December 1968, p. 69.

7. The Association, *Learning and the Teacher*, p. 33.

8. Organizing centers for subject matter content can be key ideas, people, places, materials, or ways of working.

9. Virgil E. Herrick, "Curriculum Decisions and Provision for Individual Differences," *Elementary School Journal* 62, no. 6 (March 1962).

10. Barry K. Beyer, "Individualized Learning: Students Can Do Their Own Planning," *Clearing House* 55, no. 2 (October 1981): 61–64.

11. Gerald Grant, with John Briggs, "Today's Children Are Different," *Educational Leadership* 40, no. 6 (March 1983): 4–9.

12. J. Merrell Hansen, "Understanding Youth: It's Tough Growing Up, But We Can Help," *Educational Leadership* 35, no. 7 (April 1978): 535–40.

13. The late James B. Macdonald cautioned against extending the thrust of developmental meanings too far beyond the contexts in which they were formed. See James B. Macdonald, "Myths about Instruction," *Educational Leadership* 22, no. 7 (May 1965): 574.

14. Robert J. Havighurst, *Human Development and Education* (New York: Longmans, Green, 1953).

15. Hansen, "Understanding Youth," pp. 538–40.

16. "Mainstreaming," *Today's Education* 65, no. 2 (March-April 1976): 18–29.

17. Ernest L. Boyer, "Public Law 94-142: A Promising Start?" *Educational Leadership* 36, no. 5 (February 1979): 298–301.

18. Rita S. Dunn and Robert W. Cole, "Inviting Malpractice Through Mainstreaming," *Educational Leadership* 36, no. 5 (February 1979): 302–6.

19. Ernest R. Hilgard, *Theories of Learning*, 2nd ed., 1956. Reprinted by permission of Prentice-Hall, Inc., Englewood Cliffs, N.J.

20. Goodwin Watson, "What Psychology Can We Feel Sure About?" *Teachers College Record* 61, no. 5 (February 1960). Used with permission.

21. Ibid.

22. Ibid. See also Richard C. Anderson and Gerald F. Faust, *Educational Psychology: The Science of Learning and Instruction* (New York: Dodd, Mead, 1972).

23. Ronald C. Doll, *Supervision for Staff Development: Ideas and Application* (Newton, Mass.: Allyn and Bacon, 1983), p. 256. For other suggestions concerning motivation, see Phi Delta Kappa, *Practical Applications of Research* 5, no. 1 (September 1982): 1–4.

24. Rogert M. Gagné, *The Conditions of Learning* (New York: Holt, Rinehart and Winston, 1965), pp. 31–59.

25. Jere E. Brophy, "Teacher Behavior and Student Learning," *Educational Leadership* 37, no. 1 (October 1979): 33–38.

26. Penelope L. Peterson, "Direct Instruction: Effective for What and for Whom?" *Educational Leadership* 37, no. 1 (October 1979): 46–48.

27. Marjorie Powell, "New Evidence for Old Truths," *Educational Leadership* 37, no. 1 (October 1979):45–51.

28. Ray Beck et al., *Precision Teaching Project: Implementation Handbook* (Great Falls, Mont.: Great Falls Public Schools, 1977). Reported in ERIC # ED 169 688.

29. Theodore A. Chandler, "Mastery Learning: Pros and Cons," *Bulletin of the National Association of Secondary School Principals* 66, no. 454 (May 1982): 10, 11.

30. Gary L. Taylor, "Mastery Learning: A Prescription for Success," *Bulletin of the National Association of Secondary School Principals* 67, no. 464 (September 1983):84–89.

31. Delva Daines, *Designing Instruction for Mastery Learning* (Provo, Utah: Brigham Young University, 1982).

32. Chandler, "Mastery Learning: Pros and Cons," pp. 13, 14.

33. Charles Fisher, Richard Marliave, and Nikola N. Filby, "Improving Teaching by Increasing 'Academic Learning Time,'" *Educational Leadership* 37, no. 1 (October 1979): 52–54. (This article was based on work performed at the Far West Laboratory for Educational Research and Development, San Francisco.)

34. See ERIC Clearinghouse on Educational Management, "Academic Learning Time," in *The Best of ERIC on Educational Management*, no. 65, May 1982.

35. National Association of Secondary School Principals, *Curriculum Report* 10, no. 2 (December 1980): 2.

36. See Jack Frymier, "Learning Takes More Than Time on Task," *Educational Leadership* 38, no. 8 (May 1981): 634, 649. For a discussion of research concerning time-on-task, see *Time-on-Task: A Research Review*, published by the Center for Social Organization of Schools, 3505 North Charles Street, Baltimore, Maryland 21218.

37. Louis Raths, "Sociological Knowledge and Needed Curriculum Research," in James B. Macdonald, ed., *Research Frontiers in the Study of Children's Learning* (Milwaukee: School of Education, University of Wisconsin, 1960), pp. 31–34.

38. See Benjamin S. Bloom et al., *Taxonomy of Educational Objectives* (New York: Longmans, Green, 1956).

39. Rita Dunn, "Can Students Identify Their Own Learning Styles?" *Educational Leadership* 40, no. 5 (February, 1983): 60–62.

40. Lee DeNike and Seldon D. Strother, "A Learner Characteristic Vital to Instructional Development," *Educational Technology* 15, no. 9 (September 1975): 58, 59.

41. Rita Dunn and Kenneth Dunn, "Learning Styles, Teaching Styles," *Bulletin of the National Association of Secondary School Principals* 59, no. 393 (October 1975): 37–49.

42. Rita Dunn and Kenneth Dunn, "Learning Style as a Criterion for Placement in Alternative Programs," *Phi Delta Kappan* 61, no. 4 (December 1974): 275–78.

43. Barbara Bree Fischer and Louis Fischer, "Styles in Teaching and Learning," *Educational Leadership* 36, no. 4 (January 1979): 245–54.

44. Ibid.

45. Susan S. Ellis, "Models of Teaching: A Solution to the Teaching Style/Learning Style Dilemma," *Educational Leadership* 36, no. 4 (January 1979): 274–77.

46. Rita Dunn and Kenneth Dunn, "Learning Styles: Practical Applications of the Research," *Practical Applications of Research* 1, no. 3 (March 1979): 1, 2.

47. Barbara Cooper Decker, "Cultural Diversity: Another Element to Recognize in Learning Styles," *Bulletin of the National Association of Secondary School Principals* 67, no. 464 (September 1983): 43–48.

48. Phi Delta Kappa, "Play," in *Practical Applications of Research* 5, no. 2 (December 1982): 1–4.

49. Richard M. Restak, "The Other Difference Between Boys and Girls," in National Association of Secondary School Principals, *Student Learning Styles: Diagnosing and Prescribing Programs* (Reston, Va.: The Association, 1979), pp. 75–80.

50. Herman T. Epstein, "Growth Spurts during Brain Development: Implications for Educational Policy and Practice," in Jeanne S. Chall and Allan F. Mirsky, eds., *Education and the Brain*, Seventy-Seventh Yearbook, Part II, National Society for the Study of Education (Chicago: University of Chicago Press, 1978), pp. 343–70.

51. Herman T. Epstein and Conrad H. Toepfer, Jr., "A Neuroscience Basis for Reorganizing Middle Grades Education," *Educational Leadership* 35, no. 8 (May 1978): 656–60.

52. See the four articles under the heading "Educational Implications of Recent Brain Research," *Educational Leadership* 39, no. 1 (October 1981): 6–17.

53. Mary H. Mosley and Paul J. Smith, "What Works in Learning? Students Provide the Answers," *Phi Delta Kappan* 64, no. 4 (December 1982): 273.

54. Donald E. Rush et al., "Essential Components for Effective Curriculum Development," *Peabody Journal of Education* 53, no. 4 (July 1976): 296–98.

55. For a discussion of the determination of objectives by applying psychological principles, see Ralph W. Tyler, *Basic Principles of Curriculum and Instruction*, Syllabus for Education 360 (Chicago: University of Chicago Press, 1950), pp. 24–28. For two discussions of objectives that are behavioral, see Robert M. Gagné and George F. Kneller, "Behavioral Objectives?" *Educational Leadership* 29, no. 5 (February 1972): 394–400; and W. James Popham, "Must Objectives Be Behavioral?" *Educational Leadership* 29, no. 7 (April 1972): 605–8.

56. Percival M. Symonds, *What Education Has to Learn from Psychology* (New York: Bureau of Publications, Teachers College, 1958), p. 72.

57. Goodlad and Klein have noted that both setting objectives and evaluating pupils' success in attaining them has been neglected in educational practice. See John I. Goodlad and M. Frances Klein, "What's Happening in Curriculum Development," *Nation's Schools* 77, no. 4 (April 1966): 70–73. For a view countering the current emphasis on behavioral objectives, see Donald Hogben, "Curriculum Development and Evaluation," *Teachers College Record* 74 (May 1973): 529–36.

58. Joseph F. Murphy et al., "Academic Press: Translating High Expectations into School Policies and Classroom Practices," *Educational Leadership* 40, no. 3 (December 1982): 22–26.

59. See Herbert J. Walberg, "We Can Raise Standards," *Educational Leadership* 41, no. 2 (October 1983): 4–12.

60. Association for Supervision and Curriculum Development, *Learning and the Teacher*, pp. 56–58.

61. David Elkind, "Adolescent Thinking and the Curriculum," *New York University Education Quarterly* 12 (Winter 1981): 18–24.

SELECTED BIBLIOGRAPHY

Association for Supervision and Curriculum Development. *Freeing Capacity to Learn.* Washington, D.C.: The Association, 1960.

————. *Human Variability and Learning.* Washington, D.C.: The Association, 1961.

————. *Learning More about Learning.* Washington, D.C.: The Association. 1959.

Ausubel, David P. *Educational Psychology—A Cognitive View.* New York: Holt, Rinehart and Winston, 1968.

Bloom, Benjamin S. *Human Characteristics and School Learning.* New York: McGraw-Hill, 1976.

Bloom, Benjamin S.; Hastings, J. Thomas; and Madaus, George F. *Handbook of Formative and Summative Evaluation of Student Learning.* New York: McGraw-Hill, 1971.

Bruner, Jerome S., et al. *Studies in Cognitive Growth.* New York: John Wiley, 1966.

Claydon, Leslie, et al. *Curriculum and Culture: Schooling in a Pluralist Society.* Winchester, Mass. Allen and Unwin, 1978.

Doll, Ronald C., ed. *Individualizing Instruction.* 1964 Yearbook. Washington, D.C.: Association for Supervision and Curriculum Development, 1964.

Doll, Ronald C., and Fleming, Robert S., eds. *Children under Pressure.* Columbus, Ohio: Charles E. Merrill, 1966.

Gagné, Robert M. *The Conditions of Learning.* New York: Holt, Rinehart and Winston, 1965.

Graubard, Allen. *Free the Children.* New York: Pantheon, 1973.

Havighurst, Robert J. *Human Development and Education.* New York: Longmans, Green, 1953.

Hilgard, Ernest R., ed. *Theories of Learning and Instruction.* National Society for the Study of Education, Sixty-Third Yearbook, Part I. Chicago: University of Chicago Press, 1964.

Hosford, P. L. *An Instructional Theory: A Beginning.* Englewood Cliffs, N.J.: Prentice-Hall, 1973.

Jersild, Arthur T. *Child Psychology.* Englewood Cliffs, N.J.: Prentice-Hall, 1968.

————. *In Search of Self.* New York: Bureau of Publications, Teachers College, 1952.

Johnson, Mauritz, ed. *Toward Adolescence: The Middle School Years.* National Society for the Study of Education, Seventy-Ninth Yearbook, Part I. Chicago: University of Chicago Press, 1980.

Lefrancois, Guy R. *Of Children: An Introduction to Child Psychology.* Belmont, Calif.: Wadsworth, 1973.

Mann, John. *Learning to Be: The Education of Human Potential.* Riverside, N.J.: Free Press, 1972.

Martin, John H., and Henderson, Charles H. *Free to Learn: Unlocking and Ungrading American Education.* Englewood Cliffs, N.J.: Prentice-Hall, 1972.

Meacham, Merle L., and Wiesen, Allen E. *Changing Classroom Behavior,* 2nd ed. Scranton, Penn.: Intext, 1974.

Noar, Gertrude. *Individualized Instruction: Every Child a Winner.* New York: John Wiley, 1972.

Piaget, Jean. *The Theory of Stages in Cognitive Development.* Monterey, Calif.: McGraw-Hill, 1969.

Prescott, Daniel A. *The Child in the Educative Process.* New York: McGraw-Hill, 1957.

Rubin, Louis, et al. *Facts and Feelings in the Classroom.* New York: Walker, 1972.

Thoresen, Carl E., ed. *Behavior Modification in Education.* National Society for the Study of Education, Seventy-Second Yearbook, Part I. Chicago: University of Chicago Press, 1973.

Wiles, Jon, and Bondi, Joseph, Jr. *Curriculum Development: A Guide to Practice.* Columbus, Ohio: Charles E. Merrill, 1979.

3

Social and Cultural
Forces Affecting
Curriculum Decisions

Society, the culture, and our American system of values, unclear as these values sometimes are, have a marked effect on efforts to improve the curriculum. Their impact develops at two levels: the remote but significant level of society's influence and the immediate and practical level of the community's contact with the schools.

The first portion of this chapter deals with influences from society and the culture at large. The second section discusses community influences for and against curriculum improvement. The third portion treats examples of curriculum ideas that are of current interest and that demonstrate the impingement of American society and culture on the curriculum. The final segment suggests several strategies that curriculum planners can use in dealing with social and cultural influences on the schools.

INFLUENCES FROM SOCIETY AND
THE CULTURE AT LARGE

We live in a difficult era. Sometimes the only consolation is the thought that other nations and people have lived and are living in difficult times, too. We are faced with fiscal stress within governments, problems of money management in households, deteriorating family structures, the special needs of minority populations, excessively permissive parents, youngsters out of control, and misuse of drugs and alcohol. On the other hand, we can gain courage from our ability to maintain a degree of stability, the promise of a communication revolution, and the potential residing in a population of varied and exceptional talents.

Schools are affected continually by forces and influences from American society and the culture at large. These forces and influences affect school curriculum in three major ways: by inhibiting change through the power of tradition, by speeding change that stems directly from social and cultural changes, and by applying pressures that originate in major segments of American society and culture.

The Boon and the Weight of Tradition

Tradition has sometimes been referred to as a "dead hand." Actually, it may be viewed in two ways: as a helpful preventive of attempts to discard the tried, tested, and true and as a weight that restrains desirable change.

Society has at its disposal several forces that support tradition and inhibit change. The first of these is legal authority. Laws are frequently enacted more easily than they are repealed. Hence, a law that establishes a day a year for the planting of certain trees as an exercise in conservation education may have outgrown its usefulness, but the law is likely to remain on the books anyway. A second force, which is of enduring consequence and which exercises desirable restraint, is the generally agreed upon principles of right and wrong. From our Judeo-Christian tradition we have inherited notions of property rights and individual rights that have often been considered to be immutable. Thus, education in the decent treatment of other people has become, and remains, an objective of the school. A third force, psychological resistance to change, is so potent that it gets full treatment in Chapter 7. Human beings resist change so energetically that, in some areas of their lives, they would rather die than shift their positions. Many teachers cannot prove that their curricula and methods of teaching are actually functioning for improved learning, but they will resist strenuously any effort to bring about change.

The curriculum worker must take these and other tradition-assisting forces into account. Almost daily he or she encounters people who say, "But we've always done it this way!" In a few instances, the response should be "I agree that we must continue to work in the same manner, for we are dealing here with an unchanging element of our responsibility." Matters of physical safety and the maintenance of intelligently derived morality fall within this category. In many instances, however, a question should be raised about the worth of traditionalized practices. There is nothing sacred, for example, in the methods used in the past to teach arithmetic, though the need to teach arithmetic according to some combination of methods will remain a fixed responsibility.

Consider the effect of tradition on the modern secondary school. By tradition, most secondary schools:

1. Organize pupil time in several brief and generally equalized periods
2. Emphasize a limited number of objectives in education
3. Permit pupils to elect subjects rather freely
4. Yield to established means of evaluation and accreditation
5. Subject themselves to the rigidities of the Carnegie Unit System
6. Add subjects at intervals but eliminate subjects only with the greatest difficulty.

Curriculum workers who are concerned with secondary schools should look hard at the traditions surrounding the schools. They should ask: Which traditions are imponderables? Which ought to be preserved? Which could and should be eliminated promptly? Surely numerous traditions exist today without justification or validity.

Similarly, elementary schools have their own traditions that need challenging.

SITUATION 3-1
Finding Traditions to Challenge

Imagine yourself to be a curriculum coordinator who, with a committee, has sought to identify traditions that need reexamination. The committee has elicited from teachers and laypersons several traditions that they feel should be challenged. Here are six of them:

1. Teachers in the primary grades should be women.
2. Sociology doesn't belong in the secondary school, but history does.
3. Teachers are rightly concerned only with how to teach; laypersons must tell the schools what to teach.
4. The curriculum is appropriately geared to the achievement of the upper classes in society.
5. We must continue to put a premium on verbal comprehension and verbal fluency.
6. Teachers and school board members properly represent chiefly the middle classes of our society.

Which of the six stated traditions exist in the schools you know best?

Which of the traditions that exist in the schools you know genuinely need to be questioned? Why?

The Effects of Social and Cultural Change

Society influences action for curriculum improvement in a second way— by bringing to bear upon the curriculum those changes that occur in the wider society and culture. Despite the influence of tradition in holding social forces in check, society is constantly changing. Change is accompanied by an instability that a society can tolerate unless or until instability becomes excessive, at which time disorder or revolution occurs.

In many respects, the United States is moving rapidly:

- Science and technology are continuing to advance as new discoveries and breakthroughs are made in physics, chemistry, medicine, and other fields.
- Bigness prevails in nearly everything: in government, labor, business, and agriculture.
- Improved transportation and communication have brought about travel at supersonic speeds and the transmission of messages by satellites. Additional breakthroughs in communication are yet to come.
- The family has tended to disintegrate, so that striking changes have been wrought in family patterns of living.
- Population seems to be growing out of bounds, not so much in our own country as elsewhere in the world.
- Social movements that include integration of the races, mobility of the population, and movement of people from lower socioeconomic to higher socioeconomic status are continuing, though the pace of these movements appears to have slowed.
- A value crisis has gripped youth and adults, who have become less clear about what they really believe.

Some of the changes affect school immediately. For example, when the population of a nation is on the move, new faces suddenly appear in school classrooms. Many Americans are moving each year—from cities to suburbs and, more recently, to small towns and rural areas. Movement from south to north, and later from north to south, and from Puerto Rico to the mainland has been especially marked in recent years. Schools in larger cities have been forced into curriculum reform by the influx of culturally deprived children to whom standardized tests are not applicable and to whom American middle-class experiences are foreign.

Other changes have a subtler, more gradual effect. When family life disintegrates, the school finds itself taking on more and more responsibility that the family previously assumed. Few schools now bathe children to eliminate lice, but all schools are faced daily with learning the problems of children whose parents are being divorced or of children who are feeling the effects of alcoholism or drug abuse in the home.

In the presence of these and other changes, elementary and secondary schools retain their responsibility for the cognitive development of pupils representing wide varieties of ethnicity, social status, mental ability, particular talent, and social outlook. They have become more directly responsible than ever before for affective education, a relatively uncharted domain. So-called simple education of feelings and emotions is never really simple. Today affective education is made especially complex by societal and academic disagreements about the meaning of moral development and about the determination and clarification of values. Day by day in the schools disagreements occur about matters of morality and values, often with reference to sex, drug, and alcohol education. Where homes have abdicated their responsibility for moral suasion and values setting, many people expect the schools to fill the breach.[1]

Four changes in American society that particularly affect the schools are worthy of brief discussion here.

The first change is continuing development and communication of knowledge. Growth in the so-called knowledge industry is occurring under the control of big business. Research and development in the invention and use of communication machines are well on the way to dominating the production and distribution of knowledge. As research and development help increase our capacity to learn, education for all persons is likely to take on new meaning. The storage, retrieval, and communication of information will become an even greater industry than it is now. Demand for education will increase beyond its present level.

A second change affects the financial support of the public schools. Prior to the arrival on the political scene of Howard Jarvis and California's Proposition 13, the public was getting tired of paying taxes that had steadily increased in a time of rising living costs. Many a school district was finding its annual budget and its special bond issues unacceptable to the public. Sometimes the movement against higher taxes was statewide, as when legislatures put caps on education budgets. The public was striking out against a visible, reachable opponent. Able to do very little about federal and state taxes, taxpayer groups concentrated their efforts on local property taxes. Among the effects on teachers and pupils have been numerous cutbacks in programs and courses and reduction of school activities.[2] A lesson to be learned from this experience is that in periods of extremity, the face and function of the public school as an institution are subject to surprising changes.

A third shift is in the realm of human conduct. For some time, discipline and morale in the schools have been deteriorating. As society's standards for guiding and controlling children and youth have become more and more confused, attacks on teachers and school property have increased at an alarming rate. Violence in the schools has become a frequent topic for discussion in the communication media, at education conventions, and in livingrooms. Teachers are being subjected to indignities that were unheard of two or three decades ago. A high school teacher, writing to one of her more troublesome pupils near the end of a recent school year, said to him:

> I don't know why you've acted toward me as you have. You seem to be normal, healthy, and good-looking. I think I've tried to respect you as much as I have any of the others. Certainly I've been fair with you. As you know, there have been times in school this year when I have kept you out of trouble, even when what you did was outside our classroom.
>
> You've noticed that I've had to change my home telephone number. I've asked the telephone company to leave it unlisted because of your nuisance calls in the middle of the night. I haven't enjoyed trying to start my car after you were seen putting sugar in the gasoline tank. Also, my neighbor tells me it was you who urinated against my front door.
>
> My telephone calls to your parents have yielded nothing, apparently because they think you can do no wrong. So, unless your subtle attacks stop, I shall have to take stronger action.

On reading a letter of this kind, many a teacher is constrained to say, "At least he seems not to have hit her. I wish I could say the same thing about all the youngsters in our school."

Violence has become part of the informal curriculum—in classrooms, in lavatories, in hallways, and elsewhere in schools. In some schools an atmosphere of fear that is akin to that of the jungle is affecting the lives of pupils, aides, and teachers.

A fourth recent change relates to the mobility of the population of the United States, as referred to briefly earlier in this section. People are moving from geographic area to geographic area, sometimes at a frequency of every few weeks. Their children often encounter adjustment problems in school and are enrolled in so many school systems that their total curriculum resembles a crazy quilt. Continued movement of people toward cities is being countered by movement from the inner city to the periphery. Social distance between old and new residents has increased. Assimilation of immigrants into a given culture has become less and less possible. Instead of assimilation, the key problem has been one of communication among cultures, sometimes at the most fundamental level. Children in schools, as well as their parents, now have real difficulty in understanding and accepting the values and ways of life of some of the people around them. Accordingly, education for increased cultural understanding must become one of the most prized goals of the school.

One seer has said that population shifts to the sunbelt, or extreme southern tier of states, will alter education in the United States in special ways. Education in the North and East will tend to differ from that in the South and West. In the sunbelt particularly, working mothers will be more numerous, learners will come more often from minority populations, teachers will be in shorter supply, and the pupils coming into the schools will be less well prepared. The public schools must prepare themselves to meet these and other challenges.[3]

These are but four of the several changes in U.S. society that have affected schooling. In the last analysis, the school is a miniature of the society that nurtures it. The school teaches essentially what the society expects it to teach. The values it inculcates differ little from those of the culture that supports it.

Teachers are often hard put, especially in society's fast-moving transition periods, to know what to educate for. Fortunately there are perennial goals to seek, though emphasis among the goals may change. Education continues its concern for intelligent inquiry, for developing fundamental character traits, and for training children in basic skills. Teachers must stand for principles and ideals in which they strongly believe, and at the same time cooperate with a general public that is rightly anxious and concerned about what is happening to stability in society. Though diagnosing new developments is difficult, teachers must ask, "What meaning will this societal change have for my teaching next week, next month, and in the years to come?"

SITUATION 3-2
Assessing the Effects of Specific Social Changes

The faculties of the elementary and secondary schools in Raysville thought they noted several changes in American society that have not been mentioned in the preceding discussion. These changes included increased tolerance of pornography and freedom of sexual expression, reduced interest in the classics in literature and the arts, and preoccupation with self-centered survival in an era of economic uncertainties.

How do you react to the faculties' list of changes? From your vantage point, are all three changes realistic? What other changes can you suggest?

Select two or three other changes that you consider most realistic. What impact might they have on curriculum in elementary and secondary schools in the United States?

SITUATION 3-3
What to Do about the Plight of Victimized Teachers

The principal of a school in Cranwood brought a guest to the faculty meeting. For reasons he expressed later, the guest wanted to remain anonymous. He had a story to tell the teachers. When he had told it, he wanted the teachers to react to it and to advise him about what he might do.

"What," asked the guest, "would you do about the situation I'm now going to describe? Until this year I've never had trouble with the pupils in my high school classes or around the school, but this fall a new boy arrived and soon began creating disturbances in his classes. One day in one of my mathematics classes I asked this boy to sit down. He refused, we argued, and suddenly he struck me on the chin with his fist. I fell to the floor unconscious. On my way down, according to other youngsters in the classroom, I struck the left side of my head on a chair back. After a week in the hospital with a concussion, I returned to school to find that our principal had suspended my attacker for a month, and that the boy's mother had taken the case to our board of education, protesting that a one-month suspension was too long.

"Because the case had criminal elements, it went to the municipal court, where the boy pled guilty. The judge heard several witnesses, including me, and then dismissed all of us before he passed sentence. The next morning, we at our school learned that the judge had ordered the board of education to readmit the boy immediately and had put him on probation, with a light reprimand. When the boy returned to school (as bold as brass), the morale of the teaching staff went down considerably.

"Now I've come to you as a kind of independent jury to ask what I, and possibly other people, should do immediately and in the future about situations of this kind."

If you had been a member of the faculty hearing the narration of this case, what would you have said?

Societal Pressures on the Schools

Every era brings its own kinds of pressures to bear on the schools. During the late 1950s, vocal groups in American society were demanding that our schools help us beat the Russians in the race for space and in technological sophistication. The consequence was pressure within school programs to teach "more of the same" and toughen up for the sake of keeping pupils busy. When the quality of what pupils were learning did not improve as a consequence of this kind of pressure, the funded "projects on instruction" in the sciences, mathematics, and other subjects came into vogue. Schools were urged to install enough projects to give assurance that the curriculum was being improved. Unfortunately for the planners of the projects, the incidence of project adoption was so slight that many projects did not obtain further financial support and disappeared from the scene. Many of those that remained for evaluation did not receive very favorable ratings.

Almost simultaneously, a malaise of softness, a belief that "we'll succeed somehow anyway," afflicted both the United States and a number of other nations of the world. Many parents no longer expected high-level achievement of their children; at the same time they condemned teachers for failing to "make the children learn." Falling scores in standardized tests were only the popularized symptom of a serious disease. Among nations with established educational systems, the United States rated very low in the amount of instructional time it provided pupils *in school*. As to *out-of-school* study, the average pupil in the other nations was spending 216 hours a year more on such study than a pupil in the United States. Although time spent in instruction and study is not the only criterion of learning effort or progress, time spent in learning, within school and outside it, does relate closely to level of learning.[4]

When teachers' lives are filled with numerous duties imposed from inside and outside the schools and when school leaders do not emphasize the importance of learning that is truly essential, only a brief period of time is needed for effort to diminish and even the ablest of pupils to start doing less well than they should. Such has been the situation in many a school, public and private. As an attempt to compensate for this decline has proceeded, the schools have been urged to teach the fundamentals better than before, to restore discipline, to emphasize moral and religious values, to prepare youth better for additional education and for making a living, and at the same time to reduce expenditures and to continue discharging duties that are properly within the domains of other institutions and agencies. The task of educating has become more difficult than ever.

Discussion perennially centers about the extent to which control of the schools follows the dollar. During the decades of the late nineteenth century and the early twentieth century, the funds that the public schools could not obtain from local communities came almost exclusively from state governments. In that era, the effect of financial support in determining control became unclear. The United States Constitution had left to the states the obligation and privilege of operating public school systems. Legal authority itself was nominally sufficient to accord the states the power they needed to implement control. Inevitably, however, the states granted annual appropriations to local school districts. To what extent did these appropriations specifically condition state governments' influence over policy making and management within the schools? This question has remained unanswered.

Subsequently, a new grantor of large funds, the federal government, became a competitor of state governments for the loyalty that necessarily accrues to grantors. Though the federal government had long supplied limited funds to the public schools (for instance, to support vocational education), a flood of money began to issue from Washington. As an entrant in the field of large-scale funding of public education, the federal government, especially as represented by the United States Office of Education, became a threat to school officials who resented the fact that federal grants were customarily made for limited and specific purposes that were determined by a few people at a central place. Reminding objectors to federal control that local school districts were not required to accept federal grants did not silence their complaints. Many persons in local communities feared the growth of a federal colossus whose agents might wheel and deal with friendly state officials in the interest of destroying local control by developing a national curriculum or by strengthening a state curriculum of monolithic design.

When the federal government began withdrawing from the funding of public schools through large grants, state departments of education resumed, with increased initiative, their attempt to guide the destinies of individual school systems. For a long time, state education departments had prepared curriculum guides that were meant to be what the name suggests—guides to be followed in a general way by school personnel in local districts. Inasmuch as there was never any real enforcement of the proposed use of the guides, following the guides in local districts was, in fact, optional. One could visit district after district and find untouched guides on office shelves.

During the late 1970s and the early 1980s, the accountability movement, backed by state legislation, caused departments of education to supervise the academic work of local districts more closely. The chief medium of curriculum supervision became minimum competency testing. Having established lists of pupil competencies representing the *least* that the state would require pupils to achieve if they were to be promoted or graduated, state departments of education themselves supplied, or contracted with private testing agencies to supply, measures of the achievement of the competencies called competency tests. Sometimes the appearance of rigid state control is "softened" by use of euphemisms like "state guidelines" and "the development of proficiencies." State teachers' associations and school board associations have sometimes condemned proposals of competency-based education unless the benefit from them is sufficient to compensate for the loss of local decision-making power. Teachers are beginning to feel strongly that their influence in curriculum making has seriously declined.

It may be that state departments of education still make their greatest impact on local schools by allocating funds, scheduling statewide tests, supervising pupil accounting, enforcing state laws and department regulations, and engaging in other tasks formerly regarded as almost purely administrative. Where mandates are tied directly to state grants of funds and where rigorous tests determine whether the schools in a district have "measured up," control by states is unquestioned.

When state governments dominate schools, local control is obviously reduced. The reduction sometimes occurs in subtle ways. For instance, the schools become responsible for achieving socioeconomic effects, especially for making prosperity possible. Although the culture may be imposing obligations in the education of affect, the state government insists that cognitive studies be strengthened. When the curriculum is to be improved by spending more dollars, the state government wants to control the use of the dollars it provides.[5]

ACTIVITY 3-1
How Much Federal and State Control?

One of the issues in U.S. education is the extent of control of local schools by federal authority, as opposed to state authority, that is to be permitted. Some educators have maintained that, to balance the many pressures on U.S. schools and to provide a stabilizing force in elementary and secondary education, we need a strengthened United States Office of Education or some other powerful federal agency. Too little has been said about what such an agency would do, under our governmental system of state control of schools, to make its influence fully felt without infringing upon the authority of state departments of education.

Think about ways, if any, in which you would strengthen federal influence or control in curriculum matters. What powers would you give to the Department of Education or its equivalent?

In what ways, if any, would you strengthen state influence and control?

What specific help should federal and state governments give in balancing the pressures that are applied to school systems and individual schools by groups in the society at large?

Societal and Culture-Based Developments Affecting the Curriculum

A number of developments in schooling are centered in societal situations or are culture based. One of the most noticeable of them has been declining school enrollments. When enrollment declines, school buildings are usually abandoned to purposes other than the strictly educational, and teaching staffs experience reduction in force (RIF). However, the effects on the curriculum can actually be beneficial, especially where enrollment decline is sufficiently small to prevent the closing of entire school buildings. Possible improvements include smaller class size, increased attention to maladjusted children, more opportunities for multilevel instruction, closer professional contact among teachers and other school personnel, and reduction in the duplication of effort and materials.

Other developments related to the society and the culture are

1. Admission of unorthodox subject matter content concerning events and preferences on the U.S. sociocultural scene
2. Introduction of facilities and materials that are products of a new industrial technology
3. Identification of special needs of children as seen in home and community settings
4. Increased accountability of school personnel to the American public for the quantity and quality of their work.

Reference to these four developments will be made at intervals throughout the remainder of the book.

Other developments are continuations or revivals of earlier phases of evolution in American education. The first of these is the rise of a new conservatism. Following a flurry of activity in organizing storefront and other alternative schools that tended toward reconstructionist philosophy, segments of the lay public began pushing more actively for schools representing an opposite philosophical viewpoint, that of conservatism. The new "fundamental schools," which do not always reflect the educational position of the conservative Council for Basic Education, are sometimes called the new conservative alternative. These schools emphasize discipline and cognitive achievement, sometimes using as educational means detention and paddling, homework, dress codes, repetition of grades in school, respect for adults, and observance of moral standards. Often schools of this kind are religious schools that are conservative in both moral-ethical precepts and cognitive content.[6] In an era in which a return to old values is becoming more marked, conservative education, which is of course not without its evils and excesses, is making a new appearance and a new impression.

The movement of the 1980s toward conservatism is reflected strongly in a drive to make private education public policy. The drive is directed not merely toward gaining tax relief for those who pay private school tuition and other costs involved in sending children to private schools. It is directed also toward placing control of education in the hands of parents and teachers who are free to make decisions about their own schools, with minimal interference by local, state, and federal government. Furthermore, it captures the attention and sympathy of parents who look to private schooling as a way to ensure upward mobility and economic advantage for their children.[7] We may expect to see additional private schools established in the future. In them, the roles of staff members will have to be clarified and altered as new expectations of conservative instruction are realized. The bureaucratization that has afflicted and burdened public school systems will need to be avoided.[8]

Entirely unassociated with redirection toward conservatism is the spread of partial responsibility for education from the school to persons and agencies in the community. Education at large, as opposed to limited schooling, is attracting the attention of a number of serious students of educational policy both within the schools and in the wider society. Beyond the confines of the school, pupils are expected to do *action learning* — or learning out in the community where "action" can be found. A recent yearbook identifies opportunities for action learning under the following headings: learning in the great outdoors, learning in unfamiliar cultures, learning in service agencies, learning in the professional community, learning in construction and urban renewal projects, learning on the road, learning in the political arena, and learning in the world of work.[9] The possibilities for achieving variation in pupil experiences are almost unlimited.

Another prominent development relates to diversity in ethnic status and national origin. Within recent years, when Spanish-speaking Americans in and near our large cities began their thrust for bilingual and bicultural education, they opened a range of possibilities for both recognizing and dealing with diversity and for achieving true cultural adjustment. Two major curriculum objectives became (1) fostering respect for the national background or ethnicity of each pupil and (2) helping the pupil function effectively within the common culture, within his or her own culture, and within other cultures.[10] These objectives, if carried to their limits, would materially assist in the ultimate realization of multicultural education, of which multilingualism is a part. The assumptions underlying the objectives suggest that minority cultures are unique in specific ways, but that all groups share common traits, values, and behaviors, and that individual pupils, whatever their own backgrounds, need to know and appreciate the common culture and also cultures other than their own. Furthermore, the prospects for broadened and deepened education in human relations and communication through language are improved by utilizing assumptions that lead to rejection of the melting pot theory, used for years in an attempt to "settle" minority peoples.

A significant, continuing, culture-based development can be seen also in the current impact of the labor movement on curriculum planning. Whereas business interests have influenced the curriculum for decades, the influence of labor organizations on the curriculum is relatively new. Labor groups representing teachers are now helping to make curriculum policy. Involvement of teachers in curriculum planning is regarded by teachers' unions as both a right and an obligation of professionals. The unions maintain that legislatures and business groups have often had special interests in mind when they have supported educational programs, whereas teachers' unions have the potential for promoting the general welfare of pupils. They see the entrance of teacher bargainers into the curriculum field as a safeguard against coercion by other groups in our society.[11]

The attitudes of parents toward children's use of time at home and the inroads of television in preempting children's available time form interrelated influences on the curriculum. Many parents, busy as they are with their own affairs, consign children to sit before a television tube (an assignment they readily accept), thus reducing the time spent helping with homework, discussing around the dinner table the events of the day, and reading to the children. In many American homes, little connection is made between the curriculum of the school and evening activities at home.

INFLUENCES WITHIN THE IMMEDIATE COMMUNITY

The individual community is often considered to be the real locus of decision making about the curriculum. In a sense, this is true. In classrooms, one finds teachers and pupils making fundamental day-to-day curriculum decisions. But as we have seen, master planning of educational programs of large scope and import is tending to leave the local scene. Some persons maintain that boards of education and administrators in local school districts now have little control of significant matters. Other persons, pointing out that every school district does have its own board of control, continue to insist that local decision making is much in evidence.

What the Community Wants, the Community Can Usually Get—Within Limits

Certainly communities now have, and will probably continue to have, a great deal to say about some curriculum matters in local schools. But some important curriculum decisions, such as the determination of broad educational objectives, will probably be made in the future on a state, a regional, or even a national basis. As revenue from local property taxes declines and schools' financial support comes increasingly from state and federal governments, control will almost inevitably follow the dollar. In addition, interstate programs like national testing may take from teachers and other curriculum personnel a considerable amount of control over what is taught.

It is true that some community groups favor statewide or national uniformity in the curriculum, even though so much that is known about learners and learning argues solidly against uniformity. Two major advantages attributed to uniformity are certain financial economies and educational continuity when pupils transfer from district to district and from school to school. In the American democratic system, however, development of ideas in local communities and local schools needs to be encouraged, for people grow by participating in planning. Some of the consolidations of school districts that have occurred to date have seriously limited participation in planning at the community level. Currently, the United States has a wealth of resources and facilities for planning in and through communities, and the nation must decide if it wishes to lose what de Tocqueville commended years ago—encouragement of groups of our people to volunteer for all kinds of community service.

Of course, the school is only *one* of the community agencies that contribute to education. Child development specialists say that more education than we realize occurs before the child is four years old, and observers with a comprehensive view of education report the impact of parents, youth-serving organizations, and other community groups on learners.

Curriculum workers are involved in continuing controversies as to who has responsibility for particular efforts to educate children and youth. In the areas of sex education, religion, driver training, and the social graces, for instance, they encounter many differences of opinion about the locus of educational responsibility. With some educators suspecting that the schools have already absorbed too much responsibility for child welfare from the community at large, discussions of the total role of the school are likely to increase and become more vigorous.

When asked where they acquired the learnings they consider most significant, a majority of upper elementary and secondary school pupils said their most important, durable learnings had come from sources outside schools.

The author has asked youngsters, "What could schools do to educate you in ways that no other agencies could or should?" About 200 of them provided one or more of the following answers (in paraphrase) during tape recorded interviews:

1. Put what we learn in school into a framework or system that will help us understand it better.
2. Teach us "fundamentals." Nowhere except in school are you likely to gain the tools you need for thinking and serving.
3. Give us opportunities and materials in school to help us inquire, discover and probe meaning. Getting meaning is perhaps the most important thing schools can help us do.
4. Stop attempting to compete with and destroy what we learn elsewhere. Instead, seek to coordinate what we are taught in school with what we learn outside school.[12]

Philip W. Jackson has argued that deschooling society is, of course, not a helpful way of proceeding, but learning from the vigorous critics of the school is.[13] There is a definite though evolving place for the school in the American culture complex, but it is evidently not its current place as arbiter and dispenser of education. Education itself is so universal that it needs to be thought of in broader terms than merely the institutional. A complete study of the roles of educational agencies should be undertaken to answer questions like the following: What is the full scope of current educational efforts and activities? What other useful efforts and activities might there be? What agencies should be providing education for children and youth? What responsibilities should belong exclusively to schools? How can schools best discharge their responsibilities?

American communities influence the schools in three basic ways: through the community's own needs, through the limits communities set on the curriculum of the school, and through the community's decision as to who shall receive schooling. The effect of local needs can be seen

in rural communities that insist that the pupils in their schools study vocational agriculture. It was also exemplified some years ago in a community
in which there was a high rate of school tardiness. Curriculum planners
in the community at first suspected that there were too few alarm clocks
in the homes, but a more thorough and realistic appraisal of the situation
revealed that malnutrition was unusually prevalent — children simply did
not feel like getting out of bed to go to school. Consequently, instruction
in nutrition, as part of a whole community drive for better feeding of adults
and children, became a curriculum mandate. The need for vocational
agriculture in one group of communities and nutrition in an individual
community are only samples of the numerous local needs that differ from
region to region, from section of city to section of city, and from small town
to small town throughout the nation.

The tendency of communities to determine who shall receive schooling is sometimes evident in local unwillingness to establish nursery schools
and kindergartens, even when state appropriation of funds encourages their
establishment. A less negative example is the current planning of vocational and technical high schools and community colleges throughout the
nation.

Inevitably, the curriculum is based firmly in home-school-community
relationships, and school-community planning is therefore much needed.
The great majority of American citizens live in communities of fewer than
10,000 people. Many such communities are quite isolated despite improvements in transportation and communication, and where they are not
isolated physically, the people in them are isolated psychologically, often
by their own choice. Both the traditions and the planning that touch people are grounded in local communities, so it seems unlikely that the power
and influence of the community in educational decision making will be
lost. Such power and influence are enhanced by a psychological fact:
learners are best equipped to explore and talk about their own environment, yet they need to have some aspects of it clarified for them. Accordingly, more school assignments should probably be centered in the world
of the child and fewer in the world and the universe at large. "How I
Diagnose My Own Fears" might be a more worthwhile composition title
than "What Astronauts Have Found on the Moon." One of the real obligations of the school is to help learners deal with conditions and situations
that are in or near them. To this end, community resources should claim
learners' attention in the form of resource files, directories to community
assets and points of interest, and other aids.

The legal arbiter of educational decision making in the local community is, of course, the board of education. In most instances, communities get in their board of education membership what they deserve.
If they are willing to abide the abuses that board members inflict upon
children by their shortsightedness, temporary extravagance, long-term

stinginess, or outright corruption, they perpetuate a low level of decision making that has plagued certain U.S. communities for a long time. If, on the other hand, the ablest and most responsible community members are willing to serve on boards of education, the children and the schools are sure beneficiaries.

Board members come from various occupational, religious, and ethnic groups. Naturally they reflect the predispositions and insights of other community members. Communities contain subcultural groups that hold differing views of the worth of education and its function in the lives of people of different status, aspirations, and potential. One or two subcultures value education for its intrinsic worth, its almost mystical or magical impact on the lives of people. Other subcultures value education for its practical worth and are willing to sacrifice to almost any extent to see their children enter prestigious professions and respected businesses. Still other subcultures desire rigor in education and training so that their children, divided in their thinking by their apparent potential or present socioeconomic status, may learn to do their best and may be respected for it. Unfortunately a few subcultures have little faith in the schools as agents for raising their children's position in life. The subcultural group that is perhaps most damaging to the schools is the one that seeks to intimidate administrators and teachers on the ground that parents and other taxpayers own the schools and employ, through a subservient board of education, a coterie of would-be professionals of low socioeconomic status and little influence in the community. Boards of education listen to the voices of all these, and other, groups of citizens.

Arthur Steller has suggested several ways of involving the ablest people in a community in policy making about their schools. He favors compiling a local who's who of talent, opening and using communication channels, listening to and observing community members, and preparing a "marketing framework" for convincing people of the worth of curriculum ideas. Afterward, detailed ways of proceeding to promote the ideas can be specified.[14] What Steller proposes is good public relations and good politics.

ACTIVITY 3-2
A Limited Study of One Community

Identify a community you know reasonably well. Ask public school officials in the central administrative offices to permit you to see board of education minutes of the past five years. Note what groups and individuals appeared before the board to present curriculum proposals or to discuss curriculum matters. State the points of view the groups and individuals apparently represented. What do you conclude about formal input by community members concerning curriculum concerns?

ACTIVITY 3-3
A More Comprehensive Study of the Same Community

Conduct a more comprehensive investigation of the same community. By interviewing several leading citizens, including a board of education member and a first-line school administrator, learn what forces are at work in the community to change the curriculum. Inquire about the relative influence of groups categorized as industrial, labor, political, patriotic, professional, welfare, and health.

What specific groups seem to wield the greatest influence?

How have these groups become so powerful? Who are the persons in the community who direct their activities?

What can you generalize from your findings concerning direction, strength, and necessary control of the community's influences on the curriculum?

SITUATION 3-4
When Subcultures and Social Classes Come to School

A group of teachers decided to investigate differences among their pupils attributable to subculture and social class. To do so, they took the following steps:

1. They inspected pupil records and interviewed pupils concerning their home life and general background.
2. They asked the pupils to react in small groups to experiences that the school provided through formal instruction and through informal activities.
3. They asked specific questions about the significance of photographs and ideas appearing in textbooks and other teaching materials, as these photographs and ideas reflected subculture and social class.
4. They asked the pupils to respond freely to words and expressions that might evoke particular memories and reactions: Negro, Knights of Columbus, Fundamentalist, company houses, white Anglo-Saxon Protestant, Social Register, labor union, etc.

What do you think of these methods of finding out above subcultures and social classes that pupils represent?

Would you use methods in addition to or instead of the four listed above?

What useful information would you expect to get by employing these four methods and/or your own?

The Impact of Inner-City and Rural Community Environments

The effects of social environment on children and their ability to learn are well illustrated by the impact on learners of life in the inner city and of life in what is essentially a new rural environment. Though many of the problems of inner-city and rural education have existed in the United States for a long time, the full significance of these problems is only beginning to become clear. The arrival of large numbers of migrants and immigrants in U.S. cities, their clustering for social and economic reasons in the centers of these cities, and the consequent departure for the suburbs of more privileged subpopulations have highlighted the needs of disadvantaged urbanites. At the same time, a new version of ruralism has replaced the old rural social environment in remote places throughout the United States.

The Inner-City Environment

After the waves of immigrants of the early and later twentieth century had found at least a precarious living place in U.S. cities, migrants and immigrants from numerous states and countries poured into these same cities and frequently found it necessary to accept menial employment and to occupy substandard housing facilities. These newcomers often exhibited the following characteristics: their backgrounds were rural and impoverished, their levels of formal education were low, they took commendable pride in their own cultural traditions, and they were willing to learn, but on their own terms. These people were not necessarily culturally inferior, but they *were* culturally different. To teach them, the teacher had to accept them and be accepted by them. However, several circumstances soon militated against their proper schooling:

1. Disappearing taxable property and declining values of real estate in the inner city
2. Segregation of pupils racially and, often more importantly, socioeconomically
3. Frequent displacement and consequent mobility of the poor
4. Impoverished facilities and limited personnel in inner-city schools
5. Cumulative deficits in the school achievement of children
6. Lack of community interest in problems of inner-city schools
7. Impermanence of teaching staffs and lack of preparation of school leadership to help teachers with their more difficult problems.

Efforts to overcome these circumstances have followed the point of view that the more powerful groups in society must help less powerful ones by direct assistance, education, and common involvement in lifting the downtrodden. Culture-free tests, specially prepared and diversified school staffs, an increase in the number of male teachers, textbooks devised to take into account the backgrounds of migrants, varied school experiences, summertime educational programs, work-study projects, and improved preservice and inservice education of teachers have become major devices for achieving assimilation of the culturally different.

Classroom teachers who work outside the slums of U.S. cities often believe that teaching in the slums requires the same abilities as teaching anywhere else. Conditions exist in the inner city, however, that make teaching unusually difficult. True, teachers everywhere face some of the problems one encounters in slum schools, but the inner city imposes special stress on schools and teachers because of the social realities of slum living. There is, first of all, density of population with corresponding loss of identity by residents of the inner city. In personal terms, loss of identity means that, to an exceptional degree, the slum dwellers question who they are and whether or not they are important. Slum dwellers have correctly been described as feeling anonymous, depersonalized, lonely, and hardened in their relationships with people. Big city bureaucracy, which is shared liberally by urban school systems, causes teachers and principals to make decisions for the faceless mass of pupils and then attempt to apply these decisions to individual cases. Most teachers in the slums cannot know individual children thoroughly because, as nonresidents of the community, they do not see them in family or community connections.

Furthermore, unusual feelings of powerlessness afflict inhabitants of the inner city. The big city wields big control, which creates this sense of powerlessness in the individual citizen. Forming combinations and seeking cooperation among the citizenry have become especially difficult because large numbers of markedly different people are thrown together in urban life. Both the inner-city community and its schools seem to desire to stamp out diversity. Meanwhile old-fashioned attempts at acculturation of the "melting-pot" variety no longer function because of resistances created by diverse cultural groups and because of frequent movement by families within, into, and out of the community.

To many pupils in the slum school, the curriculum seems strictly "phony" because it relates so poorly to the realities of their lives. Partly for this reason, older youngsters often show contempt for professional personnel in the schools. The individual pupil's impoverished environment contributes to development of a poor self-image and a realistic lack of confidence in his or her own future. He or she lives in a physical rather than an intellectual world, a world in which respect and personal success are needed. Communication with teachers is frequently monosyllabic, but the pupil communicates readily with peers. During the school day, the pupil is sensitive to sudden changes in routine, so disorderly and even violent conduct may occur when procedures in his or her classroom are unplanned and unorganized.

As a learner, the pupil in the inner city needs special attention and patience. This requirement is so important that it has been emphasized in the writings and oral comments of experienced teachers who have been deemed successful in slum schools. Though inner-city pupils may learn slowly, they tend to retain what they have learned if it has any meaning for them. Although they are apathetic about most of the content the schools teach, their curiosity can be aroused. Their inarticulateness should not suggest to teachers that their manipulative skills are necessarily above normal. Contrary to a popular myth, pupils in the slums are not necessarily adept in the vocational arts.

Too often the curriculum in slum schools follows patterns of schooling that are in use elsewhere. The "quality school" attains its status in the United States because it teaches the so-called basic skills with maximum success as determined by standardized tests. But the ordinary definition of quality does not apply to schooling in the inner city. The curriculum here needs to be based to a greater extent on the realities of social living in the slum—to help pupils become personally involved in the life situations in which they find themselves, to help them see options for themselves in their environment, to provide opportunities for them to perform and to act out roles in participatory citizenship. The realities of the inner city require young people to negotiate with adults, to relate to and organize people in special circumstances, and to get what they need in ways that are both civilized and effective. The schools should help them learn to do these three things.

Is there hope for the schools of the inner city? The Rand Corporation studied educational innovation in five city school districts in urban centers with a population range of 125,000 to 900,000. Rand found that innovation in these districts waxed and waned, but that the participants in innovation were learning how to do better next time.[15] The future of education in the inner city seems to depend on several factors: ideas and their dissemination, the nature of populations to be served, the political situation, economic circumstances, and social climate.

A number of urban school systems have organized to help one another with curriculum planning and supervisory strategies. The systems have achieved measurable gains in several respects, including pupils' learning of basic skills and reductions in dropout rates. The success of educational programs in the cities seems to result from the presence of strong leadership, willingness of the education hierarchy to increase principals' authority, and freedom of individual schools to change in any sensible way they desire.[16]

The New Rural Environment

In 1982 the Federal Reserve Bank of Philadelphia reported that for the first time in 150 years rural areas of the nation had outstripped in population the cities and their suburbs. Indeed, increased transportation, communication, and population migration are making the rural areas different from what they once were. The families who lived in rural regions during past decades have moved to the cities or elsewhere. They have been replaced with emigrants from cities and suburbs and with population groups arriving from outside the bounds of the United States. For some, the rural regions have become new lands of opportunity. Multilingual and multicultural influences have made the rural social scene less uniform. The seasonal presence of migrant farm workers has reduced cultural uniformity further. The establishment of new industries and the consequent failure of some of them, together with consolidation and reduction in the size of family farms, have both raised and lowered the hopes of industrial and farm workers. Shopping malls have provided employment while taxing highways with heavy traffic. All in all, the rural environment has become nondescript and filled with uncertainties.

Rural America has its indoor and outdoor motion picture theaters, along with an abundance of television sets. Its greatest cultural void is in the scarcity of libraries, museums, concert halls, and arrangements for formal continuing education. In general taste and response to advertising, the modern inhabitants of rural areas resemble people in the suburbs. In cultural sophistication, the resemblance lessens. Lack of exposure to rich and varied cultural advantages proves decidedly limiting.

Within school buildings small rural schools offer many opportunities that rival the opportunities given pupils in nonrural settings. Rural schools of limited size are, however, disadvantaged by inaccessibility to varied reading materials, by a lack of interesting places for pupils to visit, by the inability of the staff to assist pupils with special problems, and by limited opportunities for pupils to work and serve within the community. Administrators and teachers have so many and such varied responsibilities that curriculum planning tends to be neglected. The teachers often find that a public too geographically close to them makes unreasonable demands. After all, isn't the school the center of community life? On the affirmative side, however, is the fact that teachers and administrators can interact often. Similarly, pupils can interact readily with teachers, to the end that their curriculum can be individualized.[17]

In large, consolidated rural systems, the size and remoteness of school buildings have created the same general effect one sees in urban communities—poor communication and lack of understanding, which result in a loss of confidence in the schools. Because of this crisis in confidence, budgets are defeated, bond issues are lost, and the local property tax becomes a less and less acceptable base for school support.

Like the inner city, the new rural environment requires that curriculum emphases be altered. In rural pupils the idea of community and of the roles of individuals in it needs to be developed. Field trips to remote places, including centers of culture, are important, as is the study of people's ways of behaving in other cultures. Also to be emphasized is the diligent search for individual talent and for means of developing human potential.

Many rural problems that originate in poverty remind one of the poverty-based problems of residents of the inner city: facelessness, low self-esteem, and limited hope. Improvement of cognitive learning in deprived rural areas will not suffice. Carefully planned affective education is a special need.

Under the illusion that "the votes are there," politicians have favored spending money on the cities and accordingly have neglected the growing rural areas. The federal money that has helped to support rural education has gone to support primarily the disadvantaged and "special need" populations. Both federal and state programs of aid should be reformed to meet actual rural school needs, new programs should be created, and research activity in rural education should be encouraged.[18]

CULTURE-BASED CURRICULUM IDEAS: TWO EXAMPLES

Curriculum ideas do not spring from the forehead of Zeus. Orlosky and Smith say that they come from sources within school systems and from sources outside them. They categorize the external sources to include chiefly community groups, government, and foundations.[19] (Compared with earlier decades, the 1980s find the foundations to be largely out of business.) Many ideas develop but, like fingerling fish in lakes and seas, the great majority of them disappear. The ideas that are left vary in magnitude and significance; a few are called seminal, and even fewer take a nation by storm.

The ideas that genuinely succeed appear to have the support of elements of the culture and of important people in local school districts simultaneously. A little financial boost from government doesn't hurt, so community groups and government, in Orlosky and Smith's terms, are likely to be chief protagonists. The culture, however, provides the seed-bed for planting and nourishing each successful idea.

Ours is an environment in which people often feel alienated and alone. Therefore self-concept development has become a major interest. The federal grantspeople have shown willingness to fund projects with the term *self-concept development* in them. Communication, one of our greatest cultural lacks, is another reasonably sure bet. The disadvantaged, like the poor, are with us always, so the disadvantaged, handicapped, and discomfited become eligible for attention. Then there are the gifted, who, in the rush to care for the disadvantaged, have been left to get what they can from routine schooling. In a time of conservatism and the valuing of high-quality human resources, routine schooling for the gifted seems to many people to be inadequate. Special programs are again being demanded.

Some curriculum ideas are especially deeply rooted in the culture. Two of these, to be used as examples below, are development of a system of American values and career education.

Development of a System of American Values

Many Americans have been troubled during recent years by the thought that our people do not cohere more closely when they face fundamental issues that affect our existence as a nation. Often, small groups of people do not rally to the support of their fellows who face danger common to all of them. One of the basic reasons for these failures to join forces and to cooperate is the absence from people's lives of clear-cut values and value patterns. In this sense, Americans do not know what to believe because they have had too little experience in clarifying their current values and adopting new ones. To help resolve this values dilemma, which is sometimes a values vacuum, elementary and secondary schools should include in their curricula instruction in values clarification and values development, features of the individual's life curriculum that may not be available elsewhere in the culture. Such curricula would have initially a personal import for individual learners. Soon, however, they would have social import as the responses of individuals to social, political, and economic phenomena were translated into group response.

Conflicts in values are inevitable in a society as diverse and complex as ours. As conditions change, so do the people, objects, and ideas we value. Furthermore, valuing depends on a good many factors, including background, environment, and personality structure. By its diversity, our society has fostered value conflicts that complicate schooling. Nominally, for instance, we value bilingualism, but we discourage "foreignisms" in speech and writing. As teachers, we value grammatical structure at the expense of experimentation with the living, growing English language.

Although we misinterpret and misuse value patterns that exist, we are disturbed at the necessity of admitting new values or even of acknowledging their presence. Social forces have recently pushed upon us new views of old problems, one of these problems being the propagation of democracy in a basically undemocratic society. Nearly all Americans give lip service to democracy as a fundamental value. However, few of us behave consistently in accordance with democratic principles. This is especially true with reference to race and social class.

Three sources of value conflict have affected especially the work of school and community agencies. One of these is the degree of social control that has been exercised over the destinies of individuals. Big government, big business, and big labor are chief offenders in molding the attitudes and regulating the lives of individual citizens. Another source of value conflict is the so-called new morality, which is really a level of morality as old as humanity itself, now practiced in an environment of newly increased freedom. The third source is a conveyor of social effects, the mass media—television, paperback books, newspapers, magazines—

that communicate at will either diverse and unselected values or planned, prepackaged value systems. The schools, as servants of a society in which diversity exists, have felt free to support with assurance only a few limited values that allegedly promote unity in the society.

Today, our society is altering its viewpoints about the place of central government in American life, about the nation's role in international affairs, about strategies to be used in childrearing, about relationships between church and state, about the status of Far Eastern and African peoples, about depersonalization through automation, and about numerous other matters. Upward mobility through the class structure continues. Curriculum leaders must consider the meaning that each serious shift in values has for education. At the same time, all teachers need clear values of their own, especially with reference to the role of the school in society. If the school's role is to be large and omnibus, nearly every change in values must mean something to teaching and learning. If it is to be small and limited, many changes in values may be ignored.

In his lectures, Louis Raths defined the term *value* both strictly and elaborately. No one, he said, really values anything without having chosen it freely for valuing. Real valuing has not occurred unless the valuer has chosen the object from among available alternatives, has chosen it after due reflection, has prized and cherished it, has been willing to affirm its worth publicly, has incorporated it into his or her life space and pattern, and has shown his or her allegiance to it by actual behavior on repeated occasions.[20] This definition, when applied, for example, to the person who adheres to the ideas of a political party concerning welfare reform, to the person who declares himself or herself to be a Christian, or to the person who favors respecting individual pupils and teachers in schools, imposes an exacting set of standards. Persons who consider themselves to be loyal Republicans or Democrats, faithful Christians, or educational humanitarians should test themselves against these standards.

It follows from the definition that if children in schools are to learn how to value, they must be given opportunities to make free choices whenever feasible, to search for alternatives in the process of choice making, to consider the consequences of available alternatives, to think well about what they cherish and prize, to support their choices publicly, to take action in line with their choices, and to behave specifically according to their patterns of choice. According to Raths, teachers should not tell children what to value, but they should help individuals and groups to get a clear idea of the bases of what they currently believe and also of the steps they should take in making sensible, supportable new choices. Surely some of the best teaching about values occurs when teachers help children consider thoroughly the consequences of available alternatives.

Many people disagree with Raths's statement that teachers and other adults should not tell children what to value. They point out that there is no such thing as value-free education, that every school reflects a value system, and that schools should teach children what to value when no one else does.[21] A majority of these same people would probably draw the line, however, if the values to be taught in the public schools were sectarian or otherwise limited by particular religious beliefs. Most of those who would teach children what to value think specifically of civic or human relations values that all citizens should presumably accept and act upon. For example, the Salt Lake City School District has formulated twelve democratic principles that can be accepted by civilized people living in a democratic society. The list begins:

1. Each individual has dignity and worth.
2. A free society requires respect for persons, property, and principles.
3. Each individual has a right to learn and the freedom to achieve.

It is possible to identify several ways of teaching values that are currently in use. The first is *inculcation*, in which accepted values are taught with the force of ancient law. The second is *moral development*, in which moral principles and their application are highlighted. The third is *analysis of issues and situations* involving valuing. The fourth is *clarification*, the method in which Raths and others have been especially interested. The fifth is *action learning*, in which values are tried and tested concretely in the field. In addition, the approaches used by Arthur Combs and Carl Rogers may be described as *evocation*, a calling forth from the individual of personal values and the ability to value when needed in life situations.[22]

The preceding discussion indicates, of course, that both the content of instruction in values and the processes of teaching learners to value are unclear. Until we answer the questions "What values?" and "How shall we teach valuing?" we shall continue to flounder about in this central area of affective education. Curriculum workers who are seeking a challenge might profitably investigate this area of affect and propose feasible content and methods that could serve as models in the field of affective education, taking into account that the values the teacher models are often most influential, provided that the community does not reject these values openly.

ACTIVITY 3-4
A Special Problem in Recognizing and Meeting
Differences in Values

According to Louis Raths,

> The evidence is clear that in its [the school's] distribution of rewards and punishments, the former go, out of all proportion, to the middle- and upper-class students; the penalties go, out of all proportion, to the lower social

classes. There is evidence that our tests of intelligence are biased in the kinds of problems presented and in the words chosen to present these problems. The bias is in the direction of favoring the middle- and upper-class children. Participation in extracurricular activities is shown to distinguish between lower- and middle-class children. Prizes, honors, and awards go, in much higher proportion than their numbers suggest, to the middle- and upper-class children. The high grades on reports to parents and reports to colleges go to the children of the middle and upper classes in much larger numbers than their proportion of the school population. The curriculum materials, represented by the beginning primers and readers, are shown to be a product of middle-class living, hence, probably of more interest to middle-class children than to others.[23]

To what extent do these observations about the realities of school life square with the realities of social class structure in our society? How do you suppose the schools got themselves into the situation that Raths describes?

As a curriculum worker, what concrete actions might you take to develop and use teaching methods and materials designed to correspond more closely to the values held by differing social classes?

Career Education

Another culture-based curriculum idea is planning and preparing for a career. Education related to entering and pursuing careers belongs at elementary, middle, and high school levels of instruction.

Educators have shown an interest in career education for a long time. In 1918, the well-known *Cardinal Principles of Secondary Education* contained the following statement under the heading "Vocations":

> Vocational education should equip the individual to secure a livelihood for himself and those dependent upon him, to serve society well through his vocation, to maintain the right relationships toward his fellow workers and society, and, as far as possible, to find in that vocation his own best development.

In 1938, the Educational Policies Commission spoke of "the objectives of economic efficiency," including "occupational efficiency." Later, the Commission advocated development in pupils of salable skills and also appropriate career-related attitudes and understandings. Since 1970, the National Assessment of Educational Progress, popularly referred to as "national testing," has made career and occupational development one of its subject area interests in preparing tests that are administered throughout the nation.

Career education has never gained the status of a discrete subject, but it has been on the fringes of the formal curriculum since the late 1930s and the early 1940s. At that time the guidance movement was being initiated in a number of school systems after having made its first organized start in cities like Providence, Rhode Island. Guidance responsibilities were divided among the educational, the vocational, and the social. Vocational guidance was dispensed to individuals and small groups, with the later assistance of vocational interest inventories like the Strong and the Kuder. It was intended for all pupils in secondary schools. Entirely apart from vocational guidance, the schools were offering courses in vocational education, some of which were funded substantially by the federal government. Secondary school pupils who had no intention of attending college were the major clientele of vocational education programs.

After a period of quiescence, the emphasis on planning and preparing for careers revived, making an entirely new appearance under the leadership of a United States Commissioner of Education, Sidney P. Marland. Marland used the term *career education* in promoting a nationwide movement combining curriculum, instruction, and counseling. He was interested in seeing pupils prepared for economic independence, personal fulfillment, and appreciation of the dignity of work. He hoped that career education would help remove the distinction between academic and vocational preparation and would consequently affect the education of all pupils.

Interest in career education has become widespread in elementary and secondary schools. Its societal and cultural significance has seemed so obvious that articles, curriculum plans, and course guides relative to it have been created everywhere, filling ERIC files and *Education Index* listings. In kindergarten and the first four or five grades, career education usually consists of general orientation; in grades five through eight, exploration of career fields; in grades nine and ten, intense investigation of particular careers; and in grades eleven and twelve, actual preparation experiences. Vocational education itself has grown and improved vastly.

One of the major problems with career education is uncertainty as to what to teach about the careers of the future. Consequently more attention is being given to ways of making decisions about careers and to general preparation for types of careers through vocational education than to precise career opportunities and preparation for them. Current and near-future opportunities in the local community are not hard to trace, but few graduates of the local schools remain in or return to their native communities. Nevertheless career exploration in the community is frequently part of career education programs.[24]

ACTIVITY 3-5
A Study of Present and Future Career Opportunities

As a means of aiding curriculum planning in career education, teachers who are specialists in specific school subjects are sometimes asked to investigate present and future opportunities in careers that are clearly related to their subjects.

A similar possibility exists for persons who expect to become specialists in the curriculum field and are already preparing for service in it. At the higher levels of preparation, it is possible to prepare specifically in (1) the curriculum of elementary schools, (2) the curriculum of secondary schools, (3) procedures for planning curriculum, and (4) curriculum evaluation. Choose one of these four subspecialties. Review data about present and future opportunities in it, then discuss your data with others who have been conducting similar investigations. Possible information sources are ERIC materials, placement officers in universities, incumbents in positions within the subspecialty, and the literature of futurism.

STRATEGIES FOR USING SOCIAL INFLUENCES

Experience and current observation supply curriculum workers with several strategies to use in dealing with society-wide and community influences. The implication here is not that they should seek to resist these influences but that they should use them intelligently as aids to curriculum planning.

First, curriculum workers need to be as open-minded as they can be about influences that affect the schools. Although not all influences are benign, they all deserve hearing and consideration. Too often, educational leaders have been said to take a proprietary attitude toward "their" schools or to be possessive or defensive about existing programs. In the view of some commentators, they have shown too little interest in what the public has had to say, perhaps because they themselves were insecure or were insensitive to the feelings of others. A point of view that may well be taken is that the schools belong to the people, who employ professional personnel to administer and operate them. These personnel, as professionals, should be autonomous in much that they do, but they must also listen to what other citizens are saying. They must work with today's citizens, but their wisdom comes also from their knowledge of the past and their own estimates of the future.

Second, curriculum workers need to lead in using social influences. As they welcome ideas, so also must they help school staffs square the ideas with theory and practice, and see that assumptions and premises are tested. They should urge citizens who have ideas to advance them, but they must recognize at the same time that arguments as to whether two and two make four are fruitless, and that persons whose only contact with the schools occurred twenty-five years ago as pupils are definitely *not* educational authorities. When curriculum workers listen, they should also inform. The need is for dialogue rather than a hearing of witnesses.

Third, curriculum workers should consider fully the feelings of Americans about education and should act according to their best diagnosis of those feelings. Generally speaking, Americans take great pride in their schools. Most of the time they are complacent about them, but in moments of real or imagined crisis they become worried and anxious. Someone has said that Americans are satisfied in general with their schools and are dissatisfied in particular. Accordingly, the curriculum person must serve as a troubleshooter of dissatisfactions—but, not, of course, on every occasion. All of us have difficulty in knowing when to counterattack and when to remain quiescent, but school personnel seem to have been oversensitive during recent years to every wind of criticism and complaint. Basically, the public's attitudes toward the schools are often more favorable than superintendents and other school leaders believe. The public wants to know mainly whether the schools are moving forward and in what direction. Curriculum leaders should lead the planning for movement and should cause the plans to be known and talked about.

Fourth, curriculum workers should recognize that they are operating in a special dynamic. The profession that they serve has not been noted for attracting power to itself, probably because teachers behave "like teachers" and are expected to behave thus. In the past, the image of the teacher has been one of a feminine, middle-class, unmarried, white, Protestant, conservative individual without strong community influence. The curriculum person has real responsibility for encouraging teachers to move outside their own milieu, so that they may learn from other institutions, agencies, and individuals and may contribute to them. One of teachers' occupational hazards is talking too much to themselves and other teachers. The potential of teachers as both contributors and listeners to the community can scarcely be exaggerated. As teachers are seen in a new and better light, other citizens begin to help them redesign and reinterpret their role.

Finally, curriculum leaders must realize that they are deep in politics. Theirs is the politics not of the ward-heeling variety but of strategic planning, which requires balancing of pressures and cooperative making of policy. Educators should probably stop talking about the administrator's community relations when they mean political skill. Curriculum leaders are inevitably concerned with pressure groups and with allocations of public funds. These two areas of responsibility alone thrust them into the realm of politics. Gordon N. Mackenzie advanced the notion that curriculum development moves through three stages: identification of focus, development of curriculum proposals, and implementation through teaching. These stages correspond to Harold Lasswell's three stages in political decision making: pre-outcome, outcome, and post-outcome.[25]

Politicians proceed according to tried and tested beliefs about ways in which the human being as a political animal customarily behaves. Though the idea may offend some individuals, it is possible that curriculum planners will need to become increasingly adept in political behavior. Surely there are signs that curriculum improvement activities have been moving, on national and state fronts, into the realm of politics, as big projects develop and as supporting and competing interests vie with one another. Furthermore, curriculum leaders have been called upon in recent years to deal with the political ramifications of desegregation, negotiations with teachers, the rights of students, and attacks on textbooks.

In the preceding pages, curriculum workers have been urged to be open-minded about social influences, to exert leadership in using these influences, to understand people's feelings about the schools, to appreciate basic weaknesses in their own profession, and to consider themselves practical politicians. If we return to our initial discussion of society and community as they influence the schools, we see possible strategies for curriculum workers in another dimension. Beyond the attitudes and understandings they must have, they need among their strategies certain concrete strategies for dealing directly with the influences discussed in the first sections of the chapter.

Tradition is sometimes beneficient, and curriculum personnel must find specific traditions that are good and then see that these traditions are strengthened and used. For instance, certain patriotic observances fall within this category. The curriculum worker's object is to make them more impressive in educating the young in love of country and then to place them as high as seems desirable on the agenda of experiences that the school provides. Curriculum improvement should never be labeled as action to destroy the desirable learnings of the human race.

Curriculum workers should also take direct responsibility for channeling social and cultural change constructively within the school. For some persons, this action may evade the question as to whether educators should serve in their own right as social reconstructionists. Whatever their position concerning their role as social engineers, they must recognize and use influences that burst or creep upon the school from both ultimate society and immediate community.

As has been said previously in this chapter, when social values are unclear to both adults and children, curriculum workers should urge that much time be spent in helping children clarify their values. In a free society, citizens who do not know what they believe are a danger to the society and therefore to themselves. On key issues of morality, patriotism, and ethical standards, learners should be schooled in the alternatives, but where inevitably only one decision is socially acceptable, they should know what the decision is. Cheating on examinations is dishonest, whatever its causes. Juvenile delinquency is a serious social ill, and alcoholism and drug addiction are serious personal diseases with dire social consequences, whatever may have caused them. There is clearly no sense in fencing with hard reality. In order that values may be clear, the methodology of value formation and reformation should be taught. Respect for cause-and-effect relationships, testing of one's present values against evidence, and the origin and development of a philosophy of life are but three of the matters to be treated in a school where creation and re-creation of value structures are a concern.

ACTIVITY 3-6
The Site at Which Political Power Should Be Applied

"The most important election is a school board election," said a candidate for the board in his community.

"If I wanted to affect education permanently and importantly," said a candidate for Congress, "I'd try to influence governors, presidents, and members of Congress."

"Times and places determine which of you is more nearly right," said an impartial citizen.

Analyze each of these statements to determine which of them you favor. Give full reasons for your answer.

ACTIVITY 3-7
Which Will You Have?

Consider the following continuum. Only you can decide your own position along it.

|———————————————————————————————————|

| The school isolated from the community | A position somewhere between the extremes | The school involved with and busily remaking the community |

With respect to your position, answer these questions:

1. Shall the school remain as separate as possible from the community?
2. Shall the school be made to serve as a model of the community as it presently exists?
3. Shall the school help to remake the community?

Consider and discuss these related issues:

1. What shall the school do about the mores and values that large numbers of community members respect? Provide examples of mores and values you have in mind as you discuss this issue.
2. What shall the school do about treating the controversial issues that abound in our society? Be specific about particular issues.

3. What shall the school do about accepting tasks that other institutions and agencies are not performing or are performing poorly? Give examples of tasks.
4. What shall the school do about the social class values that pupils presently hold? Provide examples of values held by two or three different social classes, as listed: upper-upper, lower-upper, upper-middle, lower-middle, upper-lower, lower-lower.

Curriculum personnel should encourage community members to involve themselves appropriately in curriculum improvement. Though general guidelines to involvement can be developed, the act of skillfully involving people can only partially be described. It is easy to say, for instance, that committees of laypersons should be formed for definite purposes and with definite life expectancy, but forming and dissolving them smoothly demands almost indescribable human relations skill. One of the special responsibilities of curriculum workers in their interaction with laypersons is to help them think thoroughly about both the local and the nationwide contributions of the schools. Since control of the schools is being divided increasingly among local, state, and national agencies of government, people in U.S. communities should face the need to critically examine the whole range of authority and responsibility for schools, to determine specifically how much control is to move from the grassroots level to national and state centers.

Sometimes curriculum personnel find ways to turn hostile pressures to the advantage of their schools. Too little is known about this action, though an occasional Horatio Alger-like story is heard about turning inimical forces (which seek to counter the desirable things we know should be done for children) into helpful ones. For example, a violent opponent of a tried and tested reading or social studies program is induced to help study it, and remains to participate in modifying the program and then to support it in its revised form. In some instances, human relations skills of the high order discussed in some of the literature of industrial psychology achieve the desired result. Surely curriculum personnel need to know more and more of these skills. At times, however, they will have to stand and resist, particularly when the subject under attack is in reality a cover-up for dangerous, continuing hostility.

America is entering an era in which social forces are likely to influence curriculum planning as never before. Increase in leisure time, opportunities for continuing education, and still greater ease of transportation and communication will, in themselves, make lay participation in curriculum improvement more and more likely. Finally, social changes will probably multiply rapidly as people, machines, and influences move more speedily in the world of tomorrow.[26]

SUMMARY

Social and cultural forces have always had a strong effect in the making of curriculum decisions. Some of these forces have orginated, and continue to originate, in the wider society and culture in which people live. Still other forces develop within local communities. Sometimes they create major educational problems, like the problems involved in educating effectively those children and youth who live in the inner city and in rural areas. Education in values and in career choice relate closely to beliefs held by people in communities and the wider society. Curriculum personnel must reckon with forces without resenting them or their multiple origins, but the educator has a special responsibility to relate them to elementary and secondary education in ways that will benefit the precious clientele of the schools.

ENDNOTES

1. Michael L. Berger, "The Public Schools Can't Do It All," *Contemporary Education* 54, no. 1 (Fall 1982): 6–8.

2. See, for example, Gary Hoban, "The Untold Golden State Story: Aftermath of Proposition 13," *Phi Delta Kappan* 61, no. 1 (September 1979): 18–21.

3. Harold L. Hodgkinson, "What's Still Right with Education," *Phi Delta Kappan* 64, no. 4 (December 1982): 235.

4. Richard M. Wolf, "Achievement in the United States," in Herbert J. Walberg, ed., *Educational Environments and Effects: Evaluation, Policy, and Productivity* (Berkeley, Calif.: McCutchan, 1979), pp. 313–29.

5. Lee R. McMurrin, "Educational Change: It Can Work to Your Advantage," *Theory into Practice* 20, no. 4 (Fall 1981): 264–68.

6. For initial reactions to these schools, see Jane S. Shaw, "The New Conservative Alternative," *Nation's Schools and Colleges* 2 (February 1975): 31–39.

7. Charles S. Benson and E. Gareth Hoachlander, "The Privatization of Public Education: Implications for Educational Policy," testimony given before the House Subcommittee studying the needs of elementary, secondary, and vocational education, January 1980.

8. Stephen F. Hamilton, "Alternative Schools for the 80s: Lessons from the Past," *Urban Education* 16, no. 2 (July 1981): 131–48.

9. Vernon H. Smith and Robert D. Barr, "Where Should Learning Take Place?" in William Van Til, ed., *Issues in Secondary Education*, Seventy-fifth Yearbook, Part II, National Society for the Study of Education (Chicago: University of Chicago Press, 1976), pp. 167–75.

10. See James A. Banks, "The Implications of Ethnicity for Curriculum Reform," *Educational Leadership* 33, no. 3 (December 1975): 168–72. Proof that the education of minorities as a special function is more than a current fad can be seen in projection studies concerning the future status of non-Englishing-speaking citizens, and in references to American Indian education and the education of other less-mentioned minorities.

11. See David Selden, "How Fares Curriculum in Collective Bargaining?" *Educational Leadership* 33, no. 1 (October 1975): 28–30.

12. Ronald C. Doll, "Alternative Forms of Schooling," *Educational Leadership* 29, no. 5 (February 1972): 391–93.

13. Philip W. Jackson, "Deschooling? No!" *Today's Education* 61, no. 8 (November 1972): 18–22. See also R. W. Burns and G. D. Brooks, eds., "Designing Curriculum in a Changing Society," *Educational Technology* 10 (April 1970): 7–57; and *Educational Technology* 10 (May 1970): 9–64.

14. Arthur Steller, "Curriculum Development as Politics," *Educational Leadership* 38, no. 2 (November 1980): 161, 162.

15. John Pincus and Richard C. Williams, "Planned Change in Urban School Districts," *Phi Delta Kappan* 60, no. 10 (June 1979): 729–33.

16. James E. Walter, "Successful Program Implementation in Urban Schools," *Educational Leadership* 38, no. 8 (May 1981): 635–38.

17. See Gerald D. Bailey, *Curriculum Development in the Rural School*, November 1982. Reported in ERIC # ED 223 373.

18. See Jonathan P. Sher, "A Proposal to End Federal Neglect of Rural Schools," *Phi Delta Kappan* 60, no. 4 (December 1978): 280–82.

19. Donald Orlosky and B. Othanel Smith, "Educational Change: Its Origins and Characteristics," *Phi Delta Kappan* 53, no. 7 (March 1972): 412–14.

20. For detailed exposition of these ideas, see Louis E. Raths, Merrill Harmin, and Sidney B. Simon, *Values and Teaching* (Columbus, Ohio: Charles E. Merrill, 1966), p. 46.

21. E. Dale Davis, "Should the Public Schools Teach Values?" *Phi Delta Kappan* 65, no. 5 (January 1984): 358–60.

22. See Douglas P. Superka and Patricia L. Johnson, *Values Education: Approaches and Materials* (Boulder, Colo.: Social Science Education Consortium, 1975).

23. Louis E. Raths, "Sociological Knowledge and Needed Curriculum Research," in James B. Macdonald, ed., *Research Frontiers in the Study of Children's Learning* (Milwaukee: School of Education, University of Wisconsin, 1960), p. 21.

24. Robert I. Tobin et al., *On the Way to Work: A Report on Career Exploration in Boston Middle Schools* (Cambridge, Mass.: American Institutes for Research in the Behavioral Sciences, 1976).

25. Harold D. Lasswell, *Politics: Who Gets What, When, How* (Cleveland, Ohio: Meridian, 1958).

26. See Donald R. Thomas, *Schools Next Time: Explorations in Educational Sociology* (New York: McGraw-Hill, 1973).

SELECTED BIBLIOGRAPHY

Beck, Carlton E., et al. *Education for Relevance: The Schools and Social Change.* Boston: Houghton Mifflin, 1968.

Belanger, Maurice, and Purpel, David. *Curriculum and the Cultural Revolution: A Book of Essays and Readings.* Berkeley, Calif.: McCutchan, 1972.

Benjamin, Harold. *The Sabertooth Curriculum.* New York: McGraw-Hill, 1939.

Campbell, Duane E. *Education for a Democratic Society: Multicultural Curriculum Ideas for Teachers.* Cambridge, Mass.: Schenkman, 1980.

Claydon, Leslie, et al. *Curriculum and Culture: Schooling in a Pluralist Society.* Winchester, Mass.: Allen and Unwin, 1978.

DeNovellis, Richard, and Lewis, Arthur. *Schools Become Accountable.* Washington, D.C.: Association for Supervision and Curriculum Development, 1974.

Dunfee, Maxine. *Ethnic Modification of the Curriculum.* Washington, D.C.: Association for Supervision and Curriculum Development, 1970.

Erickson, Edsel L.; Bryan, Clifford E.; and Walker, Lewis, eds. *Social Change, Conflict and Education.* Columbus, Ohio: Charles E. Merrill, 1972.

Gordon, C. Wayne, ed. *Uses of the Sociology of Education.* National Society for the Study of Education, Seventy-Third Yearbook, Part II. Chicago: University of Chicago Press, 1974.

Haubrich, Vernon F., ed. *Freedom, Bureaucracy, and Schooling.* 1971 Yearbook. Washington, D.C.: Association for Supervision and Curriculum Development, 1971.

Havighurst, Robert J., ed. *Metropolitanism: Its Challenge to Education.* National Society for the Study of Education, Sixty-Seventh Yearbook, Part I. Chicago: University of Chicago Press, 1968.

Havighurst, Robert J., and Levine, Daniel U. *Society and Education.* 5th ed. Boston: Allyn and Bacon, 1979.

Jencks, Christopher, et al. *Inequality: A Reassessment of the Effect of Family and Schooling in America.* New York: Basic Books, 1972.

Jones, Howard L., ed. *Curriculum Development in a Changing World.* Syracuse: Syracuse University Press, 1969.

Margolin, Edythe. *Sociocultural Elements in Early Childhood Education.* New York: Macmillan, 1974.

Raths, Louis; Harmin, Merrill; and Simon, Sidney B. *Values and Teaching.* Columbus, Ohio: Charles E. Merrill, 1966.

Sharp, Rachel, and Green, Anthony. *Education and Social Control.* London: Routledge and Kegan Paul, 1975.

Sieber, Sam D., and Wilder, David E., eds. *The School in Society: Studies in the Sociology of Education.* Riverside, N.J.: Free Press, 1973.

Taylor, Philip H., and Tye, Kenneth, eds. *Curriculum, School and Society: An Introduction to Curriculum Studies.* Atlantic Highlands, N.J.: Humanities Press, 1976.

Van Til, William, ed. *Curriculum: Quest for Relevance.* 2nd ed. Boston: Houghton Mifflin, 1974.

Young, Michael. *Knowledge and Control: New Directions for the Sociology of Education,* London: Collier-Macmillan, 1971.

4

Subject Matter: Its Role
in Decision Making

Schools have always taught subject matter. This gratuitous statement would indeed be unnecessary if the notion had not been created that U.S. schools are committed to teaching *children* instead of subject matter. The prevalence of this notion was the fault, in part, of the Progressive Movement of the 1920s, 1930s, and 1940s. Progressives talked so much about the interests and needs of children that people missed what they said about subject matter. Of course it has always been impossible to teach human beings without teaching them something.

During the fifties, people became concerned about whether subject matter was "hard" or "soft" and, when it was considered to be soft, what could be done to make it harder. Some schools sought to toughen the curriculum by teaching a greater quantity of the same content more demandingly. This approach was especially noticeable in secondary education, where forty algebra problems of the same kind replaced the original twenty and where the parsing of twenty sentences was magnified into the parsing of forty. Little was being learned about selection of subject matter, because, even before the scare about the U.S.S.R.'s Sputnik, a major objective was to teach content that had been in the books long enough to be respectable. American teachers had learned that almost anything they taught could be made too difficult for pupils to learn or so easy as to prove boring, but most of them apparently did not believe, with the investigators in the Eight Year Study, that what one learned was often less significant than the way one went about learning it.

123

Of course, teachers had to face certain necessary perennial questions about subject matter. In counseling individual pupils, they had to decide in a given case whether an extra year of science would serve better than a year of home economics. Insightful teachers wanted learners to have balanced programs; by this they meant well rounded ones. At the classroom level, they were somewhat concerned with improving the quality of teacher-pupil plannning, but they showed greater interest in selecting textbooks and other aids to enrich their classroom procedures. Their decision making about content selection stemmed chiefly from two classic sources: (1) the nature of the learner and the learning process and (2) the impact of society at large and the local community upon the school. During the sixties and the seventies an additional source for decision making was more consciously tapped—the nature and uses of subject matter itself. In the early eighties, the public awakened to the fact that, though teachers had known for a long time many of the best procedures and methods of teaching all sorts of subject matter, the ease and softness that had pervaded American society generally had encouraged teachers and schools to become easy and soft. The response of the schools has been reminiscent of the reaction they had back in the fifties to charges of curriculum softness—toughening the curriculum by adding more of the same standard content.

The present chapter will concern itself with the function of subject matter alone in conditioning the curriculum. We shall return, in Chapter 5, to the whole matter of deciding what to teach in terms of bases additional to the nature of subject matter.

A NEW ERA IN THE SCHOOLS

The nature of subject matter has come to the fore as a criterion of content selection, and thus of curriculum improvement, for three major reasons:

1. Knowledge has exploded to the point that it is necessary to select for teaching those items of knowledge that seem most significant and to eliminate much that is inconsequential.
2. Subject specialists have had more to say about the nature of their fields and about the teaching of these fields.
3. Experiments are showing that subject matter, old and new, can be placed in previously unthought of locations in the life space of learners.

The effect on elementary and secondary schools of each of these factors will be discussed below.

The Explosion of Knowledge

The new era, whose significance in the annals of U.S. education is still uncertain, finds its basis in a monumental explosion of knowledge. A current estimate holds that more gains have been made in the world's knowledge in any recent year than in 100,000 years of the Stone Age. Robert Oppenheimer said that knowledge of the physical sciences can double every eight and one-half to twelve years. Anyone who views the educational scene at all perceptively can see that there is much more to be known than can possibly be comprehended, more in print than can be read, and much more that no one has time to put into writing or even to express in voice recording. The increase in knowledge is, however, only part of the problem. Knowledge is useless unless it is made grist for the mill of understanding. As knowledge increases, the time available to combine it into usable concepts decreases, so the learner asks repeatedly, "What meaning can these new findings have for my life and the lives of others?" Quandary develops from the effort to find meaning in a world of too many facts and too many affairs.

Furthermore, the process of increasing knowledge is not merely an additive one. As knowledge abounds, some of that which was known previously is negated and must be discarded. Thus physics textbooks that were completely usable years ago are partially obsolete in a new era of atomic fission, hydrogen weapons, space exploration, and space communication. Unfortunately the colleges have not prepared students to distinguish important elements of subject matter from unimportant ones. In fact, few college teachers have thought very much about the organization of the content they teach. Instead, they find it easier to follow the traditional organization of subject matter which they themselves received readymade from their college teachers. Meanwhile large blocks and little pieces of knowledge that are newly discovered overburden old plans of subject matter organization, and teachers become more and more perplexed about how they will cover all the material.

Knowledge is being compounded in a multiplicity of ways: (1) Knowledge that was once a piece of a whole has now become a whole. In mathematics, the theory of sets was once vaguely implied in the solution of certain mathematical problems. Today it is, in itself, a recognized subject entity. Like other new entities, however, it does not yet have a clear position in the whole range of subject matter. (2) Blocks of knowledge, formerly accepted, are suddenly destroyed as entities. The unaffiliated pieces remain, but they no longer form a context or design. This happened to the construct known as Newtonian physics. Part of what was believed by Newton and those who followed him is considered valid today, but Newtonian physics as an entity has been superseded by a newer physics that may conceivably be superseded in the future. (3) The number of theories and hypotheses about phenomena is increasing. Though many theories remain untested, those that are being tested suggest new combinations of the items of knowledge. Examples may be found especially in newer fields like psychology, which abounds in theories and hypotheses about individuals, groups, learning, and other concerns. (4) Specialization has become a phenomenon of modern life. More practitioners are engaging in small segments of practice, and researchers are looking more and more deeply into narrower and narrower expanses of content. A case in point is the field of biology, in which specialization has grown strikingly.

Arthur Combs points out that we cannot correctly make a curriculum that is to be required of everyone at a given level of schooling. The explosion of knowledge alone prevents such an approach. Combs notes further that the ideas that knowledge is stable and that it is entirely from the past are mythical. Persons best equipped to deal with knowledge are adaptable, problem-solving people. To develop such people, we need to educate pupils to meet change that is continuous and to explore values.[1]

The question "What knowledge is of most worth?" was posed by Herbert Spencer in 1859. It is a question that must be asked by every generation of teachers. In the mid-eighties, the question is as important as ever before. Witness the numbers of persons, professional and lay, who say that the principal function of the school is to teach the fundamentals, or basics, so well that learners can call them to use in every life situation. Witness, too, the persons who believe that the schools can teach to all pupils, regardless of background or ability, the general or liberal studies, with the expectation that every pupil will become a reasonably well educated man or woman. Witness the others who insist that knowledge that is not directly usable or functional is worthless. The types of subject matter that would be taught to satisfy each of these viewpoints obviously differ widely. Harry Broudy suggests a less simplistic way of considering knowledge than as a product of a kindergarten-through-twelfth-grade education. Broudy says learners should value knowledge in their later lives less for repeating and applying than for forming associations and interpreting phenomena. Thus learners, when mature, use the images and concepts they have become familiar with for thinking and feeling in all kinds of life situations. In this sense, the curriculum contributes the stencils or lenses through which mature learners make their interpretations of what is real in the experiences of life.[2]

The Advent of Subject Specialists

Concurrently with the reshuffling of knowledge that began with the knowledge explosion, subject specialists in greater numbers began to concern themselves directly with elementary and secondary schooling.

Previously they had been content to discover knowledge, to report it in a variety of ways, and occasionally to write textbooks and instructional manuals. Many of the textbooks and manuals were written from the viewpoint and in the vocabulary of the mature scholar and could not therefore be appreciated fully by pupils in elementary and secondary schools. The explosion of knowledge, along with other factors, caused scholars to think seriously about what subject matter is truly basic to learning additional content and especially to learning in depth. Some of the wisest scholars in subject fields are able to tell educators what is most important in the subjects, and then leave to the educators the complex task of determining where, when, how, and to whom the content should be taught. In the fifties, however, scholars were trying to design curricula for children and youth without soliciting much help from practicing educators. Said Jerome S. Bruner, in describing the situation that existed in 1959:

> Major efforts in curriculum design had been launched by leading physicists, mathematicians, biologists, and chemists, and similar projects were in prospect in other fields of scientific endeavor. Something new was stirring in the land. A tour of the United States in the summer of 1959 would have revealed a concentration of distinguished mathematicians in Boulder, Colorado, engaged in writing new textbooks for primary, junior high, and high school grades. In Kansas City, there could be found a group of first-class biologists busily producing films on subjects such as the structure of the cell and photosynthesis for use in tenth-grade biology courses. In Urbana, Illinois, there was a flurry of work on the teaching of fundamental mathematical concepts to grade school children, and in Palo Alto one might have found a mathematical logician at work trying out materials for teaching geometry to children in the beginning grades of school. In Cambridge, Massachusetts, work was progressing on an "ideal" physics course for high school students, engaging the efforts not only of text writers and film producers but also of men who had earned world renown in theoretical and experimental physics. At various centers throughout the country, teachers were being trained to teach this new physics course by others who had already tried it. Preliminary work was under way in Boulder on a junior high school course in biology, and a group of chemists were similarly engaged in their field in Portland, Oregon. Various learned societies were searching for and finding ways of establishing contact between their leading scholars and educators in the schools.[3]

Since 1959, the interest of subject matter scholars in school curriculum has risen and then abated. The scholars have found that their curricular plans for use in schools are sometimes inappropriate or too difficult, that their attempts to influence teachers and administrators are frequently oversimplified and ill-conceived, and that medium-sized and small schools are notably hard to reach and impress. On the other hand, the scholars' personal prestige has helped their cause, especially during the sixties, when much curriculum reform originated outside the school rather than within it. In general, cooperation between subject matter scholars and professional educators improved as each group recognized that the other had a special role and competence. Cooperation is still poor in situations where scholars in subject fields assume they know *how* their detailed subject matter can be used in schools.

Experiments in the Placement of Subject Matter

There has always been a certain amount of experimentation with subject matter placement, but experimentation on a larger scale has been in progress during the sixties, the seventies, and the eighties. Obviously, large-scale experimentation cannot be left to individual teachers who, in their lifetime, will achieve only a limited rearrangement of what they teach. What subject matter should be moved up the grade scale? What should be moved down? What can children learn that has heretofore seemed beyond their capabilities? These are a few of the relatively simple questions, within a range of more difficult questions, to which answers are being sought.

Various experiments in rearranging old subject matter and taking on new subject matter have been carried out. Many of these suggest that portions of content might be taught earlier in pupil development and that teachers are taking longer than is necessary to help children build certain fundamental understandings. For example, in Denver in 1962, five-year-olds were being taught basic reading skills in kindergarten. Reading readiness programs had existed in American kindergartens for years, but few kindergarten teachers had taught children to look at printed words, to listen to the words in spoken context, to think of their initial sounds, and then to decide what the words are. In Denver, parents were prepared by television and other means to teach their children reading at home.[4] More recently, parents have seen evidence that it is possible to teach young babies to read.

A second example concerns the work of the curriculum committee of the National Science Teachers Association, which recommended that pupils have experience with all science concepts before they leave elementary school. Part of the content that was formerly taught in junior high school general science courses began to be taught in elementary schools. In senior high schools, science that was formerly taught superficially to junior high school pupils was incorporated within more sophisticated science courses.

A third and even more dramatic example of altered subject matter placement occurred at the Hamden Hall Country Day School in Connecticut, where Omar Khayyam Moore had two- and three-year-olds teaching themselves how to read and write. He accomplished this by permitting the children to play with special electric typewriters until they became curious enough to form and read words. The special typewriter gave the children the sounds of letters and words they formed by striking the keys. Soon the children associated what they heard with what they wrote. Subsequently some of them listened to words they typed from lists. The children learned touch-system typing by having their fingernails painted to correspond in color with given keys of the typewriter.[5]

Other experimentation has led to the conclusion that some subject matter is being taught too early. In the "new arithmetic," for example, one conclusion was that children gain certain basic number-concepts with more understanding if these concepts are introduced later in the primary grades. Also, the field of physical education contains instances of attempting to teach physical skills before the human organism is ready for their acquisition.

During the seventies and eighties, creators of learning packages have experimented with moving subject matter up and down age and grade scales. Obviously moving instructional content vertically is only one of the ways of dealing with subject matter. Changing sequence is another. Still other ways are referred to in Chapter 5, in connection with designing and redesigning the curriculum.

Perhaps the most ambitious experiments in placing subject matter have been of a wholesale kind. When junior high schools were created, subject matter was transferred from high school and elementary schools and a minimum of new content was invented to form an educational institution that was expected to meet a serious, special need. Within the past few years, schools bearing the names "middle" and "intermediate" have been established, usually to replace junior high schools in the gap between elementary schools and senior high schools. The ninth-grade curriculum is placed in the senior high school, inasmuch as it is the first phase of the college preparatory program and inasmuch as youngsters attain puberty a year earlier than they did some years ago. Founders of middle schools or intermediate schools hope that they will not become imitations of junior high schools. To keep the middle school or intermediate school curriculum from resembling the usual curriculum of the junior high school, emphasis is placed on homemaking, the industrial arts, typing, library and media center orientation, study procedures, and other content not usually found at the same skill and understanding levels in either elementary schools or senior high schools. Block-of-time and individualized scheduling, exploratory experiences, and values studies bring the nature of the school closer to the interests and needs of preadolescents and very young adolescents. As long as middle and intermediate schools are established for philosophically clear and altruistic motives rather than merely for administrative convenience, their special curriculum is likely to fit more closely the needs of the pupils who attend them.

ACTIVITY 4-1
Finding Reasons for Changes in Subject Matter
Placement

In a time of fast-moving changes in subject matter placement, the reasons for making changes should be considered thoroughly. It is important to know as certainly as possible whether given changes are justified or unjustified.

To learn what changes have occurred, (1) talk with school principals or other persons who see the curriculum as a whole or (2) compare recently published textbooks and other teaching materials with materials published ten years ago. To get behind the facts, ask teachers why they have made specific changes in subject matter placement. Try to learn whether these changes have resulted chiefly from (1) copying what other teachers have done, (2) falling in with what seem to be national trends, (3) experimenting informally with subject matter to see whether one's pupils learn it readily and well, or (4) following the results of research that is reported in publications or that is done in one's own professional environment. Learn whether the teachers feel satisfied with the new placement of subject matter *as compared with the former placement.*

What do you conclude about the reasons that operate in subject matter placement?

What, in your opinion, should be done to make changes in placement more judicious?

SELECTING SUBJECT MATTER AS LEARNING CONTENT

The potential experience of pupils in modern elementary, middle, and secondary schools covers a respectable portion of what human beings know and understand, of what they are able to do, and of how they feel about people and things. The subject matter the schools have traditionally taught has been confined to the content of recognized school subjects. In these terms, subject matter is taught merely to be known and understood — as a layperson put it, "School is for getting something into your head." But the best modern schools teach pupils *how* to do things, and they also help them clarify how they *feel* and what they *value.*

Even today, most of what is taught in schools is to be found within bodies of organized knowledge incorporated within school subjects. But much is now being taught apart from the formal structure of school subjects — in handicrafts and in human relationships, for example. Accordingly, the meaning of school subject matter is beginning to approximate the meaning of that which is experienced within the total environment of the school. We may expect to continue teaching subject matter known and understood as *substance*. Subject matter that contributes to skill building or to values development, however, must be taught mainly as *process*. Learnings in both the substance and the process categories form the curriculum of the school. Consider the subject called history. It is now taught primarily as substance, but there is also a teachable process of creating history, in the sense of selecting historical data and then recording them understandably. This is done, for example, when pupils select and record the history that comes from interviews, known as oral history. On the other hand, teaching reading is commonly thought of as process, though that which is read is the substance called literature. Both the process and the substance are improvable.

A Range of Objectives

Liberalizing our views of what subject matter is will permit us to utilize a wider range of objectives. Since the mid-fifties, Bloom, Krathwohl, and others have formed taxonomies of educational objectives of three kinds: the cognitive, or intellectually based; the affective, based in feeling or emotion; and the psychomotor, relating mental activity with physical movement. The taxonomies are meant to embrace all the classifications of subject matter available for teaching in elementary, middle, and secondary schools.

Cognitive Objectives

The *cognitive domain*, which is the domain of intellectuality and thought process, includes:

1. Knowing, which has to do with learning and recalling facts, words, and other symbols, classifications, events, trends, principles, ways of working, and theories
2. Comprehending, which involves interpreting content, translating it to another form, and extrapolating elements from one situation to another
3. Applying, or using in new situations what one has already learned
4. Analyzing, which consists of breaking wholes into parts and noting the nature of the parts and their relationships with each other
5. Synthesizing, or putting parts together and showing creativity in combining elements
6. Evaluating, or using criteria to judge the worth of an object.[6]

Affective Objectives

The *affective domain*, which is the domain of sensing, feeling, and believing, consists of the following:

1. Receiving, or showing interest in, giving attention to, and indicating awareness of an object
2. Responding, which includes both giving willing response and replying with a feeling of satisfaction
3. Valuing, or accepting a value, preferring it, and becoming committed to it
4. Organizing values by conceptualizing them, clarifying them, and systematizing them in one's thinking
5. Characterizing values by internalizing them so that eventually they become a philosophy of life.[7]

Psychomotor Objectives

The *psychomotor domain*, the most recently described of the three domains, contains, to date, five generally accepted levels of human activity:

1. Moving physically, including walking, jumping, running, pulling, pushing, and manipulating
2. Showing perceptual ability of visual, auditory, tactile, kinesthetic, and coordinative kinds
3. Showing physical ability related to strength, endurance, agility, dexterity, and time required to react or respond
4. Making skilled, coordinated movements in games, sports, and the arts
5. Communicating nonverbally through facial movements, gestures, posture, and creative expression.[8]

Levels of Knowledge

Some of the objectives in the preceding lists deal directly with knowledge as content for teaching. Taba described knowledge for use in schools as being at four levels. The lowest, simplest, and most common level is that of *specific facts and processes*. The date Columbus discovered America is an example. Specific facts and processes constitute data to think with or means for developing basic ideas. Some teachers almost stop their teaching at this level.

Taba's second level is the level of *basic ideas and principles*, which often represent a common core of learning for all pupils. For example, a basic idea in American history is that the American frontier became a safety valve for discontent and also a stimulus to technological development.

The third level is that of *concepts*, such as the concept of human interdependence, the concept of the set in mathematics, or the concept of political democracy. Concepts are the threads of thought, or universals, that run through the curriculum. Several subjects contribute simultaneously to the development of most concepts. A teacher may never legitimately say to a pupil, "I'll give you a concept," because the pupil must develop for himself or herself each concept he or she acquires. The best a teacher can do is to arrange pupils' experiencing in ways that contribute to concept development.

The fourth level is the level of *thought systems*, which direct the flow of thought and inquiry in areas of learning. For example, in theology John Calvin developed a thought system known as Calvinism. Each thought system includes interrelated concepts, principles, and definitions. With a thought system as a base, mature pupils (especially the abler pupils in secondary schools) ask intelligent questions, relate ideas, and engage in rational and sophisticated inquiry. They become interested in ways of thinking and inquiring within their favorite subjects, as when they develop advanced machines and models for the school's science fair.[9]

The Planning of Measurable Outcomes

The two immediately preceding sections of this chapter make quite different contributions to an understanding of subject matter and its uses. The taxonomies prepared by Bloom and others provide a general mapping of large objectives. For daily, weekly, and monthly use, large objectives need to be broken into smaller, directly usable ones.

Taba's statement about levels of knowledge organizes the cognitive domain into simple to complex elements that help one to level or pitch smaller objectives to suit one's intentions and at the same time know where pupils are working within the total domain. (Unfortunately no one has organized the affective and psychomotor domains in so neat and usable a way.)

Given a level of achievement we hope to see pupils attain as they utilize subject matter, how should the small, usable objectives be stated? Perhaps a majority of persons in the curriculum field now say they should be stated behaviorally—that is, according to the behavior to be expected. A leading promoter of behavioral objectives, W. James Popham, has put it this way: "A properly stated behavioral objective must describe without ambiguity the nature of learner behavior or product to be measured."[10]

When this definition is applied literally, it leads to a "tight" method of stating objectives, now seen in *performance-based education* (sometimes called competency-based education). Objectives that are performance-based state what the learners one has in mind will do, under what conditions, and at what level of group performance if the given objective is to be regarded as having been attained. The emphasis is on intended outcomes of instruction, constituting the specific performance of pupils. Performance-based educational procedures often follow a set sequence such as the following: (1) behavioral (performance-type) objectives are stated; (2) learners' behaviors (baseline mastery of the subject matter) are assessed; (3) learners' ability to perform at an established outcome level is also assessed; (4) alternative paths to achievement of the desired outcome(s) are plotted; (5) post-assessment is used to determine the degree to which the expected performance has been attained (e.g., to a degree of 90 percent, established at the time the objective was stated); and (6) learners are passed to the next step or are asked to repeat, depending on the results of the post-assessment.

In performance-based education, the outcomes expected become definite achievement criteria. The usual achievement tests, based on national or regional norms, are not suitable for determining whether a given group of pupils has met its own definite achievement criteria. Consequently, *criterion-referenced tests* have to be designed to meet the need. These tests are expected to fit not only the objectives but also the subject matter content that has been taught. Thus criterion referencing applies to everything in the instructional procedure: content, materials, and evaluation scheme.

Performance-based education can be improved by making the statements of expected performance or competency completely clear, by paying attention to the location at which each competency fits within the curriculum, and by providing resource materials for planners.[11] Its potential seems to lie mainly in the provision it can make for such aspects of effective instruction as individualization, self-pacing, remediation, and experiences in the field.[12]

Performance-based education and criterion-referenced testing are subjected to the same criticisms that have been leveled at behavioral objectives—that they are applications of mechanistic stimulus-response learning theory; that they do not admit the variety of behaviors that occur in classrooms and therefore constitute a closed, unrealistic learning system; that the number of objectives they position behind real performance is staggering; that they make it literally impossible to attend to the needs of individuals; and that, because of the preceding handicaps, they center on a few minor, measurable bits of subject matter.[13] Some of the critics say that performance-based education will inevitably impoverish the curriculum because rich, significant elements of the curriculum will be left untouched while teachers are busy with the little pieces that the tests highlight. Nevertheless, state officials, boards of education in some communities, and numbers of laypersons continue to press for performance-based education and its associated strategies because they offer a means of holding teachers accountable for the quality of their work.[14]

Some Themes Governing the Selection of Content

An informal survey of the interests of curriculum planners in subject matter and planning processes in the mid-eighties highlighted several favorite themes. These themes include basic education, functional learning, education of affect, staff development by means of curriculum planning, and regard for futurism. The first three contribute directly to curriculum content. The last two are strategies, or process elements, that can be used in making curriculum decisions.

Basic Education

As we saw in Chapter 3, pressure to improve the teaching of the basics—skills like those needed to read, write, and do arithmetic problems, and fundamental knowledge like that in the sciences, history, or geography—has increased in recent years. Naturally persons in charge of curriculum planning have responded to the pressures by searching for ways of strengthening the teaching of the basics. Actually, methods of teaching reading and arithmetic have been thoroughly explored in the past. Therefore the essential problem as identified by curriculum coordinators has been failure of professionals in the schools to take seriously what is already known, and then to work hard in putting what is known into regularized practice.

   Though deficiencies in basic education have appeared in all geographic locations and in all segments of the U.S. population, the favorable effects of doing something about them can often be seen most readily where the deficiency has been greatest. In Appalachia, for example, improvement in basic education was brought about when two sources of help were utilized: the Appalachian Regional Commission and state-sponsored agencies.[15] In developing countries of the world, the particular need is often for skills in communication, skills that improve the quality of life, and skills that increase production.[16] Thus the meaning of the term basic skills varies in accordance with economic status and cultural background.

Functional Learning

Identification of subject matter for functional learning has been one response to the public's demand for high school graduates who not only know something but also can do something. In 1980 the Association for Supervision and Curriculum Development formed a national network of schools to redefine general education in U.S. secondary schools. The network interested itself in the broad range of learnings that are presumably necessary in a high-tech society. The schools of the network expressed a desire to achieve the following results: an increase in total requirements for graduation, more serious study by seniors, augmented mathematics and science requirements, an expectation of competency rather than of mere exposure to subject matter, and careful analysis of the nature of course content.[17] Employers, who are among the chief advocates of functional learning, have expressed themselves similarly. They have become more concerned with broad-based general education of adolescents than with their specialized education, most of which they believe they can provide on the job. Applied science has long been recognized as important functional learning. Now the applications of science are considered to include public and social policy matters and ethical issues. In biology, for instance, the emphasis has been changing from instruction in biology strictly for its own sake to instruction in biology with overtones of information management, data analysis, and decision making based on moral and ethical dimensions.[18]

Education of Affect

Education of affect, or affective education, means more than merely education in personal, religious, political, and social values. Affect, first of all, means feelings and emotions, both of which belong in the learning process. The feelings and emotions pupils bring to the learning of particular subject matter influence the facility with which the subject matter is learned and also the permanence with which it remains to function in the lives of the pupils. Arthur Combs says that the cruciality of what is learned depends on the subjective experience of the learner. He describes four preconditions for relating to and absorbing content. Put in the language of the individual learner, they are

"I think well of myself."
"I feel challenged rather than threatened by what I am to learn."
"What I value accords with what I'm expected to learn."
"I feel I belong in this situation and am being cared for here."[19]

The wisest curriculum leaders know the importance of affect. Therefore they try to meet the challenge of making room for it in planning and in teaching. Whatever they do is likely to take into account self-concept, challenge, values, and belongingness.

Staff Development by Means of Curriculum Planning

Many people think the end product of curriculum planning is a project, a program, a model, or a printed or mimeographed curriculum guide. We have known for a long time, however, that changes in the behavior of teachers and other persons who come into contact with pupils constitute the real product. With the advent of programs of staff development, curriculum coordinators have turned their attention once more to using curriculum planning intentionally to assist teacher growth.

An example of the change-in-people emphasis on a national scale is the National Writing Project.[20] The project started at Berkeley, California, in 1974 and was subsequently funded by the National Endowment for the Humanities, by an ESEA grant, and by state grants. Though it has provided for input by scholars and use of discovery learning, the project's greatest strength has been its careful and thorough involvement of teachers. In staff development groups, teachers learn to write through extensive practice and are thus prepared to teach both their colleagues and their pupils to write. The project takes the almost unprecendented step of treating teachers as professionals, and therefore differs from earlier instructional projects in which production of written materials (curriculum packages) was more important than the direct development of people.

If teachers are to use curriculum planning as a means of self-development, they must be involved in the planning from its inception; they must have sufficient time, competent help, and adequate facilites, clerical assistance, and materials; and most of all, perhaps, they must be encouraged by their supervisors to stay with the tasks of planning. When teachers work closely with a portion of a subject, identifying facts, experiences, activities, and materials and concerning themselves with scope, sequence, evaluation, and other professional matters, they use varied talents that enrich the planning process and help make the ultimate selection of subject matter especially appropriate.[21]

Regard for Futurism

One of the complaints about U.S. schools has to do with their similarity from decade to decade. For example, what is now taught in high school mathematics classrooms is remarkably similar to what was taught fifty years ago. In high school English classes, after an excursion into the teaching of questionable modern literature, teachers are returning to many of the classic literary selections that were taught a half-century ago.

The speed at which science, technology, and communication are changing suggests, however, that the curriculum of the future should be a singularly altered one. Ours is becoming the "information generation" in the fullest sense. Ready communication of data, new practical uses of number concepts, and increased dependence on machines have made this so. In the schools, the skills of reading, writing, and computation need to be supplemented with previously unknown skills.[22]

These facts have caused curriculum personnel to look to the future for clues concerning what novel subject matter to propose. Several organizations interested in future developments in subject matter fields have established agendas for the future. The futurists in mathematics believe that more comprehensive problem solving will form the focus of mathematics, that basic mathematical skills will be supplemented and extended, that calculators and computers will aid teaching more extensively, that testing will relate more closely to the new content, and that options will be increased to accommodate the ability ranges found among pupils.[23] This example concerning mathematics is only one of a series of projections into the future that will be forthcoming from subject matter organizations. Curriculum planners in school systems can ill afford to overlook the projections, though they need not take all of them literally.

Criteria for Selecting Content

Several criteria have been proposed for selecting appropriate subject matter content from an embarrassing wealth of content. They include the following:

- *The validity and the significance of the content as disciplined knowledge.* Some items of content available to learners are likely to be of little worth because they are inconsequential or trivial. Such items should be ruled out.
- *The balance that is being maintained between content for survey and content for study in depth.* Pupils need to see the broad sweep or scope of subject matter. After moving for a while on the surface of the content, however, they should have opportunities for digging deep, or "postholing." Points on the subject matter terrain at which the individual pupil postholes may be peculiar to personal needs, or they may be the same points at which his or her classmates go into depth. The problem for the teacher or other curriculum planner is to achieve a reasonable balance between scope and depth. Curriculum planners who do this best are generally those who know the most about the entire range of their subject matter.

- *The appropriateness of the content to pupil needs and interests.* Casual interest is not hard to identify. Lasting interest and the presence of need are much more difficult to determine. Only the passage of time permits curriculum planners to know pupils' enduring interests. Needs of which the pupil is unconscious appear only to outside observers, and must be assessed by those who have the necessary maturity to weigh the gravity of various needs. The value of teachers as diagnosticians of need depends on their previous experience in living as well as on the criteria they use in the identification process.
- *The durability, or lasting quality, of the elements of content that are being emphasized.* Determining how long an item of content will last as a desired and desirable element is difficult. Subject matter has changed so rapidly in fields like physics and chemistry that prediction of its durability has sometimes seemed impossible. In general, however, the closer an item of content is to a main idea or a concept, the greater is its chance of being durable.
- *The relationship of facts and other minor content to main ideas and concepts.* The last comment above concerning the criterion of durability makes contact with this criterion. The webbing that holds a body of subject matter together is big ideas and concepts. An item of subject matter devoid of contact with a major idea may conceivably be dispensable.
- *The learnability of the content.* Obviously, no attempt should be made to teach pupils that which they cannot learn. Trying to teach the same basic content to nearly all the children of all the people has been one of the major failings of the American experiment.
- *The possibility of illuminating the content with data from other fields of knowledge.* Some subject matter has potential for relating readily to content from other subjects. In modern studies of ecology, for example, ecological phenomena found in pure science have implications for the social studies and have their base in psychology, morals, and ethics. Teaching content that is capable of crossing subject lines in this way facilitates reinforcement of learning as the learner is reminded of his or her previous contact with it in other settings.

Persons especially interested in human development and other persons with a realistic view of the difficulties teachers of reluctant learners face day by day may be expected to list additional criteria: the evident needs of individual learners, their achievement status, and their expectations; the context within which the subject matter is presented; and the relevance that the learners find in the content.

As time passes, curriculum planners continue to be reminded of what John Dewey said in 1916: that knowledge is "the working capital, the indispensable resources, of further inquiry; of finding out, or learning, more things."[24] Later, Dewey wrote concerning the same theme that educators are to consider the current experience of learners, and then seek to extend that experience. What the learner knows becomes the means of opening the way to new knowledge. Educators thus serve as agents to help learners achieve connectedness in their growth.[25]

In selecting and placing subject matter, building experience on experience appropriately, as Dewey advocated, is a difficult task in itself, but curriculum leaders are called upon to help do much more. One of their additional assignments is to see that the schools accept and discharge responsibilities that are theirs, and to screen out all the unjustified responsibilities the society and the community try to impose on the schools. Another additional assignment is to encourage articulation of learning from level to level of schooling. Another is to urge strictness in the learning process when the subject matter requires strictness, and to urge relaxation and openness when the subject matter calls for exploration, inquiry, and discovery. Still another is to be the immediate source of equipment and materials that facilitate the learning of the subject matter to be taught. These assignments are so staggering in their proportions that new administrators, supervisors, and coordinators do not usually realize their magnitude and significance. Certainly persons in the lay public do not.

ACTIVITY 4-2
Planning Improved Selection of Subject Matter

Read the following questions. Ask yourself whether you know the answer to each question. If you do not, inquire within your school district or another district you know reasonably well concerning the things with which you are unfamiliar. When you report to your class or group, discuss with the members how far the school district you have studied needs to go to develop adequate bases for selecting subject matter competently, in light of your answers to the questions.

1. In this school district have curriculum planners reviewed the district's educational program to see that the schools are accepting as their responsibilities tasks that really belong to them? How have such tasks been defined?
2. In this district have administrators and other personnel tried hard to screen out tasks that obviously do not belong to the schools? What example of such a task can you give?
3. In the district have teachers, department chairpersons, and other planners tried to make sure that the subject matter taught in curriculum fields where obsolescence is common is really up to date? What example of this kind of action can you give?
4. Have systemwide planning groups attempted to achieve articulation among parts of the curriculum so that pupils' movement from developmental level to developmental level in learning is continuous and smooth? What evidence of these attempts can you give?

5. Have curriculum planners in the district made certain that the curriculum contains at every developmental level subject matter that, by its nature, must be taught rigorously and also subject matter that is rightly taught in a relaxed and open way? What evidence do you have that, under supervision, teachers are paying attention to the distinction between these two kinds of subject matter?
6. Have administrators in the district made equipment and materials available for the teaching of required and recommended subject matter? How do you know?

Learning Experiences for Achieving Objectives

No matter how wisely subject matter has been selected to aid in the achievement of objectives, teachers need to prescribe and administer subject matter to pupils. They do this by creating and using learning experiences, alone or with the help of their pupils. Teachers find several criterion questions useful in creating appropriate learning experiences:

1. Can the experiences profit the pupils we teach?
2. Do the experiences help to meet the evident needs of our pupils?
3. Are our pupils likely to be interested in the experiences?
4. Do the experiences encourage pupils to inquire further?
5. Do the experiences seem real?
6. How do the experiences accord with the life patterns of our pupils?
7. How contemporary are some of the major experiences?
8. How fundamental to mastery of total learning content are they?
9. Do the experiences provide for attainment of a range of objectives?
10. Do the experiences provide opportunities for both broad study and deep study?

Practical hints for preparing and stating learning experiences were listed by a group of teachers as follows:

1. If you are going to describe learning experiences at all, spell them out in sufficient detail to make them understandable.
2. Know the purpose or function of each experience within your curriculum plan.
3. If possible, have each experience serve more than one of your objectives. For instance, a single experience can easily serve a cognitive objective and also an affective one.
4. Try to organize each experience within a hierarchy of experiences. For example, move from the concrete and experientially close to the abstract and experientially remote, or from the easy to the difficult.

5. Make increments in experiencing "bite size." Instead of providing substantially bigger bites for bright pupils, try preparing alternative experiences for them.
6. Try rotating *types* of experiences, like the following:
   a. Experiences for intake
   b. Experiences for expression
   c. Experiences for assimilation of big ideas and of concepts, through planned practice
   d. Experiences for accommodation or restructuring of big ideas and concepts, through making them functional in real situations
   e. Experiences to sensitize or otherwise to develop feeling
   f. Experiences to stimulate intellectual growth, including gaming, puzzles, and simulation
   g. Experiences to interrelate mind and physical movement, as in sophisticated practice in sports
7. Use within the experiences varied ways of learning, including reading, writing, observing, analyzing, dramatizing, making products in the arts, working individually, working in groups, and making maps and charts. Keep a master list of possibilities like these.

SITUATION 4-1
Resolving Problems in Subject Matter Selection and
Assignment-Making

The principal of an elementary school received the following letter of complaint from the mother of a fifth-grade boy who was enrolled in the school:

Dear Mrs. Rumson:

My son Gilbert, who is in Miss Axtell's fifth-grade section, brought home a strange assignment last Friday. The assignment was given to the entire fifth grade at your school, the fifth-grade teachers having got together to make it up.

I was upset when I saw the assignment, which called for making a booklet about poets. You may already know about it yourself. Anyway, the teachers had listed twenty-four names, eight names to the column. The first column was headed 1700s, the second column 1800s, and the third column 1900s. I guess each column was supposed to contain the name of at least one poet, maybe more.

Gilbert and the others were to choose one poet from each period of time, write a biographical report about each one in script, copy at least three poems written by each poet, and make a bibliography.

I checked the lists of poets in a dictionary and an encyclopedia and found no poet in the list for the 1700s and two poets in the 1800s list that belong in the 1900s.

The poems written by many of the poets are long and hard. The kids can't understand them, and they don't want to copy all that stuff.

Didn't anybody guide the teachers in selecting the poets before the assignment went out all over town? It looks as though the teachers don't know the poets or what they wrote either.

I talked with Miss Axtell about this. She said the teachers worked very hard researching the assignment and they were going ahead with it even if it had a mistake or two. I told her nobody researched it. I have an anthology at home where I found lists of poets almost the same as the ones the teachers gave out. Some of the teachers' poets wrote only one poem.

Gilbert will complete his assignment because his mother will help him. But this does *not* solve the problem.

Other than moving or sending Gilbert to a private school, what can I do about such ignorance? What are you going to do?

Grace Oreo

1. What abuses of subject matter and pupil experiences are described in this letter?
2. What hidden abuses can you detect?
3. What *should* the principal do to help the teachers with their subject matter problems?

A CLOSER LOOK AT SUBJECT MATTER

Within recent years, subject matter as learning content has been examined more critically than ever before. There is much talk about the role of the various disciplines in learning, a *discipline* being defined by some persons both as a way of making knowledge and as the domain occupied by particularized knowledge. Thus, the phenomena of chemistry have been discovered by a given set of methods, known to the chemist as a laboratory scientist, and the content the chemist has discovered is distinctively different from the content that has been discovered by the historian or the philosopher or even by other scientists like the physicist and the biologist. Each discipline, according to the definition, has its own integrity, an integrity that is worth respecting because it has been built by the regulated efforts of so many intelligent and creative persons. A few authors, as they write about the disciplines, seem to be thinking of applications of organized knowledge, as in the field of medicine. Actually, a discipline has a history, has its own domain, follows its own rules, and should be based in testable theory.

Some of the thinking about subject matter as learning content has followed these lines: Subject matter includes what people know and believe, together with reflections of people's ideals and loyalties; subject matter may validly be selected for use in teaching and learning when it is significant to an organized field of knowledge, when it has proved appropriate down through the years, when it is useful, when it can be made interesting to learners, and when it contributes to the growth and development of our society.[26] Of these criteria, the first is highlighted within the context of the present chapter. The criterion of significance to an organized field of knowledge implies that the items of knowledge within that field must be interrelated so that the structure that the items rationally form can be seen and understood. According to this thesis, there are big and significant principles or concepts on which lesser principles, concepts, and facts depend. A first, major task of the scholar and of the learner alike is to identify clearly these big principles or concepts.[27] For example, in the view of a leading economist, there are four principles on which all of economics depends. Know these and you have the hooks on which the minor principles and the facts of economics hang. The details of economics as a discipline may change — time may retire some of them and new details may replace old ones — but the fundamental structure of economics will remain, and it is the fundamental structure that counts. Although the fundamentals often develop from observation of details in the first place, the fixity and steadfastness of the fundamentals is a basic consideration in studying the structure of a discipline. Detail is hard to remember unless it is related to the fundamentals. Transfer of training, so long argued in U.S. education, seems to proceed best when learners understand the fundamentals of what they are learning and transferring.

These ideas bring one to the thought that different elements in the structure of a discipline can be taught at different developmental levels. Thus attention must be given to more than the facts of mere readiness as a function of the human organism. Readiness for *what* becomes a central question. Piaget has maintained, in Bruner's expression, that "any subject can be taught effectively in some intellectually honest form to any child at any stage of development." This would mean, for instance, that some portions of algebra and geometry can validly be taught to children in the primary grades. These portions must necessarily be concrete. More importantly, they must accord with the child's perception of the world's phenomena. Piaget points out that children advance through three stages of development in learning subject matter and that young children tend to be at the first stage. At this stage, learners perceive phenomena in terms of their own experiences, and they try to establish relationships between their own experiences and the actions that are being taken. At the second stage, they engage in concrete operations with present phenomena, being competent enought to attempt trial-and-error experiments in their heads.

At the third stage, they go beyond working with present phenomena to work with hypothetical ones.[28] Each successive stage calls for more abstract thinking. A prime difficulty in selecting subject matter is to find content that is abstract enough to challenge without being so abstract as to frustrate. When this is done, even crudely, it is possible to build a spiral curriculum in which the same subject, but not the identical subject matter, is taught on several occasions during one's school experience. For example, selected portions of American history may be taught profitably in the fifth grade and then again in the eighth and eleventh grades of a pupil's schooling.

We know that *how* one learns, as well as *what* one learns, is very significant. The true significance of how one learns has been revealed in recent discussions of intuitive thinking and is illustrated not only in the "Oh, I see!" reaction of the person who has studied a problem for a long time and suddenly finds a solution to it but also in the making of intelligent, successful guesses concerning solutions. Geometry students have historically studied proofs and then made applications to test the validity of these proofs in similar situations. It is possible instead to discover proofs for oneself. This may be done visually, without going through all the logical steps of proof development. For example, one may memorize a formula for finding the volume of a pyramid and then apply the formula to find the volumes of pyramids of different sizes, or one may think or guess intelligently how a person might discover the volume of a pyramid. Having done so, one has no need to rely on memorization of a formula made by someone else.

When a procedure is indicated step by step, it has usually been developed through analytical thinking. When it is reached by jumping mentally over logical steps, it has been developed intuitively. Little is known about the art of intuiting, but we know that it occurs and that some people are better intuiters than others. Both analytical thinking and intuitive thinking are needed in classrooms, but we are underemphasizing intuiting in favor of analyzing, especially when the analyzing is done primarily by teachers as proxies for their pupils. In classroom after classroom, observers see teachers putting outlines on chalkboards so that their pupils may memorize them. Creating one's own outline is an experience the learners need. At times, they should be made to go behind the outline to *discover* for themselves the basic knowledge from which the outline is made.

Dewey said that when learners are ready to inquire as a prelude to discovering, they take the following steps, though not necessarily in a set order: they sense a difficulty, they locate it and define it, they suggest a possible solution, they develop by reason the details of their suggestion, and they observe and experiment until they accept or reject the suggestion.[29]

The process by which learners discover within an area of subject matter has been described by Foshay:

It is eleven o'clock in the morning . . . and the teacher has proceeded in American history to the immediate post-Civil War period. I want to suggest what she should do. She should begin—if she hadn't already done so—by remembering that history is a disciplined way of confronting the past. It deals with periods, within a chronology. It seeks consistencies with the periods, and generalizations about them. The historian constantly deals with ambiguities—with the haunting knowledge that the events he studies can never be known directly—only the records that happen to remain of these events. The historian feels his responsibility to deal with the record accurately, fully, and in a way that honestly reflects the point of view he has chosen to adopt. He knows his discipline as being in part a science; he acknowledges that aesthetic judgment plays a significant part in his decisions as historian. History, he knows, does not exist apart from the historian's interpretation of it.

Our teacher, I say, remembers these things. Now, what does she do about the post-Civil War period? If she wishes to pursue the ideal of intellectual excellence that is represented by an attempt to study the disciplines directly, she carries the children to a confrontation of the historian's problem. She asks of the children, that is, in the Progressive tradition, that they be producers of knowledge, not merely passive consumers of it. She raises with them the question, therefore, "What kinds of events after Lincoln would be most worth knowing?" (Does this seem too advanced? You should see how the children handle it!) "Now," she goes on, "how can we discover what these events were?" (Not one historian—several, for not all historians choose to deal with the same events, and the sooner we understand this, the more liberated we are from a naive view of our past and of the historian's place in understanding it.) "What are the principal ways the period has been interpreted by the historians?" "Do you, as a student, think of other ways?" "What information do you think the historians might include that they appear to have omitted?" "Why do you suppose they omitted this information? Because they couldn't find it? Because it didn't fit their interpretation?"[30]

In this way, learners "get inside" the disciplines. In France, copies of historical documents have been made available to the schools so that pupils can construct portions of the history of France de novo. An important object of the discovery process is to feel like the historian, the scientist, or the mathematician. The act of discovery can obviously be engaged in only at intervals, being time consuming and requiring special insights and materials, but it is badly needed in a society that seeks excellence in its pupils—a society in which pupils are presently able to enter college chiefly because they are effective rote-memorizers rather than effective critical thinkers. In every discipline, pupils need to understand the technology of that discipline—how it is made and put together and how it is refined and polished until it reaches a point at which the makers can be proud of it. Unfortunately, in recent years the discovery process has fallen into disuse in many of those schools in which it was once an advertised feature.

Philip H. Phenix thinks of the disciplines as being peculiarly suited for teaching and learning. He maintains that all curriculum content should come from the disciplines rather than from the needs, concerns, and problems of learners. To make knowledge useful for teaching and learning, he says, we have three needs: (1) to provide analytic simplification through which we can make understandable the classes and generalizations that are formed of particulars, (2) to provide synthetic coordination by which we make evident the patterns and relationships that exist in subject matter, and (3) to ensure the presence of dynamism, the "lure of discovery," or the force that leads us on to new knowledge. In the disciplines, says Phenix, we can find the answers to our needs, concerns, and problems. Therefore, the source of all that teachers and learners require is the disciplines themselves.[31]

Having seen what analysis of subject matter might contribute to decision making about curriculum, the educator comes full circle to the old problems of motivation, interest, and effort with which Dewey and others have wrestled. Both Phenix and Bruner express the hope that learners will find motivation in the fascination of working over subject matter that is intrinsically fascinating. But the problem of getting an "optimum level of aroused attention" from pupils must continue to challenge all who call themselves teachers.[32]

Miel raises several cautions about proposals for analysis of the disciplines. In brief, these cautions may be stated as follows:

1. There is disagreement as to the definition to be assigned to the term discipline.
2. Scholars within a given field will probably not be able to agree on what constitutes the structure of that field.
3. Structure can easily be regarded as abstract and static knowledge rather than as the dynamics of inquiry by which knowledge has been developed. Of the two, the dynamics or structure of inquiry is the more valuable for learning.
4. The structure of a discipline changes as the discipline evolves. Pupils cannot be "handed" structure; they should be helped to understand structure gradually.
5. Distinction should be made between the understanding of structure which is needed by the specialist in a discipline and the understanding needed by the nonspecialist—the pupil in a general education program.

6. Overemphasis may be given to disciplines in which structure is most obvious, e.g., in mathematics and the sciences, at the expense of other disciplines.
7. If they are not careful, those who try to teach structure will be tempted to teach adult-ordered, logical structure without regard to the pupil's perceptions and needs.
8. The problem of integrating the learnings derived from individual disciplines remains.[33]

Mauritz Johnson has pointed out that discovery is by no means new as an educational idea. He quotes William C. Bagley's statement made in 1905 in *The Educative Process*:

> The pupil is not to be told but led to see. . . . Whatever the pupil gains, whatever thought connections he works out, must be gained with the consciousness that he, the pupil, is the active agent—that he is, in a sense at least, the discoverer.[34]

Bagley owed a debt for the idea to Frank and Charles McMurry (1897), who in turn were indebted to David P. Page (1847) or else to Herbert Spencer (1860). Of course, many years earlier, Plato had referred to discovery through the asking of questions. Once again, an idea that seemed novel to many educators when Bruner advanced it has proved to be nearly as old as educational history.

Behind the search for structure and the revival of the discovery process are understandings about knowledge and its use in curriculum making that every curriculum planner should possess. The first of these understandings returns us to the problem of identifying and utilizing objectives. Most of the objectives to which curriculum committees in school systems customarily subscribe fall under the headings of acquiring knowledge, developing ability to think, effecting attitude change, and developing skills in a variety of learning areas. Of these four kinds of objectives, only the first is implemented directly through selection of content. The others are implemented mainly through stating learning activities and experiences for pupils and then stating teaching strategies for helping pupils engage in these activities or have these experiences. Also, coming to *know* something requires a different kind of learning process than does learning to think, achieving attitude change, or increasing and refining skills.

A second understanding about knowledge and its use in curriculum planning is that we can deal with the problem of having too much knowledge to teach by avoiding fact and topic teaching. Teaching should be planned around and within the largest, most significant elements of knowledge. These elements are concepts or big ideas. Within and beneath these larger elements are useful topics and pertinent facts in a variety of subjects and subject fields. If, for example, we decide to teach toward justice as a concept, we must select from the great body of available topics and facts those that will probably have the most telling effect in helping pupils make the concept their own. Some of the topics and facts may be on the frontier of knowledge and, therefore, nowhere to be found in books. No matter. It is the pertinence and potency of the topic or fact that count.

A third understanding is that subject matter content is often conveyed by means other than words. This is true today, for example, in multicultural education. Teachers' nonverbal behavior may tell more than their spoken words about their liking for or aversion to given cultural groups. Also, assumptions implicit in written content may easily be at variance with what the words of the content seem to say.

The interest of curriculum planners in the structure of knowledge has, at least for the present, declined. The discovery method, on the other hand, has continued to attract moderate interest. Occasionally, deeper investigation of subject matter gives promise of leading to useful application in the schools. For example, traditional views of subject matter for developing cognition have been considered by Joe M. Steele, Herbert J. Walberg, and Ernest R. House in light of pupils' perceptions of their own experiences with the subject matter. These researchers worked with 121 secondary school classes in four subjects, recording pupils' perceptions of the subject matter they were learning cognitively. They found that the content of the four subjects had three significant functions: convergence-divergence, syntax-substance, and objectivity-subjectivity. Mathematics was considered by the pupils to be convergent, the language arts divergent. Both the language arts and mathematics were labeled syntactical, whereas science and the social studies were thought to be substantive. Science appeared to the pupils to be objective, social studies subjective. Inasmuch as pupils seem to be learning the four subjects in these terms, Steele, Walberg, and House ask whether mathematics is in fact convergent and, if it is not, whether it must be taught convergently. They wonder whether there are syntactical aspects of science and the social studies that should be given greater emphasis and whether subjective aspects of science and objective aspects of the social studies and the humanities can be taught.[35]

ACTIVITY 4-3
Discovering What's Inside a Discipline

To help other persons become acquainted with the nature of subject matter, curriculum leaders should see for themselves what is fundamental in as many disciplines as possible. Select a discipline such as mathematics, biological science, or modern language. Learn from one or more specialists in this discipline what is considered most important to be comprehended. (You may find that the specialists disagree.) Then study the textbooks used in teaching the discipline.

When you have completed your investigation, answer these questions:

1. Can I now clearly see the fundamentals of this discipline?
2. How well are the fundamentals understood by experts in the discipline, including textbook authors?
3. What should be done to clarify for curriculum workers the meaning of the discipline for instruction in elementary and/or secondary schools?

ACTIVITY 4-4
Working with the Discovery Process

The illustration concerning discovery in history can be duplicated in other school subjects. For example, in general science, pupils can develop a test for starch and apply it to a variety of commercial products. In physics, they can approach experiments in mechanics and optics intuitively. Each experiment should be open-ended — that is, the result should be unpredetermined.

With teachers of a subject you know well, design several experiences that require pupils to discover the content of that subject. Work with the teachers as they use, refine, and evaluate the results of these experiences. Note, for your own subsequent reference, the ways teachers proceed in freeing pupils for discovery. Note also the materials they need to help individuals with the discovery process. Observe what happens to individual pupils as they discover hidden abilities of their own in mastering subject matter.

ORGANIZING AND REORGANIZING SUBJECT MATTER FOR TEACHING AND LEARNING

How educators organize subject matter for teaching and learning depends very much on their view of the uses of subject matter in curriculum planning. Some accept the "don't skip a thing, everything's important" point of view. Others think the training or discipline one gets from studying the subject matter counts most. Still others say that only "hard" subject matter is worth learning, or that the process of learning subject matter is more important than the substantive outcomes of learning it, or that subject matter is worth learning only if it proves useful in a very practical way.

In these terms, subject matter is organized around its key ideas; around materials of instruction, as in learning activity packages; around ways of working, or the processes by which one usually makes and dispenses knowledge in a subject or subject field; around significant places that are symbolic of what is being taught; or around people, as when biography is used in teaching. Someone who is especially interested in learners may organize subject matter around the centers of learners' interests; around their developmental tasks, as Havighurst has done; around social, scientific, and other problems that concern people; or around evolution in human events, treated chronologically or otherwise. In brief, the options open to us are numerous.

For use in actual teaching, subject matter may be divided into units, into themes or topics, into analyses of life problems, into cases, episodes, or anecdotes, or into incidents of real and direct experience.

The preceding discussion concerns subject matter as it is organized and then taught by classroom teachers. For curriculum planners, there is necessarily a broader prospect of what is to be taught and learned. A master planner of curriculum content must hold a definite philosophical viewpoint about what is really worth teaching and learning. Shall the content consist of that which individual subjects have to offer, of that which combinations of subjects to form fields can provide, or of something else? A half-dozen possibilities have been considered.

Organizing by Subjects

The first and most-used possibility is organizing strictly by *subjects*. This way has seemed obvious and easy to curriculum planners, who have majored in given subjects and who have had their own school programs organized in this manner. Learning subjects emphasizes the use of chronology, prerequisites, whole-to-part mastery, and deductive learning. It is considered respectable partly because it is heavy in verbal activities and utilization of logic. It permits both constants and electives to have places in the school program. It attempts to care for individual differences through extra and differentiated assignments. In the subject-centered organization, the teaching time granted to a subject depends on the alleged relative worth of that subject. Organizing by subjects tends to compartmentalize learning, to emphasize memorization, and to make the subject, rather than learners' activities and interests, central.

Organizing by Correlation

In an effort to relate proximate bodies of subject matter, curriculum planners have attempted simple *correlation* of content. Leaving subjects intact and side by side, they have correlated elements of history, geography, and literature, as in studies of the westward movement in U.S. history. They have made similar correlations between mathematics on the one hand and one or more of the natural sciences on the other. Sometimes correlation occurs fact to fact, sometimes principle to principle, sometimes viewpoint to viewpoint. Obviously correlation cannot occur without at least elementary planning. It is the first organizational step beyond the use of subjects in their "pure" form.

Organizing in Broad Fields

Becoming a bit bolder, the planners have developed the broad fields or fusion approach. This organizational plan permits surveys of subject matter within a category like the social studies or general science. Some of the subject matter in the surveys can be developed inductively by learners, who may be said to be preparing themselves in the survey process for later specialization in depth. Sometimes fusion occurs around general principles, as in courses in the problems of American democracy. The principles themselves may appear in hierarchies so that they are called on one occasion themes and on another topics. The broad fields idea actually dissolves subject boundaries by finding sensible arrangements among parts of subjects. Furthermore, it offers greater flexibility in choice of content than does subject-centered organization.

Organizing Core Programs

The plan of organization known as the core was moderately popular during the forties and fifties. Core programs were developed to allow pupils to have a core of experience with one teacher during a period of time that was longer than had been customary. This unified core of experience could be centered in subject matter on the one hand or in pupil needs and interests on the other. Four kinds of core programs came into prominence: (1) the unified studies core, closely analogous to simple correlation; (2) the culture epoch core, an attempt to study a lengthy period in human history by introducing all content that could help with understanding the period; (3) the contemporary problems core, in which subject lines were crossed to permit the study of problems in popular elections, crime prevention, modern art, and so on; and (4) the adolescent needs core, which dealt with the presumed common problems, interests, and needs of American youth, including planning one's career, establishing appropriate boy-girl relationships, and determining one's beliefs. As the last type suggests, core programs were directed primarily toward educating the adolescent population. To do this, teachers had to assume unaccustomed viewpoints concerning subject matter, pupils, and learning. One of the serious problems in core teaching and administration lay in the scarcity of teachers specifically prepared to teach in core programs. Specialized preparation of teachers is so important that without it core programs are almost certainly doomed to failure.

During the years in which the core was moderately popular, such a plethora of almost unclassifiable core programs developed that the meaning of the term core became obscured. Nevertheless two advantages of organizing core programs appeared: (1) James B. Conant and others began to advocate a somewhat similar block-of-time idea for loosening and improving the secondary school schedule, and (2) the needs, concerns, and interests of young people sometimes replaced rigidly traditional subject matter as the prominent feature of curriculum plans. In the eighties one still hears occasionally of the existence of a thriving core program.

Organizing around Persistent Life Situations

A fifth plan had its base in *persistent life situations*.[36] Initially, Florence B. Stratemeyer and other creators of the plan tried to define the characteristics of individuals and society, leading to a listing of "persistent life situations which learners face." Next, they listed these situations in detail. For example, one of the persistent life situations is need for growth in ability to deal with economic, social, and political structures and forces. Under the subhead "earning a living," there are additional subheads: "deciding what work to do" and "assuring that needed work will be done." Under "deciding what work to do" are four categories of activity listed according to developmental levels: early childhood—"assuming responsibility for simple tasks at home or at school"; later childhood—"deciding on work responsibilities with or without remuneration"; youth—"studying vocational possibilities and making vocational choice"; adulthood—"selecting and/or carrying forward chosen vocation."[37] Sample activities appear under each subhead, and there are nearly two dozen pages of subheads and activities related to persistent life situations involving growth in ability to deal with economic, social, and political structures and forces. The persistent life situations idea was a valiant effort to move attention from subject matter to the life needs of people.

Organizing around the Pupil's Experiences

Life needs are represented further in the final plan to be reported here— the *experience-centered* curriculum in which the pupil's own experience becomes the starting point for planning. In a geographically remote community, pupils may experience helping other people start a community store. As they work with others in this enterprise, they learn something of reading, writing, arithmetic, designing, group planning, human relationships, and many other "subjects." They learn the subject matter incidentally while having an exciting experience in which the learning materials are multiple and teachers' roles are decidedly nontraditional. In modern schooling few opportunities occur for experience-centered programs to flourish. Alternative schools and schools-within-schools, when organized and operated informally, present one opportunity. An additional, limited one is work experience programs in which subject matter is taught for the instrumental purpose of aiding pupils in work sponsored jointly by the school and a local business or industry. The most radical form of curriculum organization in regular use, this form has support from experimental philosophy, interactional sociology, and gestalt psychology. It promises to be used increasingly in the future. Suggestions concerning its probable future use appear prominently in the rapidly developing career education and action learning projects that school systems are undertaking.

Changing the Placement of Subject Matter and Adding New Subject Matter

Because schools are continuing institutions, the subject matter they teach needs periodic reorganization or change in placement. Perhaps the easiest way to change the placement of subject matter is to move it up or down grade scales and other educational levels. Items of subject content and major blocks of experience have been moved from one part of the school program to another. New subject matter has often been added. On rare occasions subjects and subject matter have been eliminated. The following are some well-known actions that have been taken to change subject matter placement and to add subjects:

1. Subject matter formerly taught in colleges is being taught in secondary schools.
2. Multicultural education has been added to the curriculum.
3. The kindergarten has now assumed certain of the earlier functions of the first grade.
4. Driver education has long since entered high school programs.
5. Career education has become common in the curriculum of both the elementary and the secondary school.

Curriculum reorganization proceeds on the assumption that rearranging and altering pupils' experiences can improve the quality of learning. Placing subject matter content in different sequence, substituting new experiences for old (or old for new), and combining subjects to achieve greater psychological unity can sometimes facilitate learning. Much more evidence is needed, however, concerning the results of many changes in curriculum organization. So far, the results have appeared discouraging.

The organization of the curriculum has both vertical and horizontal dimensions. Vertically, children progress from level to level on the ladder of learning experiences. Thus they move from third- to fourth- to fifth-grade arithmetic in vertical sequence and with some assurance that a thread of continuity runs through their three years of arithmetic experience. Viewed horizontally, the curriculum has breadth or scope. That is, ideally it provides sufficiently varied experiences to comprehend the child's life needs at present and, to a degree, in the future. Because all of one's life needs cannot be prepared for in a single year of schooling, specific needs must be attended to year by year according to the child's current intellectual, physical, and social development. The horizontal dimension assumes an integration of educational experiences. Integration, which must actually be achieved by the child, consists of relating experiences to one another in such a way as to create wholeness out of the collection of little pieces that constitute the usual experiences in schools. Though children must achieve integration for themselves, curriculum workers believe they can aid them by placing similar and related areas of subject matter together, as in the social studies or the language arts.

In many school systems, adding subjects and courses has resulted in a crazy quilt of offerings. Teachers themselves often find it easy to organize each new course *logically*, but there may not be much reference to the needs of learners or the structure of subject matter. Later they let relevance of course content to real-life situations diminish further as the course becomes crystallized and institutionalized. However, the curriculum has benefited from the addition of subjects and courses. Subtraction, which is often much needed, has occurred much less frequently and with great trepidation. Now the additive method of curriculum development has outworn much of its usefulness, considering the difficulty the curriculum planner has in selecting appropriate content from large bodies of knowledge.

The modern elementary school has discarded ten- and fifteen-minute periods for the teaching of twelve to fifteen separate subjects each school day. Instead, the school tends toward the scheduling of longer periods in the language arts, the social studies, the general arts (music, drawing, handicraft), arithmetic and science, and health and physical education. Similarly, the program of studies of a smaller number of up-to-date secondary schools contains broad-field offerings like general mathematics, the dramatic arts, family living, general language, and problems of democracy. The movement toward the broad-field approach often seems incidental or accidental. As a consequence some offerings have proved to be as far removed from reality for pupils as the original, fragmented subjects. Nevertheless, when they are carefully designed, offerings in the broad fields of knowledge can take the deadliness from logically organized subject matter by substituting an interesting, meaningful organization of material.

Experimentation that respects but is not limited by the differences and distinctions between subjects or disciplines has led to the creation of more varied, and often more intelligent, ways of reorganizing subject matter for sensible use. These ways tend to follow themes that are chosen because they are specially valued. Throughout the history of curriculum development in the United States, a number of themes have been tried as organizing centers for the curriculum, among them the following: the activities in which pupils may be expected to engage as adults, experiences in being a good citizen and in serving humankind, the interests and evident needs of children and youth, ways of solving problems, orientation to careers, education for work, situations in daily living that persist throughout life, and education for aesthetic appreciation. Few themes are sufficiently comprehensive to form a core of respectable learnings of both length and breadth, but they do make the traditional subjects the servants rather than the masters of the curriculum. Some themes, especially those based primarily in the humanities, become important steps on the way to formulating school programs that are both broadly and deeply educative. The struggle to reorganize the placement of subject matter will last beyond the creation of apparently satisfactory, widely accepted organizing centers, because subject matter making a marked difference in the quality of human life will continue to be discovered and will need to be put in strategic places within any schema adopted.

SPECIAL PROBLEMS IN ORGANIZING AND PRESENTING SUBJECT MATTER

Though common and pervasive problems in organizing and presenting sub- ject matter are many, some special ones demand attention. They are the deeper problems of curriculum planning and include the sequence of the curriculum, its continuity, its scope, and its balance. In general, *sequence* is the time order in which educational experiences are presented, *continuity* describes the continuousness with which the same kind of experiences are offered over a period of time, *scope* is the latitude or breadth of the cur- riculum, and *balance* defines the fit of the curriculum in providing varied but appropriate amounts of experience for learners at given times in their development.

Sequence

Sequence deals with the question "What is to follow what other learning content among prescribed, established learning experiences?" The problem of finding appropriate sequence is encountered in subject matter in which certain ideas and developments necessarily build upon others. This is the case, for instance, in mathematics and the foreign languages. It has seemed in the past to be much less the case in the social studies, a field in which an active search for sequence has been occurring. The generally accepted view of sequence is that it should depend directly on the nature and struc- ture of particular subjects and subject fields. If, instead of thinking im- mediately of subject matter, the curriculum planner were to think of developmental tasks for learners — tasks to assist their *becoming* — sequence would be determined by the competence of learners in performing tasks at various stages of their development. In this way of proceeding, sequence is associated with learners rather than with subject matter. Developmental stages might be reinterpreted as being limited to stages of mental growth or to the changing status of interests.

Traditional Attempts to Establish Sequence

Certain traditional ways of allegedly establishing sequence have been used in U.S. elementary and secondary schools. They include the following:

- Movement from the simple to the complex
- Study based on prerequisite learning
- Movement from part to whole
- Movement from whole to part
- Chronological ordering of events
- Movement from the present into the past
- Concentric movement in ever-widening circles of understanding or involvement
- Movement from concrete experiences to concepts.

One or more of these ways may seem ideal to a teacher or to a specialist in a subject, but an entirely different way may appeal to an individual pupil or a group of pupils. Actually, different sequence modes suit different pupils. For example, some children need to use manipulative materials in arithmetic for extended periods of time before they work with numerals; other children proceed almost directly to working with numerals. Spelling presents a particular problem. There are simply no ordered ways of learning to spell that can be used with all pupils or even a majority of pupils.

Sequence in the curriculum cannot be achieved by ordering topics. Why, for example, should study of the American Indian precede study of Greek civilization? Endless argument has occurred in curriculum committees because some of the members have had unfounded preferences for particular topical arrangements. There are so many available topics and possible orders of topics that only a more comprehensive basis for making choices will do.

Sequence Governed by Concept Development

The most comprehensive basis for making choices about the ordering of learning content is the concept. Once a concept has been recognized by curriculum planners as constituting a worthy educational focus, the planners may freely search for topical and other content that "feeds" the concept. Suppose we use the concept of change as a focus. Any topical or other content that helps pupils develop the concept of change is eligible for use; that is, we may provide pupils with alternative content relative to changes in people, weather, color, living conditions, economic circumstances, musical effects, preferences for clothing, and so on, and then help them make sequences to suit their abilities and their preferences. Concept development can proceed best if content is ordered so as to make the optimal contribution to it. Satisfactory sequence is often psychological rather than logical.

Continuity

Continuity inevitably relates to sequence. An established order of events in learning raises questions about how long certain events should be allowed to continue. Thus, continuity is a vertical matter affecting the continuousness with which certain experiences shall be scheduled during consecutive periods of time. In a sense, it is also a horizontal matter; it affects the continuousness of a particular kind of experience on a given school day. An example of vertical continuity is the teaching of a modern foreign language for four consecutive years. An example of horizontal continuity is teaching about the geography and history of the Oregon Trail during a two-and-a-half-hour block of time on Tuesday, January 14. Continuity also involves large questions of articulation among levels of the school system, as among elementary schools, junior high schools, and senior high schools. Articulation of school experiences among levels of schooling is so difficult that no school system has devised an ideal set of procedures for achieving it.

Like sequence, continuity is seen in unpatterned ways by children and adolescents.[38] It is patently impossible, considering what we know about individual differences, to plot a uniform plan of continuity for all children. Although the experiences of all may be continuous in time, the differences among these experiences need to be wide. In a given school system, planning for continuity may be three-way: for continuity in subjects and subject fields, for continuity between and among levels of schooling, and for continuity in experience for individual pupils. The first of these ways may be shared by planners in national curriculum projects and authors of educational materials. The second and third are clearly the onerous responsibility of individual school systems.

Possible Routes to Continuity

Alice Miel has suggested that children need to experience continuity in three respects: in developing strategic concepts, in developing ways of processing information, and in developing ways of feeling about and relating to people.[39] Development of strategic concepts was discussed briefly above. Processing information results in the development of thought processes related to three levels of tasks (an effect Hilda Taba sought to achieve when she developed her cognitive strategies). They are grouping and labeling, interpreting and making inferences, and predicting consequences. Developing ways of feeling about and relating to people involves maintaining good feelings toward oneself and other people and learning skills for improving one's interaction with other people. Schools should attempt, then, to make concept development, information processing, and learning in the area of interpersonal relationships continuous thrusts throughout children's school years.

Scope

The scope of the curriculum can be seen in the weekly program of an elementary school. The breadth of elementary school programs is usually great. Several school subjects and one or two school activities are sandwiched into the week's work so that the total program accommodates experiences in the language arts, arithmetic, the social studies, science, health, physical education, art, music, planning for and rehearsing an assembly program, and a variety of homeroom activities. The scope is so broad that many elementary school teachers, uncertain as to how to accomplish all that is expected of them, develop a kind of curriculum schizophrenia. However, the problem of scope does not end with listing subjects and activities. Each subject and activity may grow entirely out of bounds. For example, the language arts as a subject field was once heavy in reading and writing alone. Then speaking as a specific art and skill assumed increased prominence. Now listening, and to some extent the history and structure of language, has been added to the language arts area. Spelling and penmanship once took much time without being related very consciously to written composition. Now, in the face of multiple tasks to be performed within the language arts, they may be suffering from underemphasis. Problems of too-broad scope indicate again that the world of education is not afflicted with a scarcity of knowledge; rather, it needs perspective in order to fit a profusion of knowledge into limited periods of time at varied stages in the development of learners.

The scope of the curriculum can perhaps be kept within bounds most readily by cultivating allegiance to carefully selected objectives and to these objectives only. Among the prized general objectives in U.S. elementary and secondary schools are the achievement of skill in communication, skill for continuing learning, understanding of people and their world, physical and mental health, desirable citizenship behaviors, and aesthetic, moral, and ethical values. If the scope of the curriculum is to stay within bounds, the specific objectives within these general categories must be kept from becoming too numerous and diffuse.

Balance

If a learner were to enjoy a balanced curriculum at a given time, this curriculum would completely fit the learner in terms of his or her particular educational needs at that time. It would contain just enough of each kind of subject matter to serve the individual's purposes and speed his or her development. General balance in the curriculum can be partly achieved, in the sense that certain kinds of experiences can be planned for large groups of learners according to what we know about them and about the subject matter they might learn. Within the whole group, the individual learner receives an input of experiences that are of two sorts: those presumably suitable for and common to large numbers of learners and those that are tailor-made to his or her own needs and interests. However, true balance among experiences is very difficult to attain. For one thing, what constitutes somewhat acceptable balance today is imbalance tomorrow. Also, tailor-made experiences are difficult to plan in schools that have traditionally planned only for masses of pupils. Perhaps the best that can be done in working *toward* balance is to be clearer about what is valued for the growth of individual learners and then to apply these values in selecting curriculum content, grouping pupils for instruction, providing for articulation, and furthering guidance programs.[40]

The school can do much to provide a generally balanced program by seeing that all major areas of human competence are included in its curriculum. These major areas, which are comparable to those mentioned above in connection with continuity, may include skills in communication, opportunities for problem solving, understanding people and their world, knowledge of the activities of citizens, ability to care for one's mental and physical health, interest and skill in aesthetics, and recognition of specialized interests. Within each area, the individual should be permitted to perform to the maximum of his or her capacity. If the individual is to fulfill his or her obligation or to do penance to an area, he or she must be kept "in captivity" for a fixed period of time. A school program that is truly balanced for individuals can be created only with a system of flexible scheduling and within a curriculum that contains varied experiences among which the pupil is reasonably free to select. Working toward balance may involve taking actions like the following: attending to educational goals in proportion to their importance, knowing individual pupils better than we now know them, providing improved facilities and materials for teaching and learning, preventing pressures and special interests from destroying balance, and organizing pupil time around activities of appropriate kinds.

Conditions for Seeking Balance

If a school or a school system were to seek curriculum balance for individual pupils energetically, it would need to assemble a staff of professionals and paraprofessionals of varying competencies to work in a large, well-equipped learning center. The staff would work with persons inside and outside the school or school system to determine appropriate goals of schooling and out-of-school education. According to the goals that were formulated, ideas, time arrangements, facilities, and materials would be made available, the nature and needs of individual pupils would be assessed, studies made by futurists would be consulted to provide a forward look to individualized programs, the status and progress of each pupil would be carefully charted, and, after continuing reevaluation, summary data would be assembled at intervals for each pupil. This is obviously an expensive way of proceeding — according to a "hospital model" rather than a "factory model" of schooling. It seems, however, to be the only route by which curriculum balance for the individual learner can be approached.[41] Some practitioners of Individually Guided Education (IGE) have sought to approach individualization in this way, but the limited budgets within which they have operated would not permit them to proceed to the ultimate step of developing balanced programs for individual learners.

Problems of sequence, continuity, scope, and balance obviously remain largely unsolved. During the years to come, these four problems must be given more attention by curriculum planners if the much desired goal of carefully individualizing instruction is to be attained.

ACTIVITY 4-5
Becoming Acquainted with Curriculum Literature Relating
to Special Problems in Organizing and Presenting
Subject Matter

Curriculum literature abounds on the role of subject matter in curriculum planning. For example, general works on the curriculum by Hilda Taba, Virgil Herrick, and Smith, Stanley, and Shores contain information of a comprehensive sort. Some of the yearbooks of the Association for Supervision and Curriculum Development and the National Society for the Study of Education deal with more specific problems in utilizing subject matter, such as problems of continuity and balance.

Become acquainted with these and other sources. Take notes from the sources you consider most helpful.

SITUATION 4-2
Responding to the State's Criticisms of the
Yalta Pass Curriculum

For three years, the public schools at Yalta Pass had been under fire from the state department of education for providing too few learning opportunities for their pupils, considering the total amount of money being spent on the schools. Specifically, the complaint had detailed the following deficiencies:

1. Insufficient attention to the teaching of the three Rs in the elementary schools
2. Too few elective courses in Yalta Pass's small high school
3. The obsolescence of some of the subject matter currently being taught at the secondary school level
4. "Excessively compartmentalized organization of subject matter in both the elementary and the secondary schools" (each subject taught in distinct separation from every other subject)
5. The presence of too much unchallenging subject matter in the required curriculum of both the elementary and the secondary schools.

Realizing that a formal evaluation by the state department of education was to occur within two years, the superintendent of the Yalta Pass schools formed the Special Committee on Subject Matter, consisting of eighteen teachers and administrators. The committee was asked to suggest ways of meeting the state's criticisms, "ways that are likely to succeed and that can be put into effect immediately."

Yalta Pass had never been noted for its activity in curriculum planning. Lacking experience, therefore, the committee quickly developed one proposal to meet each of the state's criticisms, as follows:

1. Provide "coaching classes" to drill pupils in the three Rs. These classes, assigned to especially competent teachers, would meet partly on school time and partly after school.
2. Add elective courses to the high school curriculum in accordance with the findings in a survey of parents' opinions of the need for particular electives.
3. Form study groups of teachers (who know most about given subjects) to update the content of these subjects as they are taught in the schools.
4. Try team teaching across subject lines as a way of making the subjects interrelate.
5. Ask the administrators to urge teachers to add more difficult subject matter to what they are teaching now.

What actions can you suggest to meet the five criticisms more adequately?

THE STATUS OF SUBJECT MATTER SELECTION AND PRESENTATION

Newer developments in selecting and presenting subject matter may be discussed under three main headings: subject matter selection at local and state levels, new versions of subject matter, and special resources for presenting subject matter.

Subject Matter Selection at Local and State Levels

Subject matter selection by local school districts and by state departments of education is not an innovation. As Chapter 1 indicates, the first active curriculum planning was accomplished in city school districts. Later, state departments of education began to develop course guides that were distributed among the school districts of the states within which they were prepared.

Beginning in 1957, subject matter specialists initiated the planning of national instructional projects. Most of the projects that thrived owed their support to foundations and the federal government. A majority of them were intended to affect secondary education. Not unexpectedly, persons who planned them gave little thought to the processes that influence teachers to try new ideas. This fact helps to explain the early demise of nearly all the projects.

Some of the projects, which received their start in either elementary or secondary education, later became kindergarten-through-twelfth-grade projects or projects covering a major portion of this span. At first the projects were chiefly in the natural sciences and mathematics. Subsequently the modern foreign languages, the social studies, and the English language arts were emphasized. The National Education Association formed its Project on Instruction to sort out subject matter in selected fields and to encourage wise use of it in the schools. Some of the project sponsors and titles are still familiar: University of Illinois Elementary Science Project, Syracuse-Webster Elementary Mathematics Project, Physical Science Study Committee, Biological Sciences Curriculum Study, School Mathematics Study Group, Commission on English of the College Entrance Examination Board, and High School Geography Project.

In 1967, John I. Goodlad summarized the effects of subject-centered instructional projects to that time:

1. *Purposes:* to make order out of ranges of subject matter, to teach children how to learn
2. *Assets:* a more correct, realistic view of subject matter, greater interest in studying how children learn, and additional instructional material
3. *Liabilities:* too much concentration in the individual disciplines, imbalance in the attention given the disciplines (the humanities, for instance, being neglected), increased need to appraise curricula before they are adopted, lag in educating teachers in new curricular developments, and absence of aim in the process of development.[42]

The sciences and mathematics received more attention than other subjects or disciplines during the heyday of the projects. In 1980, when nine groups of teachers, administrators, parents, school board members, and "neutrals" were asked to comment on the curriculum reforms wrought by the National Science Foundation, they agreed that teachers had listened to the NSF proposal and then had done what they wanted to do. Teachers in the nine groups said that they were usually unaware of what was happening in other teachers' classrooms; rather, they were concerned with their own "survival" and with attaining goals that had been established in their school systems.[43]

Robert James has expressed the view that if projects and programs are to succeed, their promoters must consider the stages of teachers' concern, ranging from general awareness to specific awareness to varied thoughts about issues like the teachers' own involvement and the quality of the teachers' work with pupils and colleagues during project life. James has emphasized, too, the significance of levels of use of project ideas by teachers. Use seems to range from negligible to mechanical and routine to integration with the work of colleagues. Ignoring stages of teacher concern and levels of teacher use can result in disaster for any project or program.[44]

During the seventies, school systems and entire states varied widely in the rates at which they adopted subject-centered innovations. Many school systems abandoned their earlier commitments to projects. Through their associations and unions, classroom teachers were expressing resentment at having been pushed aside in the process of deciding what subject matter should be taught. Administrators complained that the energies of school personnel were being drawn from tasks of permanent significance so that instructional projects of uncertain worth could be staffed. The stampede for dollars that caused people to write proposals continued for a time, but other interests (such as better schooling for handicapped pupils) replaced interest in teaching "right" subject matter in "right" ways.

Studied, comprehensive effort at updating subject matter has declined during the eighties, an unfortunate circumstance in an era in which much new knowledge abounds and in which the schools could profit from capitalizing on mistakes made in connection with earlier programs and projects. The obligation to select subject matter has returned largely to local school districts and state departments of education, with occasional help from professional associations. Individual school districts, working largely alone, are plotting learning content in subject matter areas where pressures lie. Sometimes they are able to do this with financial help from federal or state governments. Too often, limited budgets prevent them from employing the help of people who know the subject fields or the planning processes under consideration, or from releasing teachers to plan together on school time.

State departments of education experience the same waves of pressure that affect the personnel of local school districts. Pressures like those to teach the three Rs better and to "do something" about the use of drugs by pupils and about the increase in pregnancies among young girls take the attention of state officials. The results are a flood of pronouncements and a few hurriedly prepared documents. Careful, deliberate planning of subject matter offerings, incorporated within updated state guides, is being neglected so that state officials may meet emergencies that are often in the areas of attitude, morality, and social relationships, elements of the curriculum for which the schools are only partly responsible.

New Versions of Subject Matter

A heritage of the instructional projects has been increased realization that the individual pupil counts. The materials developed in connection with the projects emphasized the importance of expecting teachers to monitor the progress of individual pupils. Realization has grown that learners' self-concepts need to be improved so that children are freed to learn; that curiosity and inquiry skills are well worth cultivating; that the school's responsibility includes the teaching of functional skills in valuing, thinking critically, appreciating aesthetic products, and using leisure time wisely; and that the school itself needs to be made more humane. Ways of reaching and teaching the deprived and the gifted, ways of using pupil time for more productive learning, and ways of utilizing findings about learning with reference to age, readiness, and the timing of experiences have attracted renewed interest. Drives to identify behavioral objectives to guide the selection of subject matter and the packaging of ideas and materials have constituted two simultaneous attempts to clarify what should be taught.[45] As a public school teacher said recently, "We know so much more than we have time to do."

New Selections of Subject Matter for Secondary Schools

Minicourses have been planned in secondary schools in an attempt to fill gaps in subject matter. Piecemeal efforts will not satisfy the need for curriculum reform, however. Gordon Cawelti has proposed five study areas that need further development in secondary schools: learning skills; health, physical education, and leisure; career education; cultural studies; and societal studies. He found in an investigation of secondary school practices that, although secondary schools are still subject centered, several means of opening the curriculum have been devised. These include action learning, which is learning in the community or the field, competency testing for early admission to colleges and other educational institutions, alternative schools, and community educational centers.[46] Action learning of a community service sort challenges many an adolescent to perform services like painting the living quarters of the aged and the handicapped or doing grocery shopping for people who are unable to do their own. Combined and strengthened to become comprehensive educational programs, community action experiences can provide both cognitive and affective learnings. In his statement of what constitutes a balanced and significant program of secondary education, William Van Til lists sixteen centers of experience: war, peace, and international relations; overpopulation, pollution, and energy; economic options and problems; governmental processes; consumer problems; intercultural relations; world views; recreation and leisure; the arts and aesthetics; self-understanding and personal development; family, peer group, and school; health; community living; vocations; communication; and alternative futures.[47]

Specific changes in the subject matter of secondary schools are illustrated below:

1. Addition of formal instruction in the basics, largely a result of the publicity concerning the number of pupils who enter secondary schools, and later college and work, ill prepared in subject matter fundamentals.
2. Reassessment of efforts at economic education, at a time when economic problems seem to dominate the news.[48]
3. Increased attention to global education, ranked by adults sampled in a Gallup Poll as second only to the basics.[49]
4. New attention to art and skill in writing and to interpretation of written materials.

Changes in Elementary School Programs

While secondary schools and middle schools were experiencing gradual changes in subject matter taught, the elementary schools turned first to making organizational changes that would presumably aid the teaching of subject matter. These changes included introduction of nongrading or ungrading, various patterns of departmentalization, differing versions of openness in the school environment, and funded projects that were meant to reorganize the teaching of reading, arithmetic, science, the social studies, and the arts. Affective education is now receiving some attention, and education of the handicapped, special education in general, and education of minority groups have become major interests in a number of schools.

In addition, fundamental arithmetic is being taught more rigorously, even as it replaces much of the "new mathematics" of an earlier decade. Changes in arithmetic programs represent attempts to improve the quality of basic education generally. Almost inevitably, however, an increased emphasis on basic subject matter like fundamental arithmetic will diminish the amount of attention that can be given to other elements of the curriculum.

Special Resources for Presenting Subject Matter

One of the really serious problems in presenting subject matter has been lack of, or inconvenient placement of, materials and facilities of instruction. Prominent resources for solving problems encountered in presenting subject matter are the media center, the resource room, and minicomputers.

The Media Center

The media center is sometimes called the instructional materials center (IMC) or the learning center. It is intended to maximize opportunities for learning, serving as a kind of control center for the facilities and services that can be found in the school building. Active, helpful media centers are conveniently located within school buildings and are adequately staffed. They become work centers for teachers and pupils and thus implement teaching strategies. They are storage sites for all sorts of instructional materials, print and nonprint, housing audiovisual equipment, the latest in teaching and copying machines, computer outlets, books, monographs, pamphlets, magazines, and everything else that stimulates and satisfies learning. Media centers in the newer school buildings are large enough to accommodate meetings, work space, individual study, and whatever other activities and arrangements are necessary.

The Resource Room

The resource room is separate from classrooms and the media center, but it is related to both. The interior of the resource room is arranged to be functional and to include materials of interest especially to nonacademic pupils. The room houses basic audiovisual materials, the wherewithal for gaming and simulation, and materials for art and handicrafts. Often, resource rooms contain learning centers in mathematics, reading and the language arts, social studies, science, and life skills. Experiences that cannot be had in the usual classroom for lack of time, space, and facilities are available here. Frequently the establishment of resource rooms depends on the funding of programs for the retarded and other pupils in special need of attention.

Minicomputers

Computers of small size, known as minicomputers, have come into use in elementary and secondary schools. Great expectations have developed for these machines, labeled hardware, and supplementary computer materials, called software.

As purchase of computers and software proceeds apace, use of these relatively new additions is occurring in three main ways. First, in the well-known CAI, or computer-assisted instruction, the computer serves as a tutor, employing software prepared by specialists and alleged specialists in the subject fields. When the computer presents subject matter, the pupil responds. The computer then evaluates the response, reports to the pupil how well he or she has done, makes the next presentation, and finally records how well the pupil has succeeded overall. Most school people are familiar with this use of the computer.

Second, the computer is a tool for calculating, word processing, retrieving information, and maintaining records. When properly programmed, the computer can simulate real-life problems for resolution by pupils. Examples are pressing problems in ecology and potential strategies in sports.

Third, the pupils program or "teach" the computer. Whereas in the first two uses the pupils respond rather than taking initiative, here pupils dominate the computer. Even young elementary school pupils can make simple programs. Critics of the computer as a tool have condemned this third use as involving pupils in learning more than they need to know and do.

Elementary and intermediate schools have been using computers for basic skills instruction, remediation, and enrichment of learning. Secondary schools have tended to use them chiefly in computer science courses. When pupils have learned to use computers in these courses, they are able to extend their application to other subjects and circumstances.

Large-scale purchases of computers have caused taxpayers to question their ultimate effectiveness in teaching and learning. Although the potential uses of computers in schools are great, the uses to which they have been put have proved so limited that Terrel Bell, Secretary of Education, referred to them in 1984 as "electronic page turners."[50]

SUMMARY

Although schools have never existed without teaching subject matter, the importance of the disciplines, and of ordered ways of dealing with them, has loomed larger in U.S. education within the past few years. One of the reasons for this emphasis has been the growing realization that knowledge is increasing at a tremendous rate. For a time, subject specialists became curriculum planners by demonstrating new placement of subject matter, some of it freshly discovered or developed, in elementary and secondary school programs. Also, some psychologists and educators began investigating the structure of knowledge in varied subject fields; others tried to help pupils in the process of inquiry and in ways of discovering knowledge for themselves. Because of all this activity, the disciplines assumed an unaccustomed role in decision making about the curriculum. The era during which the *nature* of subject matter was by far the leading determinant of the curriculum passed during the seventies. Subject matter within a context of pupil need has now become of increasing interest to alert curriculum planners.

ENDNOTES

1. Arthur W. Combs, *Myths in Education* (Boston: Allyn and Bacon, 1979), pp. 77–83.

2. Harry S. Broudy, "What Knowledge Is of Most Worth?" *Educational Leadership* 39, no. 8 (May 1982): 574–78.

3. Jerome S. Bruner, *The Process of Education* (Cambridge, Mass.: Harvard University Press, 1961), pp. vii, viii. Copyright © 1961 Harvard University Press.

4. *Insight*, a publication of Science Research Associates, Chicago (Spring 1962).

5. John Chamberlain, "Reading at Age Three," *Wall Street Journal*, May 12, 1961. Comments about this experiment by specialists in mental health were subsequently directed toward an increase in nervousness on the part of the participating children.

6. Benjamin S. Bloom, ed., *Taxonomy of Educational Objectives: Cognitive Domain* (New York: David McKay, 1956).

7. David R. Krathwohl, Benjamin S. Bloom, and Bert Masia, *Taxonomy of Educational Objectives: Affective Domain* (New York: David McKay, 1964).

8. See, for example, Anita J. Harrow, *Taxonomy of the Psychomotor Domain: A Guide for Developing Behavioral Objectives* (New York: David McKay, 1972).

9. See Hilda Taba, *Curriculum Development: Theory and Practice* (New York: Harcourt, Brace and World, 1962), pp. 174–81, 211–15.

10. W. James Popham et al., *Instructional Objectives* (Chicago: Rand McNally, 1969), pp. 34, 37.

11. William Habermehl, "Competency-Based Education — Will It Rob Peter to Pay Paul?" *Bulletin of the National Association of Secondary School Principals* 64, no. 439 (November 1980): 54–57.

12. Gerald D. Bailey and Robert K. James, "Competency-Based Education: Its Elements and Potential," *School Science and Mathematics* 81 (November 1981): 563–71.

13. For a critical article, see Arthur Wise, "Why Minimum Competency Testing Will Not Improve Education," *Educational Leadership* 36, no. 8 (May 1979): 546–49.

14. Note that *competency-based education* was the term first applied to the accountability movement in teacher education.

15. Mercy Hardic Coogan, "A Double Dose of Basic Skills . . . for Appalachian Alabama," *Appalachia* 14, no. 2 (November-December 1980): 24–32.

16. Abdun Noor, *Education and Basic Human Needs*, Staff Working Paper No. 450 (Washington, D.C.: The World Bank, 1981).

17. Association for Supervision and Curriculum Development, "Network Schools Define What Students Need to Know," *Curriculum Update* (October 1983): 1–8.

18. National Association of Secondary School Principals, "Public Policy,

Social Implications, Ethical Issues . . . New Emphases in Biology," *Curriculum Report* 10, no. 3 (February 1981): 1, 2.

19. Arthur Combs, "Affective Education or None at All," *Educational Leadership* 39, no. 7 (April 1982): 495–97.

20. Jane Zeni Flinn, "Curriculum Change Through Staff Development," *Educational Leadership* 40, no. 1 (October 1982): 51, 52.

21. Ronald C. Doll, *Supervision for Staff Development: Ideas and Application* (Newton, Mass.: Allyn and Bacon, 1983), pp. 172–75.

22. Irving H. Buchen, "Curriculum 2000: Futures Basics," testimony prepared for the House of Representatives subcommittee inquiry into future needs in elementary, secondary, and vocational education, January 1980.

23. See National Association of Secondary School Principals, "Mathematics in the 1980s: Recommendations by the Mathematics Community," *Curriculum Report* 10, no. 4 (May 1981): 1–8; also National Association of Secondary School Principals, "Social Studies: A Look Ahead," *Curriculum Report* 10, no. 1 (October 1980): 1–12.

24. John Dewey, *Democracy and Education* (New York: Macmillan, 1916), p. 186.

25. John Dewey, *Experience and Education* (New York: Macmillan, 1938), p. 90.

26. B. Othanel Smith, William O. Stanley, and J. Harlan Shores, *Fundamentals of Curriculum Development* (New York: Harcourt, Brace and World, 1957), chapter 6.

27. This idea and many additional ones in this section have been developed by Jerome Bruner. See also David Ausubel's theory of concept development involving subsumptive ideas, as he treats it in *The Psychology of Meaningful Verbal Learning*, published by Grune Stratton in 1963, and in other writings.

28. See Jean Piaget, *The Origins of Intelligence in Children* (New York: International Universities Press, 1953). Dewey had said earlier that children develop hypothetical thinking as they mature.

29. John Dewey, *How We Think* (Boston: D. C. Heath, 1910), p. 72.

30. From Arthur W. Foshay, "A Modest Proposal for the Improvement of Education" (Address delivered at the 1961 Convention of the Association for Supervision and Curriculum Development, Chicago, March 1961). Used with permission. See Harold Morine and Greta Morine, *Discovery: A Challenge to Teachers* (Englewood Cliffs, N.J.: Prentice-Hall, 1973).

31. Philip H. Phenix, "The Use of the Disciplines as Curriculum Content," *Educational Forum* 26, no. 3 (March 1961): 273–80.

32. Jerome S. Bruner, *The Process of Education* (Cambridge, Mass.: Harvard University Press, 1961), p. 72.

33. Alice Miel, "Knowledge and the Curriculum," in Association for Supervision and Curriculum Development, *New Insights and the Curriculum*, 1963 Yearbook (Washington, D.C.: The Association, 1963), pp. 79–87.

34. Mauritz Johnson, "Who Discovered Discovery?" *Phi Delta Kappan* 48, no. 3 (November 1966): 120–23.

35. Joe M. Steele, Herbert J. Walberg, and Ernest R. House, "Subject Areas and Cognitive Press," *Journal of Educational Psychology* 66, no. 3 (June 1974): 363–66.

36. Florence B. Stratemeyer et al., *Developing a Curriculum for Modern Living*, 2nd ed. (New York: Bureau of Publications, Teachers College, 1957).

37. Ibid., pp. 296, 297.

38. See Association for Supervision and Curriculum Development, *A Look at Continuity in the School Program*, 1958 Yearbook (Washington, D.C.: The Association, 1958).

39. Alice Miel, "Sequence in Learning — Fact or Fiction," *Elementary Instructional Service*, Stock Number 282-08810 (Washington, D.C.: National Education Association, n.d.).

40. Association for Supervision and Curriculum Development, *Balance in the Curriculum*, 1961 Yearbook (Washington, D.C.: The Association, 1961).

41. Cheryl D. Walker and Ronald C. Doll, "Curriculum Balance for the Individual Learner: A Continuing Need," *Educational Leadership* 32, no. 3 (December 1974): 208–11.

42. John I. Goodlad, "Implications of Current Curricular Change," *Education Digest* 32, no. 7 (March 1967): 12–15.

43. "National Groups Tell Why Curriculum Didn't Work," *The Teacher Educator*, Ball State University 16, no. 3 (Winter 1980–1981): 34, 35.

44. Robert K. James, "Understanding Why Curriculum Innovations Succeed or Fail," *School Science and Mathematics* 81 (October 1981): 487–95.

45. Compare this with an earlier statement of the status of the curriculum: Paul J. Klohr, "The Greening of the Curriculum," *Educational Leadership* 28, no. 5 (February 1971): 455–57.

46. Gordon Cawelti, *Vitalizing the High School: A Curriculum Critique of Major Reform Proposals* (Washington, D.C.: Association for Supervision and Curriculum Development, 1974).

47. William Van Til, "What Should Be Taught and Learned through Secondary Education?" in William Van Til, ed., *Issues in Secondary Education*, Seventy-Fifth Yearbook, Part II, National Society for the Study of Education (Chicago: University of Chicago Press, 1976), p. 197.

48. See National Conference on Needed Research and Development in Precollege Economic Education, *Perspectives on Economic Education* (New York: Joint Council on Economic Education, 1976).

49. David C. King, "Global Education," *Curriculum Update* (October 1980): 1, 2.

50. *The Star-Ledger*, Newark, New Jersey, January 19, 1984, p. 8.

SELECTED BIBLIOGRAPHY

Bruner, Jerome S. *The Process of Education*. Cambridge, Mass.: Harvard University Press, 1961.

Doll, Ronald C. *Supervision for Staff Development: Ideas and Application*. Newton, Mass.: Allyn and Bacon, 1983.

Foshay, Arthur W., ed. *Curriculum for the Seventies: An Agenda for Invention*. A report of the Center for the Study of Instruction. Washington, D.C.: National Education Association, 1970.

Grobman, Hulda. *Developmental Curriculum Projects: Decision Points and Processes.* Itasca, Ill.: Peacock, 1972.

Halverson, Paul M., ed. *Balance in the Curriculum.* 1961 Yearbook. Washington, D.C.: Association for Supervision and Curriculum Development, 1961.

Hyman, Ronald T. *Approaches in Curriculum.* Englewood Cliffs, N.J.: Prentice-Hall, 1973.

Inlow, Gail. *The Emergent in the Curriculum.* 2nd ed. New York: John Wiley, 1973.

King, Arthur B., Jr., and Brownell, John A. *The Curriculum and the Disciplines of Knowledge.* New York: John Wiley, 1966.

Krug, Mark M. *What Will Be Taught — The Next Decade.* Itasca, Ill.: Peacock, 1972.

McClure, Robert M., ed. *The Curriculum: Retrospect and Prospect.* National Society for the Study of Education, Seventieth Yearbook, Part I. Chicago: University of Chicago Press, 1971.

Overly, Norman, ed. *The Unstudied Curriculum: Its Impact on Children.* Washington, D.C.: National Education Association, 1970.

Phenix, Philip H. *Realms of Meaning.* New York: McGraw-Hill, 1964.

Piaget, Jean. *The Origins of Intelligence in Children.* New York: International Universities Press, 1953.

Progressive Education Association. *The Story of the Eight Year Study.* New York: Harper, 1942.

School of Education, University of Wisconsin. *The Nature of Knowledge.* Milwaukee: Edward A. Uhrig Foundation, 1962.

Smith, B. Othanel; Stanley, William O.; and Shores, J. Harlan. *Fundamentals of Curriculum Development.* Rev. ed. New York: Harcourt, Brace and World, 1957.

Swenson, Esther J., ed. *A Look at Continuity in the School Program.* 1958 Yearbook. Washington, D.C.: Association for Supervision and Curriculum Development, 1958.

Taba, Hilda. *Curriculum Development: Theory and Practice.* New York: Harcourt, Brace and World, 1962.

Whitfield, Richard. *Disciplines of the Curriculum.* London: McGraw-Hill, 1971.

Wilhelms, Fred. *What Should the Schools Teach?* Phi Delta Kappa Fastback No. 13. Bloomington, Ind.: Phi Delta Kappa Educational Foundation, 1972.

5

Making Decisions about the Design of the Curriculum

We come now to the difficult decision making that eventuates in the actual design of the curriculum and its subparts. In the preceding chapters consideration has been given to distinct, separate foundations on which decisions about the curriculum can be based. The present chapter is meant to interrelate foundational data and to suggest curriculum designs that can ensue. Furthermore, the chapter is intended to clarify the designing process. One of the beliefs underlying Chapter 5 is that both product and process are important in curriculum planning and neither can be separated from the other.

The curriculum planners in an elementary school interrelated the foundations discussed in the preceding chapters in the following way:

> In our school, with an eye to the general background of the curriculum movement and the traditions of our own school, we are developing a common point of view or philosophy about what is to be emphasized in our education of our children. We know our children as members of groups and, insofar as we find it possible, as individuals. Because we know also something of the ways they learn, we are trying to adjust school life to them and their learning modes. In doing this, we are influenced by what the society, the culture, and the community seem to

want of us. As we learn to work within (and sometimes in spite of) these influences, we know that we are usually encouraged and aided by them. We try to select subject matter and provide experiences for our children according to valid principles so that they learn what's worth learning, in the most effective ways.[1]

With this kind of thinking as background, the school's Committee on Curriculum Planning was ready to design proposals for improving the total school program.

THE NATURE OF DESIGN AND DESIGNING

The history of U.S. education is filled with examples of designs that fulfill the criteria of a particular definition of the term *curriculum design*. One definition says that a curriculum design is a way of organizing that permits curriculum ideas to function. Diverse ways of organizing subject matter content are exemplified by the project method, Summerhill, the open access curriculum, persistent life situations, the process approach, and the activity school. From the titles of these designs, one discerns immediately how different they are.

Another definition says that a curriculum design is a carefully conceived curriculum plan that takes its shape from (1) what its creators believe about people and their education and (2) how its creators would like to see their beliefs expressed. A curriculum design takes into account a number of interrelated and interdependent elements: what its creators want done, what subject matter they wish to use to fulfill the design's purposes, what instructional strategies they favor using, and how they will determine the success or feasibility of the design. As designers become more sophisticated, they include other elements: diagnosis of need, organization as well as selection of subject matter, and organization as well as selection of learning experiences.

Curriculum workers are sometimes confused about the distinction between curriculum design and instructional design. Curriculum design is, in a sense, the parent of instructional design. It involves a higher level of generalizing based on principles and problem solving, and encompasses fundamental beliefs, major aims, and projected outcomes. Instructional design, on the other hand, treats beliefs and aims as givens, and does the best it can to establish technologically sound teaching procedures based on the beliefs and aims. Instructional designers try hard to test validly what they have done. In this and other ways, they appear to stay closer to psychology than do curriculum designers, who call upon more than psychology to guide their actions.

Inasmuch as the designing of instruction is assuming the earmarks of a fairly careful, accurate set of procedures, why spend time on curriculum designing, which has a less favorable record in these respects? When curriculum planners fail to design, they soon begin to improvise, and improvisation leads often to chaos. Also, when they fail to design, capricious and selfish interests may easily come to govern what is done. The planners' salvation lies in their knowledge of their purposes and in their incorporation into the decision making, against a backdrop of acceptable philosophy, of three major elements: learners and learning, the society and the culture, and available subject matter.

As planners begin their design making, they must consider what kind of product they wish to develop. In their study of eighteen nations, Klein and Goodlad found five kinds of curriculum models:

1. The ideal: a curriculum the schools *might* implement, if conditions were just right
2. The formal: a curriculum expressing intended learnings
3. The instructional: a curriculum mirroring what teachers think they are doing
4. The operational: a curriculum indicating what is really being done in the schools
5. The experiential: a curriculum demonstrating what pupils actually experience, or think they experience.[2]

Only the first two kinds qualify as sufficiently forward looking for potential use as curriculum designs. The remainder fall into the general category of curriculum notation and analysis, a procedure used in an increasing number of schools in Great Britain.[3]

SOURCES OF IDEAS THAT UNDERGIRD CURRICULUM DESIGNS

Fundamental to designing the curriculum are curriculum planners' views of the nature, nurture, and destiny of human beings. In the center of the nature-nurture-destiny trilogy is nurture, or education, which expresses what can be done with and for people. What can be done with them and for them is affected by their nature, and what can be done with them and for them in turn affects their destiny. Persons who want to improve the quality of education for themselves and other people must face an initial question: What are the sources of the ideas that will determine the kind of education to be provided? The answers to this question will imply much about the curriculum improvers' view of the nature of human beings. The answers will also suggest what the curriculum planners think about some of the phenomena in their world. Most of all, however, they will suggest points of view that curriculum planners can comfortably take toward the substance and process of education.

The Bible says, "As a man thinketh in his heart, so is he." One's personal philosophy molds and determines one's thinking about the issues in planning for anything of significance. In formulating a philosophy, the individual must consider what he or she will accept as truth. In deciding what is true, one has access to sources or bases of truth.

Accordingly, in making decisions within the realm of curriculum planning, school faculties try to agree on an educational philosophy or point of view. This philosophy needs to be examined through thought and discussion to see what basic beliefs about people and things the philosophy represents.

There are several classifications of basic beliefs that underlie curriculum philosophy. In a somewhat oversimplified and rigidly stated form, these and their origins are detailed below without emphasizing any one at the expense of the others.[4] Each has its merits, and each is usable to a major extent in given situations. In general, however, the faculties of most schools would need to draw eclectically upon the classifications of basic beliefs.

Science as a Source

According to persons who rely on science as a source of belief, the scientific method is the most reliable method for establishing truth. Students should be taught to solve problems in terms of scientific procedures, and curriculum improvement itself should be accomplished scientifically; that is, valid and reliable data should be assembled in support of any curriculum change that is made. Thus, heavy reliance is placed on rational procedures, especially as found in problem-solving procedures. Judgment and valuing are of limited usefulness in strict application of scientific methodology because the results so gained are neither measurable nor certain.

Science as a source of ideas for the curriculum and its improvement enjoys much prestige in an era and a society in which science is assigned so much credence and respect. For years, scientific methods have been used in determining the characteristics of learners, the nature of their growth and development, the extent of their learning, the worth of teaching materials, and, to a degree, the effectiveness of instructional methods. It would be possible to take the position that no curriculum change should be initiated until the validity and reliability of the change have been confirmed by research and evaluation. One of the deficiencies of this position is that much of the judging and valuing that curriculum workers prize would be eliminated by the scientific method. Also, some people do not accept the premise that educational data derived by scientific means constitute the whole truth.

Society as a Source

Society may be regarded as the ultimate source from which ideas about the curriculum are to be derived. According to this view, the school owes its being to the society that has fostered it, and the school should acquire ideas from the social situation it observes. However, there are various interpretations of what society is and ought to be.

Some persons say that society's views can be determined by gathering a consensus of what people think. This consensus is usually gathered in a local community and therefore does not show the thinking of people who are geographically remote from the local scene but still highly important in a highly mobile society. Nevertheless, it would be possible to base a curriculum strictly on a series of opinion polls.

Another variation consists of thinking of government as the agent of society. Under this conception, the curriculum would be changed only by legislative enactments and the decrees of the administrative and judicial branches of government. Many persons would say immediately that a society is more than its government and that curriculum making by governmental authority limits the whole process unnecessarily.

Still another variation assumes that society in its present state is to be studied not only by curriculum makers but also by pupils in schools. The object is to perpetuate the present society by involving the pupil in studying it. A curriculum stemming from this view would be devoted to extensive study of the society both in school and out, with details of the society itself forming the subject matter.

A final variation is known as the reconstructionist view. It holds that the school's role is to remake society. The curriculum would emphasize ideas for changing the social order, and curriculum improvement would be bent toward inventing ideas for that purpose. All of these variations make society the central source of ideas about the curriculum.

Eternal Verities from the Human Past as a Source

Eternal truth, in the view of Robert Hutchins and others, can be found in the works of great persons in the past. This view has been expressed in studies of the "Great Books" in adult education and in college curricula, but it has not completely found its way, as a significant emphasis, into our elementary and secondary schools. As held today by the humanists, the notion that lasting truth inheres in the writings of the past depends on human reason for an ordering of truths in primary, secondary, and consequent importance.

A curriculum derived from this source would depend, of course, on the literature of the past. Any changes in the curriculum would call for a reordering of ideas in the hierarchy of truths. Since these truths are considered eternal, they need not be found in new experiences; therefore, reordering them would not involve reflective or creative thinking about present and current phenomena but intuitive and deductive thinking for discovery of first principles, the status of which is allegedly fixed and invariable in any age. The alleged invariability of the first principles does not prevent arguments about them: principles that are put in first position by one authority may well be put in second position by another. Furthermore, the application of fixed principles suggests that the conditions to which they are applied are unchanging, whereas change is a known rule of life. Difficulties of these kinds have prevented eternal verities from the past from becoming accepted as a guide to elementary and secondary school curricula.[5]

Divine Will as a Source

The divine will position maintains that God has revealed His Will to human beings through the Bible and especially through inspiration of the Holy Spirit of God in the lives of Christian believers. It received support in colonial New England, but its influence was subsequently weakened by the emergence of antithetical viewpoints and the divergent interests of an increasingly less uniform population. A curriculum developed according to these ideas—even if the ideas were modified to accommodate religions other than Christianity—would rely heavily on religious, moral, and ethical teachings found in Holy Writ and church doctrine. Persons who use Divine Will as a curriculum source hold that God's Will encompasses study of secular content so that learners may be prepared to fulfill His Will in their future lives. For public school systems in the United States, this curriculum source is largely unavailable because of legal sanctions against its use. For parochial and certain other private schools, it is a most important curriculum source. The use of Divine Will as a source is likely to increase if numbers of private schools with a religious emphasis are established as a consequence of the growing secularization of the public schools.

Use of God's Will as an ideational source of the curriculum is not limited to private Christian schools. It appears in private schools sponsored by Jewish congregations and also in schools maintained by religious groups separated from the Judeo-Christian tradition. The influence of religion in American life has caused this ideational source to affect the teaching about morals, ethics, and human values in public schools, even when God's existence and authority are left unmentioned.

How Particular Philosophies Relate to Sources of Ideas

The philosophies of education discussed in Chapter 1 owe their nature, in part, to the classifications and sources of ideas previously mentioned. Sometimes the relationship is clear and direct. For example, society as a source "feeds" reconstructionism. In other instances, the relationship is partial. For instance, some Perennialists use Divine Will as a definite and usually unvarying source, and some Realists make science an important source. The fact that one soon fails in an attempt to find exact relationships indicates that other thinking, much of it recent, influences philosophies of education. Thus, humanism, which was not mentioned in Chapter 1 as one of the classic philosophies, represents part of the "other thinking." Humanism and one or two other philosophical viewpoints of recent origin will be mentioned later in this chapter.

It should be clear from the preceding discussion that none of the four sources of beliefs — science, society, the eternal verities, or Divine Will — can be used exclusively to guide the making of a philosophy for a public school. Perhaps the most obvious instance of direct influence is science as a source guiding the preparation of a philosophy for a high school of science in one of our larger cities, but even in such a specialized high school eclectic viewpoints enter. Therefore one must say that differing eclectic choices guide philosophy-making in differently oriented elementary and secondary schools.

The curriculum design one advocates at a given time and place obviously depends greatly on what one wants to do for learners at that time and place. Knowing what one wants to do is, however, only a first step. The complexity of designing can be glimpsed by considering the curriculum planning operations in two school systems.

EXAMPLE 1
Decision Making under the Guise of Scientific Respectability

School System Number One was part of a suburban community inhabited by many business executives, engineers, and scientists who were employees of local industry. More than half the members of the board of education were executives and professional persons. The board members, and other citizens with whom they frequently associated, were much interested in science and its applications.

The school system staff had never taken time to state its philosophy of education. The only standard belief of teachers and administrators was that they had better do what the board and more influential people of the community wanted them to do. One of the more interested and enthusiastic members of the Parent-Teacher Council learned from a friend that listening skills were being taught as a part of the language arts program in the elementary schools of the friend's district. Soon the superintendent of School System Number One was inspired to form a committee on listening skill development to determine how these relatively unknown skills should be taught to elementary and secondary school pupils.

The committee believed that, because so little had been done anywhere to develop listening skills, the members should learn everything possible about listening as an art and skill, and that studies about listening should be accomplished by searching the literature. Eventually, teachers in the district should be encouraged to conduct some experiments of their own regarding listening. In effect, then, the committee said that the methods of science have something to offer in studying problems of this kind.

Having decided the bases on which it would operate, the committee proceeded to analyze the problem along the following lines:

Question: What sort of discipline is listening?
Answer: It is so new to us we don't know. Let's explore it.
Question: Can anyone possibly object to our studying listening? Are there, for instance, priorities of curriculum study that should delay this study?
Answer: Both questions may be answered negatively. Let's go ahead.
Question: Doesn't the nature of the learner make a difference in learning listening? What if he's a dull pupil? What if she comes from a deprived social class?
Answer: These things worry us. We'd better investigate them.
Question: Are there some listening experiences that ought to come earlier in life and some that ought to come later?
Answer: This is a matter of readiness that we may be better equipped to deal with if we know more about listening as a discipline. We'll probably find too that we'll need to know more about the learning processes involved.

After two years of investigation and discussion, the committee produced its "Curriculum Guide to Listening" and proudly gave a copy to the Parent-Teacher Council member who had suggested the study. She was no longer interested, partly because she was currently pressuring the superintendent to do something about educating adolescents against drug abuse.

EXAMPLE 2
Decision Making to Serve Two Philosophical Viewpoints Simultaneously

School System Number Two was a rural area where the residents were mainly farmers and tradespeople. These people valued what the American social system could give their children — opportunities to get ahead in the world of work and to rise in the social scale. For these utilitarian purposes, they valued the eternal verities from the human past as long as time spent with the verities did not interfere with their children's achievement in practical learning.

The teachers, and some of the administrators, in School System Number Two came and went rapidly. Most of them were young and inexperienced because the board of education discharged teachers and principals on slight provocation before they could become tenured. This, of course, was a convenient way of keeping school personnel from rising too high on the salary scale in a community where the taxpayers were happiest when the school district budget was smallest.

No one within System Number Two had time to think very much about educational philosophy, but the administrators knew that parents were clamoring for a mix of what students of philosophy would have called perennialism and pragmatism. In their eagerness to do something about curriculum reform, the administrators agreed to employ a consultant who would foster attention-getting curriculum projects to serve the ends the community seemed to desire.

After she had stimulated and indoctrinated committees and study groups of volunteer teachers, the consultant helped form a study group on helping children write creatively. The committee doubted that old, time-honored procedures for teaching English composition would produce the desired results. Accordingly, the members began a search for new ideas in books, articles, and the experiences of other teachers with whom they corresponded. Eventually they developed the hypothesis that, if learners were freed of mechanical restrictions such as neatness of penmanship, correctness of punctuation, and grammatical accuracy, they might create more worthwhile stories, poems, and essays. To test the hypothesis, the committee had to establish criteria of quality in creative writing. This led to a question: What does creativity in literature really consist of? Their experiment subsequently involved a "brakes off" approach, a freeing of learners to write as they wished. The committee worried about community opinion only to the extent of wondering what parents would say when poorly punctuated, poorly constructed papers came home. The experiment did result in considerably increased creativity according to the committee's criteria. However, the mechanical quality of pupils' writing declined to the point where an "editing and reinforcing period" was used to restore lost mechanical skills.

At the conclusion of the experiment, School System Number Two reported through the press that the experiment was indeed a success and that many youngsters in the schools were well on their way to becoming creative writers.

What Happens in the Usual Planning Operation

The planning operation in each of the two school systems was subject to influences that transcended thoughtful philosophical consideration. In each instance, philosophy was "on the back burner." Curriculum planners touched base with a system of beliefs when they perceived that system to be approved by people in the community who "mattered." Curriculum workers who feel pressed to produce results tend to look for quick, expedient, and (they hope) efficient methods of planning.

At the classroom level, if teachers are quarantined by the school administration or their union or association from outright interference by the community or, more recently, the state, they make many of their curriculum decisions according to the nature of their pupils and the ways they learn. When teachers move from their own classrooms to curriculum committee membership, however, they are faced with additional influences. In curriculum committees, they hear about social demands on the schools, the planning activities in neighboring school districts, topics at recent national conventions, and new subject matter developments. If guidelines for planning are not made available through wise curriculum leadership, teachers and other members of curriculum committees are at sea. One person's opinion then seems about as valuable as another person's opinion, and progress becomes highly uncertain. Obviously progress can be reasonably assured only by using a planning model that features matters to be thought about in preparing a curriculum design. Much of the rest of this chapter is devoted to discussion of such matters.

ACTIVITY 5-1
Thinking about Sources of Educational Philosophy
_____

If the curriculum maker takes an eclectic view of the uses of sources, the nature of practical school problems will condition the emphasis placed on given sources. Think about the problems listed below. Which of the four sources—science, society, eternal verities, Divine Will—would you utilize in solving each of the problems? Discuss your conclusions with others to discover differing viewpoints and to clarify your own thinking.

1. The senior class of a high school is planning a two-day trip to a seaside resort. Sponsors of the trip are trying to help the class make up a code of social conduct to be followed by class members.
2. The eighth-grade art class has been invited to submit plans for a new fountain

to be erected in the town's public square. Two art teachers are working with five pupils who are superior in art to determine an aesthetically desirable design for the fountain.

3. During late October, three civics classes are trying to learn about people's motives for voting in the November election. The social studies department is considering what activities and procedures should be recommended to pupils for their use.

SITUATION 5-1
Using Curriculum Foundations in Planning Improvement

Professor Morris Shamos of New York University proposed that mathematics be presented within the framework of science (*New York Times*, February 14, 1962). In Professor Shamos's view, mathematics should be incorporated within science, with examples in mathematics being "taken from the sciences rather than from the farm or the grocery store; from mechanics, for instance, or from the gas laws or geometric optics."

If you were to explore this idea further, what would you need to know about each of the following?

- The nature of mathematics
- The nature of science, with particular reference to physics
- Social demands and influences upon the teaching and learning of mathematics and science
- Relevant principles of learning
- The needs and problems of adolescents who are required to learn advanced mathematics and physics

Which of the curriculum foundations would, in your opinion, deserve greatest play in establishing a desirable relationship between mathematics and science? Why?

SITUATION 5-2
Making Further Use of Curriculum Foundations and Viewpoints

A committee of first-, second-, and third-grade teachers wished to build a social studies program to satisfy the needs of primary-grade children in their community. Key comments by the teachers about points to consider are listed below:

- "It may be that children's thinking doesn't necessarily proceed from the here and now to the there and then. Does a young child necessarily think more about home and community than he does about definite places in the state, the nation, or the whole world? Does his horizon really broaden according to a set pattern?"

- "We need to learn more about children's interests and the needs they presently feel. Shouldn't we, therefore, find ways of studying children that have special relevance to social studies experiences? What could we possibly invent for this purpose?"
- "We're free as far as demands upon us are concerned. The community doesn't care what we teach young children in the social studies. (People in the community are much more concerned about reading.) Furthermore, teachers in the fourth and fifth grades don't try to tell us what to do in the social studies."
- "We may have to develop some of our own materials to suit the program we devise."

What curriculum foundations do you consider most significant in solving this kind of problem? Do you take at face value the teachers' comments as they relate to foundations?

What inventions are needed for pioneering in using the foundations? For instance, if we do not yet know enough about the learning of social studies concepts by young children, what should be done to explore this matter?

Also, what could be done to learn more about how interests and needs of these children could be met by an improved social studies program?

THE TYLERIAN MODEL FOR CREATING CURRICULUM DESIGNS

The complexity of the designing operation caused Ralph W. Tyler to posit a series of necessary steps, which he incorporated in a syllabus at the University of Chicago decades ago; this syllabus can still be found in a classic paperbound volume.[6] The Tyler rationale has been described as a linear model for curriculum planning consisting of four elements: objectives, activities, organization of the activities, and evaluation. Tyler proposed that objectives be selected on both philosophical and psychological grounds. The objectives in turn became bases for selecting activities, often called pupil experiences. The activities were to be organized sequentially and to be interrelated. Evaluation was to be used to determine whether the objectives were in fact being attained.

The Model's Reception by Curriculum Planners

The sensible, systematic nature of this plan has made it the plan for designing curriculum in many planning centers. For example, Lawrence J. Ondrejack and David W. Cochran of Montgomery Township School District, New Jersey, say that the Tyler curriculum planning model is as American as baseball, hotdogs, and apple pie. They believe it to be the model used by most school districts, consciously or unconsciously.[7]

When the Association for Supervision and Curriculum Development polled six of its prominent members concerning the worth of the Tylerian model "for current curriculum development," four of them favored it. They said it is useful to practicing, responsible school people who need a reliable mode of thinking about the curriculum. They maintained also that its critics have failed to invent a more suitable rationale for planning.

Criticisms of the Tylerian model have centered on the author's conception of how objectives should be stated. The argument is that Tyler has provided no real basis for selecting objectives, that he has established a confining system of means-ends reasoning with objectives always the point of beginning, that he has offered a system of mechanized planning in which learning can be divided too conveniently into subparts, and that he has neglected the long view — human beings' delayed or latent response to education.

Two of the respondents in the ASCD poll criticized the model for failing to address questions of value, specifically questions of a moral, political, ethical, or aesthetic nature. In this sense, they found the model too rational and thus insufficiently real.[8] There are critics who simply do not like behavioral objectives because they limit the work of creative teachers. Still other critics prefer to style objectives in particular ways to meet standard criteria. For them, Tyler's objectives are too simplistic and crude.[9]

Changes in the Model

Over the years, Tyler's design model has been supplemented and tightened in practice. The following is a mandate, representing a revision of the model, that a curriculum steering committee might send to curriculum planners in a school system:

1. State the need for your proposed design. Base your statement on a preliminary investigation of need. Think of need as being educational, social, and/or personally developmental.
2. Indicate the objectives the design is to serve. State a few prime or major objectives of the design, making them succinct and clear. Be sure that each objective has at least two major parts: an indication of what is to be done and an indication of how you will know when it has been done.
3. Say what subject matter content will be used within the design; then say how the content will be organized for teaching and learning.
4. Provide examples of learning experiences that pupils will have — sometimes thought of as pupil activities — using the subject matter content indicated in 3, above. Show just how these experiences will be organized to profit pupil learning.

5. Say *what* you will evaluate, according to your objectives, and *how* you will evaluate it.
6. Show how you will attempt to convince other persons, including persons both in your school and outside it, that they should try the design themselves. Consider publishing the design for the benefit of others.

ADDITIONAL CONSIDERATIONS NOW AFFECTING CURRICULUM DESIGNING

As society introduces ideas or concerns that were not prominent, or even heard of, previously, curriculum planners must use their sources of ideas and the philosophies that relate to them in new ways. During the latter part of the twentieth century, the culture has produced a number of new issues. Among them are the following:

- Whether creationism or evolution should be used in the teaching of the natural sciences and literature
- Whether humanistic philosophy is a valid basis for education or an enemy of organized religion whose presence in the schools constitutes a violation of the separation of church and state
- Application of futurism in projecting curriculum needs and themes
- Application of new findings about brain functioning in learning
- Attention to the education of migrant children
- Extension of special education to impaired persons formerly overlooked in schools, improvement of education to benefit nonspecialists in particular subject matter, and re-extension of special education to the gifted and talented.

These and other issues may affect what is included in future curriculum designs. Each of the six ideas above is worthy of brief discussion.

Creationism versus Evolution

When an issue in education is brought to court on several occasions in different locations, it usually receives widespread publicity. Decades ago, Clarence Darrow and William Jennings Bryan served as attorneys in the famous Scopes "monkey" trial about the teaching of evolution in a public school in Tennessee. The presence of these two giants in the field of oratory made news, and the subject that they debated divided people clearly into advocates and opponents of the teaching of evolutionary theory.

During the 1980s the matter has been revived by individuals and organizations who favor the teaching of creationism and who urge that creationism be given the same attention as evolution. Frequently curriculum workers are caught between the evolutionists and the religionists. Unfortunately curriculum workers gain little from reminding both sides that both arguments are filled with theory and faith.

Humanism as Prevailing Philosophy in Public Schools

The term *humanism* is used in the literature of educational philosophy in two ways: (1) as the beliefs of persons who have formed what *Webster's* calls "a cult bearing allegiance to Humanist Manifesto I and Humanist Manifesto II" and (2) as the beliefs of educators of good will who would do their best to exalt and develop human potential.

The official Humanists (the first group above) are convinced that human beings determine their own destinies without intervention by a divine being. Thus they reject the miraculous, the mystical, and the supernatural. Humanist Manifesto I rejects creationism, worship, prayer, and "religious emotions and attitudes" as impediments to self-realization and personal fulfillment.[10] Humanist Manifesto II, which appeared in 1973, cast aside salvationism, faith in a prayer-hearing God, revelation of truth, divinity as a source of moral values, and puritanical views of human sexuality.[11] Persons who trust these documents follow a logical progression in believing that there is no God; that human beings therefore were not created, but evolved; that there are no moral absolutes; and that it is consequently all right to be amoral.

In many public and private schools and in much of current educational literature, humanism has become a generic term that is often confused with humaneness. Teachers who want the best for their pupils and are willing to help their pupils achieve freely call themselves humanists. Surely humanistic philosophy, as applied in the schools, has set the direction of several breakthroughs in elementary and secondary education, such as those emphasizing self-concept development and attention to the productive abilities of human beings. This is a result of what Arthur Combs calls the commitment of applied humanism to "freedom, value, worth, dignity, and integrity of persons."[12]

Some religious conservatives maintain that, largely as a consequence of court decisions against the teaching of religion in the public schools and the actual indifference of parents to what happens to their children's values, humanism has become the prevailing "religion" in many schools, replacing all others. Their views have come to the fore in the debate concerning creationism vs. evolution. When curriculum projects and materials seem to uphold what conservatives call secular humanism, objections are often loud, parents hunt for new schools for their children, and the public schools lose some of their support. Although people who call themselves humanists deny that their beliefs constitute a religion, conservatives continue to maintain that humanism has filled the gap created by the forced withdrawal of Judeo-Christian teaching, and that its presence in the schools constitutes a violation of church-state separation. Humanistic philosophy is obviously one of the themes that curriculum coordinators need to be informed about as they meet with planning groups in the schools.

Futurism as a Potential Aid in Planning

Many a scholar has been asked, "What's ahead in your field?" As more and more grandiose plans are made by scientists, practitioners of the arts, industrialists, and others, the question becomes somewhat easier to answer — but not easy enough.

Prediction of future trends has now come to curriculum planning. The available means of prediction include "genius forecasting" by specialists in the various fields; extrapolation, in which present and past developments are extended into the future; simulation, as in the making of likely scenarios or the dramatization of alternative approaches; and systems analysis, an aspect of the systems approach (see pages 211–213) which often involves the use of computers.[13] An imaginative means of predicting has been created in Scotland, where the ideas expressed by thoughtful writers of science fiction have been incorporated in making estimates of future trends in education.[14] Curriculum workers should learn all they can about the methods used in futurism so that new curriculum designs do not merely repeat the ideas and agendas of the past.

Brain Functioning As It Affects Designing

In Chapter 2 mention was made of the findings in brain research that influence our views of learning. Some of the findings have to do with brain lateralization or sidedness, and with dominance of the respective hemispheres in learning activities and life activities generally. Inasmuch as designing involves deciding what is to be learned, by whom, and at what time or times, curriculum coordinators must understand brain research data so that they can help their colleagues make wise judgments. The discrimination against left-handed children that has been practiced in the past serves as a warning against future rejection of clearcut evidence about brain functioning.[15]

The Education of Migrant Children

Some parts of our nation are especially subject to the ingress and egress of migrant populations. Immigrant processing centers, resettlement sites, and agricultural areas with quickly recurring growths of crops are a few of the places that attract and hold migrants for limited periods only. The children of migrating families have brief contacts with school after school, receiving instruction that has little continuity.

Most school systems with shifting pupil populations simply do the best they can. Tangipahoa Parish Schools in Amite, Louisiana, have developed a plan for working with migrant children. It begins with measurement of pupils' individual skill deficiencies and proceeds to instruction in the skills individuals need. Skill activities and materials are color coded according to educational level and are correlated with computer software, the National Migrant Skills List, and appropriate tests. The school system has prepared a guide containing a compendium of resource materials and suggestions to teachers.[16] The Tangipahoa plan represents the kind of attention that curriculum workers should give to pupils with special problems.

New Ramifications of Special Education

Special education of the mentally and physically handicapped has taken the attention of curriculum planners for a long time. The educables, the trainables, the blind, the partially sighted, the deaf and hard-of-hearing, the orthopedically handicapped, and many other groups have been identified and specially taught. As medical science makes the characteristics of other kinds of handicapped children and youth more clearly identifiable, and makes these youngsters more readily treatable, the schools are called upon to do something special for each of the newly identified groups. Where specialized educational offerings are needed, they should be provided, the presence of mainstreaming notwithstanding. Youngsters with nervous disorders are a case in point.

Special attention should not be reserved exclusively for victims of impairment or illness. Two groups particularly in need of attention are those pupils who need to learn all they can about a particular subject but will probably never become majors or specialists in it and those pupils who are especially gifted or talented. An example of the first group is nonspecialists in chemistry, a subject about which everyone should have some knowledge. In 1981 teachers from Japan and the United States conferred at the University of Minnesota about chemical education for nonspecialists in the subject. They identified several needs: enhanced use of the laboratory, emphasis on science processes, instruction in the special contributions of chemistry to human activity, help for mathematics-shy pupils, provision of a great variety of materials and resources, and use of interdisciplinary approaches in planning and teaching.[17] With careful thought, planners can open subjects to nonmajors in ways that have seldom been used.

The gifted and talented we have with us always, in limited numbers. Their problem is often one of finding significant subject matter to learn. Portions of curriculum designs can be devoted to content that is beyond what these pupils learn quickly in company with their classmates. In mathematics, for example, operations research, logic, statistics, and uses of the computer can provide challenging and also useful subject matter for gifted children.[18]

STRATEGIES USED IN CREATING CURRICULUM DESIGNS

Curriculum designs come in varying sizes and shapes. Most attempts at designing are made on a limited "retail" basis, within limited areas of subject matter. The titles of the following proposals suggest the limited scope of many designs.

- A Unit on Nutrition for High School Pupils
- Relating Social Studies and Science in Kindergarten
- A Plan for Peer Group Teaching
- Experiences in Sensitivity Training for High School Pupils
- New Experiences in Bilingual Education
- A Look at the Local Community: A Three-Week Minicourse for Incoming Seventh Graders
- A Plan for Parent Workshops on Drug Education
- Creating a Sixth Grade Social Studies Learning Center
- Helping Preadolescents Adjust to New School Experiences
- An Inquiry into Meanings of Success (Twelfth Grade)
- A Plan for Developing Better Eating Habits
- Experiences in Earth Science to Develop a Scientific Attitude
- Painting School Murals to Inspire Improved School Citizenship

Consider how much time during a school year might, nevertheless, be needed to fulfill the terms of each of these proposals as you perceive them from the titles.

Sometimes designing is done more comprehensively and thoroughly. The following titles of actual designs suggest the magnitude of comprehensive designing.

- A Four-Year Design for a Business Education Work/Study Program
- A Career Education Program for _____ School District
- The Secondary School Program Design for the _____ Unified Schools
- A Language Development Program for Language-Impaired Pupils (K–12)

- The Study of Mankind: A Program in Junior High School Science
- People and Culture: A Humane Approach to the Social Studies
- An Elective Program in Urban Ecology

These titles designate programs requiring much time and effort to prepare and put into effect.

Designs for both large programs and smaller projects are needed. Program development is very time-consuming, but it can, when well executed, provide for sequence and continuity in instruction. Projects, on the other hand, are often placed in little niches in the curriculum mosaic, and creating numbers of them may result in more fragmentation within the curriculum structure. Gordon Cawelti says secondary education already has a "patchwork" curriculum that lacks coherence.[19] Gail McCutcheon concludes, after a study of the curriculum in twelve elementary school classrooms, that patchwork is too charitable a term because it suggests preplanning. She suggests "emerging crazyquilt" as a more truthful description.[20]

Both programs and projects must be designed and planned with care if curriculum improvement is to occur. Curriculum leaders and major planning committees are responsible for maintaining a balance between program development and project development.

Halting, spotty, and uncertain as curriculum designing in the United States appears to be, it is at least more democratic than it is in most other nations. In this country, top and middle management administrators are not the only ones involved in planning. As Chapter 9 indicates, teachers, parents, and pupils all have their places in the planning operation. And the schools that use the completed plans and designs often provide feedback about success or failure to the planners. In their study of curriculum decision making in eighteen countries, however, Klein and Goodlad found that curriculum centers with certain allegiances to the national governments are commonly in vogue. The centers are staffed by "official planners" who develop monolithic programs, seldom consult teachers, parents, or pupils, and generally ignore feedback from the schools.[21]

Democracy does not, of course, necessarily make for proficiency. Davis and Silvernail found, for instance, that the design skills developed in future teachers enrolled in teacher education programs in Pennsylvania colleges were decidedly "uneven." The skills needed were considered to include analysis of objectives, sequencing of objectives, choosing points at which to test, preparing specific tests, and developing means of large-scale evaluation.[22] People who participate in creating curriculum designs should show particular competence because of the difficulty of the task. If their desire is to reduce differences between what is taught and what is learned, they should know possible ways of ensuring this result. If, on the other hand, they want to pose alternatives, they should know how to present them and how to be sure they are viable. The most effective designs are well-described ones that include follow-up procedures in supervision.[23]

The Importance of Preplanning

The planning that precedes creation of an actual curriculum design may be represented by a series of questions:

1. What do you think you might want to design? What are the possibilities or alternatives?
2. What level(s) of schooling are you thinking of?
3. What is the nature of the pupil population you have in mind?
4. If you're ready to narrow the possibilities, what do you think ought to be *done* under terms of the design you favor?
5. What subject matter, both classic and different from the usual, do you think you should include?
6. How might you organize the subject matter to make the best teaching possible?
7. What three or four activities or experiences occur to you as being typical of what you think pupils ought to *do*?

Whoever preplans, the cardinal rule is THINK, THINK, THINK. Thinking takes time. It is better to take a long time in the preplanning stage than to choose a design option that proves to be uninteresting or unproductive. One of the major shortcomings in the process of designing curricula in the past has been a tendency to limit the involvement of people who are to participate in the implementation of the program or project that is eventually chosen. Again, involving people takes time.

Steps to Be Taken in Designing

Once preplanning has been accomplished, the action has only begun. The yearning for a program or project may be intense, but so far no evidence has been accumulated that it is needed. Prior to elaborate goal-setting, therefore, need should be assessed. This is not the detailed needs assessment that is discussed in Chapter 8. It is the limited determination of the need to design a particular project or a major program.

Determining Need

Need determination should probably begin with an attempt by the designers to verbalize the outcomes desired. Often it is easy to think loosely and talk glibly about something that apparently needs to be done without stating, preferably in writing, the proposed outcomes. When the outcomes have been stated so that they make sense to people outside the planning group, these people—teachers, administrators, pupils, parents, and other citizens, as appropriate—should be asked what they think of the project or program in comparison with other possibilities and in light of the aims or goals of the school or school system. Next, the planners should collect evidence about the status of the pupils to be affected, lest it be found later that the pupils are already achieving most of the objectives that the proposal may help them attain. The planners then should review the local scene to gauge the community's response to a new project or program. Conversations and discussion with community groups may accomplish this purpose more readily than formal and suspicious-looking written surveys.[24]

When need seems to have been established, the planners should see to it that administrative arrangements are made for the formal steps in designing, beginning with establishing goals or aims.

Stating or Reviewing Aims

A new project or program should fit with previously established aims or goals of the school or the school system. It is necessary, therefore, that the aims be reviewed or, if aims have never been stated (as in the case of newly founded schools or of school systems that have never done serious curriculum planning), clearly prescribed.

Lists of aims are sometimes prepared by boards of education, administrators, and professional staff people, who may involve pupils and selected citizens from the community. Or they may be formulated by polling community members concerning their expectations for their schools and then stating the aims on the basis of consensus of community opinion. A third alternative, the one perhaps most common today, is for representatives of the school system and the community to rank aims previously prepared by educational organizations such as Phi Delta Kappa.

Most model lists of aims seem to be reworded versions of the Phi Delta Kappa list, which was produced by the staff of the Program Development Center of Northern California at California State University in Chico, under a grant from the United States Office of Education. The Phi Delta Kappa list calls for development by schools of skills, understandings, and attitudes in family living; management of time, money, and property; general education; character and self-respect; reading, writing, speaking, and listening; changes occurring in the world; examining and using information; a desire for learning; pride in one's work; health and safety; respecting and getting along with other people; democratic ideas and ideals; using leisure time; becoming good citizens; making job selections; and appreciating culture and beauty.[25] The Phi Delta Kappa model suggests three phases in program development. In Phase I planners are to rank the aims or goals and determine the current level of achievement. In Phase II they prepare performance objectives for the school district. In Phase III they allocate resources to achieve their aims.

Earlier the Midwest Administration Center had prepared a set of omnibus aims under four headings: intellectual dimensions, social dimensions, personal dimensions, and productive dimensions.[26] Similarly, Tyler had summarized the aims of U.S. schooling as the development of self-realization in individual learners, the making of literate citizens, provision of opportunities for social mobility in the population, preparation for the world of work, preparation for making wise choices in nonmaterial services (education, health, recreation, and so on), and instruction in learning how to learn.[27] Even earlier, the Commission on the Reorganization of Secondary Education (1918) and the Educational Policies Commission (1944) had developed standard lists of aims.

Omnibus lists provide only general guidance to curriculum planners in expressing aims for their individual schools. Every school, as a separate institution, should have its own aims, stated more specifically and clearly than the aims proposed above. Some of the individual school's aims should be identical to the aims of the system in which the school belongs; others should be adaptations of systemwide aims; still others should be distinctively the property of the individual school. Aims that will be respected and supported are formulated by representatives of all the persons and groups who are to live with the aims. Thus, representative teachers, pupils, administrators, parents, and other citizens of the school community should be involved in establishing aims for a school.

A recent resurgence of interest in the preparation of aims has raised questions about the functions of schooling that will be debated for a long time. One of the issues concerns the place of schooling in the total range of educational experience offered children and youth. Alternatives to schooling have grown up in many communities. The nature of some of the alternatives suggests that the school may in the future limit itself to activities that it is preeminently successful in performing and that must be performed in schools. Additional educational input may be provided by other media and agencies: television, paperbacks, radio, clubs, labor unions, businesses, religious education programs, community programs, and youth centers. Young people say during interviews, "School doesn't touch a lot of the real education we get." In answer to a question noted in Chapter 3, "What could schools do to educate you in ways that no other agencies could or should?" youngsters have said that schools should put learning content into a framework or system that will help them to understand the content better. Thus, they call for improved curriculum design. They have said further that schools should teach them the fundamentals they can get nowhere else; should stimulate them to inquire, discover, and probe meaning; and should stop trying to compete with and destroy what they learn elsewhere. They want the schools to help them coordinate or integrate what they learn in school with what they learn outside it.[28] Exactly who will do the coordinating of diverse contributing educational sources remains a moot point, but the schools have a responsibility for helping youngsters make value judgments about the relative worth of diverse educational experiences.

A second issue concerns central and peripheral missions of the school. The American school was originally created to educate pupils in the directions of intellectuality and values development. Subsequently the school was seen to be an agency of social interaction and uplift, and later a means of integrating different racial and cultural groups. During recent years, many of the actions taken in the field of education by high officials in state and federal government have been directed toward the aim of social uplift and the integration of peoples. The prevalence of these actions has caused some critics of the schools to suggest that the central mission of the school, as perceived by many state and federal officials, is to provide schooling less for education's sake than for improving the social status of disadvantaged subpopulations. Similarly, teachers' organizations have viewed the thrust toward accountability as being inspired by social reformers rather than by persons with fundamental interest in the quality of schooling qua schooling.

A third issue is clearly value centered. It relates to perpetuation of closed-ended aims versus the adoption of open-ended ones. The American school has traditionally served closed-ended aims by keeping pupil experiences within bounds—teaching established modes of writing, speaking, and behaving in general and assuming the rightness and the propriety of given books, songs, and conclusions in particular. Recently, the voices of a few individuals and small groups of people with different values orientations have been heard. These individuals and groups, which do not usually include parents, want school to admit experiences that enlarge the functions of the school and that sometimes fall far outside traditional functions of schooling. Experiences of the latter sort might include, for example, providing social services for the indigent and   iching pupils how to subvert the U.S. political system.

A fourth issue concerns the limits to be placed on various aspects of formal education. For instance, development of the ability to read effectively has been considered the birthright of every U.S. citizen. Experience in the teaching of reading has revealed, however, that some children never learn to read effectively regardless of the time, energies, and methodologies that are employed. Failure to recognize this fact has resulted in widespread criticism by the public and self-flagellation by teachers. Social conscience and faith in the limitlessness of human potential have kept the issue from being thoroughly considered and discussed. Without denying the wonder and the exceptionality of human potential, realists admit that although the potential of every individual is wide-ranging, covering varieties of human endeavors, the range of an individual's potential may not include effective performance in every one of the three Rs.

Still other issues and questions are age-old: Beyond basic education, shall the schools provide mainly instrumental education or mainly esoteric education? Will the American public support its schools well enough to permit them to fulfill their aims, whatever those aims may be? Are nearly all the children of all the people to receive formal education?

Stating Program or Project Objectives

Within a framework of institutional aims, it is necessary to state objectives that the program or project being designed is to meet. At first, most such objectives were vaguely stated. But notations such as "achieving correct use of language in speaking and writing" proved so general as to be confusing. A change to the pupil objective "to demonstrate in specific ways one's ability to speak and write effectively" seemed useful only to a degree. The big problem was lack of specificity. Whether a program or project objective is to be stated from the vantage point of teachers or of pupils, it should obviously be clear, definite, and limited in size. Shifting to behavioral objectives was perhaps inevitable, inasmuch as people designing programs and projects need to show clearly what pupils are to *do*.

For a program or project, then, the planners may state a general objective like "improving arithmetic learning in our upper elementary school," but to show what pupils are to accomplish specifically, they must state a series of specific objectives beneath the general one. Suppose the planners wanted to touch base with the three identifiable kinds of objectives—cognitive, affective, and psychomotor. An objective within each category might look like this:

1. *Cognitive*. To help pupils acquire an understanding of the process of division as revealed by their attainment of a 90 percent proficiency level in teacher-made tests.
2. *Affective*. To increase pupils' interest in division of numbers, as indicated by their choice, during four of every five opportunities, of "division options" during independent study periods and by their favorable comments, with the same degree of frequency, about division during interviews and group discussions.
3. *Psychomotor*. To improve pupils' perception of number size as a means of making more accurate judgments in the process of dividing, as revealed by their attainment of a 95 percent proficiency level in number estimation exercises taken from standardized and teacher-made tests.

An incidence of 90 percent, four of every five, or 95 percent is chosen on the basis of the planners' best judgment and has no other basis.

Objectives like these bear the label "behavioral" or "performance." Though they are not unmixed blessings, behavioral objectives have been instrumental in increasing learning and in relating the intent of pupils and teachers to the aims of the school. Worthwhile behavioral objectives express behaviors that are observable, and they also state the outcomes to be anticipated from behaving in given ways. Reservations about stating objectives behaviorally include the fact that not all subject matter learning can be expressed in behavioral terms, that behavioral objectives sometimes set a ceiling on learning, that objectives in general are not always products of rationality, and that objectives can perhaps be stated accurately only after instruction has occurred because they emerge only in the processes of teaching and learning.

Some of the critics of behavioral objectives point to the fact that curriculum planners who are skillful in verbalizing objectives are not always capable of formulating objectives that are worthy and attainable.[29] Values questions arise in selecting the objectives to be used. Other critics suggest that formally stated objectives should be eliminated in favor of a mutual refining of ends and means until a curriculum plan is developed that relates the best ends to the best pupil experiences available for attaining these ends.[30]

Despite the criticisms, behavioral objectives remain front and center on the curriculum planning scene. Planners are constantly searching for patterns, order, stability, efficient management, a logical approach, structure, system, and predictability.[31] Many of them believe they are achieving these effects when they prepare behavioral objectives to guide whole curriculum projects. Creators of behavioral objectives at this level should look first to the outcomes they wish to attain, make certain that the behaviors mentioned in the stated objectives are clearly observable, reduce the number of their objectives as they refine a gross list to an essential one, and distribute their objectives appropriately among the cognitive, affective, and psychomotor domains.

Whatever the method used in stating program and project objectives, the statement should be clear and precise.

Identifying Evaluation Means

"If we were to try to achieve the objectives we have just stated, how would we know when, in fact, they had been achieved?" This question should be asked at this juncture by persons designing a project or a program. The answer lies in finding or making evaluation means that will suit the requirement. Among the potential evaluation means are the following:

teachers' observations, recording of pupils' behaviors, interview schedules, rating scales, checklists, questionnaires and opinionnaires, teacher-made tests, standardized (norm-referenced) tests, criterion-referenced tests, and semi-projective instruments. Some instruments can be purchased; others must be made within the school system. Achievement standards must be made rigorous enough to make certain that achievement of the objectives has occurred. If the objectives themselves do not express achievement levels (for example, 90 percent, satisfactory performance in nine of every ten attempts), acceptable levels must be described elsewhere.

The evaluation means are put to use as the curriculum design goes into operation and continue to be used throughout its life span. (Details of program and project evaluation are presented in the next chapter.)

Choosing a Type of Design

A half-dozen design types are being used in improving the whole curriculum or part of it. They are as follows:

1. *The subject design*, which is the most common design type, follows the traditional idea of making school subjects the basis for designing. It is orderly as a consequence of its neat divisions and subdivisions of subject matter. Because of the strong presence of the Carnegie unit system, it is difficult to dislodge from high school programs. Variations of the subject design have already been discussed in Chapter 4.
2. *The societal activities and problems design* is based in perceived realities of institutional and group life. It is intended to reinforce cultural traditions and also to meet some of the community's and the society's unmet needs. Designs highlighting persistent life situations and reconstruction of the society are included here. The content generally consists of a series of social problems or human activities.
3. *The specific competencies design* has been represented in recent years by performance-based or competency-based education. Having formerly emphasized descriptions of occupations and training in occupational skills, it has been tightened in an attempt to show direct relationship among objectives, activities, and performance, especially relative to so-called essential skills. The objectives are usually stated behaviorally.
4. *The individual needs and interests design* is based in the felt and unfelt needs and the particular interests of individual pupils and small groups of pupils. It utilizes findings about human growth and development and prizes individualization of instruction. Furthermore, it recognizes what the society and the community are

doing to learners. The experiences of learners are often made a beginning point. Additional experiences are varied as they touch the needs and interests of particular learners. Curriculum planners discover these interests and needs in part by consulting and testing the learners themselves. Alternative schools often adopt this design type.

5. *The process skills design* emphasizes how to learn and how to solve immediate and lifelong problems. Development of life skills thus becomes an important component of the process skills design on the theory that if learners know *how* to confront and deal with current problems, they can continue and improve the confrontation in the future. The process skills cross subject matter lines because they are generalized—for example, observing, classifying, hypothesizing, making decisions. They extend beyond the cognitive domain to the affective, as in valuing.

Recently two supplementary design types that use portions of the five types described above have received special attention. They are humane education and the systems approach to designing, to be discussed later in this chapter. There is also a miscellany of design types that are adaptations of the original five. Many of them contain seeds of ideas for future development.

Choice of design type is governed in part by the planners' philosophical positions. It also is governed by objectives of the program or project being planned. The planners should not be surprised, therefore, if a particular project falls within a design type that is philosophically quite different from viewpoints commonly held by teachers and administrators in the planners' school.

Selecting Learning Content

"What learning content shall we select?" Aims and objectives point the way to the content that pupils are to learn. Some of the content may be formal subject matter. Part of it, especially in the affective domain, is likely to be informal and may not even be classified as content. What is the content, for example, that is to be used in teaching self-realization or civic responsibility? Much of it is necessarily drawn from the world of affairs, from the life experiences of human beings. Some of it, of course, can be found in subjects and subject fields, such as psychology and the social studies.

Selection of content taken from the subjects and subject fields has been discussed in Chapter 4. The more informal content may be said to fall within categories or domains like the following:

1. Personal development, which includes human communication, values clarification, the inventorying of interests, and self-analysis
2. Acquisition of life skills, which includes listening, discussing, analyzing issues, solving practical problems, and retrieving information (These are skills not usually taught in schools in a sophisticated manner.)
3. Improvement of human relationships, involving use of languages, practice in social interaction, participation in community affairs, and human relations trouble shooting
4. Extended development, which constitutes specializations learned by work experience, individual study, and community service.

In selection of learning content, the options are open. There is much less danger in trying varied content than in restricting learners to content that, though "tried and true," may in fact be less educative than any one of several alternatives.

Determining and Organizing Learning Experiences

"What shall our pupils do under the aegis of the design we propose?" The answer to this question depends on the answers given previously to other questions: What outcomes do we want, and what, therefore, are our objectives? What means of evaluation have we chosen to fit the objectives? What is the design type within which we are operating? What learning content shall we select? Many teachers and administrators want to determine learning experiences for their pupils before they have answered the preceding basic questions. When they do so, they are likely to select and create dead-end, irrelevant, and inappropriate experiences.

Choice of experiences deserves careful thought. Hopkins suggested these criteria:

> While all interaction of the individual with the environment is experience, the school cannot promote experiences of low educative quality. Pupils, teachers, and others can find too many of these in every walk of life. The school must be concerned with experiences of high educative quality since it should aid each individual to raise the level of his experiencing in all aspects of living. To do this, educators must have some criteria for testing incipient experiences to see whether they warrant study through the school. . . .
>
> 1. The experience must begin with and continue to grow out of the real felt needs of pupils.
> 2. The experience must be managed by all of the learners concerned—

pupils, teachers, parents, and others—through a process of democratic interaction.

3. The experience must be unified through evolving purposes of pupils.
4. The experience must aid each individual to increase his power to make intelligent choices.
5. The experience must aid each individual to mature his experiences by making progressive improvements in the logic of such experiences.
6. The experience must increase the number and variety of interests which each individual consciously shares with others.
7. The experience must help each individual build new and refine old meanings.
8. The experience must offer opportunity for each individual to use an ever-increasing variety of resources for learning.
9. The experience must aid each individual to use a variety of learning activities compatible with the variety of resources.
10. The experience must aid each individual creatively to reconstruct and expand his best experience in the developing situation.
11. The experience must have some dominating properties which characterize it as a whole and which usually give it a name.
12. The experience must close with a satisfactory emotional tone for each participant.[32]

Experiences for pupils, whatever their source or nature, need to be organized in ways that fit the curriculum designs to which they contribute. Organizing centers, around which subject matter can be learned and experiences can be clustered, should be created. Common organizing centers include life activities (ways of making a living, utilizing leisure time, and the like), pupils' needs, and pupils' interests.

Virgil E. Herrick developed a different categorization of organizing centers that was based on five qualities:

1. Significance, which meant usefulness in teaching, interest to pupils, and general worth
2. Accessibility of a physical nature, an intellectual nature, or both
3. Breadth and scope in meeting the needs of a diverse pupil population, in moving several curricular elements along together, and in serving as a stimulant in dealing with significant life problems
4. Capacity for organizing and relating so that teacher and pupils can "tie things together" in related wholes
5. Capacity for development—permitting children to "catch hold" of content and "run with it."[33]

Herrick decided that five organizing centers had the qualities noted above: ideas; materials; displays, collections, exhibits, and the like; places; and people. He developed his thesis in this way:

> The deceptive and yet enchanting thing about the whole concept of organizing centers is that, instead of qualities such as those outlined above being inherent in a given center, the center is itself described, defined, and created by the qualities. In effect, the qualities are in the mind and eye of the viewer. The milkman kicks a pebble at the doorstep, and to him it is only a pebble. The geologist residing there picks it up and enchants his children for several nights with stories of how it came to be. The girl in the match factory watches the clock and thinks of the weekend ahead, while box after box passes under her scrutiny on the production line. The woodsman picks up a single match and brings forth endless tales of woodland giants, raging fires, and reforestation. To the geologist and the woodsman, a stone and a match are organizing centers for learning and teaching. An organizing center is whatever a teacher and a class can get their hands on and their minds around to enrich the quality of classroom living. Visualizing in the center the qualities that make it worthwhile determines the usefulness of that organizing center.
>
> Since what is an organizing center for one teacher and class is not recognizable as such to another, the process of identification becomes complicated. Nonetheless, an attempt is made below to indicate some types of organizing centers for learning and teaching.
>
> 1. *Ideas.* Big ideas have traditionally served as organizing centers for learning: ideas about time, space, the future, man and his identity, the source of truth, and so on. Ideas, carefully selected, readily satisfy the requisites for good organizing centers for elementary school instruction. Ideas satisfy the criterion of development especially well; a group can take them and move with them. Problems of living are similar effective centers of attention for organizing learning.
> 2. *Materials.* On the assumption that teachers are guided more in setting up learning situations by the materials accessible to them than by any other single source of direction, most educators believe improvement of materials promises improvement of instruction. Teachers who depend heavily upon text materials, for example, are restricted by the suitability of these materials for the instructional goals they have in mind. If thinking about materials is extended to include encyclopedias, films, filmstrips, record players, and so on, it becomes obvious that materials hold much promise for classroom organization of instruction.

3. *Displays, collections, exhibits, etc.* To some, a science corner in the classroom is just a miscellaneous array of inanimate or even animate "stuff." To others, it is a source of stimulating thought and activity. Book and science collections, museums, stamp and coin collections, and so on, offer much to the teacher who is able to see their possibilities for leading children into further exploration.

4. *Places.* Use of places as organizing centers ranges from playground application to foreign travel. Classes in Atlanta make effective use of places when they visit the Cyclorama to see the Battle for Atlanta brought to life in vivid color and form; in Pittsburgh groups go to the exact site of Forth Duquesne to study the past; in Detroit pupils visit an automobile factory to study mass production; in San Francisco they visit a cruiser in the Bay to compare naval equipment of past and present.

5. *People.* Much effective learning can be tied around names such as Columbus, Galileo, Disraeli, Handel, Shakespeare, Whitman, Franklin, and Ford.

In each instance given here, the idea, material, exhibit, place, or person represents a beginning point—an opportunity to get a toehold in profitable learning. The intent to learn, however, becomes truly muddled when the vantage point, the organizing center, becomes a thing of inflated inherent value. Great names are important, yes; but the teacher who sees their potential for involving children in significant learning processes has a perspective that is fundamental to good teaching.[34]

Particular experiences can be adapted to use within each of these organizing centers. Publishers of packaged learning materials have tried interesting variations and combinations of organizing centers.

Additional discussion of learning experiences for achieving objectives can be found in Chapter 4.

Evaluating Programs and Projects

Still another step in the designing operation is determining the worth of the design. As might be expected, this action may require considerable time. The worth of the design is revealed in comprehensive evaluation of the program or project, which occurs on an ongoing basis as well as at the terminus. This is so significant a function of designing that it deserves treatment within Chapter 6.

Evaluation should reveal that the design has flaws. The question is "To what extent does the design accomplish what it was intended to accomplish?" A subsequent question is "What went right, what went wrong, and why?" One must gauge a design's worth with reference to its reason for being and its functioning with reference to the ease with which it has been initiated, implemented, and maintained.

Evaluation may result in establishment of an alternative way of proceeding in the future, or in modification of the current design.

ACTIVITY 5-2
Moving from Philosophical Sources to Objectives

Consider society as the major source of educational objectives. What particular point of view do you take toward the role of society as a source of objectives? That is, should schooling be conditioned by a consensus of citizens' views, by government on behalf of society, by the present social scene, or by a society that has not yet come into being?

Give several objectives, stated behaviorally for pupils, that you believe would stem from whatever point of view you take. For instance, if you believe that a society that has not yet come into being should condition schooling, you will value experiments by pupils that will lead them to think about establishment of a new society. Hence, several objectives written from the pupils' standpoint might begin with the words "To design experiments . . . " or "To experiment with . . . ." Suppose, on the other hand, you believe that government should condition schooling on behalf of society. You might propose objectives beginning "To understand legislation . . . ," "To acquire an attitude of acceptance toward regulations about . . . ," and so on. As you state objectives, think of the processes by which pupils are to learn, and also of the content they are to learn.

SITUATION 5-3
Selecting Evaluation Means for a Middle School Project

"Manners have really deteriorated in this school! Courtesy is a rare thing. People don't hold doors for each other. If someone drops books on the floor, no one helps pick them up. While we're thinking up projects, let's think one up on good manners."

The speaker was a member of the faculty of Cloister Middle School. The occasion: a meeting of the school's Curriculum Planning Committee.

Another member of the committee responded: "I'm for that. We need a project of that kind. It would be about as good for the teachers as for the kids."

In due time, the Good Manners Project was designed. Several objectives, mainly repetitious of one another, were stated and accepted. All of them said, in effect, "Let's treat each other in more courteous, decent ways."

Before the committee began planning project activities, the members gave much thought to a troublesome problem — how to gauge improvement in the practice of good manners when and if improvement did occur. After having spent time at home considering the problem, the members were able to suggest a number of evaluation means, five of which were determined to be most promising. They are as follows:

1. "Do before-and-after observation (by a team of teachers and pupils) of the status of our manners, with instruction or activities coming between."
2. "Give a manners test before and after instruction. See how we do."
3. "Write descriptions of several school scenes showing good and poor manners. Ask the people to comment on them before we teach and after we teach."
4. "Get the PTA to prepare and publish a manners code. Expect everyone to study it. Give a test on it."
5. "Invite three adult citizens to come in and observe our manners. Show films on etiquette in the auditorium. Have the citizens come back to observe again. Compare."

What do you think of these five ideas? How would you repair one or two of them to make them usable? If you had been a member of the committee, what else would you have suggested?

ACTIVITY 5-3
Suggesting Concrete Actions in Selecting and
Ordering Learning Experiences

From the following kinds of objectives, select one and prepare a list of actions you would take in selecting and ordering learning experiences to achieve it.

- Objectives for developing interests
- Objectives for altering attitudes and values
- Objectives for improving skills
- Objectives for developing appreciations
- Objectives for improving quality of thinking

This may well be an experience in which you would like to engage with other teachers in a group setting.

EXAMPLES OF CURRICULUM DESIGNING

The five design types mentioned in this chapter provide bases for creative designing. The special requirements of planners within diverse school systems cause particular slants to develop in the designing process. The first of the two examples below is based on the subject design. Its slant is toward extensive involvement of teachers in the planning process. The second example is based on the individual needs and interests design. Its slant is toward creation of a humane environment in which communication is prized, for the benefit of an identifiable group of pupils.

EXAMPLE 1
Organizing to Improve Subject Teaching with Maximum Involvement
of Teachers

The following procedure was used in developing curriculum in three school
districts where involvement of teachers was especially valued.

Four teams were organized of teachers who were interested in the subject matter area to be reconsidered. Where possible teachers were given
released time for planning. The first of the four teams determined why the
subject matter was important for teaching and what concepts and skills needed
to be emphasized. The second team decided on grade level content in concept development and skill development. The second team also examined
textbooks and multimedia programs that might be of use. The third team
prepared methods of evaluation. The methods included minor testing, observing, interviewing, analysis of pupils' writing, and criterion measures within
a comprehensive framework of cognitive and affective evaluation. The first
draft of a report was then prepared for distribution.

The next step was pilot testing and revision. To these ends the fourth
team tried units and subunits in classrooms, having developed criteria for
judging their worth. The fourth team also was responsible for making changes
in the design and distributing the revised version. The fourth team then
planned for implementation of the design.

The design was implemented by reeducating the school staffs on group
and individual bases. A feature of this procedure was close personalization
of inservice teaching relative to the design.

The last step called for the participation of teachers and pupils in
demonstrating at public meetings their work products under terms of the
design, which was now in reportable form.[35]

EXAMPLE 2
Creating a Humane Environment Where Communication Is Improved

Curriculum planners in Cumberland County, a rural county of New Jersey,
proposed that a project be developed to make the elementary schools of the
county more humane by improving the ability of children to communicate
with one another and with adults. The thesis underlying this approach to
humanization was that children are likely to consider their teachers and the
other adults and children in their environment humane if these persons listen
to them and otherwise appear to honor and respect them. This humane attitude on the part of others presumably causes the children to feel better about
themselves and their potential. An ability that is especially helpful in improving one's feelings about oneself is competence in communicating effectively with other people. The planners of the project thus hypothesized that

the individual child's self-concept, together with selected, related skills of communication, could be improved by implementing a program of instruction that simultaneously emphasized enhancement of the child's self-concept and improvement of his or her communication skills. The planners thought of the proposed project as being in three parts: a curriculum planning segment directly affecting pupils, a planning segment in the inservice education of teachers and administrators, and an evaluation scheme encompassing the two preceding segments.

Five assumptions about people's needs were made:

1. Many disadvantaged minority group children and other disadvantaged children in the schools of the county have poor self-concepts.
2. The low self-esteem of these children tends to generate below-normal achievement in communication skills.
3. The below-normal achievement of these children tends to affect unfavorably their teachers' expectations concerning the children's ability to learn — especially to learn communication skills.
4. Some administrators tend to think in much the same ways as the teachers about disadvantaged children's ability to learn.
5. Some teachers and administrators are partially unaware of important considerations relative to learning and cultural differences.

Evidence was sought about the validity of each assumption, and in most cases clearly discovered.

The overall, most significant objective of the project was pupil-centered: to improve the self-concepts of disadvantaged minority group children and other disadvantaged children by enhancing their ability to communicate with other people. The specific objectives of teachers, which were intended always to relate to the major objective above, were formulated at the time each teaching unit or exercise was planned.

The Human Development Program, a commercially operated program in which personal awareness, mastery of tasks, and social interaction were the central themes and in which the Magic Circle was an instrumental idea, was utilized exclusively in attempting to improve the self-concepts of the children.

Because communication skill development was not provided for directly in the Human Development Program, it was necessary to prepare a series of pupil experiences relating self-concept development to concrete development of communication skills. Accordingly, this book's author and Cheryl D. Walker developed a series of communication exercises with four themes: getting ready for better speaking, writing, and listening; communicating to develop in individual children awareness of themselves and their environ-

ment; communicating to develop in individual children self-confidence and a sense of mastery; and communicating to improve social interaction.

The inservice experiences for adults were involved directly with the ideas and materials for self-concept and communication skill development described above. A programmed series of conferences and workshops for both teachers and administrators was conducted throughout an entire calendar year.

The plan for project evaluation was divided into two parts: the formative and the summative. The entire evaluation system, formative and summative, was intended to answer three questions:

1. *To what extent have the objectives of the project been met?*
2. *How is the curriculum content of the project, at pupil level and adult level, better (or worse) for pupils, teachers, and administrators than the ordinary or routine content?*
3. *What side effects has the project had, and how are these side effects better (or worse) than the corresponding previous conditions in the schools?*

Reports of the project, with full explanation of its design, appear in the Fifth Edition of this book (1982) and in ERIC document #ED 127 229. Chief co-planners of the project were John N. Falzetta, Jean K. Nocon, William D. Fenton, Patricia Horton, and Leon Trusty.

THE PURPOSES AND THE NATURE OF NEW CURRICULUM DESIGNS

New designs like the one just described are made with the obvious intention of improving education for children and youth. Elements of the curriculum wear out and need to be replaced. New knowledge usurps old knowledge and must be incorporated into the curriculum if education is to remain realistic and functional. New ways of teaching subject matter sometimes prove more satisfactory than the old ways and should therefore be highlighted. The thrill provided by the new may constitute at least a temporary reason for emphasizing it at the expense of the old. For these and other reasons, the curriculum is changed in pieces and parts.

Curriculum planners must decide what innovations they want and why they want them. The options are numerous. Much more can be done with the teaching of subject matter than has been done heretofore. The interests and concerns of pupils always make a promising source of new curriculum ideas. Parents, too, can make significant contributions of curriculum ideas.

Instrumental materials can easily become a focus as well as a medium for planning. Moral and spiritual teachings form a basis for projects in values education. The biographies of the great suggest lessons in affective education. Experimentation can be made the means of promoting innovation. Emphasis can be placed on learning process rather than on the products of learning. Attention can be given through new curriculum materials to preserving or reforming social systems. In brief, the possibilities are limited only by the scope of life itself.

Current Choices of Design Themes

Curriculum planners today are showing interest in what they consider most important in human life and behavior. Some planners continue to put extreme faith in the disciplines; others, in preparing learners to be vocationally competent; others, in getting learners ready to engage in constructive activities of direct benefit to our society; and still others, in helping learners develop enlightened self-interest. When practitioners in the schools are given encouragement, time, and opportunity to propose curriculum projects, they can, as the following list of project titles and themes suggests, create truly functional designs.

- Implementing Performance-Based Vocational Education
- Competency-Based Curriculum Development for Rural Secondary Schools in Alaska: A User's Guide
- Resource Guide for Performance-Based Drafting Instruction
- Research and Development Project in Career Education
- Innovations in Vocational Education: Meeting the Needs of the Handicapped
- New Experiences in Conservation Education
- Education Out There: Community Service Projects for Secondary School Pupils

Attempts at Creating Exemplary Designs

Perhaps everyone who casts about for a major curriculum plan is hoping to create a grand curriculum design that will become a model. The search for a grand design has been undertaken on several major occasions in the history of the curriculum movement. One of these was preparation of the Thirty Schools experiment; another was the proposal of a plan for the General College of the University of Minnesota. The Thirty Schools experiment, commonly called the Eight Year Study, was based on an attempt to answer four questions: What is to be done within the school? What subject matter is to be used in doing it? What plans of school organization and what classroom procedures are to be followed? How are the results to be appraised? The General College project gave attention to elements necessary in making a well-balanced curriculum: philosophy of life and education of those responsible for education programs, the needs of society and resources of the school, the needs and interests of students, and purpose or outcome.

These two attempts resulted in partial rather than comprehensive designs. Curriculum design, to be comprehensive, must show a pattern of relationships among numbers of elements of curriculum. A comprehensive design defines these elements and shows their interrelationships, states the means used for selecting and organizing learning experiences, and indicates the roles of teachers and other personnel in curriculum planning. It should show the emphasis given to subject matter for its own worth or importance versus the emphasis given to the needs of pupils, since these needs also are worthy and important. Certainly it should reveal the organizing centers around which elements of subject matter are to be taught. Also, a comprehensive design should clarify the roles of teachers, pupils, and aides in continuing the curriculum planning that inevitably goes on in classrooms. Teachers naturally want to know, "How free am I? How far can I go in making changes?" About pupils, curriculum planners should ask, "Are they more than sounding boards for determining how the curriculum is functioning? What other responsibilities should pupils have in curriculum development?"

Today as previously, curriculum planners often become convinced of the worth of plans for which philosophical support seems readily at hand. Perhaps the two most prominent emphases currently are the systems approach, based on a wish for order and careful management, and humane education, based on feeling for others in the educational process. These approaches are described briefly below. Details concerning them literally fill books.

Humane Education

According to James Beane and others, about one-fifth of a child's sense of self comes from his or her school experience. As children move upward through the stages of schooling, they tend to describe themselves more harshly. Nevertheless both elementary and secondary school pupils desire positive interaction with teachers and peers.[36] Because school is so important to pupils' self-perception, something should be done to make schooling more humane than it is in many classrooms.

The humanization of education is designed to take coldness, aloofness, joylessness, and negativism out of schooling. Humane practices and procedures encourage interaction among people in schools. The real key to humanization is the willingness of teachers and administrators to change their attitudes and consequently their practices. The curriculum in a humane school highlights experiences in displaying interest in other people, in having success, in evaluating cooperatively, in inquiring and discovering, and in living closely with others. Teachers give positive attention and praise to pupils within a school atmosphere of friendliness, openness, informality, and uninhibited communication. In the literature, this sort of education is referred to as humane education, education for humaneness, or education in human values.

Arthur W. Foshay discusses curriculum design in humane education as developing at the intersection of developmental attributes, which are intellectual, emotional, social, aesthetic, spiritual, and physical, with the intentions of teachers, which he designates as fluency, manipulation, confidence/value, and persistence.[37] Actual designs in humane education are few because meanings in this approach have not been clarified as carefully as meanings in most other current options and because commitment to humane education has not been intense. A sample design in humane education is the Cumberland County Project, reported earlier in this chapter.

The Systems Approach

The systems approach is a carefully guided and tightly operated plan for improving the curriculum. The primary connotation of the term *system* is interrelatedness; the parts of a total procedure are closely related to one another. Systems of education contain interrelated components like people, buildings, books, and equipment and are designed to create carefully planned changes in people's behavior.[38]

The systems approach is helpful in making decisions among alternatives. In general, this process consists initially of gathering criterion information about each alternative, applying "decision rules" or regulations (about, for example, regard for teacher rights) that must condition the final decision, choosing one alternative, reviewing this choice of alternative, and finally confirming or rejecting the choice. Following the application of this rigorous initial thinking process, three procedures are commonly available for use.

One procedure is called the Management Information System. It is designed to provide data about current performance, to suggest modification and adjustment of objectives, and to propose additions to and deletions from the present program.

A second procedure, originally known as the Planning-Programming-Budgeting System (PPBS) and more recently renamed the Planning, Programming, Budgeting, and Evaluation System (PPBES), projects programs into the future, answering the question "What would be the effect of _____?" The programmer provides information about subject matter, educational level, the target group of pupils, the object of the effort, specific activities planned, support services, and the like. PPBS focuses on planning according to aims and objectives, considering relative costs and anticipated benefits of alternative procedures, and basing future decisions on concrete findings. Inherent in the procedure are improvements in program through elimination, expansion, revision, and addition. PPBS is heavily cost oriented and therefore offends the sensibilities of curriculum planners who like to ignore costs whenever possible in the interest of other considerations. However, in an era of budget watching, this system and others like it will inevitably be used.

A third procedure is the relatively simpler Input-Output Analysis. The questions answered by this system are "What do we give?" and "What do we get?" These questions can be answered for several programs or projects that have been tried in a given school system. The answers tend to sharpen the judgment of decision makers, who must still make value judgments about elements of cost in relation to effectiveness, benefit, or utility.

After having used one or more of the three procedures, curriculum planners may use the critical path method in determining what routes to take in implementing decisions. The Program Evaluation and Review Technique (PERT) is a commonly used critical path charting method.[39] PERT is used for ordering events in planning to meet target dates. Developed in the late 1950s by the Navy and the Lockheed Aircraft Corporation and applied to the development of the Polaris Weapon System, PERT follows a six-step procedure, as follows:

1. Significant events in the accomplishment of a desired result are selected, defined, and stated specifically.
2. The necessary sequence and the interrelationships of events are determined. The events are noted on a flow chart called a network and are connected sequentially by arrows. No event is considered to be complete until its preceding events have occurred.
3. Each action is given three time values, the values being "optimistic," "most likely," and "pessimistic."
4. The three estimates of time value indicated in (3) are used in this formula to determine the anticipated time for completing an action: $t = (a + 4m + b) \div 6$, where a is optimistic, m is most likely, and b is pessimistic.
5. A computer is used to determine "critical path" by computing expected times along every possible path on the flow chart. Only by reducing the time of the critical path can the project be completed ahead of the scheduled time. However, taking some actions at parallel times or highlighting highly critical actions may reduce the time needed to complete the project.

6. Computer printouts provide information concerning need for corrective action while the PERTing process occurs.

A variation of PERTing extends systems-oriented planning in other directions. For example, it is now possible for the central office of a local school district to learn from the state department of education or a nearby university whether the scores in arithmetic earned on a standardized achievement test by pupils in the fourth grade of a given school would be improved more by adding another fourth-grade teacher or by securing the services of an arithmetic consultant.

The systems approach provides information that is not available throug ordinary putative methods. However, like other "managed" ways of proceeding, it does not create original ideas. Instead, it offers cues that lead to idea modification.

Additional Miscellaneous Designs

Curriculum literature is filling with discussions of new ideas underlying various kinds of designs. Some of the newer designs emphasize process as opposed to product in learning; others have a values orientation; others are directed toward reforming or revolutionizing the social system; and still others depend on changing school organization.

In the field, interesting designs—many of them unknown to curriculum specialists—are being worked out by teachers and administrators. One of these is a plan for instrumental learning prepared by one of the author's former students. Given a group of upper elementary school children and a group of four partially finished buildings (double-car garages on school grounds), he pondered what could be done to provide a worthwhile educational experience for these children. Suppose the four buildings were to be used as a science center, a workshop center, a home center, and a crafts center. What kinds of experiences might the children have in finishing, decorating, and furnishing the four buildings? After the buildings were completed, what might they learn about science, the industrial arts, home economics, and arts and crafts? What could be done about enterprises in on-campus gardening, masonry, well drilling, or even rocketry? The plan answered these questions within a framework that expressed the need for the project, the objectives of the proposed design, the nature of the subject matter to be learned, the kinds of experiences open to pupils, ways of evaluating the project as it progressed and after it was completed, and media for influencing other decision makers to help bring the plan to fruition.

The fun and the challenge of creating original curriculum designs are available to teachers, parents, pupils, and administrators who are willing to think and imagine beyond ordinary limits.

ACTIVITY 5-4
Identifying Curriculum Designs

Find in use in a school or else find in curriculum literature a description of a design that is characterized by one of the following:

1. Emphasis on preselected subject matter content
2. Attention to the interests and concerns of pupils
3. Reliance on sets of instructional materials
4. Emphasis on moral and spiritual teachings
5. Dependence on biographies of the great
6. Attention to experimentation in teaching and learning
7. Emphasis on process rather than on product
8. Attention to reforming or revolutionizing the social system
9. Emphasis on letting pupils mainly do as they wish
10. Dependence on changed organizational patterns.

Discuss.

SUMMARY

Decision making about how a curriculum should be designed is a complex matter. Usually it is helpful to follow a set series of steps in the designing process, although the steps are not invariable. Sources of ideas underlying curriculum planning need to be thought of in stating educational philosophy. Ideas and themes from society, and how they relate to the sources of beliefs, must be taken into consideration. After a period of preplanning, the need for a proposed program or project is considered, as is the "fit" of the proposal with the aims of the school or school system. Subsequent steps include stating objectives of the program or project, identifying evaluation means to suit the objectives, choosing a type of curriculum design, selecting learning content, determining and organizing pupils' learning experiences, and conducting an evaluation to indicate worth and quality.

Numerous curriculum designs are being created. Many of them are to be found within two categories: humane education and the systems approach.

ENDNOTES

1. Submitted, with a wish for anonymity, by a member of the school's Committee on Curriculum Planning.

2. M. Frances Klein and John I. Goodlad, "A Study of Curriculum Decision Making in Eighteen Selected Countries," National Academy of Education, Stanford, California, September 1978. Reported in ERIC document # ED 206 093.

3. Tom Simkins, "Some Management Implications of the Development of Curriculum Information Systems," *Journal of Curriculum Studies* 15, no. 1 (January-March 1983): 47–59.

4. See B. Othanel Smith, William O. Stanley, and J. Harlan Shores, *Fundamentals of Curriculum Development* (New York: Harcourt, Brace and World, 1957), pp. 529–44.

5. For further discussion of this and other curriculum sources, see National Society for the Study of Education, *Modern Philosophies and Education*, 54th Yearbook (Chicago: University of Chicago Press, 1955). Also see John S. Brubacher, *Modern Philosophies of Education*, rev. ed. (New York: McGraw-Hill, 1950).

6. Ralph W. Tyler, *Basic Principles of Curriculum and Instruction* (Chicago: University of Chicago Press, 1949).

7. From an interview with the authors, March 27, 1979.

8. Association for Supervision and Curriculum Development, "Is the Tyler Rationale a Suitable Basis for Current Curriculum Development?" *ASCD Update*, December 1980, pp. 4, 5.

9. See James S. Fogarty, "The Tyler Rationale: Support and Criticism," *Educational Technology* 16, no. 3 (March 1976): 31.

10. "Humanist Manifesto I," *The New Humanist* 6, no. 3 (May/June 1933).

11. "Humanist Manifesto II," *The Humanist* 33, no. 5 (September/October 1973).

12. Arthur W. Combs et al., *Humanistic Education: Objectives and Assessment* (Washington, D.C.: Association for Supervision and Curriculum Development, 1978), p. 9.

13. John D. Haas, *Future Studies in the K–12 Curriculum* (Ann Arbor, Mich.: ERIC Clearinghouse on Counseling and Personnel Services, 1980).

14. Nigel Grant, "Education for A.D. 2001: Science Fiction, Futurology and Educational Planning," *Scottish Educational Review* 13, no. 2 (November 1981): 91–104.

15. See Conrad F. Toepfer, Jr., "Curriculum Design and Neuropsychological Development," *Journal of Research and Development in Education* 15, no. 3 (Spring 1982): 1–11.

16. Billie J. Pietri, *Tangipahoa Parish Migrant Education 1982–1983 Program: Guidelines for Implementation* (Amite, La.: Tangipahoa Parish School Board, 1982).

17. Michinori Oki and Robert C. Brasted, *Fundamentals of Chemistry for the Non-Major in Tertiary Education: Minimum Principles for the Non-Science Specializing Citizen* (Minneapolis, Minn.: Japan Society for the Promotion of Science, 1981).

18. John Gough, "What Mathematics Should Be Taught to Gifted Children?" *Australian Mathematics Teacher* 36, no. 4 (January 1981): 7–10.

19. *NASSP Newsletter* 27, no. 6 (February 1980): 4.

20. Gail McCutcheon, "The Curriculum: Patchwork or Crazy Quilt?" *Educational Leadership* 36, no. 2 (November 1978): 114–16.

21. Klein and Goodlad.

22. Diana J. Davis and Jean M. Silvernail, "Levels and Types of Curriculum and Instructional Design Skills Presently Offered in Pennsylvania Teacher Education Programs," an address at the annual meeting of the American Educational Research Association, Los Angeles, April 1981. Reported in ERIC document # ED 207 950.

23. Douglas D. Christensen, "Curriculum Development: A Function of Design and Leadership," *The Executive Review* 1, no. 3 (December 1980): 2–8.

24. See also John D. McNeil and Louis Laosa, "Needs Assessment and Cultural Pluralism in Schools," *Educational Technology* 15, no. 12 (December 1975): 26.

25. Northern California Program Development Center, "Goal Card" (Chico, Calif.: The Center, 1971).

26. Lawrence M. Downey, *The Task of Public Education* (Chicago: Midwest Administration Center, University of Chicago, 1960), pp. 22–26.

27. Ralph W. Tyler, "Purposes for Our Schools," *Bulletin of the National Association of Secondary School Principals* 52, no. 332 (1968): 1–12.

28. Ronald C. Doll, "Alternative Forms of Schooling," *Educational Leadership* 29, no. 5 (February 1972): 391–93.

29. Helen F. Durio, "Behavioral Objectives: Where Have They Taken Us?" *Clearing House* 49, no. 5 (January 1976): 202.

30. Robert I. Wise, "The Use of Objectives in Curriculum Planning: A Critique of Planning by Objectives" (Address delivered at the annual meeting of the American Educational Research Association, Washington, D.C., April 1975).

31. William Strong, "The Ant and the Grasshopper: A Didactic (and Somewhat Moral) Fable," *Media and Materials* 11, no. 7 (March 1975): 26.

32. L. Thomas Hopkins, *Interaction: The Democratic Process* (Boston: D.C. Heath, 1941), p. 218. Used with permission of the author. Compare Gail M. Inlow, *The Emergent in Curriculum*, 2nd ed. (New York: John Wiley, 1973).

33. Virgil E. Herrick et al., *The Elementary School* (© 1956), pp. 110–11. Reprinted by permission of Prentice-Hall, Inc., Englewood Cliffs, N.J.

34. Ibid., pp. 110–12. The origin of this material is Herrick et al., *The Elementary School* (Englewood Cliffs, N.J.: Prentice-Hall, 1956).

35. David S. Martin, "Reinventing the Curriculum Wheel," *Educational Leadership* 39, no. 2 (November 1981): 130, 131.

36. James A. Beane, Richard P. Lipka, and Joan W. Ludewig, "Synthesis of Research on Self-concept," *Educational Leadership* 38, no. 1 (October 1980): 84–89.

37. Arthur W. Foshay, "Curriculum Design for a Humane School," *Theory into Practice* 10 (June 1971): 204–7.

38. See, for example, J. Alan Thomas, *The Productive School: A Systems Analysis Approach to Educational Administration* (New York: John Wiley, 1971).

39. Carleton A. Shore, "PERT Philosophy and the Curriculum Supervisor," *Education* 102, no. 1 (Fall 1981): 77–81.

SELECTED BIBLIOGRAPHY

Association for Supervision and Curriculum Development. *What Are the Sources of the Curriculum?* Washington, D.C.: The Association, 1962.

Beauchamp, George A. *Curriculum Theory.* 3rd ed. Wilmette, Ill.: Kagg Press, 1975.

Brown, Janet F., ed. *Curriculum Planning for Young Children.* Washington, D.C.: National Association for Childhood Education, 1982.

Casciano-Savignano, C. Jennie. *A Systems Approach to Curriculum and Instructional Improvement.* Columbus, Ohio: Merrill, 1978.

Eisner, Eliot W. *The Educational Imagination: On the Design and Evaluation of School Programs.* New York: Macmillan, 1979.

Foshay, Arthur W., ed. *Considered Action for Curriculum Improvement.* 1980 Yearbook, Association for Supervision and Curriculum Development. Washington, D.C.: The Association, 1980.

Gilchrist, Robert, and Roberts, Bernice R. *Curriculum Development: A Humanized Systems Approach.* Belmont, Calif.: Fearon, 1974.

Golby, Michael; Greenwald, Jane; and West, Ruth, eds. *Curriculum Design.* New York: John Wiley, 1975.

Hooper, Richard, ed. *Curriculum: Context, Design, and Development.* New York: Longmans, 1971.

Hunkins, Francis P. *Curriculum Development: Program Planning and Improvement.* Columbus, Ohio: Merrill, 1980.

Lucas, Christopher J. *Challenge and Choice in Contemporary Education.* New York: Macmillan, 1976.

Petty, Walter T. *Curriculum for the Modern Elementary School.* Chicago: Rand McNally, 1976.

Pratt, David. *Curriculum: Design and Development.* New York: Harcourt, 1980.

Rist, Ray C. *Restructuring American Education: Innovations and Alternatives.* New York: Transaction, 1973.

Snyder, Benson R. *The Hidden Curriculum.* New York: Knopf, 1971.

Swenson, Esther J., ed. *A Look at Continuity in the School Program.* 1958 Yearbook. Association for Supervision and Curriculum Development. Washington, D.C.: The Association, 1958.

Tanner, Daniel, and Tanner, Laurel. *Curriculum Development: Theory into Practice.* New York: Macmillan, 1975.

Thomas, J. Alan. *The Productive School: A Systems Analysis Approach to Educational Administration.* New York: Wiley, 1971.

Tyler, Ralph W. *Basic Principles of Curriculum and Instruction.* Chicago: University of Chicago Press, 1950.

Warwick, David. *Curriculum Structure and Design.* Mystic, Conn.: Lawrence Verry, 1975.

Weinstein, Gerald, and Fantini, Mario D. *Toward Humanistic Education: A Curriculum of Affect.* New York: Praeger, 1970.

Wilson, L. Craig. *The Open Access Curriculum.* Boston: Allyn and Bacon, 1971.

6

Evaluation of Curriculum Programs and Projects

Chapter 5 emphasized the importance of designing programs and projects intelligently and functionally. Casual mention was made of the significance of evaluating thoroughly any program or project that is introduced. The current chapter is devoted entirely to evaluation.

Professional literature about evaluation as a general theme exists in profusion, but relatively little has been written about evaluating programs and projects intended to improve the curriculum.[1] As a consequence, ways of evaluating programs and projects have not always been as sophisticated as they might have been, and many major actions to improve the curriculum have been evaluated poorly when they have been evaluated at all. Extraneous considerations like the prestige of the author of a proposal have sometimes been permitted to replace evidence of the proposal's real effectiveness.

Two reasons are commonly advanced for the need to evaluate curriculum improvement programs and projects. One is the significance to participants of knowing what they have accomplished. This knowledge tends to improve their morale and supply guideposts by which they may plot further action. The other reason is the need to justify expenditures of time, talent, and money—expenditures about which curriculum leaders are likely to be questioned at any time.

Evaluation may be defined as a broad and continuous effort to inquire into the effects of utilizing educational content and process according to clearly defined goals. In terms of this definition, evaluation may be expected to go beyond simple measurement and also beyond simple application of the evaluator's values and beliefs. If evaluation is to be a broad and continuous effort, it must rely on a variety of instruments used according to carefully ascribed purposes.

EVALUATION AS IT IS GENERALLY KNOWN IN SCHOOLS

Teachers, administrators, and other school personnel commonly think of evaluation in three terms: the evaluation of pupil progress by teachers in classrooms; the evaluation of schools and school systems by outside agencies, usually for purposes of checkup but also as part of national, state, or regional projects; and the evaluation by the National Assessment of Educational Progress and state departments of education, often called national testing and state testing.

Evaluation in the Classroom

The classroom may, in fact, become the site of important data gathering that leads to curriculum improvement and that assists with the evaluation of programs and projects already under way. Within the classroom, curriculum leaders can help teachers administer evaluation instruments and then help them interpret the results. The instruments that are most often used fall within the following categories:

Achievement tests	Personality inventories
Anecdotal records	Projective techniques
Appreciation tests	Rating scales
Aptitude tests	Semiprojective techniques
Attitude inventories	Sociometric devices
Checklists	Tests of mental ability
Diagnostic tests	(intelligence)
Interview schedules	Vocational interest inventories
Observation schedules	

Teachers who are unfamiliar with standardized instruments in any of these categories are in obvious need of help from curriculum or guidance personnel.

Every day teachers informally evaluate on the basis of their own tests or their own subjective judgment. In its informal sense evaluation is simply a part of living. Inasmuch as we are all being evaluated with great frequency, everyone needs to become familiar with evaluation instruments that are fair and accurate. Teachers must improve their own evaluation skills and also help their pupils respond effectively to evaluation instruments. The teacher's self-evaluation of his or her own work offers one of the most promising ways of improving schools. Teachers need help in studying the differences between their intent and the outcomes they are achieving. Their objectives may need changing or amending; their methods may be faulty. To know that such circumstances exist, teachers need to observe skillfully and to record data carefully. Because the evaluation process, including self-evaluation, is probably an unfamiliar one, supervisors and administrators should be prepared to help teachers at any point in the process.

The reasoning of professional evaluators is not always understood by people in the schools. There, program evaluation and standardized testing are often considered to be synonymous. King and Thompson made a study of program evaluation as seen by school administrators, chiefly principals and superintendents. One thousand six hundred administrators were asked to participate. Of the 686 who responded to the evaluation instruments, 61 percent said that program evaluations are useful. More superintendents than principals were represented in this 61 percent; principals, especially in large school districts, were more skeptical than favorable. Most of the respondents said that information from the evaluations was being used, though 28 percent of them thought the evaluations had not succeeded in getting to what they really needed to know. It was clear that practitioners within the schools had too little contact with the program evaluators.[2]

Evaluation of Whole Schools and School Systems

Entire schools and school systems may be involved in evaluation in the form of surveys, opinion polls, follow-up studies of graduates and early school leavers, use of standard evaluation instruments, and large cooperative projects. Teachers are aware that omnibus studies are being made, but they frequently have little part in them except to answer a few questions and demonstrate their teaching skills for a few minutes. The studies are usually conducted by agencies outside the local school district; the evaluators are usually strangers.

Surveys

Comprehensive studies of schools and school systems resulting in recommendations for their improvement are called surveys. Teams of university staff members and the personnel of survey firms have customarily conducted surveys from the outside looking in. After a series of visits, conferences, and interviews, the surveyors usually prepare printed or mimeographed reports to communicate their findings and recommendations. Within recent years external surveys have been partially replaced by self-surveys and cooperative surveys.

In self-surveys, staff members of school systems organize to study their own curriculum and facilities. Often they use as criteria the objectives of teaching and learning that they have previously developed or that they have borrowed from educational literature or other school systems.

Cooperative surveys represent a compromise between external surveys and self-surveys. They call for the joint efforts of school system personnel and specially employed external surveyors. Cooperative surveys are said to avoid some of the disadvantages of both external surveys and self-surveys. External surveyors sometimes know so little about the institution being surveyed that their reports contain inaccuracies. On the other hand, self-surveys show incompleteness and improper balance because local personnel frequently lack the necessary experience and vision for the survey task. Cooperative surveys tend to bring together the understandings and skills required.

Opinion Polls

A second procedure for studying curricula of schools and school systems is relatively quick and informal. It consists of asking people within and outside the schools what they think of various aspects of schooling. Opinion polls have been used comprehensively by several polling firms. For instance, the Gallup organization regularly asks people throughout the nation what they think of their schools. In individual school districts the purpose of opinion polls is often to discover agreement regarding strengths and weaknesses of school curricula. Polls have certain public relations values, and they may set the stage for curriculum improvement. Teachers and administrators often use opinion polls to identify points along the educational front at which gains can be made with maximum public support.

Follow-up Studies

Both graduates and early school leavers are the subject of follow-up studies of educational, occupational, and personal accomplishments. These studies help to answer questions like the following:

1. What kinds of experiences do graduates and early school leavers believe the schools should offer their pupils?
2. To what extent have the schools in question offered these experiences?
3. How well has subject matter content been taught within the range of these experiences?
4. How successful have graduates and early school leavers been in applying to life situations what the schools have taught them?
5. What modifications in the school program should be made for similar groups and individuals in the future?

High school guidance personnel sometimes make statistical follow-up studies of college students and business employees who are graduates of their schools. These studies are often so superficial that one wishes more studies could be made in depth. Deeper studies could include assembling individual alumni and small groups of alumni for interviews, conferences, and meetings to reveal genuine feelings and to develop creative ideas about appropriate schooling for children and youth of varied backgrounds.

Use of Standard Evaluation Instruments

Evaluation of several areas of the curriculum may be accomplished by using standard evaluation instruments. Perhaps the most widely used is a document called *Evaluative Criteria*, which was prepared by the Cooperative Study of Secondary School Standards assisted by the American Council on Education, the National Association of Secondary School Principals, the National Education Association, and the United States Office of Education. It is applied by a half-dozen regional accrediting associations, such as the Western Association of Colleges and Secondary Schools and the comparable New England Association. The evaluators who use it review each school's curriculum organization or design, its pupil activities, its plant, its administration, its guidance and library services, and its faculty personnel. Standard questions arranged within categories are asked about every school in which the *Criteria* is made the evaluation document.

State departments of education often develop their own evaluation instruments. Regional associations like the Southern Association make cooperative evaluations of schools; the instruments they use become nationally known and are borrowed throughout the country. Study groups in New England, the Southwest, and elsewhere have tried to prepare comprehensive instruments. Standard evaluation instruments meant to be generally applicable are obviously not tailored to the evaluation needs of any one particular school. Therefore, when they are used they should be supplemented with questions and other evaluation items that conform with the situation in the school being evaluated.

Large Cooperative Evaluation Projects

School systems sometimes have opportunities to participate in evaluation and research projects that are of national, regional, or statewide scope. The federal government, universities, foundations, educational associations, and private business concerns are among the agencies now sponsoring large-scale projects. Government funds, foundation grants, and private capital have been moving increasingly into what is nominally evaluation and research activity. Developing spelling lists, experimenting with educational television, and trying out materials to be published by major instructional projects are three of the activities that have been under way in numbers of school systems at the same time.

During the past half century several large projects have been developed in elementary and secondary schools. In 1933 thirty schools engaged in a study of the relationship between high school and college that was known as the Eight Year Study.[3] The Stanford Social Education Investigation—regional in scope—was carried out by Stanford University with a grant from the General Education Board to encourage experimentation in social studies teaching and to stimulate cooperation in curriculum study between school systems and the university.[4]

National Assessment and Statewide Testing

The National Assessment of Educational Progress, begun in 1964 as an agency for nationwide testing of pupils' skills, understandings, and attitudes, has some effect on what is taught in individual schools. Governed by the Education Commission of the States, a nonprofit organization of legislators, governors, and educators financed by the United States Office of Education and the Ford and Carnegie Foundations, the NAEP has tested samplings of pupils aged nine, twelve, and seventeen, as well as young adults twenty-six to thirty-five years of age, in ten academic areas within five-year cycles. The questions asked in the ten areas—science, mathematics, reading, writing, social studies, citizenship, literature, art, music, and career and occupational development—have partly determined, in those schools where the tests are being administered, what teachers consider worth teaching.

The thoroughness with which National Assessement operates is indicated by the series of steps taken by the evaluators in developing the assessment program. The first step was the determination of educational objectives for each academic area. Every usable objective had to be considered (1) important by scholars in the academic area or subject field, (2) acceptable by school personnel for use in schools, and (3) desirable by groups of lay persons. The second step was the laborious preparation of evaluation items. The third step was the random selection of schools, pupils, and out-of-school personnel for participation in the testing. The test items, ranging from easy to difficult, are theoretically not to be used for comparison among persons, schools, school districts, or states. No norms or individual scores are reported, and the data are analyzed in census form by region of the nation, size and kind of community, parents' education, color, and sex. The NAEP releases to school systems and state departments of education numbers of test items used in recent testings. Therefore it is possible for teachers to teach subject matter in anticipation of the nature of future tests. Some curriculum personnel regard this fact as a warning that a national curriculum looms as a threat to the determination of curriculum in the individual school.

The magnitude and significance of National Assessment are reflected in the following data. In 750 school districts in thirty states, 90,000 pupils in 1,500 individual schools took assessment tests during the period from October 1983 through May 1984. The pupils tested included eighth graders and thirteen-year-olds in other grades, fourth graders and nine-year-olds in other grades, and, at high school level, eleventh graders and seventeen-year-olds in other grades. The test administrators sought to achieve a proper mix of geographic areas and ethnic backgrounds. After the testing, information about the results, "the nation's report card," was distributed in a number of ways.[5]

The efficiency with which this national program of testing and evaluation has operated has encouraged a number of the states to install programs of statewide testing. Sometimes the purpose is comparison of schools, with the hope of reducing the number of ineffective ones. Sometimes it is improvement of teaching, so that the high school diploma will have more meaning than it has had in recent years. Whatever the purpose, teachers and administrators soon feel the influence of statewide testing, and the power of state departments of education inevitably increases.

SOME PRINCIPLES AND PRACTICES OF EVALUATION

It should be obvious from the preceding discussion that evaluation has remained, for most teachers and administrators, a peripheral function in which they have had no real part. The exception, of course, has been evaluation of pupil progress in classrooms. Although teachers and administrators have participated in planning new programs and projects, the planners have too often given little thought to their evaluation. As a consequence, the curriculum has come to resemble a boat accumulating barnacles. The accretion of unevaluated material has added weight, but nothing has been done to provide streamlining. Evaluation gauges worth, thereby permitting some programs and projects to be retained and others to be eliminated.

When evaluation of programs and projects is conducted in schools, it ranges from the highly informal to the highly formal. At a basic level of informality it consists of judging, estimating, or giving opinions about the extent to which certain changes in school programs have occurred. At the more formal level it involves carefully collecting and treating data about progress toward prescribed goals. In all circumstances it has as an important characteristic the collection of evidence of some sort. This evidence may indicate merely that movement has occurred from the beginning to the end of an allotted period of time, or it may indicate the presence of carefully directed, goal-oriented movement. The difference between the two is usually a difference between aimless movement and purposeful action.

Thus, the nature of evidence varies with respect to an informality-formality continuum. For instance, an evaluator may judge informally that people's attitudes have changed in a given direction by observing one or two behavioral cues, or he or she may undertake a formal evaluation of attitude change by conducting interviews and observations and by administering attitude inventories, with all instruments having been chosen or developed to suit given purposes. Formality thus implies scholarly care.

Presence of Values and Valuing

One of the characteristics of evaluation is the acknowledged presence of values and valuing. The act of valuing—a conscious recognition and expression of the values that an evaluator holds—is a necessary initial step in the evaluation process. For instance, the Council for Basic Education values intellectual experience in the three Rs for elementary school children at the expense of certain social and emotional experiences in the school program. Accordingly the Council encourages inquiry that discovers the virtues of intellectual rigor. Whenever an evaluation project is initiated by any group, it expresses beliefs the group holds about what is worth evaluating. At the conclusion of the evaluation episode, the investigators make value judgments regarding the effects of the episode. These value judgments help determine what will be investigated next and on subsequent occasions.

Orientation to Goals

A related characteristic of evaluation is orientation to goals. Without setting a goal one cannot tell much about the nature and direction of one's progress or achievement. A thorough program of education subscribes to many goals: information getting, understanding, skill development, feeling and perceiving, critical thinking, and attitude change. When goals have been adopted, ways of evaluating their achievement should be considered immediately. Achievement of goals is accomplished by designing experiences that fit or accord with the goals; then the effects of experiences can be evaluated with reference to the goals. Consistency of both evaluation devices and learning experiences with an established list of goals is a necessity of good educational planning that is too often ignored.

Comprehensiveness

Another characteristic of effective evaluation is comprehensiveness. Evaluation must, as we have seen, be as broad as the goals to which it relates. Making it broad is not easy, a fact indicated by the difficulties one encounters in evaluating changes in attitudes and appreciations. To be comprehensive, evaluation must make use of numerous and varied media, some of which may have to be invented.

Continuity

Still another characteristic of thoroughgoing evaluation is continuity. In most education textbooks the chapter on evaluation appears at the end of the book. The consequent implication might be that evaluation comes last in an educational enterprise. Actually, it should be frequent and recurrent, continual if not continuous. It is needed at almost every stage of every enterprise, and it should be accomplished with imagination, skill, and appropriateness.

Diagnostic Worth, Validity, and Reliability

Appropriateness of evaluation suggests a need for two additional, related characteristics—diagnostic worth and validity. Instruments of evaluation must be capable of diagnosing specific aspects of educational situations. In this sense they should achieve "diagnostic fit." The instruments should also be valid; they should have the ability to describe what they purport to describe. Needless to say, many instruments in use today lack validity and also reliability, which—as applied to the curriculum—consists of ability to measure the effects of an educational experience accurately on repeated occasions.

Integration of Findings

Finally, evaluation should serve to integrate findings about educational phenomena. The ultimate object of evaluating is *not* to leave data in a diverse and unintegrated state but to combine significant findings so their real meaning is evident. Organization and interpretation of data thus become important tasks in evaluation, creating that desirable characteristic called integration.

Progress toward Goals

Inasmuch as evaluation is concerned with progress toward goals, it is important to know whether, when, how, and in what directions progress is occurring. To this end, criteria of progress like the following need to be established:

1. Are we really moving toward our goals? (*Theme:* perceptibility of movement)
2. How much movement is present? (*Theme:* time and space)
3. How fast is movement occurring? (*Theme:* rate)
4. What, precisely, can be said about direction(s) of movement? (*Theme:* directed and aberrant motion)
5. How does the general movement we have discovered relate to other movements toward change or improvement? (*Theme:* relevance within the whole complex of improvement)

These criteria have implications for the nature and the evaluation of curriculum improvement programs and projects. They imply that such programs and projects should "get somewhere" and should move as far within their allotted lifespans as possible. In the United States we expect movement to be rapid. However, movement may not always occur in a straight line—variations in movement may create significant side effects that supply new outlets for study and growth. Fundamental movement, with its variations, almost inevitably relates to other movements, and effects of the whole complex of movements should be seen in perspective.

DIMENSIONS OF PROGRAM AND PROJECT EVALUATION

The sweep of planning for program evaluation has been described by Bowers. It begins with concerns and questions with which the evaluation might deal, and proceeds to a summary of information about the program to be evaluated. Further planning includes three steps: making elements of the program clear, determining priorities for further planning of the evaluation, and arranging for the collection and use of evidence. Each of these planning steps encompasses outcomes anticipated for learners, the nature of curriculum content, the way the content is sequenced, the instructional approach used, and the extent and nature of program support.[6] When an evaluation plan has been finally reviewed, it should be ready to be put into operation.

Somewhere in the planning process, a major question must be answered: How much of a given program or project should be evaluated? This is a question of quantity or scope. It is relevant because many programs and projects are large—too large to be evaluated as thoroughly as one might like.

A parallel question is one of quality of the evaluation: What goals are being highlighted in the evaluation because attainment of these goals is believed to ensure the worth of the program or project?

The Dimension of Quantity

Programs are larger than projects because projects are meant to fit into the general scheme of things, each project being part of a program. An important decision about programs is whether one should elect to evaluate the whole program comprehensively yet superficially, or concentrate on carefully selected aspects of the program for thorough evaluation. Most projects, on the other hand, can be evaluated as a whole, but the series of steps in the evaluation is carefully limited and defined.

Evaluating the Whole Program

The amount or portion of a program to evaluate is a matter for careful consideration. It is possible to evaluate programs generally. Such evaluation is often of a survey sort and is necessarily superficial. Nevertheless the survey helps participants in curriculum improvement see "the whole forest" in which they work. When the goals of a program have been determined, criteria under general headings, such as those proposed by the Association for Supervision and Curriculum Development, should be prepared with direct reference to the goals. Under several general headings—Educational Objectives, Role Perception, Organizational Structure, Group Action and Morale, Experimentation, Communication, Resources, and Evaluation— the Association has listed specific criteria of effective leadership for program improvement. Criteria noted under the heading Group Action and Morale are typical of the specific criteria that appear under the general headings:

GROUP ACTION AND MORALE

1. Administrative officials encourage cooperative planning and deliberation by school staff and other groups.

2. Groups evidence movement toward mutually held goals, productivity in achieving these goals, and maintenance of group solidarity.
3. Individuals and subgroups evidence high morale as they work together.
4. Human relations skills are in evidence in all aspects of the school's functioning.
5. The staff acts rationally in resolving issues and in seeking solutions to problems.
6. Qualities that enhance interaction of persons in the group may be decribed in terms such as initiative, originality, communication, empathy, cooperation, understanding, cohesiveness, morale, productivity.
7. Decisions regarding program changes are cooperatively made on the basis of the most objective data obtainable.
8. The total staff is encouraged toward realizing its potential.
9. Teachers encountering teaching or other difficulties feel free to seek assistance.[7]

Criteria may be made more general than these. For example, only five general criteria were stated and justified by reference to educational literature in evaluating effects of the International Paper Company Foundation's assistance to secondary education in six school districts:

Criterion I: In the total context of the teaching-learning situation there should be provided, through varied subject matter, materials, and methods, opportunities for individual pupils to acquire habits, skills, information, and attitudes which will aid them to become contributing citizens in a democracy.

Criterion II: The organizational, administrative, and supervisory pattern, through cooperative planning, implementation, and evaluative procedures, promotes the continuous improvement of the school program and the competence of the professional staff.

Criterion III: The members of the professional staff display a unity of purpose, a sense of worth, and an appreciation of their efforts, and those of others, in the improvement of the school program.

Criterion IV: Student personnel services should result in a continuous process of pupils, parents, teachers, counselors, and other specialists working together to assist each pupil in achieving greater self-understanding, self-direction, and self-realization in a democratic society.

Criterion V: The school, through community study, interpretation of the school program, use of community resources, and working closely with lay citizens, strives to become an integral part of community life.[8]

Fenwick English has suggested a set of criteria to be used in making an educational performance audit. The criteria concern (1) the control the school district has over programs, resources, and staffs; (2) the viability of the objectives; (3) the presence of curriculum documents; (4) the uses made of data in correcting deficiencies; and (5) the evident improvement of pupil learning. Data are gathered by independent evaluators who visit the schools, interview personnel, and examine curriculum documents.[9] However, evaluation specialists find audit-taking of this sort casual and imprecise.

When criteria are too numerous, their use in evaluation becomes an unduly protracted affair. When they are too few, the evaluator may have to search out their meanings before he or she can use them concretely in evaluation.

Once an evaluator has stated his or her achievement goals and the criteria for evaluating them, he or she has taken only a limited first step in the evaluation process. Henry S. Dyer emphasizes the importance of taking all possible features of the evaluation subject and all possible influences on this subject into account when evaluation is being accomplished. Speaking of evaluating programs in reading, he says:

> One has to compare how the students are reading at any given point in their schooling with how well they were reading at some earlier point, for it is the amount of *change* in their reading ability that begins to provide an indication of the effectiveness of instruction. But this is not all. One must also know with considerable specificity the innumerable things that went on inside and outside the school that might have facilitated or impeded the change. And until one knows these things as best one may, all the agony and energy that goes into the evaluation of the schools is apt to be something less than totally fruitful in showing us how to do better tomorrow than we are doing today.[10]

So the evaluator cannot be satisfied merely with discovering that change has occurred. He or she needs to know all the conditions, or as many as possible, that have surrounded and in any way been responsible for the change. In this sense, quality of evaluation is seriously affected by the quantity of it. It is possible, as Dyer points out, to blunder seriously if only part of what should be done is done, and if the conclusions the evaluator eventually draws proceed from data in which there are large gaps.

Evaluating Component Elements of a Program

Despite the temptations and dangers, evaluators often seek to evaluate component elements of a program in depth. Here their purpose is not merely to avoid the potential sloppiness or incompleteness of whole-program evaluation or to avoid expending time and energy. They seek to "cut away clean" a section of the program so they may evaluate it with care, then possibly isolate another section for evaluation. Each section or part has, presumably, a peculiar identity or separateness about it. Sometimes evaluators make their evaluation of component elements first and then go on to evaluate the program as a whole. Evaluating a portion of the program may provide a slanted view of the whole, but careful concentration on it can yield more valid returns than whole-program evaluation usually yields.

Evaluation of parts of programs has to do with the usefulness of subject matter in achieving desired results, usefulness of materials, effectiveness of school organization and groupings of pupils, and the worth of the process by which given programs are conducted. Another way of subdividing the total evaluation task is to evaluate just learners, or educational environments, or learning, or instruction. Evaluating learners consists of studying pupil achievement and performance. Evaluating educational environments deals with characteristics of the curriculum and of school and community influences on learning in the school. Evaluation of learning is a study of changes in pupil behavior as a consequence of instruction. Evaluation of instruction includes study of pupil characteristics within a set of environmental circumstances as they affect learning. Instead of dealing directly with questions of learning and instruction, some evaluators have tried gauging programs in terms of their effects on teacher performance or their effects on teachers' attitudes toward their work.

One example of the evaluation of a part of a total program is the evaluation of a component element in a new reading program: the series of reading materials used in the program. Questions to be answered include the following: How useful is the series in helping achieve the program goals? With what segments of the pupil population is the series most effective? How does the series compare with the miscellaneous reading materials used in the program when the contributions of all the materials to the attainment of program goals are assessed?

Another program element often needing evaluation is the effectiveness of the delivery system. The question here is not "How effective has the program proved to be?" but "How effectively has the program been put into place?" To answer the latter question, evaluators should begin by selecting indicators of effective delivery. Two of the most common and most satisfactory kinds of indicators are observation of applicable teacher behaviors and observation of applicable pupil behaviors. For example, what does the teacher do to offer alternative instructional approaches, to connect new learning with former learning, to stimulate pupils to action, to supply a variety of correctives, to give pupils opportunities to show their increasing abilities? Meanwhile, what do the pupils do to demonstate enthusiasm and involvement, to ask for help when it's needed, to show ability to solve their own classroom problems, to indicate mastery of project learnings?[11] Balanced use of indicators like these can result in a complex of findings that helps to explain the effectiveness or ineffectiveness of a program.

Evaluating a Curriculum Project

A curriculum project, as defined here, is a part of a whole curriculum program, but it is a special part. For example, the curriculum program in District K had been in operation for years. In 1976 the program included the activity of four task forces and two study groups. Suddenly in 1977, funds were made available by the state department of education for a work dear to the hearts of members of the program's steering committee. The steering committee voted unanimously to have its project designers plan a special project, which was funded handsomely by the state. The special project was considered to be a part of District K's ongoing curriculum improvement program, but it was a special part with its own goals, ground rules, personnel, equipment, materials, and funding. Because of requirements made by the funding agency, it had to be evaluated separately from the program as a whole.

The process often used in evaluating a curriculum project can best be expressed in a series of steps. Assuming that needs assessment, which helps to justify the project, has already occurred, the first major step is to define the goals of the project. This step usually has two components—making a workable statement of the objectives of the project and identifying quantitative measures to be used in evaluating performance relative to the objectives. Great care is needed in stating the project objectives. The Educational Testing Service has found that the goals as first stated by program and project planners often bear only a slight resemblance to what the program or project in fact does.[12]

The second step in the process is to collect the data necessary for determining the project's effectivenes. The data may include findings about pupil characteristics; about the nature of the project and the processes used in it—its duration and the varied treatments it provides groups of pupils, for example; about the cost of resources committed to the project; and about pupil performance as revealed, for instance, by standardized test scores and dropout rates.

The third and final step is to determine the cost-effectiveness of the project. Here, levels of progress toward achieving the project's goals are noted against amounts of resources used in reaching these levels. If pouring in additional resources produces no better results, the maximum extent of desirable resource input has been reached.

The Dimension of Quality

Some Pertinent Steps

Clearly, improving the quality of evaluation is a major need. Reliable evaluation data will help the curriculum worker determine whether to continue a program or to abandon it. In the hope of ensuring quality in evaluation procedures, evaluators have sometimes used a sequence of steps:

1. The goals of the program are specified, along with the desired outcomes and alternative ways in which these outcomes might be achieved.
2. A sample of pupils is selected for the evaluation study. These pupils should be representative of all the pupils who will be exposed to the program.
3. Pupils in the sample are "measured" to determine their status with respect to relevant characteristics. For example, their levels of achievement are sought, and their learning skills gauged. Since pupil characteristics go *into* the evaluation design, they are called *input variables*.
4. The program is tried with the sample of pupils. Since alternative ways of proceeding are built into the program for the sake of evaluating it, portions of the sample of pupils will receive separate "treatments."
5. The effects of the alternative treatments are now gauged. This monitoring goes on while the program is under way and is often referred to as *formative evaluation*. Evaluation occurs also at the conclusion of the treatment process. This is *summative evaluation*. To accomplish evaluation of both kinds, tests, inventories, interviews, planned observations, and other means are used.
6. The results, or *outputs*, are reviewed, and conclusions are drawn.
7. The conclusions dictate what shall be done with all or part of the program. The program may be continued in its present form, modified according to what has been discovered in the evaluation process, or abandoned. If it is continued without change, or modified for survival, it may well be subjected to future evaluation.

Prior to the start of a program or project, judgmental data supplied by experts can be helpful in determining the probable worth of the proposal. Experts are asked to express in writing their views of the proposal, their views are assembled and a consensus formed, and modifications are made in the proposal to conform to the consensus. The modified proposal is then returned to the experts for final commentary.[13]

Formative evaluation, previously referred to in Chapter 5 as evaluation done in process to improve the quality of ongoing curriculum projects (and also to permit experimentation with evaluation instruments), has proved to be an important resource in refining evaluation procedures. In its ability to improve the quality of evaluation, the formative stage surpasses the summative stage, not only because formative evaluation is clearly involved in the development of the project but also because summative evaluation may not account for the impact on learners of "the ever-moving, ever-changing nature of curriculum."[14]

Difficulties in Managing Variables

Within the process of evaluation, there are three classes of variables: input variables—what pupils bring with them; output variables—what pupils have when they come away from instruction; and treatment variables—teaching methods, emphases in subject matter, class size, characteristics of fellow pupils, and characteristics of teachers. When output variables relate directly to the objectives of the instruction, they are called *criterion measures*. The three classes of variables interact. Thus, pupil characteristics (input) affect school climate (treatment); differing methods of teaching (treatment) affect pupil achievement (output); pupils with given characteristics (input) succeed in a given project (output). The complications are startling.[15]

Specialists in educational evaluation can usually find variables in need of control. For instance, a commentator on a social studies project in St. Louis identified eight variables and related difficulties that the project managers did not take into account: differences among districts in which the project was tried, differences among participating teachers, the effects of administrative liaison, goal ambiguity, conflicts in teacher roles, inadequacy of conceptual skills, complexities in administering the project, and defects in conceptual design.[16]

In other projects, involvement of given personnel as opposed to involvement of other potential participants, the evaluation process chosen from among alternative processes, and the particular means used to infuse the evaluation outcomes into decision making could conceivably affect the results. Obviously managers of projects must seek to control all the variables and other procedural factors they can.

A Variety of Other Difficulties

Beyond trouble with interacting variables, other difficulties appear in what would seem to be a neat evaluation sequence. First, it is hard to assign pupils randomly to the various treatments. If the lists of pupils assigned to the different treatments are not closely comparable, clashes occurring between learning environment and pupil characteristics affect outcomes. Second, it is hard to specify treatment conditions that effectively take into consideration the impact of the environment. Third, troubles with tests will appear if tests that do not measure given outcomes are applied just because they are available. Fourth, when data are collected in grouped form and then analyzed on an across-the-board basis, they hide important conditions and exceptions. Fifth, there is often the *Hawthorne effect*, resulting from the elation induced by novelty, which covers the real significance of the effort. Sixth, long-range effects of that which has been evaluated necessarily remain obscure. Finally, the nagging thought remains that funds expended for the program might better have been spent in another way.[17]

Improving the Process of Evaluation

Hulda Grobman has suggested that program evaluators may take a series of process steps to achieve better evaluation. These include the following:

1. Using tests that are valid and reliable and making one's own tests when necessary
2. Reviewing materials of the program so as to be thoroughly familiar with them
3. Making visits to the sites of programs, some visits being unstructured and others being for feedback of precise data
4. Asking teachers what they think of programs in which they are involved
5. Using questionnaires wisely to gather data
6. Utilizing small-scale tryouts of evaluation ideas.[18]

As C. M. Lindvall and Richard C. Cox point out, evaluation can become a process tool of worth in ongoing action to improve the curriculum, and it can emphasize the importance of evaluating instruction with reference to individual pupils in an attempt to distinguish between individuals who succeed and individuals who do not.[19]

Any plan of evaluation should, first of all, be workable. To be workable, it should be technically adequate. Its worth should be considered in terms of four categories: the philosophical, the psychological, the social, and the subject-related. Thus a viable plan makes contact with the foundations of the curriculum discussed in the initial chapters of this book. In addition, any viable plan must be politically feasible.

It is possible to use criterion-referenced norms to indicate the attainment of results. These norms specify levels of task performance or expert judgment rather than the norms within distributions to which test users are accustomed. They are useful indicators of status and change in a number of current curriculum projects.

Evaluators are necessarily interested in outcomes. Decker F. Walker and J. Schaffarzick analyzed curriculum projects dating from 1959 to 1972, emphasizing relative outcomes in the form of pupils' subject matter achievement under old and new curriculum plans. They found that each curriculum tended to be superior in its own terms and that students' patterns of test performance were different under differing plans, reflecting mastery of subject matter that had been included and highlighted.[20] Their findings are reminiscent of the strict test-test-test philosophy that has afflicted curriculum evaluation.

The evaluation process can often be improved by recognizing that some outcomes of the curriculum treatment given pupils are goal-free and that therefore no tests can be prescribed to measure their attainment. The quality of being goal-free means that results that are achieved have not been thought of at the outset of the project.

The evaluation process can be improved also by collecting data other than those that are specific to pupil achievement on tests—data on pupils' motor skills and attitudes, on effects of the project on teachers and schools, and on the appropriateness of given instructional objectives. Some highly informal data may prove to be extremely worthwhile.

Still other data about outcomes may be derived from sideline experimentation done by teachers as they depart from the strict terms of the project, from reexamining the design of the project in light of the participants' experience with it, and from reconsidering what is educationally valuable or even acceptable in projects of the kind. There exists a need to avoid confusing evaluation of curriculum programs and projects with evaluation of instruction. Evaluation of programs and projects opens the process to include outcomes well beyond those associated merely with pupil achievement as gauged by tests, inventories, and other routine measures.

Some evidence has been accumulated concerning what makes for really effective programs. It appears that staff expectations and morale need to be high, and that teachers need to have considerable responsibility for decision making about matters affecting teacher and pupil learning and also about the inservice education of staff. Further, the school needs to be an orderly place presided over by a capable leader and guided by a clear set of goals.[21]

DEVELOPMENT OF AN EVALUATION MODEL

An evaluation model is a widely applicable format in which the major elements in a program or project evaluation are expressed in such a way as to make their functions and interrelationships clear. One of the significant evaluation models of recent years is the Pittsburgh Evaluation Model, devised by Malcolm Provus to evaluate projects funded under the Elementary-Secondary Education Act. Using a taxonomy of program content developed by Robert E. Stake, Provus identified several steps within stages of evaluation.

Stage I has as its task obtaining a definition of the program based on the program content taxonomy. The steps within it are represented by certain questions: Is the program defined? If not, is a corrective action adequately defined? Is the corrective action installed? If not, is a corrective action defined for securing installation? Is the corrective action so defined now installed? The theme of Stage I is, then, *definition of the program.*

The theme of Stage II is *installation of the program.* Concerning implementation of this theme, the same questions that formed the steps in Stage I may be asked. Stage III has as its theme *process.* Here the key question is "Are the enabling objectives being met?" The theme of Stage IV is *product* or *outcomes,* with the key question being, "Are the terminal products achieved?" Finally, Stage V consists of *cost-benefit analysis.*

This model, complicated and systems-oriented as it looks at first, has had the advantage of appealing to practicing school administrators who wish to gather "hard" evidence.[22]

Another Model: The Analysis Package

A second model emphasizes cost-benefit — or cost-effectiveness — analysis. The steadily increasing popularity of the computer has made cost-effectiveness analysis more feasible. For example, the Analysis Package known as ANAPAC is a FORTRAN IV computer program "designed to perform a basic statistical and cost-effectiveness analysis of data from educational programs and to display the findings of the analysis in a narrative format for the use of nonstatisticians."[23] The evaluation process is divided into three steps: defining program goals, collecting pertinent data, and analyzing cost-effectiveness.

In the ANAPAC system, goals are stated with care. A distinction is made between program elements that are policy issues and those that are matters to be evaluated. The ANAPAC evaluators do not determine objectives; they are interested in how well a program achieves its objectives. They prefer objectives that are stated in terms of tangible results — higher reading ability, lower dropout rates, or improved attendance. They believe that "qualitative objectives are legitimate goals of an educational program, but to be useful they should be defined as precisely as possible."[24] A "qualitative" objective might be improving the self-image of minority groups.

A second aspect of defining program goals is identification of measures. This might include standardized achievement test results and more informal data like degree of attendance and participation in classes or use of library and other school facilities. The evaluators recognize that the data gathered will have varying degrees of "tightness" ranging from the results of administering valid tests to the judgments of educators. They believe that whatever measures they decide to use will be "acceptable indices of a program's goals only if the appropriate policy makers accept them as such. To insure acceptance, the evaluator should discuss the measures he plans to use with the policy makers."[25]

The next phase of ANAPAC evaluation is collecting pertinent data. These fall into four categories:

1. Pupil characteristics, including ethnic and socioeconomic background, age, sex, behavioral patterns, maturity, aptitude levels, and achievement levels
2. Program factors, among them the extent and nature of treatment, length and variation of treatment, and data about the program staff
3. Cost factors, including the cost of all resources committed to the program—salaries and fringe benefits for staff, training expenses, equipment, materials, use of space, rentals, leases, consultant fees, custodial costs, and administrative costs
4. Performance measures, such as test scores, grade averages, rates of attendance, promotion data, and dropout rates, and also genuinely subjective data.

Recognizing the difficulty of controlling variables, the evaluators seek to identify single factors serving as "proxies" for related variables. "For example, average program treatment time (e.g., two hours per week) might be an acceptable proxy for all the factors which constitute the overall program treatment."[26]

As a final major step, ANAPAC comes to the analysis of cost-effectiveness. Here an effort is made to trace the relationship between gains in performance achieved by pupils in a program and the resources that have been put into that program. Cost-effectiveness can be attained by minimizing resources to achieve a stated result or by maximizing the result gained with given resources. Estimated levels of progress toward achieving the program's objectives can be calculated for different levels of input resources. Points of diminishing returns might be found—the points at which addition of resources becomes fruitless.

EXAMPLE
The Use of ANAPAC

As an example, consider cost-effectiveness evaluation of a mathematics laboratory program. The objective of the program is to improve pupil com-

putational skills as indicated by gains on standardized achievement tests. During a five-month period, two plans are used for administering the program to two experimental groups of pupils. One experimental group uses the laboratory two hours a week; the other experimental group uses it four hours a week. A third group of pupils — considered the control group — receives no instruction in the laboratory. Assume the average cost per pupil for each hour of laboratory instruction to be $100 and the average gains in achievement for the control, two-hour, and four-hour groups to be four months, eight months, and nine months respectively (see Table 6-1). At a cost of $200, the two-hour group showed a gain of four months over the control group (which obviously had no cost for this specific instruction). The four-hour group produced a gain of one month over the two-hour group, at an additional cost of $200. Persons making policy might well decide that the four-hour group had not gained enough in relative terms to warrant the extra expenditure of $200 a pupil. Two hours in the laboratory seems to bring worthwhile results. Therefore, as funds permit, more and more pupils might be offered a two-hour laboratory experience.

TABLE 6-1

GROUP	PER PUPIL COST	ACHIEVEMENT GAIN	GAIN OVER CONTROL	COST EFFEC-TIVENESS RATIO
Control	—	4 months	—	—
Two-hour	$200	8 months	4 months	$50
Four-hour	$400	9 months	5 months	$80

ANAPAC states a cost-effectiveness ratio that is calculated by dividing the gain of each experimental group beyond the gain of the control group into the experimental group's per pupil cost. The cost-effectiveness figure (called a ratio) for the two-hour group is $50 for each month of achievement gain (a four-month gain divided into $200). For the four-hour group, the ratio is $80 for each month of gain (a five-month gain divided into $400). The ratio is used for comparing the effectiveness of different treatment methods within the same program. It may also be used for comparing the effectiveness of quite different programs which nevertheless have the same objectives and use the same performance measures.

Issues Concerning Process

Throughout the preceding discussion the emphasis has been on methodology grounded in experimental research. Some significant problems in attempts to evaluate projects and programs come from evaluators' unwillingness to relate cause and effect by means other than those used in experimental research. M. C. Wittrock asks whether we have "the methodological knowledge to estimate the cause and effect relations in naturalistic situations, such as instruction in schools." He reports a study by Fellows of the Center for Advanced Study in the Behavioral Sciences, Stanford, California, in which the literature of sociology, econometrics, statistics, political science, and psychology yielded cues about the uses of nonexperimental methods in making causal inferences.[27]

An approach known as path analysis—the computing of path coefficients for each chain or network of variables thought to be influencing one another in a causal way—has been tried. The search must continue for ways of collecting the hard data needed to make instructional decisions intelligently and confidently without consuming excessive amounts of time in trying to establish causal relationships.

A different issue raised by the ANAPAC case is whether project and program evaluators should do more than describe changes that occur in pupils' learning and school situations. Specifically, should they also judge whether or not the changes are acceptable? Numbers of evaluators believe that the judging of worth and acceptability need not be left to the policy makers referred to by ANAPAC.[28] This is an issue in educational decision making that social forces will continue to influence.

ADDITIONAL EVALUATION MODELS

Evaluation of projects and programs is so complicated an operation that it would be helpful if evaluators in school systems could use one or more recently developed models that would fit their own situations. Unfortunately each available model has been devised to meet the needs of a particular situation. Therefore, models are useful chiefly to provide suggestions to evaluators in solving their own design problems. Some of the more interesting though complicated-looking models are noted below.

The CIPP Model

A very significant model is Daniel L. Stufflebeam's CIPP, an acronym for Context, Input, Process, and Product.[29] From the original CIPP there developed CDPP, which represents Context, Design, Process, and Product. CIPP and CDPP have been twin bases for several other program evaluation plans. In the case of CDPP, the meaning of *Context* is investigation of pupil needs and related problems, as well as other possible context factors. *Design* suggests program development in which money, personnel qualifications, facilities, scheduling, and the like are instrumental. *Process* is actually in-process quality control monitoring of the program. *Product* means measurement of the effectiveness of the program at its conclusion.[30]

The EPIC Model

Another well-known model is EPIC, or Evaluative Programs for Innovative Curriculums. Pictured as a cube, the model shows one visible feature or panel as *Behavior*, which is subdivided into the cognitive, the affective, and the psychomotor. A second visible panel is *Instruction*, which has within it organization, content, method, facilities, and cost. A third visible panel is *Institution*, which has the following parts: student, teacher, administrator, educational specialist, family, and community. The users of EPIC reckon with five categories of variables: Category I—prediction sources, calling for examination of types of instruction; Category II—descriptive variables, including instructional techniques and institutional constraints; Category III—objectives; Category IV—behavior, instruction, and institution, as specified in the cube; and Category V—criteria of effectiveness, requiring analysis of all data collected.[31]

The CEMREL Model

A model by Howard Russell and Louis Smith, of the Central Midwestern Regional Educational Laboratory, is represented by a cube called CEMREL. The three visible panels of the cube are *focus of evaluation*, concentrated on student, mediator, and material; *role of evaluation*, or evaluation of an ongoing and of an end-of-project sort; and *data*, which are scale measures, questionnaire responses, and participant observations.[32]

Other Models

G. Atkinson has a model organized in three domains within which objectives are to fall: *structure*, or school plant, school organization, and so on; *process*, or instruction; and *product*, or pupil behaviors, which are the outcomes of learning.[33]

R. E. Stake, who follows the idea that both description and judgment are involved in evaluation, classifies data under the headings of antecedents, transactions, and outcomes.[34]

Systems analysis also constitutes a model. Within it are eight steps: stating need, defining objectives, defining major constraints, developing a number of alternative systems, selecting the best alternative(s), putting the chosen alternative into operation, evaluating the experimental system, and receiving feedback to create modifications.

Still other models have been developed by Leslie J. Briggs, Robert L. Baker and Richard E. Schutz, and Gene V Glass.[35]

These models have been presented in quick summary form to remind evaluators of some of the resources available to them. Because of the varied kinds of evaluations being conducted, other models are constantly emerging.

Applications of Models and Procedures

The ERIC Clearinghouse on Educational Management has prepared a compendium of manuals and handbooks on conducting program evaluation. The compendium refers to official publications from Oklahoma, California, Wisconsin, Australia, the Los Angeles Unified School District, and elsewhere.[36]

One example of the application of a model and procedures of evaluation is the Pitt Meadows Physical Education Project. This project, based in an elementary school in Maple Ridge, British Columbia, Canada, was evaluated with reference to eight program objectives. Data were collected by means of interviews; examination of the principal's supervisory documents and the consultant's notes; administration of a questionnaire to teachers; and collation of pupils' knowledge, attitude, and psychomotor test results. The data were subjected to content analysis, triangulation, and corroboration. Eight recommendations about implementation and further evaluation of the project resulted.[37]

Another example is the formative evaluation of the Human Sciences Program, an interdisciplinary program for children from eleven to fourteen years of age, which was conducted under the auspices of the Biological Sciences Curriculum Study. A report of the program contains evaluation instruments and instructions for evaluation utilized in 1973–1976 field tests.[38]

A third example is the development of a handbook to guide the review, evaluation, and revision of mathematics programs at school and school district levels, which was sponsored by the Oklahoma State Department of Education. In the handbook, program evaluation is described along four parameters.[39]

The Ohio State Department of Education relied on a checklist for evaluating the English language arts in Ohio's elementary schools. Seven essential aspects of an English language arts program were noted. For each of the seven aspects, a rating scale was prepared for administration in the schools. A score comparison graph for indicating program strengths and weaknesses was included.[40]

Finally, one of several available determinations of the validity of curriculum manuals comes from Oklahoma. Data from pre-tests, post-tests, and assignment sheets were analyzed after pupils had been examined concerning several of the eighteen units in a manual on distributive education.[41]

PROGRAM AND PROJECT EVALUATION IN ACTION

Programs and projects are being evaluated more frequently and more thoroughly now than they were decades ago. Much of the initiative for evaluation has resulted from the terms of grants under which projects have operated. The descriptions and evaluation schemata of several projects are detailed in Table 6-2.

Because all of these evaluation plans have to do with career education, they offer an interesting possibility for comparing evaluation methods. In discussions of methods, terms like *pre-tests, post-tests, experimental groups, control group(s),* and *nonequivalent groups* often appear. Their presence suggests the importance of making a specific evaluation design to suit each program or project being evaluated. In the following section of the chapter, making or selecting an appropriate design is discussed.

TABLE 6-2

TITLE AND DESCRIPTION OF PROJECT	EVALUATION METHODS USED	RESULTS REPORTED
A Project to Demonstrate Incremental Improvements in a K–12 Career Education Program through an Exemplary Model. (Northwestern Tri-County Intermediate Unit 5, Edinboro, Penn.). A project emphasizing career awareness, career exploration, and career preparation for pupils K–12.	Standardized tests of academic achievement in reading, mathematics, and career knowledge. Also evaluator-designed tests relating to progress toward the project objectives. Pupil sample drawn from the seventeen participating school districts. Basic control group, pre-test–post-test design used. Questionnaires administered to teachers and administrators.	Minimal differences in academic achievement between experimental and control groups. Project ideas apparently well diffused. Gains mainly in kindergarten and second grade groups. Opinions of teachers and administrators generally favorable.[a]

TABLE 6-2 (cont.)

TITLE AND DESCRIPTION OF PROJECT	EVALUATION METHODS USED	RESULTS REPORTED
An Exemplary Career Education Program in the Great Falls Public Schools, K–14 (Great Falls, Montana, Public Schools). An experience-based career education project to achieve goals in data-based implementation, improvement strategies, guidance and career decision making, placement and follow-up, basic skills, and management.	Three standardized tests, evaluator-developed means, and portions of school record data. Evaluation of the first year of the project only.	New offerings in vocational education and cooperative work experience. A work experience and career education program tried. Decision criteria created. Baselines set for evaluating future project effects. New areas for development explored.[b]
The Winona (Mississippi) Career Education Project (Winona Public Schools). A project parallel to other career education projects in the state. Nine objectives pursued. Evaluation by a third-party team.	Observation by the evaluation team. Data collection re students' attitudes toward careers and their knowledge of careers. Opinion surveys of teachers, parents, and the business and industrial community.	All objectives met to a satisfactory degree except two. Deficiencies: providing job placement and follow-up, and organizing an advisory council of enough participants chosen cross-sectionally.[c]
Project Future for Sharing Educational Success (Gerald Johnson, Bremerton School District, Bremerton, Wash.). Fourth-year evaluation of a project to provide pilot classes (four in number) at grades 3, 6, 9, and 12 with career education experiences developed by teachers and commercial agencies.	Data collected from the four classes and nonmatched control groups. Pre- and post-test data from the home-developed Career Education Inventory. Observation of videotapes showing pupils in communication exercises. Questionnaires administered to parents, secondary school pupils, and local employers.	For the Career Education Inventory, pre- and post-test increases significant at the .001 level (covariance analysis) for all four experimental groups. Most program elements considered effective by parents, students, and employers.[d]

TABLE 6-2 (cont.)

TITLE AND DESCRIPTION OF PROJECT	EVALUATION METHODS USED	RESULTS REPORTED
Secondary Career Education Project (Roseville Area School District 623, Minn.). A project emphasizing career development as a lifelong process. Committees involving thirty persons participated. One-third of district staff participated in staff development. Developed and field-tested a grade 7–12 career education curriculum to attain five pupil outcome objectives.	Questioning of pupils about their attitudes toward their experiences. Testing of pupils before and after each unit with a specially prepared unit test.	Better understanding by pupils of career-related concepts. Little difference between pre-test and post-test scores. Reaction of teachers favorable. Career learning centers established in three schools. Concentration on racial and sexual stereotyping, and on mainstreaming of the handicapped.[e]
Occupational Competence Access Project (John O. Post, Jr., Institute for Career Research, Hanover, Mass.). An occupational competence project involving a guidance system, exploratory programs in occupational preparation, and occupational employment and training opportunities. Established career information centers; developed and implemented a career guidance philosophy; introduced industrially-validated curriculum; added career development experiences to the academic curriculum; and established a community resource system.	Pre- and post-tests of all pupils at two project sites. Interviews concerning, and examination of, the system of school policy formation. Formative evaluation data collected also.	Positive influences on occupational awareness, career maturity, and decision-making abilities of pupils. Favorable influence on school personnel and policy orientations.[f]

TABLE 6-2 (cont.)

TITLE AND DESCRIPTION OF PROJECT	EVALUATION METHODS USED	RESULTS REPORTED
Regional Coordination and Support Program for Career Development (Michigan State Department of Education, Lansing, Mich.). A career education implementation project for providing coordination and technical assistance on a regional basis. Nine sub-goals identified, plus thirty-five objectives. Seven planning districts participated, with each district responsible for at least one objective in each of the three sub-goal areas.	Observation to determine how well the objectives were being attained. Criterion-referenced tests devised re career education. Statistical analyses and comparisons not possible. Experimental and control groups used.	Seventy-eight percent of objectives attained. Both experimental and control groups improved in achievement in career education.[g]

a. Reported in ERIC # ED 163 166.
b. Reported in ERIC # ED 151 507.
c. Reported in ERIC # ED 160 801 under the title "Quality Incremental Improvements in the Implementation of a Career-Centered Curriculum for Grades 1–12."
d. Reported in ERIC # ED 147 459.
e. Reported in ERIC # ED 164 770.
f. Reported in ERIC # ED 163 193.
g. Reported in ERIC # ED 163 171.

SITUATION 6-1
Evaluating an Entire Curriculum Program

To comply with terms of the Colorado Accountability Act, the Mapleton Public Schools took several steps in evaluating the curriculum program. These steps included:

1. Performing a needs assessment survey, in part by applying a needs assessment questionnaire
2. Using tests and inventories to find a "satisfaction index" and priority rank scores for each curriculum area in elementary and secondary education
3. Collecting demographic information.[42]

What else might be included in a systemwide program evaluation for the purpose of demonstrating the school system's accountability?

SITUATION 6-2
Judging the Worth of Evaluation Means

Concentrate on the middle column in Table 6-2. This column presents evaluation methods (commonly called means) used in seven different career education projects. Some of these means are obviously more appropriate to the requirements of their projects than are others. Judge the worth of the evaluation means, project by project. In doing so, consider the following questions:

1. When a project's objectives are not clearly stated, are you prevented from making a valid judgment regarding the worth of the means expressed?
2. In which two or three of the projects do the means seem most appropriate to the nature of the projects as they are described? Why?
3. What criticisms might you make of the other projects in this respect?

MAKING OR SELECTING AN EVALUATION DESIGN

In contrast with an evaluation model, which is an overall strategy, an evaluation design is a specific plan for attaining a set of objectives by following a series of implementation steps. Making a suitable design is not easy. Inasmuch as schools are not ideal laboratories because of the complexity of physical conditions and human interactions within them, the validity of the data collected under the terms of any design is subject to enough questions to make a design for experimentation in schools less than ideal. Numbers of designs have been utilized,[43] but the first three discussed below have had the widest and most enthusiastic use.

The True Experimental Design

The first is a so-called true experimental design. The pupils involved in the experiment and the pupils in a control group are randomized (randomly divided), and the teachers are selected for their similarities according to established criteria. Randomization is meant to decrease error, but it is notably difficult to achieve. After randomization, the experimental pupils are given the special curriculum treatment prescribed in the terms of the project, while the control group receives no special treatment, continuing with the customary subject matter content and educational practices. Then, evaluation of specific learning outcomes and other outcomes is conducted for both experimental and control groups by using the same evaluation strategies and instruments for both groups. Whenever the true experimental method can be utilized, it should be selected because of its relative freedom from error and because of the confidence evaluators usually place in it.

The Nonequivalent Before and After Design

The second evaluation design uses a control group that is not equivalent to the experimental group or groups—that is, no randomization is undertaken. An attempt is made to compensate for this lack by collecting both pre-test and post-test data,[44] by using multiple curriculum treatments with experimental groups in contrast to the treatment received by the control group, and by making across-the-board comparisons of outcomes for groups of pupils rather than for individual pupils. Thus, more than one experimental group is formed; pre-tests are given to all the experimental groups and to the control group; differing curriculum treatments are given to the experimental groups and, of course, to the control group; and all groups, experimental and control, receive the post-test. This design is often selected when parents might object to dramatic and obvious experimentation with their children and when the evaluators foresee difficulty in assigning teachers, some of whom might affect outcomes negatively.

The Time-Series Design

The third design is a time-series one. Again, no randomization is attempted. Also, no control group is established. If a time-series project is expected to cover two years of schooling—the years 1986–1987 and 1987–1988, for instance—the pupils involved in the project are tested, inventoried, and observed during the autumn of 1986 as the project gets under way, are given a special curriculum treatment throughout the two-year period, and are tested, inventoried, and observed in the spring of 1987 and again in both the autumn of 1987 and the spring of 1988. This design has the advantage of providing some basic data quickly, of permitting comparisons to be made within the population, and of allowing the evaluators to plot progress over a reasonable period of time (which may, of course, exceed two years).[45]

Naturalistic Designs

In Great Britain, curriculum workers are practicing *illuminative evaluation,* a form of explanatory and critical evaluation that does not rely on statistics. In the United States, the *educational criticism* movement counters the stock methods and external examination that characterize curriculum evaluation by emphasizing careful perceiving and thoughtful decision making by persons directly on the curriculum scene. Both illuminative evaluation and educational criticism admit types of data that are not accepted by more traditional evaluators.

    In the process of educational criticism, data are gathered by means of four major strategies. The first strategy is observation by skilled observers to answer the question "What is happening here?" The second is description, which should be an accurate portrayal of the situation that has been observed. The third strategy is interpretation, which is accomplished by discovering meaning relative to theoretical, historical, socioeconomic, or other standards. The fourth strategy is judgment of the worth and importance of what has been done, in answer to questions like "Was it worth doing?" and "How well was it done?"

This kind of activity is sometimes referred to as naturalistic evaluation. Departing from the technical, it capitalizes on human abilities, honed to proficiency. In answering questions about what is true and what is valuable, naturalistic evaluation encourages the participation of people in making intelligent judgments. The more the participants practice evaluation strategies with understanding and care, the greater the quality or validity of the results. The deficiencies so often found in the quantitative (or counting) methods of evaluation discussed previously in this chapter will drive many curriculum workers to try naturalistic (or quality) evaluation.[46]

Although naturalistic evaluation has strengths, it also has weaknesses. The greatest strength is often said to be the presence of informed and skilled viewers, who can act as translators and interpreters and can thus help other viewers make wise judgments. The weaknesses are thought to be as follows:

1. The curriculum is a motion picture rather than a still picture — an ongoing work of art rather than a completed one.
2. Because critics, as individuals, differ, there is no assurance that what one critic sees will be even similar to what another critic sees.
3. Standards of criticism, in themselves, necessarily vary.
4. What can be seen may easily be less than what one can test.[47]

ACTIVITY 6-1
Describing an Evaluation Design

Identify a curriculum project in your own or another school. Be sure the project you identify has a recognizable evaluation design. Describe the design in detail, noting the sequence of steps that have been taken and/or are yet to be taken in the evaluation process. Based on what you have read to this point in the chapter, what do you think of the evaluation design? What could be done to improve it?

ACTIVITY 6-2
Selecting an Evaluation Design

If you were required to select one of the evaluation designs prescribed on pages 247–248 for use in evaluating a curriculum project now operative or under consideration in a school you know well, which design would you select? Why? What deficiencies

do you find in the three designs that make you wish for an improved design? What might
be done in the designing process to meet your objections?

REPORTING THE EVALUATION OF A PROGRAM OR PROJECT

The written report of an evaluation may be an outline similar to the one
below. For some reports, not all the elements expressed here are necessary.
Nevertheless, they are included so that the interrelationship of the elements
may be made clear.

    I. A summary statement of the nature of the program or project
   II. The purpose(s) of the evaluation
  III. Basic information concerning the program or project
      A. Origin
      B. Goals
      C. Description
      D. The population of pupils involved
      E. Faculty members and other persons involved
  IV. Description of the evaluation study
      A. Evaluation design
      B. Measures of outcome(s)
         1. Evaluation instruments used
         2. Procedures used in collecting data
      C. Other evaluation measures used, with purpose(s) stated
   V. Results of the evaluation study
      A. Formal evaluation results (outcomes and all else)
      B. Informal evaluation results
  VI. Commentary and conclusions regarding the evaluation results
 VII. Cost-benefit analysis
      A. Costs of the program or project in dollars and other terms
      B. Benefits of the program or project in educational terms and
         dollar terms
VIII. Recommendations concerning the destiny of the program or
      project
      A. In the immediate future
      B. Long range

Very often, according to the King-Thompson study, evaluation reports
are not read. Nevertheless the study showed that both superintendents and
principals believe evaluation reports are the most important communication means.[48] It seems likely, however, that communication should occur

in varied ways: through news releases, informal contacts, and multimedia presentations, as well as through written reports.[49]

THE NEED FOR CAREFUL EVALUATION OF OLD AND NEW IDEAS AND MOVEMENTS

Like nearly everything in this fast-moving age, programs and practices in elementary and secondary schools are changing rapidly. Accountability, the nongraded school, differentiated staffing, packaged learning materials— what will be next among innovations and reforms? The practices, devices, and arrangements that the newer ideas and materials supplant have dominated the educational scene for years and even generations, with little evaluation to gauge their worth. Now there is danger that the innovations and reforms will themselves remain unevaluated. If this occurs, educators will be faced with another accretion of uncertain ways of behaving in a field that is so important to so many people. Despite limitations in evaluation designs, lack of skill in measurement, and educators' tendency to overgeneralize on the basis of limited data, we do know enough about ways of evaluating to insist that evaluation occur. In the process of trying to evaluate all sorts of projects and programs, educators will become more sophisticated in the evaluation process.

Consider the varied methods now being used to achieve individualization. Individualization, the most desired of the effects of curriculum change, is obviously a complex matter. Part of the problem is that there are potentially so many routes to individualization. Educators do not know very clearly what practices to uphold and what practices to abandon. Thoroughgoing evaluation, attempted from various vantage points, needs to be conducted, for we can no longer afford to be satisfied with demonstrations. We need evidence.

The object is not to resist innovation or to uphold tradition merely for the joy of doing so. The object is to validate programs and practices, whether old or new. Although this action cannot be taken on nearly enough occasions, funds *should* be set aside and personnel *should* be made available for the purpose. Otherwise, curriculum improvement programs must proceed largely by caprice. From evaluation data, curriculum workers derive not only assurance concerning what they have done and are doing but also goals that guide their future action.

The state of the evaluation art can perhaps best be seen by noting several findings which will, of course, need further checking. One finding is that what teachers do with classroom time is the most important element in determining the quality of a school. Specifically, teachers who lecture excessively or are consistently directive in other ways achieve poorer results than teachers who emphasize small-group work, individual work, discussion, laboratory work, pupil reporting, and demonstration. Another finding is that reduced class size does encourage learning. It has been possible to establish critical breakpoints that mark maximum functional sizes. Direct evidence now supports the belief that substitute teachers, most of whom perform in a "babysitting" role, have little instructional effect. This is partly because they emphasize ineffective classroom activities: test taking, watching movies chiefly for entertainment, engaging in question-and-answer recitations, and lecturing. Some evidence has appeared that having more than one adult in a classroom is less effective than the enthusiasts for team teaching used to believe it was. Further investigation is needed to discover the times of day at which pupils should have certain learning experiences and what effect the sex of the teacher has on learning.[50] These and similar questions are so interesting that failing to explore them deprives curriculum workers of half the fun of being in an exciting, fast-moving profession.

Mary Heller has reported the results of inquiries into experience with the evaluation of presumed changes in programs and projects. Although the findings are not startling, they do appear to be reliable. Among them are the following:

- Evaluation comprehends more than mere testing.
- Matters like changes in organization and changes in materials are easily caught up in the evaluation of curriculum change, as though they were all synonymous.
- Standardized testing as an evaluation means falls short because of its lack of relevance to classroom situations and the absence of useful statistical conversion tables.
- Criterion-referenced testing has therefore replaced in part older-fashioned standardized testing.
- The timing of evaluation is important. If evaluation occurs too often, it interferes with learning process. If it occurs too seldom, change progress is not properly gauged.[51]

SOME COMMONSENSE CONSIDERATIONS

Behind and beyond the technical aspects of program evaluation, there are some commonsense considerations to be observed. Some of these have been suggested by the Association for Supervision and Curriculum Development, which describes them as guidelines. Speaking of projects in instruction that were important elements of curriculum improvement programs during the 1960s, the Association says:

1. School personnel should know what is, and what is not, being evaluated.
2. School personnel should know what kinds of continuing information are available from the project center regarding evaluation procedures and data.
3. School personnel should know what materials, procedures, and suggestions are recommended and are available for evaluating according to the objectives of the project.
4. School personnel should use appropriate techniques and devices and employ properly trained observers in assessment programs.
5. School personnel should conduct assessment on a continuing basis.
6. Assessment must be sufficiently precise and comprehensive to yield the data necessary for competent judgments.

To accompany these guidelines the Association poses study questions including the following:

1. Do we have initial data on learners—their achievement, their motivation, their personalities?
2. Do we have initial data on teachers—their strategies, their motivation, their knowledge, their personalities?
3. Do we have these data at many stages during the implementation of the project?
4. What happens to learners as people and to learners as learners as a result of the project?
5. What happens to teachers as people and to teachers as teachers?
6. Are the changes which we expected occurring? Why or why not?
7. Do changes justify the time and funds expended?[52]

The guidelines are worded to express the expectation that worthwhile evaluation follows an ongoing procedure throughout the life of a project and is not merely an end-of-the-line operation.

A process element needing much more than off-the-cuff judgment is the process of decision making in curriculum change and improvement. Criteria that might be used—with considerable refining and supplementing—in evaluating decision making are set forth, with down-to-earth explanations, as follows:

Criterion 1. Curriculum decisions should be made for valid educational reasons, not for specious or noneducational ones.
Explanation. Much of our current tendency to "jump aboard bandwagons" results from our failure to ask the question "Why?" Some innovations in education originate in pressures that make no contribution to achieving quality in education. Often they proceed from

vague feelings about "what society wants or needs" or from localized, specific feelings about what community pressure groups will do if the schools fail to heed their demands. Curriculum workers need to think carefully about the consequences of the decisions they anticipate making. Are they within the context of purposes of the school? Are they likely to benefit the education of children? Do they spring from worthy and defensible motives?

Criterion 2. Curriculum decisions of a permanent nature should be made on the basis of the best available evidence.

Explanation. Most of the curriculum decisions made in the past have rested on little or no evidence. As the number of decisions we need to make increases, we shall surely need evidence to support some of these decisions. To do research concerning every proposed change in the curriculum is obviously impossible. But curriculum planners can develop a rationale for inquiry that takes into account how changes work experimentally in their own school systems, how they work in other school systems, what hard data are available concerning the quality of their function, and what other people think of the changes. Obviously, tentative decisions based on limited evidence must remain within the decision-making process.

Criterion 3. Curriculum decisions should be made in a context of broadly conceived aims of education.

Explanation. The American public will not approve of or submit to limited education of its children. Those who have asked parents about their aspirations for their children's education know that they demand much more than the three Rs. Most Americans seem to believe that citizenship education, character training, functional skill development, and improvement of social relationships come within the responsibility of elementary and secondary schools. Both education for improved thinking and education for improved feeling fall to the lot of the schools, because education is ill-conceived and limited if it does not serve objectives ranging from increasing children's understanding to developing their appreciations, and onward to helping them clarify their values.

Criterion 4. Curriculum decisions should be made within a context of previously made decisions and of needs for additional decision making so that balance and other important curriculum considerations may be safeguarded.

Explanation. Previous decisions cannot and should not be entirely discarded. There are, of course, standing in the wings, needs for decision making that may be more pressing than those the schools are now attempting to meet. The wide range of previous decisions and of needs for decision making adds to the problem of overload, which appears in the form of having too much to teach in too little time. Curriculum workers might analyze a number of pupil cases in each of their schools to determine just what educational experiences individual pupils are having.

Criterion 5. Curriculum decisions should be made by achieving a resolution of forces originating in the nature and development of learners, the nature of learning processes, demands of the society at large, requirements of the local community, and the nature and structure of subject matter to be learned.

Explanation. Bases for making curriculum decisions may be summed up in these phrases: learners and learning, social forces, and subject matter. Education that overemphasizes one of the three and largely ignores the other two is not fair to pupils. Imbalance, whatever its source, can swamp the curriculum.

Criterion 6. Curriculum decisions should be reached cooperatively by persons who are legitimately involved in the effects of the decisions, with full participation being accorded those persons who are most concerned with the effects.

Explanation. An imminent danger lies in having the curriculum imposed on classroom and school by interests outside the school. No one knows the children in a given school as well as the teachers and the principal of that school. The best those of us outside a particular school can do to improve the curriculum of that school is to provide general guidelines, data, and suggestions. Curriculum planning of a large-scale or general sort should be done cooperatively, involving as many of the users of the curriculum as possible. Although wide, continuous participation of the users is usually impossible, participation through suggestion making and tryout of ideas can readily occur. Tryout should intimately involve an underconsulted group in the body educational: our pupils. Even when pupils are too young to tell us orally how satisfactory or unsatisfactory our ideas are, they can often tell us through our own powers of observation.

Criterion 7. Curriculum decisions should take into account new facts of human life such as the proliferation of knowledge and a need for a new sense of unity within our diversity.

Explanation. Americans are living in a new era. Knowledge is increasing so rapidly that teachers cannot hope to "cover the book," for the book is already too large. More and more careful selection of content is needed.

Certain understandings, skills, appreciations, attitudes, and values may need to become universals in the United States. This fact does not make a national curriculum necessary, because behaviors people exhibit in common can be developed through a multiplicity of curriculum experiences. But a set of national goals is needed to guide education. The need for such goals becomes evident when we ask adolescents or adults to name goals or purposes around which Americans are united.

Criterion 8.   Curriculum decisions should take into account the many differences among learners, especially with reference to their potential for development, their styles of thinking, their ability to withstand pressures, and their need for education in values.

Explanation.   In the schools' anxiety to deal with groups and to make neat administrative arrangements, they have not dealt adequately with individuals. Plans for reorganizing the school and altering uses of pupil time may well stand or fall according to their success in attending to the needs of individuals. The curriculum must be made broad enough to permit development of human potential that is now going to waste. The progress being made in analyzing styles of thinking should be applied to treatment of individual learners. The schools will need to investigate further the mental and physical hazards in applying undue pressures, and they must help many confused children clarify their values.

Criterion 9.   Curriculum decisions should be made with a realistic view of certain organizational or engineering matters that can affect the quality of the decisions themselves: correlation versus separation of subjects, the distinction between curriculum content and pupils' experiences, and the uses of time, for instance.

Explanation.   Some subject matter can be correlated naturally, some cannot. Content set out to be learned obviously differs from pupils' real learning experiences. What the teacher *does* is so important in pupil experiencing that teachers should receive ample help in choosing the details of content and in setting the stage for pupils to learn in varied ways. Either lengthened or shortened periods of time may be needed to effect economy in learning effort. In sum, much depends on how teachers proceed in putting curriculum decisions into operation.

Criterion 10.   Curriculum decisions should be made with some forethought about ways in which they may be communicated and shared.

Explanation.   A curriculum decision may be of excellent quality, but unless it is appropriately communicated and shared, it may soon enter the limbo of lost ideas. In many instances, more attention should be given to a plan for communicating decisions than to their original development.

Criterion 11. Curriculum decisions should be made only with reference to subject matter and pupil experiences that cannot be offered as satisfactorily outside the school.

Explanation. The school has sometimes exaggerated its educative function. The home, community agencies, labor unions, and industry already provide more education than some people realize. The impact of extraschool agencies on total educational programs is likely to increase. The schools need to reexamine their functions to determine those exclusive to legitimate operation of elementary and secondary schools, being sure to retain functions that can best benefit children and youth.

ACTIVITY 6-3
Using Process Evaluation

Process evaluation is inquiry concerning how a program or project is proceeding while it is en route to its termination. It is meant to discover or predict, during the implementation of the project, both defects and strengths in its design and/or in ways of implementing the design. Further, it is intended to show whether changes in pupil performance under a given curriculum treatment can in fact be attributed to that treatment.[53]

Do the preceding statements mean to you that a project may be altered en route in order to strengthen it? If so, to what extent may it be altered without destroying its basic terms and intent? If possible, use an actual curriculum project as an example to demonstrate your views. If this is not possible, think of a project in which two or three changes might be made during its lifetime.

SUMMARY

This chapter emphasizes the importance of evaluating the content and process of curriculum change. The chapter begins with a statement of some understandings concerning the evaluation of curriculum programs and projects. Both the quantity and the quality of program and project evaluation raise serious technical and policy questions. A variety of evaluation designs and various evaluation models are now available for study, comparison, and possible adoption. Evaluators need to utilize designs that fit the conditions within which they work. The chapter concludes with an argument in favor of evaluating both old and new programs and projects, along with less complex educational practices, devices, and arrangements, and with a statement of common sense considerations to be observed now and in the future.

ENDNOTES

1. With specific reference to curriculum improvement activity, a *program* is a carefully planned, comprehensive, and continuing operation for improving as many elements of the curriculum as possible. A *project* is a portion of the total program, also carefully planned, but relatively limited in purpose and scope.

2. Jean A. King and Bruce Thompson, "How Principals, Superintendents View Program Evaluation," *Bulletin of the National Association of Secondary School Principals* 67, no. 459 (January 1983): 48–52.

3. Wilford M. Aiken, *The Story of the Eight Year Study* (New York: Harper & Row, 1942).

4. I. James Quillen and Lavone A. Hanna, *Education for Social Competence* (Chicago: Scott, Foresman, 1948).

5. Educational Testing Service, *Developments* 29, no. 3 (Winter 1983–1984): 11.

6. John J. Bowers, *Planning a Program Evaluation: An Educator's Handbook* (Philadelphia: Research for Better Schools, 1978).

7. Association for Supervision and Curriculum Development, *Leadership for Improving Instruction*, 1960 Yearbook (Washington, D.C.: The Association, 1960), pp. 166, 167.

8. Ben Wallace and John P. Gower, "An Evaluation of the Effects of Participation by Six School Districts in the International Paper Company Foundation's Program of Assistance to Secondary Education" (Doctoral dissertation, Teachers College, 1960), passim.

9. Fenwick W. English, "Improving Curriculum Management in the Schools." Occasional Paper 30 (Washington, D.C.: Council for Basic Education, 1980). Reported in ERIC # ED 201 049.

10. Henry S. Dyer, "School Evaluation: A Realistic Response to Accountability," *North Central Association Quarterly* 46, no. 4 (Spring 1972): 390–96.

11. Stephen F. Hamilton and Albert Mamary, "Assessing the Effectiveness of Program Delivery," *Bulletin of the National Association of Secondary School Principals* 67, no. 465 (October 1983): 39–44.

12. Samuel Ball, *Evaluating Educational Programs* (Princeton, N.J.: Educational Testing Service, 1979), p. 6.

13. See Arieh Lewy, "Utilizing Experts' Judgment in the Process of Curriculum Evaluation" (Los Angeles: Center for the Study of Evaluation, UCLA, 1973).

14. David H. Hampson, "Educational Product Development and Evaluation" (Raleigh: Center for Occupational Education, North Carolina State University, 1973), p. 19.

15. See A. W. Astin and R. J. Panos, "The Evaluation of Educational Programs," in Robert L. Thorndike, ed., *Educational Measurement*, 2nd ed. (Washington, D.C.: American Council on Education, 1971.)

16. James A. Phillips, Jr., "A Context for Considering Curriculum Research" (Paper presented at the Annual Meeting of the American Educational Research Association, Washington, D.C., April 1975). Reported in ERIC # ED 106 206.

17. Textbooks in measurement and evaluation are filled with both the joys and the hardships of evaluation. Books on evaluation procedures, such as those

by Grobman; Tyler, Gagné, and Scriven; and Wick and Beggs listed at the end of this chapter, extend the ideas presented here.

18. Hulda Grobman, *Evaluation Activities of Curriculum Projects: A Starting Point*, American Educational Research Association, Monograph Series in Curriculum Evaluation (Chicago: Rand McNally, 1968), pp. 48–82.

19. C. M. Lindvall and Richard C. Cox, *Evaluation as a Tool in Curriculum Development: The IPI Program*, American Educational Research Association, Monograph Series in Curriculum Evaluation (Chicago: Rand McNally, 1970).

20. Decker F. Walker and J. Schaffarzick, *Comparing Different Curricula: A Review of Research and Some Speculation on Its Implications* (Palo Alto, Calif., Stanford University, 1972).

21. See Stewart C. Purkey and Marshall S. Smith, "Too Soon to Cheer? Synthesis of Research on Effective Schools," *Educational Leadership* 40, no. 3 (December 1982): 64–69.

22. For details, see Malcolm Provus, "Evaluation of Ongoing Programs in the Public School System," in National Society for the Study of Education, *Educational Evaluation: New Roles, New Means*, 68th Yearbook, Part II (Chicago: University of Chicago Press, 1969), pp. 242–83.

23. Richard Vigilante, *Evaluating Educational Programs: ANAPAC User's Guide* (New York: Board of Education, City of New York, 1972), p. 4.

24. Ibid., p. 6.

25. Ibid., p. 7. This reservation stems, perhaps, from the attack in big cities on standardized achievement tests as being unfair to minority groups, and from disputes about the locus of the right and the power to make policy.

26. Ibid., pp. 8,9.

27. M. C. Wittrock, "The Evaluation of Instruction: Cause and Effect Relations in Naturalistic Data," *UCLA Evaluation Comment* 1, no. 4 (Los Angeles: Center for the Study of Evaluation, UCLA, 1969), pp. 9–14.

28. See the earlier statements of M. Scriven, "The Methodology of Evaluation," in R. W. Tyler, R. M. Gagné, and M. Scriven, eds., *Perspectives of Curriculum Evaluation*, American Educational Research Association, Monograph Series in Curriculum Evaluation (Chicago: Rand McNally, 1967); and of G. Atkinson, "Evaluation of Educational Programs: An Exploration," in W. H. Strevell, ed., *Rationale of Education Evaluation* (Pearland, Tex.: Interdisciplinary Committee on Education Evaluation, Gulf Schools Supplementary Education Center, 1967), p. 2. See also Mary Alice White and Jan Duker, "Models of Schooling and Models of Evaluation," *Teachers College Record* 74 (February 1973): 293–307.

29. See, for instance, Daniel L. Stufflebeam, "The Relevance of the CIPP Evaluation Model for Educational Accountability," *Journal of Research and Development in Education* 5 (Fall 1971): 19–25.

30. R. S. Randall, "An Operational Application of the CIPP Model for Evaluation," *Educational Technology* 9 (March 1969): 40–44.

31. R. L. Hammond, "Evaluation at the Local Level" (Tucson: Project EPIC, n.d.).

32. P. A. Pohland, "Educational Ethnology and Evaluation" (Paper presented at the Annual Conference of the American Educational Research Association, Minneapolis, March 1970).

33. Atkinson, "Evaluation of Educational Programs."

34. R. E. Stake, "The Countenance of Educational Evaluation," *Teachers College Record* 68 (1967): 523–40.

35. Their models are summarized in Marjorie E. Ward and G. Phillip Cartwright, "Some Contemporary Models for Curriculum Evaluation" (Paper presented at the Conference on Curriculum Evaluation, Cap Rouge, Quebec, August 1972). Reported in ERIC # ED 081 236.

36. ERIC Clearinghouse on Educational Management, *Program Evaluation. The Best of ERIC on Educational Management*, no. 68. (Eugene, Ore.: The Clearinghouse, 1983). Reported in ERIC # ED 226 404.

37. Peter R. Moody, *Pitt Meadows Physical Education Project: Evaluation of an Implementation Project* (Vancouver: Educational Research Institute of British Columbia, 1982).

38. James T. Robinson, *Logical Competencies and Activity Selection Patterns in Early Adolescents: A Longitudinal Study* (Boulder, Colo.: Biological Sciences Curriculum Study, 1981).

39. Eugene Hobbs et al., *Curriculum Review Handbook: Mathematics, 1981–82* (Oklahoma City: Oklahoma State Department of Education, 1982).

40. Ohio State Department of Education, *A Self-Appraisal Checklist for English Language Arts in Ohio's Elementary Schools* (Columbus: Division of Elementary and Secondary Education, The Department, 1980).

41. Don Frazier and Lyn Martin, *Validation of Distributive Education Curriculum Manual* (Oklahoma City: Oklahoma State Department of Education, 1980).

42. Mapleton Public Schools, *Educational X-ray of Mapleton Public Schools* (Denver, Colo.: Mapleton Public Schools, 1972). Reported in ERIC # ED 081 709.

43. See Donald T. Campbell and Julian C. Stanley, *Experimental and Quasi-Experimental Designs for Research* (Chicago: Rand McNally, 1963).

44. *Pre-test* and *post-test* are used here as symbols of whatever instrumentation—including tests and a variety of other instruments—is used in determining pupil status before and after curriculum treatments have been applied.

45. For a helpful discussion of the three designs described, see Maurice J. Eash, Harriet Talmage, and Herbert J. Walberg, "Evaluation Designs for Practitioners," TM Report 35, ERIC Clearinghouse on Tests, Measurement, and Evaluation (Princeton, N.J.: Educational Testing Service, December 1974).

46. See, for instance, Eliot W. Eisner, *The Educational Imagination: On the Design and Evaluation of School Programs* (New York: Macmillan, 1979); also George Willis, "Democratization of Curriculum Evaluation," *Educational Leadership* 38, no. 8 (May 1981): 630–32.

47. See Elizabeth Vallance, "The Critic's Perspective: Some Strengths and Limitations of Aesthetic Criticism in Education" (Paper presented at the annual meeting of the American Educational Research Association, Los Angeles, April 1981). Reported in ERIC # ED 163 166.

48. King and Thompson, "How Principals, Superintendents View Program Evaluation," pp. 49, 50.

49. F. Holley, "What It Takes to Win: Factors in the Utilization of Evaluation Findings for Educational Improvement," in C. B. Stalford, *Testing and Evaluation in Schools: Practitioners' Views* (Washington, D.C.: United States Department of Education, 1980).

50. See Martin N. Olsen, "Ways to Achieve Quality in School Classrooms: Some Definitive Answers," *Phi Delta Kappan* 52, no. 1 (September 1971): 63–65.

51. Mary F. Heller, "The Process of Curriculum Development: An Overview of Research," February 1981. Reported in ERIC # ED 221 938.

52. Association for Supervision and Curriculum Development, *Assessing and Using Curriculum Content* (Washington, D.C.: The Association, 1965), p. 14.

53. Daniel J. Macy, "The Role of Process Evaluation in Program Development and Implementation," *Educational Technology* 15, no. 4 (April 1975): 42–47.

SELECTED BIBLIOGRAPHY

Anderson, D. C. *Evaluating Curriculum Proposals: A Critical Guide.* New York: Halsted Press, 1981.

Association for Supervision and Curriculum Development. *Assessing and Using Curriculum Content.* Washington, D.C.: The Association, 1965.

Bellack, Arno A., and Kliebard, Herbert E., eds. *Curriculum and Evaluation.* Berkeley, Calif.: McCutchan, 1977.

Bowers, John J. *Planning a Program Evaluation: An Educator's Handbook.* Philadelphia: Research for Better Schools, 1978.

Davis, Ed. *Teachers as Curriculum Evaluators.* Winchester, Mass.: Allen Unwin, 1981.

Educational Leadership 35, no. 4, January 1978. (Theme articles on curriculum evaluation.)

Eisner, Eliot W. *The Educational Imagination: On the Design and Evaluation of School Programs.* New York: Macmillan, 1979.

Grobman, Hulda. *Evaluation of Activities of Curriculum Projects.* Chicago: Rand McNally, 1969.

Kindvall, C. M., and Cox, Richard C. *Evaluation as a Tool in Curriculum Development: The IPI Program.* Chicago: Rand McNally, 1970.

Payne, David A. *Curriculum Evaluation: Commentaries on Purpose, Process, Product.* Boston: D. C. Heath, 1973.

Rippey, Robert M., et al. *Studies in Transactional Evaluation.* Berkeley, Calif.: McCutchan, 1973.

Taylor, Peter A., and Cowley, Doris M. *Readings in Curriculum Evaluation.* Dubuque, Iowa: William C. Brown, 1972.

Tuckman, Bruce W. *Evaluating Instructional Programs.* Boston: Allyn and Bacon, 1979.

Tyler, Ralph W., ed. *Educational Evaluation: New Roles, New Means.* National Society for the Study of Education, Sixty-Eighth Yearbook, Part II. Chicago: University of Chicago Press, 1969.

———; Gagné, R. M.; and Scriven, M., eds. *Perspectives of Curriculum Evaluation.* Chicago: Rand McNally, 1967.

Wick, John W., and Beggs, Donald L., eds. *Evaluation for Decision-making in the Schools.* Boston: Houghton Mifflin, 1970.

Wilhelms, Fred T., ed. *Evaluation as Feedback and Guide.* 1967 Yearbook, Association for Supervision and Curriculum Development. Washington, D.C.: The Association, 1967.

PART TWO

Process in Curriculum Improvement

7

The General Process of Curriculum Change and Improvement

HOW DECISION MAKING RELATES TO PROCESS

In the first six chapters this book has dealt with decision making in curriculum improvement. The question now arises, "How does decision making relate to the process by which the curriculum is improved?"

We have seen that such decision making is in itself a process, which involves borrowing from various disciplines—history, psychology, the social sciences, and subject matter to be taught in schools— and then using insights derived from these disciplines in ways that are peculiar to professional education itself.

Curriculum improvement as an evolving discipline of real power and promise depends so heavily on process for its own subject matter that attention is directed in the second part of this book to certain elements of process. In the following chapters, consideration is given to how change and improvement occur, the planning process, who makes the curriculum, how communication aids improvement, and the leadership methods and strategies that can be used. These matters represent the general concerns of curriculum planners who were asked to describe the problems that trouble them in their work. Inasmuch as curriculum improvement is greatly facilitated by a thorough understanding of process, this understanding is a necessary concomitant of and supplement to the curriculum worker's knowledge of the bases and methodology of decision making.

SOME OBSERVATIONS ABOUT THE PROCESS OF IMPROVEMENT

It is obvious that curriculum improvement does not occur automatically. In most school situations, accomplishing it requires the expenditure of much time and effort within an environment rich in helpful and stimulating influences. Primarily, curriculum improvement results from improvement of individual persons and organizations of people. Their improvement follows a process that can be charted in a general way, a process with which this chapter deals. Subsequent chapters describe certain ramifications of and corollaries to the basic process.

Discussions of process tend to include reference to curriculum workers as change agents and clients, whereas discussions of decision making often refer to these persons as curriculum planners.

Curriculum Improvement as Improvement of Teachers

The learner's curriculum improves largely in consonance with improvement in his or her teacher's insights, skills, and attitudes. According to this viewpoint, emphasis needs to be placed on the growth of individual teachers, whether they are assigned to classrooms or rove about as teachers of teachers bearing the title curriculum coordinator, supervisor, or consultant. *If the curriculum is to improve, teachers must be committed to the significance of self-improvement.* Obviously some teachers are much interested in improving themselves, whereas other teachers manifest little or no interest in self-improvement. There is, of course, no teacher who cannot do his or her work better, and the basic question then becomes "How can the teacher who is more or less concerned about personal improvement be helped to improve?" This age-old question still remains partially unanswered, but a few definite guidelines and additional tentative ones, some of them simply in the form of commonsense cues, are now available.

Improvement with reference to the individual often becomes a very special problem. Consider the case of a teacher named Lucretia and her critic:

> I remember Lucretia. She and I taught in the same high school, though hers was a different generation from mine. I can recall Lucretia's long dresses, straight hair, and wan face that had seemingly never known cosmetics.

"Lucretia's the kind of teacher who defeats school bond issues singlehandedly," said a mutual friend. He may have been right. Both her appearance and her attitudes toward youngsters and subject matter were unappealing.

Lucretia expected much of her pupils but less of herself. Her understanding of her subject was limited and she obviously cared little about the adolescents she taught.

I've often thought about Lucretia since those days in Stockville High School. Where should curriculum improvement have begun in *her* classroom? With her—probably! But how and under what circumstances?

Just incidentally (and maybe it shouldn't be so incidental), I wonder what Lucretia thought of me. How might her brash young neighbor in the classroom across the hall have improved himself so that *his* pupils' experiences could have improved in turn?

The preceding vignette raises some serious questions about the process of curriculum improvement. Among them are these: Granted that Lucretia represents "a type," are there some common ways that can be used in helping people everywhere improve themselves? What different approaches are necessary and desirable for use with widely differing individuals? Are we vain enough to believe that improvement is only for persons outside ourselves? Can curriculum leaders become so preoccupied with the intrinsic worth of a proposed innovation that they forget that real improvement occurs with *people*, including *themselves*?

Meanings of Change and Improvement

The dictionary defines improvement as enhanced value or excellence. In a broader sense it is all of the following: betterment, amelioration, and enrichment. Change, on the other hand, involves a shift in position that may go in either a favorable or an unfavorable direction. One may change, for example, from total innocence of narcotics to drug addiction, but few persons would call this change an improvement. Improvements are labeled as such according to sets of values, and improvement can best be ensured by evaluating the true effects of change. In education, many changes have occurred during recent years. Certain persons, using their own systems of values, consider given changes to be improvements, whereas others may regard the same changes as backward steps. Thus, a lay committee of engineers and scientists who proposed seriously to a board of education that physical education, home economics, and all the arts be eliminated from the curriculum of their local high school made the recommendation because the committee valued a strengthening of the basic subjects at the expense of "the frills." This change was regarded by other laypersons and by organizations of educators as a decidedly backward step.

Distinguishing between Change and Improvement

Usually, precise evaluation procedures are needed to determine whether a given change is an improvement. For instance, if a plan for reorganizing elementary schools has been put into operation, planned evaluation is needed to discover whether the ultimate result has been mere reorganization of the school or actual improvement in children's learning experiences. The two are obviously not the same, though they are repeatedly being confused as U.S. education rushes into change.

In educational literature, the process of curriculum change or improvement has sometimes been referred to as educational engineering, a term that suggests the existence of a technology of improvement.[1] It has also been termed planned social change,[2] and change in the dynamics of human relationships.[3] Much of what is known about the process is of a practical or commonsense nature. Most knowledge of planned social change and the related significance of human relations comes from fields other than education. Inasmuch as improvement is really change directed toward excellence, betterment, amelioration, and/or enrichment, it should be recognized as especially worthwhile change but as change nevertheless. Whatever social scientists and educators have learned about the process of change in individuals and groups may be generally applied to the process of improving persons and institutions. With reference to improvement of the curriculum, educators must, of course, make further applications of the findings of social psychology, sociology, and the other social sciences to their own field.

HOW CHANGE OCCURS

Social scientists have stated that change probably occurs in three stages. The first stage is that of *initiation*, in which ideas for change are launched and decisions are made regarding the nature, direction, and extent of change. The second stage is said to be one of *legitimation*, in which the sentiment on behalf of change is communicated. The third stage involves *congruence* of the separate systems of values held by the person or persons seeking to create change and by the person or persons who are the targets or human subjects of the proposed change.[4] The process of change may be assisted by permissiveness and support in accordance with a helpful human relations approach. It may also be aided temporarily by manipulating extrinsic rewards such as affection, favor, promotion, and additional income. Disaster has sometimes been used as an excuse to make changes seem reasonable and necessary. In the presence or imminence of disaster, action seems necessary even when the particular action to be taken violates principles and values that are long established and widely accepted. In organizations, including school systems, change occurs as a result of (1) planning by equals, (2) indoctrination by superior officers, and (3) outright coercion by the same officers.[5] To function enduringly, change should apparently be a "deliberate collaborative process" involving the following features:

1. A joint effort that involves mutual determination of goals
2. A 'spirit of inquiry'—a reliance on determinations based on data publicly shared
3. An existential relationship growing out of the 'here and now' situation
4. A voluntary relationship between change agent and client with either party free to terminate the relationship after joint consultation
5. A power distribution in which the client and change agent have equal or almost equal opportunities to influence the other
6. An emphasis on methodological rather than content learnings.[6]

Causing Change in the Individual

Change in the individual seems to come about in the following way. Some of the stimuli in the individual's environment contribute to readiness for change by creating a felt need for something different, a dissatisfaction with what now exists. The need is met, at least in part, by a planned or fortuitous experience. Largely as a result of the experience (or series of experiences), one sees oneself and one's environment in a new light. Consequently one develops new values and subsequently new goals which may be closed-ended or open-ended. Sometimes the new goals arouse additional needs and one finds oneself in another orbit of planned change. Encouragement, help, and stimulation are needed during the entire process of change. The nearer a person's newly developed values are to the values held dear by that person, the more permanent the change is likely to be. Some persons change rapidly, others slowly. Differences in rate of change are therefore to be expected.

Applying This Concept of Change Process

This brief description, oversimplified as it probably is, contains several ideas that need examination and extension into practice in the schools. When the ideas have passed through the sieve of the educator's experience, they become a set of tentative principles like the following:

- *People improve with greatest enthusiasm when they detect the desire of the stimulator of improvement to improve himself or herself.* The argument "You need improving and I am here to improve you" has slight effect. "We have a common problem; to solve it, we should all improve our competencies" has a pleasanter, more convincing ring.

- *The direction of improvement should be determined cooperatively.* People's goals differ; however, if they are to work together effectively, they must determine cooperatively the direction their efforts are to take.
- *To achieve improvement, people must identify and examine each other's centrally held values.* This action is difficult and time consuming. It requires the best in communication—the careful listening that Carl Rogers talks about, the careful observing that Daniel Prescott recommends to teachers. It demands lengthy talking together and prolonged watching of one another's behavior, so that the persons involved may truly say, "We know each other."
- *People improve through experiencing.* The kind of teacher one is may be determined largely by the kinds of experiences one has had. School systems should seek to provide their teachers with the best of inservice education.
- *Stimulators of improvement should divide their time between contacts with individuals and contacts with groups.* Research and practice show that both individual conferences and group work are effective in helping teachers improve the quality of their work. The balance between these two general procedures cannot be predetermined; it can be judged only in consideration of prevailing situations.
- *People's resistance to the efforts of others to help them improve constitutes a major individual difference.* Not only are some people more generally resistant than others, but people vary in their resistances to specific new proposals.
- *Whenever possible, improvement should be induced in situations that involve problem solving.* People improve most when a stimulator of improvement helps them solve their own problems. Some problems pose a threat and therefore cannot be dealt with immediately and directly. For instance, teachers who have trouble with classroom control are often unable to discuss their control problems dispassionately. Curriculum workers should do their best to form such professional problems into appropriate ones for discussion and solution.
- *Stimulators of improvement should try to create and maintain a climate of freedom for those with whom they work.* This statement rests on the thesis that people improve when they feel free to improve. Where there is a feeling of restraint expressed in declarations like "My boss won't let me," that feeling should be eliminated by carefully guarded words and behavior that point clearly to greater freedom in the whole situation.
- *Stimulators of improvement should help keep channels of com-*

munication open.   Psychological static easily gets between the sender and the receiver of a message. Much of this static can be cleared away by face-to-face communication. Curriculum workers should try to ensure that they hear what others say by listening carefully, trying to understand their messages, and then repeating or rephrasing people's comments.

- *Stimulators of improvement should use their power and influence with great care.*   Educational leaders have largesse to distribute in the form of position, salary, approval, knowledge, prestige, disciplinary control, and even affection. Their status often begets in teachers an acquiescence that is easily mistaken for a genuine desire to improve. When the threat or the paternalism is gone, acquiescence disappears too.
- *Stimulators of improvement should operate on a limited number of fronts at a given time.*   Curriculum workers are learning that sweeping, comprehensive improvements rarely take place. Rather, progress is made on a broken front, a little at a time, in manageable form.

Actions to Be Taken

The preceding principles should be considered carefully by those who would improve the curriculum. They suggest the following specific actions the curriculum leader should take:

1. Work *with* people, not *over* them.
2. Show that you too desire to improve.
3. Help the people with whom you work know you and know each other.
4. Help teachers enjoy a variety of inservice experiences.
5. Work with both individuals and groups, balancing your time between individual conferences and group work.
6. Recognize that some people improve more slowly than others, both in a general sense and in specific activities.
7. Try to use problem solving as a means of improvement.
8. Help teachers feel free to improve.
9. Keep channels of communication open.
10. Use your status, whether it is real or imagined, with great care: you can easily be a threat and an impediment.
11. Be sensible and modest in your expectations, doing well that which you undertake.[7]

The curriculum leadership in the Montgomery Township Public Schools (New Jersey) has suggested similar reminders to curriculum planners:

1. Try the gradual approach.
2. Keep everyone aware.
3. Remember that awareness leads to interest which leads to involvement which leads to commitment.
4. Keep your perspective—means vs. ends, process vs. product.
5. Share the decision making with those who want a share.
6. Curriculum is a people business.
7. Careless curriculum addition is easier but it creates problems later; careful curriculum subtraction is harder now but eliminates problems later.
8. New curriculum? Pilot, don't pile it.
9. Define the banks of the stream.
10. Keep your eye on the forest. Delegate the trees.
11. Always measure and sift the *real* curriculum.
12. Remember—Ralph Tyler asks persistent questions.
13. Don't forget why we're in business—kids!
14. Budget better—your time and your money.[8]

The Importance of Care in Working with Teachers

Among the specific factors that assist change and improvement in the individual, motivation is evidently one to be reckoned with. At the beginning of the change-improvement process, the person is thought to receive motivation from "dissatisfaction or pain associated with the present situation"—dissatisfaction that results from "a perceived discrepancy between what is and what might be," external pressures to accomplish change, and an undefined "internal requiredness" that presses the individual to change.[9] After the initial stages of the process have passed, the person who is changing or improving may be motivated by a feeling of need to complete the task and to complete it with appropriate speed. He or she may be motivated further by the existence of desirable relationships between himself or herself and the stimulator of change or improvement.[10] Since these ideas are in no way final, curriculum leaders should check them against their own continuing experiences in dealing with teachers.

Motivation is thought to be inhibited at times by certain "resistance forces." These forces include opposition to any kind of change, opposition to a particular change, desire to cling to ideas or actions with which one is well satisfied, and poor relationships between the person to be changed and the stimulator of change. Sometimes change, no matter how constructive, costs "the client" more than he or she had originally expected it would, and he or she becomes discouraged with it. Sometimes, too, the client is diverted to other projects, and change is inhibited by the diversion.[11]

Arthur Combs discusses a myth that is prominent in professional education called "the myth they won't let me." Alleged prohibition by administrators and others of constructive activity on behalf of schools is, in fact, often a crutch on which teachers lean to avoid participating in curriculum planning. Combs points out that professionals employed in schools usually have more freedom than they care to believe. Frequently the prohibition does not exist,[12] but the fact that teachers and others think it exists raises questions about the ways school leaders respond to curriculum ideas and to the people who communicate them.

William Reid is not the first to assert the importance of being just in dealing with teachers. And assuming that the curriculum is something to be brought into schools from the outside, readymade by "experts," does not do justice to members of teaching staffs. To be right in relationships with teachers, curriculum planners need to see teachers as rational people, able to make choices and to improve the quality of their work. Curriculum leaders should prize and practice ethical behavior, avoiding bias against any group of people. They should view education as purposeful, though not necessarily as "preplanned purposeful." That is, they should generally eschew prewrapped curriculum packages that allow teachers little or no opportunity to participate in curriculum planning or development. At the same time, they should consider schools to be only part of a broader educational system that has a number of contributing elements in each community.[13]

Means of Encouraging Change and Improvement in Individuals

Much change and improvement occur through individualized, person-to-person contacts. However, group work also is known to have marked effect in changing people. This is true especially when the stimulator of change and the persons to be changed interact consistently in the same group. To be effective as a change medium, the group must, of course, be attractive to its members. The members accept new ideas and values most readily if the new ideas and values relate closely to those that group members already hold. The stimulator of change must diligently seek to cause the pressures for change or improvement to rest within the group itself. The more the group talks about the need to change, the more pressure for change is built within it and thus within its individual members.[14]

When they are at their best, groups engage in a high quality of problem solving. Change is believed to be created most readily by keeping problem solving openly experimental, cooperative, task oriented, and educational and/or therapeutic.[15] People who work together may be said to go through three steps in altering their views. They express compliance, usually in an effort to keep or enhance their own reputations; next, they identify with one or more other persons in their group or organization to achieve "a satisfying self-definition"; finally, they internalize the ideas and values in their environment, making these ideas and values part of themselves.[16]

The individual referred to in the preceding paragraphs is preeminently the classroom teacher. Inasmuch as change in schools occurs primarily in classrooms, and inasmuch as the classroom teacher is still in charge of the classroom, those who desire change in schools must "get to" classroom teachers, whose role automatically builds around them certain resistances. In the first place, the teacher's role is characteristically ego rewarding, for in the classroom the teacher is the cynosure of all eyes, the main font of knowledge, the chief performer. When a board of education or an administrator installs in the teacher's classroom kits of learning materials, which are advertised as being "teacher proof" and which substitute for part of the teacher's role, the teacher's resistance to the new materials is likely to be automatic.

If all the constructive work that has already been done with individual teachers in a school or school system is not to be undone, the innovations with which administrators and boards of control often become enamored must be presented to teachers with great care. The problem of moving the teacher out of a central role must be dealt with frankly and openly. Naturally, one of the first questions the teacher asks is "What's in this for the children—and for me?" The change agent must show what the proposed innovation can do to improve learning and how the teacher's time can be used more profitably in a somewhat altered assignment. Later, the teacher may ask embarrassing questions about the intentions of the innovators who devised the scheme, about which pupils are likely to gain most, about the precise gain usually attributable to the innovation when compared with doing nothing or doing something entirely different, and about the added cost of the innovation. The change agent can hardly be too well prepared to answer questions like these.[17]

The difficulties inherent in inducing change in individuals suggest that the personal characteristics of the change agent should be "special." Morin found that these special characteristics should include enjoyment of high professional esteem, ability to stimulate or to provide inspiration, openness to change in one's own ways, prudence and social awareness, ability to work well with others, and ability to lead and so to influence.[18] As is often true, this list sounds unattainable by human beings.

At its best, implementation of curriculum ideas consists of putting the ideas into operation in the most expeditious, skillful, and efficient ways possible. What actually happens when ideas affecting individual teachers are implemented in schools depends on the particulars of the situation. In Ohio, the state's Department of Education developed an implementation model for diffusing the ideas that were part of the new Environment Curriculum Adaptation Project. Later the Department assessed the factors causing success or failure in the implementation of the project. Three elements proved to be most important in causing teachers to accept ideas intended to teach pupils the importance of protecting the environment: the curriculum guides that had been produced, the interest generated by and in teachers, and the implementation workshops as an inservice device. The obstacles were largely managerial: lack of time in the teachers' work week, the higher priority placed on other curriculum content, and conflicts in crowded school schedules.[19]

In Canada, the Ontario Institute for Studies in Education traced the implementation in the schools of a packaged program designed to develop pupil skills in using concepts. Implementation was blocked in part by focusing too much on the project of instruction, or on the program's structure; by using illogical ways of diffusing the program; and by utilizing oversimplified strategies of change.[20]

The implementation process is chiefly the responsibility of curriculum leaders. Obviously they cannot be too wise in making decisions about the process.

Causing Change in Organizations

If change occurred only in one-to-one relationships and in small group settings, it would be difficult enough to understand and accomplish. But it also takes place in large organizations containing many subparts. A particular subpart—for example a subject department in a high school—may be ready for improvement while the remaining subparts lag. Another special problem of organizations is the presence of hierarchies and channels through which plans for change or improvement must pass if they are to be acceptable to the organization as a whole. Hubert S. Coffee and William P. Golden, Jr. describe the general situation:

> Institutions usually develop a formal social structure as a method of performing their work. The structure is characterized by a hierarchy of offices which have distinctive responsibilities and privileges. These are exemplified in a status system which is based on differential prestige and a prescribed set of roles and procedures. . . .
>
> The process of change can be productive within an institution only if conditions permit reassessment of goals and the means of their achievement. . . .
>
> The most significant barrier to institutional change is the resistance which persons express when such change seems threatening to roles in which they have developed considerable security. . . .[21]

Tested Processes of Institutional Change

Hierarchies, goals, procedures, and roles are all involved in the process of institutional change.[22] The existence of rigid hierarchies and standardized views of procedures and roles may inhibit change. Cooperative examination of goals does, on the other hand, encourage permanence of change provided that the altered goals are put into functional use by the hierarchy. At any rate, of the three methods of institutional change mentioned previously—planning by equals, indoctrination by superiors, and coercion by superiors—planning by equals seems to have the greatest long-term and desirable effect.

David H. Jenkins has proposed a methodology of encouraging teacher-pupil planning—and for creating other educational changes—that follows four classic steps in social engineering: analyzing the situation, determining required changes, making these changes, and stabilizing the new situation to ensure its maintenance.[23] Jenkins recognizes the existence of a "force field" (as suggested originally by the late Kurt Lewin) in which there are "driving forces" that push in the direction of change and "restraining forces" that oppose change. The present or current level of an educational situation is "that level where the sum of all the downward forces and the sum of all the upward forces are equal." An example of a driving force is the conviction that if teachers involve their pupils in planning, the teachers themselves will receive greater satisfaction from the act of teaching. An example of a restraining force is teachers' lack of skill in helping pupils plan.

In Jenkins's words, "changes will occur only as the forces are modified so that the level where the forces are equal is changed." To modify the forces, one may (1) reduce or remove restraining forces, (2) strengthen the driving forces or add to their number, or (3) change the direction of certain forces. For instance, one may remove lack of skill in teacher-pupil planning through training, strengthen or add to competence in planning, and change the direction in which the objective "good citizenship" is achieved *from* telling pupils how to be good citizens *to* planning citizenship activities with them. In analyzing the force field, the curriculum leader may seek answers to the following questions: What forces are there in the field? Can the directions of some of the forces be reversed or altered in another way? Which restraining forces can probably be reduced with least effort? Which driving forces can probably be increased?

To become permanent, says Jenkins, change must be stabilized—the stability of the new condition must be ensured. This can be accomplished by making sure that the restraining forces have been made impotent and that the driving forces continue in action.

In making a comparison of diffusion and adoption of innovative techniques in agriculture on the one hand and education on the other, Robert

G. Owens explains the relatively slow rate of change in education in the following ways. First, education has an insufficient scientific base. As a consequence, school personnel are uncertain which ideas and procedures are most valid. Second, education lacks change agents comparable to county agents in agriculture. Certainly school administrators do not create or encourage change as readily. Third, schools lack incentives to adopt new ways of proceeding. One of the important missing incentives is direct evidence that given practices work. Fourth, the U.S. public school, in particular, is a "domesticated organization" rather than a "wild" one. That is, it is protected and secure, unexposed to the risks that business organizations often encounter. As a result it develops less vigor than it should.[24] There is evidence that less vigorous organizations exhibit less desire to change.

On the affirmative side, E. G. Guba believes that it is possible and necessary to have a strategy for diffusion of innovations. As to technique, the strategy can utilize telling, showing, helping, involving, training, and/or intervening. Guba points out that a regional educational laboratory may be expected to tell, show, or involve people. A state department of education can intervene. An individual teacher can tell and show. All of these agencies need to be careful about using techniques that do not come naturally to them or are seen as being outside their prescribed roles.[25]

Very often, several categories of persons are involved in a given curriculum change. Some of them are likely to support the change; others, to resist it; and still others, to be lukewarm about it. Suppose the categories included teachers, pupils, parents, other taxpayers, local employers, college personnel, and representatives of two or three government agencies. An initial step in determining locus and degree of support can be to ask questions like the following: Which of these groups seem likely to support the change? Which seem likely to oppose it? In the former instance, why the support? In the latter instance, why the opposition? How can persons in supporting populations become most helpful in inducing opponents to support the change?

The Psychology of Institutional Change

The persons who are subjects of change may be viewed in any one of seven ways: as rational beings who can be convinced, as untrained persons who can be taught, as psychological beings who can be persuaded, as economic beings who can be paid or deprived, as political beings who can be influenced, as members of a bureaucratic system who can be compelled, and as members of a profession who have professional obligations. The way a change agent chooses to view the persons for whom he or she has responsibility depends significantly on the state or condition in which he or she wants to leave them after dealing with them.[26]

In organizations there are usually conditions that become psychological barriers to progress. One of these is the requirement that people work together when they are unaccustomed to doing so. Another is that roles become obsolete and thus preparation for existing roles becomes outdated. Another is that decision making takes time, and the passage of time builds tension in people who are waiting for the decisions. Still another is that real control is often diffused, so responsibility remains unclear, and subsequent feedback is uncertain or ambiguous.

Persons who would create change in an organization of the size and complexity of the average school system need to think of several phenomena relating to the peculiarities of people in groups. The first of these is the prospect of labeling supporters of an innovation as "good guys" and the opponents or neutrals as "bad guys." If a change agent applies the labels too prominently, the insecure opponent or neutral is likely to conclude, "If my old way of doing things is no good, then the implication is that I am no good." Polarization of supporters and detractors becomes a natural consequence, and the detractors, hoping that the innovation will fail, may actually work to defeat it. Labeling is often a subtle, even unconscious, action. The change agent should declare a given innovation to be one of the bright new prospects on the educational horizon, giving about equal time to each of the other prospects in which people in the school system have become interested.

A related phenomenon is that of "fair hairedness," or becoming an object of favoritism. Special contributors to the success of an innovation may easily be regarded by less enthusiastic and less diligent contributors as "fair haired," chosen, or specially favored. Fair-haired persons are then envied, deprecated, or hated by the rank and file. Though the fair haired are thus damaged, damage to the managerial system is even greater; distrust then becomes management's chief handicap in dealing with many of the people in the school or school system.

The so-called bandwagon effect is a third phenomenon. Teachers tend to be suspicious of the motives of administrators who continually board new educational bandwagons for short-term rides. The alleged innovations that the bandwagons represent are sometimes not innovations at all. (The bandwagon actually came through town years ago, but people have forgotten its design and the color of its trappings.) Wise school leaders control their enthusiasm for innovations until they know and understand them. This restraint helps to screen out unworthy prospects along the total range of innovations.

A fourth phenomenon peculiar to the current economic situation is the faculty's sense of insecurity. When budgets are being reduced, teachers are being dismissed, and new positions are not being approved, incumbent teachers tend to look at new projects with suspicion, especially if the projects are expensive or if they substitute in some way for service by teachers. In this situation, the facts of the matter are less important than the perceptions of faculty members. To campaign successfully for adoption of an innovation the school leader must keep the facts that support the adoption at his or her fingertips, but the real battle will be won only when the leader has worked honestly and forthrightly to correct the perceptions of the staff (if correction is needed).

Finally, a school system is what its name suggests—an organizational system with many people serving different functions. Proposals for change that cause the least disruption within the system usually have the greatest chance of being accepted and therefore of succeeding. Life in organizations is normally filled with enough disturbance to make manufactured disruptions questionable unless they are seen as contributing in the long run to constructive results.

Effecting Change in Organizations

An approach to effecting change in organizations is Organization Development (OD), which is based on some of the more humane points of view about motivation now expounded in social science literature. Organization Development attempts to change schools and other institutions from their mechanical orientation to a living, social one, thereby encouraging the reeducation of people, emphasizing learning-by-doing in confronting organizational problems, and ultimately improving the functioning of the organization. Though organizational change usually concentrates heavily on tasks, technology, and structure, OD has as its main concern the organization's human social system. It emphasizes goals and potentials, data collection and feedback, open communication, effort by a number of groups within the organization, involvement of all parts of the organization, and dedication of people, money, and time to improvement.[27] An abbreviated form of organization development known as organizational consultation uses the same strategies as OD, but it consumes less time because it is less comprehensive.[28]

Most persons who have studied the change process intensively seem to agree that people in organizations who change from old modes to new must first be made aware of the possibility of changing. Next, they must be made interested in a proposed change. Third, they must have time to consider the worth of the change. Fourth, they must try it for themselves on a small scale. Finally, if the change stands the test they apply, they accept the change for use in the future.

Problems involved in changing do not always rest with the *people* in organizations. The organizations themselves sometimes need to change to become healthier and more viable. Redefinition of the roles of personnel, training of personnel teams, improvement in communication feedback, target setting, or general troubleshooting may be needed.[29]

The Prospects for Planned Institutional Change

How will change in schools fare in a difficult era—the immediate future? People who have worked in schools throughout the past four or five decades tend to agree that the current era in elementary and secondary schooling is the most difficult one they have known. The public's faith in the schools has eroded to a significant degree. Increased imposition of minimum standards of pupil achievement has altered local curriculum requirements. This imposition is evidence of greater centralization of power in state governments, which has destroyed part of the power and influence of educators and other persons in local communities. These facts would seem to indicate that the schools can become puppets moved to and fro by outside forces, and that their destiny as mainly self-controlled institutions is dangerously uncertain.

Other factors, however, are making planned institutional change at the local level more effective and promising than ever before. In the first place, curriculum leaders are better prepared for their work. They are harder to delude. They know how to work around unwise (and sometimes downright idiotic) mandates. Whether or not they have had careful instruction in the change process, they sense the necessity of working in ways that encourage desirable change. Curriculum leaders today know more about innovations and practices that have passed both formal and experiential tests of worth. At the same time, their suspicion of quack schemes promises for the future less going-through-the-motions just for the sake of being active. They are learning gradually what better balance in programs and activities can mean in achieving high quality schooling. Accordingly, the schools themselves are becoming better planned and more nearly self-renewing institutions. As pressures change and eras pass, the substantial element in institutional change will continue to be an element that has been respected too little: constantly improving quality of personnel who operate instructional programs.[30] As Wendell Hough says more simply and directly, "Those who can make the real difference are the people in the school."[31]

The importance of increasing the competence of local school system personnel argues for improved programs of staff development. School system staffs need two kinds of development in particular: (1) reeducation, leading to a redirection and a refinement of competencies, and (2) resocialization, or realignment of roles and role relationships. In any institution, the latter tends to be more difficult to achieve than the former. People do not mind being "updated," but they dislike having their roles and functions changed and having their role relationships altered or destroyed. Nevertheless, both kinds of development are necessary, regardless of the cost in time and money.[32]

SITUATION 7-1
Resistance to Change: Trouble in a Faculty

It was October, a month after the start of Jim Downes's third year as principal of Martinsville High School. Previously he had been in charge of a similar high school in Townsend Terrace.

He came home at the end of the day much discouraged. Sitting in his favorite armchair in the living room, he looked disconsolate.

"What's the trouble, Jim?" asked Eunice, his wife. "Why don't you come to dinner?"

"I'm disheartened and disgusted," said Jim. "We had a faculty meeting again today. Our curriculum consultant from the college was there, and we thought everything would go well. I say we. Sam and I were the only two people who seemed to have any such hopes. If it weren't for Sam and his leadership of the science department, I believe I'd quit. Well, nine-tenths of the faculty members just sat there. When the consultant and I asked what problems the faculty would like to deal with during the coming year, we drew a blank."

"You mean no one said anything?" Eunice inquired.

"Well, practically so. There was a long, dead silence, and then Old Ben Oppenheimer spoke for the group, as usual. 'This is a smooth-running faculty,' Ben said. 'It's been smooth for years, Mr. Downes. It was smo-o-o-th before you came. We just don't see any need to manufacture problems.'

"That was the end of Ben's speech and practically the end of the meeting. I'm glad the superintendent wasn't there. If he had been, he'd have seen how little I've been able to jar that faculty in two years. . . ."

What might have caused the Martinsville faculty to resist change as it seems to have done?

What dynamics or forces are frequently at work in situations of this kind?

What do you suppose Jim Downes might do to reduce apathy and stimulate change?

SITUATION 7-2
Misdirected Change: The Tendency to Move in Too Many
Directions at Once

Curriculum change was popping in Plainsburg. The curriculum steering committee for the school system had invited individual teachers and groups of teachers to suggest and develop curriculum projects of any sort they wished. No machinery for selecting or screening projects had been established. The consequence was a flood of projects big and little, well conceived and ill conceived. The steering committee began to express concern as to how many of the projects represented the real needs of the school system and whether there was danger in permitting school personnel "to ride off in too many directions at once."

What is your position regarding control of the number and nature of projects leading to curriculum change?

Which of the ideas about change that appear in the initial part of this chapter relate to the problem of moving in too many directions at once and should therefore be communicated to participants in curriculum improvement?

ACTIVITY 7-1
Statements about Change Process That Are Open to Discussion

Investigate and discuss the validity of the following statements and the associated implications of the statements:

1. Parents and other groups of laypersons in most communities do not exert direct influence on the adoption of new instructional programs, but their influence is decisive on the rare occasions when it is exerted.
   Implication: In organizing new programs, it is not necessary to arouse the active enthusiasm of parents, but it is necessary to avoid their active opposition.
2. The board of education in many a community is not a strong agent in determining the path of educational innovation, but its influence is decisive when it is exerted.
   Implication: New programs must be developed in ways that will not arouse the opposition of boards of education.
3. New instructional programs are usually introduced by school administrators. Contrary to general opinion, teachers play a relatively insignificant role in educational innovation.
   Implication: It pays to convince administrators of the worth of proposed new programs and to gain their support in putting the programs into effect.
4. Classroom teachers can make only three kinds of instructional change in the absence of administrative initiative: (1) change in classroom practice, (2) relocation of existing curriculum content, and (3) introduction of single special courses of secondary school level.
   Implication: Inservice programs for teachers should be limited to the three matters indicated above.
5. The most persuasive experience a school person can have is to observe a successful new program in action. Speeches, literature, research reports, and conversations with participants are interesting but relatively unconvincing.
   Implication: Recommended new programs must be demonstrated to persons who are expected to become involved in them.
6. The most successful innovations are those that are accompanied by the most elaborate help to teachers as they begin to use the innovations.
   Implication: Instructional innovation should be accompanied by substantial continuing assistance to teachers.

PRACTICAL APPLICATIONS OF CHANGE PROCESS IN IMPROVING THE CURRICULUM

A number of models have been developed for applying the change process in practical situations.

The five classic steps in the change process—awareness, interest, evaluation, trial, and adoption—have been incorporated, with minor alteration, in the planning for curriculum improvement accomplished by several regional and local groups, including the Northwest Regional Educational Laboratory. Their plan, called Research Utilizing Problem Solving Process (RUPS), specifies the following five steps:

1. Identifying a need for change: developing awareness, sensing problems, judging who is causing and who is affected by problems, classifying problems, and specifying goals for proposed change
2. Diagnosing the situation in which change is to take place: identifying favorable and unfavorable forces and assessing the strength of each force
3. Considering alternative courses of action
4. Testing the feasibility of a plan for change: running a trial phase during which further attempts are made to understand the situation, the people who are conducting the testing are trained for it, and evaluation of outcomes and process is effected
5. Adoption, diffusion, and adaptation of successful change effort: institutionalizing successful actions, sharing successes and failures with persons elsewhere, and returning to the first step to see whether there are now new needs for change.[33]

H. S. Bhola developed the CLER model. This process model is concerned with configurations, linkages, environments, and resources. Configurations and linkages position data to achieve change; environments and resources encompass elements external to the change process itself. All are thought to be necessary for determining the domain and the time within which change is to occur, for establishing a range of action choices, and for helping with program implementation and evaluation.[34] The CLER model has been found applicable to school situations, but it is said to lack precision.[35] Perhaps it is most usable in situations outside the usual range of curriculum planning activities. For example, CLER has seemed to be helpful in improving recruitment techniques at an adult learning center.[36]

Still another practical change model is PARA, an acronym for profile, action, response, and analysis. In this approach, the first step is to make a profile of each participating teacher's aspirations in the direction of better task performance. The profile is created by asking and obtaining answers to questions such as "What do you wish to learn?" and "How do you wish to be perceived by other people in this school?" In dialog with a curriculum leader, the teacher declares his or her intention of performing a particular task that accords with the goals of the school. The second step in PARA calls for creating an action plan expressing exactly what the teacher will do within an allotted period of time. The curriculum leader assists with putting this plan into effect, and especially with identifying and overcoming obstacles to it. The plan is then put into operation. The third, or response, step consists of gathering information from pupils and other persons in the school about ways in which the plan has affected pupil behavior. The final step proceeds directly from the third. In it, action substeps are analyzed to determine whether each of them has been appropriate, readily put into effect, helpful, and necessary. Teachers find in PARA the advantage of sharing with a curriculum leader the risks involved in making changes.[37]

When elaborate proposals for change have been made, with or without the help of representative teachers, the problem of putting the proposals into effect becomes real and immediate. The public schools of Montgomery County, Maryland prepared a five-year plan for developing and installing revised systems of instruction in four subject fields. Within the latter part of the five-year period, announcement was made of a program for reeducation of personnel, incorporating a series of steps in inservice education. These steps included orienting the staff to the philosophy and nature of the proposals; instructing teachers and others about placement tests, curriculum guides, reports, and assessments; providing activities to help teachers use features of the instructional plans; demonstrating exemplary classroom practices; and teaching principals and aides what they needed to know to implement the proposals.[38]

Levels in Specific Curriculum Improvements

Changes that are judged to be improvements are produced at several levels of operation. These levels are titled substitution, alteration, variation, restructuring, and value orientation change. If, for example, a group of teachers and administrators were proposing to improve a reading program, they might simply substitute a new series of readers for the current series because the newly adopted books had features that made them superior. They might, on the other hand, use alteration by declaring that reading would henceforth be allotted thirty additional minutes of instructional time each day on the ground that increased instructional time would yield improved results. They might try variation by transferring a reading program that had succeeded reasonably well elsewhere to their own school, where conditions were such that it might have even better success. They might decide to restructure, a more hazardous means of improvement, by organizing teams of reading teachers made up of reading specialists, classroom teachers, and aides to provide maximum instructional impact. Or finally and most precariously, they might attempt value orientation change, asking classroom teachers to turn matters of routine reading instruction over to computer-assisted instruction and teacher aides while the teachers themselves became responsible for diagnosis, prescription, search for materials, and other more difficult aspects of reading instruction. Changing teachers' roles in this way requires a shift in their values, a shift that most adults make only with difficulty, though they may give temporary signs of having made it. Although the five levels may appear, for purposes of analysis, to be separate and distinctive, more than one of them may be used at any one time to promote a curriculum project.

A Study of Changes and Improvements

The aforementioned levels are represented in curriculum changes and improvements that have been underway during the past eight decades. According to a study by Donald Orlosky and B. Othanel Smith, major changes or improvements in the curriculum during the past eighty years have ascribable times of origin, sources, and ratings of success (see Table 7-1). The times of origin are specified as being pre-1950 and post-1950. The sources are internal to school systems (I) and external to school systems (E). External sources include community groups, government, and foundations. The ratings of success range from 1 to 4. The rating 1 applies to a change that has not been implemented in the schools and would be hard to find in a school system anywhere. The rating 2 means a change that has not been accepted widely but has had some influence on educational practice. The rating 3 refers to a change that has been installed in schools and is quite evident there. The rating 4 indicates a change that has successfully permeated schools and school systems.[39]

It would be interesting to conjecture what social and other forces have made for ratings of 3 and 4 in cases like driver education, safety education, and vocational-technical education. They contrast with the ratings of the core curriculum, sex education, and the famous Thirty School Experiment. Contrary to an assumption shared by many professionals and laypersons, at least as many durable innovations originate inside schools as originate outside them. Evidently, when both the pressures internal to schools and the pressures external to them operate simultaneously in favor of an innovation, its success is assured. The history of curriculum innovation shows, however, that changes in the curriculum can be discarded more readily than changes in school organization.

Orlosky and Smith came to the conclusion that planned change should be based on a combination or interaction of past experiences, current points

TABLE 7-1

MAJOR CHANGE OR IMPROVEMENT	TIME OF ORIGIN	SOURCE	RATING OF SUCCESS
Activity curriculum	Pre-1950	I	2
British Infant School	Post-1950	I	3
Community school	Pre-1950	I	2
Compensatory education	Post-1950	E	3
Conservation education	Pre-1950	E	3
Core curriculum	Pre-1950	I	1
Creative education	Post-1950	I	1
Driver education	Pre-1950	E	4
Elective system	Pre-1950	I	4
Environmental education	Post-1950	E	3
Extra-class activities	Pre-1950	I	4
Home economics	Pre-1950	E	3
International education	Pre-1950	I	3
Physical education	Pre-1950	E	4
Safety education	Pre-1950	I	4
Sex education	Post-1950	E	2
Special education	Post-1950	I	4
Thirty School Experiment (Eight Year Study)	Pre-1950	I	1
Unit method	Pre-1950	I	2
Updating curriculum content	Pre-1950	I	3
Vocational and technical education	Pre-1950	E	4

of view, and analysis of aspects of the educational field. They found that curriculum change is easier to achieve than change in methods of teaching, that adding subjects and updating content have more permanent effects than reorganizing or restructuring the curriculum. Changing an entire curriculum pattern is hazardous even if teachers support the change at the outset. Changes are made impermanent by lack of external social support and by resistance within school systems. When a diffusion plan is lacking, change is aborted. A change that causes teachers or administrators to lose power or to shift their roles drastically will probably be resisted by the very people who can make it effective. In summary, the source of a change has less to do with its success or failure than the support the change acquires and the strain it places on teachers and administrators. For example, the core curriculum and education for creativity have demanded too much of teachers, in consideration of the limited external and even internal support these innovations have received, and they have therefore had limited success. However, international education, supported moderately by school personnel and laypersons, has required so little extra effort from teachers and administrators that it has been accepted reasonably well.[40]

In supplementing the Orlosky-Smith version of what happens in the change process, Parish and Arends support the argument made by anthropologists that many innovations are put to use only when adaptations are made to the culture within which the innovations are expected to thrive. Curriculum planners need to understand the culture of each school in which they work. Within a school, teachers have their own subculture, and administrators have theirs. Therefore, if curriculum change is to begin and continue, strategies for achieving cultural change are more significant than strategies for achieving technological change, though the latter have long been emphasized.[41]

Heckman and others agree that research, development, and diffusion (the familiar RD&D) are less effective in stimulating change than is responsiveness on the part of schools to the needs of their occupants. These needs are determined in large part by looking at the sense the occupants of schools make of their settings and situations. The culture of which school people are a part is a combination of established ways of doing things and the meanings people affix to these ways. An attempt to change what school personnel do demands that they accept not only new ways of doing things but also new sets of meanings that belong with the new ways.[42]

Media and Agencies for Achieving Change

Many reports of curriculum changes do not indicate how crucial the support of administrators is to the success of curriculum innovations. However, considerable curriculum literature is available that shows that support of administrators, whatever the source of an innovation, is indeed necessary. For example, Henry M. Brickell has said:

> Major instructional innovations are introduced by administrators, not by teachers. An administrator is powerful because he can marshal the necessary authority, if not the necessary leadership, to precipitate a decision. He may not be, and frequently is not, the original source of interest in a new type program; but unless he gives it his attention and actively promotes its use, it will not come into being. The control center of the school, as things are managed today, is the administrator.[43]

This statement, written nearly three decades ago, now needs "toning down" in consideration of the effect teachers' unions and associations have had in making the curriculum a negotiable item at the bargaining table. Nevertheless, evidence increasingly shows that active support by administrators makes a real difference. The help that administrators are especially able to give includes putting teachers in contact with curriculum resources, helping teachers clarify the directions in which they wish to go with instructional projects, assisting with adaptation and development of curriculum materials, and marshaling the support of other school personnel and of community members.[44]

There is considerable evidence today that the role of teachers in creating change in schools is steadily increasing. Many professional educators are becoming convinced that teachers want greater involvement in the planning of change, and that they can contribute substantially to program planning and implementation.[45]

The Effect of Regional Centers and Teacher Centers

Relatively new agencies for curriculum change and improvement are regional education centers and teacher centers, which conduct workshops, provide consultant services, organize special events, house and lend instructional materials, prepare educational products, and maintain information retrieval systems. These centers are intended to supply classroom teachers and entire school systems with help that is otherwise beyond their reach. Reports from the field indicate that existing centers need to increase and improve the practical help they give individual teachers and schools.

Materials as a Change Medium

Materials have become a special avenue to change and improvement. For instance, packaged learning programs have come into vogue. Packages, in their simplest forms, are boxed assortments of materials; more complex packages are complicated learning systems. Packaging of learning materials holds promise of helping teachers achieve flexibility in meeting the needs of individual pupils. When the instructional objectives contained in a package tell pupils the quality of performance they should achieve, they have a standard that is seldom communicated to them by other means. Some of the activities in packaged programs are model building, large-group instruction, small-group instruction, role playing, simulation, gaming, field trips, independent study, and laboratory experimentation. Packages are, of course, only one of the kinds of materials found in multimedia centers, which also house books, slides, pictures, filmstrips, transparencies, models, telecasting equipment, instructional machines, and occasionally computers. These centers serve also as production areas or educational laboratories. Most centers are in individual schools, to be used directly by pupils and teachers. A few serve as systemwide facilities for use in inservice education, materials production and servicing, and curriculum planning. All of them contribute to school quality because wealth and availability of materials are important criteria of quality.[46]

Summer Institutes as Media

Yet another practical application of the change process has been made at the sites of summer institutes for classroom teachers who wish to update their knowledge of subject matter content. A study of institutes supported from federal funds under the National Defense Education Act revealed that the professors who taught in NDEA institutes knew little "about the limits, possibilities, and politics of teaching in the schools — about what can be changed, and how change happens in a school or a school system."[47] The study reported further that the professors were not "much concerned to learn."[48] They lectured much and listened little to elementary and secondary school teachers who had been specially chosen because of their competency. The teachers complained that they were given too little opportunity to talk back, to consider key issues, to observe ranges of teaching strategies and techniques, and to relate their newly acquired information to their own teaching. Not only did these findings lead to changes in the institutes, but the experiences of these able teachers as students in summer institutes provide insight into the importance of process in the inservice education of teachers elsewhere. Teachers need opportunities to help determine inservice agendas and procedures to be used in inservice sessions.

Inservice education can profitably be extended beyond the current institutes, conferences, workshops, graduate courses, and staff meetings to occupational experience, field trips, exchanges of teachers among departments and schools, community surveys, and professional writing, consulting, and speaking.[49]

Generally, inservice education has the earmarks of an externally imposed regimen. The idea of staff development has been formulated to "loosen" inservice education so that responsibility for teacher change and growth is placed on the shoulders of the teachers themselves. Staff development usually proves most helpful when it focuses on crucial elements of teaching such as the teacher's sense of purpose, the teacher's perception of pupils, the teacher's knowledge of subject matter, and the teacher's mastery of technique. Always the emphasis is on the teacher and his or her development, which occurs by participation, peer assistance, individual study, and the making of alternative choices. "We did it ourselves in an informal setting" is the theme of many staff development activities, in contrast to the "here's what you are to do" attitude that pervades many an inservice project.

The Potential Helpfulness of Funding Agencies

The funding agencies with which curriculum planners dealt so freely during earlier years are immediately helpful organizations of uncertain long-term effect. Federally funded projects with an evaluation plan as an important component have been proposed. However, neither federally supported projects nor other funded projects have been monitored closely enough so that anyone can know whether persons immediately responsible for the projects have faithfully collected evaluation data or whether the projects have actually proved worthwhile. Therefore too little is known about the effects of funding on curriculum change or improvement.

ACTIVITY 7-2
Teachers' Views of Curriculum Change

Teachers are obviously very important in initiating and perpetuating curriculum change. Interview a randomly selected sample of classroom teachers in an elementary or a secondary school to determine what the teachers think concerning curriculum change. A possible initial question: "If you had your way, what major change would you make in the curriculum of this school?" Formulate other questions that have to do with sources of change, reasons for acceptance of given changes, and the change process as it affects people in the school.

Share your findings with other persons in your class or discussion group.

FOUR ACTIONS THAT FACILITATE CURRICULUM IMPROVEMENT

Four actions seem to have special effect in facilitating curriculum improvement. Stated in imperative form, they are

1. Change the climate and the working conditions in your institution to encourage curriculum improvement.
2. Achieve and maintain appropriate tempo in curriculum improvement.
3. Arrange for a variety of activities that lead to improvement.
4. Build evaluation procedures into each curriculum improvement project.

Each action will be discussed in some depth.

Establish Suitable Climate and Working Conditions

Climate and working conditions, like employee morale, result from many little actions and influences. The little actions and influences within an organization may, however, be categorized under four larger headings: the general attitudes of participating personnel, quantity and quality of personnel (especially the competencies they bring to their tasks), physical resources and materials at the disposal of staff members, and absence of undue and detrimental pressure and influence.

Attitudes of Participants

Certain attitudes of participating personnel seem to be especially helpful in planning curriculum improvement. One of these is acceptance of people's right to feel and express legitimate dissatisfaction with the curriculum. Perhaps all who strive to progress in their work feel some dissatisfaction with what they are presently doing. They should harbor a feeling of legitimate dissatisfaction that does not lead to arbitrary complaining but to affirmative steps that eventually result in satisfaction. Curriculum workers should seek to learn the exact causes of dissatisfaction felt by their peers and subordinates and should encourage co-workers who feel dissatisfaction to channel it constructively into new activity.

A second attitude encourages acceptance of the contributions of many kinds of people to improving the curriculum. Obviously not all contributions of ideas and all gestures of helpfulness are of equal worth. Nevertheless, all who are at all qualified to belong to a faculty group may be expected to have unique contributions to make, if only because all are individuals. They should also be able to make certain contributions in concert with other members of the group. Curriculum workers should provide ample opportunity for all persons to express themselves and to offer their own talents in performing commonly approved tasks.

A third attitude expresses willingness to permit other persons to work on problems they themselves identify as worthy of attention. Real live problems are those that are real and live to the persons who face them and desire to solve them. Thus the principal who is concerned with his or her own problems is often certain that the teachers wish to help solve them. The teachers have their own problems, however, and may soon become impatient or even hostile if they are forced to help solve the principal's imposed or imported problems. Curriculum workers should help teachers clarify and solve problems the teachers themselves perceive as being well worth solving. The same teachers are then likely to greet with favor occasional opportunities to help solve problems for which they feel no direct personal concern. Curriculum matters do not always constitute problems in the adverse sense. Sometimes, as in the joyous expenditure of funds suddenly provided for educational materials, curriculum personnel experience pleasant challenges rather than puzzling problems. Inasmuch as so many curriculum matters require weighty problem solving, however, the term "problem" appears frequently in this text as in other curriculum literature.

A fourth attitude consists of open-mindedness about new educational decisions and practices. Perhaps every specialist in curriculum improvement agrees that the improvement process is aided materially by an attitude of open-mindedness about the new and different, as well as about the tried and tested. So little in education is known assuredly that school personnel are acting presumptuously when they cling to ideas merely because they are supported by tradition. To some persons, open-mindedness means

having an experimental attitude, a willingness to use the "method of intelligence"—commonly called the problem-solving method—in dealing
with educational problems. To others, it implies merely an attitude of
"wait and see" while other staff members try new practices. Whatever the
degree of an individual's personal involvement in a project, open-mindedness is necessary to the project's success and to prospects for future
experimentation.

A fifth attitude is one of willingness to work with other persons to
achieve common ends through commonly agreed upon means. This attitude
affects all members of every working group, leaders and followers. However
significant the contribution of the talented person working alone may be,
well-coordinated groups usually prove wiser in plotting the means and ends
of projects. Curriculum workers should become well acquainted with procedures that facilitate group work and should become competent in leading
groups of differing sizes and kinds.[50] In addition, they should seek to
reconcile the means they use with the ends they desire. One evidence of
autocracy is a tendency to use unfair means to achieve desirable ends. Even
the best curriculum workers can become careless about the means they
use.[51]

Quantity and Quality of Personnel

A stimulating, friendly climate and helpful working conditions are aided
by the presence of able personnel in sufficient numbers to accomplish
worthwhile tasks. Few school systems have too many full-time coordinators, consultants, and specialists in fields like school social work,
psychology, reading, and speech therapy. Surveys of the staffing of schools
and school systems usually reveal that more work is being accomplished
by limited numbers of persons than even the most conservative of personnel analysts expect. Nevertheless, often these persons are discharging
responsibilities that should not be theirs or discharging their responsibilities
in ineffective ways.

In spite of the fact that present-day schools are frequently understaffed
in the fields of supervision and curriculum services, the quality of assistance
that classroom teachers are receiving could be improved in at least three
respects:

- *The very best available persons should be utilized to discharge each
  major responsibility* (even though employing a new person may be
  costly). Too often, teachers or principals with full or partial work
  loads are being made part-time specialists in reading, art, music,
  physical education, speech, psychology, and other fields in which
  they may have at one time received only limited preparation.

- *The role of the school in the total community should be examined at intervals.*   This determines whether all the functions the school has adopted truly belong to an educational institution. Many teachers, administrators, and laypersons suspect that certain social-work services to children and the community at large have been preempted by the school from other institutions and agencies. Though the school may, in many instances, supply these services speedily and efficaciously, the wisdom of making the school responsible for them in the first place is questionable. Of course, children whose only source of necessary services is the school may legitimately expect the school to continue providing the services.
- *Special teachers should be assigned in different, more helpful ways.* A study by the United States Office of Education showed that varied and sometimes questionable uses are being made of special teachers in physical education.[52] Reading specialists often devote their full time to helping individual pupils instead of spending a portion of their time helping classroom teachers become competent identifiers and eradicators of common reading difficulties. Specialists should ask themselves a key question: "How can we provide the greatest long-term help to classroom teachers?"[53]

Two additional sources of personnel to improve teaching and learning are (1) the staffs of universities, state departments of education, county education offices, and school systems other than one's own and (2) well-informed laypersons who give advice strictly within their own specialties. These two sources provide part-time consultants who may be called upon for a few hours or days of assistance at almost any time. The factors that affect the success of consultants have been described in the literature; these factors should be given full consideration. Alert boards of education and school administrators are making increasing use of consultant services. Many school systems maintain resource files of community citizens who volunteer their help in instructional fields ranging from the physical sciences and the arts to citizenship education. Classroom teachers are usually the best judges of which laypersons are most effective in reaching pupils with the content they have to teach.

Of course, no substitute has been found for competent classroom teachers who work patiently and insightfully with children day after day. The quality of the schools depends chiefly on the quality of the classroom teachers who teach in them. Consequently, employing superior teachers and then helping them grow personally and professionally is the best way to ensure that American children receive excellent schooling.

The morale of able teachers can be improved by reducing the load of clerical and custodial duties that now burden many of them. Obviously professional employment carries with it responsibility for certain routine operations, but studies of the duties of classroom teachers often reveal numerous and sometimes unnecessary clerical and custodial loads. An enlightened school administration seeks to free competent persons for activity at their highest level of performance. Recent attempts to use wisely the services of teacher aides have brought revelations of their potential for helping classroom teachers with the semiprofessional and menial aspects of teaching. As "career ladders" of school personnel are built to distribute responsibility for paraprofessional, clerical, and other lower-level tasks, the role of the classroom teacher as it is now conceived will change markedly. School officials will then need to be more certain than they are at present that teachers are using their time to maximum advantage.

The individual teachers tend to feel their own role is valued if other teachers within the building are competent. In times of emergency licensing of marginally qualified teachers, the problem of maintaining mutual respect and self-respect among staff members becomes especially difficult and significant. The effect of quality of personnel on faculty morale is readily apparent.

Availability of Physical Resources and Materials

Studies of working conditions in schools have revealed that teachers feel satisfaction in having varieties of usable instructional materials at hand and in understanding how to use them. When materials and equipment accord with the requirements of the instructional program, and when the persons who use materials and equipment have a major part in choosing them, the usefulness of these resources is usually ensured.

One of the great difficulties with learning materials continues to be their failure to serve differing ability levels, socioeconomic groups, and special interests among the pupils population. Many teachers doubt that superior materials exist in quantity for children of any developmental level or status. The school that seeks to improve the curriculum for its pupils searches continuously for materials and equipment that will best take into account the range of individual differences the school encounters. The principal of a school of this sort tries to make physical resources quickly available to teachers by arranging for purchase of materials as they are needed and by moving them to points of use as speedily as possible. One of the major complaints of classroom teachers is directed against the failure of administrators and custodial staffs to move materials from storerooms according to a reasonable schedule, or even to communicate to teachers the fact that materials have arrived. An additional hazard of school administration is the tendency of principals to become overzealous about amplifying systems and electronic machinery generally and thus to spend precious funds in purchasing equipment that teachers would gladly trade for materials of more direct use to them.

Absence of Undue Pressure and Influence

Studies of teacher morale clearly show that the effectiveness of a school can be ruined by the conniving and perfidy of irresponsible politicians. Promises that are made and not kept are one of the major sources of trouble. Another is graft (which has now been eradicated from most school districts, but which is known to be present in a few and is strongly suspected in others). Tenure laws have generally been successful in preserving teachers' employment, but teachers are sometimes under pressure to behave in politically acceptable ways if they desire salary increments, promotions, and privileges. Some political scientists maintain that control of the public schools should be placed more and more in the hands of municipal and state government officials and accordingly be removed from the authority of local boards of education. It is possible that this change would create more political interference with schools and teachers than now exists. The unfortunate effects of undue influence and pressure should be reduced and avoided at almost any cost.

Both Wilbur A. Yauch and William W. Savage give helpful advice about morale and its improvement. Says Yauch:

1. Be willing to make haste slowly.
2. Take the easiest problems first.
3. Treat people as human beings.
4. Make their experiences in school pleasant.
5. Operate on the assumption that teachers can be trusted.
6. Try a little of the "Golden Rule."
7. Encourage and accept criticism.
8. Don't act like a stuffed shirt.

Savage concludes:

> Morale is important. A high level is desirable in any staff, if it is based on constructive values and attitudes. But the desire for improvement that is characteristic of the enthusiastic and professional staff member must not be confused with low morale. The possibility of "high" morale being synonymous with ineffectiveness in a school or school system staffed by mediocre persons must not be overlooked. And complacency and satisfaction on the part of incompetent persons must not be designated as the goals of administration.[54]

SITUATION 7-3
A Special Problem of Attitudes

Consider the words of a curriculum coordinator who has a complaint to make:

> Mr. Acornley, our superintendent, came to our K–12 social studies meeting and wanted the whole job we'd been working on for a long time to be done over. The teachers were all hopped up about some experiments they'd been designing. One of them was describing her plan when Mr. Acornley arrived. After about five minutes of sitting and looking wise, he turned to me and said, "Now I hope you're not misleading these teachers. I think they're getting themselves involved in things that don't concern them. I'm not much in favor of some of the ideas that teachers like to try out on other people's children. Now I'll tell you what we need—and the Board reminded me of it just last week—a good social studies course of study. Preparing one in meetings like this would be more profitable, I'll bet a cookie, than listening to each other talk, especially when the conversation is over the heads of some of the folks anyway. I'll tell you what to do: Prepare a course of study and have it ready within two months. Then you'll be making a real contribution." When he'd said all this, Mr. Acornley got up and ambled to the door. Well, you'd have thought a wet blanket had descended on that committee! All we could say was "It's time to go home."

The effect of this sort of commentary by an important leader is obviously serious and highly detrimental.

What could the curriculum coordinator and the superintendent have done to prevent this outbreak?

Is it possible that the superintendent feels somewhat threatened by the curriculum coordinator's relationship with the teachers or by the importance of the coordinator's role in instruction? How commonly does this feeling of threat prevail? If it is at all common, what should be the responsibility of curriculum coordinators in preventing it?

What might have been done in this situation to reestablish cooperation and enthusiasm among the teachers?

SITUATION 7-4
Some Common Problems in Getting and Using Instructional Materials

Mrs. Martinson, the new principal of Clemson High School, looked straight at her assistant. "Henry," she said, "in your fifteen years around here have you visited all the classrooms in the building?"

"No," replied Henry, as he fumbled with a pad of late-admission slips, "Mr. Davies had me working on administrivia—you know, administrative details—all the time. I hope things will be different under the new regime."

Dodging her assistant's hint, Mrs. Martinson explained: "Within the past eight days, I've been in all the classrooms looking for places to help improve working conditions for the teachers. I'm sure we have at least one handle to take hold of. It's the way our teachers are getting and using instructional materials. Here's a list of problems as I see them."

Henry looked at Mrs. Martinson's notebook. Half a dozen problems appeared prominently at the top of the list:

1. Most teachers seem to be using only a single textbook. In some classes there are too few copies of the single textbook to go around.
2. Teachers complain that they must order audiovisual materials a half year in advance of their use. When films and filmstrips arrive, the pupils sometimes say they have seen them two or three times in previous years.
3. A visit to the school library during almost any period of the day reveals that one could shoot a shotgun through the library without hitting any pupils.
4. Workbooks seem to be used to provide busywork or to keep pupils quiet.
5. Teachers say that many of the books their pupils are using are too difficult.
6. There seems to be a feud between the high school's audiovisual specialist and most of the department heads. The department heads charge that the audiovisual specialist is trying to "build her own little empire."

In view of the importance of adequate and well-used materials in achieving desirable climate and working conditions in a school, indicate both immediate and long-term actions Mrs. Martinson and her staff might take in dealing with each of these problems.

Achieve and Maintain Appropriate Tempo

A second major action that facilitates curriculum improvement is achieving and maintaining appropriate tempo. Curriculum workers are soon compelled to learn that the timing of curriculum improvement activities is vital. Their fundamental problem is one of maintaining balance between gradualism and rapidity. Many school systems work so gradually at improvement that they scarcely make any effort to improve at all. Eventually, groups of citizens in their communities or in the nation at large surpass the professional staffs of these school systems in thinking and planning and thus are able to create changes in the schools. Too much gradualism, or outright lack of curriculum leadership and action, has contributed to an externally planned revolution in the teaching of mathematics, physical science, and certain other subjects in U.S. schools. Teachers of these subjects have been making changes in curriculum content that they would probably have been very slow in making if they had not been "pushed." Other externally planned revolutions are obviously in the making.

The opposite of extreme gradualism is, of course, excessive and ill-founded speed. Many a noble experiment has come to grief because its supporters have moved ahead of the rank and file of classroom teachers. Many another project has been lost because popular thinking in the community in which it was initiated was not prepared for its appearance on the educational scene. Careful watching of the forces that promote or impede improvement provides the only real guide to appropriate speed. Good timing results from responding cautiously to questions like these: Are we ready for this change? How fast can we comfortably move? How does the speed at which we are effecting this change relate to the speeds at which we are making other changes? If we are not ready for a significant, timely change, how can we develop readiness for it? Are there any ideas and actions that could be helpful in sparking change?

Tempo of change or improvement relates directly to the thoughtfulness with which improvement is sought. For instance, a group of teachers may write a course guide during six weeks of occasional meetings with little effect on the practices of other teachers who are later introduced to the guide. Instead, an inservice project requiring three years may be directed to the same ends and the improvement resulting from it may be profound and long-lasting. The distinction between the two activities is not only in time expended but in careful, early consideration of the kinds of activities that might make a genuinely lasting difference. One of the major functions of leadership is to emphasize the importance of certain projects in relationship to other projects. Those that are really important to teachers' growth usually deserve the most time for completion and the most preplanning of the procedures by which they will be effected. Furthermore, the time of their initiation must depend chiefly on how soon they have to be accomplished and on the number and nature of other tasks that must be performed.

Specific Problems of Tempo

Practitioners of curriculum planning often face additional problems that affect the tempo of their work. One of these is the varying sizes of the tasks they undertake. An important duty of curriculum planners is to estimate the amount of time particular tasks deserve. If the tasks are large, one, two, or three of them may be all that a school can undertake within a year. Usually some tasks look small and others loom large. For instance, considering word analysis in the reading program of upper elementary school children is a smaller task than determining sequence in the whole language arts program. The former task might be performed rapidly in conjunction with several other activities, but full consideration of sequence in an important subject field might legitimately claim a faculty's undivided attention for at least a year. Of course, both big and small tasks are being undertaken in most school systems at the same time. It is important to keep the total number and total size of tasks small enough that curriculum study can be thorough rather than superficial.

A second problem concerning tempo relates to the manageability of projects. Some projects are so large or complicated that they simply cannot be dealt with by the personnel of a single school system. Significant experimentation with the uses of computers, for instance, usually requires large-scale financing and the cooperation of several school systems. Unwise selection of projects that are too large or too involved not only leads to frustration among personnel, but also wastes their valuable time.

A related difficulty is, of course, selecting projects that make no real difference in instructional improvement. Many tasks being performed today are unevaluated, so little is known about their relative or intrinsic worth. One may make expensive rearrangements of personnel and materials, demonstrate the materials, and advertise them widely, and still not know whether the changes make a difference to learning. Time spent on unevaluated demonstrations may easily be time stolen from other, more demonstrably useful projects.

Finally, tempo is affected by injudicious rescheduling of tasks that have been performed on one or more occasions previously. One of the common complaints of teachers is this: "Someone has decided that we ought to study the English (or some other) program again. I thought we gave it a good overhauling just three years ago." Teachers become frustrated when curriculum leaders seem to "ride" their own hobbies, calling for restudy of given educational problems at too-frequent intervals. Careful pacing of tasks is a special need in those school systems in which curriculum study has been under way for many years.

The rule, then, about tempo, timing, or pacing may be summarized as follows: *not too fast, not too slow, not too carelessly planned, not too big, not too insignificant, not too recently considered.* This is obviously a rule easier to state than to live by, but it is extremely relevant to the process of improvement.

SITUATION 7-5
The Emergencies in Pennsatonic

Pennsatonic is a big town geographically though it's not a very populous one. The principals of its sixteen schools seldom see each other except at monthly meetings in Superintendent Moody's office. Maybe it's the twenty-mile distance from one side of town to the other that makes the problems of the schools so different. Anyway, at last Tuesday's meeting two completely different kinds of problems developed. As a result of them, good old Pennsatonic may not settle down for a long time.

Ned Graves, who's in charge of Adams School, reported that he'd recently been descended upon by a group of parents who wanted to "see the curriculum of Adams School." The group was dissatisfied with the fact that ancient history is being taught in the fifth grade and that long division is postponed until near the end of the sixth grade. There were other complaints about the curriculum too. Ned found some copies of courses of study in the social studies and arithmetic and handed them to the complainants. Now he's sorry he did. The parents soon noticed that the courses of study are nearly eighteen years old. Some of the complainants want the teachers to spend their spare time during the next two weeks describing in writing what they teach in these two subjects. Later they will want the teachers to describe what they teach in other subjects too.

From the north side of town, Rita Corson had a different tale of woe. The teachers in her junior high school are up in arms because half of them are expected to do team teaching in a block-of-time program. Rita says there is likely to be a strike unless she helps eliminate the block-of-time program and makes an entirely new schedule. A few of the teachers broke up a faculty meeting last week with the complaint that Rita and two of her "favorite teachers" had planned and installed the block-of-time program during the summer without the knowledge and participation of the other teachers.

State the differences (and similarities, if any) between the two problems presented above.

What could have been done to prevent each of these problems?

What should the superintendent and the principals do both immediately and in the long run to solve each of the two problems? How could they relate their long-term actions to newly developed systemwide policies in curriculum improvement?

Select among a Variety of Activities

A third major action that assists the process of curriculum improvement is to select among a variety of activities directed toward improvement. The provision of varied activities has been referred to as a shotgun approach. When one shoots a shotgun, one is not certain what he or she will hit with any pellet. Similarly, curriculum improvers who use varied activities are sometimes unsure who will be attracted to and who will be most affected by each of several activities. The best that one can do is to narrow many possibilities to a few according to ascribed purposes and the exercise of one's good judgment. If, for instance, one wants to increase the familiarity of a given group of teachers with research procedures, a staff development project might be organized for them, an experience in using research procedures in their classrooms might be devised, or an apprenticeship to the research director of the school system might be arranged. Reason dictates that any one of these activities would prove more beneficial than merely inviting the teachers to read about research methods. But which of the three preferred activities should be engaged in by a given group of teachers? If all three cannot be utilized simply because there is not enough time to organize them or because all three are unnecessary when one would be sufficient, which one will have greatest effect on the teachers? Though a curriculum leader may judge that the least sophisticated of the activities may serve best, other considerations affect such a decision and so the answer to this question isn't self-evident.

As has been said, curriculum improvement may be equated in many respects with supervision, inservice education, or staff development. Accordingly, the activities used in these three connecting avenues to school quality are fundamentally the same. They exist in some profusion under these headings: group activities, contact with individuals, and use of literary and mechanical media. Following are some of the available activities under their appropriate headings:

Group activities

committees	clinics
study groups	institutes
workshops	courses
conferences	seminars
work conferences	

Contact with individuals

interviewing and counseling individuals	demonstration teaching by individual teachers or supervisors
observation of individual teachers in classrooms and elsewhere	inservice advisement of individual teachers
assistance to the teacher in his or her classroom	directed reading

Literary and mechanical media

written bulletins	bulletin boards
research reports	tape recordings of meetings and decisions
policy statements	
course guides	educational television

The reader will probably think of other activities belonging under these headings. Since the days when course-of-study construction was almost the exclusive activity in curriculum improvement, the problem has not been a lack of activities but uncertainty as to which ones should be used in given situations.

Curriculum workers appear to spend most of their time in activities of a group-work nature. They spend the second most amount of time interacting with individuals. In the future they will probably give more attention to the third category—literary and mechanical media—as the application of technology increases the possible uses of mechanical media. Many curriculum leaders hold that, of all the separate activities, workshops and conferences with individuals achieve most satisfactory results.

SITUATION 7-6
Homework for the General Curriculum Committee

Someone turned on the lights in the curriculum office. It was 5:45 on a Tuesday afternoon, and the general curriculum committee was torn between two requirements: leaving for dinner and other appointments, or planning to effectuate four distinct activities within the next two months.

"Since we've rejected the idea of having a subcommittee make the plans," said Dr. Stogdill, chairwoman of the general committee, "let's think about possibilities during the next two days and meet here again for an hour on Thursday afternoon."

"I'm not sure I remember all four activities," drawled Herschel Odom. "Ruth, will you put all of them on the blackboard?"

The chalk scraped and clicked as Ruth Hadley listed:

1. Sensitizing high school mathematics teachers to new content and sequences in mathematics
2. Getting teachers' suggestions about names of local citizens to add to the resource file
3. Hearing from the child study division of the State Department of Education concerning the topic "Newer Findings about the Development of Elementary School Children"
4. Presenting to all the teachers in the school system a "buddy plan" for the orientation of new teachers next fall.

Assume that you are a member of the general committee. List one or more activities you think you might emphasize in dealing with each of the four problems. Keep in mind the possibility of combining activities that belong to the three categories: group activities, contact with individuals, and preparation and use of literary and mechanical media. Discuss with a group of your fellow students the feasibility of your plans.

Build Evaluation Procedures into Each Project

A fourth major action to help the process of curriculum improvement is building into each project, from its very inception, procedures for evaluating the effects of the project. This action is taken so infrequently that the quality of both old and new educational practices usually goes unassessed. After a while, the accumulation of unevaluated practices

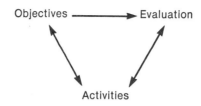

FIGURE 7-1.   The relationship among major parts of a curriculum project

becomes so large that no one can defend with assurance the ways in which schools are operated.

If the chief end of curriculum improvement is improvement of pupils' engagements in learning under auspices of the school, the significance of every important step toward this end is evident. The evaluation may, because of the pressures of time and work, be done quite informally, but it should be done nevertheless. The presence of evaluation data lends assurance to practitioners, and it supplies evidence to the people who pay school costs and want to know whether this money is being well spent.

Evaluation is meant to gauge the extent to which objectives of a project or activity have been achieved. A desirable relationship between evaluation and objectives appears in Figure 7-1. The diagram suggests that, as soon as the objectives of a project are stated, ways of evaluating the achievement of the objectives should be considered. Activities should then be chosen for their pertinence to the objectives and also with reference to possible means of evaluation. The thinking process should follow this sequence: from objectives to evaluation to activities that are useful in achieving the objectives and have effects that can properly be evaluated. Too often, curriculum workers think of activities first and then either ignore or defer consideration of objectives and evaluation.

Suppose a committee of second- and third-grade teachers wants to develop a social studies program for primary-grade children that is based less on the imaginings of adults concerning what is good for young children generally and more on the expressed interests of the children themselves in a particular school system. The committee's major objective then is to develop a program centering upon the expressed interests of given groups of children. As soon as the committee has set this objective it should raise the question "How can teachers know when this objective has been achieved?"

The answer might be formulated thus:

Teachers can know by examining the products of their work in determining children's interests within the field called social studies. One of the products will be the teachers' guide, written at the conclusion of the study. A more important product will be the choices of social studies content that teachers are observed making in their classrooms. Therefore, although we shall inspect carefully the completed teachers' guide, we shall also conduct before-and-after observations of choice making by teachers in their classrooms. Both our objectives and our methodology of evaluation imply that teacher activities like the following will be suitable: conducting interviews with children, administering a three-wishes test, asking children to draw pictures to express their wishes, recording ways in which children complete unfinished stories, and engaging children in group discussions. In this way objectives, evaluation procedures, and activities used in curriculum study become closely bound together and evaluation tends to become a continuous process.

Thus the same general principles of evaluation that were stated in Chapter 6 apply here also.

ACTIVITY 7-3
The Prevalence of Built-in Evaluation

Review several curriculum improvement projects to see whether methodology of evaluation was discussed immediately after the nature and purposes of each project were described. If you have had no direct contact with curriculum improvement projects, search for a few reports in educational literature, which can be identified by using *Education Index* or the specific directions provided by your instructor.

In how many instances have plans for evaluation been built into the projects immediately? In how many instances have plans for evaluation been mentioned at all?

What do you conclude about the esteem in which evaluation is held by those who believe they are improving the curriculum? What is your own present view of the significance of evaluation?

SITUATION 7-7
Reducing Illiteracy—A Growing Concern of the Schools

In a school district you know, an increasing number of pupils has been entering the high schools unable to read effectively and unable to interpret symbols in subject matter. High school teachers with long experience in the district are up in arms about the "lowered quality" of pupils now entering the secondary schools. The central office staff realizes that something must be done. After the staff has determined that the pupil population is in fact considerably less able to achieve in the three Rs than pupil populations of five to ten years ago and yet is only slightly less able mentally than these former populations, what basic steps should the staff and other persons take to help improve the system of teaching and learning in order to reduce illiteracy? In light of what you have read in this chapter, discuss what might be done with both the people and the equipment and materials in the learning environment.

SUMMARY

This chapter has dealt with the general process of curriculum change and improvement as it is understood today. The process follows patterns formed by interdisciplinary findings about change in individuals and institutions. Emphasis has been placed on the importance of cooperative effort in creating improvement, on the power of motivation, and on the significance of institutional arrangements. To encourage improvement, curriculum personnel have been urged to pay attention to climate and working conditions in schools, to help maintain proper tempo of improvement, to promote varied activities, and to build evaluation procedures into each project. An attempt has been made in this chapter to emphasize the importance of people in creating curriculum change and improvement.

ENDNOTES

1. B. Othanel Smith, William O. Stanley, and J. Harlan Shores, *Fundamentals of Curriculum Development* (New York: Harcourt, Brace and World, 1957).

2. Alice Miel, *Changing the Curriculum* (New York: Appleton-Century-Crofts, 1946).

3. Kenneth D. Benne and Bozidar Muntyan, *Human Relations in Curriculum Change* (New York: Dryden Press, 1951).

4. Charles P. Loomis, "Tentative Types of Directed Social Change Involving Systematic Linkage," *Rural Sociology* 24, no. 4 (December 1959): 383–90.

5. Warren G. Bennis, "A Typology of Change Processes," in Warren G. Bennis, Kenneth D. Benne, and Robert Chin, *The Planning of Change* (New York: Holt, Rinehart and Winston, 1961), pp. 154–56.

6. Bennis, Benne, and Chin, *Planning of Change*, p. 12. Some school administrators have apparently been taught to doubt the effectiveness of collaboration. Change, they say, should be initiated and prompted by administrative fiat. Hard pushes by these administrators may have been a major cause of recent counterpushes by teachers' unions and teachers' associations, whose members have seen curriculum improvement to be integral to teacher welfare.

7. The princples stated here appeared originally in Ronald C. Doll, "Our Orbits of Change," *Educational Leadership* 17, no. 2 (November 1959): 102–5. They are reproduced by permission of the editor of *Educational Leadership*.

8. From a staff memorandum provided by Lawrence J. Ondrejack and David W. Cochran, September 1980. Used with permission.

9. Ronald Lippitt, Jeanne Watson, and Bruce Westley, *The Dynamics of Planned Change* (New York: Harcourt, Brace and World, 1958), pp. 73, 74.

10. Ibid., pp. 75, 76.

11. Ibid., pp. 83, 88. See also Amitai Etzioni, "Human Beings Are Not Very Easy to Change After All," *Saturday Review*, June 3, 1972, pp. 45–47.

12. Arthur W. Combs, *Myths in Education* (Boston: Allyn and Bacon, 1979), pp. 209–13.

13. See William A. Reid, "Schools, Teachers, and Curriculum Change: The Moral Dimension of Theory-Building," *Educational Theory* 29, no. 4 (Fall 1979): 325–36.

14. Dorwin Cartwright, "Achieving Change in People," in Bennis, Benne, and Chin, *Planning of Change*, pp. 698–706.

15. Kenneth D. Benne, "Deliberate Change as the Facilitation of Growth," in Bennis, Benne, and Chin, *Planning of Change*, pp. 230–34.

16. Herbert C. Kelman, "Processes of Opinion Change," in Bennis, Benne, and Chin, *Planning of Change*, pp. 509–17.

17. See Noojin Walker, "What a Great Idea! Too Bad It Didn't Work," *Educational Technology* 16, no. 2 (February 1976): 46, 47.

18. André Morin, "An Innovator's Odyssey: How to Become a Thoughtful Change Agent," *Educational Technology* 15, no. 11 (November 1975): 43–45.

19. Dennis M. Wint and William R. Kennedy, *Strategies Affecting Successful Implementation of an Environmental Curriculum into Ohio Schools*. Reported in ERIC # ED 144 779.

20. See Ellen M. Regan and Kenneth A. Leithwood, *Effecting Curriculum Change: Experiences with the Conceptual Skills Project*. Reported in ERIC # ED 136 440.

21. Hubert S. Coffee and William P. Golden, Jr., in *In-service Education*, 56th Yearbook, Part I (Chicago: National Society for the Study of Education, 1957), p. 101.

22. See Ray Sorenson and Hedley Dimock, *Redesigning Education in Values: A Case Study of Institutional Change* (New York: Association Press, 1955).

23. David H. Jenkins, "Social Engineering in Educational Change: An Outline of Method," *Progressive Education* 26, no. 7 (May 1949): 193–97.

24. Robert G. Owens, *Organizational Behavior in Schools* (New York: Prentice-Hall, 1970), pp. 145–48.

25. E. G. Guba, "Diffusion of Innovations," *Educational Leadership* 25, no. 4 (January 1968): 292–95.

26. Ibid.

27. See, for example, Wendell L. French and Cecil H. Bell, Jr., *Organization Development* (Englewood Cliffs, N.J.: Prentice-Hall, 1973); Warren G. Bennis, *Organizational Development: Its Nature, Origins, and Prospects* (Reading, Mass.: Addison-Wesley, 1969); and Richard A. Schmuck and Matthew B. Miles, *Organization Development in Schools* (Palo Alto, Calif.: National Press Books, 1971).

28. Charles P. Ruch et al., "Training for Planning: Organizational Consultation to Design and Install Constituency-Based Planning," *Planning and Changing* 13, no. 4 (Winter 1982): 234–44.

29. Elizabeth Clark and Marvin Fairman, "Organizational Health: A Significant Force in Planned Change," *Bulletin of the National Association of Secondary School Principals* 67, no. 464 (September 1983): 108–13.

30. See also Hollis L. Caswell, "Realities of Curriculum Change," *Educational Leadership* 36, no. 1 (October 1978): 27–29.

31. Wendell M. Hough, "Power and Influence in the Change Process," *Educational Leadership* 36, no. 1 (October 1978): 59.

32. Jerry L. Patterson and Theodore J. Czajkowski, "Implementation: Neglected Phase in Curriculum Change," *Educational Leadership* 37, no. 3 (December 1979): 204–6.

33. Reported by Charles C. Jung, Northwest Regional Educational Laboratory, 400 Lindsay Building, 710 S.W. Second Avenue, Portland, Oregon 97204.

34. Ivor K. Davies, "The CLER Model in Instructional Development," *Viewpoints in Teaching and Learning* 58, no. 4 (Fall 1982): 62–69.

35. Linda S. Lotto, "Using the CLER Model in School Improvement," *Viewpoints in Teaching and Learning* 58, no. 4 (Fall 1982): 70–81.

36. Edwin E. Russell, "Use of CLER in Promoting Recruitment into an Adult Basic Education Program," *Viewpoints in Teaching and Learning* 58, no. 4 (Fall 1982): 48–54.

37. Ted R. Urich, Marlene Mitchell, and Judith P. LaVorgna, "PARA: A Mutually Reinforcing Model for Self-Directed Change," *Bulletin of the National Association of Secondary School Princpals* 67, no. 464 (September 1983): 104–7.

38. Marilyn E. Nelson, "In-Service Training for Curriculum Change," Montgomery County Public Schools, Maryland (1978). Reported in ERIC # ED 195 535.

39. Adapted from Donald Orlosky and B. Othanel Smith, "Educational Change: Its Origins and Characteristics," *Phi Delta Kappan* 53, no. 7 (March 1972): 412–14. Used with permission.

40. Ibid.

41. Ralph Parish and Richard Arends, "Why Innovative Programs Are 'Discontinued,'" *Educational Leadership* 40, no. 4 (January 1983): 62–65.

42. Paul E. Heckman, Jeannie Oakes, and Kenneth A. Sirotnik, "Expanding the Concepts of School Renewal and Change," *Educational Leadership* 40, no. 7 (April 1983): 26–30.

43. Henry M. Brickell, in W. C. Meierhenry, ed., *Media and Educational Innovation* (Lincoln, Neb.: University of Nebraska Press, 1964), p. 256. Compare with R. Farris and T. C. Ross, "A Workable Mechanism for Making Curriculum and Instructional Decisions," *Journal of Secondary Education* 46 (January 1971): 38–48.

44. Earl B. Russell, "Upgrading Curricula through Change-oriented Teachers," *Theory into Practice* 14, no. 1 (February 1975): 27–31.

45. Mary Ellen Finch, "Behind the Teacher's Desk: The Teacher, the Administrator, and the Problem of Change," *Curriculum Inquiry* 11, no. 4 (Winter 1981): 321–42.

46. See, for instance, Herbert I. Von Haden and Jean Marie King, *Innovations in Education: Their Pros and Cons* (Worthington, Ohio: Charles A. Jones, 1971), pp. 7–12.

47. Donald J. Gray, *The Lessons of Summer Institutes* (Monograph published by the Consortium of Professional Associations for Study of Special Teacher Improvement Programs, April 1970), p. 16.

48. Ibid.

49. Russell, "Upgrading Curricula," p. 28.

50. See major references on group work, two of the most helpful of which are Matthew B. Miles, *Learning to Work in Groups* (New York: Bureau of Publications, Teachers College, 1959); and Halbert E. Gulley, *Discussion, Conference, and Group Process* (New York: Holt, Rinehart and Winston, 1960).

51. Shepart and Blake speak of the importance of "interpersonal openness and a problem-solving climate" in achieving change. See Herbert Shepart and Robert Blake, "Changing Behavior through Cognitive Change," *Human Organization* 21 (Summer 1962): 88–96.

52. Elsa Schneider, *Physical Education in Urban Elementary Schools* (Washington, D.C.: United States Department of Health, Education and Welfare, Bulletin 1959, No. 15).

53. The report of a study of schools in New York State by staff members of the School of Education, New York University, suggested that superior employment practices, careful delineation of the role of the school, and wise assignment of specialist personnel are three of the main keys to school quality in that state.

54. Wilbur A. Yauch, *Improving Human Relations in School Administration* (New York: Harper and Row, 1949), pp 257–63; and William W. Savage, *Interpersonal and Group Relations in Educational Administration* (Glenview, Ill.: Scott, Foresman, 1968), p. 104. To learn from negative examples, see G. A. Griffin, "Dehumanizing the School through Curriculum Planning, or Who Needs Hemlock?" *National Elementary Principal* 49, no. 9 (May 1970): 24–27.

SELECTED BIBLIOGRAPHY

Bennis, Warren G.; Benne, Kenneth D.; and Chin, Robert. *The Planning of Change.* New York: Holt, Rinehart and Winston, 1961.

Carlson, Richard O. *Adoption of Educational Innovations.* Eugene: University of Oregon, 1965.

Corey, Stephen M. *Helping Other People Change.* Columbus: Ohio State University Press, 1963.

Foshay, Arthur W., ed. *Considered Action for Curriculum Improvement.* 1980 Yearbook, Association for Supervision and Curriculum Development. Washington, D.C.: The Association, 1980.

Fullan, Michael. *The Meaning of Educational Change.* New York: Teachers College Press, 1982.

Havelock, R. G. *The Change Agent's Guide to Innovation in Education.* Englewood Cliffs, N.J.: Educational Technology Publications, 1973.

Lawler, Marcella R., ed. *Strategies for Planned Curriculum Innovation.* New York: Teachers College Press, 1970.

Lippitt, Ronald; Watson, Jeanne; and Westley, Bruce. *The Dynamics of Planned Change.* New York: Harcourt, Brace and World, 1958.

Miel, Alice. *Changing the Curriculum.* New York: Appleton-Century-Crofts, 1946.

Miles, Matthew B., ed. *Innovation in Education.* New York: Bureau of Publications, Teachers College, 1964.

Miller, Richard I., ed. *Perspectives on Educational Change.* New York: Appleton-Century-Crofts, 1967.

Owens, Robert G., and Steinhoff, Carl R. *Administering Change in Schools.* Englewood Cliffs, N.J.: Prentice-Hall, 1976.

Reid, William A., and Walker, Decker F., eds. *Case Studies in Curriculum Change.* Boston: Routledge and Kegan Paul, 1975.

Sarason, Seymour B. *The Culture of the School and the Problem of Change.* Boston: Allyn and Bacon, 1971.

Skeel, Dorothy J., and Hagen, Owen A. *The Process of Curriculum Change.* Pacific Palisades, Calif.: Goodyear, 1971.

Verduin, John R., Jr. *Cooperative Curriculum Improvement.* Englewood Cliffs, N.J.: Prentice-Hall, 1967.

Von Haden, Herbert I., and King, Jean Marie. *Educational Innovator's Guide.* Worthington, Ohio: Charles A. Jones, 1974.

Von Haden, Herbert I., and King, Jean Marie. *Innovations in Education: Their Pros and Cons.* Worthington, Ohio: Charles A. Jones, 1971.

Wittrock, M. C., ed. *Changing Education: Alternatives from Educational Research.* Englewood Cliffs, N.J.: Prentice-Hall, 1973.

8

The Planning Process

"Let me show you our curriculum," said the principal to the visitor in his school. Proudly the principal removed from his desk a mimeographed document that told teachers what to teach, subject by subject.

The visitor scanned the document and replied, "Now let me see your *real* curriculum."

"What do you mean?" the principal asked.

"I mean that I must spend at least a few hours in your school. I need to visit several classrooms at random. I want to stand aside in hallways as the children move through them and wander through the cafeteria while children are eating and while they're talking freely. If an assembly program is scheduled for today I want to attend it. And I'd like to visit the library and then follow the children out to the playing field while they're under a teacher's supervision and while they're on their own. By doing these things I'll get at least a limited view of your *real* curriculum."

This dialogue between a principal and a visitor suggests a number of ideas about school curriculum. The first, and most obvious, idea is that the curriculum cannot actually be reduced to a lifeless sheaf of papers. A second idea is that the curriculum belongs in two categories: that of objective reality and that of mode and style. Thus, although the curriculum should be viewed as a product, it should also be viewed as process. That is, the curriculum is in part a way of working with what has been set out to be done. Inevitably the two categories become interrelated.

A third idea is that a given curriculum has a life span, determined largely by its usefulness and timeliness. Within its lifetime, a curriculum may be revised at intervals and in both major and minor ways so that its usefulness and timeliness may be increased. A fourth idea is that the real curriculum, no matter how formally and carefully planned it is alleged to be, has aspects of the unplanned. Every practicing teacher knows that what "creeps in" as a consequence of pupil-teacher and pupil-pupil interaction in the classroom goes beyond the bounds of the most carefully expressed mandates and suggestions. In addition, some of the real curriculum remains unplanned.

A fifth, and most important, idea is that the curriculum, being of the human spirit, is active and changing. It's affected by wishes, thoughts, and restraints. As we have seen in Chapter 7, to change the curriculum is literally to help people change themselves. The real curriculum of a school was defined in the first chapter of this book as "the formal and informal content and process by which learners gain knowledge and understanding, develop skills, and alter attitudes, appreciations, and values under the auspices of that school." This definition is meant to include both formal and informal aspects of schooling, what one learns (content) and how one learns (process), and products or outcomes in the forms of knowledge, understanding, skills, attitudes, appreciations, and values.

Thus the curriculum involves what happens in classrooms, auditoriums, gymnasiums, cafeterias, and hallways and—in connection with school activities—school-sponsored community service, field trips, and organized work experience programs. It is as big, broad, and all-inclusive as the lives of people in a major, thriving American institution.

The action called improvement of the curriculum may be defined as follows: *Curriculum improvement refers not only to improving the structure and the documents of the curriculum but also to stimulating learning on the part of all persons who are concerned with the curriculum.* These persons include, of course, pupils in schools, teachers, classroom aides, supervisors and administrators, and assisting parents and other community members. They have opportunities in a program of curriculum improvement to gain both cognitively and affectively. Obviously, curriculum improvement deals directly with the improvement of people.

THE BASES OF CURRICULUM PLANNING

What happens when a group tries to plan the curriculum? Obviously one has to begin with something. Many planners begin merely with the curriculum as it is, resolving to patch it here and there. Occasionally planners attempt to build something brand new, as when people first considered educating children in the use of computers. Traditionally, planners have gone into action without thinking much about fundamentals of the planing operation. These fundamentals may be called the usable bases of curriculum planning. They include the domains of planning, the characteristics of each school situation as it is, the apparent needs of the pupil population and the teachers, the curriculum problems apparent in the local school or school district, the competencies of potential participants in the planning, external and internal pressures on the planners, trends and issues affecting what is to be planned, and judicious use of human knowledge. The reader may think of other fundamentals, but these are among the prominent ones.

The Domains of Planning

The first cry of curriculum planners may be "What are we getting into?!" This expression suggests quandary, even desperation.

Most people begin to plan without knowing what it involves. A first logical consideration may well be the direction or directions in which the planners want to go. What are the aims or goals to be attained? What objectives should be achieved en route to the attainment of these aims or goals? What areas and reaches of knowledge should be tapped?

When planners have given at least preliminary answers to these questions, they should be prepared to suggest a design comparable with the curriculum designs discussed in Chapter 5. The design then requires implementation, during which process (modes of treating the design in classrooms) comes to the fore. Ways of teaching, instructional resources and media, and organization of classroom and school for learning need to be considered in planning for implementation. At intervals during and beyond implementation, planners must evaluate what has been happening in two terms: improvement, if any, in pupil learning and the worth of the curriculum plan in attaining desired aims.

Realizing that no curriculum is made in heaven, good planners make use of the feedback obtained as plans go into effect to change the answers to their original questions of intent, to alter their designs, to improve their implementation, and to modify their evaluation systems. Thus the curriculum moves, changes, lives.

The Characteristics of the Situation as It Is

Curriculum planners have to work in the situations in which they find themselves. Often they know too little about their own situations and circumstances. Surely they should know about the local scene. Planners should inquire about the qualifications of personnel, the morale of district employees, the special talents of staff members, material resources available for curriculum work, the degree of support given by top administrators, the pressures applied by the community, and other such matters.

The British have developed a scheme for situation notation and analysis known as the curriculum information system. This system performs two actions: (1) gathering and noting information about curriculum status and (2) analyzing the information collected during the first action to generate a summary showing the nature of curriculum patterns. Specifically, gathering and noting information, called *notation*, results in knowledge of what is taught, by whom it is taught, to whom it is taught, and how it is taught. Imagine the headstart knowing these things can provide! Common sources of such information used in the United States during past decades have been curriculum documents of several kinds and the recollections of a number of people in the schools, but especially of classroom teachers. The raw data constitute such a mass that one must filter them to adduce specifics about curriculum organization, sequence, and "distribution" among the pupil population. Aptly, the British call this process *filtration*.

The second action, analyzing the information, involves what the British refer to as *transformation*, or the manipulation and changing of what is taught so that it suggests design or pattern. Transformation may occur, for instance, in the focus of the curriculum or in the deployment of resources. Analyzing information with a view to taking next steps obviously represents the beginning of planning.[1]

Examination of one's work situation may be conducted in two major ways: (1) viewing the entire school or school system scene as it affects the prospect of curriculum planning and (2) learning as much as possible about the current curriculum.

The Needs of the Pupil Population and the Teachers

Inasmuch as no human institution is perfect, unmet curriculum needs obviously exist in schools. Many curriculum planners believe that the identification of curriculum needs during past decades has been casual, even careless. This fact contributes to the current popularity of formal needs assessment.[2]

Sometimes curriculum needs represent the gap between established aims and actual conditions in a school. Sometimes needs have not been recognized previously and are therefore unrelated to any established aims, in which case they must be examined carefully to determine their nature and validity and, eventually, to find some possible ways they might be met. The identification method called needs assessment permits determination of curriculum needs either in broad, general terms, with reference to several aims at a time, or in specific terms, with reference to a single, pinpointed aim. If curriculum planning in a school or school system has been either nonexistent or minimal, the broad general approach is usually followed. If the school or school system is experienced and sophisticated in planning, it may be ready for specificity. In effect, needs assessment is an evaluation of "where we are" so that planners know how to expend time and energy in planning for future activity in meeting genuine needs.

The aims or goals of the school are, then, a common takeoff point in needs assessment, though need determination in rough form may precede the setting of aims or goals. Preliminary discussion and investigation usually suggest which aims are to be attended to most closely. Possible ways of determining the current achievement of these aims may be proposed next. Partial data indicating the achievement of the aims are already at hand in, for example, pupil records, community survey reports, and curriculum documents.

The following outline suggests the kinds of data that often prove useful in needs assessment:

I.   Data about pupils
    A. Data about the pupil population as a whole
       1. The general pupil population
       2. Specific subgroups
       3. Enrollment statistics
       4. Indications of pupil progress
       5. The incidence and nature of school leaving
    B. Data about the growth and development of pupils
       1. Physical growth and development
       2. Achievement in specific school subject matter
       3. Emotional and social development
       4. Psychological needs
       5. Intellectual and creative development
       6. Personal traits
    C. Data about pupils' homes, families, and community conditions
       1. Conditions of home and family life
       2. The school's adult constituency at large
       3. Specifics concerning the nature of the community
    D. Data about pupil opportunities
       1. For current work
       2. For eventual career
       3. In terms of economic projection and forecasts
II.   Data about social and cultural matters
    A. The need to transmit and to alter the culture
    B. The need to orient and to adjust the young
    C. The need to preserve and to alter the social order

     D. The need to prepare pupils specifically for adulthood
     E. The need to relate the individual pupil to the social and cultural milieux
     F. The need to explore with pupils
        1. Values
        2. Expectations
        3. The political power structure
        4. Community issues
        5. Trends of the times
  III. Data about learning—how pupils learn
     A. What learning is
     B. What it means to be motivated to learn
     C. The nature of learning styles
     D. Problems with self-concept
     E. The nature of readiness
     F. How transfer of learning occurs
  IV. Data about subject matter—what pupils should learn
     A. What subject matter—old and new—is of most worth
     B. Criteria for selecting subject matter content
     C. How to organize subject matter
     D. Criteria for selecting and making instructional materials
     E. Criteria for determining relevance of content

A complete range of diagnostic devices is required for identifying and clarifying needs: tests and inventories of all sorts, interviews, open-ended questions and written protocols, unfinished stories and incidents, records of discussions, records of reading, sociometrics, socioeconomic analysis, reports of critical incidents, analysis of drawings, interpretations of pictures, and, of course, observation and recording of performance. The needs easiest to identify are naturally the felt, immediate ones. Needs originating in social and cultural settings are likely to be unfelt and obscure to individual pupils. In this instance, identification usually awaits the judgment of wise adults.

In most school systems, much of the data about needs that are helpful in edifying teachers, administrators, and other persons who make curriculum policy must be collected anew. These data should be useful to planners in determining whether their school or system is achieving its aims. If it is not, then the planners have two choices: (1) to re-sort the aims in order to judge whether all of them are still valid or (2) to plan what should be done about pursuing the really valid aims more effectively.

When needs assessment has proceeded to this point, the rating or ranking of unmet needs is yet to occur. This rating or ranking has usually been accomplished by largely unplanned group discussion.

The rating of needs can be accomplished by using any of the following methods:

1. *Sorting cards.*   A statement of need is put on each of a number of cards that are given to individuals or small groups to rank in order of importance. This convenient and common method is superficial because participants in the sorting need think very little about the work they are doing.
2. *Rating sheets.*   Rating sheets function like sorting cards, but they are less cumbersome to manipulate. The rating is accomplished on a single sheet or two, as in the implementation of Phi Delta Kappa's model.
3. *The critical incident technique.*   This technique requires educators, pupils, or parents to recall incidents that suggest the need for improvement (or for commendation) of the educational system. The technique works best when the incidents reported are not within just one or two aspects of educational activity.
4. *The Delphi Technique.*   To improve planning and to introduce forecasting into selecting unmet needs, the Delphi Technique requires a group leader to prepare a list of statements indicating the intentions of his or her planning group. The statements are in the form of goals, value comments, or program suggestions which are sent to curriculum specialists with the request that the specialists indicate the years in which they believe the statements will be accepted and put into use. Sometimes the statements are refined and sent to additional consultants. Summaries of the consultants' predictions may then be sent to all consultants with the request that the consultants comment on them and attempt to justify any views of their own that are markedly different from the modal respones. This procedure may be followed on several occasions until further convergence in the views of the consultants has occurred.[3] The technique provides a trend-oriented view.
5. *TARGET.*   An acronym for "To Assess Relevant Goals in Education Together," TARGET combines the Delphi Technique with gaming. People meeting in groups write their needs statements anonymously. The statements are divided into five categories and are analyzed according to the categories. Time and cost are lessened by keeping the activity within the groups, but judgment by experts is not available.
6. *Fault Tree Analysis (FTA).*   This method identifies ways in which failure in a program or project is most likely to occur. The method has been used to analyze the design of new programs prior to their implementation. Fault Tree Analysis starts with the proposal of an undesired event (UE) that people wish to see avoided in the

curriculum. Given this undesired event, the analysis leads to construction of a "logic tree," the branches of which are series of events. Small groups of participants are trained to suggest these events, which may number several hundred. Experts are assigned to consider the relative frequency and importance of the events. The shapes of the events on the tree show the relationships among the events. These interrelationships reveal the sequence of events that is likely to cause the UE. Witkin, a proponent of Fault Tree Analysis, reports that by using this technique the Seattle School District found a need for changing its mathematics program for vocational education pupils. He expresses doubt that the relationship between mathematics instruction and vocational program requirements would have been found by any other method of needs assessment.[4]

In the initial discussion portion of assessment, planners should ask one another questions about the unmet needs of pupils and teachers in the system. Needs assessment as it is being practiced calls for collection of data from many constitutents, determination of priorities by as many groups and individuals as possible, and evaluation of the gaps between what is and what might be.

Findley and Hamm point out that curriculum planners are inclined to favor practical considerations in planning at the expense of "fancier" methodology. Some of the practical questions they raise are the following: Do the teachers really want the changes we propose? How can the changes be incorporated within the curriculum: for example, by adding instructional units, by creating minicourses, by improving school activities, or by supplying new instructional materials? Does our proposal get at the problem we want to solve, or does it deal only with the symptoms? Would this proposal throw the curriculum out of balance? Would we be serving to excess only a limited pupil population?[5]

David J. Mullen has described a game called "Bonanza" that provides a baseline through which people's involvement in needs assessment can begin. The game requires each player to spend $100 twenty times. Possible goals or aims of the school are shown in comic strip form. The players spend their money on the goals they perceive to be most important. The advantages claimed for this game are simplicity, ease of administration, involvement, and inexpensiveness. One group of players chose the following curriculum emphases: the three R's, the arts, health, physical development and safety, development of the self, relationship with others, the world of work, the physical world, making choices, and the social world.[6]

Obviously, the methodology of needs assessment is due for continuing attention in an era in which resources for education are growing increasingly expensive.

Local Curriculum Problems

In curriculum planning, as in the military, the term often used for a challenge to action is *problem*. The term is meant to carry no negative connotation. It implies instead an opportunity to use one's capacities and resources in an honest effort to improve teaching and learning for children and youth. When the needs of pupils and teachers have been discovered, these needs may lead planners to specify the problems involved in meeting those needs. Like the needs, some of the problems may be identified in the teaching and learning of subject matter; others in specific pupil attitudes, behaviors and welfare requirements.

Needs having been noted, the next challenge lies in solving problems created or raised by the needs. Perceptions concerning what constitutes a proper focus for curriculum problem-solving vary from group to group. Young children view curriculum problems differently from the way adolescents view them, and teachers often see them differently from the manner in which supervisors see them. Problems that seem pressing in one school appear insignificant in another. Many ways can always be found to improve the program of a school if one looks about with care, perceptiveness, and sensitivity. Typical problems include providing for individual differences, providing experiences for minority group children, developing programs of citizenship education, and obtaining citizens' responses to what the schools are doing.

Classroom teachers may say that problems like these are big and general, and thus not concrete enough to concern the teacher "where he or she lives." Another reaction may be "None of these problems concerns us just now, but we can name a currently 'hot' and significant problem." School personnel should recognize that having problems is natural and legitimate, that not having them would suggest dullness and insensitivity. The size of a problem, whether large or small, should not make its proponent ashamed of it. If it proves to be either too large or too small to manage, it can be modified.

These facts remind one that

> Teachers and administrators frequently voice their problems in a form
> that is more respectable than real. For example, the teacher may say that
> the principal's office bothers him with frequent interruptions of his
> classroom routine and that, because of these interruptions, his pupils
> lose interest. When this respectable statement of his problem has been
> "pushed back" far enough, one may find that the teacher is really
> troubled by his own failure to vary his teaching procedures. Obviously,
> he needs help in clarifying and stating his true problem (which is in
> part his relationship with the principal) and especially in accepting it as
> being respectable and worthwhile.[7]

Teachers are often encouraged when they find that other teachers have the same or similar problems.

Numerous curriculum problems crosscut the specialized fields of supervision, inservice education/staff development, and curriculum improvement. A common question is "When should a problem be identified as a problem of curriculum improvement rather than of supervision or inservice education/staff development?" An unrealistic trichotomy has come to exist among these three elements. If the major objective of these three is seen to be the improvement of teachers in service so that the experiences of their pupils in turn may be improved, the substantive distinctions among them become less sharp. Their interrelationships are diagrammed in Figure 8-1, with large overlaps among the fields. Since the distinctions among these elements or strategies affect process much more than they affect substance, activities in supervision, inservice education/staff development, and curriculum improvement should be regarded simply as complementary means of implementing a solution or amelioration of a curriculum problem. The focus of attention should be placed on the problem itself.

A significant basis for getting started in curriculum planning is to *give attention to matters that concern teachers in their daily work*. These matters often have to do with methods of "reaching" individual pupils, selection of content for teaching particular groups of children, classroom organization of children and facilities for better learning, and ways of ensuring that children are motivated to learn. The master planning of facilities and organizational arrangements with which administrators are frequently preoccupied can make a genuine and lasting contribution to children's experiences under school auspices. However, teachers are not likely to show deep interest in such problems and proposals when they face their own distinctive problems at their respective teaching stations. Curriculum leaders should generally plan to begin with these distinctive problems.

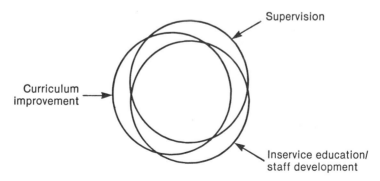

FIGURE 8–1. The interrelationship among three strategies for improving curriculum.

Problems with which to begin planning emerge from many settings. Some of them are products of given classroom situations and groupings of pupils; others are peculiar to individual schools; others stem from the developmental levels at which children are living and learning and can thus be categorized as grade-level problems; others extend from kindergarten through the top grade; still others come from community pressure groups; and still others emerge from the mandates of state governments and from the exigencies of the national scene.

There are two major steps in starting problem solution—identifying a problem and then defining it. The discussion to this point has centered on some basic considerations in problem identification. Attention will now be given to the second step—problem definition. Actually the first step merges into the second. A problem, whatever its source, is likely to be in a decidedly raw state when it is first proposed. It expresses the concern of an individual or a group about a school situation that is believed to need attention. The problem need not relate to a situation that is serious or especially troublesome. Rather, it may relate to a situation having within it great prospects for improvement because it has already proved profitable in stimulating learning. Once again it must be said that the existence of problems need have no negative implications.

As one looks critically at problems in their originally proposed state, one sees that frequently they are too big in overall size or have too many dimensions to be manageable. For instance, problems of child study are frequently proposed in such comprehensive form and with so many sources of data used in gathering initial evidence that one does not know where to take hold of them or how to handle them. On the other hand, problems may be too narrow or limited, particularly as they are seen by classroom teachers who tend to be so close to daily problems that they become myopic. Moreover, problems suggested by persons far removed from classrooms may have, for teachers, a totally unrealistic ring, so teachers resist dealing with them. The object of the initial stage in problem definition is to limit the scope of oversized problems, to extend and bolster narrow ones, to make certain that problems are real and practical, and in general to ensure the manageability and usefulness of the problems to be solved. Sometimes a problem can be described in nearly the same way as its corresponding curriculum need. Usually, however, it must be described more exactly.

Discussion of the meanings of problems can become so boring and impractical that some of the planners complain that a given problem is "being beaten to death." Or a problem may fall prey to persons with axes to grind or with tendencies to view the problem in traditional rather than fresh ways. Some of the difficulties in problem definition can be resolved by pursuing a plan that proceeds as follows:

1. The already identified problem is defined until it is judged to be single rather than multiple, manageable in size, and worth solving.

2. The problem is thought about further with a view to formulating hypotheses concerning what could be done to solve it.
3. When several promising hypotheses have been formulated, they are tested intellectually through discussion, and those that do not seem fruitful or relevant are eliminated.
4. A new problem focus now forms around the hypotheses that remain. These are tested by accumulating evidence confirming or denying their worth in solving the problem. Much of the evidence stems from the elements in decision making: children and their developing and learning, social forces that affect the schools, and the nature and structure of subject matter.
5. Now that the problem has been reasonably well defined, tasks in testing hypotheses are assigned to staff members on the basis of their competence and interest.
6. Inquiry of this kind often leads to at least a minor redefinition of the problem, as staff members find hidden factors and influences they had not previously considered. The danger here is in "going off on strange rabbit trails," which may lead too far afield and pervert the original intent of the inquiry.
7. Problems often prove to be interrelated, so that recognition of one of them speedily leads to recognition of another. This fact makes curriculum improvement a fascinating activity.

These procedures need not, of course, be followed seriatim in all situations. The indispensable ingredient in the processes of problem identification and definition is careful, critical thinking about the meanings of problems and about ways of solving them.

ACTIVITY 8-1
Finding Curriculum Needs and Related Problems in the
Field of Moral Education

The decline of the American family and several other causes have impressed upon Americans the need for moral education in their schools. Assume that moral education has been clearly identified as a need in the school or school system you know best. Convert this generalized need into statements of four or five curriculum problems that should be attacked in your institution. Worded in question form, the following are examples:

1. How can we determine what is moral and what is not and, therefore, what moral education should be?
2. How can we take stages of human development into account in planning a program of moral education?

Discuss the suggestions that are made by members of a group in answering these questions.

SITUATION 8-1
Sorting the Problems

The Curriculum Steering Committee of the sixty-eight-teacher Cormorant Unified School District was conducting its second meeting since the time of the Committee's formation three months previously. At its first meeting the Committee had decided to poll all teachers in the district to determine what pressing curriculum problems and concerns the teachers could suggest. Forty-nine teachers had responded to a simple questionnaire asking for one or more open-ended statements of problems and concerns that should receive prompt attention.

When the returned questionnaires had been read and the responses had been interpreted and categorized by a subcommittee of the Curriculum Steering Committee, the following problems and concerns were listed in rank order:

ITEM	FREQUENCY OF RESPONSE ($N = 49$)
Excessive clerical work required of teachers	30
Scarcity of locally developed curriculum guides	23
The prevalence of gum chewing in classrooms	18
Frequent interruption of classroom work because of announcements, drives, campaigns, and essay contests	17
Too much interference from community members not connected with the schools	17
Children's weakness in language skills	16
Lack of knowledge of what teachers in grades above and below are doing	15
Failure to concentrate sufficiently on the three Rs	14
Children's poor study habits	12
Uncertainty about what the principals want done	9
Poverty (lack of richness) in the arts—music and the fine arts particularly	7
Poor discipline in some classrooms	6
A top-heavy emphasis on football	3
The presence of certain incompetent teachers	2
A weak science program	2
Poor arithmetical skills	2
Lack of supplies	1
Too many chiefs and too few "Indians"	1
Ineffective leadership by the administrators	1
Limited funds for audiovisual aids	1

If you were a member of the Curriculum Steering Committee, how would you contribute to a further categorization of these problems and concerns? For instance, which of them seem to relate closely to teachers' own feelings about their jobs? What other categories can you find?

Which of the problems and concerns seem to you to be respectable cover-ups for *real* problems and concerns? Why? How could you be reasonably sure that you are right?

Select one of the problems or concerns that interests you particularly. What would you do to help teachers begin solving or ameliorating it?

If you have an opportunity to do so, conduct a similar questionnaire survey in a school with which you are familiar; then consider actions you can take in exploring teachers' initially expressed problems to determine the full and accurate meanings of these problems.

The Competencies of Participants

Much will be said in the next chapter about the roles of several categories of curriculum planners. The present discussion deals instead with the kinds of competencies needed in the planning process, without identification of the persons in whom they may be found. The competencies of participants form an important basis for planning. Naturally, some school systems have been able to employ more competent persons than have other school systems. The reasons are often salary schedules, geographic locations, and cultural advantages.

At any rate, several competencies contribute notably to the formation of the best possible plans. Effective planners are capable of planning alone, with the help of pupils, and in groups of fellow professionals and laypersons. Their competencies as a total staff should include the following:

1. Ability to create ideas. This competency may well head the list.
2. Ability to reconcile conflicting viewpoints. This ability causes planning to begin in a favorable emotional climate, and causes it to continue despite expected ups and downs in relationships.
3. Ability to contribute to the overall quality of group work. Working successfully in groups requires understanding of and skill in many aspects of group work.
4. Ability to direct and coordinate. Organizing people and things, as well as pulling people and things together, constitutes a talent definitely needed by administrators and coordinators, and also by teachers and others who have part-time responsibility for direction and coordination.
5. Ability to analyze situations and interpret actions. Often this competency falls under the category of troubleshooting.

6. Ability to recognize and choose alternatives. This competency rests on a firm base of knowledge and understanding about children, youth, learning, community influences, national trends, available philosophies, historical precedents, and developments in the subject matter fields.
7. Ability to plan and conduct experimentation and research. Special preparation is obviously required for exercise of this competency.
8. Ability to ask the "right" questions. This competency rests on a sense of where a project has been, what its prospects are for the future, and what is possible.
9. Ability to present ideas in writing.
10. Ability to present ideas orally.
11. Ability to use machines, including computers, to facilitate planning.
12. Miscellaneous abilities, including the ability to serve as recorder or secretary, to entertain visiting personnel, to anticipate people's needs.[8]

Another way of considering planners' competencies is to test their abilities, understandings, and attitudes in simulated situations. Here are three competencies, with their meanings indicated as concrete tasks:

Competency 1

Can recognize from the following list eight problems of the school or school system that belong clearly within the province of curriculum planners:

Making case studies of pupils from minority groups
Contracting with trucking firms to haul equipment from school to school
Planning a work experience program for high school pupils
Surveying pupils' attitudes toward smoking marijuana
Conferring with alumni about their experiences in the school
Providing space and other physical arrangements for a new computer
Developing a course guide in learning how to speak more effectively in public
Supervising the installation of air conditioning units in school buildings
Organizing a learning center in an old school building
Planning an interpersonal communication system to bring faculty members closer in their thinking
Plotting bus routes for the new school year
Employing a new assistant business manager for the school system

Organizing an arrangement for teacher self-supervision using videotapes

Assigning teacher aides to lavatory duty

Sponsoring a campaign for improving courtesy in the school

Organizing a research team to work on a title project using federal funds

Competency 2

(a) Can identify three of the eight problems chosen above that will probably require for solution close relationships between the current curriculum planners and other persons, such as administrators, supervisors, child study personnel, business administrators, etc. (b) In each of the three cases, can name the categories of personnel to be consulted.

Competency 3

Can suggest three ways of getting planning started that are at least as useful as the following method:

> A question was posed in writing to the faculty: "If you were to have school time for curriculum planning next year, what curriculum problems would you identify as needing most immediate attention? Name three if possible." The miscellaneous responses of the faculty were placed, with a minimum of editing, in a questionnaire that was distributed to the faculty for final response. The curriculum problems that were mentioned with highest frequency in the questionnaire returns were accepted as the problems for study.

ACTIVITY 8-2
Helping Participants Improve the Use of Their Competencies

It's never too early to think of ways in which people who are endowed with talents or abilities can be helped to use them better. Look again at the preceding list of twelve abilities. Consider possibilities for increasing, improving, or strengthening these abilities. Possibilities include (1) giving people opportunities to exercise their abilities; (2) giving suggestions for improving use of abilities; (3) monitoring use by assigning people to observe what others do; (4) providing specific learning experiences within courses, visits, conventions, institutes, and workshops; (5) recording what people do so that they may analyze their own actions; and (6) employing consultants to consider how well people's abilities are being exercised. What else occurs to you?

Pressures Outside and Inside the Self

Seeds of curriculum planning are planted consciously in numerous places. Still other seeds drop fortuitously on fertile soil. Persons and agencies that apply pressure to have curriculum improvement activities started are doing conscious planting. Many of these persons and agencies exist within school systems. They include alert superintendents, curriculum coordinators, and principals who want to see the schools move forward in using the best available knowledge of children, learning, teaching methods, subject matter, and the demands of a changing society. In addition, each school is likely to have its unofficial or emergent leaders who stimulate other personnel to improve their practices. Nearly every teacher can name one or more problems that he or she would like to see acted upon, though they may be other people's problems. Pupils themselves, the live consumers of education, demand attention, which often leads to curriculum improvement. Many a promising improvement program has resulted from administering standardized or teacher-made tests even though the data derived from the original testing may have been of doubtful worth. Teachers and other personnel become carriers of ideas from meetings, conventions, intervisitations, college and university courses, and other inservice and staff development ventures. Professional literature is now so profuse as to challenge any teacher to remain current in his or her reading, even in his or her own teaching field. These are but a few of the influences that promote improvement from within the schools.

Ours, however, is an era in which demands for change also come from many persons and organizations outside school systems. Some of them are

- Bureaus of the federal government
- Private educational testing organizations
- Private foundations
- Authors of popularly written books and articles
- Regional associations of colleges and secondary schools
- Colleges and universities
- Individual subject matter specialists and groups of specialists
- Patriotic organizations
- Trade associations and industries
- Labor unions

Impingement of such varied persons and agencies on curriculum decision making raises questions about sources of change and strategies for effecting change:

1. What should be the source of change? Staff? Research? The public? Government? Administration?

2. Is there a particular strategy for curriculum change that is appropriate for foundations? The federal government? The teacher? The principal? The curriculum director? The college? State departments of education?

3. Who are the critical decision makers in curriculum development? The teachers? The principal? The central office? The board of education? The state department of education? The federal government?

4. Does recognizing many sources of change affect the strategy?

5. How important is it for teachers or a local staff to feel that they are a part of the decision to change the curriculum?

6. Can persons in superior roles in the administrative organization influence the behavior of teachers? Do the power relationships cause resentment of authority and resistance to proposals made by the person in authority?

7. Is the strategy for attempting to make major changes in the structure of the curriculum the same as for modifying the instruction in a discipline?

8. Is the strategy the same when there is national but not local support for a change and when there is local but not national support for a change? What if there is neither local nor national support by the public or mass media?

9. Is the strategy the same at different levels? The national? The state? The school? The community?[9]

The truth of a statement made years ago by curriculum specialists is now being realized: The school that avoids improving its own curriculum will soon have its curriculum "improved" for it. Many school systems have been so negligent in planning for curriculum improvement that they have become fair game for competing interests outside the schools. Without question, many individuals and groups external to the schools are now performing beneficent and valuable services for education, but they should never be allowed to become complete substitutes for school personnel who are working with pupils day by day.

In addition to external pressures, there are pressures within the minds of potential and actual participants in curriculum planning. People conjure up all sorts of notions about how strong tradition is; about their shortages of time, energy, and resources; about what's worth doing; about difficulties in the tasks ahead; and about complications in gaining support and working with other people.

Internal pressures sometimes go even deeper. Some school people are afraid of experimenting with other people's children and with public money. Others are afraid of wasting time and energy by making wrong starts. Others feel insecure about what they might be asked to do. Still others are simply predisposed to "let sleeping dogs lie."

These enumerations do not complete the list of known internal pressures on persons who volunteer or are invited to help plan. Though many pressures are irrational, they are nonetheless real to the persons concerned. Therefore they must be taken into account throughout the planning process.

SITUATION 8-2
Whose Concerns Should Have Priority?

Orangeville Elementary School was a brand new school in a desert that had recently been made to bloom by irrigation and was accordingly attracting a number of young families. Many of the parents of Orangeville's children worked in industrial plants in a city thirty miles away. A few were skilled laborers, but the majority were scientists, engineers, or highly specialized technicians.

When the school opened a year ago, Beth Ransom, the principal, organized the Curriculum Improvement Council to identify curriculum problems and to begin dealing with several of these problems immediately. During its ten months of operation, the Council had met with all teachers who were not Council members and had identified two pressing concerns that seemed worth exploring in depth. One was the need to choose enriching materials for a school that had little more than basic textbooks. The other was the need to develop programs in art and music, inasmuch as these subjects were being largely neglected in favor of the three Rs, science, and the social studies. The Council was certain that the teaching staff was committed to pursuit of these two concerns.

Then lightning struck. A committee of parents, intent upon the opportunities of their children for college admission, called upon Beth and insisted that the previously publicized concerns of the teachers be overridden in favor of the following alleged needs:

1. Homogeneous grouping at all grade levels from first through sixth
2. Investigation of why some children do not learn to read as rapidly as others
3. Establishment of special coaching classes in the three Rs
4. The teaching of "ninth-grade general science" in the fifth and sixth grades
5. Increase in homework assignments
6. Greater competition among children in the primary grades.

Later that week, the commander of a patriotic organization discussed with Beth the importance of eliminating the social studies from the curriculum, of returning to separate teaching of history and geography, and of requiring every sixth grader to memorize the Declaration of Independence.

Indicate the degree to which the origin and intrinsic nature of each of these concerns lead you to respect it.

In this situation, what should be done by the following personnel: Beth Ransom, the Curriculum Improvement Council, and the faculty as a whole?

The Orangeville Elementary School was new and had had little opportunity to get under way. How do you account for the presence of virulent external forces at this stage of the school's career?

What principles might apply in balancing and reconciling the internal and external forces in a situation of this kind?

The Impact of Current Trends and Issues

Observers think they see a number of trends in American society and the schools that should serve as cues to curriculum planners. The deterioration of moral and ethical values has led to a decline in discipline in homes and schools and an increase in drug use, alcoholism, and sexual promiscuity. Demands have been made of the schools that they "tighten up" in many respects, but especially in the teaching of the basics. Pupils' in-school experiences have been called irrelevant to their subsequent life experiences. The purposes and formats of schooling are said to be creaking. Advocacy groups that should be helping the schools are disunited.

These and other trends sharpen issues in the fields of elementary and secondary education. Some of these issues are perennial ones; others have arisen recently. A brief list of issues follows:

- What can be done to improve the quality of new teachers and administrators who enter service in the schools?
- What can be done to help present school personnel improve?
- How can preparation in the so-called life competencies be included in the curriculum?
- How can the responsibility for forming policy about the curriculum be distributed more equitably?
- What can be done to improve the morale of school people and to heighten their desire for excellence?
- How can the real weaknesses in the curriculum be discovered and overcome?
- What can be done to coordinate the educational efforts of schools with the educational efforts of outside agencies and organizations?
- How can relationships between state education personnel and school district personnel be improved?
- How can laypersons be involved more appropriately in curriculum planning?

Beneath and in addition to general issues like these are issues that relate directly to specific planning tasks. For example, if a curriculum committee wishes to add to the school program a curriculum offering that is novel, some of the issues in the list above may apply: issues about responsibility for policymaking, identification of pertinent life competencies, and ways of preparing staffs to implement curriculum plans. Still other issues are likely to be associated with the particular subject matter content and the implementation of new projects.[10]

A Particular Use of Human Knowledge

A final basis of planning to be discussed here is an appreciation of what it means to apply knowledge. Much of the knowledge about curriculum matters that has been discussed in preceding chapters has been knowledge of *what* rather than knowledge of *how*. This chapter, on the other hand, contains procedural discussions. The distinction to be made, then, is between knowledge for background understanding and knowledge of ways of working.

Once curriculum planners think they know what it means to be an educated person and what subject matter contributes most to educating persons in given situations, they can begin to plan for optimum education. Their task is complicated by changes in subject matter and by the trends and pressures already discussed. Present knowledge of planning procedures suggests that one must follow the growth patterns of children and youth, divide total plans into learning increments, and expect that the changes sought are changes in people. A suitable plan details the steps to be taken in the planning process. Procedural knowledge suggests that the plan should consist of critical steps to be taken, should be usable by numbers of planners, and, above all, should be effective in doing what needs to be done.

WHAT CAUSES PEOPLE TO PLAN

Ideas are necessary stimulators of the planning process. Usually, worthwhile ideas evolve as a consequence of the planners' probing of the environments in which they operate. Within these environments are people's thoughts and feelings, circumstances peculiar to given situations, and other data of many kinds. To discover and sort data, planners use means like the problem census, inservice and staff development media, cooperative study and surveys, experimentation, formal evaluation, and development of philosophies and sets of objectives.

The Problem Census

A time-honored way of initiating curriculum improvement programs is to ask teachers and other personnel to state their problems orally or in writing.

At best, this procedure is operated on a face-to-face basis in an informal, unstructured situation. This procedure was used in Corpus Christi, Texas,[11] and in the Illinois Curriculum Improvement Program.[12] A more formal way of inventorying concerns and problems is to ask in writing for open-ended statements or to present a written list of possible concerns to be ranked in order of importance. These methods of census taking remain the commonest ways of locating curriculum problems and concerns. The following census form was distributed to elementary school teachers in Cumberland County, New Jersey, by the county's "helping teachers" and a team of consultants:

> As a consequence of meeting with the administrators of public elementary schools and also with a representative group of teachers in the county, we have listed below a variety of possibilities for study by teachers and administrators, and perhaps also by members of boards of education and other citizens.
>
> Will you please select from the list the four topics which you believe are most worthy of study by people who really want to benefit the schools of the county? Then please place the number 1 next to that topic which you think is absolutely tops as an important study topic. Finally, place a 2 next to your second choice; a 3 next to your third choice; and a 4 next to the topic you rank fourth.
>
> Please note that the placement of a topic in the list does not suggest the degree to which it is favored by the helping teachers or the consultants.
>
> When the returns are in, we shall report them to you, with an indication of the top preferences of all of you. You as an individual will then be asked whether you care to join a study group which you may choose freely from the several groups studying the most-preferred topics. A teacher who decides to join a study group will be working partly on his or her own time to learn all he or she can about new ideas and materials related to the topic.
>
> *Possible topics for study*
>
> _____ Learning Centers and Learning Stations
> "There ought to be places in the classroom and the school where learning is easier."
>
> _____ Developing Listening Skills
> "Why don't these kids hear anything?"
>
> _____ Ungraded School Units (Nongrading)
> "Kids don't grow in grades; they grow by years and in spurts."
>
> _____ Inquiry Training
> "What's this 'inquiry approach' all about?"

_____ Behavioral Objectives and Criterion Referencing
"Do the children and I know where we're going, and when we've got there?"

_____ Evaluation as Feedback and Guide
"How can we learn from test results, and how can we report to parents?"

_____ Gaming and Simulation in the Classroom
"How can I make it like the real thing?"

_____ Strategies for Individualizing Instruction
"How can I sort out the individuals in my group, and then do something for them?"

_____ Classroom Discipline and the Curriculum
"Does how children spend their time in school have anything really to do with their getting into trouble?"

_____ The Roles of Teacher Aides
"Lavatory patrol, hall duty, checking papers—what?"

_____ Diagnosing and Correcting Reading Difficulties
"I'm not sure how to find out, and then I don't know what to do after I've found out."

_____ Working with Underachievers
"If he isn't doing as well as he can, why isn't he?"

_____ New Developments in the Teaching of the Social Studies
"What's that about the Third World?"

_____ New Developments in the Teaching of Science
"Having competed with the Russians, there must be something else."

_____ New Developments in the Teaching of Arithmetic
"They say they can tell what kind of teacher you are by watching you teach arithmetic."

_____ Making the School a More Humane Place
"The school is an institution where people should be valued!"

_____ "Opening" the School
"How can they have new experiences without tearing the roof off the building?"

To shift from the negative emphasis, which a problem census sometimes seems to involve, faculties may use their own adaptations of the brainstorming technique, originally created for idea development in the field of advertising. Brainstorming consists of free, rapid-fire suggestion of ideas by group members, no matter how impossible the achievement of certain of the ideas appears to be. One member's suggestion is followed immediately by another member's suggestion, without critical or other comment being made by any member of the group. However, a member may elaborate, or "piggyback," on his or her predecessor's suggestion. A recorder keeps a list of the ideas, sixty or seventy of which may be proposed within a very few minutes. At some time after the brainstorming episode, a subgroup or special committee outside the group analyzes the ideas in depth for possible followup. Commonly, one or more ideas prove worthy of being put into effect. Interestingly, the accepted ideas may include those that initially seemed totally unreasonable and impossible to effectuate. Dramatic developments in program planning have been known to occur as a result of using the brainstorming technique.

Inservice and Staff Development Media

Institutes, workshops, and conferences have sometimes provided opportunities for identifying curriculum needs. At an institute, a challenging talk by a curriculum specialist may be followed by productive group discussions. One of the time-honored institute series in the nation was sponsored in the counties of Pennsylvania on prescribed "institute days." Capitalizing on another medium, some school systems have utilized workshops as a means of identifying problems and concerns that transcend the themes of the workshops themselves. National, state, regional, and local conferences have become sites for in-depth discussion of difficulties encountered in local school districts.

Cooperative Study and Surveys

Sometimes curriculum improvement starts when a faculty engages in formal or informal study of professional books and other materials. Learning centers in some of the newer school buildings are being stocked with professional materials for use in formal study by faculties. Media specialists now have the arrangements and facilities necessary for selecting useful materials for nearly any faculty effort.

Self-surveys of schools—surveys conducted by staff members themselves—and cooperative surveys involving school systems and college staffs—such as that conducted several years ago in Great Neck, New York, in cooperation with Teachers College, Columbia University—yield important topics for further study. All-purpose surveys have declined in recent years in favor of surveys to determine the progress being made in limited areas of the curriculum, such as in uses of selected resources and materials, in personalization of teaching, and in teaching of particular skills.

Experimentation

Experiments conducted by teachers individually or in small groups have led to exploitation of bigger fields for study. By beginning a program with isolated instances of experimentation, a school system can maintain the valuable "broken-front" approach, which may be described as "a little improvement here and a little there." For years the Horace Mann–Lincoln Institute of School Experimentation, Teachers College, Columbia University, sponsored experimentation based on the interests and desires of personnel in local school systems. So, in general, did the Illinois Curriculum Program. Later developments in the subject fields have encouraged teachers to try patterns of teaching created by national committees of subject matter specialists. Thus, experimentation varies in nature from the free and unstructured to the prescribed and limited. Often it prepares the way for experimental research, a rigorous form of inquiry.

Though teachers obviously cannot conduct experimentation in their efforts to solve every problem they face, every curriculum problem or issue can serve as an invitation to experimentation. To be induced and encouraged to experiment, teachers need dynamic, skilled leadership. When most of the members of a faculty experiment cooperatively under competent leadership, the faculty is likely to demonstrate growth in its insights and skills.

Formal Evaluation

The results of administering tests and inventories, particularly tests of pupil achievement, have touched off numerous efforts at curriculum change. Item analysis of test data can be especially helpful in indicating weaknesses that need correcting. When teachers readminister in October the final examinations they have given the preceding June, they often discover how shockingly ineffective their teaching has been. In general, teacher-made tests and other locally developed tests and inventories do more to convince teachers of learners' needs than do so-called national tests based on alleged national norms and prepared by remote commercial agencies. Experience shows also that teachers tend to respect their own tests more than the tests prepared in other school systems. Within recent years, National Assessment and statewide testing have had as their primary purpose revelation of deficiencies in pupil achievement that the schools can presumably remedy.

Apart from testing, ways of achieving evaluation of learning products include interviewing pupils, conducting case studies of individuals and small groups, preparing anecdotal records, diaries, and logs concerning pupils' behavior, taking still pictures and motion pictures, and using rating scales.

Development of Philosophies and Sets of Objectives

For a time, development of philosophies and lists of objectives fell into disrepute because this procedure is time-consuming and is sometimes said to keep teachers from dealing with live, flesh-and-blood problems. Subsequently, a reaction occurred when many school systems appeared to be operating in a rudderless way, devoid of acknowledged objectives. Accordingly, the mid-sixties and the early seventies saw a moderate upswing in the attention given to stating objectives. Many school systems continued to borrow statements of objectives from standard lists rather than attempting to devise their own. One of the most respected standard lists was developed by Will French and a large committee of educators in the Survey Study of Behavioral Outcomes of General Education. This so-called behavioral goals study concentrated on objectives for high schools under four headings: attaining maximum intellectual growth and development, becoming culturally oriented and integrated, maintaining and improving physical and mental health, and becoming economically competent.

Sophistication in ways of stating objectives has increased during the eighties, as people in schools have had more experience with stating objectives. Behavioral objectives have been written to express outcomes anticipated or desired as a direct result of instruction. Although behavioral objectives have been both defended and attacked, they are favorably regarded in current efforts to make teachers and other school personnel accountable for the outcomes of their work.

Miscellaneous Additional Ways of Starting

In the realm of techniques for the curriculum worker, Jeff West suggested numerous specific ways of getting planning started. Following are several promising ones:

1. Help teachers identify one general area of emphasis for the year.
2. Set aside a day a week. Call it "Teacher Day" and use it for conferences with teachers about their problems.
3. Utilize a school and community pupil-personnel survey.
4. Keep publications like the *Encyclopedia of Educational Research* handy for teachers' use as they puzzle about problems.
5. Display recent books and other materials and aids where teachers can see them.
6. Encourage teachers to develop small experimental projects in their classrooms.[13]

Even the smallest school may be too complex an institution to rely for very long on just one procedure for initiating curriculum planning.

Teachers with searching minds think of varied ways of pursuing the common objective of improvement. Following are narratives of the beginning stages of three improvement programs:

> *Program 1:*   The curriculum coordinator conferred with the superintendent and other administrators regarding the budget, aims, and underlying principles of the new program and concerning the present condition of the curriculum. A council of administrators prepared a general plan for the program, and "study committees," consisting chiefly of teachers, identified problems for study. A "pilot committee" then looked for materials that would be helpful in solving the problems. In addition, a review of the present curriculum was undertaken.[14]
>
> *Program 2:*   The faculty of a high school formed a Curriculum Improvement Committee charged with referring specific problems to special committees. In its first year the Committee made several proposals for curriculum revision, reviewed present course outlines, led several research-type projects, revised school brochures, helped plan an inservice program, tried to keep abreast of national developments, and served in a continuing curriculum advisory capacity.[15]
>
> *Program 3:*   It its early stages this program featured a concentrated effort to locate needs and resources of the school system. Its leaders accomplished their purpose by conducting a census of teachers' problems, consulting administrators, utilizing testing programs, sponsoring classroom visitations, conferring with individual teachers, using parent contacts, and analyzing personnel records.[16]

Other ways in which planning has been initiated are as follows:

1. A school system established a committee on inservice education to plan college extension courses, workshops, and local courses to suit the interests of its teachers.
2. Another system allotted funds to permit teachers to attend selected national conventions of professional associations. It required reports in the form of "ideas worth pursuing."
3. A school dedicated half its faculty meetings to brainstorming solutions to major instructional problems.
4. Another school established an instructional materials allocation of twenty-five cents a pupil to be spent cooperatively by teachers for improvement projects.

5. Still another school scheduled its outstanding teachers to conduct inservice courses and key faculty meetings.
6. A school system planned quarterly clinic sessions concerning the
   educational needs of atypical pupils.
7. The schools of a rural region conducted a twice-yearly show-and-
   tell program for reporting and demonstrating experimental, innovative projects.
8. The "myth and error conference" at a county high school revealed
   untruths about public education that were being reported in popular magazines and newspapers and then stimulated a search for
   needed changes and corrections in programs and procedures in
   the schools.
9. A city school made Saturday a day of informal schooling during
   which children's interests were explored. Jewelry making, the
   molding of ceramics, and other activities eventually came into
   the formal curriculum and the pupil activities program as a result
   of a few Saturdays of exploration.
10. A group of school systems applied measures of quality developed
    by a regional school study council and a state department of
    education.
11. A school system provided "alertness experiences" for teachers by
    sending them on interstate trips to visit selected schools and
    teachers.
12. Another school system established, in cooperation with a college,
    a curriculum study center in which teachers could investigate pos-
    sible solutions to instructional problems.
13. An alliance of schools planned cultural workshops for teachers
    on the theory that teachers' personal development is at least as
    important as their professional development.
14. A school district paid selected teachers for summer work in plan-
    ning experiences for children, and these were tried out during
    the following scholastic year.

The variety of approaches employed in these programs shows how
unwise it is to pattern one program after another. Varying situations call
for creating new ideas and using differing combinations of procedures.

Initial identification of curriculum concerns has often proved to be
a crude and invalid process. Criteria can be preestablished for analyzing
concerns with some care in order to accept or reject them for treatment.
Among possible criteria are these:

1. Will dealing with the identified curriculum concern prove worthwhile? Is it really worth the necessary expenditure of time and

resources? How meaningful could the process and the results be to the participants?

2. Can the concern be properly dealt with at this time? Is the timing appropriate?
3. Is dealing with the concern within the competence of the participants? Specifically, is it any of their business, and *can* they deal with it?
4. Is the plan for dealing with the concern of such size and scope as to be manageable?
5. If help is needed, is competent help available?

Staffs of schools and school systems have real difficulties in setting priorities among the concerns to be dealt with. The values held by participants in curriculum study are, of course, important in determining priorities. These values should be permitted to surface during lengthy periods of probing, questioning, and conferring. Great danger to morale and productivity lies in assuming that values emerge quickly and that problems that are finally identified are being considered in their appropriate order of importance. In their haste to get projects and programs under way, curriculum planners must not fail to take time for initial deliberation.

SITUATION 8-3
Procedures to Fit the Situation

Glovers Central School District has been in operation seventy-two years. Recently a superintendent of twenty-eight years' tenure retired. During his regime, only occasional and sporadic activity to improve the curriculum occurred. The following additional facts have also become evident:

1. Few of the 329 teachers have taken any inservice courses within the past five years.
2. The community has recently experienced a wave of conservatism that has resulted in the defeat of two bond issues to pay for new school buildings.
3. A local resident has created disturbances at board of education meetings about the presence of "radical" textbooks in the schools.
4. The teaching staff likes to think of itself as a collection of individualists.
5. John Dewey's name is generally despised in the schools and, where it is known, in the community at large.
6. Teachers' concerns are directed largely toward improvement of reading and of English composition.
7. An evaluation committee from the regional association of colleges and secondary schools has recently called Glovers High School "twenty-five years behind the times in program and in understanding by teachers of what constitutes a modern program."

Assume that you have been appointed curriculum coordinator in charge of the school system's curriculum program and that the teachers' concerns about reading and English composition are bona fide. Assume that the new superintendent is a forward-looking person who has given you a free hand. What would you do to probe these concerns in depth?

Which of the procedures enumerated in this section of the chapter do you think might prove helpful in opening a wedge to improvement?

Whom would you need to work with in making decisions about the procedures to be used? How, exactly, would you hope to proceed?

CUSTOMARY PLANNING MODES

Since the 1920s, when formal planning of the curriculum was begun in some of the larger U.S. cities, a number of factors to be considered in planning have emerged. Among them are the nature of pupil populations, the importance of teachers as change agents, participation by parents, establishment of program goals and objectives, quality of evaluation procedures, and the presence of what Mary Heller has called "sequence interlock" to ensure that planning steps are carried out in rational order. Heller points out that planners have developed systems of renewal strategies that provide for continuous input by different categories of people, careful planning of staff development projects, and full recognition of people's expressed needs and concerns.[17]

Some school systems have tried to do their planning in yearly cycles during which goal-setting, actual curriculum planning, and application of accountability measures occur.[18] A few systems are preparing scenarios as planning tools. Used frequently in the social sciences, the scenario is a visionary projection of what conditions may be years hence.[19] Whatever the procedures used, curriculum planning is regarded in both developed and developing nations as being of paramount importance to progress.[20]

Despite the availability of newer planning procedures, most school systems follow customary planning modes. Representations of customary modes appear below.

School system A has

1. Described a proposal briefly, specifying its purpose or intent.
2. Considered the actual need for this proposal.
3. Made a list of aims or goals for the proposal.
4. Had the aims ranked by numbers of participants.
5. Had the aims restated so that each of them expressed a desired learning outcome and proved capable of subdivision into functional objectives.

6. Reexamined the aims to see whether they "covered" the intent of the program.
7. Added and deleted several aims.
8. Stated usable objectives that belonged under the aims to which they seemed to relate.
9. Thought how the staff would know when each of the objectives had been attained.
10. Described experiences or activities for pupils.
11. Determined evaluation means for checking pupil achievement and also for gauging the worth of the proposal.
12. Communicated the proposal in the form of a curriculum guide.

This school system has obviously spent a great deal of time setting and clarifying aims and objectives.

School system B has

1. Developed guidelines for planning.
2. Organized a systemwide curriculum review committee.
3. Established goals and objectives, general in nature.
4. Required the review committee to prepare forms for submitting curriculum proposals.
5. Found representative personnel to staff curriculum committees.
6. Asked these committees to submit concrete proposals to the review committee for its approval.
7. Valued uniformity in programs and proposals followed in schools throughout the system.

This school system has apparently relied heavily on a centralized approach to planning.

School system C has

1. Designated a curriculum coordinator to supervise all planning.
2. Decided to revise each part of the program every four or five years.
3. Prepared time lines for the accomplishment of planning tasks.
4. Appointed a central curriculum council.
5. Searched for ideas and supporting materials.
6. Decided via the central curriculum council just what to plan, from kindergarten through twelfth grade.
7. Adopted an evaluation system.
8. Gathered teaching/learning materials and evaluated them.
9. Determined inservice needs of the staff.
10. Filed, at intervals, summaries of what has been done.
11. Evaluated the planning operation annually.

This system seems to have assumed some large tasks in a cavalier manner, perhaps without knowing their magnitude.

School system D has

1. Identified general curriculum aims or goals.
2. Stated goals specifically for subjects.
3. Made scope and sequence charts.
4. Identified the competencies of staff members for planning.
5. Stated instructional objectives, subject by subject.
6. Prepared and distributed curriculum guides in a number of subjects.
7. Considered means of evaluating parts of the curriculum.
8. Planned for subsequent curriculum revision.

Placing a heavy emphasis on subjects, School system D has seemingly only scratched the surface, after the manner of curriculum planners in the 1920s and 1930s.

School system E has

1. Formulated a logical design for planning.
2. Stated within each facet of the design a series of tasks.
3. Begun planning by analyzing what might be done.
4. Proceeded to design several new proposals.
5. Elaborated on the proposals so that each of them could be used by teachers.
6. Observed teachers while they put the proposals into effect.
7. Provided evaluation means (chiefly questionnaires) for assessing the worth of each proposal.
8. Sought feedback often during implementation of each proposal.
9. Searched for ways in which each proposal might be revised.

This school system has worked carefully in utilizing the design it has created.

The customary planning modes used by school systems evidently differ widely.

A SCHEMA FOR PLANNING

What has been said so far in this chapter suggests several steps that are essential to effective planning. These steps may not all be required at a given time, or in the order in which they are expressed below. Nevertheless, all of them are eligible for inclusion in the planning process. They include surveying the scene, assessing needs, identifying and defining problems, making and evaluating proposals, preparing designs, organizing the work force, supervising the planning process, utilizing the products of planning, applying evaluation means, and anticipating the future.

Surveying the Scene

Surveying the scene involves knowing what makes a particular school system the same as other systems and what makes it markedly different from the rest. Included in the curriculum scene are tradition, expectations, people, funds or the scarcity thereof, school system organization, and several other features. What has been said previously about the domains of planning is relevant.

Assessing Needs

Needs can be thought of in two ways. The first is singular: need for any change. The second, or plural, form expresses the needs of pupils and teachers. Pupils have their recognizable educational needs; teachers have needs related to performing their work effectively and improving their own functioning.

Identifying and Defining Problems

As a result of assessing needs, planners can identify problems of teaching and learning. Additional problems not initially identified in the needs assessment may be discovered as the planning process proceeds. Any curriculum problem that is deemed worth solving and that can be managed should be defined to clarify its meaning and implications.

Making Proposals—and Evaluating Them

The most promising problems can form the basis for making proposals for curriculum change. Some of the proposals can eventuate in carefully developed designs. Proposals can be evaluated informally by determining whether they conform to aims or goals and then formulating critical questions about them, which are then answered by the most competent school system personnel and, if possible, by outside consultants.[21]

Preparing Designs

Designing that capitalizes on the most promising proposals usually follows steps like those that appear in Chapter 5: stating program or project objectives, identifying evaluation means, choosing a type of design, selecting learning content, determining and organizing learning experiences, and evaluating the program or project summatively.

Organizing the Work Force

Organizing the work force requires finding the best available personnel to perform designated tasks, and then judging how to organize these personnel so that their talents are used well. Constant scouting or inquiry among present staff members is needed for personnel search. Occasionally, new personnel can be brought in to provide certain necessary abilities. The identified personnel are then organized into study groups and committees to do the most difficult part of the planning and to perform the easy tasks too.

Supervising the Planning Process

Planning cannot proceed smoothly without direction. Central steering committees often make policy and arrange for resources. Daily direction usually comes, however, from leaders such as curriculum coordinators and school principals. The special functions of leaders are discussed in Chapter 11.

Utilizing the Products of Planning

Whatever has been planned needs to be implemented. Implementation, or the act of putting plans to intelligent use, usually is done by classroom teachers. Because that which is new or different is likely to be puzzling, teachers need help and encouragement from supervisors who know what to expect in the implementation process.

Applying Evaluation Means

Applying evaluation means could be called applying the test of reality and other tests. Many projects and programs look good on paper, but the crucial question is "Do they work?" This question often yields offhand judgments, only some of which are valid. The validity of a judgment can be checked by formal evaluation of the project or program, as described in Chapter 6. It is impossible to tell what a plan has accomplished in action without applying appropriate evaluation means.

Anticipating the Future

The future begins with feedback of information regarding the apparent success of a plan. This information includes data from formal evaluation as well as little items of news about the experiences that teachers and pupils have had with the plan. When conditions change rapidly, as when the details of subject matter change, the plan should be revised. Looking to the future can be systematized by projecting revision schedules in subject matter fields and other curriculum areas.

SITUATION 8-4
What Was Done in the Planning Process?

Consider the steps in planning that have just been described. Think of a program or a project that has been planned during the past five years in your school system or in a system you know. Learn which of the steps were actually used in the planning. In what order were they used? Which of them were omitted for good reason? How successfully were some of the steps used? Were there actions taken that cannot be classified under any of the steps?

What is your final conclusion about the quality of the planning that was done?

Organization for Putting the Schema into Effect

The schema described above can be put into effect only if an organization is developed for allocating and assigning people and material resources. Experience in curriculum planning offers several guidelines that are helpful in organizing people and materials:

1. Start small by involving only a few persons at first.
2. Choose these people carefully. They should be interested, able persons who are eager to see the schools improved.
3. Hold planning sessions when they are needed, having due regard for the time schedules of the planners.
4. Give credit to the planners, rewarding them sensibly and openly.
5. Provide the planners with necessary time, resources, and materials.
6. Fix responsibility for the subparts of the planning operation.
7. Establish time limits for completing portions of the work, but do not rush the participants.
8. Help the planners see what's important by personally emphasizing the important as opposed to the trivial.
9. Have some criteria for determining what's to be done. For example, the first proposals should help solve commonly recognized problems, and should be of the right size and complexity to be pursued successfully.
10. Encourage participants to get the job done well—without stress—

remembering that what happens during the first attempt colors or conditions subsequent attempts.

One of the theses of this book has been that curriculum improvement occurs chiefly where the teacher is—in the individual school. This would imply that most organizational arrangements should be centered at the building level. To a large extent this is true, but the need for developing programs vertically for the sake of sequence and continuity, the importance of articulation among educational levels, and the necessity for teachers to associate with teachers in other schools at the same grade or educational level mandate that the organization for curriculum improvement be bigger than an individual school.

Thus it is unwise to center organization either in individual schools or in central offices. Rather, a centrally coordinated approach is needed in facing both those problems originating in the individual school and those problems that are of concern to the total system or to a level within the system. The centrally coordinated approach encourages activity in either the central office or the local building, depending on the kind of problem being attacked. For example, the central office may be concerned with teacher morale throughout the system, while the local school wishes to develop a social studies program for children of a given socioeconomic background.[22] Small school systems containing only one or two schools tend to operate according to a local building or decentralized approach, and some traditionally oriented systems retain strong central control. But the centrally coordinated approach is the most common today.

In individual schools, teachers organize in grade-level groups, departments (secondary school), teams, school councils, planning committees, and working (ad hoc) committees. Sometimes large schools are broken down into schools within schools. In the individual school the leadership of the principal is obviously very important. Committees in individual schools develop resource units, adapt outlines and course guides to the school's needs, consider schoolwide problems like the quality of assembly programs and the power to be given to pupil government organizations, and perform a multitude of other local functions.

In whole school systems, curriculum planning is initiated by means of systemwide faculty organizations, central steering committees (as well as vertical ad hoc committees), lay advisory committees, and central office supervisors, to mention only a few of the groups in the organization. Central organization often provides guidelines for planning, general curriculum leadership, machinery for getting under way, duplicated or printed curriculum materials, and means of evaluating the programs.

Centrally coordinated organization makes almost mandatory the formation of a central steering committee, sometimes called a districtwide or central curriculum committee. Much attention has been given in the literature to the functions of central steering committees and to ways of forming them. Common tasks for these committees are

- Surveying curriculum needs
- Getting action started
- Facilitating communication
- Approving the accomplishments of ad hoc committees
- Locating help—personnel, facilities, time, and materials
- Coordinating activities
- Arranging for and guiding evaluation
- Maintaining relationships with individuals and groups outside the committee and also outside the school system.

Committees to perform special functions, called ad hoc committees, should be organized to fulfill clearly defined purposes such as preparing a system for reporting the work of junior high school pupils. Obviously, these committees should arise from definite, pressing concerns and should not be organized because of a preconception that they are essential to a thriving program. Membership should be based on competence and interest and should terminate at a definitely prearranged time. Someone has said that it is easy to form committees but difficult to get rid of them. Committee members should be helped to see their task broadly, in the context of a program that has other facets. Furthermore, they should know the scope and the probable duration of their task.

Ad hoc committees come in varied sizes and organizational forms. Some are short-term task forces; others attack problems of such importance that they become long-term enterprises. These committees tend to deal with problems of substance or content and to ignore problems of process. They find process problems unfamiliar, mysterious, and hard to resolve.

Ad hoc committees provide maximum opportunity for increasing the involvement of personnel, including laypersons. In the past, maximum involvement of competent people has seldom been made a goal. Today, however, most curriculum authorities consider that goal highly desirable. Because of the significant work ad hoc committees do, they will probably remain the backbone of curriculum improvement programs. Much attention should be given to the quality of their functioning.[23]

SITUATION 8-5
The Shortcomings of the Curriculum Steering Committee

To listen to the teachers in the Mannheim School District, one would think that everything was wrong with the newly organized Central Curriculum Committee. In teachers' rooms and other out-of-the-way places, the comments went like this:

"Whoever said we needed a big committee to tell us to do what we're already doing?"

"It's the group of administrators who thought of the idea. I notice that no teacher was in the group that made the decision to have a Central Curriculum Committee."

"I think each school can take care of its own business. We don't need a big central committee, even though there are twelve schools in the system."

"There is some need for a central committee. I say that because I believe every fifth grade all over town should be doing the same thing at about the same time. Someone or some group has to police the teachers."

"The big trouble with a group like the Central Curriculum Committee is that it becomes a debating society—all talk and no action."

"Why doesn't the superintendent spend more time preparing the principals to do their jobs? Then they could take the leadership in developing curriculum instead of having the leadership centered in a group like this."

"In the eight months it's existed, the Committee hasn't done a thing to help the eight groups that were already started in an informal way before the Committee was organized. I know. I'm a member of the committee on reporting to parents."

"I guess someone on the inside is bucking for promotion."

Which complaints seem to you to represent the real shortcomings of the Committee? Why?

How do you account for the presence of each of the comments that you rejected?

What democratic principles of organization for curriculum improvement can you adduce?

THE COMPUTER AS A PLANNING INSTRUMENT

The work of committees can be aided considerably by new technology. People in schools today know very well that we have entered the computer age. Computers, which for a quarter of a century have been an aid to business, industry, and universities, have come into homes and schools. In fact, development of the microchip has made a box-on-the-desk, purchased at reasonable cost, an attraction to pupils in elementary and secondary schools—such an attraction that even reluctant pupils come to school early.

Many teachers and pupils think of computers only as instructional tools. They have seen sales of microcomputers to schools increase remarkably, as computer-assisted instruction (CAI) has become common. Many a pupil is aided in learning elements of the three Rs by a microcomputer. The degree to which pupils benefit from using microcomputers in learning basic skills and other curriculum content remains, however, in some doubt. As has been said previously, in 1984 Terrel Bell, the Secretary of Education, criticized available computer software as contributing to mere "electronic page-turning." The need, he said, was for programs capable of analyzing pupil responses, offering remediation, and helping pupils to new levels of learning.[24]

To many people in schools, the computer is obviously more than a fad in need of refinement. They consider it useful enough to favor expending the public's money on the inservice education of staff members in computer operation and programming. The vastness of national and regional organizations promoting computerization is astounding. For school personnel who want to do more with computers than they are now doing, help is on the way.

In a chapter on curriculum planning, discussion of computer uses needs to emphasize the planning operation itself. Just how helpful are computers in curriculum planning?

In beginning to answer this question, one may note the school management uses to which microcomputers have already been put. They include storing and retrieving information according to given requirements; printing this information in varied displays like lists, charts, and graphs; preparing forms to suit particular purposes; correcting records of people's performance by deleting invalid and outdated information and inserting new data; and sorting and putting in order the records currently in files. These uses are obviously more facilitative than dramatic, but they are time savers.

Larger computers in the central offices of some school districts have been performing four separate functions. The commonest one is financial management, in which electronic spread sheets show budget projections and fund accounting. A second function, and one of greater interest to curriculum planners, is information management. Information kept in data bases is retrieved for use in making inventories, scheduling classes and programs, assembling grade reports, indicating attendance records, and maintaining personnel records. An interesting third function called telecommunication permits users to contact computers far away by using a telephone to "call up" the computer. (The present revision of this book, as well as the preceding revision, was made possible in part by contact between a computer in New Jersey and a master computer in California.) A fourth function is word processing for producing form letters, updating mailing lists, editing manuals, and preparing guides. A less used function, now in its infancy, is simulation of situations or conditions by means of graphics.

Using Computers in Initial Curriculum Planning

Whereas computer-assisted instruction (CAI) is utilized chiefly in tutoring pupils, computer-managed instruction (CMI) is used in curriculum planning and other management operations. At the grassroots or local school level, microcomputers can help to retrieve and assign goals and objectives, to recall test and observational data, to link objectives with performance, and to display achievement data for program evaluation. Obviously what one puts into a computer is what one gets out, though the information may be treated and then exhibited in different forms. In both individual schools and entire school systems, computers help primarily with planning tasks like surveying the scene, assessing the needs of pupils and teachers, and identifying and defining curriculum problems. In addition, they can effect certain statistical treatments.

Numerous examples have been reported of the use of computers in initial planning steps. The armed forces have experimented with varied training sequences, have formed data bases for indicating transitions from one objective to another, and have identified "natural" groupings of objectives by means of mathematical analysis.[25]

Vertinsky and Thompson have reported an attempt to use a computer to find links between a physical education program and the socioeconomic environment in which it was offered.[26]

A needs assessment plan described by Masinton and others is ready-made for computerization. Data of three kinds can be entered with a view to subsequent summary and retrieval: interviews with pupils, parents, other community citizens, and school staff members; descriptions of the curriculum; and a profile of the pupil population.[27]

The planning done by individual teachers can be improved by permitting the teachers to use computers for recording answers to test items; analyzing pupil achievement status, item by item; and determining pupil averages.

The examples so far have dealt largely with "local data." Ideas, trends, and developments of national scope also have relevance for curriculum planning. A competent librarian can help planners become familiar with the Educational Resources Information Center (ERIC), the National Information Center for Educational Media, and the Exceptional Child Education Resources. The publications *Resources in Education* and the *Thesaurus of ERIC Descriptors* are used daily in libraries. Many an agency throughout the country can make contact with database sources like ERIC centers. Within the agency, a search analyst conducts "on line searching" to aid the client in learning what data are available about given topics. The client may then limit, broaden, or refine the data until he or she can specify just what is needed. The desired articles, speeches, and other data are then printed at the distant center and sent to the client.[28]

Can More Be Done?

Some planners apparently begin to use a computer with the idea that this instrument can think for them. The expectation often originates in the rumor that there is such a thing as "artificial intelligence." The psychologist Eugene Galanter points out that a quarter-century ago the hope of inducing artificial intelligence attracted considerable attention. The computer was the means by which this hope was to be realized. The fact is that computers can work for planners but they cannot substitute for them.[29] As Howard Peelle puts it, we have a partnership in teaching in which computers do their work well in conjunction with teachers who in turn do their work well.[30] There is no question as to which partner does the more difficult work. A goal for the future is development of computers that can "understand" subject matter and its uses, but the future is yet to come. The instrument for difficult planning, designing, and decision making is obviously the human mind.

Meanwhile, however, planners keep trying to use computers in more sophisticated ways. For example, the schools in Gilbert, Arizona, wanted to develop a program in which "curriculum unification" (uniformity) would be achieved. The equipment at hand in the Gilbert schools consisted of a used IBM System/34 computer and a new optical scanner for reading answer sheets. The planners stated and monitored objectives from grade one to grade twelve in reading, English communication, science, mathematics, and the social studies. A record of pupils' performance in achieving the objectives was then plotted, stored, and printed. The objectives themselves were distinguished as being "milestone" and "minimum" objectives. The former represented essential learnings; the latter, minimal learnings to permit graduation. Information became available about pupil performance status and the efforts made by teachers in working toward curriculum unification. In addition, gifted pupils took criterion-referenced tests to determine their progress, and data about other pupils in the special education program became clearer and more accurate. For planners who want to keep the curriculum continuous, uniform, or "intact," this procedure seems to hold possibilities.[31]

At the college and university level, use of computers in the planning of parts of courses has been going on for some time. At the University of Delaware, for instance, a four-step arrangement has been developed for participation by faculty members in planning courses with the help of minicomputers. An individual faculty member makes a proposal about which other personnel consult, and the proposal is reviewed by an advisory committee. A design is then created by faculty, designers, and programmers, and is reviewed by a "lesson review group." Next, the programmers produce a program that is reviewed by the lesson review group and a code review group, and is then tried and critiqued by students and faculty. When the program is believed to be ready for publication and dissemination, it is reviewed extensively again and then finally distributed to libraries and other user sites. Using the PLATO system, faculty members at Delaware

have prepared dozens of instructional lessons. One may judge from the
following titles the general nature of the lessons:

In accounting, Accounting Sample Test
In art, Optical Letterspacing
In biology, Somatic Cell Genetics
In counseling, Exploring Careers: The Theory
In education, Factors in Reading Comprehension
In languages, The French Verb Test
In mathematics, Graph Theory
In music, Competency-Based Interval Drill
In physical education, Ingredients of Fitness
In physics, The Positions of the Planets
In psychology, Direct Scaling[32]

Stanley Pogrow observes that when computers are used to greatest
advantage, they reduce personnel time and improve teaching effectiveness.
There is considerable doubt as to whether computer-managed instruction
has any direct effect in increasing pupil achievement. However, the time
teachers use in doing paperwork can be reduced through the use of
minicomputers.[33] Robert Gagné has said that there is profit in computerizing basic data as a means to undertaking higher level thinking.[34] In the
future, computers will probably do more complex work than they are now
doing.

At present, computers cannot assemble data, enter them, or modify
them. These three tasks must be performed by human beings. If they cannot be performed rapidly, they may render some of the uses of computers
uneconomical of time and consequently of money. If computers are
to prove economical, they must process substantial amounts of information. Furthermore, the planners who use them must be able to enter
and retrieve data quickly, and also to make necessary data changes
quickly.[35] In working with computers, planners must become acquainted
with (1) programs that involve database management for keeping records,
filing them, and ultimately retrieving them; (2) programs that require treatment of large amounts of numerical data which appear on spread sheets;
and (3) programs that involve word processing, to help with the preparing and editing of written materials.

The Role of Software

People who learn about computers soon become aware that hardware (the
computer and its related equipment) has to be supplemented with software

(computer programs of the three kinds mentioned in the preceding paragraph). Programs are really sequences of information stored on disks, diskettes, or cartridges that are utilized in the computer. In effect, the disk, diskette, or cartridge tells the computer what to do. Curriculum planners with microcomputers have the option of buying software or of making their own. Because so little has been done to prepare software commercially for use in curriculum planning, planners must make most of the programs they insert into the computer. For this function, they or persons associated with them must have acquired skills in programming. Cautions to be exercised in both buying and making software can be found in more sophisticated discussions than the present one. An excellent source of information about software used in education is the Minnesota Educational Computing Consortium, 2520 Broadway Drive North, St. Paul, Minnesota 55113. Special attention has been given to the uses of computers in educational administration by the Management Information Services, Florida Department of Education, 275 Knott Building, Tallahassee, Florida 32301.

SITUATION 8-6
Beginning to Use the Computer in Planning

In your own school system there are probably curriculum proposals that offer opportunities for using microcomputers or larger computer units in planning. Identify one or more of these opportunities by testing them, through discussion, with reference to the following criteria:

1. The curriculum proposal is large and important enough to make computerization worthwhile.
2. At the same time the proposal is small enough to make computerization manageable.
3. The proposal has in it elements that can be treated or managed in part by computerization.
4. Computerization would apparently be economical of the planners' time and energy.
5. Commercial software is obtainable for at least a minimal portion of the programming.
6. One or more persons are available to program the computer(s) further.
7. The proposal chosen seems to provide satisfactory content for a first effort at computerizing curriculum planning.

THE IMPORTANCE OF THOUGHTS AND FEELINGS

Personal feelings have proved to be very important in curriculum planning. The initial stage of organized curriculum improvement, like the course of true love, does not always run smoothly. As we have seen in Chapter 7, people tend to resist change in varying degrees in different areas of their living. At the same time, most persons wish to appear desirous of conforming to vogues having the support of superior officers. Teachers find conforming behavior less troublesome and upsetting than resistance.

Because of these facts, locating problems that represent real concerns is difficult, and interest in curriculum study is often feigned. In many a school, the following sort of dialogue has passed between teachers:

Teacher A: Why did you volunteer to join the social studies committee? Were you really interested?

Teacher B: No, I wasn't interested, but sooner or later I'll have to accept a committee assignment of some kind. This might as well be the one.

It is easy to say that persons like teacher B should be removed from schools if they persist in their present attitudes. However, one of the biggest challenges in education lies in helping teachers become alert and alive so that they do more than "keep school." Besides, some of the attitudes curriculum leaders encounter have resulted from their own fumbling, from the unproductiveness of much curriculum work in the past, and from already adverse attitudes toward certain school administrators.

Actually, curriculum leaders have oversimplified the reasons teachers become involved or fail to become involved in new curriculum projects. The reasons are numerous and complex. Leaders should make it easy for personnel to accept or reject specified opportunities for service. Often staff members are already performing important responsibilities other than the one immediately at hand, and they may justifiably reject new responsibilities.

Practical experience with the emotional element in initiating curriculum improvement leads to these conclusions:

1. Nothing of significance is likely to happen until teachers' real concerns come out. The climate of the school and school system can contribute greatly to the emergence of these concerns.
2. The behavior of educational leaders can help or hinder both initial and eventual progress.
3. The notion must be conveyed that educational engineering requires time and persistence.
4. The whole spirit must be one of working *with* people rather than of causing people to work.
5. Feeling tends to improve as curriculum groups become "in-groups" to which the members feel they belong.

Bayne Logan confirms the idea that some teachers feel they belong and others feel they do not. He calls the former inner-directed; the latter, outer-directed. Inner-directed teachers feel secure, sensing that they are directed by resources within themselves. Outer-directed teachers tend to be insecure because they are subject to varied external forces.[36]

SITUATION 8-7
How the Teachers Felt
_____

William A. Fullagar conducted an investigation of teachers' feelings about a newly started curriculum improvement program.[37] Among the statements he collected from teachers were these:

"Look at the beginning of the program. It didn't come from any suggestion of ours. It was thought up by the board of education or someone else at the top. They get the ideas but expect us to do the work."

"After the program was decided upon, no one gave us any clear picture of what it was all about."

"We would have gotten more out of our program if we could have met in groups made up of those who teach the same grade."

"Speaking of the administration, they contributed their share of problems for us. Some of our principals were quite open in their hostility to the program and criticized the ideas we brought back from our meetings."

"In a sense we were our own worst enemy. We were suspicious of the motives of those who were working with us—the consultants and the administrators."

On the basis of your own experience with teachers, select one or two of these comments that sound like remarks made by teachers you know. How are feelings like these acquired?

What other feelings might teachers be expected to express at the start of an improvement program? Which of these feelings are legitimate and to be expected?
_____

EXPECTATIONS, AND AN EYE TO THE FUTURE

Curriculum planning is most likely to succeed if certain expectations are kept in mind:

1. Persons in local schools and school systems should accept responsibility for planning. This responsibility should be distributed among numbers of people.
2. Feelings of personal security and worth, as well as satisfactory interpersonal relations, are essential.
3. Adequate time, facilities, and resources should be provided.
4. Curriculum workers should attempt to solve problems that seem real and important.

5. Effective communication about plans, policies, procedures, and achievements should be established and maintained among persons who have a stake in the projects.
6. Curriculum development should be considered a continuous, normal activity and not a stop-and-start activity.[38]
7. All persons concerned in a given project should be involved in it in some way.
8. Nothing of real importance should be undertaken without developing an understanding of its purpose.
9. Continuous evaluation of improvements should be built into the design of each project.
10. Balance must be achieved in both the loci and the types of activities to be performed.
11. Consistency must be maintained between the means and the ascribed ends of each project.

Persons who undertake curriculum improvement should not expect that great changes will necessarily occur within a period of a few months. Initially, growth may come only in the form of people's sensitization to themselves, to one another, and to the nature of the curriculum and its changes. Values, attitudes, and skills change to some extent almost immediately, but progress of lasting significance takes time.

Planners can rely on the authority of persons, the significance of knowledge, or the stringencies of a system.[39] Reliance on the first of these has been overused by zealous principals and superintendents who have wanted to see quick progress. Reliance on the second, based in research and well-communicated practical experience, has been used to a limited extent. Reliance on the third, which is relatively new, usually focuses on a particular way of proceeding. The keynotes of the first and third are power; the keynote of the second is information.

If planning is to have a suitable knowledge base, competent people must be assembled to provide input. For example, personnel from the City University of New York examined the health occupations education programs in New York State by holding meetings of members of the health professions and persons representing high schools, colleges, technical institutes, and regional agencies.[40] County school systems in New York State enlisted the help of competent people in testing a "futures envisioning process," called ED QUEST, to identify educational trends, to assess their significance, and to adopt strategies for coping with them.[41]

An interesting way of projecting the curriculum into the future is to raise questions concerning how the curriculum is to be viewed. Answers to the questions may suggest metaphors that can determine the focus of planning. Anglin and Dugan have projected five metaphors: (1) the curriculum as medicine for educational ills; (2) the curriculum as a greenhouse that encourages growth; (3) the curriculum as a route for traveling to a destination; (4) the curriculum as a means of production; and (5) the curriculum as a resource for developing and using human abilities.[42]

SUMMARY

This chapter has described ways in which people plan the curriculum. Beginning with an explanation of the bases of planning, which include knowledge of the planning environment, of people's needs, of curriculum problems, and of external and internal pressures, the chapter moved to discussions of what prompts people to plan, a presentation of the usual planning modes, and a scheme for planning. A feature of the chapter was an assessment of the computer as a planning instrument. In the final pages, the importance of people was highlighted once again.

ENDNOTES

1. See, for example, Tim Simkins, "Some Management Implications of the Development of Curriculum Information Systems," *Journal of Curriculum Studies* 15, no. 1 (1983): 47–59.

2. Note that the *need* for a specific program is different from the *needs* of learners for curriculum experiences. In the former instance, the question is "Is this program needed?" In the latter, the question is "What are the needs of our pupils for elements of educational experience within broad ranges of potential experience?"

3. See Kae Hentges and Michael C. Hasokawa, "Delphi: Group Participation in Needs Assessment and Curriculum Development," *Journal of School Health* 51, no. 8 (October 1980): 28–32.

4. B. R. Witkin, *An Analysis of Needs Assessment Techniques for Educational Planning at State, Intermediate, and District Levels* (Hayward, Calif.: Office of the Alameda County Superintendent of Schools, 1975).

5. Dale Findley and Russell Hamm, "The Bandwagon Approach to Curricular Innovation: Look Before You Leap," *Bulletin of the National Association of Secondary School Principals* 61, no. 411 (October 1977): 57–60.

6. David J. Mullen, "Involving Parents, Students, and Staff in Determining a Needs Assessment of Educational Priorities" (Paper delivered at the annual convention of the National Association of Elementary Principals, April 1974). Reported in ERIC # ED 093 036.

7. Association for Supervision and Curriculum Development, *Research for Curriculum Improvement*, 1957 Yearbook (Washington, D.C.: The Association, 1957), pp. 260, 261. Used with permission.

8. See Ronald C. Doll, *Supervision for Staff Development: Ideas and Application* (Newton, Mass.: Allyn and Bacon, 1983), pp. 172–182.

9. Adapted from Association for Supervison and Curriculum Development, *Strategy for Curriculum Change* (Washington, D.C.: The Association, 1965), p. 9. Used with permission.

10. See Louis Rubin, "The Current Scene in Curriculum," Occasional Paper I (Austin, Tex.: Southwest Educational Development Laboratory, 1980); also, Keith Goldhammer, "An Agenda for Education for the Next Generation" (Paper prepared for the House Subcommittee on Elementary, Secondary, and Vocational Education, January 1980).

11. Corpus Christi, Texas, Public Schools, "Curriculum Bulletin," mimeographed, October 2, 1951, p. 1.

12. Harold C. Hand, What People Think of Their Schools (New York: Harcourt, Brace and World, 1948), pp. 195–217.

13. Jeff West, "Improving Curriculum Procedures," Bulletin of the National Association of Secondary School Principals 43, no. 244 (February 1959): 77–82.

14. Itrice E. Eubanks, "Initiating a Program of Curriculum Improvement," School and Community 46, no. 9 (May 1960): 21.

15. Eugene Kitching, "Curriculum Improvement in Action," Educational Administration and Supervision 43, no. 3 (March 1957): 165.

16. Jack Rand and Robert Burress, "Case Study of a Curriculum Improvement Program," School Executive 73 (April 1954): 50–53.

17. Mary F. Heller, "The Process of Curriculum Development: An Overview of Research," February 1981. Reported in ERIC # ED 221 938.

18. Victor J. Ross, "To Achieve the Kind of School Operation You Need, Use This Step-by-Step Goal-Setting Plan," American School Board Journal 167, no. 9 (September 1980): 30, 31.

19. Christopher Dede and Dwight Allen, "Education in the 21st Century: Scenarios as a Tool for Strategic Planning," Phi Delta Kappan 62, no. 5 (January 1981): 362–66.

20. Boris K. Kluchnikov, "Reflections on the Concept and Practice of Educational Planning," Quarterly Review of Education 10, no. 1 (1980): 27–39.

21. See also J. Harvey Littrell, "Here's How to Evaluate Proposals for Curriculum Changes," American School Board Journal 167, no. 1 (January 1980): 30, 46.

22. Ronald C. Doll, A. Harry Passow, and Stephen M. Corey, Organizing for Curriculum Improvement (New York: Teachers College Press, 1953), pp. 1–10.

23. For interesting information about curriculum councils and committees, see Donald R. Grossnickle, "An Administrator's Guide for Effective Committee Work," Bulletin of the National Association of Secondary School Principals 67, no. 466 (November 1983): 78–80; John J. Lane, "Is This Meeting Necessary? An Application of Decision Theory," Bulletin of the National Association of Secondary School Principals 65, no. 446 (September 1981): 85–89; and Elaine McNally Jarchow and Karilee K. Watson, "Utilizing the Steering Committee in the Needs Assessment Process," Education 101, no. 2 (Winter 1980): 148, 149.

24. Quoted in the Newark Star-Ledger, Newark, New Jersey, January 19, 1984, p. 11.

25. Thomas R. Renckly and Gary Orwig, "Curriculum Viewed as a Binary System: An Approach to the Determination of Sequence" (Paper presented at an interservice and industry conference on training and equipment, Orlando, Florida, November 29–December 2, 1981). Reported in ERIC # ED 222 172.

26. Patricia A. Vertinsky and William A. Thompson, "Cross-Impact Computer Simulation of Physical Education Program Priorities: A Systems Perspective," Research Quarterly 51, no. 2 (May 1980): 389–406.

27. Harry W. Masinton, Johanna Smith, and Dudley Solomon, "A Three-Prong

Approach Takes Mystery Out of Needs Assessment," *Bulletin of the National Association of Secondary School Principals* 65, no. 448 (November 1981): 11–18.

28. See Ray Gerke, "Instructional Strategies through Computerized Information Retrieval," *Clearing House* 55, no. 1 (September 1981): 9–11.

29. From an address at Columbia University in 1984.

30. Howard A Peelle, "Computer Metaphors: Approaches to Computer Literacy," *World Future Society Bulletin* 16, no. 5 (November-December 1982): 9–16.

31. Bradley K. Narrett and Michael J. Hannafin, "Computers in Educational Management: Merging Accountability with Techonology," *Educational Technology* 22, no. 3 (March 1982): 9–12.

32. Fred T. Hofstetter, *The Eighth Summative Report of the Office of Computer-Based Instruction* (Newark, Del.: The University of Delaware, 1983).

33. Stanley Pogrow, *Education in the Computer Age* (Beverly Hills, Calif.: Sage Publications, 1983), pp. 107–110.

34. Robert M. Gagné, "Developments in Learning Psychology," *Educational Technology* 22, no. 6 (June 1982): 11–15.

35. Pogrow, *Education in the Computer Age*, pp. 124–27.

36. Bayne Logan, "Teacher Self-Perception and Curriculum Innovation," *Phi Delta Kappan* 63, no. 10 (June 1982): 705, 706.

37. William A. Fullagar, "The Teacher and Curriculum Improvement Programs," *Educational Administration and Supervision* 40, no. 2 (February 1984): 110, 111.

38. These six expectations have been taken from Doll, Passow, and Corey, *Organizing for Curriculum Improvement*, pp. 16–27, 29, 30.

39. James L. Martin, "Building Curricula When You Don't Have the Answer" (Paper presented at the annual meeting of the American Educational Research Association, New York City, March 1982). Reported in ERIC # ED 216 978.

40. The City University of New York, *Examination of the Health Occupations Education Curriculum from a Futurist Perspective: II* (Albany: New York State Education Department, 1981).

41. Thomas B. Mecca and Charles F. Adams, "ED QUEST: An Environmental Scanning Process for Educational Agencies," *World Future Society Bulletin* 16, no. 3 (May-June 1982): 7–12.

42. Leo W. Anglin and Therese Dugan, "Teachers' Perception of Existing and Ideal School Curriculum: An Analysis of Metaphors" (Paper presented at the annual meeting of the American Educational Research Association, New York City, March 1982). Reported in ERIC # ED 217 037.

SELECTED BIBLIOGRAPHY

Anderson, Walter A., and Young, William E., eds. *Action for Curriculum Improvement*. 1951 Yearbook, Association for Supervision and Curriculum Development. Washington, D.C.: The Association, 1951.

Brubaker, Dale L. *Curriculum Planning: The Dynamics of Theory and Practice.* Chicago: Scott, Foresman, 1982.

Caswell, Hollis L., et al. *Curriculum Improvement in Public School Systems*. New York: Bureau of Publications, Teachers College, 1950.

Doll, Ronald C. *Supervision for Staff Development: Ideas and Application.* Newton, Mass.: Allyn and Bacon, 1983. Especially pages 172–82.

Doll, Ronald C.; Passow, A. Harry; and Corey, Stephen M. *Organizing for Curriculum Improvement.* New York: Teachers College Press, 1953.

Eisele, James E., et al. *Computer Assisted Planning of Curriculum and Instruction.* Englewood Cliffs, N.J.: Educational Technology Publications, 1971.

English, Fenwick, and Kaufman, Roger A. *Needs Assessment: A Focus for Curriculum Development.* Washington, D.C.: Association for Supervision and Curriculum Development, 1975.

Florida Department of Education. *Handbook for Educational Planning in Florida Schools.* Tallahassee: The Department, 1974.

Gress, James R. *Curriculum: An Introduction to the Field.* Berkeley, Calif.: McCutchan, 1978.

Macdonald, James B.; Anderson, Dan W.; and May, Frank B. *Strategies of Curriculum Development.* Columbus, Ohio: Charles E. Merrill, 1965.

McNally, Harold J., and Passow, A. Harry. *Improving the Quality of Public School Programs.* New York: Bureau of Publications, Teachers College, 1960.

Pratt, David. *Curriculum: Design and Development.* New York: Harcourt Brace Jovanovich, 1980.

Verduin, John R., Jr. *Curriculum Building for Adult Learning.* Carbondale, Ill.: Southern Illinois University Press, 1980.

9

Participants and Their Roles in Curriculum Improvement

As a curriculum improvement program begins, the question soon arises, "Who shall participate in curriculum planning?" Today, problems of defining roles of participants in curriculum improvement loom larger than they ever have before. The key issues concerning participants' roles include the following: What responsibilities should various personnel take in planning and improving the curriculum? What special backgrounds, skills, and abilities do they need? How may the talents of participants be used in coordinated ways? These and related issues are sharpened by widespread criticisms that are being leveled against the schools. Persons who have worked for years in professional education have sometimes been replaced in curriculum planning today by nonprofessionals whose programs for changing schools and school curricula receive wide publicity. Indeed, media coverage makes some of the most complex problems of teaching and learning look easy enough for professional educators to have solved years ago. As broadly based participation in curriculum planning increases and intensifies, however, intelligent participants develop more respect for the complexity of problems with which they must deal.

Curriculum planners from varied segments of the population tend to see the curriculum strictly as a product. As long ago as 1927, curriculum planners in Long Beach, California, rightly saw that "the chief value of curriculum revision does not lie in the product made, but in the process of the making."[1] To the school people at Long Beach, the process contributed especially a "rekindling of the intellectual life" of the participants. This rekindling is of course most important in those who are "closest" to the curriculum day by day: teachers, pupils, principals, and others in individual schools. Of these, teachers and principals are clearly most closely involved in curriculum decision making.[2]

INPUT COMING FROM MANY SOURCES

So many sources contribute ideas and impetus to curriculum planning that lists of contributors are always long. The contributors include individuals, small groups of people, institutions, agencies, and the documents produced by these persons and organizations. Influences from the sources are often attitudinal rather than substantive. Consider a list composed by two curriculum workers:

> National studies
> Administrators' attitudes
> Board members' concerns
> Ideas of theoreticians
> Teachers' proprietary rights
> National/state testing
> Other districts' curricula
> Old or traditional curricula
> Needs assessments
> Pressures from universities
> Grants
> State curriculum frameworks
> Graduate education requirements
> Published materials
> Proficiency inventories
> Parents' concerns
> Teachers' concerns[3]

Another more limited list of participants specifies minority groups, boards of education, superintendents, other administrators, children and adolescents, teachers, community citizens, colleges and universities, the United States government, state legislatures and governors, state education departments, and the courts. The fact that the two lists differ as they do indicates diversity in ways of thinking about participants' roles. Pat Cox has identified three categories of "assisters" in the planning process: the principal, the change agent from outside the school district, and the central office staff. These assisters focus in part on the content of curriculum change and in part on the context of it. The latter has to do with approval, resources, facilities, and personnel.[4]

Misjudgments about roles in curriculum improvement are easy to make. In times of real or imagined emergency, people assume roles that, on reconsideration, seem entirely inappropriate for them. Also, in times of emergency more people accept roles than in times of calm and the role-takers come from more varied backgrounds. As more people become interested in the curriculum, the likelihood of maintaining productive dialogue among them diminishes. In general, participants in curriculum improvement activities fall into two large classifications: those who operate within local school districts and those who operate outside the districts. It is possible to identify other classifications such as those of professional and nonprofessional personnel, but the crucial issues of the times tend to center about the respective roles of community personnel, both professional and lay, who are willing and able to exercise local control, and persons and organizations beyond the confines of local communities.

ROLES OF INDIVIDUALS AND ORGANIZATIONS WITHIN LOCAL SCHOOL DISTRICTS

Persons responsible for curriculum improvement activities within local school districts should be held sensibly and appropriately accountable for the quality of their work in improving the curriculum. The individuals and organizations within local districts who have special roles in improving the curriculum are teachers and their aides, pupils, administrators and supervisors, boards of education, and individual laypersons and groups of laypersons.

Teachers and Their Aides

There is little need to reemphasize the fact that classroom teachers and their aides largely determine the details of the curriculum. Regardless of the curriculum plans, when the classroom door is closed, the insight and skill of teachers determine in large measure the quality of learners' school experiences.

Teachers perform three major tasks that make them effective improvers of the curriculum: (1) they work and plan with pupils, (2) they engage in individual study, and (3) they share experiences concerning the curriculum with other teachers. By learning from children, from books, and from one another, they grow in insight and skill so that they may provide better experiences for their pupils. Among these three tasks, teachers most often prefer group activity with other teachers. Teachers in elementary schools like grade-level meetings; teachers in secondary schools, department meetings. Perhaps the loneliness and isolation of the teacher's life cause this predilection for group work with peers. To influence curriculum planning on a broad front and in favorable ways, teachers need to pool their thinking, for only by knowing, acccepting, and promoting the goals of their schools can they be lastingly helpful in curriculum planning. Group thinking, of course, does not always result in wise decisions, but it does create higher morale, maintenance of interest, and willingness to change. The quality of group problem solving, including that of the evidence collected during the problem-solving process, determines the quality of the decision making and hence the extent of improvement.

What happens in the group should transfer in part to the classroom and to individual teachers' planning. By the same token, what happens in the classroom and teachers' planning should enrich the life of the group. In performing the three tasks, teachers should keep a central goal in mind: to improve the quality of decision making as they come to educational crossroads on frequent occasions during each day. Much more needs to be learned about ways in which teachers' ability to make decisions can be improved and enriched by both preservice and inservice education.

Teachers continue to make their presence felt in group meetings for curriculum improvement. After all, they know best what happens in classrooms, and their understanding of the needs of individual pupils is the most accurate. Furthermore, their status as members of strong associations and unions has caused their voices to be heeded more readily than they once were.

It has often been assumed that teachers are willing to make all the curriculum decisions they are asked to make. Questions have arisen from time to time, however, as to how much decision-making power teachers really want. For example, Robert Kroop and Robert O'Reilly asked 192 secondary school teachers in six Ontario school districts to consider methods of making decisions about selecting textbooks in a school subject, planning curriculum for the subject, and evaluating the curriculum in the subject. The possible methods were described as (1) decision making by one person—the principal, the department head, or the teacher; and (2) decision making by a group: (a) the group engages in discussion but leaves the final decision to one person, (b) the group makes the decision on the basis of majority vote, and (c) the group decides on the basis of consensus.

In general, the teachers did not want the principal to decide alone, and they downgraded decision making by department heads, yet they themselves wanted less involvement if they were expected to make decisions as individuals. For textbook selection, the teachers favored group method (2a) above. For curriculum planning, they chose group method (2c), with method (1) a close second. For curriculum evaluation, they selected group methods (2b) and (2c) with equal enthusiasm.[5]

Ways Teachers Participate

How teachers become involved in curriculum projects and how they participate from that point onward makes an interesting study. A two-year case analysis of the participation of eight teachers seemed to show that there are five steps in the process of participation: orientation of the teacher to his or her role, orientation to particular "choice points" and alternatives, orientation to practical application of what has so far been theoretical, actual use by the teacher of the theoretical-practical ideas of the project, and modification by the teacher of his or her choices and actions in light of interaction in the classroom and outcomes for pupils.[6]

Leslee J. Bishop describes the customary involvement and participation of teachers as occurring in the following sequence. The teachers hear about the ideas, the policy, the design, the materials, and the process to be used in putting a project into effect. They have probably attended meetings about the project and have been made to feel the pressures for change and for their own participation. Their personal commitment to the project depends on the degree to which they accept project ideas, the compatibility of the project with their own ways of working, and their estimate of the project's efficiency in their own classrooms. If they agree with the project and believe they can do what it requires, they comply with its terms and endorse it. Teachers' overt responses range from token moves to enthusiastic participation. As Bishop says, if conditions are just right and the teachers participate, the project is now in operation and the change has come into effect—almost.[7]

David Crandall and others, in their organization called Network, studied the implementation of 61 innovative practices in the schools and classrooms of 146 school districts. They found that teachers were the chief implementers of the new practices, and that they were implementing them successfully. The identifiable factors in the implementation proved to be commitment by teachers, the extent to which teachers found practices exemplary, training of teachers in utilizing the practices, and leadership by administrators. Interestingly, commitment occurred largely *after* implementation, whereas the conventional wisdom holds that teachers become committed first and then willingly implement. This finding suggests that, in cases where curriculum planners know practices will work, they can follow a "try it, you'll like it" philosophy with teachers. Once teachers have tried the practices and liked them, they will become committed to them.[8]

Jere Brophy says that teachers do not perform successfully in setting objectives, preparing really useful curriculum materials, and evaluating instructional outcomes. One reason is that they lack time. When they meet in planning groups, they tend to adopt, adapt, and select as they encounter ideas and materials. They seek help for the "intended curriculum" by consulting publishers' manuals and locally made curriculum guides. Improving these materials, says Brophy, would be a constructive measure.[9]

All of this does not negate the fact that no curriculum plan is teacherproof. In their own familiar environments, away from other professionals and laypersons, teachers are usually masters of the ideas and materials they have received from others. Just how teachers respond within the privacy of their classrooms has been overlooked too long.

Suppose we put into teachers' own words some of the statements about teacher roles that have come into the literature directly from classrooms:

Teacher 1 says: "I identify and evaluate a variety of curriculum materials under a given theme or topic. Then I select what seems appropriate to what I want to do in the classroom."[10] This statement suggests a paucity of imposed plans.

Teacher 2 declares: "I identify and evaluate a variety of curriculum materials, too, but I see myself as a free person, an authority figure in my own right, a manager, a decision maker, an individualist. Also, I'm a producer, not a mere consumer. I interpret what seems at first glance to wear a 'mantle of nobility and righteousness.'"[11] Here's a teacher with extreme initiative, one who is probably difficult for the principal to direct.

Teacher 3 announces: "In planning I don't like the 'objectives first' way of proceeding. I can enrich planning by calling to mind my preparation in teaching, my interests, the materials I know, and what the administration will let me do. Stating objectives can follow in due time."[12] This teacher would please the growing body of educators who favor free as opposed to structured planning.

Teacher 4 remarks: "I'm influenced by my own beliefs, but I recognize that I have to yield to pressures coming from outside myself. I don't really know how I balance personal belief and pressure."[13] Ambivalence is characteristic of uncertain persons in an unstable profession.

Teacher 5 states: "I know what I value. When an idea comes along that is close to my values, I can accept it immediately. I'm then seen as a cooperative person. But I have trouble with ideas that are far removed from what I value—enough trouble that I balk and drag my feet. Then I'm considered subversive."[14] Perhaps this is a reminder to planners and administrators that they should know teachers' values and at least *begin* by working in accordance with these values.

Finally, Teacher 6 expresses herself thus: "When something new comes along, I usually try it. One thing bothers me, though. I don't want to give up old curriculum content for new. It doesn't seem right to meet new requirements and, at the same, time, discard the good in traditional ones."[15] "Preservers of the faith" are found outside the bounds of religion.

The six teachers obviously differ in their exact perceptions of their role. All of them would probably agree, however, that they are important gatekeepers relative to what is taught in their classrooms. The shyest of them would say that he or she has at least an advisory function in curriculum decision making. Studies show that the actual roles of teachers depend on the teachers' positions, their teaching (grade) levels, the social organization of their schools, the areas of decision making in which they are to voice judgments, the professionalism of their fellow teachers, and the size and wealth of their school districts.[16] Though much planning is done in groups, teachers like to act informally and privately because they are often uncertain how much influence they have in the arena of curriculum policy making.[17] Two influences on teachers' behavior seem to predominate: their own philosophical beliefs and their own versions of their roles.[18]

Pupils

Changes have occurred in the role of pupils, especially at secondary school level, in planning the curriculum. The revolutionary movement in colleges of the sixties had almost immediate effect on many high schools and indeed on some elementary schools. Student rights came to include the right to participate with adults in planning the uses to which pupils' time in schools was to be put. Though this right had existed in some better-known schools for many years and had been advocated to a limited extent by authors in the curriculum field, it now meant permission to speak freely and at length in curriculum meetings, often on a footing equal to that of experienced adults. To some teachers and principals, pupils' newly acquired status represented a refreshing view of human potential and a deserved position in the educational hierarchy; to others it seemed an especially time-consuming and plaguing form of contemporary insanity. Without question, pupil participation was sometimes carried to ridiculous limits. The student rights movement, as it developed during the seventies, was generally supported by the courts, which by their decisions gave courage to persons who wished to extend participation by children and adolescents.

Methods of Participation by Pupils

Children and youth may be said to be the consumers in the educational process. As such they deserve to be consulted informally at intervals as teachers plan with them. They also may be consulted formally and at length at various times in formal curriculum planning.

Consultation with pupils may take several forms, including oral questioning beginning "How do you feel about . . . ?" At times, pupils may be requested to fill out questionnaires, engage in group discussions of curriculum proposals, or subject themselves to intensive interviews. The older the pupil, the more formal and sophisticated his or her participation may become.

But pupils can do more than give quick reactions. They can participate for periods of time in certain curriculum studies. In a junior high school in which the teachers felt especially secure, selected pupils who had suggested that they and other pupils were sometimes disorderly because the teachers "talked too much" in their classroom lectures were asked by a curriculum committee to help the teachers find ways of reducing their lengthy oral contributions in classrooms. The consequent study resulted in teachers' discovering teaching methods they had not previously considered or tried.

Robert L. Loar has suggested that secondary school pupils can participate by helping parents conduct surveys, by conducting their own surveys, by serving on curriculum committees when selected agenda items are discussed — especially matters like discipline and dress codes — and by working on a paid basis when committees function during the summer. Among the special duties of pupils may be contributing during brainstorming sessions, writing their own ideas, and criticizing existing programs.[19] In addition, pupils can "model" the behaviors required in new projects, take tests containing unaccustomed items, and use innovative materials. As pupils work in these ways, they exhibit skills and other learnings that they have not exhibited previously.

Schooling that ignores what learners think and feel does more than create deep-lying resentment — it inhibits the learning that is possible when the teacher knows the thoughts and values of the learners. One of the interesting ways in which educators can learn what schools are doing to and for youngsters is by "shadowing" individual pupils as they move through one or more days of school life. Shadowing consists of observing individual pupils' behavior in classrooms, corridors, lunchrooms, and elsewhere within schools. One of the conclusions often drawn by panels of observers after they have shadowed secondary school pupils is that the pupils talk little in classrooms and much more elsewhere in the school environment, whereas their teachers talk almost incessantly in classrooms. Down-to-earth findings of this kind can be helpful in starting curriculum improvement where it can be of real practical use to the participants. A publication prepared by the Association for Supervision and Curriculum Development, *The Junior High School We Saw*, is helpful in demonstrating what careful observing in schools can contribute to curriculum study.

A final word of caution is needed. Asking children and youth to go beyond their depth in helping with curriculum planning is of advantage to no one. The maturity and experience of participants should be taken into account in assigning tasks. Two additional ideas are worthy of note: involvement does not mean dictation, and a curriculum that is not created in part by learners may be weak.

Administrators and Supervisors

Administrators and supervisors of school programs have very special roles to fulfill. Though they administer the curriculum remotely while teachers administer it directly and immediately, the impetus they provide has an important effect in making programs succeed. Evidence has been accumulating that the power of money in stimulating curriculum improvement has definite limits. When additional money, expended for a variety of purposes, no longer makes any real difference, forward movement can result chiefly through bringing new and effective leadership personnel to the task. Truly effective administrators and supervisors know teaching-learning processes, have an understanding of learners and of the intellectual disciplines, and possess knowledge and skill as educational leaders. They invite the persons with whom they work to participate freely in making decisions, both big and little. During recent years, one of the valid criticisms of administrators and supervisors has been their tendency to "take the play away" from teachers and other important participants. Administrators and supervisors perform best when they stimulate, suggest, and guide without controlling and dominating.

Leaders in the Central Offices

In the forefront of administrators and supervisors is of course the superintendent, who must simultaneously keep things going and inspire change. He or she provides opportunities for participation in curriculum planning, lends active support to curriculum projects, aids communication among personnel, and values efficient problem solving. Specifically, the superintendent must establish organization for improvement; interpret the revisions in program to the board of education; seek funds, personnel, and materials; and facilitate lay participation. If improvement programs are to work, superintendents must give them personal attention. When superintendents see themselves almost exclusively as business administrators, trouble tends to develop in their instructional programs.

General supervisors and curriculum coordinators have been assuming roles as superintendents' delegates in curriculum matters. They have sometimes been considered the most active and important agents of curriculum change. Frequently they surpass superintendents and principals in their alertness to trends and developments in the curriculum field. Generally, they have more time and opportunity to think and take action about the curriculum. Their preparation has improved in quality and specificity. Numbers of the better qualified specialists in curriculum coordination have, unfortunately, lost their positions because of revised educational policy and budget stringency, but employment opportunities for lower echelon coordinators are apparently increasing. The most knowledgeable supervisors and coordinators find new ideas and resources, assist with staff development, and do the encouraging and troubleshooting that are so important to their functions.

Leaders in Individual Schools

Their proximity to teachers and pupils makes school principals the first-line gatekeepers of curriculum improvement. They serve as interpreters of the culture, professional leaders on the educational frontier, supervisors of instruction, stimulators of local community enlightenment, and managers of important educational enterprises. More specifically, they try to employ able teachers, arrange reasonable teacher loads, orient new staff members, encourage teachers to evaluate their own performance, support changes in the school program, stimulate teachers to inservice growth, help their staffs understand school goals, and facilitate the improvement process in other practical ways. These listings of roles and responsibilities assume more understanding and ability than many principals now possess. The heavy instructional responsibilities that superintendents and community members place on principals call for a thoroughness of preparation in curriculum and instruction that colleges and universities have not always provided.

A survey of the studies of principals' actions and behaviors indicates that, though their contributions are many, principals apparently do not have direct effect on the school achievement of pupils.[20] A major direct contribution of principals, however, is serving as chief protagonist in maintaining desirable curriculum change. Principals who are willing and able to interact with teachers about curriculum matters seek the help of their central offices and of outside agencies in providing incentives for maintaining change.[21]

SITUATION 9-1
Achieving Balance in Participation

Monegan High School had just been evaluated by its regional association of colleges and secondary schools. Its school plant had undergone some serious criticism, as had its teaching staff and its library. Among the subjects taught at Monegan, the social studies had been listed as being in greatest need of improvement. According to the evaluators' report:

1. Teachers are using single antiquated textbooks and are using them to excess. Supplementary reference sources are badly needed.
2. Classroom procedures need varying; the lecture method predominates.
3. The social studies program should be in reality a citizenship education program. Youth should involve themselves, under the auspices of the school, in

community affairs. They should learn firsthand what active citizenship means, not merely within their school but in the community at large.

In what ways do teachers, pupils, and administrators have roles to assume with regard to the above-mentioned three curriculum needs?

Boards of Education

Boards of education are legally responsible for the schools under their direction. Formed generally of laypersons, they provide responsible lay participation in legislating for and guiding the schools. With reference to the curriculum, the responsibilities of board members have often been (1) to inform themselves about the curriculum, (2) to articulate the values of the present curriculum, (3) to affirm and help to extend the goals of schooling, (4) to inquire about and propose new curriculum content, (5) to enact general curriculum policies, and (6) to vote funds to put curriculum policies into effect.

Boards of education are subject to three dangers in particular as they help to implement curriculum planning. One danger lies in making extreme decisions, either reactionary or revolutionary in nature. Another danger is in making decisions into which they have been pressured by special interest groups. A third danger is in casually, even carelessly, approving proposed curriculum changes without studying them or having anyone else study them.[22]

Intelligent board members soon learn how complex teaching and learning really are. If they are to make wise decisions, they must learn from members of the staff (in addition to superintendents and principals) by attending teachers' meetings, inservice courses, and informal discussions of school problems, and by browsing in professional libraries. At the least, they need to comprehend matters of legislation and finance as they affect the curriculum.

When boards of education use definite, sensible criteria for making curriculum decisions, they serve their communities and states well by resisting the pressure and avoiding the capricious decision making that have caused many boards to blunder into unwise judgments. Beyond the bounds of simple blundering, some boards of education have been known to take unto themselves authority and responsibility for basic work in curriculum planning, ignoring the functions of superintendents and other staff professionals.

During recent years, being a board of education member has become an especially onerous, thankless task. When communities are in ferment, board members are sometimes subjected to insults and even physical abuse. Service on a board of education should be considered a dignified, responsible assignment within which curriculum matters deserve preeminent attention.

Laypersons

Lay individuals other than members of boards of education have been assuming increasing roles in guiding the destinies of U.S. schools. Most practitioners in the public schools would agree that the feasibility of lay participation is no longer a debatable issue. Community sharing in the making of major curriculum decisions *is* desirable because changes prove more durable if they are understood and supported by the public, and because those who are to be affected by policies should share in their development.

The question, then, is not *whether* laypersons other than board members should participate but *to what extent* and *how* they should participate. Certainly no group of laypersons "without portfolio" should constitute itself a rival board of education. In their relationships with the board, lay groups should serve as aides, resources, and advisers. The generalization has been made that lay groups should work on real problems, be sponsored by boards of education or school administrators, elect able officers, maintain a supply of resource personnel, agree on their own recommendations, and submit their findings directly to the board of education or to sponsoring administrators.

One way to assess laypersons' potential for helping the schools is to think of learning sites at which they could be helpful, of the particular laypersons who might be most helpful at those sites, and of the capacities in which they might serve. For example, consider the great outdoors as a learning site. The laypersons who might be most helpful at that site are perhaps foresters, botanists, zoologists, and farmers, to name a few. They might be most helpful in conducting field trips, assembling and explaining exhibits, and demonstrating procedures in plant and animal culture.

Numbers of other sites might be suggested. They could include ethnic neighborhoods, service agencies in the community, offices of practitioners in a variety of professional fields, construction projects, on-the-road historical and other centers, political and governmental offices, and work sites of many sorts. This method of involvement taps the resources represented by individual laypersons. Most school administrators agree that involving individuals causes little conflict or other difficulty. It is committees and other groups that sometimes need "special handling."

Parents usually rank first among laypersons concerned with the schools. In 1983, an opinion research organization employed by the Grolier Society asked parents whether they wanted to have a say regarding curriculum in their children's schools. Eighty-eight percent responded affirmatively, indicating that their involvement should be moderate to great.[23]

Continuity in home-school relations seems to do much to improve pupil achievement.[24] A Johns Hopkins University study revealed that 85 percent of parents want to be involved in their children's learning at home. Eighty percent said they could spend more time on this cause if they knew specifically how to help.[25]

Organizing Citizen Committees

M. Chester Nolte has discussed how boards and administrators can keep their prerogatives intact by organizing citizen advisory committees more meticulously. He recommends that cross-sectional committees be selected, that only the board appoint committees officially, that the advisory nature of committees be emphasized, that the board and school personnel cooperate with committees, that these personnel remain open-minded about committee actions until the actions are completed, and that committees be disbanded when their work is done.[26]

The lore associated with forming and working with advisory committees and other lay groups has compounded during recent years. The Illinois State Office of Education has pointed out how important careful selection of committee members is, indicating that specialist members are more often needed than generalist members and that a selection committee may well be organized to select members of other committees.[27] Notice has been taken also of how difficult it is to recruit interested and helpful lower-income parents, a search group often being needed for the hunt.[28] Frequently advisory committees should be given inservice education before they undertake their assignments.[29] Generally, according to a rather common view, it pays to have a layperson rather than a school person chair meetings of lay groups. The schools, however, have a clear obligation to serve lay groups faithfully by providing meeting places and amenities, by offering secretarial help, by preparing materials and making duplicating arrangements, and by sending out notices as requested.[30] The success of school personnel in finding and using the services of lay group members often depends on skillful recruitment, the making of specific assignments, and proper orientation.

Of course, school personnel do not always behave as they should in their dealings with lay groups. For example, Jenkins reports a tendency on the part of principals to try to create definite, favorable impressions of themselves in the minds of advisory committee members. Called "impression management," this ploy does not seem to fool most lay group members.[31] Without question, many school people resent the presence of laypersons during deliberations about some curriculum matters. Sometimes they show it.

The search for an appropriate role for laypersons continues. School personnel who have worked at length with laypersons say that the most competent of them perceive the levels at which they should be involved. Thus they avoid preempting the authority, either intellectual or legal, of persons who have made the study of the curriculum their life work. Occasionally, of course, one encounters lay people who have been reading unrealistic books and articles about education, who have learned somewhere to dislike teachers, who think educators are plotting against the welfare of children, or who oppose on general principles what the schools are trying to do. Special patience and skill are needed in working with these persons.

Additional Considerations in Working with Laypersons

Many of the current difficulties with lay participation result from failure to think about the extent and manner of participation. Much lay participation has occurred on too broad a front, with inadequate definition of both the nature and the duration of committee assignments. Furthermore, school officials have too often involved lay members merely to defend present practices. When these same members have suggested possible improvements, the officials have resisted mightily and the laypersons have gone away saying "Educators are too hard-headed; we can't work with them."

Laypersons obviously differ in the power and influence they wield on behalf of good causes. Ralph Kimbrough, writing in a publication of the Association for Supervision and Curriculum Development, tried to identify the real "men of power":

> Prior to the findings in recent studies of power, there was a popular belief that the men at the top of the power echelons of the different institutional sectors of society were the rulers. Power was based upon position—position of wealth, social prestige, and government officialdom. Yet, when we analyze the evidence, this assumption is not supported universally. . . .
>
> I think that we can make only one generalization concerning those whom we might expect to be influential. I am impressed with the fact that businessmen have the greatest influence in the power structure of most school districts.
>
> The economic community is overrepresented in comparison to other institutional sectors of society. Callihan appears to be on safe ground when he contends that many so-called curricular innovations are made on the basis of business principles rather than upon educational principles.[32]

School personnel working with laypersons should keep in mind the public relations aspect of this work. Public relations specialists continue to urge that the people operating schools earn the public's confidence by what they do rather than by what they say. At the same time, the public needs and deserves full information about the schools it supports. In the thrust toward good public relations, every school employee can play an important part in forming and modifying attitudes. The mystery of attitude formation makes inservice education of school personnel in this specialty very important.[33]

Possible Levels of Involvement

If one remembers that the public schools belong to the citizens and that coordination between the schools and other community agencies has become a genuine necessity, four levels of involvement seem reasonable and workable, wherever the centers of power now appear to be:

1. Involvement on as broad a front as a White House Conference (central lay committees on the curriculum perform this function on a continuing basis, making some of their best contributions in helping to determine objectives)
2. Provision of resource help by lay individuals (human resource files have become common in the larger school systems)
3. Participation in decision making in individual schools (lay cabinets and advisory committees constitute prime examples of this mode of participating)
4. Utilization of lay assistance to teachers on a regular basis (the help that parents give in school libraries and elsewhere in the school has sometimes proved indispensable.)

SITUATION 9-2
How Much Involvement for Laypersons?

The new curriculum improvement program in Terrytown had been under way for nearly a year. Ned Stanley, the curriculum coordinator, had recently told the curriculum steering committee that he felt the need for lay participation but that he didn't know quite how to get it.

"Let's begin by informing our PTAs about the five study groups we've organized," one of the members of the steering committee had suggested. After some discussion, the other members of the committee had concurred. Accordingly, a "package program" containing a common message to the PTAs had been prepared. For twenty minutes, three or four members of the steering committee were to tell each association what the teachers and administrators had been doing to improve the curriculum in the Terrytown Public Schools.

Tonight was the third time Ned had spoken to a PTA. As usual, Ned told about several interesting study projects, about the released time that teachers were receiving for doing their curriculum study, and about the favorable attitudes of participants. Then he asked the same question he'd asked twice before: "What do you parents think of what we're doing to improve our schools?" Result: two or three harmless and noncommittal replies. Then the vice-president of the Terrytown Trust Company responded: "I don't think we know whether you're doing anything worthwhile or not. Why don't you professionals decide things like this for yourselves?"

What kinds of curriculum projects could the banker legitimately say belong exclusively to professionals?

What kinds of projects naturally call for the participation of parents?

Think of two differing situations in curriculum planning—one in which parents should be involved continuously and another in which parents should have absolutely no part at any time. Think of still another situation in which parents should be involved to a certain point.

SITUATION 9-3
Competency in Role Determination

In these days of competency-based and performance-based education, curriculum coordinators are called upon to state specifically the roles of participants in curriculum planning.

A curriculum coordinator is asked, in connection with his or her candidacy for the position of assistant superintendent in charge of instruction, to respond to the following exercise concerning the role of laypersons in planning. How should the coordinator respond?

Competency

Can recognize the bounds within which laypersons may legitimately work in most school systems in assisting the curriculum planning operation. Specifically, can recognize four functions in the following list that are commonly considered to be "out of bounds" for laypersons.

1. Planning with teachers and administrators an accountability system for teachers, parents, and others in school and community
2. Participating as an elected member of the parent council on a goals-for-the-school-system committee
3. Sitting in a child's classroom during the school day without permission from the teacher and the principal
4. Raising questions about the appropriateness of the curriculum for a given group of children
5. Specifying the methods of teaching reading that should be used in School X
6. Organizing to oppose a program in sex education
7. Refusing to send one's child to school because the school is not "satisfactory"
8. Joining a school board–appointed committee on one's own initiative

9. Operating as members of a taxpayers' association to keep school costs down
10. Suggesting a list of goals and requirements for the school that one's child attends.

Beyond the four "out of bounds" functions, which functions may be considered marginal?

ACTIVITY 9-1
Looking to the Future of Lay Participation

Participation in curriculum planning by laypersons needs improving. With an eye to the future of the schools with which you are familiar, specify the following:

1. What are the constructive, forward-looking ways of working with laypersons that your experience has taught you?
2. Think especially of laypersons who, for a variety of reasons, are not likely to participate in education programs either within or outside schools. What are some constructive, forward-looking ways of relating to them?
3. In the future, how can laypersons make constructive contributions to the cause of elementary and secondary education beyond anything they have done in this direction heretofore?

Consider saving a summary of your discussion contributions for future reference.

ROLES OF PERSONS AND ORGANIZATIONS OUTSIDE LOCAL SCHOOL DISTRICTS

The literature of curriculum improvement contains ascriptions of roles to certain categories of curriculum planners—administrators and laypersons working at the local community level, for example. It tells little about the roles being assumed today by persons new to the educational scene. So much has happened to shift roles and to create new ones that recent history and the current scene provide the best sources of information about who is making curriculum decisions.

Role-Takers Who Are Becoming More Influential

Among the out-of-district role-takers, those that appear to be in ascendancy are state boards of education and departments of education, legislators, regional associations, producers of educational devices and materials, and test-makers. Some of the others, such as the federal government, remain strong, but their recent influence has either declined or remained stable.

State Agencies

The interest of state governments in accountability, performance-based teacher education programs, revision of tenure laws, and statewide testing has put state boards of education and departments of education at the forefront of contemporary educational movements. Furthermore, the revived philosophy that management of education truly belongs to the state, together with a decrease in the funds available from the federal government, has augmented the state's role.

Some local boards of education and administrators now see state boards of education and state departments of education as a real threat. Personnel at the local level fear that decision making will become centered excessively at state government level. Control by state departments of education has, in the past, affected financial reimbursement of local districts and regulation of bonding, insurance coverage, pupil transportation, and like matters removed from the curriculum field.

Robert L. Buser and William L. Humm, after studying the practices of state education agencies in thirty-two states, found that superintendents, principals, and curriculum personnel had decided that the following four state practices were having the greatest effect in influencing curriculum in local school districts: (1) providing financial reimbursement on a program or project basis, (2) granting or withholding accreditation, (3) granting or withholding financial reimbursement in cases of nonaccreditation, and (4) enforcing state legislation. The administrators gave a much lower ranking to such allegedly helpful actions as sponsoring curriculum workshops, providing school visitation by state personnel, promulgating educational policies and enforcing minimum standards, and conducting inservice institutes.[34] The conclusion may be that the state's money has had more influence than the state's attempts at providing leadership.

Legislatures

In 1983 the Education Commission of the States saw state input in seven terms: staff development, statewide curriculum guides, new accreditation standards, improvement of whole schools, technical assistance and information dissemination, new pupil tests, and parent and community involvement. State agencies in full-time operation provided these services. Behind the agencies there exists the power of legislatures charged with ultimate responsibility for education within the state. Ewald B. Nyquist, former Commissioner of Education in New York State, has argued convincingly that state legislators now largely determine the curriculum. Noting that pupils are busy learning subject matter that has been legislated for them at a remote center, the state capital, Nyquist has cataloged some of the legislated requirements, state by state:

1. In Florida, the metric system
2. In California, guidelines for programs for preventing genetic diseases
3. In Louisiana, the free enterprise system
4. In Oregon, the contributions of organized labor
5. In Washington, manners, honesty, honor, and industry; kindness to all living creatures
6. In Michigan, kindness and justice to animals
7. In New York, nature and effects of alcoholic beverages (within courses in physiology and hygiene)
8. In Connecticut, humane treatment of animals and birds.[35]

Luther Kiser confirms the increased input by state legislatures and proposes two ways of enhancing local control of the curriculum. It is important, first, for local personnel to have curriculum ideas worthy of being promoted. Local persons should see that these ideas appear so essential and so strongly supported by force of personality that they are permitted to go into effect. Second, local persons must become better organized and more politically aware so that they make contact with legislators and influence them.[36] Although the quantity of state legislation concerning education has increased during the past few years, educators have not become more adept at working with legislators to ensure that legislation most beneficial to schools is being enacted.

Regional Organizations

Voluntary agreements reached by groups of states sometimes result in curriculum development on a large-region basis, as do voluntary cooperation by school systems and the continuing work of regional accrediting associations. Regional improvement centers or laboratories constitute the newest form of regional organization. Regional organization has the dual advantage of encouraging participation by local personnel and discouraging people from duplicating each other's efforts. Regional organizations can provide for economical planning of projects too insignificant for larger government and association units but too large or specialized for local school districts.

Makers of Educational Materials

Materials and devices used in the learning process have become more numerous and varied. Although the textbook continues to hold its place as the chief learning tool in schools, packaging of materials has become a thriving new business. When curriculum materials express the values and ideals of their producers, the producers become increasingly important curriculum makers.

With schooling beginning in the nursery and continuing through adulthood, and with almost half the population falling into an age bracket in which schooling is most likely to occur, the market for educational materials and devices has become one of the major markets in the U.S. economy. Unlikely and unexpected mergers are occurring between producers of materials and companies entirely outside the educational materials business. The self-teaching materials, including computers, that business organizations produce are sure to have a continuing impact on life and learning in schools, homes, and communities. Educational television continues to hold promise, and devices for simulation and gaming are proving their worth.

The Test-Makers

Designers and publishers of tests have long had an influence on some aspects of elementary and secondary education; they have influenced what has been taught and have helped to determine college admission practices. But testing from highly centralized sources has only recently affected large numbers of U.S. school children. Not only has the coming of National Assessment and of related statewide testing of children at given grade levels in the public schools made testing a bigger business; it has directly increased the influence of test-makers over the curriculum. It is too early to say just what will be done with the results of nationally administered and state-administered tests, but large scale teaching-to-the-tests seems assured.

Miscellaneous Groups

Individual authors like Silberman, Holt, and Kohl; colleges and universities, with their admission standards, extension programs, and consultant service by professors; pressure groups and producers of sponsored teaching aids that contain particular propagandistic or public relations messages; and subject matter specialists continue to influence the curriculum in their respective ways. As groups bearing influence, they have maintained a steady impact, though the messages they convey have varied from time to time.

Role-Takers of Declining Influence

Colleges and universities, concerned during recent years about their own numerous problems, have discontinued some of their pressure to upgrade high schools according to their perceptions of the upgrading process. National pressure groups differ somewhat from those prevalent a decade ago. Perhaps the greatest change in out-of-district groups and organizations has occurred in the federal government, in teachers' organizations, and in foundations with a particular interest in education. Teaching aids sponsored by special interest groups in the economy and political life are somewhat less numerous than they were during the sixties and seventies. Subject matter specialists, now lacking the monied instructional projects through which they spoke, tend to operate individually or through their professional organizations. No individual either outside or inside education has attained the influence that James B. Conant wielded several years ago.

The Federal Government

The federal budget for education has come on evil days, especially with regard to the well-publicized projects it supported during the sixties and the seventies. The federal government has become especially interested in funding projects for improving the lot of minority group children, but the number of projects carefully earmarked for given purposes has decreased. Some of the federal funds not specially earmarked may therefore be used more widely and generally to help local school districts and have been distributed through state governments. Because the tax dollar is still considered to have "gone to Washington," the issue concerning ways of sharing federal revenues with states and municipalities remains prominent.

Roles that have been assigned to the federal government, at least in people's thinking, include projecting issues, promoting research, recommending applications of knowledge, and proposing guidelines for the education of specialists in education. Thomas Shannon suggests fc.... reas in which the federal government should interest itself in the future: financing high-cost programs of national importance, financing special educational needs, supporting the cause of civil rights, and acting as a communication channel and clearinghouse for educational research.[37]

Teachers' Organizations

National and state teachers' organizations, including unions, have lost some of the power and influence they had during earlier years. In the past, both the National Education Association, with its affiliated subject and topical organizations, and the American Federation of Teachers have sought to strengthen teachers' impact on decision making about the curriculum. State affiliates of the National Education Association have helped local districts set instructional improvement goals. In this connection, as well as in drives for improved salaries and working conditions for teachers, state affiliates of the National Education Association have used methods commonly used by labor unions. In some states, the demands made by state associations and by their competitors, the teachers' unions, have become so nearly identical that joining one organization is comparable to joining the other. Choosing between the two organizations has become possible, especially in the larger cities.

Union and association groups have sometimes made the curriculum a negotiable element in the drive for new contracts, an effort that has come under vigorous attack by some boards of education, administrators, and laypersons. Teachers argue that if the curriculum is the heart of the school's life and purpose, and thus a central concern to teachers who spend their time implementing and administering it, then, time being money, their organizations should negotiate for ways of using instructional time. Persons outside the teaching profession argue that the curriculum, important as it is to so many people's destiny, should not be made an element in the negotiations of any special interest group including either teachers or administrators.

Because opponents of the teachers' cause seem to the teachers themselves to be everywhere, association and union groups do everything they legitimately can to increase their power, including specific power over determination of the curriculum. Recently, a shortage of public funds has curtailed many of the efforts and has limited the successes of unions and associations.

The Foundations

The foundations concerned with education have recognized that they have made mistakes. In the past, many of them have eschewed research and experimentation in favor of large-scale, expensive demonstrations. Some of their fondest projects have come to naught. Still a potential source of help to education, the foundations are now seeking to use their learnings from experience to place their funds where they can do more good.

ACTIVITY 9-2
Developing a Perspective Concerning Outside Agencies

Agencies operating in differing times and places assume varied roles. For instance, this year in your community the three agencies with greatest power to remake the curriculum may be a regional accrediting association, a powerful industry, and the state board of education. Analyze your community situation by methods of inquiry and reflection. Then respond to the following questions:

1. Which three of the agencies discussed in this chapter have the most powerful influence in remaking the curriculum in your community?
2. Which two or three have changed most in role and function during the past five years? What are the directions of these changes?

3. Which two or three agencies would you like to see strengthen their roles during the next few years? Why?

4. Compare your responses with those of other persons.

ACTIVITY 9-3
Identifying New Agencies and Combinations of Agencies

It is possible that in your community additional agencies or combinations of agencies are forming to participate in curriculum planning. If so, discuss the nature and status of these independent or combined agencies. If not, are there additional or combined agencies you would like to see formed. Why? How, at this point, do you view the contributions and the dangers coming from the actions of persons and groups outside local school districts?

ACCOUNTABILITY AS A DETERMINANT OF ROLE ASSIGNMENTS

A dictionary definition of accountability is "the circumstance of being answerable or liable to being called upon to render an account." People are accountable for aspects of educational programs according to their role assignments. Determining accountability becomes more complex for the persons who are trying to assign it when they realize that expectations of an incumbent's role differ among his or her constituents. Thus the curriculum coordinator in a school district is expected by the superintendent to say the "right" things to board of education members about the great progress that is being made in curriculum planning within the district; is expected by principals to supply teachers with ideas that are "solid," acceptable to the teachers, and not too upsetting of school routines; and is expected by the teachers to provide materials and ideas that are usable in classrooms and in term papers for graduate courses — and to provide them quickly. Of course the expectations do not stop here. When administrators and teachers become more or less patient members of the central curriculum committee, they expect the curriculum coordinator to "make things move," eliminate troublesome committee members, and specify the agenda for each meeting, unless they have not had sufficient input in helping formulate it. Because the role assignments of administrators and teachers are both varied and variable, the behaviors they expect of the curriculum coordinator are compound. Meanwhile, other people have their own expectations of the coordinator. These people include parents as parents, parents as PTA officers, parents as fellow members of the coordinator's church or social club, and parents as taxpayers who are having a hard time with their family finances. Think, too, of the expectations developed as the coordinator associates from time to time with pupils, supervisors, board members, politicians, and peers in neighboring school districts. The list does not include, to this point, the coordinator's spouse, children, intimate friends, or inlaws.

Here we have the concept of role family or "role set," as Katz and Kahn call it.[38] Warren Bennis has illustrated role set with a school principal as center of interest, or Pivotal Role Player. The role occupants who hold expectations concerning Bennis's principal are the Superintendent, the Board of Education, the Department of Secondary Education, Principal #3, the PTA President, Parents, the Student Council President, Teachers, Department Chairman #2, Department Chairman #1, Principal #2, and the Assistant Superintendent.[39] The number of persons could obviously have been increased. In these terms, is it hard to see why assigning accountability definitely and in detail causes problems?

Conflicts further compound the problem. Role conflict, or "mutually contradictory expectations,"[40] easily develops. Any role-defining group, such as teachers, is sure to have within it people who have differing expectations concerning what the coordinator should do. The result is what is known as intra-role conflict. The coordinator says, "Whatever I do, I can't please them."

Then there is inter-role conflict, which occurs when the coordinator occupies two or more roles, the expectations concerning which are mutually contradictory. Consider the teachers again. In curriculum work, the coordinator is expected to function with the teachers on a strictly cooperative basis. He or she is a leader who does not force or compel. Part of the coordinator's function, however, is to report teachers to the business office when they fail to appear for work for which they are to be paid. The coordinator is, in the eyes of the teachers, a monitor. Someone, it would seem, has to serve as monitor, so most of the teachers are not offended by this subrole of the coordinator. Now comes a budget crunch during which the coordinator is required by the superintendent to serve temporarily as an evaluator of the classroom work of teachers. In this subrole, the coordinator is no longer seen as a familiar cooperator or as a benign monitor, but as a role-taker with potential for depriving more or less worthy teachers of their bread and butter. This kind of role conflict causes a great deal of trouble within school systems, not the least of which is in the area of determining accountability and balancing its aspects.

School personnel have long been said to be generally *responsible* for the learning accomplished by children in schools. Responsibility, with the accompanying sense or feeling it engenders in human beings, has always been considered commendable. But responsibility has remained voluntary, vague, and unassessed. In an age of systems and technology, it would seem logical that sooner or later a system of accountability would be proposed that would include an independent, unbiased, reportable assessment of the effectiveness of people and of the evidence of value received for dollars spent.

Some of the critics of accountability believe that "personal responsibility is to fiscal accountability as lovemaking is to gynecological examination."[41] Thus they criticize the relatively unfeeling, mechanistic nature of some of the evolving schemes for holding people accountable for their behavior in schools. The author of the preceding description remarked further:

> If I'm to be held accountable for my students' performance, then I must be granted powers far exceeding any ever accorded teachers heretofore— to control the materials purchased, the methods permitted, learning sites, scheduling, grouping and mixing, style and atmosphere, and to abolish censorship, centralized adoption and curriculum determination, grammar teaching (though it cost the superintendent his job), and grades and testing (though it render accountability itself difficult to implement).[42]

The quarrel of most objectors to accountability is not with the importance of the concept itself but with certain ways in which it is being applied.

Educators' Views of Accountability Systems

Pressure to establish accountability systems has been increasing for several reasons. First, the factory model of the school persists in people's thinking. According to this model, schools, like factories, turn out "products," which can be planned for, produced, and then measured for quantity and quality when they come off the assembly line. Furthermore, educators have encouraged people in this kind of thinking by talking too little about pupils as individuals (for we do not really know them well enough) and talking too much about the importance to school quality of input in dollars and material things as opposed to outgo in the form of accomplished, genuinely educated human beings. Also, the costs of public education have been escalating wildly. This cost increase has occurred during a period of permissiveness, when people have been unsure of the values they hold and the voices raised have been respected just because they were voices.

Thoughtful educators find themselves able to accept several features of the argument for accountability. They like its proposed emphasis on individualization, with objectives thought of as being individualized and evaluation centered on the individual's progress toward his or her own objectives. They like its forward look, its emphasis on progress rather than on failure, and its recognition of gains yet to be made. They like the wide variety of pupil experiences it can foster. They like its increased attention to the outcomes of schooling, in particular the planned feedback of data about pupils that teachers and their aides can use.

On the other hand, they object to talk of "management," systemization, and assured consequences of schooling because they believe the education of individuals is too complex to be managed, systematized, or assured. They wonder how systemization will really take human differences into account. They are uncertain as to how generalized goals can be converted into specific objectives. Above all, they resent having measured pupil progress become the criterion of their own and other people's success in educating children because it is usually uncertain just where in their total environment children have learned given content. The school, they say, should not be held accountable for what pupils learn, except perhaps within limited areas of content that are specifically and even exclusively taught in school; but the school should be held accountable for the processes by which learning proceeds, in consideration of the limitations that individual pupils bring to learning tasks. They believe it is foolish to talk about children never failing in school, unless the school gives them only those learning tasks in which they *can* succeed; under these terms, the curriculum would be broadened and no single task would be mandated for all learners unless all learners *could* succeed in it.

Attempts to Achieve Accountability

Attempts to make educators accountable have assumed several forms. They include the voucher plan, according to which parents are given vouchers representing quantities of education for their children, to be used or cashed at the schools the parents choose. They also include performance contracting, a scheme by which contracting firms or organizations agree to produce a fixed amount of education for a fixed number of dollars.[43] Both plans seek to fix responsibility for results, in the first instance on the school accepting a voucher and in the second on the contractors who, if they do not deliver according to the terms, are usually assessed a portion of their prescribed fees. Uses of the voucher system and of performance contracting, respectively, occurred in Alum Rock, California, and Texarkana, Texas. Neither plan proved very acceptable and neither has been widely used.

Criticisms of Methods Used

Arthur Combs, who recognizes the worth of accountability as an essential idea in education, criticizes the methods by which persons both outside and inside professional education are attempting to make educators accountable. He points out that since one's behavior is probably never the result of any one stimulus or set of stimuli prepared by another person (because human behavior is more complex than that), no one can be held responsible for the behavior of another person except under three unusual conditions. The first of these conditions occurs when the other person is too ill or too weak to be responsible for himself or herself. The second condition exists when the other person becomes dependent on his or her mentor. The third is when the mentor's peculiar role demands responsibility, as in the instance of a prison guard's being responsible for a prisoner. Since the proper role of a teacher is to help and facilitate rather than to direct and control, these three conditions do not apply primarily to teaching. But teachers may be held accountable for five things: knowledge of the subject matter, concern for the welfare of their pupils, understanding of human behavior, the purposes they seek to carry out, and the methods they use in carrying out their own and society's purposes.[44] If, as teachers' associations and unions say, it is unfair to assess a teacher's work in terms of what pupils learn, inasmuch as the universe of their learning encompasses so much more time and space than mere schooling can occupy, then the five factors of professional competence listed by Combs become significant centers of attention.

The presence of Combs's five factors in teachers' behavior is not easy to determine, but since when has evaluation of teachers' effectiveness been easy to accomplish? It is possible, with carefully devised systems of observation, to sample teachers' knowledge of subject matter, to infer their purposes, to judge their methods, and to gauge their concern for the welfare of their pupils and their understanding of human behavior. When the implications of the five factors are considered, they are readily seen to be sufficient for assessing teachers' accountability.

The accountability of teachers may rightly be based in what teachers are required and officially expected to do within the bounds of their prescribed role. In the last analysis, parents apparently want to know "What does this teacher do to stimulate and help our sons and daughters so that they show new and additional evidences of intelligent behavior?" It is obviously unjust of state agencies or boards of education to demand of teachers behaviors that are clearly outside their role, as when boards send "accountability experts" into schools to gauge teachers' competence according to inappropriate, mysterious criteria. Like all major attacks on morale, this kind of action damages the curriculum improvement process.

Another aspect of accountability that few persons have considered is interrelationships among the "accountables" in performing tasks for which several categories of role-takers are to be held accountable in part. That is, some of the major tasks in school systems require the efforts of teachers, several categories of administrators, parents, other community citizens, librarians, secretaries, and consultants from colleges and universities. These efforts are made on a part-time basis by numbers of people who are expected to cooperate in attaining a common ultimate goal. Some of the efforts are distinctly those of given categories of personnel, or of individual persons, who should then be held directly accountable for them. Other efforts are cooperative ones, across the categories. Only the group as a whole should be held accountable for these. For example, consider a plan that was designed for preparing California school district personnel in career education. The plan involved forming a "cadre" of personnel to lead inservice education. The cadre devised a transportable package of learning materials and proposed organizational procedures for an inservice program.[45] The cadre should be made accountable for the worth of these two products. Individual members of the cadre or teams of individuals should be held accountable only for any individual, significant contributions to which they had the right to sign their names.

ACTIVITY 9-4
When People Are Held Accountable

State the terms of an "accountability contract" you would be willing to sign because you believe you could—as a responsible professional—conform to it. Mention only those aspects of your performance or behavior you think should be included in an evaluation of your work.

Discuss your contract with others who have prepared contracts for themselves.

ASSIGNING ROLES AND ACHIEVING BALANCE AMONG THEM

People assume roles in schools for definite reasons. A worthy reason is to improve learning conditions for children and youth. Usually teachers and their aides, abetted by administrators and supervisors, have this reason in mind when they participate in curriculum planning. However, people being human, motivations that are less than worthy sometimes appear. When laypersons are added to planning groups, the real reasons for the presence of both laypersons and professionals become more numerous and varied. In a contemporary curriculum planning group observed over a year or more, one is likely to see drives for power by both lay members and professionals, the appeal of the dollar in setting priorities that should be set according to other considerations, and a kind of hysteria that has resulted from the overwhelming growth of subject matter content the schools are expected to teach.[46]

The varied roles and role perceptions that appear in the preceding sections of the chapter suggest how difficult the tasks of assigning and balancing roles can be. Role adjustments and reallocations should usually be made at the site of role performance—the local school district. Teachers, administrators, and sometimes pupils, aided by boards of education and other adult citizens, should determine what functions, originating either within or without the school district, should be discharged by the schools and who in the schools should discharge them. In the last analysis, assigning and balancing roles becomes a question of values, which can be resolved only by persons who have determined what values in schooling they will accept and uphold.

When the locus of authority for role assignment and balance is the school system, personnel in each system can take three important steps in establishing roles:

1. They can plan to cover all necessary assignments according to their view of the purposes of the schools.
2. They can strive to remove conflict among role-takers and duplication among the roles themselves.
3. They can seek to ensure convergence of perceptions regarding particular roles.

Ways of taking each of these steps will be discussed briefly.

Planning Coverage

U.S. schools badly need a reexamination of their purposes. A few school districts have followed the work of "little White House Conferences" in their communities with a careful plotting or replotting of purposes. Most districts, however, have tended to drift and shift with the pressures without benefiting from comprehensive planning. Only when purposes are known can roles be listed. Curriculum leaders in many communities need to help local personnel decide the directions in which the schools should go, and also help them see what specific tasks the purposes imply and who should perform the tasks. By agreement during meetings, staff members who share an area of responsibility can divide among themselves area segments to be assigned to individuals.

For example, when a guidance director was first employed in the West Orange, New Jersey, Public Schools, the superintendent assembled all persons who were concerned in any way with guidance as an area of responsibility. In a series of meetings, these persons determined the bounds of guidance responsibility and allocated portions of the responsibility among classroom teachers, counselors, librarians, principals, the guidance director, and assistant principals. For each major classification of staff members (for example, counselors) two levels of responsibility were assigned—primary responsibility, which was exclusive to persons in that classification, and cooperative responsibility, which was to be shared with persons of other classifications. Allocations of responsibility were put in writing and were altered as changing conditions required.

The 1976 yearbook of the National Society for the Study of Education contains another example of dividing large-scale responsibility for curriculum planning among a number of role-takers. In this instance the Curriculum Coordinator has responsibilities that are distinct from the responsibilities of the Professional Team Leader, of the Lay Participant in Planning, of the Classroom Aide, and of the Pupil Representative. (The selection of these five role-takers for purposes of illustration is not intended to imply exclusion of other important role-takers such as classroom teachers and building administrators.)[47]

Don Davies mentions three phrases that characterize the main difficulties with role coverage: lack of ownership of a role, role overload, and role confusion.[48]

Removing Conflict and Duplication

However carefully conceived the plan of allocation, differences are likely to arise among staff members who have differing perceptions of their roles and different temperaments. One of the major disputes among curriculum personnel has now become almost classic—the dispute between new curriculum coordinators and veteran principals. Whenever a new position is created, conflicts about roles are likely to arise. Differences must be recognized and accepted and a reasonable plan of action developed.

> An example of this is to be found in the case of a newly appointed helping teacher who came into conflict with a veteran reading consultant because the helping teacher had begun to assist elementary school teachers with grouping and materials in reading. The director of instruction met with the two specialists involved in the conflict. He asked each specialist to state her perception of her own function with respect to reading as well as her view of any other areas of present or potential conflict. As the two staff members talked about their perceptions of their distinctly different roles, they found their own grounds for agreement with little help from the director of instruction. They seemed to find satisfaction in recognizing their differences in perception and then in testing these perceptions against reality. They succeeded in citing instances in which overlapping efforts to help teachers had confused the teachers. At their second and third meetings, they agreed on specific actions concerning instruction in reading which each would take, and they then role-played the methods they would use in referring teachers from specialist to specialist for assistance.[49]

Not all stories of this sort end so happily. In this situation there was no hidden agenda of smoldering dislike, since the specialists had not known each other very long.

Reduction of both conflict and duplication can be achieved only by giving the warring parties enough opportunity to talk about their differences. Sometimes they can settle the differences alone; at other times they may need the intervention of a third or a fourth party or even of a policy committee. It is often the duty of administrators to mediate disputes of this kind. One should realize that conflict about roles is not necessarily unfortunate; it often serves to clear the air and results in a more definite and happy clarification of roles. By troubleshooting in cases of conflict, curriculum leaders can achieve greater balance and harmony among roles.

Encouraging Convergence of Role Perception

The present chapter has referred at intervals to varying perceptions of a given role. Each occupant of a role, if he or she becomes sensitive to problems of role perception, asks interrelated questions: How do I see my own role? How do others see my role? How do I think others see it? Perceptions can be converged through study of similarities and differences in perceptions. When direct attention is given to areas of difference, these areas often tend to diminish.

The difficulty in getting perceptions to converge is demonstrated by the confusions that pervade complex organizations. These confusions result from such factors as changed and changing situations, differing personality patterns and self-concepts, inadequate preparation of role occupants, the tendency to assign several roles to one person, and the presence of subgroups within organizations.[50] Case studies and sociodramas, as well as discussion of role perceptions, should be used to merge differing views of roles so that staff members can work together with less conflict and greater productivity.

ACTIVITY 9-5
The Conflict between Principals and Curriculum
Coordinators

"I thought curriculum planning was *my* job!"

This statement is frequently made simultaneously by principals and curriculum coordinators in the same school district. Interview one or more principals and one or more curriculum coordinators to learn their respective perceptions of ways in which this conflict has arisen.

When you have assessed the situation, state what you believe might have been done to avoid conflict. State also what actions should be taken in the future to prevent further conflict.

SUMMARY

Against a backdrop of systems of accountability, people assume roles in the planning and implementation of the curriculum. We have lived through an era in which responsibility for the curriculum has shifted from the shoulders of persons within school districts to the shoulders of persons outside them. Both types of role-takers remain prominent in curriculum planning. Within each of the two classifications role-takers may take the form of individuals, small groups, and larger organizations. The categories that were ascendant years ago are not necessarily ascendant today. Thus, at any given time some role-takers may be assuming added importance while others are diminishing in importance. The difficult tasks of assigning and balancing roles require coverage of assignments, removal of conflict among role-takers, removal of role duplication, and convergence of people's perceptions concerning particular roles. Teachers and school administrators are expected to be accountable for their actions and also for failing to act. Confusion occurs, however, when role-takers develop differing versions of accountability.

ENDNOTES

1. From Long Beach, California, curriculum records.

2. Mary P. Tubbs and James A. Beane, "Decision Making in Today's Schools: Who Is Involved?" *Bulletin of the National Association of Secondary School Principals* 66, no. 456 (October 1982): 49–52. See also Richard D. Kimpston and Douglas H. Anderson, "A Study to Analyze Curriculum Decision Making in School Districts," *Educational Leadership* 40, no. 2 (November 1982): 63–66.

3. An edited version of the list presented by Marilyn Winters and Babette Keeler Amirkhan at the national convention of the Association for Supervision and Curriculum Development, New York City, March 10–13, 1984.

4. Pat L. Cox, "Complementary Roles in Successful Change," *Educational Leadership* 41, no. 3 (November 1983): 10–13.

5. Robert Kroop and Robert O'Reilly, "Participative Decision Making in Curriculum" (Private report of an investigation conducted in Ontario, Canada). Reported in ERIC # ED 102 684.

6. Michael F. Connelly and Barbara Dienes, "The Teacher as Choice Maker in Curriculum Development: A Case Study" (Toronto, Canada: Ontario Institute for Studies in Education, 1973). Reported in ERIC # ED 083 241.

7. Leslee J. Bishop, *Staff Development and Instructional Improvement: Plans and Procedures* (Boston: Allyn and Bacon, 1976), pp. 138, 139.

8. David Crandall, "The Teacher's Role in School Improvement," *Educational Leadership* 41, no. 3 (November 1983): 6–9.

9. Jere E. Brophy, "How Teachers Influence What Is Taught and Learned in Classrooms," *Elementary School Journal* 85, no. 1 (September 1982): 1–13.

10. See Virginia Chaimbalero, "Developing Original Curriculum: What One Teacher Can Do," *Clearing House* 55, no. 4 (December 1981): 165–68.

11. Diane L. Common, "Who Has the Power to Change Schools?" *Clearing House* 55, no. 2 (October 1981): 80–83.

12. Diane Wells Kyle, "Curriculum Decisions: Who Decides What?" *Elementary School Journal* 81, no. 2 (November 1980): 77–86.

13. John Schwille, Andrew Porter, and Michael Gant, "Content Decision Making and the Politics of Education," *Educational Administration Quarterly* 16, no. 2 (Spring 1980): 21–40.

14. Sheldon F. Katz, "Curriculum Innovation: Teacher Commitment, Training, and Support" (Paper presented at the annual conference of the American Educational Research Association, Los Angeles, April 1981). Reported in ERIC # ED 200 546.

15. R. E. Floden et al., "Responses to Curriculum Pressures: A Policy-Capturing Study of Teacher Decisions About Content," *Journal of Educational Psychology* 73, no. 2 (April 1981): 129–41.

16. Paul D. Hood and Laird R. Blackwell, "The Role of Teachers and Other School Practitioners in Decision Making and Innovation" (Report of the Far West Laboratory for Educational Research and Development, San Francisco, 1980).

17. William M. Bridgeland, Edward A. Dunne, and Mark E. Stern, "Teacher Sense of Curriculum Power in a Suburban School District," *Education* 102, no. 2 (Winter 1981): 138–44.

18. Bruce Thompson, "The Instructional Strategy Decisions of Teachers," *Education* 101, no. 2 (Winter 1980): 150–57.

19. Robert L. Loar, "Curriculum Committees—Can Students Be Involved?" (Paper delivered at the Annual Convention of the National Association of Secondary School Principals, Dallas, Texas, February 1973). Reported in ERIC # ED 089 450.

20. Joan Shoemaker and Hugh W. Fraser, "What Principals Can Do: Some Implications from Studies of Effective Schooling," *Phi Delta Kappan* 63, no. 3 (November 1981): 178–82.

21. H. Dickson Corbett, "Principals' Contributions to Maintaining Change," *Phi Delta Kappan* 64, no. 3 (November 1982): 190–92.

22. Harold V. Webb, "School Boards and the Curriculum: A Case of Accountability," *Educational Leadership* 35, no. 3 (December 1977): 178–82.

23. In the public press, September 22, 1983.

24. Robert L. Sinclair et al., "A Two-way Street: Home-School Cooperation in Curriculum Decisionmaking" (Report by the Institute for Responsive Education, Boston, 1980).

25. The Center for Social Organization of Schools, The Johns Hopkins University, *Effects on Parents of Teacher Practices of Parent Involvement* (Baltimore, Md.: The Center, 1983).

26. M. Chester Nolte, "Citizen Power over Schools: How Much Is Too Much?" *American School Board Journal* 163, no. 4 (April 1976): 34–36.

27. Illinois State Office of Education, *A Guide for Planning, Organizing, and Utilizing Advisory Councils* (Springfield, Ill.: Division of Vocational and Technical Education, 1975).

28. Gordon E. Greenwood et al., "Citizen Advisory Committees," *Theory into Practice* 16, no. 1 (February 1977): 12–16.

29. Angelo C. Gilli, *Improving Vocational Education through Utilization of Advisory Committees* (Houston: Texas Southern University, 1978).

30. Joseph T. Nerden, "Advisory Committees in Vocational Education: A

Powerful Incentive to Program Improvement," *American Vocational Journal* 52, no. 1 (January 1977): 27–30.

31. Jeanne Kohl Jenkins, "Impression Management: Responses of Public School Principals to School-Community Advisory Councils" (Paper presented at the convention of the American Educational Research Association, Chicago, April 1974).

32. Ralph B. Kimbrough, "Community Power Structure and Curriculum Change," in Association for Supervision and Curriculum Development, *Strategy for Curriculum Change* (Washington, D.C.: The Association, 1965), pp. 64, 65. Used with permission.

33. John H. Wherry, "Building Public Confidence in Education," *Educational Leadership* 36, no. 8 (May 1979): 533.

34. Robert L. Buser and William L. Humm, "Curriculum/Instructional Change through State Education Agencies" (Paper presented at the convention of the American Educational Research Association, Washington, D.C., March 1975). Reported in ERIC # ED 103 971.

35. Ewald B. Nyquist, "So You Think Schools Make the Curriculum!" *New York Times*, November 11, 1979, p. 37.

36. Luther L. Kiser, "When Mandated Courses, Mandated Programs Control the Curriculum," *Educational Leadership* 35, no. 3 (December 1977): 187–90.

37. Thomas A. Shannon, "The Emerging Role of the Federal Government in Public Education," *Phi Delta Kappan* 63, no. 9 (May 1982): 595–97.

38. Daniel Katz and Robert L. Kahn, *The Social Psychology of Organizations* (New York: McGraw-Hill, 1966).

39. Warren Bennis, *Changing Organizations* (New York: McGraw-Hill, 1966).

40. See Thomas J. Sergiovanni and Fred D. Carver, *The New School Executive: A Theory of Administration* (New York: Harper & Row, 1980), pp. 210–18.

41. From a paper by James Moffett presented to a discussion group at the Annual Conference of the National Council of the Teachers of English, Las Vegas, November 1971.

42. Ibid. See also Hannelore Wass, "Educational Accountability Here and Abroad," *Educational Leadership* 29, no. 7 (April 1972): 618–20.

43. A critic has facetiously reported the history of performance contracting in reverse chronology from the contract made for the St. Valentine's Day Massacre in 1929 to Judas's contract to betray Jesus Christ. See H. G. Vonk, "Performance Contracting from Chicago to Calvary," *Clearing House* 48, no. 6 (February 1974): 365.

44. Arthur W. Combs, *Educational Accountability: Beyond Behavioral Objectives* (Washington, D.C.: Association for Supervision and Curriculum Development, 1972), pp. 33–40.

45. Charles C. Healy and James Quinn, *Project Cadre: A Cadre Approach to Career Education Infusion* (Los Angeles: University of California, 1977). Reported in ERIC # ED 170 479.

46. Ronald C. Doll, "The Multiple Forces Affecting Curriculum Change," *Phi Delta Kappan* 51, no. 7 (March 1970): 382–84. See also G. L. Kincaid, "Curriculum for the 70's: Cooperation Is the Name of the Game," *English Journal* 61, no. 5 (May 1972): 723–27.

47. Ronald C. Doll, "How Can Learning Be Fostered?" in William Van Til,

ed., *Issues in Secondary Education*, Seventy-Fifth Yearbook, Part II, National Society for the Study of Education (Chicago: University of Chicago Press, 1976), p. 283.

48. Don Davies, "School Administrators and Advisory Councils: Partnership or Shotgun Marriage?" *Bulletin of the National Association of Secondary School Principals* 64, no. 432 (January 1980): 62–66.

49. From material supplied by the author for use in the 1960 Yearbook of the Association for Supervision and Curriculum Development. See Association for Supervision and Curriculum Development, *Leadership for Improving Instruction* (Washington, D.C.: The Association, 1960), pp. 84, 85.

50. See J. W. Getzels and E. G. Guba, "Structure of Roles and Role Conflicts in the Teaching Situation," *Journal of Educational Sociology* 29 (September 1955): 30–40.

SELECTED BIBLIOGRAPHY

Burdin, Joel L., and McAulay, John D. *Elementary School Curriculum and Instruction: The Teacher's Role*. New York: Ronald, 1971.

Combs, Arthur W. *Educational Accountability: Beyond Behavioral Objectives*. Washington, D.C.: Association for Supervision and Curriculum Development, 1972.

DeNovellis, Richard L., and Lewis, Arthur J. *Schools Become Accountable: A PACT Approach*. Washington, D.C.: Association for Supervision and Curriculum Development, 1974.

Dickson, George E., and Saxe, Richard W. *Partners for Educational Reform and Renewal*. Berkeley, Calif.: McCutchan, 1974.

Doll, Ronald C. *Supervision for Staff Development: Ideas and Application*. Newton, Mass.: Allyn and Bacon, 1983.

Gross, Neal; Mason, Ward S.; and McEachern, Alexander W. *Explorations in Role Analysis*. New York: Wiley, 1958.

Leithwood, Kenneth A., ed. *Studies in Curriculum Decision Making*. Toronto, Canada: The Ontario Institute for Studies in Education Press, 1982.

Lessinger, Leon M., and Tyler, Ralph W., eds. *Accountability in Education*. Worthington, Ohio: Charles A. Jones, 1971.

Mallery, David. *A Community School Venture: Top Professionals Work with School Students*. Boston: National Association of Independent Schools, 1963.

Miller, Richard I., ed. *Perspectives on Educational Change*. New York: Appleton-Century-Crofts, 1967.

Rogers, Frederick A. *Curriculum and Instruction in the Elementary School*. New York: Macmillan, 1975.

Storen, Helen F. *Laymen Help Plan the Curriculum*. Washington, D.C.: Association for Supervision and Curriculum Development, 1946.

Tanner, Daniel, and Tanner, Laurel. *Curriculum Development: Theory into Practice*. 2nd ed. New York: Macmillan, 1980.

Van Til, William, ed. *Curriculum: Quest for Relevance*. 2nd ed. Boston: Houghton Mifflin, 1974.

10

The Massive Problem
of Communication

"We worked a whole year but no one knew about it."

"How can I convey to the other teachers in my school what I've learned in recent months?"

"All that we do in Ramsey Elementary School seems to involve very few people."

The preceding comments are typical of many remarks one hears about lack of communication among staff members of U.S. schools. It is true that many years may be required for an educational idea to move from its source to common practice, but it is also true that many promising ideas are annually lost because they are never launched into communication channels of any sort. How can ideas move freely within schools and school systems and then move out into the educational world at large? How can countering ideas be fed back to the sources of the original ideas to modify, correct, and improve them? In brief, how can the news about developments in education be distributed quickly and easily so that practice will evolve with the speed that befits a thriving profession? Providing appropriate answers to these questions could materially aid the process of curriculum improvement.

COMMUNICATION: A COMPLEX ENTERPRISE

Human communication, which has been defined as transmission of facts, ideas, values, feelings, and attitudes from one person or group to another, has been called the number one problem of school administration. It may also be the greatest problem of curriculum improvement. Merely transmitting the simplest of information from sender to receiver without undue loss or confusion becomes a major task. The complexity of messages about the curriculum, the intertwining of networks through which messages move, and the uncertain readiness of receivers to accept the messages all increase the problem.

The process of human communication has been described as conforming to the model in Figure 10-1. The model suggests something of the complexity of communication. Like most complex problems, human communication has been oversimplifed by lay individuals. "The prevailing thought is that all the sender has to do now is transfer his ideas from his mind to the receiver's mind. He bundles his ideas into a neat package and sends them off on an unperilous journey to be opened and digested whole."[1] Actually, the model reminds one of Harold Lasswell's pithy question "Who says what to whom via what channel with what effect?" The question suggests the agents of and elements in communication: *who*, the sender; *what*, the message; *whom*, the receiver; *what channel*, the communication medium and the structure of human relationships through which the message is transmitted; and *what effect*, the evaluation of results. The first four of these agents or elements can either facilitate or impede communication.

FIGURE 10-1

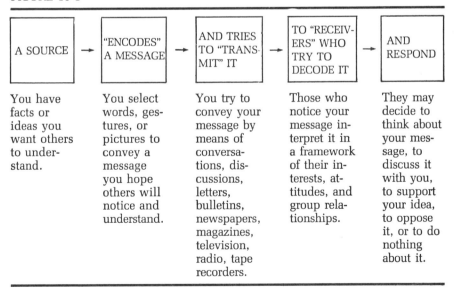

A SOURCE	"ENCODES" A MESSAGE	AND TRIES TO "TRANS-MIT" IT	TO "RECEIV-ERS" WHO TRY TO DECODE IT	AND RESPOND
You have facts or ideas you want others to understand.	You select words, gestures, or pictures to convey a message you hope others will notice and understand.	You try to convey your message by means of conversations, discussions, letters, bulletins, newspapers, magazines, television, radio, tape recorders.	Those who notice your message interpret it in a framework of their interests, attitudes, and group relationships.	They may decide to think about your message, to discuss it with you, to support your idea, to oppose it, or to do nothing about it.

From Gordon McCloskey, "Principles of Communication for Principals," *Bulletin of the National Association of Secondary School Principals* 44, no. 257 (September 1960): 17–23.

Several barriers to effective communication in schools have been identified. All of them relate to the three kinds or levels of communication problems noted by Shannon and Weaver in an early study. First there are technical problems that affect the accuracy with which symbols are transmitted. Then there are semantic problems, affecting the precision with which meaning is conveyed by the symbols. Third, there are effectiveness problems, or problems involved in getting perceived meaning to influence human conduct desirably.[2] With these three problems as a base, barriers or difficulties like the following become worthy of note. People are different, so they have differing values. They also have their own vested interests and prejudices. Accordingly, they perceive the very same situation differently. Sometimes, because of lack of intellectual capacity or because of a physical, mental, or emotional blockage, the meaning of a situation or a statement about it does not "get through" to them. Then, personal insecurities will not let people receive certain communications. Often people do not hear the whole message because they start evaluating the first part of the message content while the remainder is being communicated. Sometimes potential receivers of messages just feel too negative about almost everything to receive almost anything. Finally, the words and other symbols people receive mean different things to them as individuals.

What Schools Do to Communicate

In schools, people communicate with one another to inform, to teach, to change attitudes, to get recognition, to urge participation, and to tap each other's ideas and creative energies. Schools rely a great deal on printed materials to convey their messages. When administrators and teachers encounter one another face to face, they may easily threaten one another by force of personality, status, or behavior. They may seem impatient, gruff, or harsh. They may engage in duplicity or attempt to manipulate others. Receivers of communications, called *communicatees* in the literature, are affected by fatigue, conflicting demands on their time, varying backgrounds of experience, and specific anxieties. Considering the formidable nature of these barriers, it is remarkable that communication, whether attempted in writing or attempted in person, proceeds as well as it does.

The length or extent of communication can be viewed in at least two ways. Some communicatees desire messages that are thorough and complete, whereas other communicatees want messages that are superficial and only generally informative. Messages of the former sort are for persons who are deeply involved in the task with which the message deals. Messages of the latter kind are for persons who merely want to hear about what is happening without becoming directly involved.

It is possible to concentrate on spreading facts that most people want to know, or to go into depth by conveying assumptions, values, and points of view. Thus a message may differ not only in the nature of its content but also in its depth. Facts may be communicated by means of letters, books, bulletins, or speakers. Assumptions, values, and points of view, which are much more difficult to convey, require interactive media like workshops, meetings, role playing, and demonstrations. Multiple interactive media provide reinforcement through direct contacts among human beings. Either a simple or a complex message may be subject to differences in perspective. These differences develop not only with reference to the differing roles of communicator and communicatee but also according to the position each occupies in the organizational hierarchy.[3]

Related Research

Research in human communication within the fields of political science, psychology, semantics, and sociology suggests additional ideas about the nature, importance, and complexity of communication in schools:

- Much communication occurs informally, outside the neat, formal channels we prepare.[4] We should expect this situation to exist as a plain fact of human behavior.
- True communication occurs only when we have given ample opportunity for feedback of ideas from communicatee to communicator. Research on feedback has shown, for instance, that "as the exchange of ideas, or feedback, increases, speed, accuracy, and morale of the communicators also increase."[5]
- Communication does not automatically teach. In Cincinnati, "an extensive, long-term effort to familiarize the population with the United Nations achieved very little new learning, in spite of maximum use of radio, press, films, and other media."[6] The process of curriculum improvement (Chapter 7) requires teaching of the highest order. Thus communication for curriculum improvement must emphasize effective teaching, the methodology of which needs careful study and development.

Ideas and sets of values seem to be conveyed faster and more accurately in "settled" professions like medicine than in education. Several reasons for this phenomenon might be advanced: a vast body of respectable learnings—against which new ideas must be evaluated—has been accumulated; sources such as the leading professional journals command great respect; practitioners, though they frequently work alone, work cooperatively on certain important occasions; and the practitioners themselves are less secretive about professional lore. Teachers "talk shop" almost unremittingly, but they talk much more about problems than about reliable solutions to problems. In a new profession, especially one that involves the uncertainties of the social sciences, respect for what is communicated comes slowly. This is a fact with which communicators in education will have to reckon for a long time to come.

Several causes of communication breakdown have been identified. One is message competition. When a message one wants to communicate has to compete with other messages—a common phenomenon in these complex times—the intended message is almost certain to suffer from the competition. A second cause of communication breakdown originates in the ego or the status of the communicatee. A message that threatens the communicatee's ego or status in any way is not likely to be appreciated or even understood. A third difficulty is called erroneous expectation. People often "listen past" what a communicator has to say because they expect a message different from the one they are receiving. Finally, organizations are inclined to arrange complex communication systems in which so many links or separate communicators are placed in each communication chain that both the accuracy and the impact of messages are damaged.

Jerry L. Pulley suggests that there are five major interference points in communication within schools. The first point is the source—for example, individuals and groups with information to share. The second point is the message, encoded in words, graphics, body language, and other symbols. The third is the delivery system—print, electronic devices, conversations, or gestures. The receiver of the message constitutes the fourth point, where the message is beclouded by varying perceptions of individuals and groups. Reaction to the message is the fifth interference point. The receivers' reactions, which result in acceptance or rejection of the message, are naturally as variable as the people who do the receiving.[7]

Research data developed in schools, businesses, and industries indicate that people who communicate best understand that real communication starts with what other people need. Of course, effective communicators also concern themselves with presenting their own ideas clearly and with whether communicatees can take in what has been said. They know that, because communication is a form of exchange, they must have feedback from communicatees by whatever means seem promising.

SITUATION 10-1
Communication Backfire

Bill Akers, the superintendent of schools, was talking with one of his assistants about a communication mixup in the school system.

"But I never said that," bellowed Mr. Akers.

"*I* know you didn't," his assistant replied. "The committee of teachers and principals doesn't know it though. Someone told the the committee that you said their plan for improving the arithmetic program was ridiculous, and now the committee members believe you said it."

"What I said by telephone to one of our principals was that organizing a lot of meetings of teachers to talk about what's new in the teaching of arithmetic is largely unnecessary. Maybe we need an occasional short meeting, but nothing as elaborate as the committee wants: three workshops, each two days long, and partly on school time besides. The Board won't stand for it, and I won't stand for it either. Not when we have good teachers' guides that explain the new ideas in the arithmetic textbook series. I maintain that teachers who can read will get ideas from the guides and then can put them into practice on their own initiative. How long are we going to spoon-feed teachers and try to redo what the colleges are supposed to have done?"

"I guess you'll have to put more of your thoughts in writing," said the assistant.

"I suppose so," replied Mr. Akers. "When you're in a position like mine, you're likely to be wrong whatever you say and however you say it. The trouble is with people. Most of the time they don't want to understand."

According to what you now know about communication, wherein do you agree and wherein do you disagree with Mr. Akers and his assistant in their views of effective communication?

What additional considerations should personnel in this school system take into account in the future with reference to (1) Mr. Akers's behavior and staff members' perceptions of his behavior, (2) the problem of word meanings in whatever message is conveyed by Mr. Akers to his staff, and (3) the special difficulties that communicatees face, at their end of the communication range, in receiving, interpreting, and responding to the messages sent to them by Mr. Akers?

COMMUNICATION THROUGH LITERARY AND RELATED MEDIA

In U.S. schools and school systems, communication of facts, ideas, values, feelings, and attitudes occurs by two principal means: through literary and audiovisual media and through face-to-face contact by staff members and laypersons as individuals or as members of groups. The first is the concern of this section of the chapter; the second is the concern of the following section.

Curriculum Documents That Communicate

In the early days of organized curriculum improvement programs, the chief method of formal communication was the writing and "installation" of courses of study, which were conceived as detailed and prescriptive statements of the required activities of teachers and pupils in classrooms and, occasionally, in other sites in and about the school. The customary procedure was to "have a committee of representative teachers . . . meet with one or more of the assistant superintendents and with the director of the subject, if there [was] a director. The course thus prepared [was] submitted to the board of superintendents for approval and this [went] to the school committee (board of education) for authority to print as a school document."[8] The course of study was then "installed" by transmitting to school staffs a mandate from a highly placed school official and sometimes by conducting meetings to emphasize the importance of the document.

The real problem with courses of study has been that they have too often found their way into the bottom drawers of teachers' desks rather than into their nervous systems and thus into the ongoing activities of teachers and pupils. Despite this, prescriptive courses of study continue to be produced in a sizable number of U.S. school systems both large and small. Theoretically, at least, curriculum workers now believe it is as foolish to legislate educational experiences for a large group of children simultaneously as it is to prescribe physical treatment aimlessly for numbers of children who are suffering from malnutrition. They recognize that courses of study tend to be repetitious of other courses of study, matching the tables of contents of leading textbooks. Scissors and pots of paste are too often the chief tools with which unthinking, uncreative "curriculum builders" borrow ideas formulated by other people. Rigid courses of study are still being perpetuated partly because administrators find them useful in achieving uniformity (or alleged uniformity) in educational experiences, in facilitating the orientation of new teachers, and in pacifying critical lay groups who want to be certain about "what our children are learning." The wise administrator knows that, after a limited period of taking instruction, teachers are likely to do what they want to do when the classroom door is closed. There is no such thing as idea-tight, uniform administration of the curriculum.

The need in any era is for curriculum documents that truly communicate. Armstrong and Shutes have prepared a Curriculum Document Assessment Instrument that they invite curriculum workers to use freely; it is not copyrighted or otherwise legally protected. The instrument consists of twelve criteria that should prove helpful in assessing the quality of documents. They are

1. Legitimacy of the document
2. Credibility of the developers
3. Specification of intended learners
4. Specification of intended users
5. Specification of document purpose
6. Scope of document coverage
7. Labeling of contents
8. Consistency with other curriculum documents

9. Clarity and usability of format and organization
10. Maintenance of internal consistency
11. Specification of intended document use
12. Evidence of professional editing and reproduction.

The meaning of each of the criteria is expounded in the article in which the criteria appear.[9]

The documents that communicate curriculum ideas include curriculum guides; statements of philosophy, aims, and objectives; policy statements; resource units; research reports; lists of teaching materials; newsletters; and booklets and brochures. Of this long list, curriculum guides have attracted most interest and effort.

Curriculum Guides

Curriculum guides, which are intended to be less prescriptive than courses of study, enunciate principles, guidelines, and suggested actions. They contain hints and aids of all sorts, such as lists of books, brochures, articles, and audiovisual materials. Students of curriculum planning should examine several guides and several courses of study to see the distinction between the two kinds of documents. Neither guides nor courses of study are, in themselves, capable of providing curriculum sequence, and their contents usually are not based on research findings. In special education, early childhood education, drug abuse education, and alcohol education, a number of guides have been produced. A redeeming feature of guide-making is that teachers are being involved increasingly in idea production and tryout. In fact, the keynote of guide-making is involvement of staff. Because it is difficult to communicate to others either the substance or the spirit of an experience, staff members of school systems should be involved at different levels of operation and in different ways in experiencing the development and communication of ideas. Schools should search for methods of involving staff members freely and vitally. The staffs should be helped to suggest ideas, try them, and describe them in writing, in addition to participating in meetings for planning, preparing, and evaluating innovative guides, and feeding back suggestions for improving the guides. Most curriculum guides should contain blank pages on which teachers can write their reactions and suggestions, which can then be communicated to the persons mainly responsible for guide-making.

The tendency of teachers to ignore guides has caused curriculum planners to give greater attention than they did originally to the quality of the guides being produced. Guides can be improved through meticulous need determination, careful selection of writers, early communication with potential recipients, and tryout of finished documents.[10]

The most useful guides are usually planned in great detail before pen is put to paper. The kind of guide to be prepared, what is to be included in it, how use of the guide can be encouraged, and how its real worth can be gauged become important considerations.[11] The final test of a guide is its emphasis on freeing teachers to think, on extending their range of operation, on developing their teaching skills, and on challenging them to try ideas that are new to them and then to report results.

Statements of Philosophy, Aims, and Objectives

Beliefs about the role and purpose of a school or school system appear in statements of philosophy, aims, and objectives. These beliefs should be restated occasionally in revised form to help prevent the school or school system from stumbling along without direction under changing social conditions.

Philosophy in this instance reflects the general beliefs about education held by people who are concerned with schools. Aims of a school indicate the direction or directions in which persons responsible for that school (including lay individuals) think the school should go. Objectives express the intentions of the persons most intimately involved in teaching — teachers and their aides — and in learning — the pupils.

Policy Statements

The policy handbook or policy guide has become fairly common in school systems. Policy statements are frequently enunciated by committees or task forces that compile instructional and other policies from school system records and from the expectations of school and community personnel. Today an abbreviated kind of policy statement, a summary of important committee decisions, is being produced. The more open the system under which teachers and others do their curriculum planning, the shorter and less stringent policy statements are likely to be. General agreements, which can be altered without major difficulty, usually suffice in guiding curriculum development. Teachers' unions sometimes add to "official" policy statements their own statements highlighting particular terms of contracts they have negotiated.

Resource Units

Resource units are "master" units designed as resources to which teachers may refer in devising and tailoring units for use in their classrooms. Individual teachers and groups of teachers write resource units that contain sections like the following: the nature of the unit problem, purposes of the unit in developing understandings, skills, and attitudes, sequence of the subject matter content, nature of pupil experiences within the unit, methods of teaching the unit, resources (written and other) for learning, and ways of evaluating the learning experiences. State departments of education and the education departments of industries prepare resource units that form valuable starting points in developing more precise and usable teaching units.

Statements of learning rationale help to make resource units more realistic by identifying worthwhile instructional tasks. These statements clarify what learners are to do to master subject matter content. Furthermore, they set a level of quality that is to be achieved in the teaching-learning process, and they point to needed changes in curriculum plans.[12]

Research Reports

Reports of research activities assume varied forms: articles in journals, mimeographed statements for staff distribution, and survey reports, to mention a few. For a number of years grants from foundations and the federal government spurred issuance of printed reports on subjects such as team teaching and educational television. Obviously, most school system research reports originate in systems that can afford the time, energy, and money required to conduct research.

Lists of Teaching Materials

Teaching materials lists are often formulated in a materials center in a school or school system for use throughout the organization. Names of books, magazines, films, filmstrips, still pictures, tape recordings, and other aids to learning are presented to teachers on annotated master lists. Nationally, the Association for Supervision and Curriculum Development has periodically distributed lists of the newer teaching and learning materials of interest to curriculum specialists.

Newsletters

Newsletters have become more common as communication has become more informal. They contain items of interest, briefly stated. Sometimes they are humorous; sometimes they achieve a personal tone by referring to staff members by their first names. One of the advocates of newsletters as a communication device recommends that they approach discussion topics positively, be printed or duplicated on paper of an appropriate color, and begin with a superior first issue.[13]

Booklets and Brochures

Booklets and brochures serve numerous purposes, from orientation of new teachers to development of lay understanding of instructional programs.

They are time-consuming and costly to prepare, and they should therefore be written only when their existence can be justified.

Booklets and brochures need to be "brightened" to make them more attractive to readers. The Iowa Department of Public Instruction has prepared a handbook of ideas for curriculum improvement that is attractively presented. Headings like these invite readership: "Where Does One Begin—And How Much at Once?" and "Good News—Change Can Be Planned."[14]

Other Forms

Written communication in education has also taken the form of the following devices:

1. *Manuals supporting training programs.* In Kentucky, for example, a manual was produced to guide a five-day career education conference. It detailed events proposed for the five days and emphasized human relations experiences for the participants in curriculum designing.[15]
2. *Planning guides.* A guide to planning processes in health education was prepared in Wisconsin.[16] In New York, the Department of Education produced a guide to planning the curriculum in elementary school social studies, and to organizing classrooms for more effective instruction.[17]
3. *Consultants' packages.* Packages of materials for use by consultants in career education workshops were developed in West Virginia. They describe career education as subject matter and suggest methods of implementing career education programs.[18]
4. *Implementation guides.* The Oregon implementation guide to career education discusses career education as a field, then describes the career education program in Vale School District #15 as a prototype. The guide concludes with suggestions to other school districts for implementing career education programs.[19]
5. *Guides to be used in field testing.* In North Dakota, a field tester's guide describes ideas and materials in the industrial arts and presents instructional units in five cluster areas. The guide was used in field testing in eight school settings.[20]

Basic Problems with Written Materials

In a culture in which there is already so much printed material that people are overwhelmed by it, written materials should be developed more selectively. The principal's brief daily bulletin is not read by numbers of teachers. Surely then, many inch-thick documents will be consigned to the same fate. School systems that have expensive publications programs with uncertain effects should employ expert help to improve this aspect of their communication programs.[21]

Audiovisual Materials

Many of the newer, more effective materials are audiovisual rather than literary. Media like films and filmstrips allow the viewer to identify closely with the scene being presented, especially when the scene is realistic and dramatic. Marshall McLuhan refers to our electronic age as being dominated by the auditory rather than by the centuries-old lineal and pictorial. Some of the research concerning inservice education demonstrates that audiovisually provided experiences for adults can increase learning better than experiences provided in literary form.

The changes in communication resulting from use of audiovisuals are demonstrated by two developments. First, learning centers in schools have become much more than libraries housing books and magazines. They are in fact centers where all sorts of instructional materials can be found. Second, the computer is appealing increasingly to persons who are in a hurry to gain statistical information or summaries of information in verbal form.

The Process Called Diffusion

The accumulation of educational ideas has brought diffusion or distribution of these ideas on a large scale. Because the distribution has needed to be wide and, on occasion, deep, a variety of means have been used. For wide distribution, written materials, with some help from radio and television, have proved most useful. For development of meaning in depth, face-to-face communication of the kinds discussed in the next section of the chapter has proved necessary. One of the first wholesale distributors of ideas to its member school districts was the Associated Public School Systems. Communication in depth, on the other hand, was attempted by the promoters of instructional projects, with their conferences and workshops of the sixties and seventies.

Some people have tried to make diffusion equivalent to instructional change. Myers points out that mixing the two has prevented both diffusion and instructional change from succeeding. As a remedy, he recommends cooperative planning by teachers and supervisors, school system personnel, change agents from outside the district, and specially designated diffusers.[22] Similarly, Marker says that role specialization that distinguishes designers and testers of innovations from diffusers who demonstrate and disseminate the innovations is possible. Marker also suggests three other ways of achieving diffusion. One of these is a social interaction model that emphasizes the informal social channels through which ideas move, such as in small discussion groups and conversations. The second way, called the problem-solver model, focuses on the problems of the client using the ideas to develop local commitment to the ideas. The third way is termed the linkage process because it emphasizes the openness of channels between idea creators and users. Back-and-forth flow of information between the two may make this the most usable method of all.[23]

An interesting study of diffusion by a variety of means was made by Arnold Grobman. The diffusion Grobman discusses is international in scope. He reports that diffusion of educational ideas occurs most rapidly among heavily populated countries that spend the most money on public education. Diffusion is discouraged, however, when the goals of a receiving, participating school district are different from the goals specified in the model materials. Other discouraging influences are barriers to open information exchange, limited publishing technology, and domination of educational programs by government officials and entrepreneurs.[24]

One of the great diffusion efforts of recent years has been that of the Nuffield Science Teaching Projects in Great Britain. P. J. Kelly reports a followup study of the Nuffield effort that considered who adopts ideas and how the ideas come to the attention of these people.[25]

The eclectic use of varied means in the diffusion process requires an understanding of face-to-face communication, which is discussed next.

SITUATION 10-2
How Can They Present It Most Effectively?

The kindergarten-through-twelfth-grade Language Arts Committee of the Eberville Consolidated Schools has been conducting experiments in the teaching of linguistics. Individual members of the committee have found that pupils in the fifth, eighth, and tenth grades—the grades in which experiments have been tried—are making unusual progress in understanding and interpreting the structure of English. On a Tuesday afternoon in January they meet in the office of Mrs. James, the language coordinator, to plan means of attracting the interest and enthusiasm of other teachers on the Eberville staff.

"We can't possibly describe what we've done," says a tenth-grade teacher.

"No, we can't," replies an eighth-grade teacher. "The method we've used is strange enough to make analysis of English look like analysis of a strange language. Just the vocabulary we use presents a problem: *determiners, verb signals, patterns of writing*, and so on. Maybe we should buy copies of the books by Paul Roberts, Henry Lee Smith, and Charles Fries, and ask the teachers to read them so they'll understand what we're talking about. I'm convinced that the linguistic approach to teaching the structure of English is just what we need, but I've almost given up trying to convince other people who are entirely new to it."

After some discussion, Mrs. James suggests that the committee think about its communication problem between now and the next week. "Concentrate on written and pictorial ways of communicating with our teachers," Mrs. James suggests as the meeting concludes.

What is the first step you would take in helping people who have used a formal grammatical approach for many years to become acquainted with a new method of language analysis?

What written or pictorial material would you hope to see prepared to give teachers an opportunity for careful study of the new method?

What additional long-term learning opportunities would you need to provide?

COMMUNICATION VIA PERSONAL CONTACT

Much evidence indicates that, where geography, time, and facilities permit, the most effective communication occurs through personal, face-to-face contact. This oldest form of communication is unlikely ever to be displaced by the other media. As a matter of fact, the mass media are usually most helpful when they reinforce communication by word of mouth. Many persons believe that nothing should be put in writing or otherwise widely publicized until it has been discussed, analyzed, and, if possible, experimented with. Discussion, with feedback to further discussion, greatly facilitates communication. Philip H. Phenix has referred to communication as a "personal transaction"; thus "the real barriers to communication are not technical, but personal.[26] Interpersonal communication between two individuals conferring alone is subject to fewer hazards than communication between the same two individuals in a group setting.

Personal decision making is influenced most by what the members of one's intimate group are saying and doing.[27] People communicate most readily with individuals they like and trust.[28] Each person tends to find within his or her own group one or more friends with whom he or she can communicate easily. Also, people who share common interests often communicate effectively about matters affecting their interests. They feel an "emotional kinship" with, and are usually geographically close to, the persons with whom they communicate. All of this seems to make eminently good sense and is supported by findings in sociology and social psychology.

Toward Depth in Interpersonal Communication

The depths of communication through personal contact have been too little explored. Decades ago, Carl Rogers presented a paper that has remained a classic in the field of interpersonal communication. Rogers argued that the basic difficulty with human communication is our tendency to judge and evaluate—promptly and recklessly—the comments made by other people. The result is that people "miss each other in psychological space," failing to understand each other because each person is busy evaluating what the other person has said. Rogers suggested that real communication occurs only when people pause to listen to each other with an attempt at understanding. To achieve ability to listen, he suggested the following experiment:

> The next time you get into an argument with your wife, or your friend, or with a small group of friends, just stop the discussion for a moment, and for an experiment, institute this rule. "Each person can speak up for himself only *after* he has first restated the ideas and feelings of the previous speaker accurately, and to that speaker's satisfaction." You see what this would mean. It would simply mean that before presenting your own point of view, it would be necessary for you to really achieve the other speaker's frame of reference — to understand his thoughts and feelings so well that you could summarize them for him. Sounds simple, doesn't it? But if you try it, you will discover it one of the most difficult things you have ever tried to do. However, once you have been able to see the other's point of view, your own comments will have to be drastically revised. You will also find the emotion going out of the discussion, the differences being reduced, and those differences which remain being of a rational and understandable sort.[29]

The listener needs both a sensitive ear and the ability to observe carefully. He or she should concentrate not only on the meanings of words but also on the meanings of behaviors. What does body posture tell? What are the hands of the conferee saying? What emotional tone does the voice quality communicate? Are there silent symbols in eye contacts, pauses, and hesitations? Does the behavior of the speaker suggest that he or she is relaxed, or tense, or threatened? What would the speaker say if he or she sincerely expressed what he or she is feeling and thinking? Are there clues about subconscious motivation?

Investigations of the meanings of people's body language have revealed patterns of their use of hands, eyes, eyebrows, facial expressions, and postures to communicate ideas. One psychologist estimates that the emotional impact of a message may be 7 percent verbal, 38 percent vocal, and 55 percent facial. Clothes and hairstyles are thought to tell more than we once realized about people's viewpoints and values. Experimenters have played back recorded voices with the sound filtered in order to study voice tone independently. Some observers report that Americans tend to "dim their lights" (shift their gaze) when they walk along crowded streets; that the English customarily stare and blink when conversing; and that Oriental conversationalists scarcely look at each other. A keen observer comments about a friend, "You think Sam is calm until you watch his left foot."

The examples above are classified as *proximics* when they refer to the personal space individuals need when they associate with each other, and as *kinesics* when they refer to body language.

In listening to what other people say, the curriculum worker needs to avoid six bad habits described in a leading book on listening:

1. Faking attention, or pretending to listen
2. Listening for facts without considering broader meanings
3. Overconcentrating on physical appearance and delivery at the expense of attending to verbal content
4. Yielding to distraction
5. Dismissing content as uninteresting
6. Ceasing to listen because the content is hard to comprehend.[30]

In both conversations in the teachers' rooms of school buildings and formally organized meetings for reporting progress, effective listening can contribute greatly to staff development.

Role playing is an important means by which communication on a person-to-person basis can be facilitated. There is often a real advantage in reversing the roles to which two individuals are accustomed so that the participants may begin to perceive a situation from each other's viewpoint. For instance, a teacher who has participated in and supported an experimental project may defend it blindly while a nonparticipant who has had absolutely no contact with the project may attack it bitterly. If the two agree to reverse their roles in a discussion of the project, each may be led to modify his or her extreme point of view, and they may then be able to talk together more cogently.[31]

The principal of a school is in a unique position to help create a climate in which people can communicate, as well as to take a personal interest in problems that have groupwide interest. The subtleties of communication within the individual school remain, in part, a mystery. The story is told of a principal, who thought he was on the best of terms with his staff, saying "Good morning" to a teacher, only to overhear her ask a co-worker, "Now what did he mean by that?"

Face-to-face communication with persons who are elevated in the hierarchy or shifted in assignment is even more difficult than most other communication because distance increases psychological static. Teachers often imagine strange things about other teachers and administrators whom they seldom see. A common if secret question is "I wonder how I stand with my fellows and my bosses?" Social science research has shown that communication is improved by knowing how one is viewed by others, especially by persons in authority. It is improved also by knowing which actions are permissible and which are taboo. One of life's most frustrating experiences is to find, belatedly, that a decision that an individual or a group has laboriously reached is beyond the authority and responsibility of that individual or group.

Ernest R. House has stated several propositions concerning influence that leads to innovation in schools and consequently to curriculum change. The first two state that diffusion of innovations depends on face-to-face personal contact and that "transportation routes," or channels of communication, and the ways schools are organized help to condition face-to-face personal contact. Another of his propositions suggests that innovation can be increased or decreased by interpersonal contact.[32] Certainly in a world in which people mingle freely with each other, face-to-face communication will remain without equal as a medium for transmitting subtle cognitive and affective content. The quality of face-to-face communication must, however, be improved radically in times like these, when ideas and values are undergoing rapid change.

It is important for curriculum leaders to know how they appear to others during interpersonal contacts. Five possibilities were identified in connection with designing the Administrator Empathy Discrimination Index. The leader may appear evaluative, behaving as a commander-in-chief; instructive, behaving as a know-it-all; placating, being a consoler; probing, serving as an interrogator; or understanding, thereby appearing to level himself or herself to the position or status of the other person.[33]

The effectiveness of contact between individuals depends a great deal on the interdependence they develop. Interdependence comes from sharing, which can be brought about by teaming people, providing for their frequent and regular interaction, and assigning responsibilities to them commonly or jointly.[34]

SITUATION 10-3
The Storms at Stoneham Center

The April faculty meeting at Stoneham Center Elementary School was about to get under way. At least the clock said it should. But Ed Ringo, the new young principal, had not yet arrived.

"He must have had a flat tire again," remarked Elsie Kingsland, the oldest member of the group.

"Always excusing Mr. Ringo's actions, aren't you?" retorted Mr. Kermit.

Mr. Kermit's remark proved to be the gun that opened another battle. When Ed Ringo arrived breathlessly thirty-five minutes later, he found a donnybrook in progress. Ed had already learned that there were two or three troublemakers in the faculty of twenty-four, and Mr. Kermit was one of them. Originally he had hoped to team the teachers in groups of three or four so they could exchange ideas, engage in some simple experimentation, and ease the problem of continuity among grade levels. Abstractly the idea was excellent, but it apparently could not work at Stoneham Center. Not right now, anyway.

Next, Ed thought of organizing informal grade-level meetings simply to share ideas about good teaching. Miss Perry, who seemed to be a ringleader for evil causes, had sabotaged that idea by remarking at the February faculty meeting, "I wouldn't be caught giving my best ideas to anyone. Let other people learn for themselves. I always erase my blackboard as promptly as I can so no one will have a chance to borrow what I do."

"Face-to-face communication!" thought Ed. "Only twenty-four teachers and I can't get most of them to have anything to do with one another. What can I do?"

Discuss the Stoneham Center problem as you see it.

Ed asked the question "What can I do?" How should he behave just to keep the situation from growing worse?

What other question or questions might Ed have asked?

If you were in Ed's place, what long-range plans would you make for improving interpersonal communication among the twenty-four teachers and the principal?

ACTIVITY 10-1
Interpersonal Effects of Some
Interpersonal Communications

Indicate orally or in writing the responses you think a supervisor might expect and deserve from teachers to whom she has written the following individual communications:

Perhaps you and I could confer about ways children can spend their time in classrooms so they stay out of trouble. I'm convinced the real curriculum of the classroom genuinely affects discipline. Do you want to talk with me about some ideas you and other teachers have used in selecting what children are to learn?

Beginning Tuesday at 9 A.M., please send your plan book to me through your grade leader. Every other Monday hereafter your plans will be due. For information, see your copy of our "General Rules for Planning and Use of Plan Books."

Teach something new today! Innovation will make a big difference to your pupils, believe me! We are all being paid to innovate.

Forms for Interpersonal Communication

Face-to-face communication sometimes begins with one-to-one conferences. Thence it may move to group conferences, presentation of ideas with subsequent comparison of notes, and group work of the kinds described in Chapter 11. Schools in New Haven, Connecticut, used four media for achieving face-to-face communication among staff and parents: citywide curriculum forums, curriculum advisory councils, a Parents' Center, and

Curriculum Monday. The first two media are being utilized in a number of school systems. The other two are almost unique. The Parents' Center, housed in an old building near Yale University, was opened to increase communication among parents, teachers, and supervisors, who did what they could to make it a nonthreatening environment. The third Monday of each month was declared Curriculum Monday, a day on which subject matter supervisors visited the schools to talk about curriculum matters with staff members.[35]

DEALING WITH TWO MAJOR BARRIERS
TO GOOD COMMUNICATION

Action for curriculum improvement, like many activities in educational supervision and administration, faces two major barriers to good communication. One of these is the manufacture and spread of rumor; the other is commonly known as "filtering" of information conveyed by curriculum leaders and other persons.

Rumor as a Communication Barrier

A rumor is a report without foundation or basis in fact. It may be a fabrication out of whole cloth, an educated guess about an impending event, a "leaked" preannouncement of a circumstance that later becomes a reality, or a product of wishful thinking. A famous ex-general in the United States Marines is alleged to have said, "Dame Rumor is the biggest liar in the world."

A rumor does the most damage when the situation in which it originates is unsettled, as when a former curriculum leader leaves and a new one is just beginning his or her tenure, when important information has been concealed from curriculum personnel who should have received it, or when insecurity and distrust have run rampant in the school or school system.[36] Politicians and others have been known to spread rumors purposely as "trial balloons" and then to turn the rumored circumstances into reality. A rumor may become more pointed or brief as it spreads, since the communicators usually focus on a detail that suits them and the content they decide to emphasize depends both on their interests or motives and on what they think their hearers want to hear.

Countering rumors is schools and elsewhere is never easy. First, the curriculum leader in a school or school system must form a pattern of attending to all interpersonal and group relations that he or she has the power to affect. This action is, of course, more easily talked about than done. It means keeping fellow workers informed and involved, analyzing rumors to see what they really suggest concerning ways of helping the organization, and contradicting rumors with accurate information. Merely quelling rumors will not eliminate the effects they have already created. The ideal solution is to prevent rumors from starting and spreading in the first place. At best, this solution can be achieved only in part.

Filtering as a Barrier

Filtering, the second major barrier to good communciation, is the process of eliminating or screening out important information that should be passed along a given communication chain. Filtering occurs in upward, downward, and horizontal communication among school personnel. Frequently it is most troublesome in large organizations, such as large school systems. Subordinates are sure their superiors do not welcome certain ideas, responses, and criticisms so they filter them out of their communications to superior officers. Superiors soon learn they are not hearing the whole truth from subordinates. Meanwhile, they in turn withhold information from their subordinate officers. Superiors may adopt open door policies to encourage their subordinates to talk with them, and sometimes they call for written suggestions from subordinates, being reasonably sure that all suggestions will be discreetly given. However, if the suggestions are seldom considered, the sources of them will soon dry up. People tend to filter out reports of their failures (data that would make hearers react unfavorably to their pet projects), favorable information about their enemies, and unfavorable information about their friends.

How can curriculum leaders reduce filtering? Perhaps by employing the most moral, ethical, and psychologically secure persons they can find. Perhaps by keeping the working environment of the school open so that teachers and others can admit their failures and state their problems. Perhaps by making it very clear that not all available information can be distributed to school staffs freely and indiscriminately at any one time.

Suppose a popular middle management curriculum leader is discovered altering achievement test scores to favor a given group of pupils. Interviews with him conducted by the superintendent and an assistant superintendent reveal that he has altered school records repeatedly during the preceding five years. A lengthy discussion among the three individuals results in the offender's volunteering to resign and leave the school system immediately. What, if anything, should be said publicly about the reason for this man's sudden departure? The ethical questions involved are complex. Curriculum workers who discuss questions of this kind can understand that information may sometimes be filtered with perfect justification.

ORGANIZING FOR BETTER COMMUNICATION

Let us now turn our attention to marshaling and integrating forces for communication to improve the curriculum in the school and school systems. Most communication activities today are hit-or-miss, not part of a comprehensive plan. Occasionally, however, a school system organizes a committee on communication that plans and coordinates a series of communication activities. In general, the planning should take into account criteria like these:

- *The media of communication used to disseminate information about curriculum projects should depend on the special purposes to be served.* Brief written reports may be used for one purpose, tape recordings for another, individual contacts with staff members for another, news bulletins for another, and meetings for still another. As Forsdale has said, "Appropriate communication behavior in one situation, with one audience, for one kind of purpose, is not necessarily appropriate in another setting with another audience for another purpose."[37]
- *Communication units should be kept small.* This criterion applies in both large and small school organizations. Groups with a membership of over forty persons tend to have problems with communication. Seven to ten persons may constitute optimum size for a group. However, some different viewpoints and talents should be sought in groups, because they enrich feedback, which in turn produces further improvement in communication.
- *Messages should usually be brief, direct, and pointed.* There is no sense in using more words than necessary. Several brief messages are often more effective than a single comprehensive one.
- *Ample time for communication is decidedly necessary.* Face-to-face contacts, the preparation of written messages, and the use of electronic devices all require time.
- *Both formal and informal communication channels should be employed.* An example of the former is the prearranged faculty meeting for sharing understandings and insights; an example of the latter is permitting teachers to assemble where they wish, in groups of differing sizes and constituent personnel, to discuss curriculum problems that concern them.
- *Lines of communication should be kept short.* This criterion applies especially to vertical communication, which is aided by decreasing the number of hierarchical levels through which the message must go from bottom to top and from top to bottom in the organization. For example, what happens in a faculty meeting in School X could

easily be reported to the Curriculum Steering Committee without being told and retold to numerous intermediaries.

- *Some persons or groups should watch over communication activities in the school or school system.* Without supervision and perspective, planning and coordination are likely to go awry. Perhaps the best answer is formation of a central committee on communication. However, much care should be exercised to ensure that members of such a committee are not merely unwilling representatives of faculties or departments.
- *Emergent communicators should be sought among members of the staff.* Experience indicates that certain personnel do very well as communicators. They need only an invitation to serve an ongoing organization whose purpose is improved communication.
- *Invention is needed in developing new communication practices.* So little has been reported during recent years concerning communication practices in school systems that persons responsible for communication are finding it increasingly necessary to develop new practices of their own.

In the West Orange, New Jersey, curriculum improvement program of the early fifties, a committee on communication reported that the following methods of communication were in use:

- Brief written reports are issued at intervals to persons who request them. Frequently these are summaries of the recent work of action groups.
- Teacher members of the Central Curriculum Committee confer with teachers and principals in the schools they represent. Often the conferences are in the nature of informal conversations held wherever people meet. Sometimes there are small groups meeting in lunchrooms. At other times, they are more formally organized portions of faculty meetings. One of the advantages of conferences in the local school is that they capitalize on face-to-face, two-way communication.
- Members of the CCC are instrumental in maintaining curriculum bulletin boards in local schools and in displaying curriculum materials on office counters, in school libraries, and in teachers' restrooms.
- Leaders and other key persons in action groups are sometimes invited to attend meetings of the Central Curriculum Committee to report for their groups and receive advice and promises of assistance. Hearing the reports and the discussions of reports of action group members is helpful to communication between groups, between groups and the CCC, and between CCC members and the staffs of local schools.
- Other agents of communication include status persons who discuss curriculum projects in meetings and in less formal situations. The supervisor

of elementary education, for example, attends many action group meetings and subsequently, in supervisory meetings which she herself calls, encourages participants in curriculum activities to share information and insights with nonparticipants.

- Action group recorders have been given limited training. Reports of meetings prepared by recorders are sent to the central curriculum office where they are duplicated and forwarded to CCC members, Institute [Horace Mann-Lincoln Institute of School Experimentation] personnel, and action group members who are directly concerned with the matter being reported.
- Tape recordings are sometimes made of summaries of group decisions, curriculum proposals, or teacher-made units. Recordings which might be of interest to large groups of staff members are then transferred to discs for playback in local schools. An example is a disc reporting the development of a social studies unit.
- An informal news bulletin is issued irregularly to all staff members. This bulletin would have more attention if communication committee members felt that written materials had a great deal of value for communication purposes, but the tendency has been to distrust the written word as a communication medium.
- One work conference has been tried, partly as a communication device. The evaluation of the work conference on reading held in February 1951 showed that it was valuable enough to be worth repeating. Similar conferences, and even more elaborate ones, are tentatively scheduled for the future.[38]

The methods described above seem to have been suitable in the West Orange situation; variations on these communication procedures may prove useful in other school systems. Research has revealed several additional ideas that may affect organization for communication:

- Theoretical communication structures are not necessarily the actual ones. Considerable study is needed to determine just how communication is occurring.[39]
- Big schools and school systems do not necessarily suffer from malcommunication because of their size. In a study of school administration, "communication problems were reported somewhat less frequently in the larger schools than in the smaller schools.[40] This is true because larger schools may be better organized.
- Curriculum planners should become acquainted with the teaching situations of the members of planning groups so that they may know the experiential backgrounds that influence the members' words and actions.[41]
- Status affects communication. Information and ideas initiated by top-

level administrators move into channels of communication more readily than information and ideas initiated by teachers.[42]
- Of the means of communication, individual school faculty meetings are primary.[43]
- If communication is to proceed upward, downward, and horizontally, the organizational structure of the school may have to be adjusted to permit a wide-ranging flow of messages.[44]
- Several key actions need to be taken initially in planning communication systems. They include making clear statements of goals to be achieved, assessing specific needs for communication, designating responsibility for communication activities, striving to build credibility, determining staff members' communication rights, and opening the most suitable communication channels.[45]

Wedemeyer and Bossert have taken a future view of the designing of communication systems. Defining transportation as moving people to experience and telecommunication as moving experience to people, they say that the basic physical and psychological welfare of people should be the first consideration in developing a communication system. Other, more specific considerations are giving attention to personal or private threats, providing facilitation via telecommunication, arranging for data storage and retrieval, keeping information current, and putting the receiver in definite control of the media. When the receiver (recipient) is in control, he or she is operating within a "demand-pull" rather than a "supply-push" system.[46]

There are several practical steps that creators of communication systems may take in opening a school to free communication. The first is to observe what channels of communication presently exist. Some channels are natural and obvious, others are hidden. One of the usual channels is a pattern of relationships among teachers who have known and trusted one another a long time. When a promising channel has been identified, a way of entering it must be found. Frequently the medium of entry is a faculty member who is experienced, knowledgeable, and respected. Next the channel must be put to use. Much of the use is necessarily vertical, with messages coming from the top of the organization down or going from the bottom up. Thus the person serving as the medium for the communication of a message may receive that message from the principal or other top administrator, or he or she may receive it from new faculty members whose uncertain status puts them at the bottom of the hierarchy. The message can easily be blocked by the malfeasance or misfeasance of persons anywhere in the channel. Hypersensitivity on the part of the top administrator to disturbing messages is especially likely to bring about blocking. Finally, as a means of assessing the quantity and quality of communication, a system of evaluation needs to be established.

Experience in curriculum work suggests the following summary guidelines for organizing improved communication arrangements:

1. Emphasize good human relations. This is fundamental.
2. Make exchange of ideas the major goal of the system.
3. Communicate with people at the levels of their interest and understanding.
4. Be as sure as possible that a message that is sent is received.
5. Use varied communication media.
6. Decide whether a message should be talked about or put in writing.
7. Provide needed facilities, materials, and services.
8. Schedule time for communication.
9. Make every message clear.
10. Make the materials that convey each message attractive.

SITUATION 10-4
Influencing the Eighty-Nine, Less Seven

As a school leader, you have worked with a committee in your school to achieve ungrading (nongrading). You and the committee hope that next year the pupils in your school will be grouped three ways: in large groups to receive mass instruction, in small groups to explore meaning, and in two- to three-person teams to complete projects. The former school grades will be ignored to permit newly organized groups of learners to include pupils of widely differing ages.

You and the committee need to influence the other members of your school faculty to accept this proposal and to cooperate in making the necessary changes. The total teacher population of the school, including aides, numbers eighty-nine. How can you and the committee members, consisting of seven teachers, communicate with the remaining eighty-two so that they are constructively influenced?

SITUATION 10-5
A Plan for Banksdale

Banksdale Central School District had two high schools, five junior high schools, sixteen elementary schools, and a pupil population of about 15,750. Under the guidance of an assistant superintendent in charge of curriculum and instruction, thirteen recognized curriculum projects were under way. "Recognition" of the projects was the responsibility of a central curriculum committee. The members of the committee knew that, in addition to the thirteen acknowledged projects, there must be numerous other more informal ones, chiefly at the individual school level. Like many central steering committees, the Banksdale committee discovered that not only were they and other school personnel ignorant of such curriculum improvement activity in schools other than their own, but few school faculty members were even acquainted with faculty members of other schools in the district.

Some of the discussion in a central committee meeting went as follows:

Member A: How is it I'm just hearing of the work the teachers in Pleasant Valley School are doing in science? Science is my own field.

Member B: The bigger the system becomes, the worse off we'll be. Imagine trying to keep track of all the things happening in the different schools. I guess we'll just sit here and talk to ourselves without knowing what's going on.

Member C: Stewartsville has solved the whole problem. They have a staff publication that tells what's happening. I recommend that we get someone to serve as editor of a publication of our own. Each of us could be a news representative.

Member A: I have a better idea. People don't want to read. Let's tape reports of what's going on and mail the tapes each month to every school for playback in faculty meetings.

Member D: But the teachers in our schools don't even know one another! Hadn't we better begin by introducing ourselves to one another!

Indicate which of the comments made by the committee members seem to you to make sense.

What other ideas can you think of? Simply list them without any effort to organize them into a communication complex.

In a school system the size of Banksdale, what steps do you consider absolutely essential in organizing a program to improve communication about instructional matters? If your proposals can be expressed in chart form, make a chart of your organization for communication.

SUMMARY

Communication of curriculum matters is complex chiefly because human beings and their interactions are so complex. Curriculum workers show a desire to communicate symbolically through literary media such as curriculum guides, statements, reports, and brochures; they have done less to explore the possibilities in communicating through audiovisual materials. Even though face-to-face communication is the most natural and, apparently, the most effective means of communication, curriculum personnel have done little to develop it into a lively, useful art. Communication seems to proceed best when it is carefully planned according to tested principles.

ENDNOTES

1. Fred R. Dowling, "The Teacher and Communication Theory," *Education* 81, no. 3 (November 1960): 182.

2. Claude E. Shannon and Warren Weaver, *The Mathematical Theory of Communication* (Urbana: University of Illinois Press, 1949), p. 96.

3. J. J. Richards, "People Problems: The Human Component in PPBS," *Bulletin of the National Association of Secondary School Principals* 56 (October 1972): 50–59.

4. Wilbur Schramm, "Educators and Communication Research," *Educational Leadership* 13, no. 8 (May 1956): 503–9. See also Stanley Elam, "Attitude Formation: Direct Experience Best," *Bulletin of the National Association of Secondary School Principals* 58 (January 1974): 38–40.

5. Dowling, "Teacher and Communication Theory," p. 148.

6. W. Phillips Davison, "Modern Mass Communication – Trends and Prospects," *National Elementary Principal* 39, no. 6 (May 1960): 40–43.

7. Jerry L. Pulley, "The Principal and Communication: Some Points of Interference," *Bulletin of the National Association of Secondary School Principals* 59, no. 387 (January 1975): 50–54.

·8. National Society for the Study of Education, *The Foundations and Technique of Curriculum Construction – Part II: "The Foundations of Curriculum Making" (Bloomington, Ill.: Public School Publishing, 1926), p. 121.

9. David G. Armstrong and Robert E. Shutes, "Quality in Curriculum Documents: Some Basic Criteria," *Educational Leadership* 39, no. 3 (December 1981): 200–202.

10. Bill Lamperes, "Is There Life After the Curriculum Guide?" *Curriculum Review* 21 (May 1982): 133–37.

11. See J. Harvey Littrell and Gerald Douglass Bailey, "Administrators, Teachers: Stop Writing Curriculum Guides That Won't Be Used!" *Bulletin of the National Association of Secondary School Principals* 65, no. 443 (March 1981): 29–32.

12. Lowell E. Johnson and Carolyn P. Casteel, "The Learning Rationale Statement as a Component of Instructional Materials: A Generic Model for Development," *Educational Technology* 23, no. 4 (April 1983): 22–25.

13. Barry S. Sigmon, "Informal Newsletter Improves Communication, Staff Meetings," *Bulletin of the National Association of Secondary School Principals* 63, no. 429 (October 1979): 122, 123.

14. Iowa State Department of Public Instruction, *A Handbook of Ideas for Curriculum Improvement* (Des Moines: The Department, 1981).

15. Robert Ruoff et al., *Humanistic Career Education Training Manual* (Frankfort: Kentucky State Department of Education, 1976). Reported in ERIC # ED 158 025.

16. Chet E. Bradley, ed., *Health Education: A Planning Resource for Wisconsin Schools* (Madison: Wisconsin State Department of Public Instruction, 1977).

17. New York State Education Department, *Planning for Social Studies in Elementary Education* (Albany: Bureau of Elementary Curriculum Development, 1974).

18. Reported in ERIC # ED 137 622.

19. Jean Lewis et al., *Implementation Guide to Career Education* (Vale, Ore.: Vale School District #15, 1976). Reported in ERIC # ED 138 801.

20. Myron Bender, *Development of Instructional Materials for Industrial Arts Education in North Dakota* (Grand Forks: North Dakota University, 1976). Reported in ERIC # ED 134 822.

21. William Goldstein, "How to Communicate with Simplicity, Clarity," *Bulletin of the National Association of Secondary School Principals* 66, no. 451 (February 1982): 53–59. Goldstein's pithy article focuses on common errors in writing, "language malfunctions," and steps to take in improving one's writing.

22. Charles B. Myers, "'Diffusion' Does Not Equal 'Instructional Change'" (Paper presented at the annual conference of the National Council for the Social Studies, Cincinnati, Ohio, November 1977).

23. Gerald W. Marker, "Spreading the Word: Implementing Alternative Approaches in the Diffusion of Instructional Materials" (Paper presented at the annual conference of the National Council for the Social Studies, Cincinnati, Ohio, November 1977).

24. Arnold B. Grobman, "Factors Influencing International Curricular Diffusion," *Studies in International Evaluation* 2, no. 3 (Winter 1976): 227–32.

25. P. J. Kelly, *Outline Report: Curriculum Diffusion Research Project* (London: Chelsea College of Science and Technology, 1975).

26. Philip H. Phenix, "Barriers to Academic Communication," *Teachers College Record* 59, no. 2 (November 1957): 88.

27. Elmo Roper, in Elihu Katz and Paul F. Lazarsfeld, *Personal Influence* (New York: Free Press of Glencoe, 1955), p. xv.

28. George C. Homans, *The Human Group* (New York: Harcourt, Brace and World, 1950).

29. Carl R. Rogers, "Communication—Its Blocking and Its Facilitation" (Paper presented at the Centennial Conference on Communication, Northwestern University, October 11, 1951).

30. Ralph Nichols and Leonard Stevens, *Are You Listening?* (New York: McGraw-Hill, 1957).

31. For further development of this idea, see Kenneth D. Benne and Bozidar Muntyan, *Human Relations in Curriculum Change* (New York: Dryden, 1951), pp. 272–82.

32. Ernest R. House, "The Micropolitics of Innovation: Nine Propositions," *Phi Delta Kappan* 57, no. 5 (January 1976): 337–40.

33. Andrew V. Beale and William A. Bost, "Improving Communication Skills of Administrators," *Bulletin of the National Association of Secondary School Principals* 63, no. 426 (April 1979): 31–39.

34. H. Dickson Corbett, "To Make an Omelette You Have to Break the Egg Crate," *Educational Leadership* 40, no. 2 (November 1982): 34, 35.

35. Nicholas P. Criscuolo, "Communicating with the Staff and Public about Curriculum," *Educational Leadership* 40, no. 2 (November 1982): 25.

36. See Bernard M. Bass, *Organizational Psychology* (Boston: Allyn and Bacon, 1965), p. 311.

37. Louis Forsdale, "Helping Students Observe Processes of Communication," *Teachers College Record* 57, no. 2 (November 1955): 128.

38. Ronald C. Doll, A. Harry Passow, and Stephen M. Corey, *Organizing for Curriculum Improvement* (New York: Teachers College Press, 1953), pp. 63, 64. Used with permission.

39. George E. Ross, "A Study of Informal Communication Patterns in Two Elementary Schools" (Doctoral dissertation, University of Illinois, 1960).

40. F. H. Knower and P. H. Wagner, *Communication in Educational Administration* (Columbus, Ohio: Center for Educational Administration, Ohio State University, 1959). Communication in larger schools is now being aided by the presence of carefully organized schools-within-schools.

41. Marcella R. Lawler, *Curriculum Consultants at Work* (New York: Teachers College Press, 1958), p. 107.

42. Ralph M. Peters, "The Effectiveness of Internal Communication in Selected School Systems in East Tennessee" (Doctoral dissertation, University of Tennessee, 1960).

43. Ibid.

44. Patricia S. Kusimo and David A. Erlandson, "Instructional Communications in a Large High School," *Bulletin of the National Association of Secondary School Principals* 67, no. 466 (November 1983): 18–24.

45. Walter St. John, "How to Plan an Effective School Communications Program," *Bulletin of the National Association of Secondary School Principals* 67, no. 459 (January 1983): 21–27.

46. Dan J. Wedemeyer and Philip Bossert, *Communication, Earth 2020 Workshop* (Honolulu: University of Hawaii, 1974).

SELECTED BIBLIOGRAPHY

Bereday, George Z. F., and Lauwerys, Joseph A., eds. *Communication Media and the School*. The Yearbook of Education, 1960. Tarrytown-on-Hudson, N.Y.: World, 1960.

Berlo, David. *The Process of Communication*. New York: Holt, Rinehart and Winston, 1960.

Doll, Ronald C. *Leadership to Improve Schools*. Worthington, Ohio: Charles A. Jones, 1972, Chapter 10.

Eisenson, Jon; Auer, J. Jeffery; and Irwin, John V. *The Psychology of Communication*. New York: Appleton-Century-Crofts, 1963.

Harms, L. S. *Human Communication, the New Fundamentals*. New York: Harper & Row, 1974.

Kelly, P. J. *Outline Report: Curriculum Diffusion Research Project*. London: Chelsea College of Science and Technology, 1975.

Maidment, Robert. *Straight Talk: A Communication Primer*. Reston, Va.: National Association of Secondary School Principals, 1980.

McCloskey, Gordon. *Education and Public Understanding*. New York: Harper & Row, 1972.

National School Public Relations Association. *Communication Ideas in Action*. Washington, D.C.: The Association, 1970.

Nichols, Ralph, and Stevens, Leonard. *Are You Listening?* New York: McGraw-Hill, 1957.

Nostrand, Peter F., and Shelly, Richard W. "An Educational Leadership Listening
    Model." Privately published, 1973. Reported in ERIC # ED 087 100.
Pearce, W. Barnett. "Trust in Interpersonal Communication." Paper presented at
    the Annual Meeting of the International Communication Association, Mon-
    treal, 1973. Reported in ERIC # ED 087 069.
Schramm, Wilbur, ed. *The Process and Effects of Mass Communication.* Urbana,
    Ill.: University of Illinois Press, 1954.
Sereno, K. K., and Mortensen, C. D., eds. *Foundations of Communication Theory.*
    New York: Harper & Row, 1970.
Winters, Marilyn. *Preparing Your Curriculum Guide.* Alexandria, Va.: Associa-
    tion for Supervision and Curriculum Development, 1980.

11

Curriculum Leadership:
Its Nature and Strategies

How can one describe leadership that facilitates the curriculum improvement process? What are some of the important actions curriculum leaders take to make curriculum planning effective? These are the questions this final chapter of the book is designed to answer. Having seen how decisions about the curriculum are made and what process is used in effectuating them, we come to the place at which we need to think about how to lead other people in planning.

People who have worked in schools are sure they have seen both effective and ineffective leaders. They are often hard put, however, to explain just what has made their favorite leaders effective. Actually, superstitions and fallacies about the nature of competent leadership continue to abound in schools as elsewhere. Among the common ones are the following:

- Leaders are *born*; we cannot hope to develop them, only to embellish them.
- Conformity and uniformity in thinking should be stimulated by competent leaders.
- Leaders should be so far ahead of their followers in quantity and quality of ideas that few followers can hope to catch up.
- Leaders should always be found in the act of "leading"; quiescence is for followers.
- Leaders should not tolerate conflict, even when it "clears the air."

Perhaps the epitome of what leaders do in democratic organizations is to help their co-workers identify worthwhile goals, and then help the co-workers achieve these goals. As helpers, leaders provide service. As models of appropriate speech and behavior, they teach. *What* they do is important, and *how* they do it is just as important. Some of the what and much of the how are, in fact, invisible, and are therefore beyond description.

What leadership *ought* to be, according to our best understanding, differs from what many people will accept it as being. People have both culturally based and individual notions of what desirable leadership is. Furthermore, the theories that have been propounded have often failed to stand the test of careful investigation in varied situations. Leadership as an area of inquiry has thus been plagued with "theory trouble." In fact, even defining leadership accurately causes difficulty. The author of a yearbook chapter has called educational leadership "that action or behavior among individuals and groups which causes both the individual and the groups to move toward educational goals that are increasingly mutually accept-able to them."[1] Then he says that "leadership action is more than words can describe—it is a quality of interaction which takes on added meaning for people as they live and study its significance."[2]

THE NATURE OF CURRICULUM LEADERSHIP

Curriculum leadership performs a particular function within the general realm of educational leadership. Effective curriculum leadership is characterized by the ability of leaders to hold to clear and viable curriculum principles, and by their willingness to make long-term commitments af-fecting the curriculum, unswayed by the politics of the moment. Such leadership is found too seldom among middle management personnel, not only in education but also in business and industry. Too many leaders are afraid to make commitments according to principles in which they really believe, lest they be blamed for failure or left "holding the bag" and so lose status. Effective leaders have ideas of their own—and the courage to ad-vance them.

These statements, taken alone, might suggest that curriculum leaders should operate dictatorships. That notion runs counter to the ideas about democratic curriculum leadership that have been advanced for decades. Mackenzie and Corey, writing in the early 1950s, spoke of four ways of exercising leadership: by force, by bargaining, by paternalism, and by deter-mination of mutually acceptable goals and means. Of the four, they opted for the last.[3] More recently, Karolyn Snyder has suggested a school improve-ment procedure highlighting cooperative planning, specific development of teachers and programs, and careful assessment of results. According to this procedure, leaders emphasize cooperative envisioning of what is possible and consequent thinking and acting with school staffs.[4] Even those who would achieve increased "productivity" in schools by applying the much-heralded Theory Z recognize that trust and participative decision making are essential.[5]

Three Theories of Leadership

In years past, three major leadership theories have influenced our views of curriculum leadership: the traits theory, the group theory, and the situational theory.

More than a hundred studies have been made of leaders' traits. In the findings, only a few traits appear again and again. They are (1) empathy, or identification with the emotional needs of others; (2) surgency, or enthusiasm, geniality, alertness, expressiveness, cheerfulness; (3) group recognition, or obvious ability to fit the norms of the group without seeming different or odd; (4) helpfulness, or ability to give practical, direct assistance; (5) emotional control, or ability to give the appearance of serenity or poise; (6) intelligence, including verbal and social adeptness as well as academic brightness; and (7) interest in leading, or full-heartedness in assuming leadership responsibilities. We do not know which of these traits are most important to the success of curriculum leaders. Probably the list does not exhaust the possibilities. For instance, a leader's reputation for transmitting information freely and accurately or for refusing to take self-serving actions may be as important as any of the other traits. Probably the traits that strengthen a leader's position in one situation may damage his or her position in another. Also, leadership traits usually admired by Americans are not always the traits admired by people of other nations and cultures, or even by people of certain American subcultures.[6]

The group theory, on the other hand, emphasizes solid achievement of the goals accepted by staff groups, and accordingly downplays the characteristics and actions of individual leaders. According to this theory, leadership in a group is shared by members of the group for the sake of reaching commonly determined goals in a cooperative manner. An experiment reported by Kimball Wiles illustrates diffusion of leadership within a group:

> We did a study of our students in P. K. Yonge High School at the University of Florida. There were 240 students in it at the time. We asked them questions like these: Suppose all the football equipment had burned up—which person would you choose to head a campaign to buy new equipment? Suppose we were going on the radio to explain our school program to the public—which people would you choose to be on the panel? There were seven types of activities like this in which a

person's leadership could be identified. We guessed that 25 to 50 students would be selected. Over 200 out of the 240 were identified by their fellows as the persons they would choose.[7]

Some leaders are appointed by their groups for at least temporary action, whereas other leaders emerge, or rise to the occasion. Modern leadership theory has prized emergence as a means of getting the best contributions from people while they develop their own potential. Apparently, assertive leaders are tolerated best by large groups; leader behavior varies according to the nature of the task; and emergent leaders can succeed more readily than status leaders by being forceful and individualistic. Always, however, the ultimate emphasis should be on working *with* people, not over them.[8]

According to the third theory, the situational theory, a given situation calls for leadership of a given kind. Out of the situation and the need it engenders there arises a demand for leadership that can deal effectively with that situation. Therefore, the leadership considered competent in one circumstance may not be considered competent in another, and the image of the monolithic leader is thus inappropriate. The ingredients or factors in a given situation include the structure of interpersonal relations within the organization, the nature of the culture in which the organization exists, and the physical conditions and tasks with which the organization must reckon.[9]

Both task performance and human relations are present in the situational theory. Numbers of studies have been made in an effort to relate these two leadership dimensions. Within the situational theory there has also been included a third dimension: the maturity level that followers achieve in performing a given task. Maturity is exhibited by setting high but attainable goals, by showing willingness and ability to take responsibility, and by demonstrating the effects of relevant education and experience. When followers show increased maturity, the leader should presumably reduce the number of his or her behaviors designed to get the task done, and should increase the number of his or her behaviors designed to secure better relationships with the followers. When a follower shows decreased maturity, for example after having been shifted to an unfamiliar job assignment, the leader should probably offer additional socio-emotional support and then increase the supervision of the follower's task performance.[10]

As the curriculum leader moves from school to school and from group to group within the school system's organization, different situational ingredients operate. According to the situational theory, no single status leader can hope to perform effectively with extreme initiative in all the groups with which he or she meets. In this sense, the significance of emergent leadership and release of leadership potential in others is forced upon the status leader.

If the nature of leadership could be explained adequately by forming a happy combination of the three theories, much time could be saved in future study. However, other factors with which the three theories do not reckon enter the scene. These factors include the nature of the social organization within which leadership is to be established, the value systems that exist within organizations, and differing expectations of leadership behavior and role. The words of Murray G. Ross and Charles E. Hendry still express the basic truth:

> Perhaps the best we can say at this point is that any comprehensive theory of leadership must take into account the fact that roles in groups tend to be structured, and that the leadership role is probably related to personality factors, to the attitudes and needs of "followers" at a particular time, to the structure of the group, and to the situation. . . . Leadership is probably a function of the interaction of such variables, and these undoubtedly provide for role differentiation which leads to the designation of a "central figure" or leader, without prohibiting other members in the group from performing leadership functions in various ways, and at various times, in the life of the group.[11]

An updated version of the interaction of the three theories may be said to contain the following statements:

1. While educational leaders cannot be said to have common traits or characteristics, they do have traits or characteristics that make a difference in the quality of their performance.
2. It is true that leadership in any democratic group or institution is, in fact, widely distributed. Thus, leadership that emerges has its place.
3. Of course, the situation, defined in such terms as nature of environment, kinds of tasks, distribution of power, and priority of goals, makes a vast difference.
4. Curriculum leadership is being subjected to more study today than leadership in school administration.[12]

The three theories discussed above provide background for answering the question "What makes leaders effective?" but they have been unable to offer a direct answer. Of the three, the situational theory has been extended most in studying the effectiveness of educational leaders. The situation or setting in which educational leaders exercise their skills with greatest effect appears to be one that supplies trust, caring, mutual respect, cohesiveness, high morale, effort at improvement, use of people's input, and continuing academic and social gains. Fred Fiedler, who developed the Contingency Theory of Leadership Effectiveness, has found that three factors determine how favorable work situations are for leaders: the quality of leader-member relations, the degree to which tasks are structured, and the amount of formal power the leader has. Fiedler discovered, however, that there is no simple relationship between the favorableness of leadership situations and the effectiveness of leaders. Task-oriented leaders seem to be most effective in situations that are either very favorable or very unfavorable. Human relations–oriented leaders are apparently at their best in moderately favorable situations.[13]

ACTIVITY 11-1
Assigning Values to Leadership Traits

In general, what traits or characteristics do you wish to see in your leaders? The following is a list of leadership traits. If you tend to like a given trait, place a plus next to it. If you tend to dislike it, put a zero next to it. If you are not certain, record a question mark. When all class members have assigned values to the traits, discuss the possible reasons for the differences among individual class members in assigning values.

Adaptive	Informal
Aggressive	Impersonal
Assertive	Laissez-faire
Autocratic	Paternal
Benevolent	Recessive
Brave	Resistant
Democratic	Rigid
Despotic	Soft
Determined	Stimulating
Distant	Strict
Efficient	Strong
Empathic	Sympathetic
Fairminded	Thoughtful
Firm	Tough
Friendly	Warm
Imaginative	Willful
Impulsive	

SITUATION 11-1
Leadership without Equilibrium

Leona Riordan was new at her position as elementary school coordinator. In the view of many of her fellow teachers, she should never have been appointed coordinator, but politics had accomplished it. Today she felt newer and more inexperienced than usual. "Something's wrong either with them or with me," said Leona. ("Them" referred to the teachers in Graves School with whom Leona had to work.)

"They tell you a lot of things in college and university that are of no practical use," Leona continued. "Here on the job someone is always thinking up something for you to do or to avoid. Keeping it all in balance is a real problem. Yesterday I told some of our teachers to meet this afternoon in Room 104. Fewer than half of them arrived for the meeting. In meetings I often run into real trouble. Last week in the meeting on science, one of the fourth-grade teachers asked me what I thought of experimentation with electricity in fourth-grade classrooms. I didn't reply. The next day in a meeting on reporting to parents, the question was whether children ought to be compared with each other according to national achievement test norms. What are the teachers trying to do—test *me*? Then of course there's the weekly complaint that we don't know what direction we're taking in the elementary schools. And so it goes until I don't know which way I'm expected to turn."

How does Leona's conception of educational leadership compare with the theory that leadership is the property of the group? How does it compare with the conception you now hold? What does Leona seem to need to gain equilibrium and security in her position?

ACTIVITY 11-2
Finding Situational Factors That Affect Leadership

Every curriculum leader who has large responsibility meets with numbers of groups and individuals. In doing so, he or she encounters situational differences of many sorts. Identify a responsible leader, such as the principal of a large school or the general supervisor or coordinator in a school system. Ask this leader to recall the events of his or her professional life during the past week. Make notes while he or she talks about the differences in situations that seemed to affect the quality of his or her leadership.

If others in your class or group carry out this activity, pool your findings with theirs.

FACTORS AFFECTING CURRICULUM LEADERS' WORK

A number of factors affect the quality of curriculum leaders' work. They include the perceptions that people have of curriculum leadership, the roles of curriculum leaders, leaders' styles, leaders' behaviors and behavioral orientations, difficulties appearing in leaders, the need for authority to accompany responsibility, and the attitudes and competencies of curriculum leaders themselves.

Varied Perceptions of Curriculum Leadership

There are so many gaps in our understanding of curriculum leadership that further inquiry will be needed during the years ahead. One of the greatest needs is for increased discernment concerning the precise roles of elementary and secondary school principals in instructional improvement. The center of activity for improvement continues to be the individual school. Therefore, everything possible must be done to build the authority, security, and competence of principals and their assistants. This observation raises the question "What can be done to increase the confidence and the competence of persons who lead staffs and programs in individual schools?"

The first question leads promptly to another. Much that has been done in directing instructional improvement programs in the past has included patterning and copying of ideas. There is a growing need for leaders who can stimulate creativity and discovery in themselves and others. The question then is "What ways of thinking and what educational experiences do leaders need if they are to be encouraged to create and inquire?"

Many leaders are uncertain about what it means to behave democratically, according to teachers' perceptions of democracy. Actually, teachers do not have a clear image of the democratic leader. They are much better at describing what a democratic leader *is not* than at describing what he or she *is*. Since they cannot identify him or her clearly, and since they have given little real thought to the advantages of democratic leadership, can it be that, at the present time, they do not really wish leaders to be democratic? At times teachers seem to want autocratic leaders to do some of their work for them. This is not meant to suggest that teachers are perverse or lazy: their reaction is often a natural effect of being uncertain about where an unknown quantity called "democratic leadership" might place them. One may advance the thesis that a leader can be democratic only to the extent to which the staff of the school or school system is willing to assume both new and old responsibilities. These comments return us to some really basic questions:

1. What do we mean by democratic leadership?
2. What responsibilities and obligations might result from enjoying democratic leadership?
3. Is democracy in schools really somewhere between autocracy and laissez-faire, as it has often been pictured? Or is it "softened autocracy" and/or "organized laissez-faire"?

These questions need to be pondered by all persons who aspire to, or are already engaged in, curriculum leadership. To answer them, teachers and status leaders need to consider the possible effects of democratic behavior and then watch for those effects as leaders behave democratically.

The Roles of Curriculum Leaders

Views of curriculum leaders' roles obviously differ widely. One study indicates that leaders in individual schools do not have accurate perceptions of the total concept their staffs and their superintendents have of the leader's role, that closer agreement exists between the principal and the staff than between the principal and the superintendent regarding concepts of the principal's ideal role, and that principals are seen by their staffs as over-emphasizing public relations and strictly administrative functions at the expense of curriculum functions. Role definition, as it affects curriculum leaders, will need better clarification in the years to come. Already leaders in individual schools have much autonomy in instructional matters, but they are both unclear as to their roles and overinterested in "housekeeping" functions.[14]

Superintendents and other persons who supervise the work of leaders in the schools should help them decide whether they should be *nomothetic* leaders, who emphasize institutional requirements and conformity to role expectations, or *idiographic* leaders, who minimize role expectations in favor of the requirements of individual personalities. Idiographic leaders are likely to be much less "neat" in their leadership performance and to behave less as "good boys and girls" in the opinion of central offices.

Continuing studies show that where leadership is weak or lacking in continuity, curriculum programs are likely to fail. Some of the most useful findings about the actual roles of leaders in individual schools have been developed by David B. Austin and his associates.

Leaders' Styles

Every leader has a style of his or her own. An individual's style is very difficult to change. From the time of the Ohio State studies by John Hemphill and others, educational researchers have tended to think of leadership style under two headings, the task-oriented and the human relations–oriented, but practitioners have tried to say more definitively what they mean by style. For example, they describe particular leaders (mainly principals) as follows:

- "He acts like an executive secretary, so we form committees to make decisions."
- "Of course he behaves paternalistically. He is, after all, the father of our school family, and father knows best."
- "People call her pseudodemocratic because she solicits ideas freely, rejects most, and acts on a few to suit herself."
- "I suppose I am autocratic. The buck stops on my desk, so the decision is mine."
- "He leads by whim. Nearly every need to make a decision calls forth an unpredictable emotional reaction."
- "She leads by threat, often engaging in demeaning chastisement of those who are in disagreement with her."

- "She jawbones, explaining and explaining but never helping us decide. She's pleasant, but she gives no straightforward answers. Somehow she reminds us of too flexible, overcooked spaghetti."[15]

Fiedler's Contingency Theory emphasizes the importance of having a leader's style fit his or her situation. Inasmuch as style changes with great difficulty, it pays to seek changes in the situation.[16] Also, as new leaders are appointed, persons with particular styles should be designated to work in situations that suit their styles. As an elementary school teacher once said, "Good leader here is not necessarily good leader there!"

Recent considerations of style have gone beyond the teacher's situation-related comment. For instance, Gene Hall and others have thought of the curriculum leader as initiator, manager, and responder. If the leader wants to achieve success in implementing ideas, he or she should be a responder to requests for help. If the leader wants to develop morale among teachers, he or she can "manage" by monitoring teachers' work, keeping close contact with teachers, supporting them, and minimizing their problems. If the leader wants to prove that he or she is "on top of the situation," he or she can serve as an initiator by anticipating needs, gathering usable information, supervising implementation of ideas, and generally knowing what's happening to learners.[17] Because purposes change, merge, and blur, consistency of style is not always to be prized.

Leaders' Behaviors and Behavioral Orientations

The behavior of curriculum leaders is readily noticed by teachers. John Hemphill and others at the Ohio State University, reporting in their *Situational Factors in Leadership*, discussed leadership behavior as involving both showing consideration to others and initiating structure within the organization. Through the years, showing consideration has often been highlighted at the expense of initiating structure. This emphasis has suggested to many students of leadership that school administrators, coordinators, and supervisors should give more attention to "being nice" than to getting jobs done. Recently, however, Kunz and Hoy have sought to determine effectiveness of leader behavior by isolating a single measure, the leader's success in having his or her directives followed. They identified three domains in which a leader might give orders: maintaining the organization/operation of the school, guiding (regulating?) teachers' personal behavior, and guiding teachers' professional behavior. They found that teachers would accept leaders' orders affecting organizational maintenance, but would reject their mandates about personal behavior. Regarding teachers' acceptance of leaders' guidance of their professional behavior, the variation was so great that Kunz and Hoy considered teachers' professional behavior to be the zone within which leader effectiveness could really be seen.[18] It is, of course, the zone in which curriculum leaders are greatly interested.

Kunz and Hoy report that teachers are most willing to accept the professional directives of leaders who are high in *both* showing consideration and initiating structure.[19] Of the two, they found initiating structure to be more significant. This finding continues to gain support.

Though teachers want more in their status leaders than friendliness and congeniality, they do want to participate in decision making that affects them and the quality of their work. A number of investigators have found that groups of people who have a stake in the results of decisions make decisions of better quality than individuals can make. For example, Donald Piper found that the involvement of several people resulted in better decisions than could be made in what he called his "one man deciding alone" model.[20]

The tug in almost any leadership situation is between the human relations dimension of performance and the productivity dimension. Good human relations emphasizes mutual respect, good will, faith and trust in others, and recognition of the dignity and worth of other people. One of the best-known studies of leader behavior pictures the leader who practices good human relations as finding time to listen, doing favors for others, making things pleasant, seeking to understand and to be understood, looking out for people's welfare, treating people as equals, showing willingness to make changes, making people feel at ease, and putting other people's suggestions to use.[21] The present author has found that school leaders demonstrate human relations skills — according to the perceptions of teachers and parents — when they are involved in the following:

1. Meeting prominent psychological needs of teachers and other persons in schools
2. Guarding and guiding their behavior and words
3. Recognizing the worth of other people
4. Helping other people
5. Coordinating the work of teachers and other people.[22]

To stimulate productivity, the school leader evidently needs to do such things as make his or her viewpoints clear, help try out new ideas, conscientiously criticize poor work, maintain standards of performance, develop staff role assignments, emphasize the meaning of deadlines, and try to make certain that staff members are working to capacity.[23] Rigorous as one or two of these actions may look, they are instrumental in moving commonly agreed upon projects forward. Some actions within the productivity dimension call for unilateral action by the leader; more of them require cooperation between the leader and his associates.

From industry comes a catalog of leadership actions often labeled "best" by personnel at the middle management level. One of the first actions mentioned is making it clear to people that they are expected to have problems. There are also concerns about improving the quality of group work so that meetings lead to results and not merely to more talk, so that group goals become clear, and so that regular time can be provided for important and worthwhile meetings. Other actions have to do with making decisions cooperatively about performance standards and with helping personnel achieve progressive growth in responsibility and independence.[24]

Difficulties Appearing in Leaders

Many of the difficulties encountered by leaders are indeed in the nature of the people around them, but some of the difficulties are within the individual leader himself or herself. Three of the leader's personal difficulties are expressed in the following questions: To what extent can I be liked and still do an effective job? To what extent do I fear failure? To what extent do I actually fear success? These questions imply conflicts within the person which are characteristically American. We Americans want to be liked, but as leaders we do not wish to be merely likeable or lovable. We want to produce. Consequently, we fear failure. At the same time we may fear success because the presence of success brings us guilt feelings about displacing other people or leaving them behind.

The Need for Authority to Accompany Responsibility

Books on school administration sometimes discuss *administrators* and their *authority*. Books on curriculum and instruction tend to discuss *leaders* and their *responsibilities*. Under an ancient concept of leadership still in evidence today, authority resides in the superintendent of schools and those staff members to whom he or she delegates it. Frequently, superintendents do not delegate authority to instructional personnel, though they do delegate it to business managers. In these instances the business of a school district appears to be more important than the curriculum.

Major modification of this concept is needed. First, delegating authority increases "the number of levels of authority and thus results in a pyramidal rather than a flat organizational structure. This type of organization has often been authoritarian rather than democratic and has not promoted a free flow of communication."[25] Authority, a term used to describe institutionalized power, should sometimes be shared rather than delegated. "Shared decisions make it possible for the staff to be importantly involved. . . ."[26] As William F. Whyte puts it, the problem is not that of eliminating authority but of weaving authority and participation together.[27] Delegation may be regarded as giving authority to another person or other persons for tentative or limited use, whereas sharing suggests continued, cooperative control of an enterprise by both a status leader and his or her co-workers. Inasmuch as, within the structure of U.S. school systems, superintendents are responsible to boards of education for total administration of the schools, superintendents are directly responsible to their boards for instructional programs. If they want the best instructional programs, however, superintendents will share their concerns, responsibilities, and authority for curriculum planning with members of their staffs.

Responsibility without authority tends not to produce results. As Caswell says, "It is much more effective to have the responsibility for curriculum work accompanied by authority over matters that fall within the curriculum area. This arrangement will foster cooperative and effective work in curriculum development."[28] Both individuals such as directors of instruction, principals, department chairpersons, coordinators, and classroom teachers and groups such as curriculum committees should have authority to plan for and make improvements in instructional programs. The extent and nature of the responsibility and the authority that accompanies it should be made clear to those who are to perform duties in schools. Where there is any possibility of conflict of interest among groups and individuals, the conflict should be foreseen and resolved as early in the life of a project as possible.

Attitudes and Competencies of Curriculum Leaders

From beyond the walls of school buildings have come points of view about people in organizations that are shared by curriculum leaders. Here, for example, are three such points of view.

The first may be termed the *utopian*. It holds that people are inherently good and that they proceed naturally toward self-actualization, but if the structure and values of an individual's work situation block him or her in the attempt to achieve self-actualization, the individual will join with his or her fellows to resist authority. The remedy is to restructure or otherwise correct the situation or system.

A second point of view about the functioning of people in organizations is *individualistic*. According to this view, people are neither good nor bad, but they do have particular needs that must be met. Preeminently, they need freedom and opportunities to make choices. They should be helped and developed within a congenial person-organization interaction. Where tension exists, action for release of tension should occur; satisfaction of needs will ensue.

A third position may be termed *moral-ethical*. It holds that people are inherently bad, particularly in the sense that they are self-centered. They need reorientation toward more constructive, cooperative, selfless behavior. Thus the problem is first with people and then with the organization. A chief function of the leader is to make reorientation possible; turning people toward goodness will improve the organization, and the organization will become beneficent because of the quality of the people in it.[29]

The basic attitudes that curriculum leaders hold concerning their co-workers (and themselves) can affect how they proceed with their work. Thus success may be based in attitude and then be realized in competency.

Specific competencies that curriculum leaders need include the abilities to

1. Practice good human relations
2. Adhere to principles of human growth and development
3. Know when, where, and under what conditions curriculum change occurs
4. Use group process techniques
5. Relate quickly to other people
6. Develop the creative abilities of other people
7. Invent new plans for organizing personnel and facilities
8. Know how to solve educational problems
9. See themselves as others see them.

Innovative spirit, imagination, and follow-through are apparently features of leadership that get results. In late 1972 the Ford Foundation admitted the failure of its $30 million ten-year attempt to improve education through its Comprehensive School Improvement Program. Among the Foundation's findings were the following: The hold of the single textbook can be broken, paraprofessionals are valuable assets, large-scale change occurs more easily when both grantor and recipient agree on specific purposes of a project, the size of a grant has little to do with a project's success, and change occurs faster in small schools but is more durable in medium-sized suburban ones. However, the most important finding was that quality leadership makes the greatest difference when that leadership stays on the job.

SITUATION 11-2
Choosing the Principal's Assistant

Woodhaven School District was finally going to give high school principal Matthews an instructional assistant. Matthews had just visited the superintendent who, busy with the building program and a bond issue, had turned the problem of selecting an assistant over to the principal himself. Back at his office, Matthews shuffled through the sets of employment credentials and came up with two leading candidates.

The basic requirements of the assistantship seemed clear enough to Matthews and to five or six of his staff members whom he had consulted. They were

1. Ability to secure a state certificate in the general supervision of secondary education
2. A broad educational background
3. At least two years' experience in a similar position elsewhere
4. Special competency in leading groups and counseling individuals about instructional matters
5. Ability to coordinate warring groups and diffident personalities.

Matthews and his consultants had been afraid to go further in listing job requirements. Like almost any other instructional position, this would be a difficult one to fill.

As he looked at the list, the principal muttered to himself, "I think I'll take a new tack. I'll look for the man or the woman who has what it takes to fill the position." Accordingly, he made a list of the characteristics of his two leading candidates by inferences from their credentials and from his interviews with them:

Candidate Smathers	*Candidate Rink*
Very enthusiastic about professional advancement	Moderately enthusiastic about professional advancement
Reserved in her social contacts	Outgoing in his social contacts
Broadly experienced in supervisory work	Somewhat experienced in supervisory work
Excellent academic record	Satisfactory academic record
Fair ability to adjust to differing groups with which she works	Superior ability to adjust to differing groups with which he works
Interested in some of the facets of her past professional work	Interested in most of the facets of his past professional work
Almost icily self-controlled	Sometimes lacking in self-control
Generally well accepted by other staff members	Generally well accepted by other staff members

Which candidate do you think principal Matthews should favor?

What else should Mr. Matthews seek to know about these and other candidates?

ACTIVITY 11-3
Interrelating Human Relations and Task Performance in Curriculum Leadership

Mention has been made of the human-relations and task-performance aspects of leadership. These two elements of the leadership act should function simultaneously. That is, while educational leaders are trying to be pleasant and cooperative in their dealings with their associates, they should, at the same time, be doing important work to get educational jobs accomplished.

The following sociodramatic episodes are meant to emphasize the simultaneous interaction of human-relations and task-performance skills. Staff these episodes with players, play the episodes, and discuss them with reference to the quality of human relations and of task performance.

Sociodrama 1

Five complaining parents arrive outside the principal's office to protest the new program in drug education being offered in the high school. Their basic argument is that the program does not *prevent* drug abuse; rather, it informs youngsters about how to use drugs and therefore encourages them in drug abuse.

The principal, after inviting the parents into her office, defends the school's drug education program chiefly on the basis that the high school has a legal and moral right to provide it. Behind the principal sits her "conscience," making comments that run counter to some of the principal's public arguments. The principal is aided in making her public, official arguments by the assistant principal in charge of instruction, who knows most about the content of the drug education program.

The objects in this episode are (1) to resolve the immediate situation tentatively and thus to "cool" it and (2) to pose possibilities for permanent resolution of this and similar conflicts.

Total number of actors: 8.

Sociodrama 2

Three teachers representing a majority of the total teaching staff of an elementary school meet with the principal and others to object to the workshop in reading instruction that has been conducted in the school every other Thursday afternoon since September. The main thrust of the teachers' complaint about the workshop, which was planned by the principal and an outside consultant in reading programs, is that it is largely a waste of time and, at any rate, should not have been planned without the teachers' participation.

The principal takes the position that, as principal, he knows the needs of the faculty and has both a right and an obligation to plan for the teachers' in-service education. The outside consultant defends the nature and quality of the workshop. A reading consultant from the assistant superintendent's office bewails the conflict between her point of view about reading instruction and the point of view taken by the outside consultant. The union delegate is present to determine whether the teachers can make a grievance case of this situation.

The purposes here are to highlight the importance of leaders' ways of working and to note the complications created by input from persons with differing motivations and objectives.

Some of the roles of actors may be reversed part way through this episode. Total number of actors: 7.

SITUATION 11-3
What Shall We Do to Improve Our School?

Staff and conduct the following role-playing episode:

The Characters

1. The principal, who has just returned from an administrators' convention and who now advocates a plan for teaming teachers in teams of three.
2. The union steward, who automatically resists all attempts to manipulate teachers.
3. The chairperson of the school's curriculum steering committee, who insists that the three curriculum projects involving teachers are already "set" for the year and should not be moved aside now in the month of March.
4. The principal's stooge, a teacher currying favor for unknown reasons, who maintains that the remainder of the year should be devoted to trying the principal's team-teaching idea.
5. The unofficial leader of the school faculty, a popular habitué of the teachers' rest rooms, who wants nothing to succeed that would give the principal additional power or publicity.
6. A sincere and somewhat naive teacher who wants "what is best for our children" regardless of whether the principal's plan is implemented or not.
7. A bright young teacher who is bucking to become a curriculum coordinator in the administrative district and who is interested in promoting curriculum projects which he or she can later defend.

Description of the Scene

1. This is a meeting of presumably interested persons who have responded to the principal's call to the faculty to attend a voluntary session concerning a "new" idea the principal has garnered at a recent national convention.
2. The principal opens the meeting by pushing his plan, which consists basically of dividing the faculty of sixty-six classroom teachers into twenty-two teams of three teachers each, allocated wherever possible by the teachers' personal preferences, but certainly by competence in subject matter and special skills.
3. The plan would lead to alteration of teachers' schedules so that trios could plan together an hour each day, work in unison at times, and continue working in self-contained classrooms most of the time.

4. The curriculum steering committee already has scheduled three projects involving three-fourths of the teachers: one in corrective reading, another in improvement of pupils' self-esteem, and a third in consumerism.

When the episode has been played, discuss its implications for curriculum leadership.

SITUATION 11-4
The Curriculum Leader without Authority

The Branchville Consolidated Schools had an active, thriving curriculum improvement program. Thirteen curriculum committees and five study groups were under way in the eight schools of this rural district. The curriculum coordinator, Lillian Dinsmoor, was busier than usual. She had recently helped the superintendent make a cooperative arrangement with the state university to begin curriculum experimentation for which the school district and the university would share the costs. Mrs. Dinsmoor had many responsibilities, but the superintendent saw to it that she was strictly a staff officer, lacking line authority to make decisions.

At 3:30 on a Thursday afternoon, Mrs. Dinsmoor telephoned three of the principals of the Branchville schools to ask whether they could find substitutes for a previously selected teacher from each of their schools for the full day one week from the following Monday. The purpose, Mrs. Dinsmoor explained, was to secure teacher representation on a new committee that would help her and Dr. Campbell, of the state university staff, plan for curriculum experimentation in Branchville. The first two principals called readily agreed to release their teachers. Mr. McKay, the third principal, refused. "What kind of school do you think I'm operating?" he asked. "We have important things for Mrs. Fineman to do here on that day." Mrs. Dinsmoor knew that she had the responsibility for organizing the committee, which was to meet partly on school time, but no one had told her what to do when principals refused to release teachers to serve during the school day. She concluded the telephone conversation with Mr. McKay as quickly and as graciously as she could.

What, if anything should Mrs. Dinsmoor do immediately about her problem?

What should she do over the long term?

How should her own actions relate to the possible actions of others in the school system who might help prevent similar situations from developing in the future?

LEADERSHIP STRATEGIES FOR IMPROVING THE CURRICULUM

A strategy is a comprehensive plan or series of maneuvers for achieving a result. As curriculum leaders think of what should be done to improve the curriculum over a period of years, they attempt to find strategies. The strategies they choose should fit their particular situations.

A strategy likely to come to mind immediately is careful planning from the vantage point of the central offices of the school system. This strategy, which comprehends planning for the whole system that none except central office leaders are likely to initiate and continue, is called *master planning*.

A second strategy requires shifting the focus of attention from large-scale, centralized planning to planning at numerous local sites within the school system. The leaders immediately involved in this strategy are usually the principals of individual schools, though they may also be district or zone administrators. When the strategy operates at its best, one or more central office leaders coordinate the planning done in numbers of local schools, as well as its implementation. The purpose is to prevent each school from "going off on its own," without taking into account the plans made and the actions taken in other schools. This strategy may be termed *coordinated local planning*.

Many curriculum leaders prefer a third strategy. Operating according to the belief that the curriculum cannot improve unless teachers and other professionals in charge of the schools improve their own understandings, skills, and attitudes, they emphasize reeducation of personnel. The third strategy is therefore comprehensive *inservice education and staff development*.

A fourth strategy is based in the concept that the curriculum is where teachers and pupils are, so improvement of teachers' day-by-day decision making is most important. Leaders who emphasize this strategy urge careful development of *planned programs of supervision* that highlight decision making in classrooms to improve the real curriculum.

Large numbers of principals and other administrators believe that the curriculum improves when organizational conditions in schools make improvement possible. Accordingly, they emphasize the need to make changes in the organizational structure of schools. The strategy involved is *school reorganization*.

Leaders in elementary and secondary education have maintained for a long time that an important means of improving the curriculum is involving teachers and other school personnel in conducting sensible experiments and in undertaking research. Of all the strategies, this one relies most on the scientific method. It is referred to as *educational experimentation and research*.

Leaders may think of other means of promoting curriculum improvement, but the means they propose will probably not have the magnitude and significance of the strategies noted above. Two or more strategies may, of course, receive emphasis in a school system at a given time and for overlapping periods of time. Each strategy obviously has its own contribution to make. Each differs so much from the others that danger of duplication among them is minimal.

The most recent studies of the competencies needed by curriculum leaders with systemwide responsibilities show that ability to coordinate the entire curriculum enterprise is central and most significant. As a team of authors put it, the curriculum leader in the central offices "must be able to keep straight the relation of the trees and the forest" while causing the contributions of people to mesh well. New demands facing systemwide coordinators today include dealing with public discontent with the schools and adapting technological resources like computers to meet the needs of schools. Still other demands have to do with responding to economic trends, knowing management procedures of promise, applying knowledge from the behavioral sciences to working with people, and finding ways of meeting the educational needs of disadvantaged pupils.

Strategy 1: Master Planning

Master planning for a whole school system or an administrative district of a large city involves establishing purposes, policies, and criteria to guide curriculum improvement. This action is accomplished by individuals and groups based either temporarily or permanently in places of central authority. We have seen in earlier chapters that most of the work accomplished in the curriculum field during the twenties and the thirties was done in central offices of school systems. Though the site of planning has moved increasingly to the individual school, the central office has retained its functions of initiating, leading, and guiding major actions for curriculum change. Several arguments have been advanced for giving the central office a maximum of authority. One is that a systemwide approach brings the schools close to the community as a whole, with the result that citizens appreciate where the entire teaching staff stands on important educational issues. Another argument is that "across-the-board activity" is administratively neater and easier to manage. A third is that communication is improved because there are fewer conflicting actions and procedures. Other arguments are these:

1. People who "know" are usually housed in the central office.
2. Time is saved by avoiding detailed analysis of the needs and problems of individual schools.
3. There is maximum assurance that a given project or product has received the blessing of the powerful central office.
4. Coordination and comprehensiveness can be made keynotes of systemwide activity; hence, things can run smoothly and handsomely on a large scale.
5. A major result of systemwide activity is continuity—the presence of a common thread in the curriculum.

In the past, much of the planning done in the central offices of school districts was unsystematic. Currently, there is a stronger emphasis on system, order, and series of sequential steps in making major plans, and an occasional use of the systems approach to planning. With or without this approach, however, central offices are exercising increased care in planning, partly because of the demand for stricter accountability. To this end, Walter St. John has developed a guide for setting priorities, as well as a priority planning chart.[30]

Actions Commonly Taken

Actions taken by central office personnel to achieve master planning on behalf of entire school systems or major divisions of large systems include the following: conducting large staff meetings, issuing directives and memoranda, preparing policy statements, organizing major projects for study and research, preparing course guides and unit plans, considering and announcing school system aims and general objectives, collating annotated lists of materials, producing booklets, pamphlets, and brochures on numerous topics, and preparing packages of learning materials. The function of each of these actions is given below.

- Large staff meetings are conducted as often as once a month, and though they are of doubtful worth for making policy, the meetings may increase understanding of systemwide procedures and may bring together staff members who seldom see one another.
- Directives and memoranda are issued when the matters to be presented seem to need no discussion or further elaboration.
- Policy statements express guidelines for curriculum planning in entire school systems.
- Organizing major projects for study and research involves doing careful, centralized planning, then making contacts and contracts with individual consultants, government agencies, universities, and foundations.
- Preparing course guides and unit plans has often been a central office responsibility, with some of the necessary talent being drawn from individual schools in the district.
- School system aims and general objectives have real impact when they are considered and announced by the central office.
- Collating annotated lists of materials helps to broaden the selection of materials by teachers, thus avoiding the stereotyping of materials to be used by pupils.
- Producing booklets, pamphlets, and brochures can become an

important staff development activity that gives a school district a distinctive flair.

- Locally prepared packages of learning materials that suit the district's particular needs can be an effective supplement to commercially prepared materials.

Centralized planning works best when it accomplishes those tasks that do not rightfully belong to the individual school. Some actions should be undertaken by an individual—for example, a superintendent or an assistant superintendent in charge of instruction—or a small group of people on behalf of all personnel in the system. These actions should be accomplished chiefly for three reasons: coordination, desirable uniformity, and economy of time and effort. The case for coordination needs no pleading. The expression "desirable uniformity" suggests that some uniformity in school systems is *not* desirable. Therefore, those who would encourage uniformity should determine whether it is really needed. "Economy of time and effort" refers to the importance of having certain tasks performed by one agency so as to bypass unnecessary duplication by several agencies. Duplication of effort is one of the great ills of organizations, and it needs to be rooted out of school systems that have existed for years without analysis of roles or even the most elementary time study.

With these cautions in mind, one must acknowledge that centralized activity will and should continue in school systems. The best leadership and facilities are often found in central offices. Master planning can be made effective by several means, including: (1) designating someone to have the responsibility and authority for systemwide activity, (2) organizing a central steering committee to guide this activity, (3) working closely with lay advisory committees or other groups of citizens, and (4) forming special-interest committees or task forces to assume the responsibility for particular systemwide assignments.

Some Dangers and Difficulties

There are, of course, certain dangers in master planning. One is failure to involve enough professional personnel and laypersons in the decision-making process. Another is the well-known tendency of central offices to overemphasize paper work. A third is the unfortunate temptation to make systemwide comparisons of teachers and children. A fourth is the compulsion to issue military-like directives. These dangers are theoretically reduced by bringing the planners and the planned-for together in individual schools. In practice, some school systems, which are alleged to be most forward looking, have in charge superintendents and other top-echelon personnel who seem to believe that improving the curriculum depends solely on accepting the wisdom dispensed by leaders of national curriculum projects and the status leaders of school systems. This limited view of the process of curriculum improvement can in the long run lead to impoverishment of the curriculum and to the rise of insurgent movements among teachers who have learned that participation on a systemwide basis is both possible and productive.

ACTIVITY 11-4

Finding Evidence of Master Planning in a School System

Identify a school system or a district of a medium to large city system in which you will be permitted to inquire about the curriculum planning that is conducted centrally. Keep in mind the examples of master planning given above, but do not limit your inquiry to these. Ask one or more responsible persons in the central offices what phases of the curriculum are determined centrally. Inquire about the ways in which decisions about the curriculum are communicated to the schools and ask to see documents that are used in the communication process. If you compare your findings with those of another inquirer, you will both learn much about master planning.

Strategy 2: Coordinated Local Planning

When the teacher closes the classroom door, much of the *real* curriculum of the school goes into operation. Most of the best curriculum improvement that occurs anywhere is accomplished where teachers and their pupils are. In classrooms of the individual school, teachers and pupils live together five or six hours each school day. Here the differences among children are revealed. Here the teachers, no matter how stringent the supervisory authority of the school, are free to try some of their own ideas and ways of working and to put into practice what they have learned elsewhere. Here is the "cutting edge," the real frontier of education.

In the individual school, teachers of similar children or teachers with like professional problems can meet most readily. In faculty meetings or in small, informal groups, they can discuss their problems, share information about possible methods of solving them, and design investigations in an attempt to find new solutions. Unless a domineering principal, an equally domineering central office, or the community itself ignores the concerns of the faculty, the problems selected for consideration are likely to be the real and immediate ones of the faculty itself. The real problems might be what to do with certain troublesome discipline cases, how to talk with parents during parent-teacher conferences, and what supplementary books to order with the dollars allocated for this purpose. Some of the real problems of teachers—such as the fatigue of children who watch television too late at night—originate in the community and require that teachers cooperate with parents and other school patrons. Other problems, such as those connected with methods of teaching spelling to intermediate grade children, require attention by teachers only.

One of the special advantages of the individual school as a curriculum planning unit lies in the smallness of many faculty groups. Small faculties engage in much face-to-face contact and can easily get together. In large high schools, teachers often meet in departmental groups, with occasional interdepartmental meetings. In large elementary schools, teachers assemble according to grade level and according to location in the school.

Conducting Staff Meetings

Under thoughtful leadership, meetings of several kinds may be used in the individual school for curriculum planning. Teachers may meet as a whole faculty, by grade levels, by departments, as building task forces, and as members of steering committees. When it seems appropriate and desirable, adult laypersons and pupils may attend some of the meetings. Depending on who attends, meetings may be called to consider policy for the whole school, details of subject matter by grade level or age grouping, the program of a teacher's own department as it relates to the programs of other departments, the advisability of using certain business-sponsored teaching aids in the school, and numerous other matters. In large schools the principal sometimes organizes a cabinet or steering committee, which represents the faculty and acts for it with respect to issues that need not or cannot immediately claim the attention of the whole staff.

For all staff meetings in the individual school, there are certain common ground rules that teachers and principals should know and observe:

1. Call meetings when teachers are alert.
2. Arrange for social contacts and refreshments before or after meetings.
3. Devote meetings on a continuing basis to one or more important topics rather than staging "one-shot performances" in single meetings.
4. Encourage faculty participation in planning the meetings.
5. Seek out subject matter of real concern to the persons who participate.
6. Keep the meetings "on the beam."
7. Apply what has been learned about effective group procedures; for example, arrange for clarification of the problem or situation under discussion, encourage requests for information, urge a search for facts rather than mere opinion, plan frequent summaries of progress made during the meeting.

8. Evaluate meetings by means of discussion or prepared evaluation forms, then use the data in planning subsequent meetings.

Decisions about meetings that leaders of local schools need to make include those associated with how to prepare for meetings, who should plan the meetings, where and when meetings should be held, what topics and concerns should be discussed, and how meetings can be evaluated. Background for making these decisions can be found in references on group process in school situations. Basic discussion of many matters belongs in the individual school. The discussion channel should often run from the individual school to the central offices and then back to the individual school.

Freeing Teachers to Plan

Teachers need to be freed to plan, inasmuch as real curriculum improvement frequently begins with teachers. Teachers plan in three ways: individually, with pupils, and with professional colleagues. The products of their efforts may be any of the following:

1. Resource units, which are master plans on which teachers may draw in making unit plans and functional units
2. Unit plans, which are written with groups in the pupil population in mind
3. Functional units, specifying learning experiences for carefully identified pupils
4. Minicourses, or courses of short duration that deal with limited themes or topics
5. Ways of individualizing instruction.

The Need for Coordination

One may wonder whether the emphasis placed on the importance of the individual school in curriculum planning implies that every school should develop its own exclusive and different curriculum. To expect the individual school to stand completely alone in curriculum planning would be foolhardy. There are at least two important reasons for this:

1. Similarities as well as differences exist among schools in the same system; these similarities should be capitalized on through central or systemwide planning.
2. Improving the curriculum from the ground up in each building would prove wasteful of time and funds. Whatever can be done

legitimately in a central place should be done there. The remainder will be sufficient to keep the staffs of individual schools more than amply occupied.

School people and parents often worry about differences among the curricula of schools within the same system. What happens, they wonder, when a fifth-grade child moves from School D to School A and finds that fifth graders in the new school are learning something quite different in the social studies? Worries of this kind have doubtless been exaggerated. The pace and content of learning in Schools D and A may correctly vary, as they may indeed among several fifth-grade classrooms within a large individual building. Furthermore, a given experience in the social studies or in any other subject may, within limits, be as valuable as another experience.

The most important question is whether the diverse experiences contribute directly to goals of education that have been set for the system and for the individual school. The question then is *"What experiences best serve definite purposes?"* If concepts and major ideas are learned, then the details of subject matter contributing to their learning may safely differ from classroom to classroom and from school to school. In an era in which knowledge abounds to such an extent that it has become unmanageable, concepts must be made the uniform core of the curriculum, and details that contribute most to concept development must be sought more diligently.

ACTIVITY 11-5
Some Practical Problems in Local Planning

In planning educational experiences, there are several alternatives to developing units of instruction. One alternative is to follow a topically or chronologically organized textbook. Another is to use a "grasshopper approach," hopping from topic to topic without any long-range plan. Can you think of other, more constructive alternatives? Are there situations in which unit planning should not be used? If so, describe such a situation.

Now think how you would proceed to help a teacher who exhibited the following symptoms of poor planning: (1) a tendency to skip from subject matter item to subject matter item without regard to sequence and (2) a failure to identify and follow cues from pupils that indicate the pupils are confused by the subject matter and are losing interest in it.

Strategy 3: Inservice Education and Staff Development

Curriculum leaders have clear responsibility for directing activities that belong under the headings of inservice education and staff development.

If the curriculum is to be improved, teachers must have the necessary insights, skills, and attitudes for planning and implementing curriculum change. They gain these insights, skills, and attitudes by being educated or reeducated on the job. If the education tends to be formal, stringent, and mandated, it is usually called *inservice education*. If it is informal, free in nature, and guided by teachers toward their own need satisfaction, it is usually called *staff development*. The justification for engaging in both inservice education and staff development activities rests on the assumption that learners' lives will not be changed very much unless the professional and personal lives of their teachers are made ever richer with fruitful experience.

Teachers have professional problems that well-conducted inservice and staff development programs can help them solve, though, naturally, these problems do not fall neatly into premade topics. The problems in their original formulation are crude; they need reformulation and explication. They cover a broad spectrum, and they require limitation of content to what can appropriately be discussed in inservice situations.

It is possible to reeducate teachers using a variety of means and media. It is possible, for instance, to reeducate teachers by a behavior modification process—by giving a teacher special privileges in return for increasing the number and variety of his or her teaching procedures or by penalizing a teacher for refusing to increase the number and variety of procedures used. Or teachers may be asked to observe and criticize their own teaching behavior after it has been videotaped and also observe and criticize the work of a versatile teacher. The author believes that by using procedures of behavior modification we tend to keep teachers in bondage, and by using a system of observation and criticism, especially self-criticism, we help to liberate them, though we are uncertain of the precise direction they will take in their liberated state.

If we want teachers to possess a broad repertory of teaching procedures—evidence now indicates that having such a repertory aids teachers in helping pupils learn—we should similarly have a broad repertory to use in the reeducation of teachers. If we want teachers to behave differently, we must reeducate them to believe differently. One route to helping teachers believe differently is to convince them that what they are being reeducated to do is indeed practical and useful.

Such reeducation must also be *practiced*. On this point, Rubin says:

> New modes of behavior develop when particular actions are rehearsed again and again until they become an organic part of the individual. Accordingly, in-service education must begin with perception, kindle the freedom and the lust to change, then provide a method and support, and end in the confirmation of newborn habits. In this form, professional growth becomes self-transcendence.

> Where the desired change is a matter of ritual, the difficulties are
> minor. Where it is a matter of value, or belief, or master craftsmanship,
> there is no easy way. . . .[31]

The studies of inservice and staff development programs show that leaders serve best when they involve teachers in planning and operating the programs; when they see to it that program activities are scheduled carefully; when they help arrange sequences of events, with feedback from experienced people; when they bring in consultants who know professional development processes; when they provide opportunities for teachers to view simulations and actual situations; when they make individual schools the usual sites of the activities; and when they insist on adequate levels of funding for employment of instructors and purchase of materials. Leaders should attend to both the content and the delivery of programs. If either content or delivery lacks quality, the whole effort can fail.[32]

Actions Leaders Can Take

The following lists contain twenty-one staff development actions that directly benefit individual teachers and twenty actions that benefit groups of teachers, with ultimate application to the needs of many individuals. For descriptions of these actions, see Doll, *Supervision for Staff Development.*[33]

Actions for the direct benefit of individuals

Making educational platforms
Doing coteaching (teaming)
Participating in peer supervision
Using a laboratory approach to learning
Analyzing artifacts
Developing a portfolio
Participating in guided educational travel
Receiving microcounseling
Doing summer session and extension teaching of adults
Engaging in professional writing
Attending professional conventions
Studying independently (sometimes via correspondence courses)
Receiving classroom observation by a supervisor
Conferring individually with a supervisor
Receiving assistance in the classroom from a supervisor
Practicing individually
Training paraprofessionals
Engaging in internships

Engaging in intervisitation
Receiving advisement for personal and career development
Doing directed reading

Actions for the benefit of groups, for application
to the needs of individuals

Joining a "floating faculty"
Engaging in practica
Receiving programmed instruction
Engaging in group analysis of recorded teaching episodes
Trading classrooms
Engaging in community (sociological) study
Taking on-campus courses and seminars
Taking courses offered on commercial television
Attending conferences or work conferences
Attending institutes
Participating in study groups
Attending clinic sessions
Participating in workshops
Attending demonstrations
Participating in T-groups and sensitivity training groups
Participating in retreats
Engaging in cooperative educational research
Utilizing the services of consultants
Gaining information and ideas from bulletins and bulletin boards.

The curriculum leader should have a "speaking acquaintance" with each of the items in the list. Some of them he or she would probably not recommend or advocate. Some are obscure and a few are new, but most of them have been tried in inservice or staff development programs. For instance, institutes, conferences, and study groups have been organized and conducted in a number of school systems. One action, the workshop, has been genuinely tried in a limited number of places. It has often been abused by organizers who have called activities workshops when they were not. Teachers consider the well-conducted workshop so useful that it requires full description.

The term *workshop* recalls the spiritual containing the words "Everybody who talks about heaven ain't goin' there." Not everyone who thinks he or she is conducting or attending a workshop is doing so, because all sorts of educational meetings have been called workshops. The workshop has been defined by Earl C. Kelley as differing from meetings, gatherings, and classes by including planning sessions, work sessions, and sessions for summarizing and evaluating.[34] This definition implies that the workshop is a democratically organized and rather lengthy medium of inservice education. It permits varied activities, which may include listening to consultants, discussing common problems, reading professional literature, assembling materials, watching film presentations, playing roles, filling evaluation forms, and picnicking. Not the least important of the workshop's features is the social proximity and the good feeling that can be developed among participants. Another feature is the devotion to solving problems that seem most significant to the participants.

Workshop sessions may be held on consecutive days for several weeks, as during the summer months. Sometimes sessions are conducted at intervals ranging from a few days to a week. In any event, time is scheduled so that programs like the following can operate:

- *First hour:* General Session (singing, whole-group planning, listening to consultants, viewing films)
- *One-and-a-half hours:* Special Interest Groups (discussion by each group of a subject of special interest to it)
- *One-half hour:* Informal Conferences (with staff and other workshoppers)
- *One hour or more:* Study and Planning Period (study, research, planning, trips and tours)
- *One hour or more:* Activities (social events and sports).

A program of this kind may stretch to fill a full day or it may be condensed to occupy a shorter period. Workshop participants should be given responsibility for helping to plan their own programs.

Organized programs of inservice education and staff development may be said to serve as one of the two or three major direct stimuli to curriculum improvement. By organizing the programs, teachers and administrators consciously set aside time for activities that promote curriculum change. The blocks of time they reserve pay off in great or slight progress depending largely on two factors: the concern staff members feel for the idea or subject being dealt with and the cooperativeness and good feeling engendered by the program. The twin sparkplugs of concern and cooperativeness can fire the whole curriculum program in a school system. Cooperative study helps to reveal hidden problems, and organizers of the best programs encourage staff members to work on those problems that, after due consideration, prove to be most significant to the members' own thinking. Then they watch for ways of working together to encourage good human relationships. Programs based on the viewpoint mentioned above are an excellent takeoff point for further curriculum study and planning because effective programs contribute what a thriving curriculum improvement program needs: a cadre of interested, motivated teachers and insightful, prepared leaders.

ACTIVITY 11-6
Themes and Procedures for Planning Inservice and Staff
Development Projects

Inservice projects organized in various school systems within recent years include the following:

- In Baltimore, Maryland, "How can we develop leadership among our staff members?"
- In Aberdeen, South Dakota, "Let's find out what our goals should be and then make them visible through concrete action."
- In Nyack, New York, "We need wide involvement of the people who should become fully aware of our more pressing problems."
- In Van Dyke, Michigan, "We must plan a variety of helpful, coordinated activities designed to meet teachers' needs."

Who should determine the theme of a project or a program? What should be the deciding factors in determining the theme?

When the theme has been determined, how would you help decide which inservice media (institutes, workshops, and so forth) to use?

Strategy 4: Planned Programs of Supervision

In this section of the chapter, the leader will be termed *supervisor*. Here, the emphasis is on development of programs of supervision that foster close educative contact between the supervisor and the supervised so that learning experiences for pupils may be improved. The supervisor faces a formidable array of tasks. He or she is expected to help teachers improve their use of numerous procedures and techniques in the classroom.

When supervisors become familiar with teachers' special needs for help, they often discover that the needs fall into a half-dozen categories:

- The need to improve long-term and day-to-day planning with reference to objectives, pupil motivation, homework, and ongoing curriculum projects within the school system
- The need to improve use of pupils' time by achieving variety in classroom activities, relating learning theories to activities, adopting appropriate teaching procedures, relating classroom activities to schoolwide activities, and reassessing homework policy
- The need to improve understanding of the dynamics of classroom groups with respect to ways of grouping, what really happens in group situations, classroom control, and humanization of the classroom
- The need to give attention to individuals, with reference to actions

and materials that assist personalization, and to ways in which
creativity can be fostered
- The need to use available resources wisely, in consideration of use
  of facilities and materials, organization of the classroom for learning,
  and use of human talent
- The need to improve the quality of evaluation, with reference to objectives, comprehensiveness in the evaluation process, development
  of test items, and the planning of marking and reporting practices.

Leaders who serve as supervisors need conceptual skills that permit
them to help plan; to organize people, time, and resources; to lead by stimulating, communicating, and making suggestions for moving ahead; and
to monitor what is happening. Of course they need interpersonal skills also,
so that their own and others' relationships may become smooth enough
to facilitate progress.[35]

At one time, school personnel seemed to think of supervision as being distinct and vastly different from curriculum improvement. Supervisors
were originally employed to inspect teaching and to build programs of instruction that teachers would closely follow. With the advent of curriculum
specialists, supervisors were assigned to "supervise," and curriculum coordinators were designated to direct curriculum planning. Experience has
shown, however, that the duties of supervisors and curriculum coordinators inevitably overlap and that people who carry these titles should constitute a service team for better teaching and learning.

Traditionally, teachers have disliked what some of them call "snoop-
ervision." Old-style supervision has emphasized inspection and rating of
the teacher's work. According to the perceptions of the supervised, inadequate effort has been expended in helping teachers with the problems that
concern them. The day the supervisor comes to visit the classroom is still
regarded in some schools as a black day of fear and distrust. Adverse feelings about supervision have caused teachers to perpetrate all sorts of artful
dodges, like changing suddenly to a specially prepared lesson or "passing
the red book" to announce to other teachers the supervisor's arrival in the
building. Fortunately, the role of the supervisor is shifting in many school
systems to that of a helping teacher or consultant. Teachers and supervisors
should work cooperatively to improve the quality of pupils' experiences.

School systems that can afford them often develop unusually strong
supervisory programs. These programs depend significantly for their success on quantity and quality of the supervisors and on functions they serve.
In some states, county offices of education provide supervisory services
through specially staffed service centers.

Perhaps the most natural and productive situations calling for the
teamwork of supervisors and teachers grow out of ongoing curriculum
study. For example, development of a course guide in the social studies

may require classroom experimentation with content, methods, and materials. Two or three central office supervisors, several principals, and a score of teachers may involve themselves in the project, working in classrooms, meetings, and conferences and planning both the experimentation and the guide. In situations of this kind the fear and the artificiality that have often characterized supervision tend to disappear.

Supervisory Tasks

A good program of supervision serves many functions, all of which relate to the educational welfare of pupils. Teachers may expect to find their supervisors engaging in activities like these:

- Holding meetings and group conferences
- Conferring with individual teachers
- Visiting classrooms
- Working on curriculum committees
- Organizing and conducting inservice programs
- Helping teachers select textbooks, audiovisual aids, and other materials
- Working with teachers on plans and units
- Helping select and use standardized tests
- Speaking to parents and other lay groups
- Maintaining relationships with teacher education institutions and the state department of education
- Orienting new teachers to their jobs
- Writing policy statements and other curriculum materials
- Arranging intervisitation
- Conducting workshops, institutes, and conferences
- Attending meetings of professional organizations
- Helping teachers develop tests and instructional materials
- Planning demonstration teaching
- Interviewing candidates for teaching positions.

Alert supervisors recognize that they must work differently in different situations—with experienced teachers, with first-year teachers, with parent groups, with fellow supervisors and administrators, and with varied groups of teachers in a kaleidoscope of settings. Supervisors are regularly involved in curriculum improvement activities so diversified as to challenge their adaptability and ingenuity. In general, however, supervisors are concerned with three giant tasks: (1) helping to determine purposes of education and helping to see that these purposes are adhered to in daily practice, (2) giving democratic instructional leadership, and (3) keeping channels of communication in school organizations open. If they are not careful, supervisors fall into the habit of manipulating teachers to achieve the ends that the supervisors themselves consider desirable. Patience and willingness to see the other person's point of view are among the fundamental qualities that supervisors should possess. Four leadership roles of supervisors have been classified by the Webster Groves (Missouri) Public Schools: leadership to meet individual differences among pupils, leadership for faculty growth, leadership for coordination of programs and services, and leadership in integrating school and community life.

Of the numerous procedures that supervisors have developed, a few have become very popular. These include classroom observation, supervisor-teacher conferences, group work, and demonstration teaching.

Other supervisory procedures, some of which are similar or akin to procedures used in organized inservice education, are intervisitation, directed reading (in which professional reading is planned for and with teachers), preparation of written bulletins, exhibits and bulletin displays, courses, professional conventions, and selection and development of teaching materials.

Teachers seem to consider supervision effective when it supplies stimulation, encouragement, ideas, materials, and skill in troubleshooting. As a strategy of curriculum improvement, supervision has the advantage of dealing with down-to-earth situations, building consciousness of highly specific needs for improvement, and keeping close to the feelings of teachers.

Newer Developments in Supervision

Supervision is sometimes considered a likely prospect for application of the systems approach. A systems model in supervision usually has three phases: input, process, and output. Input involves determination of needs, setting of goals, and identification of strategies for meeting the needs. Process consists of implementing and monitoring the strategies. Output is determined by evaluating the effectiveness of the strategies in light of the goals. The output phase may involve suggesting modifications in the system. Kathryn V. Feyereisen and others have developed a supervisory system that includes designing curriculum, providing teachers with advice, and helping an instructional staff with problems of teaching and learning. These authors recommend the systems approach because it integrates elements of supervisory strategy into a single plan.[36]

The discussion of educational supervision in the preceding pages has been limited largely to supervision for improving the curriculum. Other purposes of supervision include inspection of classrooms and schools and evaluation of teaching. Some of the facets of supervisory strategy mentioned above have been combined by Morris L. Cogan, Robert Goldhammer, and others within a development called "clinical supervision," in which the sequence may be preobservation, observation of teaching, analysis and strategy, conference, and postconference analysis.[37]

A newer development of promise is *human resources supervision*, which is not to be confused with human relations supervision. The human resources supervisor places first emphasis on important and meaningful work. In accomplishing this work, teachers gain the kinds of satisfaction that the advocates of human relations supervision desire and place first in priority. The need to emphasize the work involved in improving the curriculum (at a time when the work ethic is again looming larger) makes human resources supervision a potential asset.[38]

Both human relations supervision and human resources supervision are concerned with teacher satisfaction. The former calls for action that will increase teacher satisfaction so that the teachers are easier to work with and to lead, and so that in the long run schooling becomes more efficient and effective. Human resources supervision, on the other hand, sees satisfaction as an end toward which teachers aspire if they have important and meaningful work to do. The accomplishment of worthwhile work is the way to efficient and effective schooling.[39]

During the late 1970s and the early 1980s, many leaders with responsibility for supervision were urged by state departments of education and presumed public opinion to emphasize evaluating or monitoring teachers' work. As the pendulum swung in this direction, a flurry of interest in evaluation devices, merit pay plans, alternative routes of entry into teaching, and other means of compulsion and extrinsic reward became evident. A countermovement emphasizes a longer view of the improvement process, with supervision focusing on careful and thorough development of current staff who, under the tenure laws, are likely to serve in the schools for years to come.[40]

ACTIVITY 11-7
Surveying Teachers' Needs for Supervisory Help

The late J. Minor Gwynn, an authority in the field of supervision, surveyed teachers along the Atlantic coast to learn ways in which they believed their supervisors could help them best. The top five needs for help which these teachers identified were associated with: (1) planning, (2) finding teaching materials, (3) evaluating pupil progress, (4) establishing discipline or control, and (5) solving professional, community, and social problems.

Conduct a similar survey of your own, even though your sample of teachers will necessarily be smaller. Combine your findings with those of your fellow students.

How do your combined findings compare with those of Dr. Gwynn? What implications do your findings have for the organization and nature of supervisory programs?

ACTIVITY 11-8
Getting to Know Teachers' Strengths

Considering that attempts at making studies of teachers' work have often ended in conflict, perhaps we should try *describing* teaching episodes we see, emphasizing not only how teachers currently perform but also what their teaching can become. The following questions may be pertinent:

1. What can this teacher do well in his or her teaching? What strengths do you recognize?
2. How do you describe the nature and degree of control this teacher has over what he or she can do?
3. What is your description of the fit this teacher achieves between what he or she does and the teacher's objectives?
4. What is your description, based on your experience with this teacher, of the teacher's ability to learn from work in the classroom so that he or she may have special competence in helping with an aspect of curriculum development?

If you are in a position to do so, study the work of a teacher in these terms as a means of determining the particular strengths of the teacher and the teacher's probable potential for helping to improve the curriculum and instruction in your school.

Strategy 5: School Reorganization

The assumption has been widely made in recent years that the curriculum can be improved to a marked degree by reorganizing the school. Reorganizing a school can affect its personnel, its buildings, its facilities and materials, and its entire way of operating. For some time, educational planners outside local school systems have been asking, "What will happen if pupils' and teachers' time is used differently because the school has been reorganized? What will occur if teachers have altered responsibilities and novel kinds of help? What about changing the basic organizational structures within which people work?"

Reorganizing the school requires making changes in factors like the duration of time teachers spend with given groups of pupils, kinds and sizes of instructional groups, teaching by individuals versus teaching in teams, amount of aid by paraprofessionals and other persons on the "career ladder," and close grading versus nongrading of pupils. Some of the means that have already been used to create varied effects through reorganization are team teaching, teacher aides, large- and small-group instruction, nongraded elementary and secondary schools, and departmentalized elementary schools.

Some of the ways leaders may propose to reorganize their schools are specified below.

Team teaching has now been accepted as a fundamentally sound idea. Implementing it has proved to be the real problem. Committed teachers, appropriate space, and the necessary facilities are all requisites. Team teaching permits pupils to gather information in large groups, to explore meaning in small groups, and to pursue their individual interests. To make team teaching work, the people involved must believe in the importance of individualization, be willing to work together and to plan extensively, and cherish flexibility and creativity.

The present is a time of increased *differentiated staffing*. At first, aides in the classroom tended to perform routine chores for teachers and pupils. Currently, the "career ladder" has on its levels paraprofessionals, cadet teachers, teachers in charge of research, and teachers in charge of curriculum development. Both educators and the lay public are at least partially convinced that staff differentiation can increase efficiency in classrooms. However, the roles of all interrelated personnel need further defining, standards need to be established for choosing personnel within categories, and improved programs for preparing categories of personnel must be established.

In a limited sense, *nongrading* is as old as the one-room school. Modern nongrading is intended to remove the labeling that has accompanied assigning pupils to grades, and to permit children to achieve mastery of subject matter before they move to another level in the educational hierarchy. Nongrading is meant to enhance our recognition of children as individuals and thus to improve their self-concept. Naturally, effective nongrading requires committed, skilled teachers who realize that the individual child has such varied potential in performing the different tasks the school sets before him or her that "grading" each individual becomes a practical impossibility.

The *middle school*, originally designed in many communities as an expedient for accommodating a rapidly increasing school population, is beginning to have its own purposes and programs. A search is being made for relevant content, with the thought that the middle school can, without due care, go the way of the junior high school by becoming a miniature high school. Presumably, the middle school, if it provides appropriate experiences for children, can meet the needs of earlier developing adolescents, whose physical maturation and peer interaction patterns are those formerly associated with pupils higher on the age scale. Programs emphasizing individualization, varied group activities, inquiry, helpful guidance, and subject matter that permits pupil action give promise of helping the middle school succeed.

Flexible scheduling permits a loosening of school organization so that pupils can use their time in more varied ways. Dividing the school day into more blocks of time and altering time allocations assigned to given school experiences are means of increasing flexibility.

Open space schooling permits pupils to have varied experiences throughout the school building and beyond.

New building designs depart from the traditional by providing areas and rooms for activities constituting additions to the curriculum. At best, the new designs are created specifically to accommodate new and carefully planned reorganizations of the curriculum.

New learning facilities and materials, ranging from recorders to computers, make implementation of curriculum ideas easier. The general learning center occupies a crucial place in schools where the newer facilities and materials are prized.

These innovations are only examples of means for reorganizing schools as institutions. Prospects for improving pupils' learning within reorganized schools seem to depend on a significant condition: If teachers are given more time away from the routine duties or away from duties they lack competence to perform, they should spend this time productively in performing professional tasks. These tasks might include becoming better acquainted with individual pupils, working closely and more insightfully with alienated or disadvantaged learners, and helping pupils improve the quality of their thinking and the clarity of their values. A great danger in focusing on reorganization of schools is that it may become equated with curriculum improvement. The two may or may not be the same in any given situation. Much depends, after all, on how profitably pupils and teachers spend their time *within* the reorganized institution with its new arrangements. Where these considerations are taken into account, reorganizing schools as workplaces seems to increase the fruitfulness of staff development activities and the general effectiveness of teaching and learning.[41]

ACTIVITY 11-9
An Investigation of Local Trends and Tendencies in
Reorganization

Note the numerous ways of reorganizing schools that have been mentioned above. Learn what is being done under the heading of reorganization in a school or school system you know well. What advantages and what deficiencies do you see in the plans for reorganization that are now in operation and that are projected? Compare your findings with those of other investigators.

SITUATION 11-5
Improve Curriculum Design or Change the Organization
of the School?

The superintendent and the principals of the Bellevue Public Schools had spent nearly a year studying plans for altering the allocation and use of pupils' and teachers' time.

In the process, they had considered core-type programs, plans for team teaching, the employment of teacher aides, and part-time use of programmed learning. It was time now to decide what should be done both to improve the curriculum and to impress the community. Sometimes the latter objective seemed to take precedence over the former. At a crucial meeting, Principal Anna Jones said: "We can talk about improving the organization of the curriculum, or about improving the organization of the school, but the two actions are not necessarily the same. Manipulating external things is often popular and sometimes easy; improving the experiences of children may be difficult and even unpopular. I hope we're concerned about experiences and that we'll ignore gadgetry and moving people around."

To what extent do you agree with Principal Jones's point of view? Suppose you made organizational changes in the school itself. How could you tell whether these changes had improved the quality of children's learning experiences? Be specific as to the change or changes you have in mind and as to methods of determining their effect.

Strategy 6: Educational Experimentation and Research

Educational experimentation is an important means of moving educational practice out on the frontier. It is a medium for trying new content and procedures and for testing ideas in action. It does not, in the manner of research, provide definitive data on which one can rely, but it does offer many cues to improved practice.

Research, on the other hand, is systematic inquiry that helps solve instructional problems. It consists of conjecturing intelligently about steps to be taken in solving a given problem, taking one or more actions in line with the conjecture, and then observing whether the actions have brought the results that were predicted or anticipated in the conjecture.

Research comes less naturally to teachers than experimentation. So little research has been conducted in U.S. classrooms that data about even the most important facets of education—the learning process, the learners, and methods of teaching—are fragmentary. Occasionally teachers are involved cooperatively in broad-scale research in the teaching of reading, spelling, and other school subjects. In the past, this research has been sponsored by the university groups and by individual professors, or else by research bureaus in the larger school systems. Actually, the quantity of well-directed research involving classroom teachers has been small.

Though few teachers have had opportunities to engage in formal research, they do experiment informally. At a low level of experimentation they often move pupils from seat to seat to quell disruptive behavior. The teacher who wishes to be more certain of what is happening when he or she creates change uses procedures of operational research, or *action research* as it is sometimes called. *Action research* has been defined by Corey and others as research conducted "in the heat of combat." It has been called by others controlled experimentation by means of which practitioners study their problems to guide and correct their decisions and actions. The elements of the overall action research design are

1. Identification of a problem area about which an individual or a group feels enough concern to take action
2. Selection of a specific problem and formulation of an "educated guess" (hypothesis or prediction) that states a goal and a way of reaching it
3. Careful taking of action, recording of action, and collection of evidence to determine the degree to which the goal has been reached
4. Drawing conclusions or making generalizations from the evidence as to the worth of the actions in reaching the desired goal
5. Continuous retesting of the generalizations in practical school situations.[42]

Consider an example of the use of this process.

EXAMPLE

A teacher became disturbed about the disinterest and poor performance of her eighth-grade pupils in written composition. She made the hypothesis that if writing were more closely related to the real-life experiences of children, both the children's interest in writing and the quality of their writing would improve. She learned from her pupils by interview, by a specially prepared inventory form, and by observation what they thought of their present composition projects. She also analyzed, from the viewpoint of fluency of expression and technical quality, two or three samples of each pupil's written work. She then arranged excursions to an airport, a construction project, and the United Nations center in New York. Subsequently, she encouraged the children to write about one or more of these excursions, inquired by the methods indicated above about their interest in describing the excursions, and analyzed the new compositions for fluency and technique. The evidence showed improvement in both interest and performance, with interest showing more improvement than performance. The teacher generalized that a writing project originating in real-life experience resulted, at least for her group of pupils, in improved interest and performance in writing. She realized that this was a tentative conclusion that merited additional testing in her own and other classroom situations.

The procedures in research or experimentation of this kind have been attacked as lacking the tightness and neatness of more careful research, but they may be defended as providing the classroom teacher with some evidence on which to base decisions. Perhaps the greatest handicap to performing action research is a lack of the understanding and skill required—an experimental outlook, understanding of the research process, and skill in formulating testable hypotheses. In the immediate environment the leader-researcher should have a supportive administrative staff, favorable community climate, adequate resources, and open lines of communication. The classroom teacher should become familiar with at least the better-known references concerning research—*Encyclopedia of Educational Research; Review of Educational Research; Education Index*, which does for education what *Readers' Guide to Periodical Literature* does for general literature; *Bibliography of Research Studies in Education*; compilations of research studies by Phi Delta Kappa, an honorary fraternity-sorority in education; and the ERIC materials.

The problems that research and experimentation help to solve usually come from one or more of the following sources: the teacher's own feeling of need, criticisms by lay people of the program of the school, and evidence of shortcomings revealed by evaluation. The teacher who feels dissatisfaction with conditions as they are is ready—psychologically at least—to undertake reasoned inquiry.

The teacher's self-evaluation of his or her own work offers one of the most promising ways of improving schools. Teachers need help in studying the differences between the nature of their intent and the outcomes they are achieving. Their objectives may need changing or amending; their methods may be faulty. To know that such circumstances exist, teachers need to observe carefully and to record data carefully.

Attention has been directed recently to a way to identify problems that need further study—the Quality Circle idea created by Japanese industrialists to improve the postwar output of their industries. The Quality Circle consists of ten to fifteen volunteers who meet weekly for one hour to identify problems that block high-quality work and to discover sources of information about them. A Circle in the school or the school system could prove useful also in formulating hypotheses leading to further inquiry and eventual problem solution.[43]

Research and experimentation can open the door to curriculum improvement. They are useful to the extent to which the evidence they turn up is used to advance improvement. Much depends, then, on the willingness of school personnel to employ data for functional purposes in the improvement process.

SITUATION 11-6
A Guide to Research by Classroom Teachers

John B. Barnes, writing in *Educational Research for Classroom Teachers*, suggests nine questions to be asked by school leaders before they encourage teachers to undertake projects in research and experimentation:

1. Does the school problem which you have in mind definitely limit the operation of your school or decrease the value of your educational program?
2. Can your educational program be improved by concerted study, reflection, and research on this problem?
3. Are the various school publics—students, teachers, school board members, parents, and general public—aware of this educational problem?
4. Have teachers and parents discussed the problem and failed to solve it?
5. Has the school board discussed this problem at a regular board meeting?
6. Is this educational problem one that seems perennially to cause concern?
7. Have you carefully identified, described, and analyzed the problem?
8. Do you see its parts, its ramifications, its possible causes?
9. Can you list on paper the effect which this school problem has on the educational program?[44]

Which of these questions seem most important in the evaluation, research, and experimentation projects you have in mind?

What are these projects? Make a written plan for conducting the evaluation, research, or experimentation in one of the projects.

IMPLEMENTING THE STRATEGIES

Leaders need to act specifically and precisely in implementing the six strategies that have been discussed. What they do necessarily conforms to the powers and constraints that go with their positions. Among the prominent status leaders with particular assignments of duty are systemwide curriculum directors or coordinators, principals of schools, and local school coordinators and chairpersons. Other status leaders, such as superintendents and supervisors, have particular assignments also, but most of the responsibility for overseeing curriculum planning and implementation falls to the three kinds of functionaries whose cases can be used as prototypes.

Some general leadership tasks are, however, distributed among numbers of status leaders and other persons:

Task 1: To help the people of the school community define their educational goals and objectives. In the early days of activity for curriculum improvement, defining goals and objectives was a frequent first step. Because many school systems did not get beyond this step, goal definition fell into some disrepute. The attention of curriculum workers turned to the problem census, the isolated experiment, the demonstration project, and other steps as a means of starting improvement. The result has been an absence of purpose-centered education and an eventual realization in some quarters that without vision the people in schools, as elsewhere, perish. When they fail to set goals and objectives, curriculum workers do not know what educational values they stand for, where they are going, or how to evaluate what they have accomplished. Definition of goals, then, is a fundamental task in curriculum improvement; this task is to be shared with laypersons.

Task 2:   To facilitate the teaching-learning process; to develop greater effectiveness in teaching.   Task 2, which formerly resided chiefly in the central offices of school systems, now belongs more and more in individual schools under the status leadership of building principals. It is accomplished by whatever means the staff decides to emphasize from year to year—programs of supervision, the newer studies of subject matter, projects in inservice education and staff development, experimentation and research, testing programs, and curriculum planning activities of many kinds. We are in danger of seeing this task, in its full meaning, obscured by easy panaceas and nostrums, the use of which impedes serious study of teaching and learning and supervisory assistance to individual teachers.

Task 3:   To build a productive organizational unit.   The importance of building organizational structure should be self-evident. An appropriate organizational unit has as its essentials cooperative planning and group deliberation. It releases people to examine their own and one another's roles, and to decide calmly who has the power and qualifications to assume particular responsibilities. In addition, this organizational unit keeps the channels of communication clear and arranges for finding out how well pupils are attaining the goals set for them and for the schools.

Task 4:   To create a climate for growth and emergence of leadership.   Much of the previous discussion has stressed the importance of freeing teachers and other personnel to express themselves and to ask for help. In addition, task 4 highlights the importance of providing opportunities for staff members to accept and discharge various leadership responsibilities. It calls for emergent leaders to enrich the work of the school by their contributions and to free status leaders for assignments they could not undertake without help from emergent leaders. For heavy responsibilities, teachers who emerge as leaders need released time. However, when problems of the school are seen as *our* (the whole staff's) problems rather than *his* or *her* (the administrator's) problems, teachers are more willing to share freely in the minute tasks of planning and operating the instructional program.

Task 5:   To provide adequate resources for effective teaching.

Teachers have more resources at their disposal than they realize. Some are personnel in the school and the community. Others are material in nature—homemade, commercially produced, or borrowed. Leadership must keep alert to lapses in the utilization of presently available resources and also must search continually for new resources that make teaching lively and practical.[45]

These tasks are broad and general enough to fit any situation, and they are shared by many persons. As narrower leadership tasks are talked about, they are seen to belong to specific persons who have strong leadership roles. One of the common expectations concerning democratic leaders is that, although they should share many responsibilities with others, certain responsibilities should be affixed to them as individuals of special competence and with special license to act.

Accordingly, the whole range of responsibilities divides into three categories. Some responsibilities for curriculum planning are shared freely by all who have any stake in the planning. Others are shared cooperatively by status leaders and certain selected or representative staff members, as in curriculum steering committees. Still other responsibilities belong strictly to status leaders who bear such titles as superintendent, assistant superintendent in charge of instruction, director of instruction, curriculum coordinator, or some other title that suggests comprehensive curriculum leadership; and to other leaders with narrower but more concentrated responsibilities—principals, special subject supervisors, coordinators who bear aegis over a portion of the instructional program, and department heads in secondary schools.

What Curriculum Leaders with Systemwide Assignments Do

The general leadership of curriculum programs falls to persons in the central offices of school systems who bear such titles as assistant superintendent in charge of curriculum and instruction, director of curriculum, director of instruction, and curriculum coordinator. Inasmuch as they are often regarded as surrogates for the superintendent of schools, these persons usually do in the area of curriculum and instruction what the superintendent would presumably do if he or she had the necessary time, inclination, and expertise. Many times they make their positions what they want them to be, subject to the will of one or more higher administrative officers. They have varying degrees of authority, so that their positions range from powerful line assignments to weak staff or advisory posts. At any rate, they must share many of their responsibilities with other personnel. Which responsibilities are shared and which are retained by general curriculum leaders depends so much on organizational patterns in school systems and the personal preferences of the leaders themselves that one cannot distinguish, by general rules, between responsibilities that should be shared and responsibilities that should be retained. No one but the curriculum leader with systemwide responsibilities is likely, however, to accept leadership in achieving curriculum balance, in seeking the elimination of contradictions in the total curriculum, in trying to improve curriculum design and organization, in urging continual evaluation, in serving as a curriculum change specialist, and in retaining a total view of all curriculum matters.

The preceding list of large responsibilities does not, of course, represent what most curriculum leaders do day by day. They are found more often meeting with supervisors and faculty groups about other matters, serving as consultants to principals and teachers, helping make policies of all sorts, arranging for exhibits and demonstrations, representing the superintendent at ceremonial functions, working with community groups, and helping interview candidates for positions. Important as the latter tasks may be, they do not tax the abilities of most curriculum leaders. It is easy, therefore, for the superintendent to send his or her front-line curriculum leader to do work that is less than worthy of the leader's abilities while important curriculum tasks are left untouched.

Using the strategies discussed earlier in this chapter, the leader with systemwide responsibilities finds much to do in guiding master planning, in helping coordinate local planning, in establishing and presiding over programs of inservice education and staff development, in supervising the supervisors, in helping plan school reorganization, and in giving general direction to research activities. International scholars in the curriculum field honor systemwide leaders for their demonstrated abilities in developing ideas, in alerting their school systems to needs and trends, and in making accurate predictions of things to come. In brief, a well-prepared generalist in curriculum study not only has a promising career ahead but also occupies the role of prime curriculum expert in his or her community.

SITUATION 11-7
The Responsibilities of a New Curriculum Leader

The president of the Wasson Board of Education turned to Superintendent Rogers at the conclusion of the Board's regular monthly meeting. "What are your specifications for the new position of director of instruction?" she asked.

Rogers was caught flat-footed. "We haven't really determined the specifications," he had to admit.

"Don't you think you ought to—right away?" the president asked.

Early the next morning, Rogers assembled several of his aides to help him establish a set of responsibilities for the directorship. Within an hour or two they had the basic responsibilities listed to their satisfaction. The trouble came in trying to assign approximate percentages of the director's time to the responsibilities. "Maybe we can't do it very accurately," Superintendent Rogers had said, "but I'd like to see each of you put on paper a percentage figure to indicate the amount of time the director should spend on each responsibility." When the proposed allocations of time had been assembled by the superintendent's secretary, they looked like this:

	TIME ALLOCATIONS (IN PERCENT)				
ACTIVITIES	AIDE #1	AIDE #2	AIDE #3	AIDE #4	AIDE #5
1. Attending curriculum meetings	30	20	0	50	10
2. Visiting individual classrooms	10	2	40	8	60
3. Conferring with individual teachers	10	15	10	10	2
4. Employing new teachers	20	10	30	5	10
5. Attending teachers' social functions	3	2	0	10	0
6. Reviewing lesson plans	2	5	15	0	10
7. Conducting meetings, workshops, and other inservice activities	25	45	2	15	3
8. Ordering and assembling materials and supplies for teachers	0	1	3	2	5

What do you think of the perception of the curriculum director's role that is evidently held by Rogers's aides?

If, as the new director of instruction, you felt obliged to accept the list of activities as constituting your basic responsibilities, how (abstractly) would you want to allocate your time among them? Tell why you would favor your plan of allocation.

What School Principals Do

The pivotal, firing-line position on the curriculum scene is often said to be the school principalship. Principals have the advantage of serving at a middle management level where they can make certain that proper attention is given to both goals and people. Principals who want to be influential in curriculum planning and implementation proceed by helping provide teachers with intrinsic rewards, by influencing teachers' beliefs about curriculum matters, and by making certain that teachers are involved in crucial decision making.[46] They can do a great deal to set new norms for their schools that are directed toward increased achievement by both teachers and pupils.[47] Principals who head high-achieving schools have been found to emphasize achievement, to identify instructional strategies, to keep the school environment orderly, and to show a real interest in evaluating pupil progress.[48] Thus their schools have what has been called a "positive instructional atmosphere."[49]

The role of principals as improvers of teaching and learning is of such classic, historic importance that it has, until recent years, remained unquestioned. Lately some critics have been raising their voices against the principalship as an instructional leadership position. They would relegate it to institutional management. The justification for perpetuating the principalship as a significant position in the administrative hierarchy, however, depends on continuing to place the principalship at the center of the instructional leadership system and on improving the education of both new and experienced principals.

Principals who are truly effective leaders in curriculum planning know the bases that support curriculum decisions. They understand curriculum design, and they function well as organizers and coordinators. They know how people are helped to change their behavior and what they themselves can do to encourage worthwhile change in others. As persons who keep activities in perspective and balance, they lead people both within their schools and in their communities. They are close to the needs and concerns of teachers and pupils, and they are able to translate ideals into day-to-day realities. In short, they epitomize the best in leadership by manifesting executive ability and maintaining desirable human relations. Significantly, they accomplish their work in the most important place in the school system—the individual school. They adapt master plans to fit their schools, guide and coordinate local planning, tailor inservice education and staff development to the needs of their own teachers, supervise teaching, suggest and implement evaluation plans, and help with experimentation and research.

ACTIVITY 11-10
What the Best Principals Do

Identify by professional reputation two or three principals who are believed to have done a great deal to help improve the curricula of their schools. Inquire as deeply as you can into the reasons for their reputations. Do this by asking persons who know them professionally what the principals have done to merit recognition as curriculum improvers. Then talk with the principals directly about their accomplishments.

What do you conclude that these principals have done to assist with curriculum planning?

As you compare your findings with those of classmates who have inquired about other principals, what do you discover that the best principals do to make curriculum improvement possible and effective?

What Local School Coordinators and Chairpersons Do

Coordinators in elementary and secondary schools and department or division chairpersons in secondary schools are closest to the sites at which curriculum is implemented. They are close to curriculum needs as expressed by teachers and others in immediate learning environments. Thus their input is essential to careful, thorough curriculum planning.

Local coordinators and chairpersons need to know all they can about the details of curriculum. They should know the subject matter both within the range of their supervisory responsibility and beyond. In addition, they should make themselves as expert as possible in the process of curriculum change, in techniques of teaching varied kinds of learning content, in organizing instruction, and in dealing with great varieties of instructional problems. No one in the local school environment should be expected to know more about available instructional materials, their selection, and their use. Increasingly the emphasis in school operation has fallen on coordination. Therefore coordinators and chairpersons are relied on heavily for assisting people and interrelating subject matter to the end of coordinating elements of the curriculum.

Characteristically, local coordinators and chairpersons assume leadership in the following areas of responsibility:

1. Setting instructional goals pertinent to the work of their instructional units
2. Designing units of instruction
3. Adapting to local use selected curriculum plans devised elsewhere
4. Developing new curriculum proposals and plans for their departments and divisions
5. Evaluating and selecting learning materials
6. Producing new learning materials specific to local needs
7. Evaluating the long-term effectiveness of learning materials
8. Reassessing goals and objectives
9. Preparing change strategies.[50]

From the weekly log of a coordinator serving two elementary schools within a given school district, the following tasks relative to curriculum matters have been excerpted from the total range of tasks performed by the coordinator during a week in April: recommended textbooks for adoption following a series of staff meetings on textbook needs; sent away for sample curriculum materials in elementary school science; conferred with other coordinators about curriculum proposals affecting the work of all of them; and advised a school librarian about purchases of children's books and other materials. Although not all the weeks in a school year are filled with so many significant tasks, this example highlights some of the major responsibilities that fall to coordinators.

Most coordinators and chairpersons participate in implementing at least four of the six leadership strategies discussed previously.

SITUATION 11-8
How Far Does Competency in Leadership Extend?

When the Blankton Valley Schools employed Dana Jenkins as general supervisor, they found the best supervisor in the whole state. Dana seemed to have all the personal qualities, skills, and understandings anyone could ask for in an instructional leader. Members of the Board of Education were impressed with her knowledge of curriculum problems, as was Superintendent Roush. However, Mr. Roush had always had one reservation about Dana. "How," he'd asked several people, "can someone know about instruction from kindergarten all the way through the twelfth grade?"

Superintendent Roush felt that his reservation had been a wise one when the "Adams case" developed at the high school. Miss Adams, a second-year teacher, was, in the words of the high school principal, "doing only fairly well." The principal asked Dana to visit Miss Adams's French classes, and she did so on three separate occasions. Dana concluded that Miss Adams was not doing at all well. Miss Adams was almost sadistic in her treatment of the pupils, ridiculing and embarrassing them and assigning them unreasonable loads of work. In addition, she was using antiquated and questionable methods of teaching. Accordingly, Dana wrote an adverse report and conferred with Miss Adams and the principal about it.

Miss Adams, who was the daughter of the town's most influential and wealthy merchant, prided herself on her knowledge of French. Having been in France on nine separate occasions and having secured a master's degree in the teaching of French, she knew that she was, technically, an excellent French teacher. When she faced Dana in the presence of the principal and the superintendent and later in a Board of Education dismissal hearing, which was attended by her father's two lawyers, Dana had to admit that she knew no French. The superintendent, the board members, and nearly everyone else in the Board of Education room began to question Dana's competency to judge Miss Adams's teaching.

What should Dana have said to the Blankton Valley Board of Education about her qualifications for judging Miss Adams's work? What rather typical lay points of view about teaching and learning was she encountering?

To make a well-rounded estimate of Miss Adams's performance in the classroom, what help should Dana have had? Where might she have secured this help?

What, apparently, was Superintendent Roush's viewpoint about the qualifications a curriculum leader should have? What, then, was probably his view of curriculum leadership?

SUMMARY

Curriculum leadership, like leadership generally, has in it elements of mystery. We know, however, that the words *principle, commitment, cooperation,* and *skill* figure prominently in any definition of curriculum leadership. Three theories of leadership have been formulated, highlighting, respectively, leader traits, group leadership, and leadership according to specific situations, but no one of them taken alone explains just what curriculum leadership is. Obviously, however, several factors do influence the quality of curriculum leaders' work. They include, for instance, the leaders' roles, styles, and behaviors, and also the outside factor of people's perception of leaders and leadership.

A half-dozen strategies for improving the curriculum have become the obligation and responsibility of curriculum leaders. They are master planning, coordinated local planning, inservice education and staff development, planned programs of supervision, school reorganization, and educational experimentation and research. Within these strategies, three categories of personnel find their major leadership functions: leaders with systemwide assignments, principals of schools, and local coordinators and chairpersons.

ENDNOTES

1. Association for Supervision and Curriculum Development, *Leadership for Improving Instruction,* 1960 Yearbook (Washington, D.C.: The Association, 1960), p. 27.

2. Ibid.

3. Gordon N. Mackenzie and Stephen M. Corey, *Instructional Leadership* (New York: Bureau of Publications, Teachers College, 1954), pp. 23–30.

4. Karolyn J. Snyder, "Instructional Leadership for Productive Schools," *Educational Leadership* 40, no. 5 (February 1983): 32–37.

5. See James O'Hanlon, "Theory Z in School Administration?" *Educational Leadership* 40, no. 5 (February 1983): 16–18.

6. Some of the most helpful and interesting references concerning the traits theory are as follows: Graham B. Bell and Harry E. Hall, Jr., "The Relationship Between Leadership and Empathy," *Journal of Abnormal and Social Psychology* 49 (January 1954); Raymond B. Cattell and Glen F. Stice, *The Psychodynamics of Small Groups* (Urbana: University of Illinois, 1953); and F. Loyal Greer, Eugene H. Galanter, and Peter G. Nordlie, "Interpersonal Knowledge and Group Effectiveness," *Journal of Abnormal and Social Psychology* 49 (July 1954). Also see William E. Martin, Neal Gross, and John G. Darley, "Studies of Group Behavior: Leaders, Followers, and Isolates in Small Organized Groups," *Journal of Abnormal and Social Psychology* 41, no. 4 (October 1952): 842; Launor F. Carter, "Some Research on Leadership in Small Groups," in Harold Guetzkow, ed., *Groups,*

Leadership and Men (Pittsburgh: Carnegie Press, 1951), p. 151; and Fillmore H. Sanford, "Leadership Identification and Acceptance," in Guetzkow, *Groups, Leadership and Men*, p. 174.

7. Kimball Wiles, "Human Relations Approach to Supervision," *Baltimore Bulletin of Education* 37, no. 1 (November 1959): 19. (Address to Baltimore supervisors.)

8. Valued references concerning group theory include John K. Hemphill, *Situational Factors in Leadership* (Columbus, Ohio: Bureau of Educational Research, Ohio State University, 1949); Gordon Lippitt and Warren H. Schmidt, *My Group and I* (Washington, D.C.: Arthur C. Croft, 1952); and Muzafer Sherif and M. O. Wilson, eds., *Group Relations at the Crossroads* (New York: Harper & Row, 1953).

9. Cecil A. Gibb, "Leadership," in Gardner Lindzey, ed., *Handbook of Social Psychology* (Cambridge, Mass.: Addison-Wesley, 1954), vol. 2, p. 901.

10. Philip E. Gates, Kenneth H. Blanchard, and Paul Hersey, "Diagnosing Educational Leadership Problems: A Situational Approach," *Educational Leadership* 33, no. 5 (February 1976): 348–54.

11. Murray G. Ross and Charles E. Hendry, *New Understandings of Leadership* (New York: Association Press, 1957), p. 36.

12. See Gerald R. Firth, "Theories of Leadership: Where Do We Stand?" *Educational Leadership* 33, no. 5 (February 1976): 327–31.

13. Fred E. Fiedler, "The Effects of Leadership Training and Experience: A Contingency Model Interpretation," *Administrative Science Quarterly* 17, no. 4 (December 1972): 453–70.

14. Article after article and book after book support this statement. See, for example, James M. Lipham and James A. Hoeh, Jr., *The Principalship: Foundations and Functions* (New York: Harper & Row, 1974), pp. 134–47, and E. G. Bogue and Robert L. Saunders, *The Educational Manager: Artist and Practitioner* (Worthington, Ohio: Charles A. Jones Publishing Company, 1971), pp. 190–205.

15. From descriptions proposed by practitioners in the author's classes.

16. See Fred E. Fiedler, *A Theory of Leadership Effectiveness* (New York: McGraw-Hill, 1967).

17. Gene Hall et al., "Effects of Three Principal Styles on School Improvement," *Educational Leadership* 41, no. 5 (February 1984): 22–29.

18. Daniel W. Kunz and Wayne K. Hoy, "Leadership Style of Principals and the Professional Zone of Acceptance of Teachers," *Educational Administration Quarterly* 12, no. 3 (Fall 1976): 49–64.

19. Ibid.

20. Donald L. Piper, "Decisionmaking: Decisions Made by Individuals vs. Those Made by Group Consensus or Group Participation," *Educational Administration Quarterly* 10, no. 2 (Spring 1974): 82–95.

21. Andrew W. Halpin, *Theory and Research in Administration* (New York: Macmillan, 1966), pp. 88, 89.

22. Ronald C. Doll, *Leadership to Improve Schools* (Worthington, Ohio: Charles A. Jones, 1972), pp. 40–54.

23. Halpin, *Theory and Research*, pp. 88, 89.

24. From an inspection of literature in industrial relations.

25. Roald F. Campbell and Russell T. Gregg, *Administrative Behavior in Education* (New York: Harper & Row, 1957), p. 280.

26. Ibid.

27. William F. Whyte, *Leadership and Group Participation*, Bulletin No. 24 (Ithaca: New York State School of Industrial and Labor Relations, Cornell University, May 1953), p. 41.

28. Hollis L. Caswell et al., *Curriculum Improvement in Public School Systems* (New York: Bureau of Publications, Teachers College, 1950), pp. 81, 82.

29. See the treatment of the first two viewpoints by Abraham Zaleznik in *Human Dimensions of Leadership* (New York: Harper & Row, 1966). Zaleznik favors the Freudian view, which is the second viewpoint.

30. Walter St. John, "Effective Planning, Delegating, and Priority Setting," *Bulletin of the National Association of Secondary School Principals* 66, no. 451 (February 1982): 16–24.

31. Louis J. Rubin, ed., *Improving In-service Education: Proposals and Procedures for Change* (Boston: Allyn and Bacon, 1971), p. 276.

32. See, for example, Phi Delta Kappa, *Practical Applications of Research* 5, no. 3 (March 1983): 1–4; Peter A. Williamson and Julia A. Elfman, "A Commonsense Approach to Teacher Inservice Training," *Phi Delta Kappan* 63, no. 6 (February 1982): 401; and National Association of Secondary School Principals, *Tips for Principals* (October 1982): 1.

33. Ronald C. Doll, *Supervision for Staff Development: Ideas and Application* (Newton, Mass: Allyn and Bacon, 1983), pp. 195–99. With the permission of the publisher.

34. Earl C. Kelley, *The Workshop Way of Learning* (New York: Harper & Row, 1951), p. 137. Kelley's book is a classic in its field.

35. Doll, *Supervision for Staff Development*, pp. 81–84. See also National Association of Secondary School Principals, "How to Be a Better Supervisor," *Tips for Principals* (February 1983).

36. Kathryn V. Feyereisen, A. John Fiorino, and Arlene T. Nowak, *Supervision and Curriculum Renewal: A Systems Approach* (New York: Appleton-Century-Crofts, 1970).

37. See, for example, Morris L. Cogan, *Clinical Supervision* (Boston: Houghton Mifflin, 1973); and Robert Goldhammer, *Clinical Supervision: Special Methods for the Supervision of Teachers* (New York: Holt, Rinehart and Winston, 1969).

38. See Thomas J. Sergiovanni and Robert J. Starratt, *Supervision: Human Perspectives*, 2nd ed. (New York: McGraw-Hill, 1979).

39. Ibid.

40. Doll, *Supervision for Staff Development*, passim.

41. Judith Warren Little, "The Power of Organizational Setting: School Norms and Staff Development" (Paper presented at the annual meeting of the American Educational Research Association, Los Angeles, April 1981).

42. Stephen M. Corey, *Action Research to Improve School Practices* (New York: Teachers College Press, 1953), pp. 40, 41.

43. Thomas O'Neill Dunne and Rick Maurer, "Improving Your School Through Quality Circles," *Bulletin of the National Association of Secondary School Principals* 66, no. 457 (November 1982), 87–90. More detailed information is available from the American Society for Quality Control, 161 West Wisconsin Avenue, Milwaukee, Wisconsin 53203.

44. John B. Barnes, *Educational Research for Classroom Teachers* (New York: G. P. Putnam's, 1960), p. 211.

45. For further discussion of these tasks, see Association for Supervision and Curriculum Development, *Leadership for Improving Instruction*, 1960 Yearbook (Washington, D.C.: The Association, 1960); see also Doll, *Leadership to Improve Schools*, pp. 130–328.

46. See John A. Ross, "Strategies for Curriculum Leadership," *The Australian Administrator* 2, no. 5 (October 1981).

47. See ERIC Clearinghouse on Educational Management, *Research Action Brief*, no. 23 (February 1984).

48. James Sweeney, "Research Synthesis on Effective School Leadership," *Educational Leadership* 39, no. 5 (February 1982): 346–52.

49. D. Hugh Ferguson, "The Principal as Instructional Leader," *Contemporary Education* 52, no. 3 (Spring 1981), 163–66.

50. See Thomas J. Sergiovanni, *Handbook for Effective Department Leadership: Concepts and Practices in Today's Secondary Schools* (Boston: Allyn and Bacon, 1977), pp. 283–320. See also the second edition of this handbook dated 1984.

SELECTED BIBLIOGRAPHY

Campbell, Roald F., and Gregg, Russell T. *Administrative Behavior in Education.* New York: Harper & Row, 1957.

Carlson, Evelyn F., ed. *Role of Supervisor and Curriculum Director in a Climate of Change.* 1965 Yearbook, Association for Supervision and Curriculum Development. Washington, D.C.: The Association, 1965.

Cogan, Morris L. *Clinical Supervision.* Boston: Houghton Mifflin, 1973.

Combs, Arthur W., et al. *Helping Relationships: Basic Concepts for the Helping Professions.* 2nd ed. Boston: Allyn and Bacon, 1978.

Corey, Stephen M. *Action Research to Improve School Practices.* New York: Bureau of Publications, Teachers College, 1953.

Cunningham, Luvern L., and Gephart, William J. *Leadership: The Science and the Art Today.* Twelfth Annual Phi Delta Kappa Symposium on Educational Research. Itasca, Ill.: Peacock, 1973.

Doll, Ronald C. *Leadership to Improve Schools.* Worthington, Ohio: Charles A. Jones, 1972.

———. *Supervision for Staff Development: Ideas and Application.* Newton, Mass.: Allyn and Bacon, 1983.

Granger, Robert L. *Educational Leadership: An Interdisciplinary Perspective.* Scranton, Penn.: Intext, 1971.

Griffiths, Daniel E., ed. *Behavioral Science and Educational Administration.* National Society for the Study of Education, Sixty-Third Yearbook, Part II. Chicago: University of Chicago Press, 1964.

Gross, Neal, and Herriott, Robert E. *Staff Leadership in Public Schools: A Sociological Inquiry.* New York: John Wiley, 1965.

Halpin, Andrew W. *Theory and Research in Administration.* New York: Macmillan, 1966.

Harris, Ben M. *Supervisory Behavior in Education*. 2nd ed. Englewood Cliffs, N.J.: Prentice-Hall, 1975.

Hass, Glen, ed. *Leadership for Improving Instruction*. 1960 Yearbook, Association for Supervision and Curriculum Development. Washington, D.C.: The Association, 1960.

Kelley, Earl C. *The Workshop Way of Learning*. New York: Harper & Row, 1951.

Ross, Murray G., and Hendry, Charles E. *New Understandings of Leadership*. New York: The Association Press, 1957.

Rubin, Louis J., ed. *Frontiers in School Leadership*. Chicago: Rand McNally, 1970.

————, ed. *Improving In-service Education: Proposals and Procedures for Change*. Boston: Allyn and Bacon, 1971.

Saylor, J. Galen, and Alexander, William M. *Planning Curriculum for Schools*. New York: Holt, Rinehart and Winston, 1974.

Schaffarzick, Jon, and Hampson, David. *Strategies for Curriculum Development*. Berkeley, Calif.: McCutchan, 1975.

Sergiovanni, Thomas J., and Starrett, Robert J. *Supervision: Human Perspectives*. New York: McGraw-Hill, 1979.

Spears, Harold, *Curriculum Planning through In-service Programs*. Englewood Cliffs, N.J.: Prentice-Hall, 1957.

Speiker, Charles A. *Curriculum Leaders: Improving Their Influence*. Washington, D.C.: Association for Supervision and Curriculum Development, 1976.

Unruh, Glenys G. *Responsive Curriculum Development: Theory and Action*. Berkeley, Calif.: McCutchan, 1975.

Wilson, L. Craig. *School Leadership Today: Strategies for the Educator*. Boston: Allyn and Bacon, 1978.

Zaleznik, Abraham. *Human Dilemmas of Leadership*. New York: Harper & Row, 1966.

Name Index

Anglin, Leo W., 355–356
Arends, Richard, 287
Armstrong, David G., 401–402
Atkinson, G., 241
Austin, David B., 433

Bagley, William C., 148
Baker, Robert L., 242
Barnard, Henry, 14
Barnes, John B., 465–466
Beane, James, 210
Bell, Terrell, 5, 168, 347
Bennis, Warren, 383
Bhola, H. S., 283
Bishop, Leslee J., 364
Bloom, Benjamin S., 60, 63, 65
Bossert, Phillip, 418
Bowers, John J., 227
Brickell, Henry M., 287
Briggs, Leslie J., 242
Brophy, Jere, 364–365
Broudy, Harry, 20, 126
Bruner, Jerome S., 60, 127, 144, 147, 148
Bryan, William Jennings, 186
Buser, Robert L., 377

Caswell, Hollis L., 437
Cawelti, Gordon, 165, 191

Cochran, David W., 184
Coffee, Hubert S., 275
Cogan, Morris L., 458–459
Combs, Arthur, 126, 136, 187, 273, 385–386
Conant, James B., 152–153, 380
Corey, Stephen, 426, 463
Cox, Pat, 361
Cox, Richard C., 235
Crandall, David, 364

Darrow, Clarence, 186
Davies, Don, 389
Davis, Diana J., 191
Dewey, John, 11, 16–17, 139–140, 145, 147, 338
Dugan, Therese, 355–356
Dunn, Kenneth, 66
Dunn, Rita, 66
Dyer, Henry S., 230

Elkind, David, 80
English, Fenwick, 230

Falzetta, John N., 208
Fenton, William D., 208
Feyereisen, Kathryn V., 458
Fiedler, Fred, 429–430
Findley, Dale, 317

479

Flanagan, John C., 60
Forsdale, Louis, 415
Foshay, Arthur W., 145–146, 211
French, Will, 335
Fries, Charles, 407
Froebel, Friedrich, 10
Fullagar, William A., 354

Gagné, Robert, 61, 351
Galanter, Eugene, 350
Gesell, Arnold, 41
Glass, Gene V., 242
Golden, William P., Jr., 275
Goldhammer, Robert, 458–459
Goodlad, John I., 163, 175, 191
Grobman, Arnold, 407
Grobman, Hulda, 235
Guba, E. G., 277
Gwynn, J. Minor, 459

Hall, Gene, 434
Hamm, Russell, 317
Havighurst, Robert, 42, 45, 54, 150
Heckman, Paul E., 287
Heller, Mary, 252, 339
Hemphill, John, 433, 434
Hendry, Charles E., 429
Herrick, Virgil, 50, 161, 201–203
Hilgard, Ernest R., 56–58
Hopkins, L. Thomas, 30–31, 200
Horton, Patricia, 208
Hough, Wendell, 280
House, Ernest R., 149, 411
Howe, Harold, 5
Hoy, Wayne K., 434–435
Humm, William L., 377
Hutchins, Robert, 177

Jackson, Philip W., 101
James, Robert, 164
James, William, 11
Jarvis, Howard, 91
Jenkins, David H., 276
Johnson, Mauritz, 148
Judd, Charles, 15

Kahn, Robert L., 383
Katz, Daniel, 383
Kelley, Earl C., 453
Kelly, P. J., 407
Kimbrough, Ralph, 373
King, Jean A., 220

Kiser, Luther, 378
Klein, M. Frances, 175, 191
Kroop, Robert, 363
Kunz, Daniel W., 434–435

Lasswell, Harold, 116, 396
Lewin, Kurt, 276
Lindvall, C. M., 235
Loar, Robert L., 367
Logan, Bayne, 354

Mackenzie, Gordon N., 7, 116, 426
Mann, Horace, 14
Marker, Gerald W., 406–407
Marland, Sidney P., 114
Massinton, Harry W., 349
McCloskey, Gordon, 396
McCutcheon, Gail, 191
McLuhan, Marshall, 406
McMurry, Charles, 148
McMurry, Frank, 148
Miel, Alice, 147–148, 158
Moore, Omar Khayyam, 129
Morin, Andre, 274
Mullen, David J., 317
Myers, Charles B., 406

Nocon, Jean K., 208
Nolte, M. Chester, 372
Nyquist, Ewald B., 377–378

Olson, Willard C., 42
Ondrejack, Lawrence J., 184
O'Reilly, Robert, 363
Orlosky, Donald, 285
Owens, Robert G., 276–277

Page, David P., 148
Parish, Ralph, 287
Parker, Francis, 15
Peelle, Howard, 350
Phenix, Philip H., 147, 408
Piaget, Jean, 45–46, 60, 144–145
Piper, Donald, 435
Plato, 148
Pogrow, Stanley, 351
Popham, W. James, 133
Prescott, Daniel, 42, 270
Provus, Malcolm, 237
Pulley, Jerry L., 399

Raths, Louis, 65, 111–113
Reid, William, 273
Roberts, Paul, 407
Rogers, Carl, 270, 408–409
Ross, Murray G., 429
Rousseau, Jean Jacques, 10
Rubin, Louis J., 451–452
Russell, Howard, 241

St. John, Walter, 445
Savage, William W., 295
Schaffarzick, Jon, 6, 236
Schutz, Richard E., 242
Shamos, Morris, 183
Shannon, Claude E., 397
Shannon, Thomas, 380
Shores, J. Harlan, 161
Shutes, Robert E., 401–402
Silvernail, Jean M., 191
Smith, B. Othanel, 161, 285
Smith, Henry Lee, 407
Smith, Louis, 241
Snyder, Karolyn, 426–427
Spencer, Herbert, 126, 148
Stake, Robert E., 237, 241
Stanley, William O., 161
Steele, Joe M., 149
Steller, Arthur, 103

Stratemeyer, Florence B., 153
Stufflebeam, Daniel L., 240
Sturges, A. W., 37
Symonds, Percival M., 77

Taba, Hilda, 66, 132, 159, 161
Thompson, Bruce, 220
Thompson, William A., 249
Thorndike, Edward L., 11, 15
Trusty, Leon, 208
Tyler, Robert W., 184–186, 194

Van Til, William, 166
Vertinsky, Patricia A., 349

Walberg, Herbert J., 149
Walker, Cheryl D., 207
Walker, Decker F., 236
Watson, Goodwin, 56–58
Weaver, Warren, 397
Wedemeyer, Dan J., 418
West, Jeff, 335
Whyte, William F., 436–437
Wiles, Kimball, 427–428
Witkin, B. R., 317
Wittrock, M. C., 240

Yauch, Wilbur A., 295

Subject Index

Ability grouping, 17
Academic Learning Time, 64
Academic press, 78
Academies, 14, 15, 21
Accountability, 94, 97, 362, 377, 382–384
  attempts to achieve, 385–387
  educators' views of, 384–385
  group, 387
Action learning, 98–99, 112, 165
Action research, 463–465
Activity curriculum, 286
Activity program, 17
Administrator Empathy Discrimination Index, 411
Administrators, in curriculum improvement, 368–370
Affective education, 10, 19, 91, 109, 112, 132, 136–137, 166, 209
Aims of education, 27–28, 193–196, 199, 403, 445
Allocated time, 64
American Federation of Teachers, 380–381
American values, 108–113
Analysis Package (ANAPAC), 237–240
Analytical thinking, 145
Apperception, 15, 60
Artificial intelligence, 349–350

Association for Supervision and Curriculum Development, 136, 185, 228–229, 252, 367, 404
Authority, versus freedom, 27, 29

Balance, 79, 80, 160–162, 469
Basic ideas and principles, 133
Basics, 4–5, 20, 95, 135
Behavioral objectives, 133–135, 185, 196–197, 335
Behaviorism, 60
Bilingual education, 99
Boards of education, 370–371
"Bonanza," 317
Booklets, 404–405, 445–446
Brain, 188
  development of, 69–70
Brainstorming, 332–333, 367
British Infant School, 286
Brochures, 404–405, 445–446
Building design, 462

Cardinal Principles of Secondary Education, 113
Care, importance of, 272–273
Career education, 108, 113–115, 154, 243–246, 405. See also Vocational education

CDPP (Context, Design, Process, and Product), 240–241
CEMREL, 241
Change
  administrator support of, 287–288
  driving forces for, 276
  in individuals, 269–275
  materials as medium for, 288
  media and agencies for, 287–290
  models of process, 283–284
  in organizations, 275–284
  practical applications, 283
  psychological resistance to, 88
  resistance forces and, 272
  restraining forces and, 276
  teacher involvement in, 288
Changes, in American society, 91–93
Children, characteristics and needs of, 43–45, 47, 53–54
CIPP (Context, Input, Process, and Product), 240–241
Classroom, as organizing center for learning, 79
CLER model, 283
Climate, 290
  and absence of pressure, 295
  and appropriate personnel, 292–294
  and attitudes of personnel, 291–292, 296
  and availability of resources, 294–295, 296–297
Cognitive objectives, 131
Colleges, and curriculum improvement, 379–380
Commission on Excellence in Education, 4–5
Communication
  backfire of, 399–400
  barriers to, 413–414
  breakdown of, 399
  communicatee, 397–398
  defined, 395
  feedback in, 398
  interference points, 399
  listening, 408–410
  via media, 400–408, 411
  nonverbal, 409–410
  organization for, 415–420
  via personal contact, 408–413
  problems with written materials, 405–406
  process of, 396
  research on, 398–400, 417–418

role playing, 410
in schools, 397–398
Community colleges, 102
Community school, 286
Compensatory education, 286
Competency-based education, 63, 96, 134–135, 198
Competency tests, 96, 165
Comprehensive School Improvement Program, 438
Computer-assisted instruction (CAI), 167–168, 347
Computer-managed instruction (CMI), 348–349
Computers, 347–352, 406
Concept development, 59
Concept learning, 61
Concepts, 133, 139, 157–158
Congruence, 268
Connectionism, 60
Conservation education, 286
Conservatism, 98
Consultants' packages, 405
Content, selection of, 135–141, 199–200
Contingency Theory of Leadership Effectiveness, 429–430, 434
Continuity, 79, 80, 158–159
Cooperative education, 222–223
Core curriculum, 285, 286
Core programs, 152–153
Correlation, 79, 80
Cost, of education, 3, 4
Cost-benefit analysis, 237–240, 250
Cost-effectiveness ratio, 239
Council for Basic Education, 98, 225
Courses of study, problems with, 402
Creationism, versus evolution, 186–187
Creative education, 285, 286
Criterion measures, 234
Criterion-referenced norms, 235
Criterion-referenced tests, 134, 252, 350
Cross-sectional approach, 41
Curriculum
  acknowledged, 7
  adult-organized, 10, 11
  analyzing concerns about, 337–338
  changes in, 12–21, 360–361. See also Curriculum improvement
  child-centered, 10, 11, 16, 34
  defined, 6–8
  effect of television on, 99

formal, 7, 8
hidden, 7, 8
historical foundations of, 3–26
influence of labor organizations on, 99
informal, 7, 8
metaphors for, 355–356
organizing center for, 3
philosophical foundations of, 26–39
planned, 7, 8
real, 310–311, 447
scope, 3, 4
stability, 3, 4
systems approach to, 211–214
trends in, 21
uniformity of, 3, 4
unplanned, 7
updating of, 286
Curriculum decisions
  criteria for, 253–257
  directions in, 76–78
  influence of American culture on, 87, 109–115
  influence of local community on, 87, 100–109
  politics of, 116–117
  psychological bases for, 41–86
  reform, 80–81
  relationship to improvement process, 265–266
  role of subject matter, 123–172
  school experiences, 78–80
  social and cultural influences on, 87–122
Curriculum design, 173, 312
  community input, 193
  definitions, 174
  examples of, 205–208
  versus instructional design, 174
  new, 208–214
  preplanning for, 192, 342–343
  versus reorganization, 462–463
  sources of ideas for, 175–182
  steps in, 192–205
  strategies for, 190–208
  Tylerian model for, 184–186
  types of, 198–199
Curriculum Document Assessment Instrument, 401–402
Curriculum evaluation, 203–205, 218–219
  in the classroom, 219–220, 224
  comprehensiveness, 226

continuity, 226
cooperative projects for, 223
criteria, 228–230
design of, 247–250
dimensions of, 227–236
formative, 203, 233, 234
illuminative, 248
integration of findings, 226–227
orientation of goals, 225–226
Pittsburgh Evaluation Model, 236–237
planning of, 227–228, 302–304
principles and practices, 224–227
of a project, 230–232
reporting, 250–251
of schools and school systems, 220–222
summative, 203, 233
validity, 226, 247
values in, 225
Curriculum guides, 402–403
Curriculum improvement, 12–26, 266–268, 284–287, 319, 355
  accountability, 362, 377, 382–387
  actions to facilitate, 290–304
  assigning and balancing of roles, 387–390
  defined, 311
  leadership, 425, 442–474
  and local participants, 362–376
  and outside participants, 376–382
  planning for, 425, 444–450
  sources of input, 361–362
Curriculum information system, 313
Curriculum issues, 5
Curriculum leadership, 425
  attitudes and competencies, 437–438
  behaviors, 434–436
  effective, 426
  factors affecting, 431–442
  general tasks, 466–468
  nature of, 426–431
  perceptions of, 431–432
  roles, 432–433
  strategies, 442–474
Curriculum models, 175
Curriculum planning, 22–26
  ad hoc committee for, 345–346
  bases for, 311–330
  central steering committee, 345–346
  computer as instrument in, 347–352
  customary modes, 339–341
  data as base, 42–47

expectations, 354–356
importance of thought and feelings, 352–354
products of, 137
schema for, 341–347
sources of ideas for, 330–339
staff meetings, 448–449
teachers' roles, 24, 25, 26, 99, 447–449
Curriculum problems, 318–323, 349
Curriculum unification, 350

Dalton Plan, 17
Data, useful, 314–315
Delphi Technique, 316
Design. See Curriculum design
Development, Piaget's levels of, 45–46
Developmental characteristics, 54
Developmental tasks, 54
Differentiated staffing, 461
Direct instruction, 61–62
Discipline
  as domain of knowledge, 143, 147–150
  in the schools, 91–92, 98
Discovery, 145–150

Education
  humaneness of, 210–211
  quality of, 3, 4
Educational criticism, 248–249
Educational dimensions, 79
Educational directions, 76–78
Educational experiences, 78–80
Educational goals, 76, 225–226, 466–467
Educational issues, 27, 29
Educational leadership
  authority and responsibility of, 436–437, 442
  defined, 426
  democratic, 432, 457, 468
  idiographic, 433
  nomothetic, 433
  styles of, 433–434
  theories of, 427–430
Educational objectives, 76–77, 148, 303, 466–467
  evaluation of, 77, 303
Education Commission of the States, 5
Eight Year Study, 123, 209–210, 223, 285, 286
Elective system, 286

Engagements, 7, 8
Enrollment, decline in, 97
Environment, influence on education, 104–109
Environmental education, 286
EPIC (Evaluative Programs for Innovative Curriculums), 241
Ethnicity, 99
Evaluation
  of curriculum. See Curriculum evaluation
  models for, 236–243
  of pupil progress, 77, 197–198
  of schools, 220–227
Evaluative Criteria, 222
Evolution, versus creationism, 186–187
Expectations
  of pupil achievement, 76
  of the schools, 5, 17, 103
Extra-class activities, 286

Faculty. See Teachers
Faculty psychology, 60
Family disintegration, effect on schools, 90–91
Fault Tree Analysis (FTA), 316–317
Federal aid, 16, 95–96, 114
Filtration, of curriculum information, 313
First principles, 178
Flexible scheduling, 461
Follow-up studies, 221–22
Force field, 276
Foreign languages, 5
Formative evaluation, 203, 233, 234
Foundations, and curriculum improvement, 381
Franklin's Academy, 13
Free public schools, 13, 15
Functional learning, 135–136, 165
Fundamentals. See Basics
Funding, of schools, 16, 95–96, 100, 114
Funding agencies, 289–290
Futurism, 137–138, 186, 188, 355–356

Gender-based differences, 68–70
General College project, 209–210
Gestalt-field theory, 60
Gestalt psychology, 154
Goals, 57, 58, 276
  progress toward, 227

Government, and curriculum
    improvement, 377–378, 380
Graduation requirements, 5
Group theory, of leadership, 427–428
Growth factors, interrelatedness of, 42
Guidance, 114

Hawthorne effect, 235
History, as source of truth, 177–178
Home economics, 286
Homework, 5, 52
Human Development Program, 207
Humane education, 210–211
Humanism, 178, 179, 186, 187–188

Idealists, 32–33
Illuminative evaluation, 248
Indirect instruction, 62, 68
Individual, change in, 269–275
Individualization, of learning, 51–52,
    160–162, 165, 198, 251
Individualized conditioners, of learn-
    ing, 48
Individually Guided Education (IGE),
    161
Initiation, 268
Inner-city environment, 104–107
Input-Output Analysis, 212
Input variables, 233, 234
Inquiry skills, teaching of, 62
In-school study time, 94–95
Inservice education, of teachers, 56,
    236, 270, 271, 289, 301, 319
   in attitude formation, 374
   and audiovisual materials, 406
   in computer operation, 348
   as leadership strategy, 440–445
Instructional design, 174
Instructional materials center (IMC).
    See Media center
Intelligence, defined, 49
International education, 286
Intuitive thinking, 145

Judeo-Christian tradition, 88, 178–179,
    188
Junior high school, 16, 21, 129

Kindergartens, 102, 154
Knowledge
   explosion of, 124–126
   levels of, 132–133

Laypersons, 31, 135
   involvement of, 24–25, 98, 119, 282,
    293, 329, 346, 370–376, 446
Leadership. See Curriculum leadership
Learners, growth and development of,
    41–56
Learning
   experiences, 79, 141–143, 200–203
   individualization of, 51–52
   and pupil insight, 72–75
   to think, 65–66
   types of, 61
   understanding of process, 56–72
Learning center. See Media center
Learning styles, 66–68
Learning theory
   application of, 59–72
   generally accepted principles, 56–58
   older models, 60
   and practice, 58–59
Legitimation, 268
Longitudinal method, of studying
    learners, 42

Magic Circle, 207
Mainstreaming, 19, 55–56, 189
Management Information System, 211
Master planning, 443–447
Mastery learning, 63–64, 461
Measurable outcomes, 133–135
Media Center, 167, 406, 462
Merit pay, 459
Middle school, 21, 129–130, 461
Migrant children, 188–189
Minicomputers, 167–168
Mobility, of American population, 92
Morrill Acts, 15
Motivation, 56–59
Motor chaining, 61
Multicultural education, 149, 154
Multiple discrimination, 61

National Assessment of Educational
    Progress (NAEP), 113, 219,
    223–224, 334, 379
National curriculum, 96, 100
National Defense Education Act, 18,
    289
National Education Association, 163,
    380–381
National Institute of Education, 6
National Science Foundation, 18, 163
National Writing Project, 137

Naturalistic evaluation, 248–249
Needs assessment, 192–193, 313–317, 342, 349
Neobehaviorism, 60
Newsletters, 404
Nongrading, 460, 461
Normal schools, 15
Notation, of curriculum information, 313

Open school, 11
Open space schooling, 462
Opinion polls, 221
Organizational consultation, 279
Organizational Development (OD), 279
Organizations, change in, 275–284
Organizing centers, 201–203
Outcomes, measurable, 133–135
Out-of-school study time, 95
Output variables, 233–234

PARA model, 283–284
Perennialists, 31–32, 179, 181
Performance-based education, 63, 96, 134–135, 198
Performance criteria, 19
Phi Delta Kappa, 193, 316, 465
Philosophical positions, 26–30
Phrenoblysis, 69–70
Physical education, 286
Pittsburgh Evaluation Model, 236–237
Planning guides, 405
Planning process, 310–311
    bases of, 311–330
    causes of, 330–339
    and expectations, 354–356
    modes for, 339–341
    role of computers in, 347–352
    a schema for, 341–347
    and thoughts and feelings, 352–354
Planning, Programming, Budgeting and Evaluation System (PPBES), 211–212
PLATO system, 350–351
Policy statements, 403
Positive instructional atmosphere, 471
Pragmatists, 34–35, 181
Precision teaching, 62
Principle learning, 61
Problem census, 330–333
Problem solving, 61
Process evaluation, 257

Program Evaluation and Review Technique (PERT), 212–213
Program objectives, 196–197, 204
Progressive Movement, 123
Progressivists, 26–30
Project method, 17
Project on Instruction, 163
Project Talent, 60
Proposition 13, 91
Psychoanalysis, 42, 60
Psychomotor objectives, 132
Public high schools, 14, 15
Public relations, 221, 373–374, 433
Pupil competencies, 96

Quality, in curriculum evaluation, 233–236
Quality Circle, 465
Quantity, in curriculum evaluation, 228–232

Realists, 33–34
Reconstructionists, 27, 35–36, 177, 179
Reform, of school practices, 76, 80–81
Regional educational centers, 288
Religion, in education, 12–13, 178–179, 186–187
Remediation, 62
Research reports, 404
Research Utilizing Problem Solving Process (RUPS), 283
Resistance, to change, 88
Resource room, 167
Resource units, 403–404
Role of schools. See Schools, role of
Role set, 383
Rural environment, 104, 107–109

Safety education, 286
Scholastic Aptitude Test scores, 20
Schools
    communication in, 397–398
    evaluation of, 220–224
    morale in, 91–92, 236, 290, 293–295, 329, 338, 386, 434
    public expectations for, 5, 17, 103
    role of, 95, 101, 111, 118–119, 140, 293, 403
Science, as source of truth, 176–177
Scientific method, 176
Scope, 79, 80, 159

Scopes "monkey" trial, 186
Self-concept, 48, 109, 187, 206–208
  role in learning, 48, 136–137, 165
Self-realization, 10, 187, 199
Sequence, 79, 80, 156–158
Sex education, 285, 286
Signal learning, 61
Situational theory, of leadership, 428
Social and cultural change, effects on
  curriculum, 90–94
Social engineering, 276
Societal pressures, on schools, 94–97
Software, 351–352
Special education, 189–190, 286
Special teachers, 293
Staff development, 23, 137, 280, 289,
  301, 319, 444, 450–455, 459. See
  also Inservice education, of
  teachers
Standard evaluation instruments, 222
Standardized tests, 94, 219–220
Stanford Social Education
  Investigation, 223
Stimulus-response learning, 61
Study skills, 5
Subject matter, 123–124
  experiments in placement of, 124,
    128–130
  knowledge explosion and, 125–126
  as learning content, 130–143
  organization of, 10, 125, 150–162
  as process, 131
  resources for presenting, 166–168
  for secondary schools, 165–166
  selection of, 162–166
  uses of, 27, 29
Subject specialists, 124, 126–128, 163
Summative evaluation, 203, 233
Summer institute, 288–289
Supervision, 319, 343, 455–460
Surveys, 220–221
Survey Study of Behavioral Outcomes
  of General Education, 335
Systems analysis, 241
Systems approach, 211–214

TARGET (To Assess Relevant Goals in
  Education Together), 316
Taxonomies, of educational objectives,
  131–132
Taxonomy of Educational Objectives,
  65, 131

Tax reduction, effect on schools, 91,
  100
Teacher centers, 288
Teacher-pupil planning, 276
Teachers
  and curriculum improvement,
    362–366, 380–381
  and curriculum planning, 24, 25, 26,
    99, 447–449
  decisions by, 50–51, 182
  effective, 80
  improvement of, 266–267
  reeducation of, 23, 451–452
  self-respect of, 294
  as stimulators of motivation, 58–59
  stress on, 106
Teaching
  direct, 61–62
  efficiency of, 64–65
  indirect, 62, 68
  materials for, 404
  styles of, 67
Team teaching, 461
Technical high schools, 102
Television, 73, 99, 108, 110, 194
  educational, 379
Textbook adoption, 5
Theory Z, 427
Thinking strategies, 66
Thirty Schools experiment. See Eight
  Year Study
Thought systems, 133
Time-off-task, 64
Time-on-task, 64
Time-series evaluation, 248
Tracking, 28
Tradition
  as inhibitor of change in curriculum,
    88–90
  beneficent, 117
Traditionalists, 26–30
Training program manuals, 405
Traits theory, of leadership, 427
Transformation, of curriculum
  information, 313
Treatment variables, 233–235
Truth, sources of, 175–179, 204
Twentieth Century Fund, 5
Tylerian model, 184–186

Undesired event (UE), 316–317
Unfoldment, 60

Unit method, 17, 286
Unit system, 16
Universities, and curriculum improvement, 379–380
Upward mobility, 4

Values
  clarification, 112, 113, 117, 130
  exploration of, 126, 129, 388
  provided by schools, 91, 93,
    110–113, 117–118, 209, 308
Verbal association, 61
Violence, in schools, 92, 93–94
Vocational education, 13, 16, 114, 285, 286. *See also* Career education
Vocational high schools, 102

Winnetka plan, 17
Working conditions. *See* Climate
Work skills, 5